Untold Stories

Untold Stories

A Canadian Disability History Reader

Edited by
Nancy Hansen, Roy Hanes,
and Diane Driedger

Toronto | Vancouver

Untold Stories: A Canadian Disability History Reader
Edited by Nancy Hansen, Roy Hanes, and Diane Driedger

First published in 2018 by
Canadian Scholars, an imprint of CSP Books Inc.
425 Adelaide Street West, Suite 200
Toronto, Ontario
M5V 3C1

www.canadianscholars.ca

Copyright © 2018 Nancy Hansen, Roy Hanes, Diane Driedger, the contributing authors, and Canadian Scholars.

All rights reserved. No part of this publication may be reproduced, stored in a retrieval system, or transmitted, in any form or by any means, without the prior written permission of Canadian Scholars, under licence or terms from the appropriate reproduction rights organization, or as expressly permitted by law.

Every reasonable effort has been made to identify copyright holders. Canadian Scholars would be pleased to have any errors or omissions brought to its attention.

Library and Archives Canada Cataloguing in Publication

Untold stories : a Canadian disability history reader / edited by Nancy Hansen, Roy Hanes, and Diane Driedger.

Includes bibliographical references.
Issued in print and electronic formats.
ISBN 978-1-77338-046-9 (softcover).--ISBN 978-1-77338-047-6 (PDF).--ISBN 978-1-77338-048-3 (EPUB)

1. People with disabilities--Canada--History. 2. Sociology of disability--Canada--History. 3. Disability studies--Canada--History. I. Driedger, Diane, 1960-, editor II. Hansen, Nancy, 1957-, editor III. Hanes, Roy, 1953-, editor

HV1559.C3U58 2018   362.40971   C2018-901560-8
                                                      C2018-901561-6

Cover image: *My Will Remains* by Diane Driedger, 2006, mixed media, 2 × 4 × 2 feet
Text and cover design by Elisabeth Springate

Printed and bound in Canada by Webcom

CONTENTS

Introduction   1
    Nancy Hansen, Roy Hanes, and Diane Driedger

SECTION I: SETTING THE STAGE

Chapter 1   "Out from Under": A Brief History of Everything   8
    Kathryn Church, Melanie Panitch, Catherine Frazee, and Phaedra Livingstone

Chapter 2   Posthumous Exploitation? The Ethics of Researching, Writing, and Being Accountable as a Disability Historian   26
    Geoffrey Reaume

Chapter 3   Uncovering Disability History   40
    Nancy Hansen

SECTION II: CONFEDERATION TO THE EARLY TWENTIETH CENTURY

Chapter 4   "Blindness Clears the Way": E. B. F. Robinson's *The True Sphere of the Blind* (1896)   53
    Vanessa Warne

Chapter 5   The Education of "Good" and "Useful" Citizens: Work, Disability, and d/Deaf Citizenship at the Ontario Institution for the Education of the Deaf, 1892–1902   66
    Alessandra Iozzo-Duval

Chapter 6   "An Excuse for Being So Bold": D. W. McDermid and the Early Development of the Manitoba Institute for the Deaf and Dumb, 1888–1900   91
    Sandy R. Barron

Chapter 7   Remembering the Boys   110
    Caroline E. M. Carrington-Decker

Chapter 8 "Someone in Toronto ... Paid Her Way Out Here": Indentured Labour and Medical Deportation—The Precarious Work of Single Women   121
Natalie Spagnuolo

Chapter 9 Service Clubs and the Emergence of Societies for Crippled Children in Canada: The Rise of the Ontario Society for Crippled Children, 1920–1940   140
Roy Hanes

SECTION III: INTO THE MID-TWENTIETH CENTURY

Chapter 10 Work, Education, and Privilege: An Alberta City's Parasitical Relationship to Its Total Institution for "Mental Defectives"   163
Claudia Malacrida

Chapter 11 Disability as Social Threat: Examining the Social Justice Implications of Canada's Eugenic History   179
Phillip B. Turcotte

Chapter 12 The Impact of Ventilation Technology: Contrasting Consumer and Professional Perspectives   196
Joseph Kaufert and David Locker

SECTION IV: THE 1960S TO THE 1980S

Chapter 13 Je me souviens: The Hegemony of Stairs in the Montreal Métro   207
Laurence Parent

Chapter 14 Organizing for Change: The Origins and History of the Manitoba League of the Physically Handicapped, 1967–1982   221
Diane Driedger

Chapter 15 The Council of Canadians with Disabilities: A Voice of Our Own, 1976–2012   243
April D'Aubin

Chapter 16 Building an Accessible House of Labour: Work, Disability Rights, and the Canadian Labour Movement   268
Dustin Galer

Chapter 17 The Habeas Corpus of Justin Clark   282
Marilou McPhedran

SECTION V: TO THE END OF THE TWENTIETH CENTURY AND BEYOND

Chapter 18 Winnipeg Community Centre of the Deaf: Program Development as Community Development   297
Charlotte Enns, Bruce Koskie, Rita Bomak, and Gregory Evans

Chapter 19 History of Science and Technology and Canadians with Disabilities   306
Gregor Wolbring and Natalie Ball

Chapter 20 "Like Alice through the Looking Glass" II: The Struggle for Accommodation Continues   320
Vera Chouinard

Chapter 21 Triple Jeopardy: Native Women with Disabilities   339
Doreen Demas

Chapter 22 The Community Inclusion Project in Manitoba: Planning for the Residents of the Pelican Lake Training Centre   345
Zana Marie Lutfiyya, Dale C. Kendel, and Karen D. Schwartz

Chapter 23 Living in the Midst: Re-imagining Disability through Auto/biography   356
Kelly McGillivray

Contributors   368
Copyright Acknowledgements   374

INTRODUCTION

Nancy Hansen, Roy Hanes, and Diane Driedger

People with disabilities tend to be invisible in Canadian society. This volume, *Untold Stories: A Canadian Disability History Reader*, is an attempt to put disabled people back into the history of Canada, to show their rich and diverse relationship with the rest of Canadian society from Confederation to the present and beyond.

Disability has always been part of the diversity of humanity. It is an undeniable part of the human experience across all social sectors; however, the experiences and stories of disabled people are rarely included in the historical record. Where are disabled people? The World Health Organization (WHO) estimates that there are more than a billion disabled people worldwide.[1] Despite this significant number, disabled people remain invisible compared to their non-disabled peers. The degree of anonymity experienced by disabled people is not simply a natural consequence of impairment. Lack of social acceptance resulting from a combination of fear and ignorance that reflects myths and misconceptions about the "abnormality" and "dysfunction" of disability has resulted in centuries of segregated housing, education, and employment away from mainstream society.[2] Disabled people are among the world's socially, politically, and economically disadvantaged minorities.

Disabled people make up nearly 14 percent of the Canadian population, and those 3.4 million people compose one of the largest minority groups in Canada.[3] Disability has always been part of the diversity of the Canadian heritage; however, the richness and complexity of disabled people's lives remains largely overlooked and undocumented. Where they are acknowledged, disabled people often occupy one of two stereotypical extremes: tragic victims of circumstance or heroes overcoming adversity.[4]

In the 1970s, taking a cue from the American Civil Rights Movement, disabled people and their allies began to see the lack of social positioning as a social justice issue rather than a consequence of impairment. The Coalition of Provincial Organizations of the Handicapped (COPOH, now the Council of Canadians with Disabilities [CCD]) was founded in 1976.[5] Disabled Peoples' International was established in 1981.[6]

Adopting a rights-based focus, Disability Studies has evolved over several decades as an interdisciplinary approach to disability and disability issues. Disability history illustrates the growth and development of this discipline; however, disability history is not simply an extension of Disability Studies. Disability history has also become part of the larger *history* discipline.

Like other historically marginalized groups before them, such as Indigenous people, women, racialized persons, and LGBTQ people, disabled people are now beginning to tell their stories on their own terms. They are identifying and filling gaps in the historical record. Disabled people, scholars, and historians have begun peeling back the layers, uncovering disability or putting it back into the historical landscape. The following volumes trace the steady growth of the subject area.

Stiker's *A History of Disability* (1999) was the first to examine disabled people's place in history, tracing the historical treatment of disabled people in a Western European context from biblical times through to post–World War II rehabilitation.[7] In *The Last Civil Rights Movement: Disabled Peoples' International (DPI)* (1999),[8] Driedger traces the rise of an international disability rights movement. *The New Disability History: American Perspectives* (2001),[9] edited by Longmore and Umansky, examines disabled people's daily lives at key points in American history, from the Civil War to the present day. With "Disability History: Why We Need Another 'Other'" (2003),[10] Kudlick was among the first of a small group of American historians who advocated the value of exploring disability history. Stienstra and Wight-Felske's *Making Equality: History of Advocacy and Persons with Disabilities in Canada* (2003)[11] brings together a diverse collection of disabled people's and their allies' voices, representing many different provinces and the disparate ways that disability has been experienced and organized in Canada over the years. Evans's *Forgotten Crimes: The Holocaust and People with Disabilities* (2004) looks at the eugenic extermination of disabled people in Nazi Germany, which had previously received limited scholarly attention.[12] Similarly, Schweik's *The Ugly Laws: Disability in Public* (2009) documents how discriminatory public policy restricted the movements of disabled people in public space (sidewalks and parks, for example) on the grounds of public decency in several US cities from the late nineteenth to the late twentieth century.[13] Nielsen's *A Disability History of the United States* (2012) looks at disability in America from first European contact through to the present-day disability rights movement.[14]

Wheatcroft's *Worth Saving: Disabled Children during the Second World War* (2013) explores how disabled children were differentially treated in Britain during the war.[15] Finally, Burch and Rembis's *Disability Histories* (2014) takes a global perspective of disability history, moving both geographically and philosophically beyond European and North American conceptualizations of disability to include not only histories from the United States but also Africa, Asia, and the Global South.[16] This is particularly important given that the majority of people with disabilities are located outside North America.

Disability history is gradually coming into its own as a discipline; however, many of Canada's stories of disability are yet to be told. The first specifically Canadian texts that document institutional histories include Reaume's *Lyndhurst: Canada's First Rehabilitation Centre for People with Spinal Cord Injuries, 1945–1998* (2007) and *Remembrance of Patients*

Past: Patient Life at the Toronto Hospital for the Insane, 1870–1940 (2009).[17] Institutional histories are important because, until very recently, as a result of restrictive public policy and inaccessible housing, transportation, education, and employment, institutions were the only places where most disabled people could be found outside the family home. Wheatley's *"And Neither Have I Wings to Fly": Labelled and Locked Up in Canada's Oldest Institution* (2013) and Malacrida's *A Special Hell: Institutional Life in Alberta's Eugenic Years* (2015) document the harsh, unyielding reality of life in Canadian disability institutions of the period.[18]

Durflinger's *Veterans with a Vision: Canada's War Blinded in Peace and War* (2010) and Wright's *Downs: The History of a Disability* (2011) mark the first efforts of Canadian historians to incorporate a critical social perspective to examine the history of specific impairments beyond a purely medical context.[19]

Most recently, Rose's *No Right to Be Idle: The Invention of Disability, 1840s–1930s* (2017) discusses how in the United States people with disabilities moved from being contributors at home and in the wage market to being seen as needing care and support during that time period.[20] Economic changes meant that they did not fit the mainstream definition of a worker who could be like other workers. This resulted in social policy shifts that deemed disabled people unproductive citizens who needed to be cared for in separate institutions and subject to different social policies.

There is still a great deal of disability history yet to be uncovered and explored. *Untold Stories* is the latest effort to bring to light and illustrate current interdisciplinary developments in the field coupled with increasing attention from new disciplines. This book presents a series of snapshots in time of the lives of disabled people in Canada, documenting and recounting instances of agency, resistance, and activism. With this in mind, it is important to note that, throughout the book, the reader will encounter terminology that in today's world may be viewed as inappropriate or derogatory; however, the language used is true to the period. The book is organized chronologically into five sections: Section I: Setting the Stage, Section II: Confederation to the Early Twentieth Century, Section III: Into the Mid-twentieth Century, Section IV: The 1960s to the 1980s, and Section V: To the End of the Twentieth Century and Beyond.

Untold Stories is an interdisciplinary approach to disability history that brings together a diverse group of scholars to highlight the experiences, richness, and diversity of disabled people's lives over more than a century. This book gives a voice to populations of disabled people whose stories remained silent for many generations. We hope it will prove a useful resource both to scholars, students, and individuals interested in disability issues and to those who have yet to discover them.

NOTES

1. World Health Organization, *Summary World Report on Disability*, (Malta: WHO, 2011), http://apps.who.int/iris/bitstream/10665/70670/1/WHO_NMH_VIP_11.01_eng.pdf.
2. Nancy Hansen, "Passing through Other People's Spaces: Disabled Women, Geography, and Work" (PhD diss., University of Glasgow, 2002).

3. Statistics Canada, *A Profile of Persons with Disabilities among Canadians Aged 15 Years or Older, 2012*, last modified February 15, 2017, http://www.statcan.gc.ca/pub/89-654-x/89-654-x2015001-eng.htm.
4. "Common Portrayals of Persons with Disabilities," Media Smarts, accessed August 3, 2017, http://mediasmarts.ca/diversity-media/persons-disabilities/common-portrayals-persons-disabilities.
5. "History," Council of Canadians with Disabilities, accessed August 3, 2017, http://www.ccdonline.ca/en/about/history.
6. "Welcome to Disabled People's International," Disabled Peoples' International, accessed August 3, 2017, http://www.disabledpeoplesinternational.org.
7. Henri-Jacques Stiker, *A History of Disability*, trans. William Sayers (Ann Arbor: University of Michigan Press, 1999).
8. Diane Driedger, *The Last Civil Rights Movement: Disabled Peoples' International (DPI)* (London and New York: Hurst and St. Martin's Press, 1999).
9. Paul Longmore and Lauri Umansky, *The New Disability History: American Perspectives* (New York: New York University Press, 2001).
10. Catherine Kudlick, "Disability History: Why We Need Another 'Other,'" *American Historical Review* 108, no. 3 (June 2003): 762–93, https://doi.org/10.1086/ahr/108.3.763.
11. Deborah Stienstra and Aileen Wight-Felske, *Making Equality: History of Advocacy and Persons with Disabilities in Canada* (Concord, ON: Captus Press, 2003).
12. Suzanne E. Evans, *Forgotten Crimes: The Holocaust and People with Disabilities* (Chicago: Ivan R. Dee, 2004).
13. Susan M. Schweik, *The Ugly Laws: Disability in Public* (New York: New York University Press, 2009).
14. Kim E. Neilsen, *A Disability History of the United States* (Boston: Beacon Press, 2012).
15. Sue Wheatcroft, *Worth Saving: Disabled Children during the Second World War*, Disability History Series (Manchester: Manchester University Press, 2013).
16. Susan Burch and Michael Rembis, *Disability Histories*, Disability Histories Series (Urbana: University Of Illinois Press, 2014).
17. Geoffrey Reaume, *Lyndhurst: Canada's First Rehabilitation Centre for People with Spinal Cord Injuries, 1945–1998* (Montreal/Kingston: McGill-Queen's University Press, 2007); Geoffrey Reaume, *Remembrance of Patients Past: Patient Life at the Toronto Hospital for the Insane, 1870–1940* (Don Mills, ON: Oxford University Press, 2009).
18. Thelma Wheatley, *"And Neither Have I Wings to Fly": Labelled and Locked Up in Canada's Oldest Institution* (Toronto: Inanna Publications, 2013). Claudia Malacrida, *A Special Hell: Institutional Life in Alberta's Eugenic Years* (Toronto: University of Toronto Press, 2015).
19. Serge Marc Durflinger, *Veterans with a Vision: Canada's War Blinded in Peace and War* (Vancouver: University of British Columbia Press, 2010); David Wright, *Downs: The History of a Disability* (New York: Oxford University Press, 2011).
20. Sarah F. Rose, *No Right to Be Idle: The Invention of Disability, 1840s–1930s* (Chapel Hill: University of North Carolina Press, 2017).

BIBLIOGRAPHY

Burch, Susan, and Michael Rembis. *Disability Histories*. Disability Histories Series. Urbana: University Of Illinois Press, 2014.

Driedger, Diane. *The Last Civil Rights Movement: Disabled Peoples' International (DPI)*. London and New York: Hurst and St. Martin's Press, 1999.

Durflinger, Serge Marc. *Veterans with a Vision: Canada's War Blinded in Peace and War.* Vancouver: University of British Columbia Press, 2010.

Evans, Suzanne E. *Forgotten Crimes: The Holocaust and People with Disabilities.* Chicago: Ivan R. Dee, 2004.

Hansen, Nancy. "Passing through Other People's Spaces: Disabled Women, Geography, and Work." PhD diss., University of Glasgow, 2002.

Kudlick, Catherine. "Disability History: Why We Need Another 'Other.'" *American Historical Review* 108, no. 3 (June 2003): 762–93. https://doi.org/10.1086/ahr/108.3.763.

Longmore, Paul, and Lauri Umansky. *The New Disability History: American Perspectives.* New York: New York University Press, 2001.

Malacrida, Claudia. *A Special Hell: Institutional Life in Alberta's Eugenic Years.* Toronto: University of Toronto Press, 2015.

Neilsen, Kim E. *A Disability History of the United States.* Boston: Beacon Press, 2012.

Reaume, Geoffrey. *Lyndhurst: Canada's First Rehabilitation Centre for People with Spinal Cord Injuries, 1945–1998.* Montreal/Kingston: McGill-Queen's University Press, 2007.

Reaume, Geoffrey. *Remembrance of Patients Past: Patient Life at the Toronto Hospital for the Insane, 1870–1940.* Don Mills, ON: Oxford University Press, 2009.

Rose, Sarah F. *No Right to Be Idle: The Invention of Disability, 1840s–1930s.* Chapel Hill: University of North Carolina Press, 2017.

Schweik, Susan M. *The Ugly Laws: Disability in Public.* New York: New York University Press, 2009.

Statistics Canada. *A Profile of Persons with Disabilities among Canadians Aged 15 Years or Older, 2012.* Last modified February 15, 2017. http://www.statcan.gc.ca/pub/89-654-x/89-654-x2015001-eng.htm.

Stienstra, Deborah, and Aileen Wight-Felske. *Making Equality: History of Advocacy and Persons with Disabilities in Canada.* Concord, ON: Captus Press, 2003.

Stiker, Henri-Jacques. *A History of Disability.* Translated by William Sayers. Ann Arbor: University of Michigan Press, 1999.

Wheatcroft, Sue. *Worth Saving: Disabled Children during the Second World War.* Disability History Series. Manchester: Manchester University Press, 2013.

Wheatley, Thelma. *"And Neither Have I Wings to Fly": Labelled and Locked Up in Canada's Oldest Institution.* Toronto: Inanna Publications, 2013.

World Health Organization. *Summary World Report on Disability.* Malta: WHO, 2011. http://apps.who.int/iris/bitstream/10665/70670/1/WHO_NMH_VIP_11.01_eng.pdf.

Wright, David. *Downs: The History of a Disability.* New York: Oxford University Press, 2011.

SECTION I

SETTING THE STAGE

How have the current historical oversights regarding disability developed? We begin by looking at cultural invisibility. In "'Out from Under': A Brief History of Everything," Church, Panitch, Frazee, and Livingstone document the difficulties and triumphs associated with researching, mounting, and presenting the first Canadian disability history in cultural space. This chapter traces the manner in which students and instructors from Ryerson University's Department of Disability Studies developed an exhibit of objects of significance to disability history in Canada. From this emerged a "museum display" of items, first hosted at the Royal Ontario Museum in Toronto, which has received national and international recognition.

Reaume's "Posthumous Exploitation? The Ethics of Researching, Writing, and Being Accountable as a Disability Historian" notes the difficulties associated with uncovering disability, candidly raising questions about the ethical challenges related to using personal material in the form of files, charts, and personal letters. Reaume also notes his own standpoint as a "psychiatric survivor"; this perspective is undoubtedly the cornerstone of his concern that disability historians treat their subject matter with dignity and respect.

Hansen's "Uncovering Disability History" discusses how history and what is perceived as valuable have been "culturally curated"—that is, how historians, archivists, and museum curators determine what is and is not valuable and worthy of note, with a particular focus on spaces of culture such as museums and galleries.

CHAPTER 1

"Out from Under": A Brief History of Everything*

Kathryn Church, Melanie Panitch, Catherine Frazee, and Phaedra Livingstone

INTRODUCTION

From September 2006 to July 2008, the School of Disability Studies at Ryerson University in Toronto produced an exhibit of activist disability history titled *Out from Under: Disability, History, and Things to Remember*. The authors of this chapter were involved: Catherine, Melanie, and Kathryn as co-curators, Phaedra as one of 14 exhibitors.[1] In this chapter, we narrate our way from the invitation that sparked the school's engagement, to the exhibit's initial installation in a disability arts festival, to its further installation in a premier Canadian cultural venue.

As we go, we imagine the disabled artists and performers who are creating disability arts and culture as an increasingly dynamic force for change in Canada and abroad.[2] We imagine disability activists whose stories, individually and collectively, gave *Out from Under* its energy and direction. And we imagine students of Disability Studies—our own students—who are learning and negotiating disability politics, as well as practices of activist and arts-informed inquiry. What have we learned that can assist these audiences? Having navigated our way into a major museum, what is revealed from a position of disability presence rather than absence? Beyond exhibit construction, what are the complexities of how a completed work is interpreted to and received by the public? Finally, what are the implications for practitioners located in museums and other cultural organizations?

While contemplating this writing, we were flooded with the enormity of attempting to convey the history we have lived with *Out from Under*. For two years, every action we took to move the exhibit ahead required us to negotiate the politics of disability representation—less as high drama than as treacherous "tucks" in a relentless progression of mundane tasks and decisions. For this reason, our chapter gives you a broad sweep of the whole process, foregoing for now the pleasures of probing its nooks and crannies. We glance back in time to the exhibit's origins, peer behind the scenes to reveal its key deliberations and turning points, and highlight the ways in which exhibiting involves risk and discovery, celebration and remembrance, social inquiry and political action.

ORIGINS: A CURATORIAL NARRATIVE

In 2006, organizers for the Abilities Arts Festival[3] approached the School of Disability Studies[4] with a request that we contribute a Canadian disability history exhibit to their autumn 2007 event. This invitation signifies the beginning of a broader process of community-university connection that is woven through the project. Who we are is one strand of that pattern. Arriving late to academic careers, each of us trails a long history of paid and volunteer work with community-based organizations, both local and national. Each of us lives in, fosters, and/or draws from networks of relationship to disability worlds: physical, intellectual, and/or psychiatric. Each of us chips away at an activist agenda. We are border-crossers, hybrid rather than "pure" scholars, and this subjectivity was a key ingredient of our project. As we are neither historians nor museum specialists, our particularities remain central to the broader account of disability history that we mobilized together.

We begin by recounting the origins of *Out from Under* in a voice that could be called the "curatorial we." It conforms to the shape that we—Catherine, Melanie, and Kathryn—have given to our labours in the ebb and flow of "trialogue" at each stage of this project.

Invoking the Classroom

Established in 1999, the School of Disability Studies is expanding and maturing as part of a downtown university positioned by its current president as a "city builder."[5] In the winter of 2007, with the clock ticking on our Abilities Arts invitation, we introduced a Special Topics course titled "Exhibiting Activist Disability History," designed to take up critical questions such as "What is history?" and "Who gets to make it?" The end product would be an exhibit with an activist stance, one that would profile resistance to discrimination and marginalization of disabled people. One of our innovations, then, was to jump-start exhibit development through the reciprocal learning and teaching of the classroom.

The strength of this move lay in adopting a forum in which disability representation is already on the agenda. As a school, we marinate continuously in the struggle to address the invisibility of disabled people in and across a range of situations without reproducing or reinforcing "that telling glance"[6] or "the stare" that turns people with disabilities into objects of curiosity.[7] Working with this dilemma is front and centre in everything we do, from academic programming to public education, from student recruitment to corporate fundraising, from student awards to event titles,[8] from interdisciplinary networking to bureaucratic interactions, and from research production to media spin. So, although exhibit development was new on our list, it made sense that we would favour our own expertise.

There were, however, limitations to this approach. Although we knew we would "air" the exhibit at least once in the disability community, we had no reassurance that our project would ever find an audience with the general public. Working without a museum partner, we had limited access to the display and production skills that abound in these institutions, nor could we call upon their financial resources. Conversely, by containing the development process, we buffered museum personnel from exposure to the political sensitivities surrounding disability until after the exhibit was fully developed. Had they worked with us from the ground up, they would have confronted more "harshly" situations and positions that we introduced "softly" at a later stage in the process.[9] On the one hand, our relative isolationism prevented the direct transfer of representational expertise to the museum itself, and thus was less effective in altering taken-for-granted practices. On the other hand, it permitted our exhibitors to proceed boldly, without the censorial inhibitions of institutional oversight.

Engaging the Students

As other contributors to this volume argue, making exhibit production more responsive to diverse communities is not just about choosing new or different artifacts, but also about making new social relations. In England, for example, Dodd and colleagues recruited disabled individuals who were also experts in the field to constitute a "think-tank" for their project.[10] Our "think-tank" was composed of people who assembled for the course, a group that assumed some unusual features. It included several students of Disability Studies who registered for credit. Active as undergraduates in our program, these individuals are simultaneously full- and/or part-time workers with disability-related job histories. As word of the project spread, we acquired significant others: alumni yearning to return to our hothouse of activist scholarship, a researcher with a national independent-living organization, and scholars from other universities. We enhanced and extended the group by inviting recognized leaders of the disability movement to join us.

Quite naturally, these people hooked us into disability as it is transacted and negotiated in the environments they inhabit, from large congregate care settings to community organizations and service agencies, from school systems to trade unions. The disability activists strengthened our grounding in the lived history of their work while connecting us to representative organizations. They contributed decades of experience with education, career, and advocacy initiatives as well as irreplaceable knowledge of human rights campaigns and public policy battles. To press the meaning of representation, then, it was not so much who each member represented that mattered as the fact that each one took on the task of representing what we were doing to the key groups and audiences in their networks. Our work radiated out from this human centre.

Thus, we did not follow the more conventional practice of selecting participants in order to represent a particular range of disability experiences and/or organizations. Instead, we created an opportunity for collective work that expressed our actual circumstances and invited membership to form around it.[11] By stretching the definition of *student* in unusual ways, we built a group—primarily women—whose members extended and complicated the project's portrait of participation.[12] Our task was to work across diverse locations and mixed embodiments in the creation of an exhibit. What we shared was a point of view as protagonists and participants in, and allies to, progressive social movements in Canada.

Gleaning a Collection

Out from Under started with a group of people rather than a collection. In order to establish a material base for exhibition, each participant in the course was asked to bring an object that s/he felt was significant to disability history. Trusting our decision to "fall into" rather than drive the project, we had no idea what things would turn up;[13] however, we found that we had provoked a collection of 13 objects: a shovel, photos of three early residents of a psychiatric hospital, a poster, a sweatsuit, an IQ test, a program from the Shrine Circus, a trunk, a portable respirator, a death certificate, a Braille watch, a bulletin board, a photo of a disability activist, and a Canadian flag.

Looking back, it is clear that we sidestepped two dilemmas: one of working with pre-established collections and another of choosing some objects over others. We simply accepted all of the objects that participants brought to class. In this way, object selection became a social process rather than a curatorial task. In the course of searching some/thing out, each person not only helped generate a collection but also developed a stake in it. All of us were delighted to encounter the objects that other participants had serendipitously "found." By the time the class met, these objects carried tracings of their relation to the contributors as well as to the histories of disabled people. The "how I found it" stories became, unexpectedly, an important genre that we later incorporated into exhibit materials. Retaining and honouring these relations is evidence of the feminist methodology that lay, implicitly, at the heart of our project. The narrative and reflexive "turns"[14] enabled us to savour the particularities of local stories while searching out their extra-local significance.[15]

Teaching for Discovery

The course on exhibiting disability history was held over two weekends using a form that we call "an intensive." Our approach was to excavate hidden disability histories through a process of presentation and amplification. During the first session, we orchestrated a "go-round" with all participants at the table, having them introduce their object and tell us why they thought it was important. Having dug deeper into their objects, participants arrived for the second "go-round" bearing not just the thing itself but a mock-up installation.

In both sessions, we relied on participant knowledge, impressions, and associations to move explorations along. We worked from the particular object to the general context without erasing the links between them. We traced the connections between the objects and the people who owned or used them: past and present, individuals and groups. While we were preoccupied with objects from start to finish, we worked towards a "peopled" exhibit alive with disabled characters, their families, friends, and allies.[16] Much creativity was at play here. In fact, we generated more ideas than we could use, as we would later find out.

The process was not without risk.[17] The exhibit might be too particular. Rooted in personal narratives, it might fail to communicate the broader patterns of disablement shaping the stories we told.[18] The exhibit would not be comprehensive of all disability movements, visionaries, and watersheds, and would almost certainly fail to communicate the breadth and fullness of Canadian disability history. Worse, it might be considered elitist or exclusionary.

What constitutes "history" in this context? This question was an active piece of our problematic. On the one hand, we were familiar with interdisciplinary scholarship, Canadian and international, that could inform class discussions and exhibit themes. Indeed, we assembled this material for two course readers. On the other hand, we knew that the written record on disability history—especially the activist history to which we aspired—is missing, fragmented, or hugely compromised both by medical fixations on deviance and pathology and by the cultural tropes of tragedy and heroism.[19] Given this circumstance, we could not use objects merely to reflect or illustrate a pre-existing and pre-authorized history. Instead, we drew what we could from scholarship that was aligned with our purposes even as we worked to fill scholarly silences by discovering and producing a fresh account.[20]

Out from Under arrived at a general history.[21] Our almost random collection of objects opened into a much larger story of people with disabilities: generations of lives dominated by demeaning labels and life-altering categorization, by segregation and forced confinement, by the monotony and uniformity of institutional life, by unpaid labour and bodily harm, by the good intentions of charitable benefactors. Surfacing throughout are significant acts of individual achievement as well as the growth of national disability movements struggling to claim power, dignity, and full citizenship rights.[22]

That said, we have never viewed *Out from Under* as completely representative of disability history in Canada. Even when the exhibit was finally ready for installation, we understood it as a work-in-progress. Rather than definitive or comprehensive, the project was invitational. We used the objects we collected and the stories we derived from them to invite visitors and other potential exhibitors into a process of discovery that had only just begun. Clearly stated on the final text panel of the exhibit and repeated in the exhibit catalogue, our message remains the same. Our project is intended to spark further discoveries and reflections that advance the ongoing work of making disability history *public* history.

DELIBERATIONS AND TURNING POINTS: MULTIPLE NARRATIVES

In this section, we tease out various strands of labour whereby the authors engaged with the making of *Out from Under*. In the following exchanges, we break the "curatorial we" in favour of singular voices. While creating an exhibit required tremendous collaboration from all of its participants, each also has his/her own story.

Designing: Kathryn

By July 2007, our project had reached a point where participants from the "exhibiting course" were ready to present their winter's work to the student body at the school's annual

Summer Institute. Each tableau occupied its own table, told a complete and complex story, and had a unique visual style that expressed its presenter's flair for display. This pilot presentation—not yet titled—excited audience members with both its historical assemblage and its method of working from objects. Some still prefer the immediacy and vitality of this iteration to those that came later. As people mingled and chatted after the event, someone new circulated amongst them: drifting from table to table with notebook in hand was a design consultant named Debbie Adams.[23]

Debbie was present because, as curators, we had reached a crucial turning point with our work. The course was over; our participants were drifting away to embrace the brief glow of summer. With a scant three months remaining before our Abilities Arts opening, the exhibit was still uncomfortably reminiscent of a high school science fair. We knew that an amateur production would not be taken seriously. Given that disabled people have long been treated as second-class citizens, we firmly believed that nothing less than top-notch would suffice.

From a design perspective, Debbie's major concern was to create a cohesive "look" for the exhibit, an instant signal to visitors that all of the installations belonged to the same storyline. She insisted that each installation revolve around a single object rather than the clusters that some had become. She pressed us to clarify the primary message that each would contribute to the whole. I bounced back and forth between designer and participants until we reached agreement over what to keep, what to ditch, and what might be added to each display.

It was a significant transition, and not always comfortable. On the one hand, participants lost a measure of control over their work; on the other, their installations were enhanced in useful and exciting ways. The process ended well for two reasons. While she sharpened the work done by participants, our design consultant respected and did not dislodge it. Participants retained the final say, even as they were pressed to find the critical essence of their installations.

The summer passed in a blur. My days were organized around email and telephone exchanges with Debbie and tasks arising from our formidable checklist, repeatedly revised as we inched towards the deadline. We plotted the exhibitors on a grid, charting everything that had to be assembled to complete each installation. Having "de-cluttered" the project, Debbie now wanted to enhance its core objects by adding supporting materials: photos, archival documents, lists, letters, stickers, and clippings, for example. These had to be collected afresh or manufactured. We measured each item so that Debbie could figure it into her plan. We took digital photos of each object in low and high resolution so that she could scan them into her computerized graphics program.[24]

While crafting a design that was sophisticated and flexible, Debbie also researched a display system to suit our needs. Her choice comprised aluminum rods and connectors, magnetic "push-fit" joints, and lightweight metal trays; she reassured us that they were "like giant Tinkertoys." The manufacturer, Burkhardt Leitner, markets the system as "a convenient means of developing complex spatial structures and visualizing them in three dimensions." Indeed, it turned out to be perfect for amateur and professional preparators alike. We assembled it ourselves the first time out, snapping the text panels that Debbie produced onto the framework with special screws and elastics. Taken with its practicality, we did not expect the pedagogical "lift" the system gave to our modest collection. The effervescence of the tubular structure—its bird-like bones—allowed viewers to perceive and absorb the weighty social chronicle that it carried.

Crystalizing: Catherine

As the enthusiasms of our intensive sessions built, a mosaic of contributor voices and styles found expression in installation titles. Some were ironic, while others were bittersweet. "It's a Miracle!" wryly chided the hucksters of cure. "Great Expectations" spoke wistfully of engagement in reform campaigns that yielded only symbolic results. Some were evocative, while others were declaratory. "They Fed and Clothed Each Other" summoned the spirit of solidarity among asylum inmate-labourers. "A Billboard Is a Site of Struggle" drew attention to activist utterings pinned to workplace corkboards. Some were polemic, while others were rhetorical. "No Voices, No Choices" challenged institutional clothing practices that stifled individuality. "What's in a Name?" traced the eugenic history of medical categories carried forward into today's language of taunt and insult.

But would the intended ironies translate beyond "insider" circles? Would these titles beckon audiences accustomed to histories spoken in "neutral" tones? Would they soothe where they sought to unsettle? Were they adequately calibrated for a liberal reader, a militant reader, a literal reader, a bigot? Did they leave enough, or too much, of the interpretive work for audience members to do themselves?

Our design consultant helped us to appreciate the complexity embedded in these titles, and impressed upon us the need for a harmonious, unified approach. Ever vigilant to the perils of too much creativity, especially with an exhibition of such diverse perspectives, emotions, and eras, she urged a rethinking, a higher-level curatorial venture in titling.

On a conference call at summer's end, we brainstormed. It seemed an impossible task. Paring down the titles we had might well reduce the chaos factor, but at what cost? Bland or button-down would be intolerable. We resisted sacrificing the singularity of these assembled histories and the powerful agency of their origins. As we contemplated how to generate some sense of movement and purpose in our titles, we stumbled upon the possibility of single action words. A list of present participles began to emerge: "Fixing." "Aspiring." "Labouring." "Struggling." "Dressing." "Naming." One by one, we warmed to the idea.

"Breathing" clinched the deal. An installation featuring a cuirass (a 1950s innovation in portable ventilator technology) had presented a particular challenge of focus. Originally titled "Maverick Minister on the Move," this installation profiled the intrepid volunteerism of a pastor-turned-repair mechanic who determined that his own daughter—and the sons and daughters of every community visited by polio—should live securely at home. The contributors, one of whom was a ventilator user with deep activist credentials, were clear on a message of liberation. But we worried that the overlays of benevolent service that audiences would likely bring to this narrative could eclipse the disability perspective necessary to understand the installation. "Helping" was not the story here. The revolutionary act of *breathing* was the story, supported by threads of resistance, ingenuity, and alliance. "Breathing" was everything we could wish for in a title: simplicity paired with subversion, translating the everyday act of respiration as defiant and autonomous. The text crafted to accompany the installation would arc back to the title, leaving no room for misinterpretation:

> This installation honours the man, the movement he nurtured and each and every breath of freedom and flourishing in Independent Living.

Musing: Phaedra

The *Out from Under* exhibitors brought a diverse range of identities, allegiances, and interests to the project.[25] I contributed as an exhibitor and offer here my reflections on the experience as a museologist/museum professional with activist experience. For some time before learning about the project, I had been researching a collection of archival photographs documenting a 1924 exhibition on mental health and early psychiatry in Canada. The question of how one might interpret their staged and offensively labelled images to contemporary museum audiences stymied me. Ethical concerns raised by the photos included the following: How might they be thoughtfully used today to address our history of discrimination against disability? The standards of care have changed, and the young patients depicted would not be photographed today—can their right to privacy be balanced with the desire to show how their condition was framed and labelled in 1924? Will displaying them outweigh the risk of offending viewers?

This project was a fortuitous opportunity for my study. Neither collections-based research nor "best practice" in museum representation could resolve my questions. Conducting exhibit development in this unique classroom setting, I was not limited by conventional museum interpretation expectations, such as a focus on authenticity and provenance. The approach of *Out from Under* liberated my interpretation, allowing me to experiment with a shift from a material history analysis to arts-informed inquiry. I was able to address the ethical dilemma by transforming the original artifact into an artifact-cum-artwork.

Setting out with an exhibit agenda (i.e., to present disability history as an activist intervention) rather than an interpretive plan facilitated my process. As a group conceptualizing art installations, we did not have to debate and come to consensus on a grand narrative of disability history to which we would each subscribe in our work; we could focus on the development of our own piece, independent of the others. Given the huge diversity of issues, moments, and interpretations in Canadian disability history that could be presented, this avoided possible conflicts about priorities and privileging of some topics over others.

I took the photograph of a poster as my object, and selected one image as the detail I would use. The girl in this image returns your gaze and asserts her social being. Her anonymous portrait's inscription is now an inflammatory label: "Moron (high grade feeble-minded)." Drawing on my experience and research in museum learning, I knew that the sensational nature of the poster demanded purposeful engagement with the viewer in order to stimulate self-reflection. Using a mirror somewhere in the display would inscribe the viewer in the presentation, causing at least literal reflection. My concern for purposeful display through viewer engagement was addressed by the same measure that addressed concern for the girl's privacy: with a cut-out, reminiscent of the "black box" treatment in later medical photos. While simply covering her eyes would have dehumanized her, when seeing our own eyes in her face, we cannot help but identify with the girl's ghostly image overlaid on the mirror.

With the portrait now reframed and transformed, the poster's antique medical terms still require viewer reflection. How could I keep the viewer from turning away from the emotionally charged terms and prompt thinking about medical labels and negative attitudes colluding over time to become colloquial slurs or "bad names"? I attempted a flip-book layering of chronologically labelled images, envisioning time-lapsed projections, to demonstrate shifts over time in medical terminology related to intellectual disability.

My display text read:

What's in a Name?
Over the last century, the medical terms for intellectual disabilities have changed a lot.
How would you feel if you were called one of the names used in the pictures here?

The resulting prototype was an interactive but distracting experience. Intent on a constructivist display[26] employing experiential learning, I subsequently opted to simply use the mirror and add the list of "names" under a redraft of the above text. I submitted my mirror, label text, and a supplementary artist's statement for the Abilities Arts Festival exhibition, assuming my art installation would remain as I had created it.

In the months leading to the festival, a designer was hired and the decision made to unify the displays textually and visually. Being minimal, it was decided that my display needed more content to blend in. Although I resisted it, the archival image I had drawn from was added to the display. I was told some text from my artist's statement would also be added. Shortly before the opening I was emailed the revisions—the leading question had been replaced with a text focused on the poster and sarcastic in tone. While I understood the intention behind the changes, the use of irony and the overshadowing of the engagement I had tried to create were frustrating. Although production had begun, a last-minute addition of the text I had submitted was made, in small font under the mirror.

The display bears my name, but through design and curatorial choices, the final version is really a hybrid of two displays with different genres. In particular, the scale and prominence of the sensational poster competes visually and affectively with the mirror. The added text and image shift the display back from a history-informed art piece to artful social history; rather than experiencing ideas through a constructivist engagement, the display is shifted to a didactic and expository engagement of the viewer's attention.[27] Showing the poster reintroduces ethical dilemmas I had chosen to avoid. This shift served the goals of exposing disability history and developing an overall aesthetic for the show, but I wonder if the compromise limits the transformative potential of the "Naming" installation.

"Naming" is one of 13 displays informed by unique objects, narratives, and a range of interpretive approaches. Mine is a museum perspective and just one of the many stories exhibitors could tell about the complex process of creating an *Out from Under*.

Negotiating: Melanie

In October 2007, *Out from Under* premiered at the Abilities Arts Festival where it was extraordinarily well received. By working our networks, we made sure that two highly placed members of the Royal Ontario Museum (ROM) were in attendance: one was the senior director of exhibit planning and the other was a museum trustee named Christine Karcza. A corporate champion for accessibility and a woman with a disability, Christine was already lobbying on our behalf. Our negotiations started right there on the exhibit floor. Reading the texts, the exhibit planner searched for her preferred sense of "balance," encountering instead a "point of view." She had misgivings. How might a residential worker react to the critique of her workplace depicted in "Dressing"? Our response—that it had been written by someone who had worked in an institutional facility for many years—seemed only marginally reassuring. Yet the exhibit planner was unable to resist the exhibit's striking design. If a "balanced perspective" was elusive, the stunning look of *Out from Under* was seductive. Shortly after this key encounter, we were invited to mount a 12-week run at the ROM.

A number of intersecting dynamics kindled that invitation. It came at a transitional moment when the ROM was, in the words of its chief executive officer William Thorsell, creating a "radical re-imagination of architecture, function and public space." He spoke of its role as "the new Agora, the common space, the new city square."[28] Daniel Libeskind's artful Crystal addition had opened a new front door to the ROM, provoking animated public conversation about the museum's engagement with the city. For Christine Karcza, the time was ripe for our exhibit. She recognized it as the perfect vehicle to drive her activist message home to the board of trustees. And she had in her corner the newly appointed president of the ROM's board of governors, a one-time provincial government minister under whose watch the landmark Accessibility for Ontarians with Disabilities Act (2005) became law, a woman who recognized that welcoming the exhibit and its point of view could also be part of her legacy. Such was the terrain from which the invitation arose to bring *Out from Under* inside. But there were material forces, too. Compelled by the expense of the ROM's reinvention in the face of declining government operating support, the ROM was searching for bigger crowds and, of course, tickets at the door. In *Out from Under* they began to envision a new market.

Our adventure in search of history called upon negotiating skills at many turns: as teachers, we invited our students to negotiate the politics of display; as an academic collective, we negotiated the concept of history itself; and as Disability Studies scholars, we negotiated the very use of the word *activist*. However deftly we may have maneuvered the various twists and turns to this point, the negotiating skills required to carry out the next phase of work were by far the most complicated and taxing. I likened the relationship to planning a wedding—with the ROM as our prospective in-laws. "How do WE stay in charge?" I demanded in a marginal note to myself after only the second meeting.

At the root of this tension was an encounter between two worlds. On the one hand was the enduring, long-standing, and permanent reality of Canada's oldest and most established museum; on the other were the elastic, dynamic, and gritty worlds of disability. Negotiating the ground between them permeated every arrangement we made with the ROM. Indeed, the museum's "tried and true" blue ribbon practices set us up for marginalization, broken promises, and inequities on a number of fronts, from exhibit space to opening ceremonies to communications strategies.

Our first adventure was a narrow escape from cramped quarters. Initially, we were offered a small room with three doors that attracted a steady traffic flow of ROM employees. Disappointed, we began the process of shrinking our layout, but voiced concerns about accessibility. It was later that the penny finally dropped for the ROM. Eager to showcase their accessibility agenda, the critical question suddenly dawned on them: How would VIPs comfortably view the exhibit in that tiny space on opening night? Concerned that they would be "severely criticized" for a lack of accessibility, they found an alternative—overnight. If we delayed the opening by two months, we could have the more generous "west wing." We were grateful. We needed the time. And they saved themselves the embarrassment.

Having won that battle, we proceeded towards a grand opening. The invitation to bring the exhibit into the ROM had come with an explicit promise of an evening celebration. Deep into planning, however, we were confronted with a last-minute proposal to replace the much-anticipated evening gala with a scaled down midday coffee party. Was it because ours was a community exhibit (not a blockbuster), and we were a disability group (not prospective donors), that the promise of a gala could be so easily rescinded? If the word "negotiate" is large enough to contain within it elements of protest, anger, disappointment, and betrayal, this is what we expressed to our ROM partners. A reversal of fortune was ultimately assisted by a successful approach to our university president, who saw the strategic importance of the gala and offered to share the costs.

Designing the guest list was another contested arena. Both sides agreed to submit an equal number of names. But almost immediately this 50-50 split did not feel equitable. The museum's list included prominent citizens and members of boards and committees who frequently receive invitations to openings and decline a good many. On the community/ university side, invitations of this sort were rare and eagerly sought-after. We tried but failed to get a larger share. It was only when the electronic invitation was circulated that we saw our chance and seized it, snowballing the evites to swell our numbers and fill the gallery to capacity. RSVPs flooded into central booking from guests whose names appeared on no list at all, our allies and friends who were determined to be part of this historic moment.

On opening night, the gala welcomed 350 people, many from the disability community, who rolled up on the red carpet and took the Crystal elevator to the third floor where they were greeted like royalty. It was a ritzy event with a menu that boasted an "upscale take" on some old classics, all passed around by servers. At our behest attention was paid to allergies and food ingredients, to bi-level cruiser tables, café tables, bars at various heights, and hors d'oeuvres requiring minimal dexterity. As the celebration soared, only a handful of us knew that this extraordinary evening came perilously close to not happening.

Arriving: Catherine

Linton describes one effect of disabled people's arrival in the public commons as "upping the ante on the demands for a truly inclusive society."[29] One major curatorial contribution to this "upping" unfolded in our quietly activist efforts to set a high bar for exhibit access. All texts were produced in Braille, large print, and audio formats. Supplementary verbal descriptions of the exhibit's visual elements were prepared precisely and evocatively, in a way that mirrored the tone and content of each installation.[30] Video and audio podcasts of American Sign Language (ASL)[31] and visual descriptive components were produced for the Web, YouTube, and Facebook distribution. Replica artifacts[32] had been procured by contributors and would be available for tactile examination by audience members with visual impairments. Supplementary programming would include a major public lecture on "Blindness at the Museum" by international author and scholar Georgina Kleege,[33] followed by a live staged reading of exhibit descriptions and texts. Our ASL translation represented a breakthrough in Deaf cultural content:[34] the interpreters were themselves culturally Deaf, their translation achieving a level of depth and fluency impossible in the signed English that is customary for such productions.

But a partnership forged in the pressure cooker of eleventh-hour coordination buckled under the stress of an "ante" unilaterally—and perhaps somewhat naively— "upped." Weeks passed before a mounted flat-screen monitor could be pressed into service for our ASL video in an anteroom adjacent to—but not inside—the exhibit. Wall-mount boxes for Braille materials took a heartbreakingly long time to appear, and, once installed, their contents were easily carried off and could not be promptly restocked. Touch-table displays could not be secured and were therefore locked away and brought out only when volunteers were present to supervise their handling; the scheduling of these tactile opportunities remained sporadic and mostly inscrutable. Exhibit-specific training of volunteers was overlooked until a chance encounter with one of the exhibit curators made such training an urgent concern.[35] Audience members turned out to be not in the habit of downloading podcasts to their own iPods before visiting the museum, and of the two units available for loan at the museum information desk, one that disappeared early in the exhibit's run was never replaced. Many visitors were unfamiliar with iPods, and unable for various reasons to operate them successfully to access the exhibit text; many Deaf visitors who were highly savvy at text messaging did not own video-capable units. Visitors with cognitive and learning impairments experienced the exhibit as "textually dense" and "too difficult to penetrate without significant support."[36]

Still, *Out from Under* offered us a glimpse of an utterly dazzling ante. As gala guests poured in to the foyer of the steel and glass ROM Crystal—an extraordinary 10-storey structure of self-supporting crystalline shapes with no right angles and only one vertical surface[37]—they encountered a 4,800-square-foot projection onto a massive overhead wall. There, in the soundless eloquence of ASL, the premiere screening of our magnificent video privileged Deaf visitors with a sneak preview of what was to come and signalled to all, in proportions equal to the moment, a clear triumph of upstart prerogative.

Arriving, evidently, is merely where the journey begins.

CONCLUSION

To conclude, we return you to the exhibit's opening gala, a scene that Melanie set with her delicious backstory. This was our finest hour. As the champagne flowed, in our finale for the formal ceremony, Christine and Catherine riffed through a kind of syncopated spoken-word anthem, free-associating from the phrases "We remember," "We celebrate," and "We welcome." With a sly grin, Catherine called out, "Tonight, we remember that we belong, and that *belonging looks good on us*."

Intended as radical incantation, the words affirmed the pride and place of an uppity rabble. We had arrived in significant number, and our presence was unmistakably consequential. There was much in this occasion to evoke Simi Linton's now-classic narration of a community having summoned "the temerity to emerge":

> We have come out not with brown woolen lap robes over our withered legs or dark glasses over our pale eyes but in shorts and sandals, in overalls and business suits, dressed for play and work—straightforward, unmasked, and unapologetic. We are, as Crosby, Stills, and Nash told their Woodstock audience, letting our "freak flag fly."... We may drool, hear voices, speak in staccato syllables, wear catheters to collect our urine, or live with a compromised immune system.... We have found one another and found a voice to express not despair at our fate but outrage at our social positioning.[38]

Out from Under at the ROM was not business as usual. That much was clear as our guests strutted their stuff on the red carpet, hooted their approval when Catherine spoke of celebrating "our kick-ass spirit," and generally revelled in the superlatives of the occasion. Together, we were celebrating not so much the opening of an exhibit as the rise of a body politic.

NOTES

* An earlier version of this chapter was published in *Re-Presenting Disability: Activism and Agency in the Museum*, edited by Richard Sandell, Jocelyn Dodd, and Rosemarie Garland-Thomson (London and New York: Routledge, 2010). Our acknowledgement to Julie White, whose chapter entitled "Looking Back: A Brief History of Everything" in *Equity, Diversity, and Canadian Labour* (Toronto: University of Toronto Press, 2008) provided the inspiration for our chapter title.

1. *Out from Under* was created by 14 exhibitors working with 13 objects. They are as follows: Terry Poirier ("Digging"), Ruth Ruth Stackhouse ("Labouring"), Phaedra Livingstone ("Naming"), Sandra Phillips ("Dressing"), Carrie Fyfe ("Measuring"), Ryan Hutchins ("Fixing"), Sarah May Glyn Williams ("Packing"), Audrey King and Karen Yoshida ("Breathing"), Cindy Mitchell ("Remembering"), Kim Wrigley Archer ("Trailblazing"), Christine Brown ("Struggling"), Jihan Abbas ("Leading"), and Jim Derksen ("Aspiring").
2. Jihan Abbas et al., "Lights…Camera…Attitude! Introducing Disability Arts and Culture," occasional paper, Ryerson-RBC Institute for Disability Studies Research and Education, Ryerson University (2004); Catherine Frazee, "Disability Pride within Disability Performance," *Canadian Theatre Review*, no. 122 (Spring 2005): 10–12; Leslie G. Roman and Catherine Frazee, eds. "The Unruly Salon," *Review of Disability Studies* 5, no. 1 (Special Issue 2009).
3. http://www.abilitiesartsfestival.org.
4. The organizational vehicle we used for this work is the Ryerson-RBC Institute for Disability Studies Research and Education. The institute's contributions in cultivating both opportunity and audience for disability arts and culture are documented at www.ryerson.ca/ds/activism/performance.
5. Sheldon Levy, "Address to the Canadian Club of Toronto" (March 8, 2009).
6. Lennard Davis, *Bending Over Backwards: Disability, Dismodernism & Other Difficult Positions* (New York: New York Press, 2002), 35.
7. Rosemarie Garland-Thomson, "Ways of Staring," *Journal of Visual Culture* 5, no. 2 (2006): 173–92.
8. See Melanie Panitch, "Vision. Passion. Action: Launching an Activist Poster," *Abilities* (Fall 2004): 47.
9. Thanks to our colleague Tim Diamond for the phrasing.
10. Jocelyn Dodd et al., "Rethinking Disability Representation in Museums and Galleries," Research Centre for Museums and Galleries (RCMG), University of Leicester, 2008.
11. We had already experimented with this approach in several research projects of the Ryerson-RBC Institute for Disability Studies Research and Education. Instead of conventional

statistical sampling, which troubled us because of its underlying positivist assumptions of populations, norms, and categories, we worked with the notion of allowing participants in various environments to select themselves into (or out of) the "empty category" of disability. We then attended as part of our data collection to how that empirical category "filled up." (For more on the notion of using an empty category, see Making Care Visible Working Group, *Making Care Visible: Antiretroviral Therapy and the Health Work of People Living with HIV/AIDS* [Toronto: MCVWG, 2002]).
12. Asked to give a keynote address about this project to the Canadian Association for Women and Public History (2008), Kathryn discovered that the exhibit can also be interpreted "as an account in which gender and disability are present together, as they are in life."
13. Kathryn Church, "Making Disability History Public History: Can a Body of Activist History Find a Home in the Museum?" (Keynote address, annual conference of the Canadian Association of Women and Public History, Ottawa, November 2008).
14. Catherine Kohler Riessman, "Analysis of Personal Narratives," in *Handbook of Interview Research: Context and Method*, ed. Jaber F. Gubrium and James A. Holstein (Thousand Oaks, CA: Sage, 2002), 696, provides a useful summary of the "burgeoning literature on narrative [that] has touched almost every discipline and profession." We refer people to her chapter for more extensive referencing.
15. Dorothy Smith, *The Everyday World as Problematic: A Feminist Sociology* (Toronto: University of Toronto Press, 1987); Dorothy Smith, *Institutional Ethnography: A Sociology for People* (Lanham, MD: AltaMira, 2005); Marjorie DeVault and Liza McCoy, "Institutional Ethnography: Using Interviews to Investigate Ruling Relations," in *Handbook of Interview Research: Context and Method*, ed. Jaber F. Gubrium and James A. Holstein (Thousand Oaks, CA: Sage, 2002).
16. Melanie Panitch, *Disability, Mothers and Organization: Accidental Activists* (New York: Routledge, 2008).
17. Esther Ignagni and Kathryn Church, "One More Reason to Look Away? Ties and Tensions between Arts-Informed Inquiry and Disability Studies," in *Handbook of the Arts in Qualitative Social Science Research*, ed. Ardra Cole and J. Gary Knowles (Thousand Oaks, CA: Sage, 2008).
18. Michael Oliver, *The Politics of Disablement* (London: MacMillan, 1990); Carol Thomas, *Female Forms: Experiencing and Understanding Disability* (Buckingham, UK: Open University Press, 1999); Carol Thomas, *Sociologies of Disabilities and Illness: Contested Ideas in Disability Studies and Medical Sociology* (Houndsmills, Basingstoke, Hampshire: Palgrave MacMillan, 2007); Michael J. Prince, "Review Essay: Disability, Disability Studies and Citizenship," *Canadian Journal of Sociology* 29, no. 3 (2004): 459–67.
19. Tom Shakespeare, "Cultural Representation of Disabled People: Dustbins for Disavowal?" in *Disability Studies: Past, Present and Future*, ed. Len Barton and Mike Oliver (Leeds, UK: The Disability Press, 1997); Tom Shakespeare, *Help* (Birmingham: Venture Press, 2000); Richard Rieser, *Disabling Imagery* (London: British Film Institute, 2004); Tanya Titchkosky, *Reading and Writing Disability Differently* (Toronto: University of Toronto Press, 2007).
20. Melanie Panitch and Karen Yoshida, "Out from Under: Making Disability History Visible" (Inaugural Conference on Disability History: Theory and Practice, San Francisco State University, August 2008).
21. Historian Timothy Brook, *Vermeer's Hat: The Seventeenth Century and the Dawn of the Global World* (Toronto: Viking Canada, 2008), 9, describes this approach as follows: "When we think of paintings as windows, we treat the objects in them as two-dimensional details showing either that the past was different from what we know today, or that it is the same, again as though a photograph has been taken.... If we think of the objects in them not as props behind

windows but as doors to open, then we will find ourselves in passageways leading to discoveries about the seventeenth century world that the paintings on their own don't acknowledge, and of which the artist himself was unaware."

22. It is interesting to note how closely the exhibit mirrors the history told by other curators using more deductive means. We are thinking specifically of Dr. Sharon Snyder and Dr. David Mitchell, who were the moving force behind an exhibit of disability history in Chicago. Although our methodologies worked in opposite directions, each arrived at similar events, debates, and struggles. The exhibits mirrored each other across two nations.

23. An instructor at the Ontario College of Art and Design, Debbie Adams is also principal and creative director of Adams and Associates. In 2008, the Association of Registered Graphic Designers of Ontario recognized Debbie and her team with a design award for their work on *Out from Under*.

24. The curators wish to thank Jijian Voronka and Jenn Paterson, who were of invaluable assistance on a range of essential tasks through this period of time.

25. It is beyond the scope of this chapter to explore these commitments; however, their range is illustrated in the artists' statements found in the catalogue produced for the Royal Ontario Museum installation of the exhibition.

26. George Hein, *Learning in the Museum* (London: Routledge, 1998).

27. Hein, *Learning*.

28. William Thorsell, "The Museum as the Public Agora" (address to the Empire Club, Toronto, May 3, 2007).

29. Simi Linton, *Claiming Disability: Knowledge and Identity* (New York: New York University Press, 2008), 3.

30. Christine Brown, contributor of the installation titled "Labouring," authored a complete visual description of the exhibit after consultation with blind stakeholders and fellow contributors. David Reville, faculty member at the School of Disability Studies, subsequently performed an audio recording of these texts for CD and podcast distribution.

31. DVD: *Out from Under*, ASL Translation, produced by Ryerson University, School of Disability Studies, Toronto, 2008. ASL interpretation by Donovan Cooper and Giulio Schincariol, ASL/English consulting by Penny Schincariol and Gus Mancini.

32. Notable in this collective effort were the eBay bidding skills of Ryan Hutchins, contributor of the installation titled "Fixing." After Catherine suffered a crushing defeat in a bidding war for a rare and vitally important 1960 Stanford-Binet intelligence testing kit, Ryan saved the day when an eleventh-hour auction offered us one more chance to procure an exact replica for our touch table display.

33. Georgina Kleege, "Blindness at the Museum," (lecture presented at the Royal Ontario Museum, May 24, 2008).

34. For her creative vision, her expert guidance, and her meticulous efforts to preserve the poetics and nuanced meaning of the exhibit texts, we are grateful to Penny Schincariol, project coordinator.

35. On an informal visit to the exhibit one afternoon, Kathryn encountered a volunteer docent entertaining a small cluster of visitors at the "Labouring" installation. The man was explaining to his audience that the lives of the three women featured were likely quite different from the account that we advanced in our profile of 150 years of collective unpaid labour. "Notice that they lived to be quite old," he intoned. "They had food and a roof over their heads, which is more than many women had at that time. They did quite well for themselves; they were probably happier in the asylum than they would have been on the street." Needless to say, we insisted that he be moved to a different section of the museum.

36. Esther Ignagni and Jihan Abbas, "Media and Messages: Exploring Old and New Worlds of Developmental Disability and the Media," *Journal on Developmental Disabilities* 14, no. 3 (2008): 90; Jennifer Patterson, Tess Vo, and the Compass Youth, "Out from Under: Disability, History and Things to Remember," *Journal on Developmental Disabilities* 14, no. 3 (2008): 98–100.
37. Royal Ontario Museum. "Michael Lee-Chin Crystal," last modified May 2008, https://www.rom.on.ca/en/about-us/rom/michael-lee-chin-crystal.
38. Linton, *Claiming Disability*, 3–4.

BIBLIOGRAPHY

Abbas, Jihan, Kathryn Church, Catherine Frazee, and Melanie Panitch. "Lights…Camera…Attitude! Introducing Disability Arts and Culture." Occasional paper, Ryerson-RBC Institute for Disability Studies Research and Education, Ryerson University, 2004.

Brook, Timothy. *Vermeer's Hat: The Seventeenth Century and the Dawn of the Global World*. Toronto: Viking Canada, 2008.

Church, Kathryn. "Exhibiting as Inquiry: Travels of an Accidental Curator." In *Handbook of the Arts in Qualitative Social Science Research*, edited by Ardra L. Cole and J. Gary Knowles, 55–70. Thousand Oaks, CA: Sage, 2008.

Church, Kathryn. "Making Disability History Public History: Can a Body of Activist History Find a Home in the Museum?" Keynote address, annual conference of the Canadian Association of Women and Public History, Ottawa, November 2008.

Davis, Lennard. *Bending Over Backwards: Disability, Dismodernism & Other Difficult Positions*. New York: New York Press, 2002.

DeVault, Marjorie, and Liza McCoy. "Institutional Ethnography: Using Interviews to Investigate Ruling Relations." In *Handbook of Interview Research: Context and Method*, edited by Jaber F. Gubrium and James A. Holstein, 751–76. Thousand Oaks, CA: Sage, 2002.

Dodd, Jocelyn, Richard Sandell, Debbie Jolly, and Ceri Jones. "Rethinking Disability Representation in Museums and Galleries." Research Centre for Museums and Galleries (RCMG), University of Leicester, 2008.

Frazee, Catherine. "Disability Pride within Disability Performance." *Canadian Theatre Review*, no. 122 (Spring 2005): 10–12.

Garland-Thomson, Rosemarie. "Ways of Staring." *Journal of Visual Culture* 5, no. 2 (2006): 173–92.

Hein, George. *Learning in the Museum*. London: Routledge, 1998.

Ignagni, Esther, and Jihan Abbas. "Media and Messages: Exploring Old and New Worlds of Developmental Disability and the Media." *Journal on Developmental Disabilities* 14, no. 3 (2008): 90.

Ignagni, Esther, and Kathryn Church. "One More Reason to Look Away? Ties and Tensions between Arts-Informed Inquiry and Disability Studies." In *Handbook of the Arts in Qualitative Social Science Research*, edited by Ardra Cole and J. Gary Knowles, 625–38. Thousand Oaks, CA: Sage, 2008.

Kohler Riessman, Catherine. "Analysis of Personal Narratives." In *Handbook of Interview Research: Context and Method*, edited by Jaber F. Gubrium and James A. Holstein, 695–710. Thousand Oaks, CA: Sage, 2002.

Levy, Sheldon. "Address to the Canadian Club of Toronto." March 8, 2009.

Linton, Simi. *Claiming Disability: Knowledge and Identity*. New York: New York University Press, 2008.

Mactavish, Joan. *Bravo Miss Brown!* Toronto: Cavu, 2001.

Making Care Visible Working Group. *Making Care Visible: Antiretroviral Therapy and the Health Work of People Living with HIV/AIDS*. Toronto: MCVWG, 2002.

Oliver, Michael. *The Politics of Disablement*. London: MacMillan, 1990.

Panitch, Melanie. "Vision. Passion. Action: Launching an Activist Poster." *Abilities* (Fall 2004): 47.

Panitch, Melanie. *Disability, Mothers and Organization: Accidental Activists*. New York: Routledge, 2008.

Panitch, Melanie, and Karen Yoshida. "Out from Under: Making Disability History Visible." Inaugural Conference on Disability History: Theory and Practice, San Francisco State University, August 2008.

Patterson, Jennifer, Tess Vo, and the Compass Youth. "Out from Under: Disability, History and Things to Remember." *Journal on Developmental Disabilities* 14, no. 3 (2008): 98–100.

Prince, Michael J. "Review Essay: Disability, Disability Studies and Citizenship." *Canadian Journal of Sociology* 29, no. 3 (2004): 459–67.

Rieser, Richard. *Disabling Imagery*. London: British Film Institute, 2004.

Roman, Leslie G., and Catherine Frazee, eds. "The Unruly Salon." *Review of Disability Studies* 5, no. 1 (Special Issue 2009).

Sandell, Richard, Annie Delin, Jocelyn Dodd, and Jackie Gay. "Beggars, Freaks and Heroes? Museum Collections and the Hidden History of Disability." *Journal of Museum Management and Curatorship* 20, no. 1 (2005): 5–19.

Shakespeare, Tom. "Cultural Representation of Disabled People: Dustbins for Disavowal?" In *Disability Studies: Past, Present and Future*, edited by Len Barton and Mike Oliver, 217–33. Leeds, UK: Disability Press, 1997.

Shakespeare, Tom. *Help*. Birmingham: Venture Press, 2000.

Smith, Dorothy. *The Everyday World as Problematic: A Feminist Sociology*. Toronto: University of Toronto Press, 1987.

Smith, Dorothy. *Institutional Ethnography: A Sociology for People*. Lanham, MD: AltaMira, 2005.

Thomas, Carol. *Female Forms: Experiencing and Understanding Disability*. Buckingham, UK: Open University Press, 1999.

Thomas, Carol. *Sociologies of Disabilities and Illness: Contested Ideas in Disability Studies and Medical Sociology*. Houndsmills, Basingstoke, Hampshire: Palgrave MacMillan, 2007.

Thorsell, William. "The Museum as the Public Agora." Address to the Empire Club, Toronto, May 3, 2007.

Titchkosky, Tanya. *Reading and Writing Disability Differently*. Toronto: University of Toronto Press, 2007.

White, Julie. "Looking Back: A Brief History of Everything." In *Equity, Diversity, and Canadian Labour*, edited by Gerald Hunt and Derek Rayside, 25–48. Toronto: University of Toronto Press, 2008.

CHAPTER 2

Posthumous Exploitation? The Ethics of Researching, Writing, and Being Accountable as a Disability Historian

Geoffrey Reaume

INTRODUCTION

Reading psychiatric patients' files includes looking at the most private information likely in existence about an individual, including personal letters by and about the person whom the file documents. This is something that I have done and continue to do as part of my work as a historian who has researched hundreds of patient files of people who were patients at the former Toronto Asylum for the Insane during the late nineteenth and early twentieth centuries.[1] Given my own personal psychiatric history during my teens and involvement in the Toronto psychiatric survivor community, I approach this topic from interconnecting personal, academic, and activist angles. A few people have asked over the years whether this kind of historical research is a form of therapy. My response is usually, "No. It is not therapy. It is history." It is no more a form of therapy than someone from any particular background researching aspects of a history with which they are personally engaged to gain some understanding and knowledge of a group of people whose perspectives have been under-represented. One wonders, for example, whether working-class historians who write labour history are asked if they focus on this topic as a form of therapy. Let's hope not. The assumption is that the archives reading room has become a metaphorical therapist's couch.[2] If that is the case, then a lot of historians, well beyond disability history, are in therapy by dint of researching topics that have touched us personally at some point in our lives. In any case, the underlying point is that personal experiences inform research topics, and so too does our emotional and ethical response to what historians find and write about. There is nothing wrong with this; in fact, it is a good thing and it is not unique to any particular area of history. But it should not be pathologized as being a form of *therapy*, a term that is particularly patronizing for someone doing disability history.

When thinking about the ethical issues that are the focus of this paper, it helps to remember the comments a fellow historian made to me during my doctoral dissertation defence when we were discussing the ethics of reading private patient records found in the archives: "Historians are nosy." How much is our nosiness influenced by a desire to unearth the lived experiences of forgotten disabled people while at the same time trying to bring the past to a wider audience in the hope of changing attitudes about the people we write about? To what extent are we as disability historians accountable to the communities from which this history originates?[3]

Before addressing the ethical issues behind these questions, it is important to acknowledge that this topic is not new. The administrative interception of personal letters written by insane asylum inmates and the right to have some control over what is recorded in one's medical file were areas of concern for patients' rights advocates from the second half of the nineteenth century. Activists in the Alleged Lunatics' Friend Society in Britain during the mid-1800s demanded that asylum inmates have the right to record their own views in their files about whether they should be confined, while ex-asylum-inmate activist Elizabeth Packard campaigned in the United States for unimpeded letter mailing rights of patients following 1863 when she was released.[4] They were thus demanding that their histories be written from their own perspectives long before the field of disability history existed. Asylum authorities rationalized the confiscation of private letters on the basis of a person's mental state, claiming they were either doing the person a favour—particularly female patients—by preventing their mad thoughts from being read by correspondents, should they ever be released and returned to the world outside. Letters were also regularly confiscated with the claim that such documents provided valuable insights into a person's clinical state. Needless to say, one of the prime unwritten reasons letters were confiscated was because they often reported on abuses within the asylum and gave otherwise unflattering details of daily life there.[5]

Ironically, this material, originally taken from both the authors and whomever they were writing to, now exists to document the lives of people whose voices would, in most cases, be lost to us had these letters not been confiscated. This is hardly a reason to be grateful for this act of emotional cruelty on the part of the asylum superintendents and their staff. It is, however, a compelling reason to ensure such letters are used with the utmost care and respect. It also raises ethical issues for everyone who uses such records. In my own research, people who have been psychiatric patients, past and present, have raised the issue of whether such private confiscated letters or any kind of confidential material should ever be used, in contrast to published work, such as a personal memoir intended for a reading public. This question of whether to use or not to use confiscated letters relates as well to all documents in a person's clinical file. The contrast between the value of first-person accounts in case files needs to be juxtaposed with the fact that these confiscated letters written by asylum inmates to a spouse, sibling, child, parent, or relative of any kind, as well as to friends and lawyers, among others outside the institution, were never intended by their authors to be seen by anyone except those to whom these letters were addressed. This chapter will argue that confidential private documents can and should be carefully used by researchers to uncover disability history, so long as this work is integrated into the community to whom this history belongs. Doing so will make historians more accountable to people who have, heretofore, been left out of the historical record, and will instead include them in the discussion of what this history means for people most directly affected today.

SENSITIVE SOURCES: SELECTION OF PERSPECTIVES PAST AND THE ETHICS OF CHOICE

Selecting sources for any historical project is fraught with methodological minefields in which self-selectivity can slant an interpretation in particular ways that show a person in the best—or worst—possible light. In regard to disability history, and mad people's history in particular, it is essential to avoid the great person point of view, or one that presents people to whom we may otherwise be sympathetic, in a rosy light devoid of prejudices and moral failings. Ultimately, all primary source research used in any study is a matter of selective choice, but in the case of using confiscated letters, the choice also relates to either liberating a voice ruthlessly silenced by administrative fiat or continuing the silence perhaps forever unless someone else uses these same sources. Even the term "liberated" needs to be used with care. How do we know that people whose letters were confiscated would want their letters to be "liberated" for all to read long after they are dead? It can reasonably be assumed that some of these people would not have wanted their letters published, even anonymously. What about people whom we have developed an admiration for in certain respects but who express bigotry or are recorded in physically degrading situations? I will admit that in some instances, I chose to not include primary source information that, I felt, would have degraded the memory of certain patients—for example, in the case of two people who were recorded as consuming parts of their own human waste and bodily fluids. It appeared to me unnecessarily voyeuristic to record this about individuals whose lives were being discussed at the Toronto Asylum, and it would add nothing further to their own stories beyond what had already been included in the historical narrative about them.

On the other hand, after much thought, I included a reference to a rat literally chewing at the remains of 23-year-old Evelyn F. the night she died in 1909, while also degrading and disgusting, to indicate the wretched conditions under which patients lived and died and to give an idea of the overall lack of hygiene in the asylum.[6] These choices were editorial decisions; in the first instance, the decision was meant to prevent the denigration of particular patients in a way that would not have added significantly to the stories of who they were as people. In the second instance, admittedly degrading evidence was introduced into the historical published record in a way that showed the institution in a particularly poor light given the conditions under which Evelyn F. died and how her remains were left in such a disrespectful state. As the study was intended to be a respectful, and critical, interpretation of the lives of inmates, rather than an honorific discussion of the asylum, primary source evidence was selected in this case to understand the last hours of a forgotten patient in the wider context of a cold institution. These are not so much lost voices from the past, but are lost experiences that need to be recorded if the conditions of the asylum are to be more fully understood. At the same time, it needs to be acknowledged that undertaking this work can be "difficult hunting," as Matthew Warshauer and Michael Sturges wrote about their two-year struggle to obtain access to Connecticut state asylum records for Civil War veterans who experienced post-traumatic stress disorder.[7] Even though research like this is intended to *lessen* the posthumous and contemporary prejudices towards people with disabilities, privacy and confidentiality laws can have the effect of perpetuating discrimination by the guardians of such records, who claim offence may be taken by families if people knew their descendants who had been in an insane asylum were written about in a historical study, and thus stopping such research from taking place.[8] Part of this ethical conflict relates to power dynamics over who has control of these primary sources; however, part of it is also related to the emotional response readers have to reading this history, and that applies to primary source researchers who find this material as well.

THE INFLUENCE OF EMOTIONAL IMPACT ON DOCUMENT SELECTION

It is important to note the emotional impact of primary source records on researchers in regard to how we make our choices as disability historians. The emotional impact of some records can stay with a researcher long after reading them and can influence whose stories are included in a historical narrative. Take photographs for instance. Since most of the patient files examined for my study on the Toronto Asylum are about people who were admitted in the late nineteenth and early twentieth centuries, most of these case files do not include photos of asylum inmates. With a very few exceptions, nearly all of the photos that do exist in these files are of elderly men and women that were taken in the 1930s, not long before their deaths in most instances. The photos were placed in the front of their files for identification purposes. Immediately upon opening some of these records, a grainy black-and-white photo of the person about whom the file concerned presented itself to the reader. Whenever such photos were found in a file, I kept them directly in front of me while reading and compiling information, kind of like someone who keeps a memorable photo of someone on their desk at home or in an office. Looking at their images, and having them "watch me," so to speak, while reading about them, provided a connection and sense of empathy for the person whose life I was peering into. It was also rather humbling to see them right in front of me knowing that I had access to records about them that they would never even have even seen themselves, such as clinical entries and letters sent to administrators about the individual from people outside the hospital, including family members.

It was, however, the letters, particularly confiscated patient letters, that had the greatest impact upon my reading them. Some letters contained humour, as was the case with Mary A., who wrote a poem after her release (which was therefore not confiscated) in which she gently chided her former doctor for his practice of staring at people—an ex-inmate's critique of the medical gaze.[9] Not surprisingly, most letters from inmates were not humorous, but instead expressed mental anguish about their situation or discussed abuse in the asylum. It was therefore particularly poignant to read and reflect upon letters intended for people who never had the opportunity to see them, from individuals who would never receive a response. Considering that letters were written by patients and intended for recipients who often had neither the resources nor time to travel to the asylum on a regular basis, particularly rural families who lived outside Toronto, it is hard to imagine the distress of inmates who waited for a response to a letter their correspondent never received. But if a researcher is to begin to understand history from the perspectives of confined people, imagine this anguish is what they should try to do. It is considerations like this that help to motivate the inclusion of a letter in a historical study, such as that from Ralph M. to "My very Dear Wife," which she did not receive before his death at the age of 70 in 1911 and which was found in his file over 80 years later.[10] Thinking about the unknowable anguish of Ralph, who sent a letter to his wife whom he clearly loved and never received a response to this letter because it was confiscated, is a motivating factor in choosing this document to illustrate his life as an asylum patient, although we can never really know what kind of anguish he and his wife endured because of this letter that was stolen from both of them.

The same is true for patients like Alex C., who complained about their writings being confiscated in letters that were then taken from them and placed in their files, where they were found decades later. Alex wrote dozens of letters campaigning to be released; these letters exist for 5 of the 38 years he was confined. Coming across these letters decades later elicits sympathy for a man whose thoughts were hidden away in his file, never to reach those for whom they were intended, something he commented on in some of his letters when he wondered about what happened to his earlier writing. Yet, reading Alex's overall file also elicits other feelings that are anything but sympathetic. His anti-Catholic prejudices and his abuse of his wife, Louisa, which prompted his confinement, present him as someone for whom it is difficult to feel sympathetic when all of the evidence is placed in front of us.[11] When reading a file about a person like Alex for whom sympathy is engendered in some areas—confiscation of his mail and intense mental anguish—while offence is engendered elsewhere—spousal abuse and religious bigotry—it is important that selectivity does not exclude the frankly repellent side of a person whose past we are recording. To do otherwise is to create, at best, a selective, romanticized, one-sided version of individuals like Alex for whom sympathy would be easy to create if the unsavory aspects of his life were excluded. What is needed when writing a history that is predicated on an empathetic foundation is a portrait that presents disabled people as multi-faceted individuals, who could be and were as offensive as anyone else. Empathy needs to avoid making disabled historical subjects solely into victims of administrative fiat, as Alex certainly was in regards to the way his letters were confiscated. He was also a person who victimized people around him, not least his wife, which led to a 30-year estrangement, only for them to visit again in his last years, along with the Catholics whom this ardent Orangeman loathed, though this too trails off as he gets older. In short, Alex was not a very nice man to be around. It might seem odd to make this point when mad people have generally been portrayed in history as less than pleasant, and indeed much of this history is to counter gross stereotypes from the past.[12] Yet, in countering such stereotypes, historians also need to avoid romanticizing disability history by filling in previously blank pages, or stereotyped images, with selective positive portrayals of those we write about empathetically when evidence creates a less than flattering portrait.

For researchers who are intent on showing a far different perspective, however, one in which mad people were not and are not the violent people that they have so often been depicted as, nor disabled people more generally as objects of both pity and scorn, this does not mean leaving out unpleasant aspects of the story that we should not be surprised exist among a group of people we seek to show in a more dignified way.[13] Dignity does not mean denial of historical evidence, no matter how much it challenges our own desire to write a history that gives a fuller, more positive understanding of those we research and write about. Accuracy is a basic requirement of this work if a full, honest, and rigorous history of neglected people from the past is to be recorded. Only by ensuring that unsympathetic as well as sympathetic aspects of a person or group of people are included in our histories will it be possible to combat the negative stereotypes that portray mad and disabled people as caricatures rather than like everyone else, with the positive attributes, faults, and grey areas that make up most of what it means to be human.

It is also important to note that the stories of the people we are writing about can be inspiring or worthy of respectfully acknowledging in some way, an idea that some disabled people regard as patronizing.[14] While individuals have every right to make such a criticism of how disabled people are viewed today, it is worth reflecting on how this critique needs to be reconsidered when placed in historical perspective. There is a lot to be gained by looking with admiration upon the lives and struggles of people in disability history in a way that avoids romanticizing them while also recognizing their usually ignored contributions within their own communities. In doing so, we can find ways of ensuring our collective mad and disabled past is read and understood by people who would otherwise have learned nothing about those who had been previously ignored. Revealing various sides of a person, including negative aspects, only shows how much disabled and mad people are like the rest of humanity as multi-faceted human beings. Uncovering our past should never be about hagiography, but should always be about revealing history in all its complexity and difficulty; this applies to the stories of disabled people whom we might otherwise admire and wish to portray sympathetically. It is also a way of ensuring that disabled people are included in standard historical references, such as the *Dictionary of Canadian Biography*, where Alice G., who was an inmate of the Toronto Asylum for the Insane for 45 years until her death in 1938, is included along with well-known politicians, artists, and industrialists, among others, whose establishment credentials were beyond anything she could have known in her lifetime.[15] The ethics of choice also refers to what to include for publication and where to try to get published in an effort to ensure that this history is not only for the "converted" but also available in places where disability history has not previously appeared.[16]

WHO DO RESEARCHERS THINK WE ARE TO USE PRIVATE DOCUMENTS ABOUT DISABLED PEOPLE?

All of this about the need to recover and write about our past sounds very good. But how do we respond when some people to whom this history belongs do not want to have this history uncovered—not, at least, by using unpublished records of deceased disabled people who had no say in what happens to these records? This raises the issue of accountability within the disability and mad communities. Academic research has historically been an inter-elite enterprise involving peers and institutions, such as universities and archives, that, in most cases, do not include people with disabilities in making decisions about who has access to the primary source material of deceased people from state-run institutions.[17] This has led to criticism about the ethics of this work.

About a decade ago, a person who identified as having a psychiatric history asked me, in so many words, "Who are you to use patient files without the permission of people whose lives they describe?" No matter how careful, sensitive, and respectful a researcher may be about the lives of people we write about, this person argued, it will always be unethical to use this material about people who have no choice in how their lives are written about, even with identifiers removed as required by privacy legislation. Furthermore, academic researchers, like myself, with self-interest were criticized for making a career, and hence money, off the lives of individuals who can never benefit materially from academic research given that they are long since dead. Thus, one could argue that all the talk about liberating our past and empowering ourselves to use this history does not escape the fact that latter-day researchers are exploiting the written remains of the very people we research and write about, many of whom were exploited while they were alive. Therefore, historical research using information from psychiatric patient files of any kind—including intercepted letters and clinical reports—is a form of posthumous exploitation.

How to address these criticisms? First, it has to be admitted that there is much substance to this criticism. Academic historians and researchers of any kind who use the files of disabled people confined in institutions, like the private unpublished writings of any person, are trying to tell a story that benefits us as we proceed to research, publish, and speak about the individuals we study, no matter what part of the past we examine. Such a criticism could also be levelled at a researcher studying any aspect of history that includes use of confidential, private documents. Yet, this criticism has a particular resonance for disability history, and in the case of the work I have been primarily engaged with, mad people's history. This is because of the well-known exploitation of people deemed mad or mentally disabled, and the historical exclusion of asylum inmates from any form of decision about their treatment.

While I have argued in presentations and papers that using this material is a way of liberating buried histories of mad people who were ruthlessly silenced in their own lives, there is no doubt that this work is done without the permission of the people whose histories are being described and upon whom academics, like myself, are building our careers.[18]

The liberation of patients' past stories can just as easily be construed as an imposition upon those who never asked to be so freed from the mists of time by an academic who employs such heroic terminology as a historical rescuer to justify my own academic career. One could further argue that leaving deceased asylum inmates in peace, which few of them had in their own lifetimes, is fairer to their memory and dignity than using them in public venues where none of them chose to participate.

One response to these criticisms is to argue that the very nature of historical scholarship involves writing about people who have not given permission to be written about, other than those who are engaged in public activities of any kind and can expect some kind of historical accounting, or who have participated in contemporary research such as oral histories. Most historians from any field of study, however, write about people who are dead and who are never going to have a say in how or whether they wish to be remembered. Indeed, most social history, where mad people's history and disability history springs from, engages histories of neglected peoples and by its very nature seeks to publicly discuss those social groups whose lives have heretofore been hidden from public view or seriously under-represented. This includes the urban working class, subsistence farmers, slaves, prisoners, Indigenous populations, ethnic and racialized communities, women and gender minorities, and gays, lesbians, and transgendered people, among many others. With the exception of the most privileged members of some of these communities who left published memoirs and participated in public life while alive—a tiny minority of these groups—it is a safe bet to assume that large numbers of previously neglected people whose experiences and lives researchers seek to understand would not have given permission for their histories to be told, especially when it comes to details deemed private or personal (acknowledging that such concepts are fluid and have changed significantly over time and place). They would not have even been asked for such permission during their own lifetimes since the officials who compiled such material were unlikely to care about seeking consent for the views of marginalized people. Instead, often the major problem is locating such stories in the first place, as so much was not recorded, especially prior to the late nineteenth century when literacy rates were quite low for the majority of people. Thus, such historical records about socially marginalized people, especially rare first-person accounts, are considered to be a gold mine by historical researchers like myself.

But does this desire to right a historical wrong by taking seriously those who were dismissed or ignored during their own lifetime and, further, to try to combat prejudices that persist about people who belong to such groups today by telling these stories respectfully justify use of such material without the permission of those whom it is about? If permission by the deceased were the litmus test for the use of unpublished records created by or about dead people, there would not be much history left to tell. All that would be left is the publicly available material created by elites throughout most of history. Even in this regard, there is documentary evidence created by elites, such as private correspondence, which the creators did not leave permission for later researchers to use.[19] Yet, there is likely to be far more will to protect the privacy of the mass of poor people whom these questions concern, who never had any material or class advantages in their life, as was the case with most asylum inmates in public institutions. There is a moral imperative to protect from posthumous exploitation people at the bottom of the social ladder in history, no matter what their background, that is far more compelling than exists for elites who, after all, did so much of the exploiting. Indeed, it can be argued that there is no comparable analogy between using the private records of elites and those of, or about, socially marginalized peoples in history since the former had advantages in life that the latter did not. Thus, using such records is also influenced by the nature of whose lives we are looking at, rather than solely the issue of private documents in themselves.[20]

DEVELOPING AN ETHICS OF ACCOUNTABILITY IN DISABILITY HISTORY RESEARCH AND WRITING

While no response will satisfy those on all sides of this issue, an argument can be made that there is an ethics of accountability that is being developed by those who ask very difficult questions of historians—just who do we think we are to access such private material about deceased socially marginalized people who have no choice in who sees their posthumous records and how they are portrayed in public accounts? While I do not agree that such access, when safeguarded by privacy legislation, is itself unethical and can never be justified, it is important to understand where these arguments come from and what can be done to address them, even if not to everyone's satisfaction. As mentioned previously, the criticisms mentioned above stem from the long history of exploitation and abuse of confined mad people and from personal experiences of having one's views and ideas dismissed, of having personal privacy violated within the psychiatric system, and of having little or no say in what happens in terms of one's personal treatment.[21] Vulnerability to further lack of control over one's own experiences, in this case posthumously as written up by a historian, is what forms the basis of this criticism regarding the use of private, unpublished psychiatric patient records. It also relates to who researchers are accountable to among the community these documents represent. No one has elected a historian, such as myself, to go into an archives, research private medical files, and tell this history. While one could argue that we are accountable to our professors and peers in the academy, if that is where this research originates as a dissertation, thesis, or other form of publication afterwards, this limits the discussion to the academic elite of which we are a part.[22]

It is important to widen this accountability circle to include people beyond the academy for whom these documents are not a distant historical memory turned into contemporary scholarship, but part of their life today. This includes, at its most basic and obvious, making presentations in communities that are directly affected by this history, which should be done in a way that is accessible to all (e.g., avoiding academic jargon). It is also essential to work with people who want to interpret this history, including individuals to whom this history most directly belongs—in this case, psychiatric patients, consumers, survivors, and mad people. The practicality of how to do this involves years of work within the communities concerned and should avoid a top-down attitude of "historians (or academics) know best." Being involved with grassroots groups where it is acceptable to do so—recognizing that there will be times when it is not acceptable to be a part of such groups, given the long-justified suspicions about academic researchers' motives—is important to develop trust and working relationships over a long period. Historians who work for years researching and writing about disabled or mad people's pasts should strive to become a part of that community by attending public events and engaging people with their history in a way that makes them feel they have some connection to it. It is through this sort of "active history" within the communities we write about that a sense of accountability can be developed by ensuring that our work is integrated as part of the group of people we are writing about today and is not an outside product delivered to those who might otherwise be expected to be passive partakers of what is their own historical heritage.[23] At the same time, it is recognized that it will not always be possible for some researchers to work with people in a community over many years due to geographical distance or life circumstances, such as family responsibilities, financial difficulties, or disabling experiences of various kinds, which can prevent this sort of direct engagement. Yet, perhaps, sharing information over the Internet (assuming such technology is available, though this is not always so) or holding on-site meetings to discuss this historical work over time will allow some form of dialogue and accountability to develop. There is also an additional challenge for researchers whose studies are geographically dispersed rather than localized in a particular place (like the Toronto Asylum), which raises further issues of sharing of information and fostering accountability. Whatever form sharing this knowledge takes, criticism from outside of the academy from the people about whom our history is focused should be part of the accountability process and should be actively encouraged through public dialogue.

Naming people is also an essential part of this interpretation, even where a pseudonym is legally required to publish information about an asylum inmate as it is in Ontario for 100 years after their death. In her article on the Canton Asylum for Insane Indians with a particular focus on a Dakota woman, Elizabeth Alexis Fairbault, who was an inmate there from 1915–1928, Susan Burch describes ethical issues involved in this research: "What and how much to reveal remains an ethical challenge for those privileged with access to these sources.... Although the names of members held at the Canton Asylum are available to the public in various sources, this work only includes actual names in the cases where family members have granted me permission to use them. This is guided by ethical considerations and attention to the histories of conquest, genocide, oppression, and dislocation that the people described in this work—and their communities—have experienced and the ways that academic disciplines have contributed to this marginalization. Descendants of Elizabeth Alexis Fairbault wanted me to use their relatives' names."[24] In other jurisdictions like Ontario, where it is illegal to contact family members of people whose asylum records are found in the archives, asking relatives' permission to use family names is not possible. Nevertheless, it is possible to make the existence of these histories more widely available in the hope that family members and communities to which they belonged will be able to reconnect and honour disabled and mad people's contributions to our understanding of the past.[25]

What this involves is a never-ending process. The attempt to engage people with their own history should continue as long as we care about how we practice our craft and who is able to access a collective past that belongs on the street corner and in local community centres as much as in a university lecture hall or on a library shelf. How to interest people in this history is also part of our job. There are plenty of disabled people who are interested in their history and who have much to add to what academics are doing if we take the time to engage them by using our mutual skills and knowledge to benefit our interpretation of this past, including those to whom it belongs. In other words, we must get away from the idea that the way in which we do historical work is only accountable to other academics. Instead, historians of disability need to engage disabled people outside the academy with regards our ethical obligations to people whose history we are researching and writing. This will not resolve the critique that forms the basis of this paper regarding the posthumous exploitation of mad people's asylum records. There are also times when such efforts to create community historical engagement will not work for a variety of reasons; this can be a learning experience to improve upon, and it can at least be acknowledged that an effort at accountability has been made, which is better than no attempt at all. Ultimately, disability historians need to engage people from the communities we are studying today to ensure we listen to their critical voices about the nature and purpose of our work, just as we strive to document disabled people's voices from the past.

NOTES

1. Geoffrey Reaume, *Remembrance of Patients Past: Patient Life at the Toronto Hospital for the Insane, 1870–1940* (Toronto: Oxford University Press, 2000; University of Toronto Press, 2009, 2010).
2. In the seven years that I saw psychiatrists, psychologists, and social workers, I never once saw, let alone lay down on, a therapist's couch. The appointments took place in regular chairs.
3. For a related discussion on research in various types of cases files, see Karen Dubinsky, "Telling Stories about Dead People," in *On The Case: Explorations in Social History*, ed. France Iacovetta and Wendy Mitchinson (Toronto: University of Toronto Press, 1998), 359–66.
4. Nicholas Hervey, "Advocacy or Folly: The Alleged Lunatics' Friend Society, 1845–63," *Medical History* 30, no. 3 (July 1986): 258; Barbara Sapinsley, *The Private War of Mrs. Packard* (New York: Paragon House, 1991), 180–82, 190–92, 212. See also Linda V. Carlisle, *Elizabeth Packard: A Noble Fight* (Urbana: University of Illinois Press, 2010), 172, 174–75.
5. Reaume, *Remembrance of Patients Past*, 73–91; Geoffrey Reaume, "Accounts of Abuse of Patients at the Toronto Hospital for the Insane, 1883–1937," *Canadian Bulletin of Medical History* 14, no. 1 (1997): 65–106.
6. Reaume, *Remembrance of Patients Past*, 239–40.
7. Matthew Warshauer and Michael Sturges, "Difficult Hunting: Accessing Connecticut Patient Records to Learn about Post-Traumatic Stress Disorder during the Civil War," *Civil War History* 59, no. 4 (December 2013): 419–52. While their efforts were ultimately successful for the research they were undertaking, the authors note that the state legislature soon thereafter

passed a new law that removed access to these records for future historical investigation.
8. Warshauer and Sturges ("Difficult Hunting," 435–36) record how it was pointed out to Connecticut state officials that their research focused on Civil War veterans, most of whom had been dead for over 100 years, and that there was no reason for the public to take offence at the knowledge that post-traumatic stress disorder occurred among these soldiers. It was also pointed out to state authorities that this historical research is a matter of public interest in terms of trying to understand the history of a mental disability that was little understood at the time and that continues to be a source of public concern.
9. Mary's poem was as follows: "Oh my Dr Clare why do you stare/At the people whom you meet/It is so rude for you to glare/at them in the Street/and when you have done your staring/I am sure you must be tired/To have to do so much Glaring/at every little child." Reaume, *Remembrance of Patients Past*, 220.
10. Ralph M.'s letter is dated "Decr 9th" but there is no year. It was found in his file, along with other confiscated letters from the time of his confinement, 1898–1911 (Reaume, *Remembrance of Patients Past*, 77–78).
11. See references to Alex C., his letters, and his wife, Louisa, in Reaume, *Remembrance of Patients Past*, 67, 89–90, 220–22, 285–86 note 111, 315 note 416; and also in Geoffrey Reaume, "Keep Your Labels Off My Mind! Or 'Now I Am Going to Pretend I Am Craze but Dont Be a Bit Alarmed': Psychiatric History from the Patients' Perspectives," *Canadian Bulletin of Medical History* 11, no. 2 (1994): 408–12.
12. For a discussion of stereotypes about mad people in historical accounts, see Geoffrey Reaume, "Portraits of People with Mental Disorders in English Canadian History," *Canadian Bulletin of Medical History* 17, no. 1/2 (2000): 93–125.
13. Reaume, "Portraits of People with Mental Disorders."
14. Harilyn Rousso, *Don't Call Me Inspirational: A Disabled Feminist Talks Back* (Philadelphia: Temple University Press, 2013).
15. Geoffrey Reaume, "Alice G" (1854–1938, Toronto Asylum Inmate Labourer), *Dictionary of Canadian Biography, Volume XVI (1931–40)* (University of Toronto/Université Laval, 2016). Accessed on March 8, 2017, http://www.biographi.ca/en/bio/g_alice_16E.html.
16. For an early disability historiographical survey from the United States about the need to publish in standard historical references, see Catherine J. Kudlick, "Disability History: Why We Need Another 'Other,'" *American Historical Review* 108, no. 3 (June 2003): 763–93.
17. I am only referring to documents contained in archives that were created about disabled people in state institutions. I am not referring here to more recent collections of oral history transcripts and recordings that have involved the willing participation of people with disabilities who were and are interviewed for such purposes. See, for example, Karen Hirsch, "Culture and Disability: The Role of Oral History," in *The Oral History Reader*, ed. Robert Perks and Alistair Thomson (London: Routledge, 1998, 2000), 214–23.
18. Geoffrey Reaume, "Toronto Asylum Walls of Remembrance," *Disability History Association Newsletter* (Fall 2006): 8–11; Geoffrey Reaume, "Psychiatric Patient Built Wall Tours at the Centre for Addiction and Mental Health (CAMH), Toronto, 2000–2010," *Left History* 15, no. 1 (Fall/Winter 2010–2011): 129–48.
19. For one example among many, see Roger Fulford, ed., *Beloved Mama: Private Correspondence of Queen Victoria and the German Crown Princess, 1878–85* (London: Evans, 1981).
20. This point needs also to underline that protection of the personal privacy of people who are from the elite is justified in certain circumstances, in which it is as important for these individuals as it is for everyone else. For example, the private case files of rich psychiatric patients in history deserve, and are subject to, the same protection offered by privacy legislation in the

Province of Ontario to the poorest patients. The records I am talking about regarding elites are of those who were never socially marginalized in state-run institutions, such as asylums, but who lived in their own homes, while also acknowledging that members of the elite could be marginalized within their own social class, such as the marginalization that women have historically been subjected to.

21. Since this is the population group that my work concerns and about which I have received critiques from within the group of psychiatric survivors, consumers, and mad people, I will limit my discussion to these records, though one could easily apply this same critique to confidential records about people categorized as having different disabilities.
22. While there are disabled people who are part of academia, most disabled people have no say in the questions raised in this article about the historical disposition and use of personal records created about them.
23. The term *active history* is borrowed from the website ActiveHistory.ca, which "connects the work of historians with the wider public and the importance of the past to current events.... We define active history variously as history that listens and is responsive; history that will make a tangible difference in people's lives; history that makes an intervention and is transformative to both practitioners and communities. We seek a practice of history that emphasizes collegiality, builds community among active historians and other members of communities, and recognizes the public responsibilities of the historian." Accessed March 8, 2017, http://activehistory.ca/about/.
24. Susan Burch, "'Dislocated Histories': The Canton Asylum for Insane Indians," *Women, Gender, and Families of Color* 2, no. 2 (Fall 2014), 143.
25. Since my first book was published in 2000, numerous descendants of asylum inmates have contacted me by email asking for advice on how to research their relatives' files either from the former Toronto Asylum or from an institution located elsewhere in Ontario. A few people have asked if I came across their relatives' files in my research, in which case I would check my records to inform them one way or the other. In this latter instance, since the contact was initiated by a relative of a deceased person, I was not breaking laws by letting them know if I had seen the file of a person in question and, if so, I directed them to the Archives of Ontario for further information to request access to the file.

BIBLIOGRAPHY

Burch, Susan. "'Dislocated Histories': The Canton Asylum for Insane Indians." *Women, Gender, and Families of Color* 2, no. 2 (Fall 2014): 141–62.

Carlisle, Linda V. *Elizabeth Packard: A Noble Fight*. Urbana: University of Illinois Press, 2010.

Dubinsky, Karen. "Telling Stories about Dead People." In *On The Case: Explorations in Social History*, edited by France Iacovetta and Wendy Mitchinson, 359–66. Toronto: University of Toronto Press, 1998.

Fulford, Roger, ed. *Beloved Mama: Private Correspondence of Queen Victoria and the German Crown Princess, 1878–85*. London: Evans, 1981.

Hervey, Nicholas. "Advocacy or Folly: The Alleged Lunatics' Friend Society, 1845–63." *Medical History* 30, no. 3 (July 1986): 245–75.

Hirsch, Karen. "Culture and Disability: The Role of Oral History." In *The Oral History Reader*, edited by Robert Perks and Alistair Thomson, 214–23. London: Routledge, 1998, 2000.

Kudlick, Catherine J. "Disability History: Why We Need Another 'Other.'" *American Historical Review* 108, no. 3 (June 2003): 763–93.

Reaume, Geoffrey. "Keep Your Labels Off My Mind! Or 'Now I Am Going to Pretend I Am Craze but Dont Be a Bit Alarmed': Psychiatric History from the Patients' Perspectives." *Canadian Bulletin of Medical History* 11, no. 2 (1994): 397–424.

Reaume, Geoffrey. "Accounts of Abuse of Patients at the Toronto Hospital for the Insane, 1883–1937." *Canadian Bulletin of Medical History* 14, no. 1 (1997): 65–106.

Reaume, Geoffrey. "Portraits of People with Mental Disorders in English Canadian History." *Canadian Bulletin of Medical History* 17, no. 1/2 (2000): 93–125.

Reaume, Geoffrey. *Remembrance of Patients Past: Patient Life at the Toronto Hospital for the Insane, 1870–1940*. Toronto: Oxford University Press Canada, 2000; University of Toronto Press, 2009, 2010.

Reaume, Geoffrey. "Toronto Asylum Walls of Remembrance." *Disability History Association Newsletter* (Fall 2006): 8–11.

Reaume, Geoffrey. "Psychiatric Patient Built Wall Tours at the Centre for Addiction and Mental Health (CAMH), Toronto, 2000–2010." *Left History* 15, no. 1 (Fall/Winter 2010–2011): 129–48.

Reaume, Geoffrey. "Alice G." (1854–1938, Toronto Asylum Inmate Labourer) *Dictionary of Canadian Biography, Volume XVI (1931–40)*. University of Toronto/Université Laval, 2016. http://www.biographi.ca/en/bio/g_alice_16E.html.

Rousso, Harilyn. *Don't Call Me Inspirational: A Disabled Feminist Talks Back*. Philadelphia: Temple University Press, 2013.

Sapinsley, Barbara. *The Private War of Mrs. Packard*. New York: Paragon House, 1991.

Warshauer, Matthew, and Michael Sturges. "Difficult Hunting: Accessing Connecticut Patient Records to Learn about Post-Traumatic Stress Disorder during the Civil War." *Civil War History* 59, no. 4 (December 2013): 419–52.

CHAPTER 3

Uncovering Disability History

Nancy Hansen

A long-standing philosophy of segregation has meant that disabled people lived, worked, and were educated in segregated spaces away from public view. Western society has developed, for the most part, without consideration of the needs or perspectives of disabled people.[1] Disability and impairment are largely understood as individual deviations presented in terms of defect and illness in need of correction or treatment.[2] Consequently, the presence of disabled people in public spaces (shopping centres and theatres, for example) is often unforeseen. Accommodation of disability is often on the fringes of the social mainstream. We, disabled people, are usually perceived as solitary individuals whose presence is often disruptive to the "natural" speed, space, and time elements that impact the rhythm of life's daily activities.[3] It is as if our invisibility and exclusion are (at least until very recently) somehow natural.[4]

NATURAL ABSENCES

The absence of disability in spaces of public culture (such as museums and art galleries) appears quite natural. There are an estimated one billion disabled people worldwide,[5] and almost 14 percent of Canada's population have some form of disability or impairment.[6] Yet, the history of disabled people is for the most part undocumented.[7] As with other marginalized groups (e.g., Indigenous people, women, LGBTQ and racialized groups), disability history appears to have been considered undeserving of documentation.[8] The naturalness of exclusion is reflected in cultural space. That is, disabled people are rarely represented or depicted in museums or art galleries (and if disabled people are present in cultural settings they are objectified as curiosities or medical anomalies).[9]

Western society has yet to develop a level of comfort with the diverse "messiness" that constitutes the richness of humanity.[10] This discomfort is apparent in the many negative associations still attached to our understanding of disability, which is often linked to language that stresses its ugliness, defectiveness, or abhorrence.[11] Indeed, the so-called "ugly laws" passed in late nineteenth- and early twentieth-century North American cities were geared to keeping the "unsightly" out of public spaces and in their place so as not to offend public sensibilities.[12]

Many times throughout history, and well into the twenty-first century, the nature of our humanity (i.e., what it is and means to be human) has been questioned.[13] It appears that the presence of disability in public life remains disruptive in that it is capable of unsettling long-standing conventions about what belongs in cultural spaces and what does not.[14] This chapter chronicles the efforts of disabled people and their allies in an ongoing cultural reclamation project at the local, national, and international levels. It seeks to challenge the social exclusion of disabled people while promoting the public circulation of representations of disability in places of culture.

Society does not usually perceive disability as a minority or human rights issue.[15] Rather, cultural understandings of disability tend to be highly medicalized, focusing on defect, weakness, and available means of "correction."[16] Much of what is known about the history of people with disabilities has been written by non-disabled scholars from descriptive, clinical, or medicalized perspectives.[17] These objectify disability by recording differences and impairments in a manner that reflects dominant medical, defect, or pathological models.[18] Atypical, physically non-conformist, and unique bodies such as those belonging to "General Tom Thumb" (Charles Sherwood Stratton) or the "Elephant Man" (John Merrick) characterize the freakish "abnormality" and objectification historically associated with disability.[19] This view of disability maintains existing stigmas and stereotypes, and thus serves to keep disability remote from the population at large.[20]

In her book *Staring: How We Look*, Rosemarie Garland-Thomson explores the influence of the regulatory social stare, and considers its influence on the cultural absences that people with disabilities experience. Accepted socio-cultural rules of engagement with strangers often do not apply to people with disabilities. Disabled people are regularly asked deeply personal questions in public by complete strangers or discussed as if they are not there.[21] Throughout history disabled people have been ever-present, yet socially invisible.[22] The social distancing and spacing provides an implied safety or comfort zone, a distinct dividing line between disabled and non-disabled people.

CULTURAL "CORRECTNESS"

Historically conservative, museums are both the reflection and guardian of culturally dominant understandings.[23] Museums play a vital role in determining both what is culturally valued and worthy of preservation.[24] They determine what belongs and what does not. Curators can be highly selective regarding what is remembered or recorded, as well as the manner in which it is presented.[25]

Whereas curators have made progress incorporating richer accounts of marginalized populations within museum collections with regard to issues of race, gender, and Indigenous issues, disability issues have yet to be viewed along the same continuum, and therefore represented with the same care.[26] Charged with safeguarding what is finest and best, museum curators are perplexed as far as disability is concerned because of its dominant negative socio-cultural associations with impairment.[27] Our place in the cultural-historical landscape has been largely overlooked.

The primary focus of disability at museums is usually limited to physical access (wheelchair ramps, elevators, accessible toilets, and eating areas).[28] Some progress has been made with institutions developing touchable exhibits for individuals with vision impairments;[29] however, as yet there is little understanding of disabled people's actual *place* in the dominant, non-disabled historical narrative, perhaps because there is a perceived risk of offending public sensibilities in dealing with what some may perceive as *difficult* history.[30] Slavery, conflict, and holocaust history collections have caused similar misgivings among museum curators.[31] Perhaps disability and impairment cause greater difficulty, as they are often greeted with fear and loathing in the wider culture.[32]

SELECTIVE MEMORY

At present, few if any museums contain any references to the lives, history, or experience of disabled people.[33] There is a high level of socio-cultural unease associated with impairment,[34] and curators may believe themselves to be in a difficult position, caught between fear of insult and the objectification of disability.[35] The Lowry, the principal gallery housing the collection of noted painter L. S. Lowry, is reluctant to display prints of his painting or giftware depicting *The Cripples* (1949) for fear of being labelled insensitive.[36]

Some of Western culture's most revered political leaders, writers, and artists had and have some form of disability. To name just a few examples, Franklin D. Roosevelt was a wheelchair user as a result of polio, yet the wheelchair was rarely shown or discussed; Winston Churchill and Virginia Woolf both experienced depression; and artist Frida Kahlo had chronic illness and physical disability resulting from a vehicle accident.[37] However, with the exception of Kahlo, who openly wrote about and depicted her disability, this aspect of their lives has been largely expunged through a form of social deletion.[38] It is as if their skill, accomplishments, and status are somehow diminished if attention is drawn to each individual's disability or impairment.[39] Similarly, aspirational models of beauty such as the Venus de Milo, although armless, is not represented as having a disability.[40] Almost every image of Lord Nelson, a noted nineteenth-century British admiral and war hero, openly depicts him without an arm, yet he is rarely characterized as disabled despite the loss of an arm and an eye.[41]

If reference is made to impairment in museum settings, it is usually incidental.[42] Consider as an example of this reductionist approach to impairment the Ulster Folk and Transport Museum's treatment of Sampson Towgood Roch, an Irishman who was profoundly deaf and also arguably one of the finest watercolourists and miniaturists of late eighteenth- and early nineteenth-century Britain. In the catalogue description of his *Piper and Dancers*, it is noted that, "as he was deaf, Roch would not have been able to enjoy the sound of the pipes but in this wonderful painting he certainly captures the immediacy of the scene that confronted him."[43] This is the only reference to Roch's deafness in the exhibit, and it is presented in a rather trivial manner. Only his inability to hear music is negatively reflected upon. The overarching socio-cultural dissonance is present in this description.[44]

SHIFTING PERSPECTIVE THROUGH A DISABILITY LENS

Cultural representations of disability (or the lack thereof) have a direct impact on how mainstream society understands disability.[45] Nevertheless, the richness and texture of the disability community is arguably absent from the vast majority of these representations.[46] Just as gender, race, and sexual orientation are now sources of cultural pride, so too is disability.[47]

People with disabilities are engaged in a cultural reclamation project. No longer content to be absent citizens in the cultural landscape, disabled people throughout the world are laying claim to cultural spaces on their own terms.[48] The socio-cultural script governing disability-related concerns is changing, and is becoming more responsively informed by disabled users' perspectives. Crutches, wheelchairs, and hearing aids are no longer simply items with medical utility that fade and disappear into the background; instead they have become points of disability culture and pride. Complete with colour and style, these assistive devices are now unique spaces of self-expression and social change.[49]

POWER SHIFT

The socio-cultural subtext of disability is being rewritten, the landscape is slowly shifting, and the invasive stare is being gradually pivoted to become a form of engagement, the emergence of disability culture and politics. The stare is being reclaimed and knowledge is present where, to this point, it was unknown or unrecognized.[50] The narrative of disability, the way in which disabled bodies are ideologically framed and responded to, is quite literally being reshaped through a new emphasis on dignity and human worth.[51] Cultural representation can be a reflection of acceptance and lead to wider social rights.[52]

It would seem that as portrayals of disability change, perceptions of disability gradually transform and the understanding of human difference shifts, along with ways of seeing and understanding. This in turn reshapes the social lens and narrative of disability and disability rights. Bonnie Sherr Klein, noted disabled filmmaker, states the following:

> It's scary for anyone to admit our own power, scary in our culture to use the word artist, with its connotations of elitism, or God-given talent—or not. Scary in particular for a person with disabilities, a blatant contradiction to the messages of weakness, imperfection, and revulsion which we internalize and sometimes fulfill. To give permission to the artist within your disabled body is an outrageous act of defiance.[53]

As asylums and institutions for physically and intellectually disabled people close in Canada and around the world, valuable pieces of a historical archive (annual reports, correspondence, and log books, for example) are often destroyed, lost, or left behind. These items, which may appear to have limited worth, can provide valuable insights into institutional life; however, their importance is not readily understood or recognized in the rush to move beyond, progress, and leave a difficult past behind. As a result, much of our history has been lost.[54]

We, disabled people, are starting to build and rebuild from the ground up, working to create a new understanding of disabled people's history, creating and reframing the cultural narrative. This history is becoming available in fragments and pieces, in anonymous photographs with blacked-out eyes, charity boxes, clipped phrases in patient and inmate logbooks, and forgotten institutional and legal files.[55]

At present, few museums in Canada contain permanent representations of the presence or histories of people with disabilities. There are few, if any, archivists and curators with experience in disability-related memorabilia.[56] Museums and archives contain material relevant to the retrieval of the hidden history of disability and disabled people, and this history will be written following the examination and analysis of existing collections from a Disability Studies perspective; however, the difficulty often lies in persuading museum personnel to recognize the value in doing so.[57] My meetings with museum personnel in Canada and in Britain are punctuated by a reluctance to spend time on such activity when faced with funding cutbacks and the need to host special travelling exhibitions that are profitable and responsive to public sensibilities. In this latter regard, museums operate under the belief that disability history would appeal to only a small minority of individuals.[58]

In my own research, I have found that early census forms, ships' passenger manifests, annual reports from charities and hospitals' poorhouses, and private photographs can all provide fodder for researchers to work with, as in these locations "difference" was often documented or recorded in some manner.

No longer are we with disabilities content to be remote and disassociated from the objects and materials that mark our everyday lives. Disabled people and our allies are providing needed substantive context and substance to these items, which we encounter daily. A fine example of this process is the award-winning 2011 British multimedia exhibition entitled *Re-framing Disability: Portraits from the Royal College*. Britain's Royal College of Physicians has a collection of rare seventeenth- and eighteenth-century prints of disabled people,[59] but little was known of the people depicted in the prints, so curators embarked on a two-tiered project of *reframing* disability. First, they uncovered information about these lives beyond specifying the nature of each person's bodily physical differences.[60] Second, they adopted a social model orientation, which permitted the analysis of disability from a social environmental perspective rather than an individual medicalized one.[61] People with disabilities were substantively involved in the project as expert consultants from the outset. They (disabled consultants) were asked for their impressions of the depiction of disability in the prints and understanding the disabled body in a modern socio-cultural context. Finally, the consultants had their photographs taken on their terms and in a manner defined by them.[62] Through this practice, a person who was formerly the subject of objectification became relocated to a position of pride, power, and, most importantly, control. Yet another example of this re-examination is the

BBC Radio 4 series *Disability: A New History*, in which historians document the daily life experiences of disabled people in the eighteenth and nineteenth centuries through careful reading of archival documents.[63]

In a Canadian context, *Out from Under: Disability History and Things to Remember* lies at the vanguard of contemporary curatorial practice, marking the current moment of disability history at museums in Canada. Originally a disability history and arts project developed by the School of Disability Studies at Ryerson University, it draws from objects and materials representative of disability-related history in Canada.[64] Monochrome tracksuits, a shovel, a stuffed toy, a travel trunk, psychological testing equipment, and a Braille wristwatch are a few of the items collected and submitted by students for exhibition. Text written about the objects reflected the daily activity of those to whom they belonged.[65] More than a dozen of the submissions were exhibited, complete with accompanying descriptive text, at the Royal Ontario Museum from April to August 2008.

The museum was initially somewhat uncomfortable with displays that might be perceived as politicized, activist subject matter.[66] "Museum culture" barriers were gradually dealt with, and the exhibit went forward. It was tucked into a side wing of the museum, however, and a sign reading "This Way to the Bronze Age," complete with an arrow pointing in the opposite direction, was positioned immediately outside it. When I went to the exhibit there were very few signs noting its existence, full stop. I stood on my crutches in the middle of the exhibit with tears of pride and validation rolling down my cheeks. It was the first time in my life that the realities of life for disabled people were being recognized in cultural space.

The group of people with physical, intellectual, and sensory disabilities in Canada who were educated in segregated "special school systems" and/or housed in provincial institutions is aging rapidly. (At present, Manitoba is one of the few remaining provinces with large institutions for people with intellectual disabilities that are not scheduled for closure.) Their histories and experiences as disabled people and the lessons those contain will be lost over the next several decades. The parallel universe inhabited by this demographic is unknown to most non-disabled Canadians. Recording and recovering these experiences before they are largely gone forever is crucial.[67]

The Freedom Tour, a co-operative film project between People First Canada and the National Film Board, can be characterized as part of this recovery process, although it was not envisioned as such when the project began. This documentary film records the cross-Canada Freedom Tour, documenting the experiences of people with intellectual disabilities who had lived in provincial institutions in Western Canada.[68]

CULTURAL INCLUSION

The existing cultural narrative around disability is slowly changing. *Re-framing Disability*, *Out from Under*, and *The Freedom Tour* all play an important role in this process. Together they illustrate a definitive, substantive philosophical shift driven in large measure by people with disabilities and their allies. Museums can play a pivotal role in presenting and understanding all manner of differences and changes. Shaping and reshaping the socio-cultural comfort zone surrounding disability history and disability rights in cultural spaces like museums has just begun. The Canadian Museum for Human Rights (CMHR) is a prime example of this work in progress. The CMHR has incorporated disabled people's milestones into the human rights timeline and the experience of people with disabilities within its Holocaust gallery. In addition, a portion of the above-mentioned *Out from Under* collection is in its permanent collection. Furthermore, disabled people's perspectives are included through strong partnerships, substantive commitment, and a genuine desire for understanding. The journey ahead now appears far less daunting.

NOTES

1. Nancy Hansen, "'Passing' through Other People's Spaces: Disabled Women, Geography and Work" (PhD diss., University of Glasgow, 2002).
2. Michael Oliver, *Understanding Disability: From Theory to Practice* (London: Palgrave, 1996).
3. Nancy Hansen and Chris Philo, "The Normality of Doing Things Differently: Bodies Spaces and Disability Geography," *Tijdschrift voor Economische en Sociale Geografie* 98, no. 4 (2007): 493–506.
4. Tanya Titchkosky, *The Question of Access Disability, Space, Meaning* (Toronto: University of Toronto Press, 2011).
5. World Health Organization, *World Report on Disability* (Malta: WHO, 2011).
6. Statistics Canada, "Disability in Canada: Initial Findings from the Canadian Survey on Disability," modified November 30, 2015, http://www.statcan.gc.ca/pub/89-654-x/89-654-x2013002-eng.htm.
7. Geoffrey Reaume, *Remembrance of Patients Past: Patient Life at the Toronto Hospital for the Insane, 1870–1940* (Toronto: Oxford University Press, 2000).
8. Reaume, *Remembrance of Patients Past*.
9. Rosemarie Garland-Thomson, *Staring: How We Look* (New York: Oxford University Press, 2009).
10. Ato Quayson, *Aesthetic Nervousness: Disability and the Crisis of Representation* (New York: Columbia University Press, 2007).
11. Garland-Thomson, *Staring*; Tobin Siebers, *Disability Aesthetics* (Ann Arbor: University of Michigan Press, 2010).
12. Susan M. Schweik, *The Ugly Laws: Disability in Public* (New York: New York University Press, 2010).
13. Peter Singer, *Rethinking Life and Death: The Collapse of Our Traditional Ethics* (New York: St. Martin's Griffin, 1995); Martha Nussbaum, *Frontiers of Justice: Disability, Nationality, Species Membership* (Cambridge, MA: Belknap Press of Harvard University, 2006).
14. Richard Sandell and Jocelyn Dodd, "Activist Practice," in *Re-Presenting Disability: Activism and Agency in the Museum*, ed. Richard Sandell, Jocelyn Dodd, and Rosemarie Garland-Thomson (New York: Routledge, 2010).
15. Sandell and Dodd, "Activist Practice."
16. Nancy Hansen, "Remapping the Medical Terrain on Our Terms," *Aporia* 1, no. 3 (2009): 28–34.
17. Reaume, *Remembrance of Patients Past*.
18. Oliver, *Understanding Disability*.

19. Annie Delin, "Buried in the Footnotes: The Absence of Disabled People in the Collective Imagery of Our Past," in *Museums, Society, Inequality*, ed. Richard Sandell (London: Routledge, 2002).
20. Jocelyn Dodd et al., "Buried in the Footnotes: The Representation of Disabled People in Museum and Gallery Collections" (Leicester, UK: Research Centre for Museums and Galleries, University of Leicester, 2004), http://www2.le.ac.uk/departments/museumstudies/rcmg/projects/buried-in-the-footnotes/BITF2.pdf.
21. Garland-Thomson, *Staring*.
22. Garland-Thomson, *Staring*; Nancy Hansen and Diane Driedger, "Art, Sticks and Politics," in *Living the Edges: A Disabled Women's Reader*, ed. Diane Driedger (Toronto: Inanna, 2010).
23. Delin, "Buried in the Footnotes."
24. Sandell and Dodd, "Activist Practice."
25. Ana Carden-Coyne, "Ghosts in the War Museum," in *Re-Presenting Disability: Activism and Agency in the Museum*, ed. Richard Sandell, Jocelyn Dodd, and Rosemarie Garland-Thomson (New York: Routledge, 2010).
26. Sandell and Dodd, "Activist Practice."
27. Carden-Coyne, "Ghosts in the War Museum."
28. Sandell and Dodd, "Activist Practice."
29. Kathryn Church et al., "'Out from Under': A Brief History of Everything," in *Re-Presenting Disability: Activism and Agency in the Museum*, ed. Richard Sandell, Jocelyn Dodd, and Rosemarie Garland-Thomson (New York: Routledge, 2010).
30. Delin, "Buried in the Footnotes."
31. Carden-Coyne, "Ghosts in the War Museum"; Heather Hollins, "Reciprocity, Accountability, Empowerment," in *Re-Presenting Disability: Activism and Agency in the Museum*, ed. Richard Sandell, Jocelyn Dodd, and Rosemarie Garland-Thomson (New York: Routledge, 2010).
32. Dan Goodley, *Disability Studies: An Interdisciplinary Introduction* (London: Sage, 2017).
33. Sandell and Dodd, "Activist Practice."
34. Delin, "Buried in the Footnotes."
35. Sandell and Dodd, "Activist Practice."
36. Nancy Hansen, research notes, 2011.
37. Delin, "Buried in the Footnotes"; Sharon Snyder and David Mitchell, *Disability Takes On the Arts*, DVD (Chicago: Brace Your Self Productions, 2005).
38. Delin, "Buried in the Footnotes."
39. Dodd et al., "Buried in the Footnotes."
40. Ann Millett-Gallant, *The Disabled Body in Contemporary Art* (New York: Palgrave Macmillan, 2010).
41. Delin, "Buried in the Footnotes"; Dodd et al., "Buried in the Footnotes."
42. Delin, "Buried in the Footnotes."
43. Ulster Folk and Transport Museum Facebook page, https://www.facebook.com/ulsterfolkandtransportmuseum/photos/a.365179496886976.83054.153658808039047/1513133722091542.
44. Delin, "Buried in the Footnotes."
45. Rosemarie Garland-Thomson, "Picturing People with Disabilities: Classical Portraiture as Reclamation Narrative," in *Re-Presenting Disability: Activism and Agency in the Museum*, ed. Richard Sandell, Jocelyn Dodd, and Rosemarie Garland-Thomson (New York: Routledge, 2010).
46. Reaume, *Remembrance of Patients Past*.
47. Jihan Abbas et al., "Lights…Camera…Attitude! Introducing Disability Arts and Culture" (Occasional paper, Ryerson-RBC Institute for Disability Studies Research and Education, Ryerson University, 2004).
48. Garland-Thomson, *Staring*.

49. Hansen and Driedger, "Art, Sticks and Politics."
50. Garland-Thomson, *Staring*.
51. Abbas et al., "Lights...Camera...Attitude!"
52. Michel Foucault, *Archeology of Knowledge* (London: Routledge, 2002).
53. Bonnie Sherr Klein, "The Art of Disability: Some Ideas about Creativity, Health and Rehabilitation" (John F. McCreary Lecture, University of British Columbia, October 11, 2000), 5.
54. Darby Penney and Peter Stastny, *The Lives They Left Behind: Suitcases from a State Hospital Attic* (New York: Bellevue Literary Press, 2009).
55. Reaume, *Remembrance of Patients Past*.
56. Nancy Hansen, "(Dis)Ability and Its Discontent" (project proposal, Ireland Canada University Foundation, Dublin, 2006); Church et al., "'Out from Under': A Brief History of Everything."
57. Sandell and Dodd, "Activist Practice."
58. Church et al., "'Out from Under': A Brief History of Everything."
59. Bridget Telfer, Emma Shepley, and Carole Reeves, *Re-Framing Disability: Portraits from the Royal College of Physicians* (London: Royal College of Physicians, 2011).
60. Telfer, Shepley, and Reeves, *Re-Framing Disability*.
61. Oliver, *Understanding Disability*.
62. Telfer, Shepley, and Reeves, *Re-Framing Disability*. See also the video "Re-framing Disability: Portraits from the Royal College of Physicians," February 23, 2011, http://www.youtube.com/watch?v=PALIKx1PFes.
63. See "Disability: A New History," http://www.bbc.co.uk/programmes/b021mdwt.
64. Church et al., "'Out from Under': A Brief History of Everything."
65. Church et al., "'Out from Under': A Brief History of Everything."
66. Church et al., "'Out from Under': A Brief History of Everything."
67. Hansen, "(Dis)Ability and Its Discontent."
68. People First of Canada, *The Freedom Tour*. DVD (Ottawa: National Film Board of Canada, 2008), http://www.youtube.com/watch?v=13y4BI0Lets.

BIBLIOGRAPHY

Abbas, Jihan, Kathryn Church, Catherine Frazee, and Melanie Panitch. "Lights...Camera...Attitude! Introducing Disability Arts and Culture." Occasional paper, Ryerson-RBC Institute for Disability Studies Research and Education, Ryerson University, 2004.

Carden-Coyne, Ana. "Ghosts in the War Museum." In *Re-Presenting Disability: Activism and Agency in the Museum*, edited by Richard Sandell, Jocelyn Dodd, and Rosemarie Garland-Thomson, 64–78. New York: Routledge, 2010.

Church, Kathryn, Catherine Frazee, and Melanie Panitch. "Out from Under: Disability History and Things to Remember." http://www.ryerson.ca/ofu/.

Church, Kathryn, Melanie Panitch, Catherine Frazee, and Phaedra Livingstone. "'Out from Under': A Brief History of Everything." In *Re-Presenting Disability: Activism and Agency in the Museum*, edited by Richard Sandell, Jocelyn Dodd, and Rosemarie Garland-Thomson, 197–212. New York: Routledge, 2010.

Delin, Annie. "Buried in the Footnotes: The Absence of Disabled People in the Collective Imagery of Our Past." In *Museums, Society, Inequality*, edited by Richard Sandell, 84–97. London: Routledge, 2002.

Dodd, Jocelyn, Richard Sandell, Annie Delin, and Jackie Gay. "Buried in the Footnotes: The Representation of Disabled People in Museum and Gallery Collections." Leicester, UK: Research Centre for Museums and Galleries, University of Leicester, 2004. http://www2.le.ac.uk/departments/museumstudies/rcmg/projects/buried-in-the-footnotes/BITF2.pdf.

Foucault, Michel. *Archeology of Knowledge*. London: Routledge, 2002.

Garland-Thomson, Rosemarie. *Staring: How We Look*. New York: Oxford University Press, 2009.

Garland-Thomson, Rosemarie. "Picturing People with Disabilities: Classical Portraiture as Reclamation Narrative." In *Re-Presenting Disability: Activism and Agency in the Museum*, edited by Richard Sandell, Jocelyn Dodd, and Rosemarie Garland-Thomson, 23–40. New York: Routledge, 2010.

Goodley, Dan. *Disability Studies: An Interdisciplinary Introduction*. London: Sage, 2017.

Hansen, Nancy. "'Passing' through Other People's Spaces: Disabled Women, Geography and Work." PhD diss., University of Glasgow, 2002.

Hansen, Nancy. "(Dis)Ability and Its Discontents." Project proposal, Ireland Canada University Foundation, Dublin, 2006.

Hansen, Nancy. "Remapping the Medical Terrain on Our Terms." *Aporia* 1, no. 3 (2009): 28–34.

Hansen, Nancy, and Diane Driedger. "Art, Sticks and Politics." In *Living the Edges: A Disabled Women's Reader*, edited by Diane Driedger, 195–203. Toronto: Inanna, 2010.

Hansen, Nancy, and Chris Philo. "The Normality of Doing Things Differently: Bodies Spaces and Disability Geography." *Tijdschrift voor Economische en Sociale Geografie* 98, no. 4 (2007): 493–506.

Hollins, Heather. "Reciprocity, Accountability, Empowerment." In *Re-Presenting Disability: Activism and Agency in the Museum*, edited by Richard Sandell, Jocelyn Dodd, and Rosemarie Garland-Thomson, 228–43. New York: Routledge, 2010.

Millett-Gallant, Ann. *The Disabled Body in Contemporary Art*. New York: Palgrave Macmillan, 2010.

Nussbaum, Martha. *Frontiers of Justice: Disability, Nationality, Species Membership*. Cambridge, MA: Belknap Press of Harvard University, 2006.

Oliver, Michael. *Understanding Disability: From Theory to Practice*. London: Palgrave, 1996.

Penney, Darby, and Peter Stastny. *The Lives They Left Behind: Suitcases from a State Hospital Attic*. New York: Bellevue Literary Press, 2009.

People First of Canada. *The Freedom Tour*. DVD. Ottawa: National Film Board of Canada, 2008. http://www.youtube.com/watch?v=13y4BI0Lets.

Quayson, Ato. *Aesthetic Nervousness: Disability and the Crisis of Representation*. New York: Columbia University Press, 2007.

Reaume, Geoffrey. *Remembrance of Patients Past: Patient Life at the Toronto Hospital for the Insane, 1870–1940*. Toronto: Oxford University Press, 2000.

Sandell, Richard, and Jocelyn Dodd. "Activist Practice." In *Re-Presenting Disability: Activism and Agency in the Museum*, edited by Richard Sandell, Jocelyn Dodd, and Rosemarie Garland-Thomson, 3–22. New York: Routledge, 2010.

Schweik, Susan M. *The Ugly Laws: Disability in Public*. New York: New York University Press, 2010.

Sherr Klein, Bonnie. "The Art of Disability: Some Ideas about Creativity, Health and Rehabilitation." John F. McCreary Lecture, University of British Columbia, October 11, 2000.

Siebers, Tobin. *Disability Aesthetics*. Ann Arbor: University of Michigan Press, 2010.

Singer, Peter. *Rethinking Life and Death: The Collapse of Our Traditional Ethics*. New York: St. Martin's Griffin, 1995.

Snyder, Sharon, and David Mitchell. *Disability Takes On the Arts*. DVD. Chicago: Brace Your Self Productions, 2005.

Statistics Canada. "Disability in Canada: Initial Findings from the Canadian Survey on Disability." Modified November 30, 2015. http://www.statcan.gc.ca/pub/89-654-x/89-654-x2013002-eng.htm.

Telfer, Bridget, Emma Shepley, and Carole Reeves. *Re-Framing Disability: Portraits from the Royal College of Physicians*. London: Royal College of Physicians, 2011.

Titchkosky, Tanya. *The Question of Access Disability, Space, Meaning*. Toronto: University of Toronto Press, 2011.

World Health Organization. *World Report on Disability*. Malta: WHO, 2011.

SECTION II

CONFEDERATION TO THE EARLY TWENTIETH CENTURY

During the period from 1867 (Canada's Confederation) to the early twentieth century, many people with disabilities contributed to their family's household chores and farms, as we can extrapolate from Sarah Rose's history of people with disabilities in the United States from the 1840s to 1930.[1] Other persons with various disabilities were housed in institutions and poorhouses.[2] Research remains to be done on these early years in Canada. This time period also saw the beginnings of the movement for disabled people to become educated and trained to be "useful" and to be contributing members of Canadian society. In this process, people with disabilities began to tell their own stories, as is discussed in "'Blindness Clears the Way': E. B. F. Robinson's *The True Sphere of the Blind* (1896)," in which Warne addresses the education of blind persons living in late nineteenth-century Ontario by utilizing an autobiographical text written in 1896. The chapter highlights many of the positivist views of sighted writers about the blind students of the Ontario School for the Blind, which opened in 1872.

Iozzo-Duval's "The Education of 'Good' and 'Useful' Citizens: Work, Disability, and d/Deaf Citizenship at the Ontario Institution for the Education of the Deaf, 1892–1902" examines the experience of deaf students at a similar point in time, documenting how early Deaf education in Ontario reflected an underlying belief that deaf students lacked the ability to be productive citizens.

Barron's "'An Excuse for Being So Bold': D. W. McDermid and the Early Development of the Manitoba Institute for the Deaf and Dumb, 1888–1900" traces the development of the institute from a private to a publicly funded educational institution. Furthermore, this chapter examines state education as part of social citizenship. The institute is presented as a space of early social resistance promoting the use of deaf sign language rather than oralism (teaching speech). During this period, there were doubts that people with disabilities could be contributing members of society. Carrington-Decker's "Remembering the Boys" documents the history of the Victoria Training School in Mimico, Ontario. It explores the Victorian ideology, policies, and procedures behind the historical segregation of those labelled "deviant," the conditions under which they lived, and the school's eventual downfall.

Spagnuolo's "'Someone in Toronto ... Paid Her Way Out Here': Indentured Labour and Medical Deportation—The Precarious Work of Single Women" takes a critical look at how eugenically informed and racist immigration and employment policies negatively impacted women of colour. Working in conjunction with numerous government agencies in the 1920s, these policies served to enforce a form of state-sponsored social purging.

As the twentieth century moved on, it became apparent that people with mobility disabilities needed services as they lived longer due to advances in medicine. Hanes's "Service Clubs and the Emergence of Societies for Crippled Children in Canada: The Rise of the Ontario Society for Crippled Children, 1920–1940" examines the rise of the crippled child movement in Canada during the early twentieth century. This chapter examines the development of the Ontario Society for Crippled Children as part of the rise of scientific medicine and the service club movement. It not only focuses on care and treatment, but also connects the rise of specialized programs for crippled children as a broader concern for social and moral reform and how the care of cripples was linked to concerns about the greater good of society.

NOTES

1. Sarah Rose, *No Right to Be Idle: The Invention of Disability, 1840s–1930s* (Chapel Hill: University of North Carolina Press, 2017).
2. Rose, *No Right to Be Idle*, 1–2.

CHAPTER 4

"Blindness Clears the Way": E. B. F. Robinson's
The True Sphere of the Blind (1896)

Vanessa Warne

In the decades following the 1872 opening of the Ontario Institution for the Education of the Blind (OIB),[1] a curious Canadian public turned to newspapers and magazines for information about the school and its students. Articles appearing in a range of publications described the OIB's scenic grounds in Brantford, the housing of its male and female pupils, and the types of instruction available there: on the one hand, the academic study of subjects such as literature, mathematics, and geography, and, on the other hand, vocational training in willow-work, piano tuning, sewing, and knitting. Praising the extension of free public schooling to Ontario's visually disabled citizens, these articles are uniformly positive, characterizing the OIB, in the words of one reporter, as a monument to "the enlightened statesmanship and wise liberality of the Ontario Government."[2] Reporters were equally enthusiastic about the accomplishments of the school's students. Their mastery of subjects such as geography was noted in a number of articles, one of which explained that "well-informed visitors often find themselves wanting in knowledge concerning their own county or province which the blind student supplies without a moment's hesitation."[3] The same article described the students' examination by touch of raised sectional maps, explaining how "the finger traces with almost unerring accuracy the lines of railroad or the courses of rivers."[4] Interested in the education of blind people and, more narrowly, in the role that touch plays in their education, sighted commentators divided their attention between the academic attainments and haptic skills of Ontario's blind students.

This chapter explores the education of people with visual disabilities in late nineteenth-century Canada but takes as its focus the impressions not of sighted observers but of a visually disabled graduate of the OIB, Edgar Bertram (Bert) Freel Robinson. Robinson, who was born in 1872, attended the OIB from 1883 to 1890; he went on to graduate from Trinity University with a BA in 1893 and an MA in 1903. Robinson was an organizer and active member of several associations, including the Blind Man's Self Help Club in Toronto, and was, at the time of his early death in 1908, librarian of the Canadian Free Library for the Blind, founded in 1907, a circulating library based in Robinson's father's home in Markham.[5] In 1896, Robinson published *The True Sphere of the Blind*, a book about the educational and professional prospects of blind people and a valuable record of the ideas and opinions of a visually disabled, middle-class man living in Canada in the late nineteenth century. In what follows, I analyze *The True Sphere*'s campaign for the recognition of the intellectual potential of visually disabled people, I explore Robinson's recommendations regarding improvements to the OIB, and I discuss the reception of his book. Taking as my focus Robinson's claim "that blindness clears the way for a more intense mental life,"[6] I propose that Robinson's championing of the intellectual superiority of blind over sighted people is not only a direct response to the limited educational and professional opportunities available to blind people, but also a reaction against the sighted community's interest in the purportedly heightened sense of touch of visually disabled people—interest that can, in turn, be attributed to two key developments in the nineteenth-century history of visual disability: the opening of schools for blind students and the related proliferation of literacy among Canadians with visual disabilities.

Historians who turn to Robinson's book for biographical information about a key figure in the early history of blind activism in Canada are likely to be disappointed.[7] Neither memoir nor autobiography, *The True Sphere* is an inquiry into the educational and professional prospects of visually disabled people in late nineteenth-century North America. On the rare occasions when Robinson offers information about himself, noting, for instance, on the title page of the book that he was "Philosophy Prizeman of Trinity University in 1893," he does so in support of a central goal: the fostering of a new awareness of the unrecognized intellectual potential of blind people. Befitting Robinson's training in philosophy, the book contains chapters on such topics as the "General Nature of Blindness and Tendencies of its effects upon the Life of the Soul." It also contains information on more pragmatic matters, such as the best kind of cane to use when walking city streets. In both the philosophical and the practical chapters, Robinson's central point is that "blindness tends to intensify and strengthen the higher mental powers."[8] Blind people are, he argues, more intellectually inclined than the sighted and are consequently better suited to academic pursuits. Of work in professional fields, Robinson observes, given that "the whole secret of success in scholarship and learning lies in concentration and application, the possession of these powers in a highly developed degree is bound to insure ... ultimate triumph."[9] He goes on to explain: "I do not contend that every blind man is a born thinker, but only that their peculiar situation renders it more likely than not that they will succeed in vocations requiring thought."[10]

Significantly, as Robinson discusses the intellectual life of visually disabled people, he develops for his readers a model of the human sensorium as a kind of circulatory system of mental energy. "Man is," he proposes, "endowed with a certain amount of energy and ordinarily this finds an outlet in the pleasures obtained through the eye. In the blind however it is forced back into the higher mental activities."[11] Characterizing a blind person's intellect as fuelled by a force not lost to vision, Robinson imagines an economy of mental energy in which energy is either productively conserved by blindness or consumed by vision. With this model, Robinson promotes a reconsideration of the value of vision and its contribution to intellectual life. Similarly, when he characterizes blindness as the cause of an intensification of mental power, he calls for a reconsideration of visual disability as a beneficial condition whose advantages are not available to those with vision.

If Robinson conceives of vision as a threat to productivity, as a loss of energy otherwise productively preserved for mental work, he also imagines blind people as a resource not fully utilized by society. Robinson identifies himself not as an activist for blind people but as an economist with a cautionary message for Canadians: "Were it not for the great economy of employing the vast mental energy of the blind and not allowing it to waste, it would hardly be my place to plead our cause, since in my work, I do not pretend to be a philanthropist, but an economist."[12] Promoting an appreciation of the education of blind people as an economically responsible rather than merely charitable undertaking, Robinson advocates for a reallocation of resources from vocational to intellectual training. He observes the following of contemporary Canadian society:

> While some should toil with their hands, others should work with their brains. It is to this latter class I conceive that the blind belong. Not so much because they are unfitted for manual labour but from the nature of the limitation they are peculiarly adapted to follow the intricate windings of a mental labyrinth. The blind are undistracted, undisturbed in the midst of varying petty details of the visible world. No matter where the blind man be no chance stroke of the eye can call up an irrelevant chain of associations.[13]

Confident about the intellectual potential of blind people, Robinson develops his model of mental energy, portraying vision loss as an escape from the distractions of sight, from petty visual details and irrelevant associations. "The blind should," he proposes, "follow those pursuits which depend on the brain and not on the hand. They should earn their right to citizenship by virtue of what they know, not for what they do."[14] Rejecting vocations such as basket- and broom-making, activities central to the training provided in educational institutions for blind students in North America and Europe in the nineteenth century, Robinson looks instead to professions that require advanced education, proposing, among other possibilities, the likely success of blind obstetricians and surgeons. He also offers examples of his own success as an insurance agent, and of the success of a blind lawyer in his acquaintance who is "rapidly working himself into a good practice."[15] Documenting the achievements of blind people in professional fields, Robinson reiterates his assessment of blindness as an advantage for those pursuing advanced studies and intellectually engaging careers.

With observations of this kind, Robinson argues for both the reformation of current practices in the education and employment of blind people and the development of new ideas about both blindness and vision. Robinson's characterization of visual disability as a state that preserves mental energy involves a related reconfiguration of vision as a threat to intellectual activity, an idea that challenged well-established notions of sight as the most valuable sense and, specifically, as the sense most supportive of intellectual activity. While belief in the pre-eminence of vision is so central to nineteenth-century culture as to require little by way of demonstration, an example from the writing of a commentator on blind education well known to Robinson, A. H. Dymond, principal of the OIB during Robinson's time as a student there, may prove useful here.

In an 1886 essay entitled "Education of the Blind in the Province of Ontario," Principal Dymond praises the accomplishments of the students of his school but expresses noteworthy pessimism about the potential of blind people to equal, let alone surpass, sighted people in academic or professional endeavours. He explained this position in a discussion of the dedication of sighted teachers of blind students and of the inventive methods used by them:

> Let it never be forgotten, when we come to ascertain results, that no teaching, however skillful or devoted, can absolutely compensate for the loss of sight. No instruction, however ingenious, can ever fully atone for the absence of the educating power and functions of the eye. The eye is, to a large extent, an involuntary teacher, but it is an ever present and ever active one nonetheless. It may be wonderful that the blind can be taught so much, but it should be an ever active stimulant to efforts to teach them all they can acquire, to know how little with the best help they can, as compared with the seeing, know and do after all.[16]

A paean to sight and a grim assessment of the limits that blindness places on intellectual accomplishment, this passage is, like the larger essay of which it is a part, an expression of conventional notions of visual disability and vision. In addition to his position as the principal of Ontario's first (and, at that time, only) educational facility for blind students, Dymond was also president of the American Association of the Instructors of the Blind. The fact that this statement was made by Dymond, an individual with knowledge of and, more importantly, significant influence over the education of blind students, demonstrates the hold that the pre-eminence of vision in the hierarchy of human senses had on late nineteenth-century culture and hints at the detrimental effect that ideas like these had on the daily lives of people with visual disabilities.

Robinson's assertions regarding the special intellectual gifts of blind people and his denigration of vision as a distraction can be read as a direct response to opinions of this kind. Vision, identified by Dymond as the primary sense involved in education, is, according to Robinson, a threat to the very same endeavour. Robinson's prioritization of intellectual aptitude over haptic ability, discussed above in relation to his championing of pursuits of "the brain" versus those that depend "on the hand,"[17] can also be read as a reaction to contemporary ideas about blindness and blind education. While the success of efforts to educate blind people challenged the popular conception of sight as the primary sense involved in learning, it did not challenge the widespread understanding of heightened touch as a compensatory gift common to blind people. Again, this is a well-established convention but examples of it, taken from Robinson's realm of experience, demonstrate the prevalence of this idea in late nineteenth-century Canadian culture and also suggest its detrimental effect. Reports on the OIB appearing in the periodical press in the last decades of the nineteenth century document popular interest in visually disabled people's experience of the sense of touch. In 1885, a *Pleasant Hours* reporter explained to sighted readers that students at the OIB "read with their finger-tips almost as readily as we read with our eyes."[18] Intrigued by the entry of blind people into literacy, the reporter turned to conventional theories of compensatory skill to understand their accomplishments, observing of the blind students that "the defect in one sense seems to be accompanied by the increased efficiency of the others."[19] Striking a similar note, the *Journal of Medicine and Surgery* reported in 1898 on the "marvelous skill and dexterity" of the OIB's students, praising their handicrafts and asserting that "no sighted worker could excel in this line some of the blind girls at Brantford."[20] Responses of this kind are particularly well represented by the work of a *Brantford Expositor* reporter who described "the wonderful power of touch" he observed in use at the OIB, giving as an example an object lesson in which students handled varieties of wheat.[21] "By the mere sense of touch," he explains, "they could tell spring from fall wheat. It was more than I could do by looking at them."[22]

Yet another article, this one from *The Canadian Mute*, a publication of the OIB's sister institution, the Ontario Institute for the Deaf and Dumb, takes enthusiasm about blind people's sense of touch to a revealing extreme. In it, the anonymous author states of blind students he observed at work at the OIB that "their sense of touch is developed to a degree that is quite inconceivable to other people."[23] From this observation, he turns, disturbingly, to a discussion of autopsies on blind people that have purportedly investigated the relationship between vision loss and a heightened sense of touch:

> It is asserted that very often when the fingertips of blind people have been dissected a deposit of gray brain matter has been found there constituting a sort of nerve centre independent of the brain itself.[24]

For the article's author, the academic achievements of the OIB's students offer support for a scientifically preposterous but culturally significant claim. Noteworthy for its conception of a physical connection, if not cellular sameness, between the fingers and the brains of blind people, the anecdote imagines a biological difference between visually disabled and sighted people that is notably unrelated to the eye and its function. Increasing the distance between blind and sighted people by adding a new element of bodily difference to the public profile of visually disabled people, this anecdote conflates the intellect with the body, literally locating in the hands of blind people their facility for intellectual achievement. Attributing academic success to an exceptional bodily state, the article is representative of the penchant of sighted observers to focus on the bodies of blind people, to find in their bodies evidence of difference, and to identify not just the disabilities but also the aptitudes of blind people as bodily in nature.

Of course, the fascination with blind people's sense of touch, demonstrated here, is not a nineteenth-century phenomenon. Interest in this aspect of blind experience predates the invention and proliferation of finger reading, but it gained new force with the late eighteenth-century invention of books for the blind and the nineteenth-century spread of blind literacy, both of which were extensively covered by the popular press. The finger reading of books, and also of maps, fascinated sighted visitors to educational institutions for the blind who found in the new methods and successes of blind education evidence of the compensatory heightening of touch in the wake of vision loss. While new optimism regarding the ability of touch to fully compensate for the lack of vision had progressive effects, fuelling enthusiasm for the education of blind people and inspiring efforts to adapt printed text and other learning materials to the perceptual needs and preferences of visually disabled people, optimism about touch also heightened already strong interest in the disabled body. Popular fixation on the bodies of blind people had the effect of limiting options for education, training, and employment. A group understood as characterized by unusual tactile skill and manual dexterity was also understood as a group best suited to manual labour—to the making of brushes, brooms, mattresses, and chairs. While sensitive touch was recognized as an aid to students in the acquisition of literacy, its most obvious application for nineteenth-century observers was in the space of the workshops whose central place in schools for blind people repeatedly threatened to reduce schools to asylums, a term regularly used to describe the OIB in the decades following its founding.

There were other effects of the popular fascination with the sense of touch. The physicality of blind literacy, of reading with the finger rather than the eye, prompted or, perhaps more accurately, licensed sighted observers to focus on the bodies rather than the minds of blind students and, in doing so, to focus on difference rather than sameness. When commentators fixated on the sensitive touch of blind students, they chose not only to take the body as their focus, but also to prioritize difference over the new common ground of blind and sighted people: their collective possession of literacy, their shared pursuit of formal education, and their study of the same topics and texts. Identifying skilled and sensitive touching as the defining ability of blind persons and emphasizing bodily difference over intellectual and cultural sameness, sighted commentators prioritized not the proximity of sighted and blind experience in the wake of the acquisition by blind Canadians of the now shared skill of literacy, but the differentiating feature of the "how" of blind reading: the practice of finger reading. The result was twofold: the addition of exceptional skill to exceptional lack as defining features of blind identity and the related retention of the focus on bodily difference instead of intellectual, emotional, or social sameness. With the addition of tactile sensitivity to the absence of vision in a list of blind people's bodily differences, the public response to the proliferation of blind literacy and the opening of schools for the blind was a doubling of the difference of blind people in the popular mind, further differentiating blind and sighted bodies and blind and sighted people.

As mentioned above, Robinson responds to this development by trying to shift attention away from touch and toward thought. Of course, what media reports on the OIB and more generally on the proliferation of blind literacy have in common with Robinson's book is their interest in the exceptional skills of blind people, skills that sighted communities identified as bodily but that Robinson insists are intellectual. Robinson's book, which makes almost no mention of touch, challenges the notion that blind people are compensated for the loss of vision with a heightened sense of touch and are, as such, remarkable not for their intellect but for their tactile sensitivity. Aware that ideas of this kind—ideas that characterize blind ability as bodily rather than intellectual and that emphasize the difference rather than the sameness of blind and sighted people— matter because of the limits they place on blind people, Robinson tries to end the fascination with the disabled body, both its limits and its aptitudes, that informed the underemployment of, and inadequate provision of education to, blind Canadians. When sighted audiences shaped a historical development that could just as easily be understood as a reduction of the distance between blind and sighted experience into evidence of difference and distance, Robinson responded by countering the tendency to embody, if not over-embody, the blind student. Conscious that what seems like praise is, in fact, problematic—for its focus on body and bodily difference, for its lack of attention to vocation and future, and for its overshadowing of intellectual potential—Robinson uses *The True Sphere* to work toward a kind of escape from the body, from both its sensory deficiencies and its sensory strengths. Intervening in the fascination with the disabled body and identifying the compensatory abilities traditionally associated with blindness as intellectual rather than sensorial in nature, he argues for a different kind of difference and develops a model of blind ability in which thought rather than touch figures centrally.

While *The True Sphere* is very much a book about ideas, it also contains a number of pragmatic recommendations, many of them related to the operations of schools for the blind, including, not surprisingly, the one with which he was most familiar, the Ontario Institution for the Education of the Blind. Robinson's comments on the school range from polite acknowledgement of his connection to it to detailed criticisms of its management and of its failure to accommodate the intellectual appetites and aptitudes of blind students. Robinson, who attributes many of his ideas about institutional reformation to a group of blind men with whom he has discussed the topic of blind education, presents a series of recommendations aimed at reducing the differences between schools for the sighted and schools for the blind. They include requests regarding reading materials, with Robinson calling not only for "increasing the number of embossed books largely"[25] but also for the adoption of specific books. "The blind should," he argues, "be taught the art of reading from the same text-books as the sighted and should take up these text-books in the same order and series."[26] The chief importance of this is, he explains, to establish "a bond of sympathy between blind and sighted children" and "to unite them in thought, memories, hopes and ambitions."[27] Unlike sighted observers, Robinson is not interested in the method of reading but in what is available to be read; the emphasis, for him, is not on difference but on connection.

Additional recommendations are similarly directed at bringing into closer proximity blind and sighted educational practices. He states that his chief objection to the OIB is that it is, unlike so-called normal schools, under the management of the Provincial Inspector of Prisons, Asylums, and Hospitals. Robinson explains: "It seems to me high time that the institution for the education of the blind should be transferred to the Education Department, where it rightly belongs. The blind are neither idiots nor criminals and no matter how well qualified persons may be to superintend prisons and asylums it does not follow that they know how to deal with the blind."[28] He also asks for a reconsideration, if not elimination, of the vocational training undertaken at schools for blind students. Concluding that basket-making, for instance, is "useless as a means of support,"[29] he dismisses the vocational training undertaken at the OIB as a failure. Here and elsewhere, his intention is, as Robinson phrases it, "to show how the education of the blind should and can be made like that of the sighted."[30] He also notes the success of institutions that have hired blind teachers, such as the Halifax School for the Blind, and campaigns for the OIB to follow their lead.

Perhaps most significant is his recommendation of "a careful inquiry ... into the after success of the blind trained in the special schools and of those trained in the ordinary schools,"[31] an inquiry that Robinson hopes will be undertaken by an organization "of the intelligent blind in all parts of the world."[32] Questioning the success of special schools for the blind and raising the possibility of their elimination and of the consequent placement of blind students in mainstream schools, Robinson explains: "As far as text-books are concerned, there is no longer any reason why they should not receive the same education as is given to the sighted. Are there other reasons which make it necessary to give them a special training? That question really means, do the blind need special schools?"[33] While Robinson has concrete suggestions for the improvement of the OIB and similar schools, he will ultimately direct readers' attention beyond schooling to the foundation of independent organizations of blind people: "It is not upon the improvement of the schools that the amelioration of the blind depends, but upon the formation of associations of the intelligent blind themselves. Without this cooperation the institutions can accomplish little."[34]

It is a telling historical development when a blind author can not only argue that blind people are naturally inclined toward scholarship but can also question the need for special schools for the blind a mere 25 years after the founding of the first school for blind students in Ontario. Demonstrating the rapidity of developments in the field of blind people's education, Robinson's declaration of the intellectual aptitude and professional potential of blind people and his critique of existing schools for blind people mark a new era in blind culture in Canada, one in which a blind Canadian can not only author and publish a book but can also use that book both to question the need for separate schools for blind students and to promote a new model of the blind student as not just capable of academic training but as more likely to succeed in it than a sighted person.

The reception of Robinson's book was mixed. A positive review of *The True Sphere* by James Cooke Seymour in *Methodist Magazine* in 1897 summarized Robinson's key points on blind education and praised the book as "excellent."[35] Seymour observes: "Mr. Robinson ... has treated this subject very fully. He has shown conclusively that most of the trades taught the blind have proved comparative failures, at least so far as enabling them to make a living by them."[36] Seymour accepts Robinson's argument that "it is not in the line of handicrafts at all that the blind find their best field for the use of their powers, but in the region of intellectual work,"[37] and he adds that "our author Mr Robinson is an excellent proof that a blind man can write a capital book."[38]

One might logically assume that a principal of a school for the blind would share this reviewer's enthusiasm and be eager to advertise the publication of a book by a highly accomplished former student, especially given the book's detailed engagement with the issue of education of visually disabled people. That was not, however, the case. Principal Dymond of the OIB used his annual report for 1896, the year in which *The True Sphere* was published, to defend the OIB and to challenge Robinson's arguments. Although he leaves both Robinson and his book unnamed, Dymond addresses the criticisms Robinson makes regarding the OIB's underestimation of blind students and the inadequate training provided them by it. Engaging Robinson's notion of blind people's possession of exceptional potential, Dymond explains: "I wish it to be distinctly understood that this Institution is equal to all reasonable possibilities; and, on the other hand, that whatever exceptional talents and advantages may here and there have done for a blind man, to the achievements of the blind as a class, the possibilities have pretty well-defined limits."[39] Writing in direct contradiction to the central arguments of Robinson's book, Dymond goes on to insist on the unlikelihood of a blind person's success in "professions or employments of an intellectual character."[40] Industrial training is, he insists, the intelligent blind man's best hope. Demonstrating the distance between the assessment of a former student and of a staff member of the OIB of the potential of blind people, Dymond refutes Robinson's ambitious agenda of reform and rejects his optimism about the future of blind people.[41] While he concedes that a blind man may achieve professional success, that is, "if assisted by highly educated sighted attendants and costly appliances, or under altogether exceptional advantages,"[42] he concludes that the professional blind man is "terribly handicapped if not hopelessly disadvantaged."[43] It is a telling phrase, disturbing both for its content and its confident tone. Clearly, Dymond and Robinson's difference of opinion regarding the central role of vision in education finds a parallel in their difference of opinions regarding both the operations of the OIB and the employment prospects and intellectual potential of blind people.[44]

Given Dymond's recalcitrant position, it is not surprising that Robinson's recommendations regarding the OIB appear to have gone largely unheeded. While Robinson did lobby successfully for a transfer of the OIB from the Provincial Inspector of Asylums, Prisons, and Public Charities to the Department of Education, a change that took place in 1905, a series of publications by two students of the OIB, Walter A. Ratcliffe and Arthur W. Beall, suggest that the OIB itself remained largely unchanged in the years immediately following the publication of *The True Sphere*. In pamphlets titled "An Appeal for the Blind" and "The Ontario Institution for the Education of the Blind: Its Management and Mismanagement," published in 1900 and 1901, Ratcliffe and Beall presented to their fellow Ontarians a long list of concerns about the mismanagement of the OIB. Their grievances range from arguably trifling complaints regarding cafeteria menus to disturbing and significant complaints about the failure of the school's administration to stop the sexual abuse of young male students by senior students. Of particular significance to this essay is the fact that Ratcliffe and Beall also echo key recommendations concerning the OIB made by Robinson in *The True Sphere*, most notably his request for the introduction of embossed versions of the standard textbooks of the Ontario curriculum.

While the influence of *The True Sphere of the Blind* was limited, it remains an important document of the nineteenth-century history of visual disability in Canada, valuable both for its philosophical content and its practical recommendations. It is, however, only a part of Robinson's legacy, which includes his publication of a Canadian magazine for blind readers, *Gleams of Light*, and, as noted above, his founding of the Canadian Free Library for the Blind. This library, which was amalgamated with the CNIB in 1919, circulated embossed books, many of them from Robinson's personal collection. These books were sent to readers by mail, Robinson having lobbied successfully for free postage for books for the use of blind readers within Canada. With the library, Robinson bypassed schools for blind students and their administrators, providing access to a wide selection of books and, in doing so, feeding the intellectual appetite that he identified in members of his community. Sadly, his work as a librarian and, more generally, his efforts to improve the public perception and educational and employment opportunities of blind people ended suddenly with his death at the age of 35 from typhoid fever. A contributor to a print culture that tended to over-embody the blind reader and to respond to the intellectual accomplishments of blind people with discussions of sensitive fingertips, Robinson wrote, instead of being written about. In doing so, he demonstrated the extent to which the spread of blind literacy, a development that while fuelling popular interest in visual disability and difference, provided visually disabled Canadians with new possibilities for self-representation and social influence.

NOTES

1. For a history of changes to the name of this school and abbreviations used to refer to it, please see Chapter 45 of Margaret Chandler Ross's *A Century of Challenge: The History of the Ontario School for the Blind* (Belleville, ON: Mika, 1980).
2. "Ontario Institution for the Blind, Brantford," *Canadian Mute* 7, no. 7 (January 2, 1899): 2.
3. "Ontario Institution for the Education of the Blind," *Canadian Journal of Medicine and Surgery* 3, no. 1 (January 1898): 29.
4. "Ontario Institution for the Education of the Blind," *Canadian Journal of Medicine and Surgery*, 29.
5. For more information on Robinson's role in the founding of the CFLB and for a detailed history of the CFLB, see Janet B. Friskney's "From Gleam of Light to Seedbed of a National Institute: The Canadian Free Library for the Blind, 1906–1918," *Papers of the Bibliographical Society of Canada* 50, no. 2 (2013): 187–237.
6. E. B. F. Robinson, *The True Sphere of the Blind* (Toronto: William Briggs, 1896), 20.
7. There are a number of surviving documents that record details of Robinson's life. They include a *Globe* newspaper report identifying Robinson as the secretary of a New Self Help Club; a program of the OIB listing a Bertie Robinson as a participant; a brief account of his life

prepared by his widow, Marion Robinson, who managed the library and its move to Toronto after her husband's death, held by Library and Archives Canada; and information gathered by CNIB historians, also held by Library and Archives Canada, whose efforts resulted in the erection of three plaques acknowledging Robinson's contribution, one in Toronto and one in Markham erected in 1956 to commemorate the 50th anniversary of the establishment of the Canadian Free Library for the Blind and one at his former home in Markham erected in 1980.
8. Robinson, *True Sphere*, 76.
9. Robinson, *True Sphere*, 106.
10. Robinson, *True Sphere*, 107.
11. Robinson, *True Sphere*, 20.
12. Robinson, *True Sphere*, 199.
13. Robinson, *True Sphere*, 22.
14. Robinson, *True Sphere*, 18.
15. Robinson, *True Sphere*, 230.
16. A. H. Dymond, "Education for the Blind in the Province of Ontario," *Special Report by the Bureau of Education: Educational Exhibits and Conventions at the World's Industrial and Cotton Centennial Exposition, New Orleans 1884–85*. Part I. Catalogue of Exhibits (Washington: Government Printing Office, 1886), 537.
17. Robinson, *True Sphere*, 18.
18. "The Ontario Institution for the Blind," *Pleasant Hours* 5, no. 15 (1885): 118.
19. "The Ontario Institution for the Blind," *Pleasant Hours*, 118.
20. "Ontario Institution for the Education of the Blind," *Canadian Journal of Medicine and Surgery*, 31.
21. "A Day in the Ontario Institution for the Blind: A Study of Present-Day Methods." *Methodist Magazine* 40, no. 6 (1894): 556.
22. "A Day in the Ontario Institution for the Blind," *Methodist Magazine*, 556.
23. "Ontario Institution for the Blind, Brantford," *Canadian Mute*, 2.
24. "Ontario Institution for the Blind, Brantford," *Canadian Mute*, 2.
25. Robinson, *True Sphere*, 81.
26. Robinson, *True Sphere*, 148.
27. Robinson, *True Sphere*, 148.
28. Robinson, *True Sphere*, 205.
29. Robinson, *True Sphere*, 205.
30. Robinson, *True Sphere*, 158.
31. Robinson, *True Sphere*, 100.
32. Robinson, *True Sphere*, 99.
33. Robinson, *True Sphere*, 99.
34. Robinson, *True Sphere*, 167.
35. "A Day in the Ontario Institution for the Blind," *Methodist Magazine*, 229.
36. "A Day in the Ontario Institution for the Blind," *Methodist Magazine*, 229.
37. "A Day in the Ontario Institution for the Blind," *Methodist Magazine*, 229.
38. "A Day in the Ontario Institution for the Blind," *Methodist Magazine*, 230.
39. Dymond, "Education for the Blind in the Province of Ontario," 15.
40. Dymond, "Education for the Blind in the Province of Ontario," 13.
41. More direct criticisms of Dymond may have also played a role in his decision to leave Robinson's book unnamed. Unlike former students Beall and Ratcliffe, whose publications, mentioned below, are notable for their vehement attacks on the personality and the professional competency of Dymond, Robinson is careful in his criticisms, noting for instance, politely

but suggestively, that "in his last report, Mr Dymond makes an admirable defense of the institution, its staff, its expenditures and its usefulness. I must say that in most particulars his points are well taken" (181). When Robinson addresses problems with the management of schools of the blind, he tends to generalize his comments, referring, for example, not to Dymond specifically but to unnamed sighted managers who understand schools for the blind as comfortable sinecures for themselves rather than as educational institutions. He takes a similar approach when he accuses, again without naming Dymond, principals of schools for the blind of putting their own desire for a large per capita grant ahead of the best interests of students when they fail to encourage students to graduate promptly.
42. Dymond, "Education for the Blind in the Province of Ontario," 13.
43. Dymond, "Education for the Blind in the Province of Ontario," 14.
44. A final anecdote in regards to Robinson's former principal: an announcement in *The Educational Journal* for September 15, 1890, noted that an unnamed blind youth had qualified for entry into Trinity University. The student in question was almost certainly Edgar Robinson:

> Among the successful candidates for Matriculation at the late examinations in Trinity University, was a blind youth of eighteen, educated at the Ontario Institution for the blind, at Brantford. This young man is said to have taken a very good position, when the difficulties he had necessarily to contend with are considered. That those difficulties are very great, we can well believe. (137)

The announcement is noteworthy for the information it provides not only about Robinson's success but also about his former principal's understanding of it. Surprised by the entry of a blind student into university, the *Educational Journal* turned to the principal of the OIB for information about his former student's academic success:

> As Principal Dymond suggests, it is not easy for one endowed with sight to really understand how much patient effort on the part of the teachers and how much steady application and persistence from the student is demanded when every subject has to be mastered by blind methods. (137)

Dymond's comments emphasize effort, the labour performed by both the student and his sighted teachers, to master material using "blind methods," which included the use of embossed print books, adapted maps, and writing frames, but relied heavily on oral modes of instruction. In *The True Sphere of the Blind*, when Robinson proposes that blindness brings about a heightening of the intellectual powers of visually disabled people, Robinson counters Dymond's portrait of industry and effort with an insistence on the innate ability of blind people to succeed in intellectual work.

BIBLIOGRAPHY

Announcement in *The Educational Journal* 4, no. 9 (1890): 137.

Beall, Arthur W. "The Ontario Institution for the Education of the Blind: Its Management and Mismanagement." 1901.

Chandler, Margaret Ross. *A Century of Challenge: The History of the Ontario School for the Blind.* Belleville, ON: Mika, 1980.

"A Day in the Ontario Institution for the Blind: A Study of Present-Day Methods." (Abridged from the *Brantford Expositor.*) *Methodist Magazine* 40, no. 6 (1894): 549–57.

Dymond, A. H. "Education for the Blind in the Province of Ontario." *Special Report by the Bureau of Education: Educational Exhibits and Conventions at the World's Industrial and Cotton Centennial Exposition, New Orleans 1884–85*. Part I. Catalogue of Exhibits. Washington: Government Printing Office, 1886. 537–40.

"The Ontario Institution for the Blind." *Pleasant Hours* 5, no. 15 (1885): 118.

"Ontario Institution for the Blind, Brantford." *Canadian Mute* 7, no. 7 (1899): 2–11.

"Ontario Institution for the Education of the Blind." *Canadian Journal of Medicine and Surgery* 3, no. 1 (1898): 25–31.

Ratcliffe, Walter A., and Arthur W. Beall. "A Further Appeal for the Blind." 1901.

Robinson, E. B. F. *The True Sphere of the Blind*. Toronto: William Briggs, 1896.

Seymour, James Cooke. "The Blind and their Achievements." *Methodist Magazine* 45, no. 3 (1897): 226–31.

"Twenty-Fifth Annual Report of the Inspector of Prisons and Public Charities upon the Ontario Institution for the Education of the Blind Brantford being for the year ending 30th September, 1896." Toronto: Warwick Bro's & Rutter, 1897.

CHAPTER 5

The Education of "Good" and "Useful" Citizens: Work, Disability, and d/Deaf Citizenship at the Ontario Institution for the Education of the Deaf, 1892–1902[*]

Alessandra Iozzo-Duval

In 1870 the Ontario Institution for the Education of the Deaf and Dumb (OIED), the first publicly funded residential school for the d/Deaf1 in the province, officially opened its doors. The OIED was mandated to provide a basic elementary education and an industrial training program guided by a specific d/Deaf pedagogy. The curriculum was imbued with specific citizenship messages echoing the public school system's that characterized "good" Canadian citizenship as consisting of respect for the existing social hierarchy, loyalty to the British Crown, diligent work habits, and self-sufficiency in adulthood. All Ontario school children were subject to such citizenship messages, in both subtle and overt ways. The students at the OIED, however, received particularly strong messages around ideas about work and self-sufficiency. These were emphasized and reinforced through the trades curriculum, which set out to ensure that OIED students, male and female, were well prepared to support themselves in adulthood. This emphasis on work, I argue, was integral to a broader citizenship project focusing on a reconstruction of "deafness": the hearing administration, policy-makers, reformers, and elite d/Deaf associated with the OIED sought to distance the d/Deaf from broader associations of disability that cast the d/Deaf in dependant roles. The OIED simultaneously emphasized that it was only through this specialized education that the province's d/Deaf could be taught to be "good" and "useful" citizens, at once legitimizing their own social value and that of the school as the newly designated "experts" of d/Deaf education.

Using the OIED as my focal point, I engage with the school's newspaper, *The Canadian Mute*,[2] to understand how notions of work and self-sufficiency—both practically and ideologically—were part of a specific citizenship project aimed at OIED students within a broader citizenship project of reconstruction. Canadian scholars of children and childhood have demonstrated how paid and unpaid work has always been a part of childhood for most children.[3] While ideas around labour and disability are being explored, the bulk of the secondary literature tends to focus on workers who become injured on the job, or who developed disabilities as a result of exposure to dangerous job conditions.[4] Paul Longmore and David Goldberger, for example, in their study of the physically handicapped during the Great Depression, point to the medical model of disability, viewing disability as a personal and medical construct rather than a social or ideological one. Like Longmore and Goldberger, much of the previous work on disability and labour has focused on occupational health.[5] Despite the depth of such work, no one has yet linked ideas about disability, d/Deafness, childhood, education, and citizenship. I focus my examination on the first decade of publication of *The Canadian Mute*, from 1892–1902.[6] My questions are straightforward: In what ways were constructions of work and d/Deaf citizenship represented in *The Canadian Mute*? In what ways did these representations contribute to, or detract from, dominant messages about "good" citizenship? Finally, in what ways did the student writing in *The Canadian Mute* reinforce, adapt, or reject these messages?

Disability Studies scholars such as Catherine Kudlick, Susan Burch, Ian Sutherland, and Douglas Baynton have demonstrated the importance of understanding how constructions of disability have been defined in the past, change over time, and shape how we engage with questions of disability today.[7] Understanding historical constructions of disability and d/Deafness is particularly important in the Canadian context given the paucity of work in Canada integrating education, citizenship, and d/Deaf history within a larger Disability Studies framework. As a social construction, "disability" and its meanings and definitions are contingent on historical processes, making it crucial to understand the social, political, and economic context in which questions of "good" d/Deaf citizenship arose.

In Ontario during the years of the late nineteenth and early twentieth century examined here, notions of disability embodied particularly negative connotations around ideas of danger, immorality, intellectual deficiency, and financial dependency—on both the family and the state. A key component of reconstructing "deafness" was an emphasis on the d/Deaf person as a capable and willing worker and therefore a self-sustaining citizen. To distance the d/Deaf from the disability category, the OIED insisted that its d/Deaf graduates could contribute positively to society in a number of important ways. Consequently, the notion of working ability was directly linked to, and often emphasized in, a reconstruction of the d/Deaf as closer to "normal" than "disabled." This reconstruction made up an important part of the OIED discourse on "good" citizenship. At the same time, the OIED administration maintained that if the d/Deaf were not educated at a specialized institution such as theirs, they would likely succumb to immoral and criminal behaviour—often defined as synonymous—and endanger both themselves and society at large. There were, they argued, social and economic consequences to failing to educate d/Deaf children at the OIED, further legitimizing the school as a base of d/Deaf "experts" and educators.

Industrial training was held in high regard and widely promoted at the OIED because the acquisition of a skilled trade countered the fear that d/Deaf students would become burdens on the family or the state in adulthood. As Dustin Galer notes in his study of disabled workers in Victorian Ontario, disabled bodies were perceived to be non-working unproductive bodies.[8] While the OIED sought to engage its students in a citizenship discourse similar in many ways to that of the public schools, its administrators directly correlated citizenship with productive labour. The need and desire for the d/Deaf to be armed with employable working-class skills was thus the priority. In June 1893, *The Canadian Mute* praised its graduating class, contending that "with them the state of dependency has been succeeded by one of active independence and self-reliance. They must take their places in the great army of workers, and compete for a share of fortune's gifts."[9] The product of the trades curriculum was "an army of workers" important to attaining "good" d/Deaf citizenship, and, indeed, "good" Canadian citizenship. This reflection highlights the administration's strong belief in training its students, male and female, for the "battle of life" and providing the ultimate shield against the disability stigma—earning one's own livelihood.

Reconstructing "deafness" in relation to d/Deaf children was congruent with the newly reconstructed Canadian childhood,[10] which included a series of state-regulated, -funded, and -organized institutions meant to protect this newly vulnerable group including, but not limited to, the establishment of the Children's Aid Society,[11] development of a separate system of juvenile justice,[12] and compulsory education.[13] In a period where systematic sorting soothed middle-class anxieties regarding the perceived upheaval and danger brought on by rapid industrialization and urbanization, the establishment of d/Deaf education was but one more saving effort directed at children. Canadian scholars of education have identified that public education involved not only basic academic skills—the three Rs—but also an ongoing lesson in citizenship, particularly as it related to instilling a common sense of identity rooted in social values that favoured loyalty, self-sufficiency, and respect for social order.[14] In particular, subjects such as history and geography, which in contemporary language fall under the category of social studies, were particularly suited to delivering citizenship messages about the greatness of Canada and Britain and the individual's civic duty to maintain such "greatness."[15] Education, in all its forms, was always at the core of reconstructing childhood, including d/Deaf childhood.

The OIED officially opened October 20, 1870, on 86 acres of land outside of Belleville.[16] The school was open to all d/Deaf Ontario children who were free from contagious disease and between the ages of seven and nineteen, for a period of seven years. The OIED opened using the combined system, a pedagogical approach that taught d/Deaf students to communicate through a combination of finger spelling, sign language, and oral articulation. During the years 1892 to 1902, the school remained committed to this system.[17] In conjunction with these vital communication skills, an academic and industrial training curriculum were pursued. The school operated as a residential institution where children remained on site from September to June, unable to return home on weekends or for holidays for fear they would bring back contagious disease.[18] Although the OIED was a non-denominational institution, a strong Christian structure similar to that of the public school was observed.[19]

The OIED administration was adamant that the OIED was first and foremost a school, and not an asylum or prison. This was a significant distinction, as the OIED fell under the jurisdiction of the Provincial Inspector of Prisons and Public Charities until 1905 when, after much lobbying, the school was finally subsumed under the Department of Education.[20] The distinction between education and reformation was made repeatedly, as the OIED's administration sought to distance the students from associations with criminality, dependency, and lunacy, all perceived markers of "bad" citizenship. There was also constant comparison, in school documents and in the school newspaper, between OIED students and their hearing counterparts in the public schools. The rhetoric emphasized that the students were "normal" schoolchildren who were merely deprived of hearing, and that the OIED itself was an educational institution equal to the best of the province's public schools.[21] There was evident tension in the administration's attempt to normalize the d/Deaf as potential citizens who merely lacked the sense of hearing while also classifying OIED students as different, and therefore in need of a specialized education. In this way, "good" d/Deaf citizenship was constructed as a goal that could only be reached through a school staffed by experts, such as the OIED.

According to the school administration, the OIED had two principal objectives: the first, to cultivate the mind through an education similar to that of the public school, and the second, to teach the d/Deaf various trades and industrial skills.[22] This two-pronged approach to d/Deaf education highlights the important role that work played in educating citizens and demonstrates how the academic and industrial curricula at the OIED were intertwined.[23] Schooling, then, had overt economic underpinnings at the OIED. It was imperative to the overall construction of the d/Deaf citizen to ensure that students could support themselves and their families in adulthood. The belief that ideas about disability would precede the d/Deaf worker to the workplace prompted the OIED to push its students to be seen as equal to, or having advanced skills over, the average hearing worker. Mediocre work would not make one a good candidate in an increasingly industrialized and capitalist society. Disability historian Catherine Kudlick argues that capitalism and disability are inseparable: "The rigors of the industrial workplace created more disabilities while the capitalist system had less patience for those who failed to conform to its highly specified demands."[24] In the industrial age, a disabled body was hard to ignore. Mitigating the perceived unproductiveness of d/Deaf students and alumni was a critical step in reconstructing the d/Deaf person as a "good" and "useful" worker, and hence a "good" citizen.

The OIED operated under the belief that two areas of work especially suited the d/Deaf: agriculture and mechanical trades,[25] reflecting the belief that the d/Deaf would generally stay within the working class.[26] During the first year of operation, the school offered training in carpentry and farming.[27] Tailoring was offered for the first time during the 1872–1873 school year, when 20 boys were employed in the trade.[28] Baking, which always attracted a smaller attendance than the others, was also offered during this period. The most popular trade for the first two decades of operation was shoemaking. The shoe shop opened during the 1872–1873 school year and subsequently filled an order of 250 boots for the Cobourg Central Prison, in addition to supplying some boots and shoes for the Toronto and London Prisons.[29]

While more options existed for male than female students, the curriculum reflected the belief that girls too needed to be prepared for a productive life in adulthood. As early as the first year, girls were engaged in work training under the supervision of the Matron:

"They are employed in sewing, knitting, and such other household work as they are fitted to perform."[30] As the years went on, sewing became more formalized and dressmaking and tailoring were pursued so that the girls would be able to complete not only household sewing but also work in dressmaking, millinery, and tailor shops. When tailoring opened at the school during the 1872–1873 school year, Principal Palmer noted that "several of the older girls will be placed in the tailoring department during work hours, which will give them an opportunity to learn to cut and make clothing of various kinds."[31] Given the limited sphere of employment open to women during this period, particularly those who were seen to be disabled, this working-class skill was deemed an important one in terms of future self-sufficiency.

Boys were generally employed in the shops by the fourth or fifth year of study for about three hours a day, including Saturday mornings,[32] meaning that boys as young as 10 or 11 could begin their training far in advance of what was being offered in the public schools at the time. Girls too were in the sewing room during designated industrial training hours.[33] During this period, the children began their days in the shops, proceeded to the academic classrooms, and returned to the shops after school for an hour or two.[34] In addition, The OIED allowed students who had finished the academic curriculum to come back for a year or two of trades training. This was further explained in an 1896 editorial in *The Canadian Mute*:

> Our pupils put 4 ½ hours per day in the class rooms and from 1 to 1 ½ hours at evening study; in the shops they work about 3 hours per day and half a day on Saturday. In addition to this there is the post graduate course for pupils who have passed the school limit and these work 8 ½ hours each week day except Saturday. We notice that in many schools this post graduate course is finding favour.[35]

This last year of extended study again emphasized the importance of making the d/Deaf "good" workers, while acknowledging that this was difficult to accomplish in a few hours a day. Again, the students were educated to enter the working class.

Although trades training commenced at the OIED in 1870, manual training for boys and domestic science for girls were not introduced into the public schools until the late nineteenth century. By 1900, work had become an important element of the New Education movement. The New Education incorporated subjects such as manual training, domestic science, agriculture, nature study, and physical education into the larger academic curriculum.[36] Between 1870 and 1890 the urban population and the number of employees in manufacturing doubled as the country became increasingly industrialized and urbanized, with Ontario as the manufacturing heartland of the nation.[37] This shift from agriculture and small-scale craft enterprises to increasingly larger manufacturing operations shaped educational policy. No longer would basic mechanical skills be provided solely through apprenticeships.[38] The 1889 report of the Royal Commission on the Relations of Capital and Labour admonished the public school system for leaving boys unprepared for the rigors of industrial life, a void that could only be filled by incorporating mechanical training into the regular curriculum.[39] The pressure from industrialists pushed the provincial governments to re-evaluate the curriculum. Manual training for boys and domestic science for girls became a growing part of Ontario schoolchildren's education. Manual training for boys was typically geared toward training the "eye, hand and mind" of the boy[40] and focused on basic woodworking rather than the skills involved in shoemaking, baking, or printing, as offered at the OIED. While scholars have examined the socio-economic and political forces at work in promoting technical education,[41] what remains to be considered is how questions of trades education intersected with notions of disability, and specifically d/Deaf education at the OIED.

It is particularly significant that the OIED offered this specialized training at the elementary level, decades before anything similar appeared in the province's public schools. In 1889, as the annual report of the Inspector of Prisons and Public Charities noted, "Industrial training in the common schools is one of the questions of the day for hearing children. For the deaf in Ontario it has been in operation since the establishment of this institution, and the good accomplished leads me to hope for its extension."[42] In 1910, national concern led to the establishment of the Royal Commission on Industrial Training and Technical Education, which strongly influenced the passage of the Ontario Industrial Education Act in 1911.[43] It was not until 1914, however, that trades training for hearing boys became a standard offering of the senior elementary curriculum in most urban schools.[44] The OIED was a frontrunner, roughly 40 years ahead of the trend, with its dual curriculum of academic and trades education as of 1870. In particular, specialized technical education for hearing children, as opposed to basic manual training, was more frequently provided at the secondary school level, whereas formalized trades training in the OIED shops began much earlier. The need at the OIED for students to acquire employable working-class skills was a priority. This does not mean, however, that the OIED neglected to follow the trend of the public school system, a system that they sought to emulate in all regards. Indeed, Sloyd—a version of manual training in basic woodwork as opposed to carpentry—was introduced in 1899, and domestic science officially became a part of the OIED curriculum in 1902, although it existed in various less organized forms for years prior.[45]

While shoemaking, carpentry, baking, and farming had deep roots at the OIED, it was not until 1892 that the print shop was added to the industrial trades curriculum. Many schools in the United States had print shops, and printing was believed to be a good trade for the d/Deaf as it allowed the students to become better schooled in the English language as well as capable of earning a living.[46] Although the majority of those who learned the printing trade were boys, during the first year of operation the OIED's print shop employed two girls. One of these went on to obtain work in a print shop a year later.[47] This break in the gendered divisions of trades education indicates that the notion of the d/Deaf becoming financially self-supporting was the ultimate goal. As such, blurring traditional gender lines was an acceptable concession in view of the objective to recreate the d/Deaf as capable and willing workers.

The main product of the print shop was the school newspaper, *The Canadian Mute*, which became a bi-monthly event in the lives of both students and alumni. It was first published on February 15, 1892. The official purpose was to teach typesetting to some students, to provide interesting reading material for the d/Deaf, and to serve as a medium of communication between the school and parents and friends of the pupils and alumni.[48] *The Canadian Mute* is a useful analytic tool because it allows some historical insight into popular ideas about disability, d/Deafness, citizenship, gender, and work during this particular period of time. It is also the outcome of the work objective itself, as it constituted the product of the trades training at the institution, and was certainly distinct from anything that the public schools were doing. *The Canadian Mute* had a wide circulation among parents of students, d/Deaf alumni, and those connected and/or interested in the OIED.[49]

For the purposes of this paper I focus on three features of the newspaper, which appeared, with limited exceptions, in each edition: the editorial, the Home News, and the Pupils' Locals. The editorial provides insight into the "official" word from the institution, representing the OIED's stand on matters relating to d/Deaf education and other national and local matters. From February 1892 to May 1894 the editorial was in the hands of teacher J. B. Ashley, with Superintendent Mathison as co-editor, although it was claimed he did not write the editorials.[50] After Ashley died in the spring of 1894 (and to the end of this study period in 1902), teacher George F. Stewart was listed as editor with Mathison listed as managing editor.[51] The Home News column consisted of point-form notes regarding the daily goings-on at the school. This column was written by William Nurse, a d/Deaf man who was an active member of the Ontario Deaf Association and the school's shoemaking instructor. The Pupils' Locals, like Nurse's Home News, were also presented as point-form notes about items that interested the students and often provided insight into the daily lives of the children within the classrooms, shops, and playground. The Pupils' Locals were written by senior students. Both the Home News and the Pupils' Locals are more casual in nature than the editorial and, as often noted, were the columns that parents most looked forward to reading:[52] "We know that many small things that go to make up our locals are of little account to those who have no connection with our school, but to those who have a dear little boy or girl here every little item is noticed, hence we pen them."[53] For parents separated from their children for almost 10 months of the year, these Locals were a line of communication.

In reading the newspaper, I seek the OIED's students' perspectives or voices; however, I am keenly aware that the newspaper was firmly in the control of adults and even more firmly in the hands of a hearing administration funded by the provincial government with a specific citizenship mandate. In her work using letters written by Canadian children to newspaper clubs during the early twentieth century, Norah Lewis warns that although we are "hearing" the child's "voice" via their written words, their submissions had to meet particular editorial standards regarding the quality of their penmanship and the content of their letters.[54] The student "voice" in the Pupils' Locals was also subject to adult approval, as explained in a spring editorial in 1894:

> The "pupils' locals" that appear in the columns of THE CANADIAN MUTE are subjected to editorial revision, not so much for the correction of errors in language, as to guard against license of expression that young persons are apt to take. They are simple brief references to persons and events, of local interest to the pupils.[55]

While useful, consequently, the Pupils' Locals cannot be taken to represent the authentic lived experience of students at the OIED. Regardless, they remain an important tool as so few records are left behind by children in the past.

My reading of these three columns, from 1892 to 1902, focuses on how ideas about work and citizenship were portrayed and the ways in which these constructions contributed to the ideas of a reconstructed d/Deaf citizen who was, in the end, a "good" and "useful" member of society. In particular, I examine how the newspaper expressed pride in the school's trades curriculum, provided past students success as proof of "good" d/Deaf citizenship, and chastised notions of d/Deaf dependency characterized primarily around the image of the d/Deaf beggar or peddler, and how the newspaper and the students who contributed to it reflected, adapted, and rejected dominant notions about work and "good" d/Deaf citizenship.

The industrial trades curriculum was an essential part of an OIED education and an important contributor to a reconstructed d/Deafness primarily because it encouraged good work habits and prepared students for their adult life as workers. In the spring of 1901, as George Stewart editorialized,

> to inculcate self-reliance should be one of the great aims of the school, and in order that this shall be attained the pupils should be thrown as much as possible on their own resources. A child that is always carried will never learn to walk.[56]

As discussed, this belief in the importance of an OIED education to develop "good" worker d/Deaf citizens was rooted in the schools origins in 1870; however, by the period under study (1892–1902), it was also a reflection of the New Education movement influencing the public schools. Legislation allowing individual school boards to establish technical schools if they wished was met with favour, as expressed by George Stewart in a spring editorial in 1897: "It is surely as much the prerogative of the State to compel children to learn how to earn their own living as it is to compel them to learn history or arithmetic."[57] Although he does not speak directly to questions of d/Deafness or disability, the implication is clear: arming a student to earn their own livelihood was important to every Ontarian.[58]

The desire for the d/Deaf to become self-reliant citizens was often linked to notions of masculinity underpinning the breadwinning role. The male body as "disabled" had particular significance during this period, as Dustin Galer observes: "The disabled body as an incomplete body meant that people with physical impairments did not have a proper claim on manhood."[59] Therefore, the administration sought out trades and skills that they believed would suit the d/Deaf male citizen both socially and practically and would enable them to support themselves and their families in adulthood.

The emphasis on the manliness of the boys as future breadwinners ultimately cast the girls in roles as future wives and mothers.[60] Just prior to Christmas in 1897, Nurse reflected on how well the girls' cooking classes were going, and observed that perhaps more could be done for the future breadwinners of the school as well:

> With the establishment of the cooking class the girls have opportunities for increased usefulness. When Mr. Mathison first spoke of it in the chapel most of the pupils thought it a little joke of his when he said he wanted the class and hoped it would fit them to be better wives and mothers, but the class is now going on and doing well. Perhaps it will be the boys' turn next to be given more opportunities for preparations as bread winners when they leave school. They cannot get too much of that kind of learning and we are glad to see that they recognized it more and more.[61]

The notion of educating girls for motherhood and domesticity and boys for the provider role reflected the public school rhetoric of the period, but extra pains were taken at the OIED to ensure that, for the years prior to marriage, or for the girls who remained unmarried, they were able to support themselves, usually as domestic servants, seamstresses, or dressmakers. An article appearing in *The Canadian Mute* in the spring of 1893 makes note that not only working-class girls but girls of all backgrounds needed to be able to take care of themselves:

> Every daughter should be taught to earn her own living: the rich as well as the poor require this training.... Skill added to labour is no disadvantage to the rich and is indispensable to the poor. Well-to-do parents must educate their daughters to work: no reform is more imperative than this.[62]

This article speaks to the notion that, while the OIED recognized the working-class backgrounds of a great deal of its students, it stressed the fact that work was a virtue for every student—and all citizens. In this way, overcoming "disability" trumped class.

The students, as well as the material products that they made, were also highlighted by the newspaper. The quality of the shoes and boots produced by the schools' shoe shop was a particular source of pride.[63] Not only were these boots often sent to asylums and institutions throughout the province,[64] but parents of OIED students were encouraged to have their children's footwear produced at the shop, as the quality, they maintained, was far superior to that of cheaper factory-made products.[65] There was a consistent belief that the boys in the shoe shop had a distinct advantage over hearing boys because of the depth of the trades training available through the shoe shop.[66]

On the practical side, the OIED also emphasized how the trades curriculum contributed to the operation of the school. The carpenter boys, in particular, were useful in installing and removing storm windows; building new seating for the classrooms, shops, and dormitories; making snow shovels and other tools; building fences; and even building an ice house.[67] The print shop, in addition to publishing the newspaper, also did all the printing for the school.[68] Similarly, the bakeshop provided all the bread and baked goods for the institution and, in the spring of 1893, when the baker took ill, two of the baking pupils stayed up all night just to get the bread done.[69] The practical benefits to the OIED, including cost efficiency, were certainly part of what made the industrial trades courses a success for the administration.

Although not all students participated in the industrial trades curriculum, all students were required to contribute to the school's daily upkeep through chores—another avenue to instill the value of a "good" work ethic. Shovelling snow, digging fence-post holes, building and maintaining sidewalks, mending fences, chopping and stacking firewood, sweeping the dormitory, waiting on tables in the dining room (on rotation), tidying the grounds, and doing farm work were among the chores the boys were expected to complete.[70] Girls were expected to help in the laundry room, including ironing, and to wash dishes and complete basic kitchen work and cleaning.[71] These chores reflected the gendered work that they would have been expected to do at home. All children performed gender-specific chores, but those who were not in the shops, particularly the larger and older boys, were tasked with extra chores to keep idleness at bay and ensure diligent work habits.[72] In the spring of 1897, Nurse noted disapprovingly of the number of "large boys with 'no ambition to learn a trade' so rather than have them lounge around they are now required to work on the farm. The boys were surprised but the farmer wanted a new field and he'll keep these boys busy in 'healthy work.'"[73]

The extended course, in which pupils were readmitted for a year or two of trades training after their academic training was completed, was also a source of pride for the OIED and was certainly unique in the province.[74] As Nurse noted in 1896, "Those who leave may not be finished mechanics or needlewomen but the foundations are well laid to build experience upon, and none need lack a livelihood who turn what they have learned to practical account."[75] Again, pride in the industrial curriculum was tied to notions of having the students well prepared to earn a living after they left school. If the OIED was to justify the public expense of its services for these children and young people, it was imperative that they produce citizens who would be self-sustaining in adulthood.

Portraying success among OIED alumni was important, as it served to prove that the graduates, thanks to their education, were able to find and retain employment. It was also important to identify the graduates as "good" citizens who were eager to work and financially self-supporting, and thus valuable to employers and society at large. Finally, the success of past pupils served to justify the establishment and maintenance of the OIED, as well as those experts associated with it. Pride in their alumni often found its way into *The Canadian Mute*, as this 1902 editorial indicates:

> It is with no little pride and gratification that we can point to the fact that at least ninety-five per cent of these have attained to a reasonable degree of prosperity in life, and that, with possibly one or two exceptions, all of them are industrious, law-abiding citizens, enjoy, as they merit, the confidence and respect of their fellows.[76]

This editorial exemplifies the school's praise for its graduates, once again correlating "good" citizenship with prosperity and industry. The graduates, once having left the school, were well aware of the reputation they were expected to uphold and equally aware that if they were seen to fail in any regard, the administration and the d/Deaf community at large would learn about it.

Although such official comments represented important "proof" to the school's administrators, it is likely that the words of the alumni themselves carried the most weight with the students and the d/Deaf community. The pages of the newspaper include comments and quotes, often taken from letters from graduates, about job "situations," homes, and lives.[77] For example, Elsie Garden's contribution to the Pupils' Locals informs us, "Miss. Ethel Irvine, one of our young friends who left here last year, has got work at Mr. Mills' tailoring shop in the city, and we all sincerely wish her every success."[78] The links between "good" citizenship were made clear: "Messers. P. Fraser and J. Flynn are two knights of the awl and have steady situations at W. B. Hamilton's factory, which they have held for quite a number of years. They are both good citizens and it is needless to say that they are also old Belleville Institution pupils."[79] These pieces of news kept the d/Deaf community connected while also serving as a reminder to its members that attaining employment was not only possible but also expected.

If holding down a job was proof of "good" d/Deaf citizenship, acquiring property and other material goods was equally important. Alumni also used *The Canadian Mute* to demonstrate their success in this regard. For example, in the winter of 1893 it was reported that former student Marshall Simmons was "proud as he has a horse and buggy of his own. He also owns two houses, two barns, and over three acres of land."[80] Similarly, in 1901 alumni Thomas Hazelton submitted a photograph of his shoe shop and home as a symbol of his success and inherent "good" citizenship.[81] Public declarations of material success were important to demonstrate that the d/Deaf were capable "good" workers, and that parents should believe the "experts" at the school and entrust their education to them, as it would ensure job security.

There was also a concerted effort by the OIED to portray its students and graduates as skilled tradespeople to future employers. The newspaper eagerly reported on any requests from employers for more workers from its shops. In 1898, for example, Nurse observed the following:

> It pleases us to know that the graduates of our shops are in demand and that many of them have won the respect of those who employ them. A little while

ago we received from a Georgetown firm a request for the addresses of some of the graduates of our shoe-shop as they wish to employ a couple more in their factory. One of our former pupils, Sam Beattie, has been with them several years and is one of their most valued employees.[82]

The fact that a former student had a job was a great source of pride, but having employers contact the school asking for similarly trained students was a huge boost to the school's faith in its industrial trades curriculum. These requests also served as evidence that the d/Deaf were considered "good" workers and were making progress in distancing themselves from broader disability labels.

Despite such confirmation that their objectives were being realized, the OIED did have to acknowledge that prejudice toward the d/Deaf was very real. The fact remained that many employers, as well as members of the public, did not always view the OIED graduates as being as capable as their hearing counterparts. In the spring of 1898, Nurse acknowledges,

> In these days when so many avenues are closed against the deaf for gaining a living, the success of a number of our old boys in running small shoe repairing shops of their own in various parts of the country should rouse others to the possibilities in this direction. We have received several excellent reports from them, and it is proved that deafness is not a bar to their success, that a capable pushing boy can remove and be independent of employers in a little business of his own.[83]

For this reason, the OIED encouraged the d/Deaf to practise trades in which they could maintain an element of control or autonomy. They argued that the trades curriculum would prepare the students to run a small shop, thereby ensuring their independence from any employer.[84] Not surprisingly, they identified whom they believed represented good examples of this type of success:

> J. A. Isbister has been working the cutting and fitting department of our shoe-shop through the winter, and purposes to start in business for himself next Fall. It would be well for them, if more of our pupils who have the ability followed his example.... By such a course they would be independent of hearing employers, and a comfortable livelihood would be assured them.[85]

There was interesting tension that in their desire to reconstruct the d/Deaf into an image of a "normal" citizen, they acknowledged that they would likely be more successful if they did not have to depend on the hearing for employment. If they could not start their own businesses, however, there was a sense of community in working alongside fellow d/Deaf people: "Mr. George Young, who was a pupil here about 11 years ago, has bought a farm about five miles from Belleville. The farm contains 400 acres and he paid $6000 for it. He wants to hire a deaf-mute on his farm and perhaps one of our big boys will go and help him."[86] Here, the newspaper also acted as a means to attain employment, connecting members of the d/Deaf community with opportunities to work together.

The newspaper occasionally printed letters from alumni reporting that they could not find employment, but that they hoped something would turn up soon. We learn from a letter submitted to the newspaper in 1892 by J. R. Byrne, who graduated from the OIED after learning the shoe trade, that he wished that the printing trade had been available to him when he was at school: "I only wished I had learned it before I left; it would have saved me many hardships that I have gone through owing to the dullness in the shoe trade, due to cheapness of machinery made boots and shoes, which is a great drain of revenue from the poor cobbler."[87] These contributions to the newspaper demonstrate that obtaining work was not always as easy as the OIED proposed. Good intentions and a trades education would only carry students so far in a society where disability remained an important status identifier.

The demonstrations of job success and property acquisition by OIED alumni in the pages of the newspaper as representations of "good" d/Deaf citizenship set those unable or unwilling to work as examples of "bad" d/Deaf citizenship. In particular, those who supported themselves and their families through peddling or, worse, begging were openly chastised. In the wake of a series of peddling incidents in 1895, a former student lamented,

> I am surprised that the deaf-mutes, knowing that it is a disgrace not only to themselves, their friends and schoolmates as well, go all over peddling.... I am sure that all the mutes who hold responsible positions in large establishments, as all are well aware that there are deaf printers, lithographers, cabinet-makers, shoemakers, carpenters, etc., will agree with me that it is better than peddling. Let all the mutes who are at present peddling think the matter over for a while, and change their positions, and act like gentlemen and work at something better. Then their friends would speak in the highest terms of them.[88]

The notion of reputation comes to light as the writer, who calls him or herself "A Graduate," is deeply troubled that a few acts of peddling will overshadow the successes of the majority of the d/Deaf. Peddling was equated with begging in many ways, and the less than "respectable" impression this gave was a detriment to all d/Deaf people.[89] In this way the d/Deaf community also contributed to the reconstruction of d/Deafness as its members sought to distance themselves from ideas about pauperism, charity, or incivility.

It is interesting, however, that allowances could be made for those who had no choice but to peddle, as was the case for former pupil Thomas Hill who received a reprieve, of sorts, due to his extra disability of poor eyesight. In the Home News column in the fall of 1894, Nurse reports,

Thos. Hill one of our old pupils gave us a call lately. He is on the road peddling. His eyesight shuts him out from many fields of labor. We don't object to peddling when it is done honestly—something useful is sold and an equivalent for the money received; but we draw the line at the sale of trashy articles that are of no value to anyone. If Tom must peddle, we are glad that it is something useful, and hope he will tide over the hard times. He is the first of our pupils to take to the business.[90]

The final comment, that he was the first of the graduates to take up such business, puts distance between him and the other peddlers, identifying Hill as an exception. Four years later, in regards to another d/Deaf peddler, the newspaper took a stronger stance, declaring that "such characters should receive no pity from the hearing public, they are a disgrace to their kind."[91] There was a strong desire on the part of the administration, as well as some members of the d/Deaf community, to distance themselves from the characterization of the d/Deaf as incapable of attaining honest work. If the education they received could not prepare them to earn a livelihood and thereby to assimilate into hearing society as productive citizens, the entire system of d/Deaf education was in danger of falling into question.

Under the veil of humour, the newspaper also began to print jokes and funny stories about hearing people posing as d/Deaf peddlers. For example, in December of 1902 the newspaper reprinted this comical anecdote:

A beggar was standing on the corner of a street with a large card on his breast with the words: "I am deaf and dumb." Two gentlemen came along, and one of them said he would like to give the poor man a dime if he was sure that he was deaf and dumb. The beggar quickly leaned over and whispered in his ear: "Read the card."[92]

Not only did this put a humorous spin on a threat to the reconstructed d/Deaf citizen, but it also pointed an accusatory finger at the hearing. Highlighting that a hearing person impersonated a d/Deaf person for the purpose of begging meant that it was the hearing person who was the "bad" citizen by not working.

Peddling had particularly negative connotations when linked to notions of "good" citizenship and masculinity in which the breadwinning role was exalted. In 1898 Nurse reported that a "tramp" had come to the school and asked to have his shoes repaired. The school allowed the boys to do this, but Nurse reasoned that the "tramp" must have told others because there was suddenly a deluge of "tramps" coming to the school. The practice was stopped and they were no longer allowed to fix shoes.[93] I suspect that had as much to do with the financial strain as the negative influence these "tramps" were perceived to have on the students. This is reflected in an observation in *The Canadian Mute* regarding a number of "tramps" that had been calling at the back kitchen doors of the institution in search of food: "The larger boys do not too look with much favor on such mendicants, as they have been taught lessons of industry and frugality."[94] Within a carefully constructed and implemented citizenship framework, ideas around "good" citizenship and masculinity were tightly controlled. For example, Nurse related that in the spring of 1901,

> a number of our pupils visited a moving picture exhibition given in the city opera house last week. The Queen's funeral and many interesting views of South Africa were shown, also several comic combinations which our boys enjoyed immensely. The big boys paid for the admission but at the Saturday afternoon matinee a crowd of our little fellows who had not the cash were invited in and given free seats by the manager. Our boys voted him a jolly good fellow.[95]

While it was acceptable for the younger boys—children—to accept the free seats it was certainly not acceptable for the larger boys to accept this form of charity. That this point was emphasized in the paper was as much a declaration to the public as it was to the boys themselves.

Although "good" d/Deaf citizenship manifested itself through constructions of work as a civic duty, there were also many references to work contributing to personal happiness. Making work a natural or normal characteristic, particularly in reference to masculinity, cast those who did not enjoy work as abnormal. A prescriptive story in April of 1895 informed readers of *The Canadian Mute* that it was physiologically impossible to work too much and that it was a hardship for "manly" men to not work.[96] This was reinforced by contributions to the Pupils' Locals such as the report that "Harmudas Forgette is still compelled to lay off from school and shopwork on account of his eyes. To an active, industrious boy this is a great hardship."[97] Girls, too, were encouraged to find personal happiness through work such as cleaning and keeping house, as in the following excerpt from a prescriptive story appearing in the newspaper: "Perhaps the reason why housework does so much more for women than games, is the fact that exercise which is immediately productive cheers the spirit. It gives women the courage to go on living, and makes things seem really worthwhile."[98] That both girls and boys were encouraged to believe that work was good for them mentally and physically reinforced the intended reconstruction of the d/Deaf worker citizen.

The Pupils' Locals generally reflected the dominant discourse about the value and virtue of hard work. Statements such as "All labor is honorable"[99] and "Industry is the best policy"[100] were commonplace within the Locals and speak to the degree to which notions about work were integrated into the daily discourse. In the spring of 1902 a student in Mr. Coleman's class noted, "We will be glad and happy to go home once more. Will you help your parents to work when you go home? You should be glad to do so."[101] Helping at home, a common occurrence in most homes of the period, was also an element of constructing "good" workers and demonstrated the reach of the OIED rhetoric. Even during the summer months, the ever-present mantra equating "good" citizenship with "good" work habits would guide the students. The dominant discourse remained with the students after graduation, especially, I suspect, if one wanted their letter to appear in the newspaper, as demonstrated in this excerpt from a former pupil's letter, submitted to *The Canadian Mute* in 1893 after he had relocated to Manitoba: "I am glad to say that my education has been a great benefit to me. I must prepare for the future, and must earn my own living. I am now doing my best."[102]

The student reflections are also interesting in that they reflect the degree to which parents still maintained some control over their children's education, despite the OIED's "best interest" philosophy, which cast the state and the school administration as the experts, although during this period attendance at the OIED was not compulsory. For example, in January of 1896 it was reported, "Nelson Wood has left the printing office on account of his mother wanting him to learn drawing every day so as to become an artist when he is through school."[103] A year later the Pupils' Locals reported that he was doing well as a portrait artist.[104]

The newspaper routinely points to the working lives of those graduates who are making a living as a measure of success and proof that an OIED education would result in graduates who were willing and capable workers. This is not to say that the students necessarily accepted all such discourses wholeheartedly and without question. Despite the dominant discourse that work was good, healthy, and natural, the children themselves sometimes offer a dissenting perspective. In the June 15, 1892, issue of the paper, an item from the Girls' Locals read, "The girls are generally saying: 'We will soon be speeding our way home, 'Home, Sweet Home'!' they say the boys don't care much about going home, and that they know the reason. They say it is because the boys have to help their fathers work on the farm, and it is hard work. Do you think it is so?"[105] This comment highlights the gendered expectations of life after school, while also acknowledging that d/Deaf children, like other children in farm and working-class families, already understood that work formed a large part of their daily lives, and that, moreover, they seldom had any choice but to work. Yet the financial independence of graduates served to justify to parents that an OIED education would benefit their children and was worth the emotional cost of separation and the material loss to the family economy. It was equally important to assure the government and the public that maintaining the OIED was a good investment. Finally, it was essential to inform potential employers that the d/Deaf were qualified diligent workers whose skills were equal and, in some cases, superior to those of their hearing counterparts.

A reading of *The Canadian Mute* from its inception in the winter of 1892 to the end of 1902 demonstrates that the OIED was firmly committed to presenting a version of citizenship that was in line with that of the public schools and general societal sentiments about a citizen's value as a worker and ability to be self-sustaining. The degree to which this was reinforced, through the residential nature of the school and by the publication of their own reading material, is significant in that it worked to shape a particular version of what the OIED believed made a "good" d/Deaf citizen. Through the shops and chores associated with daily life at a residential school, practical and ideological ideas about work, within a working-class framework, coalesced to form a distinct citizenship framework in which work was not only one's civic duty but also a path to one's own personal happiness. Work, in both the ideological sense and practical sense, was integrated into all aspects of school life, in and outside of the curriculum. That the d/Deaf could be "good" workers and support themselves and their families rather than rely on the state or their own family and friends for assistance in their adult years was paramount to "good" d/Deaf citizenship. The productive body was central to the reconstruction of the d/Deaf person as citizen outside of the category of "disabled."

NOTES

[*] This paper stems from a conference paper, based on my early doctoral research and analysis, presented at the Canadian Disability Studies Association–Association Canadienne des Études sur l'Incapacité, in Waterloo, Ontario, in 2012. The final dissertation, published in 2015, provides an extended form of this research and covers the period from 1870–1914.

I would like to thank Lorna McLean for reading early drafts of this paper and her continued support for my work. I would also like to acknowledge the financial support of the Nursing History Research Unit–Unité de recherche sur l'histoire du nursing and Marie-Claude Thifault for her interest and support of my research.

1. I have adopted the practice of using d/Deaf in reference to people who have varying sensory degrees of deafness as well as those who are culturally Deaf. For more on this debate, see Brenda Jo Brueggemann, "Think-Between: A Deaf Studies Commonplace Book," in *Signs and Voices: Deaf Culture, Identity, Language, and Arts*, ed. Kristin Lindren, Doreen DeLuca, and Donna Jo Napoli (Washington, DC: Gallaudet University Press, 2008), 30–42.
2. In 1913 the school would undergo a name change from The Ontario Institution for the Education of the Deaf and Dumb to The Ontario School for the Deaf. At this time the newspaper dropped the "Mute" from the title of the paper, deeming it an offensive term. From 1913 onward the newspaper was titled *The Canadian*.
3. See, for example, Neil Sutherland, "'We Always Had Things to Do': The Paid and Unpaid Work of Anglophone Children between the 1920s and 1960s," *Labour/Le Travail* 25 (Spring 1990): 105–41; James Bullen, "Hidden Workers: Child Labour and the Family Economy in Late Nineteenth-Century Urban Ontario," in *Canadian Family History*, ed. Bettina Bradbury (Toronto: Copp Clark Pitman, 1992); Bettina Bradbury, *Working Families: Age, Gender and Daily Survival in Industrializing Montreal* (Toronto: University of Toronto Press, 1993); Joy Parr, *Labouring Children: British Immigrant Apprentices to Canada, 1869–1924*, 2nd ed. (Toronto: University of Toronto Press, 1994); Robert McIntosh, *Boys in the Pits: Child Labour in Coal Mines* (Montreal: McGill-Queen's University Press, 2000).
4. See, for example, Nancy Forestell, "'And I Feel Like I'm Dying from Mining for Gold': Disability, Gender, and the Mining Community, 1920–1950," *Labor: Studies in Working-Class History of the Americas* 3, no. 3 (2006): 77–93; Sarah Rose, "'Crippled' Hands: Disability in Labour and Working-Class History," *Labor: Studies in Working-Class History of the Americas* 2, no. 1 (2005): 27–54; Rick Rennie, "The Historical Origins of Industrial Disease: Occupational Health and Labour Relations in the Flourspar Mines, St. Lawrence, Newfoundland, 1933–1945," *Labour/Le Travail* 55 (2005): 107–42.

5. Paul Longmore and David Goldberger, "The League of the Physically Handicapped and the Great Depression: A Case Study in the New Disability History," *Journal of American History* 87, no. 3 (December 2000): 888–90.
6. I will study the paper from the first issue, February 15, 1892, to December 15, 1902.
7. See, for example, Douglas Baynton, "Disability: A Useful Category of Historical Analysis," *Disability Studies Quarterly* 17 (1997): 82–96; Douglas Baynton, "Disability History: No Longer Hidden," *Review in American History* 32 (2004): 282–93; Susan Burch and Ian Sutherland, "Who's Not Yet Here? American Disability History," *Radical History Review* 94 (Winter 2006): 127–47; Catherine Kudlick and Paul Longmore, "Disability and the Transformation of Historians' Public Sphere," *Perspectives* 44, no. 8 (November 2006): 8–12; Catherine Kudlick, "Disability History: Why We Need Another 'Other,'" *American Historical Review* 108, no. 3 (June 2003): 763–93.
8. Dustin Galer, "A Friend in Need or a Business Indeed?: Disabled Bodies and Fraternalism in Victorian Ontario," *Labour/Le Travail* 66 (Fall 2010): 35.
9. J. B. Ashley, "Editorial: Our Graduates," *Canadian Mute*, June 15, 1893, 2.
10. Neil Sutherland's seminal work examined how childhood, as a social category, was reconceptualized through a series of middle-class "child saving campaigns" and state initiatives, which became the focus of anxieties about the family and the future of Canada. See Neil Sutherland, *Children in English Canadian Society, 1880–1920: Framing the Twentieth-Century Consensus* (Toronto, 1976; reissued by Wilfrid Laurier University Press, 2000). See also Neil Sutherland, "Children and Families Enter History's Mainstream," *Canadian Historical Review* 78, no. 3 (September 1997): 379–84.
11. For more on the emergence of the Children's Aid Society in Ontario, see Alan Jones and Leonard Rutman, *In the Children's Aid: J. J. Kelso and Child Welfare in Toronto* (Toronto: University of Toronto Press, 1981); Patricia T. Rooke and R. L. Schnell, *Discarding the Asylum: From Child Rescue to the Welfare State in English Canada, 1880–1950* (Lanham, MD: University Press of America, 1983); Xiaobei Chen, *Tending the Gardens of Citizenship: Child Saving in Toronto, 1880–1920s* (Toronto: University of Toronto Press, 2005).
12. For more on the emergence of the juvenile justice system in Ontario, see Susan Houston, "Victorian Origins of Juvenile Delinquency: A Canadian Experience," in *Education and Social Change: Themes from Ontario's Past*, ed. Michael Katz and Paul Mattingly (New York: New York University Press, 1975); Susan Houston, "The Role of the Criminal Law in Defining 'Youth' in Mid-Nineteenth Century Upper Canada," *Historical Studies in Education* 23, no. 3 (1994): 39–55; Paul Bennett, "Turning 'Bad Boys' into 'Good Citizens': The Reforming Impulses of Toronto's Industrial Schools Movement, 1883–1920s," *Ontario History* 78, no. 3 (1986): 77–101; Paul Bennett, "Taming 'Bad Boys' of the 'Dangerous Class': Child Rescue and Restraint at the Victoria Industrial School, 1887 to the 1920s," *Ontario History* 78, no. 3 (1988): 71–96; Bryan Hogeveen, "'You Will Hardly Believe I Turned Out So Well': Parole, Surveillance, Masculinity and the Victorian Industrial School, 1896–1935," *Histoire Sociale/Social History* 37, no. 74 (2004): 201–27; Bryan Hogeveen, "'The Evils with Which We Are Called to Grapple': Elite Reformers, Eugenicists, Environmental Psychologists and the Construction of Toronto's Working-Class Boy Problem, 1860–1930," *Labour/Le Travail* 55 (2005): 37–68.
13. For an overview of early education in Canada, including the move to compulsory schooling in Ontario, see Paul Axelrod, *The Promise of Schooling: Education in Canada, 1880–1914* (Toronto: University of Toronto Press, 1999); Alison Prentice, *The School Promoters: Education and Social Class in Mid-Nineteenth Century Upper Canada* (Toronto: McClelland and Stewart, 1977).
14. Prentice, *School Promoters*.

15. Kenneth Osborne, "Citizenship Education and Social Studies," in *Trends & Issues in Canadian Social Studies*, ed. Ian Wright and Alan Sears (Vancouver: Pacific Educational Press, 1997), 55.
16. Clifton Carbin, *Deaf Heritage in Canada: A Distinctive, Diverse, and Enduring Culture* (Toronto: McGraw-Hill Ryerson, 1996).
17. The OIED opened under the combined system of education in 1870 and remained under this system until early 1907 when an oral approach was gradually implemented.
18. When Superintendent Robert Mathison took over in 1877 he changed the policy so that students could not go home, except for the summer holidays, for fear that they would bring back contagious disease and sickness. Parents were permitted to visit the school as often as they wished but those parents who lived far away often only saw their children during the summer months.
19. Carbin, *Deaf Heritage in Canada*.
20. "Report of the Minister of Education Province of Ontario for the Year 1905. Part I. Appendix L.—Report of the Superintendent and Principal of the Ontario Institution for the Deaf and Dumb."
21. "The Institution for the Education of the Deaf and Dumb," *Twenty-Second Annual Report of the Inspector of Prisons and Public Charities upon the Ontario Institution for the Education and Instruction of the Deaf and Dumb, Belleville, Being for the year ending September 30th, 1892*, 43; "Report of Literary Examiner," *Twenty-Fifth Annual Report of the Inspector of Prisons and Public Charities upon the Ontario Institution for the Education and Instruction of the Deaf and Dumb, Belleville, Being for the year ending September 30th, 1895*, 47.
22. Wesley Palmer, "Report of the Superintendent of the Ontario Institution for the Deaf and Dumb, Belleville," *Twenty-Third Annual Report of the Inspector of Prisons and Public Charities upon the Ontario Institution for the Education of the Deaf and Dumb, Belleville, being for the year ending 30th September, 1893*, 16.
23. This is apparent in the following observation made by Inspector Chamberlain in 1898: "The industrial improvements of late years have kept pace with the literary work." Robert Chamberlain, "Inspector's Summary of the year's operations." *Twenty-Eighth Annual Report of the Inspector of Prisons and Public Charities upon the Ontario Institution for the Education of the Deaf and Dumb, Belleville, being for the year ending 30th September, 1898*, 9.
24. Catherine Kudlick, "A Profession for Every Body," *Journal of Women's History* 18, no. 1 (2006): 164.
25. William Nurse, "Mechanical Pursuits for Deaf Mutes," *Thirteenth Annual Report of the Inspector of Prisons and Public Charities upon the Ontario Institution for the Education and Instruction of the Deaf and Dumb, Belleville, Being for the year ending 30th September, 1883*, 59.
26. Wesley Palmer, "Report of the Principal of the Institution for the Deaf and Dumb, Belleville," in "First Annual Report of The Ontario Institution for the Deaf and Dumb, at Belleville Ontario for the Fiscal year ending 30th September, 1871." *Fourth annual Report of the Inspector of Asylums, Prisons, &c., for the Province of Ontario, 1870–71*, 168–69.
27. Palmer, "Report of the Principal," *Annual Report, 1870–71*, 169.
28. Wesley Palmer, "Ontario Institution for the Education of the Deaf and Dumb, Belleville. Reports of the Principal and Surgeon," in *Sixth Annual Report of the Inspector of Asylums, Prisons, &c., for the Province of Ontario, 1872–73*, 194.
29. J. W. Langmuir, "Ontario Institution for the Education of the Deaf and Dumb, Belleville." in *Sixth Annual Report of the Inspector of Asylums, Prisons, &c., for the Province of Ontario, 1872–73*, 39.

30. Wesley Palmer, "Report of the Principal of the Institution for the Deaf and Dumb, Belleville," *First Annual Report of The Ontario Institution for the Deaf and Dumb, at Belleville Ontario for the Fiscal year ending 30th September, 1871*, in *Fourth annual Report of the Inspector of Asylums, Prisons, &c., for the Province of Ontario, 1870–71*, 169.
31. Wesley Palmer, "Ontario Institution for the Education of the Deaf and Dumb, Belleville. Reports of the Principal and Surgeon," *Third Annual Report of The Ontario Institution for the Deaf and Dumb, at Belleville Ontario for the Fiscal year ending 30th September, 1873*, 194.
32. Robert Mathison, "The Superintendent's Report," in *Thirty-Third Annual Report of the Inspector of Prisons and Public Charities upon the Ontario Institution for the Education of the Deaf and Dumb, Belleville, being for the year ending 30th September, 1903*, 12.
33. Robert Mathison, "Report of the Superintendent of the Ontario Institution for the Deaf and Dumb," in *Nineteenth Annual Report of the Inspector of Prisons and Public Charities upon the Ontario Institution for the Instruction and Education of the Deaf and Dumb Belleville, Being for the year ending 30th September, 1889*, 27.
34. Mathison, "Report of the Superintendent," *Annual Report, 1889*, 27.
35. G. F. Stewart, "Editorial," *Canadian Mute*, December 1, 1896.
36. George Tomkins, *A Common Countenance: Stability and Change in Canadian Curriculum* (Toronto: Prentice-Hall Canada, 1986), 115–28.
37. Alison Taylor, "Education for Industrial and 'Postindustrial' Purposes," *Educational Policy* 11, no. 1 (March 1997): 6. For more on industrialization and labour, see seminal works by Bryan Palmer, *Working-Class Experience: The Rise and Reconstitution of Canadian Labour, 1800–1980* (Toronto: Butterworth, 1983); Greg Kealey, *Toronto Workers Respond to Industrial Capitalism 1867–1892* (Toronto: University of Toronto Press, 1980).
38. Kael Sharman and Larry Glassford, "The Appeal of Technical Education in Tough Times: A Comparison of the Toronto and Windsor Experiences, 1890–1930," *Historical Studies in Education* 23, no. 2 (Fall 2011): 55.
39. Axelrod, *The Promise of Schooling*, 107.
40. Tomkins, *A Common Countenance*, 117–19.
41. Robert Stamp's (1972) classical view argues that the rise of technical and vocational education was rooted in the decrease of apprenticeships as working-class parents sought employable futures for their children and this coincided with capitalist interests for a qualified workforce, all of which overlapped with the "New Education." For Stamp, secondary level technical education was broadly supported. Alternatively, historians such as John Bullen and Terrance Morrison have argued that the foundations of manual training and technical education can be connected to attempts to control the urban youth crime "problem" of the period. The industrial schools movement in Ontario for the province's "bad" boys and girls resulted in an amendment of the 1871 School Act allowing school boards to establish industrial schools. Likewise, Alison Taylor has examined the drive for state-sponsored technical education at the secondary level and argued that it was rooted in an industrial crisis characterized by technical change, an unstable economy, and labour-management conflicts. See Sharman and Glassford, "The Appeal of Technical Education in Tough Times," 55–56. See also Robert Stamp, "Urban Industrial Change and Curriculum Reform in Early Twentieth Century Ontario," in *Studies in Educational Change*, ed. Richard Heyman, Robert Lawson, and Robert Stamp (Toronto: Holt, Rinehart & Winston, 1972), 11–87; Robert Stamp, *The Schools of Ontario, 1876–1976* (Toronto: University of Toronto Press, 1982), 51–96; John Bullen, "Children of the Industrial Age: Children, Work, and Welfare in the Late Nineteenth-Century Ontario" (PhD diss., University of Ottawa, 1989); Terrance Morrison, "Reform as Social Tracking: The Case of

Industrial Education in Ontario 1970–1900," *Journal of Educational Thought* 8 (1974): 87–110; Taylor, "Education for Industrial and 'Postindustrial' Purposes," 11.

42. Robert Mathison, "Report of the Superintendent of the Ontario Institution for the Deaf and Dumb," in *Nineteenth Annual Report of the Inspector of Prisons and Public Charities upon the Ontario Institution for the Instruction and Education of the Deaf and Dumb Belleville, Being for the year ending 30th September, 1889*, 26.
43. Sutherland, *Children in English-Canadian Society*, 198–201.
44. Axelrod, *The Promise of Schooling*, 107.
45. Robert Mathison, "Report of the Superintendent of the Ontario Institution for the Deaf and Dumb, Belleville," in *Thirty-Second Annual Report of the Inspector of Prisons and Public Charities upon the Ontario Institution for the Education of the Deaf and Dumb, Belleville, being for the year ending 30th September, 1902*, 7.
46. "Untitled," *Canadian Mute*, February 15, 1892, 2.
47. "Untitled," *Canadian Mute*, February 15, 1892, 5; Mary Lynch, "Letters from Former Pupils," *Canadian Mute*, December 15, 1893, 3.
48. J. B. Ashley, "Editorial: Salutatory," *Canadian Mute*, February 15, 1892, 2.
49. For example, in 1893 it was reported that circulation of the newspaper reached 1,200 copies for each issue during the first year and that already 100 names had been added to the new subscription list. William Nurse, "Home News," *Canadian Mute*, March 15, 1893, 5.
50. Although Superintendent Mathison had a background in journalism and was integral in setting up the print shop and the newspaper, the first edition of the paper makes it clear, at least "officially," that "the control and management of 'THE CANADIAN MUTE' will after this issue be in charge of Mr. J. B. Ashley, one of our teachers whose ability for the task all will recognize." "Untitled," *Canadian Mute*, February 15, 1892, 5. See also the April 16, 1894, edition of the newspaper where Mathison and Ashley are listed as "Associate Editors." For the purposes of this research I will credit J. B. Ashley as the author of the editorials from February 1892 to May 1894.
51. It appears that Mathison retained the title of "co-manager" as an overseer of sorts: "Mr. Mathison is the managing editor and supplies a little copy occasionally for the MUTE, some teachers and officers contribute original and clipped matter from time to time, but a number of the best and brainiest articles that have been printed in the paper were from the versatile pen of 'G. F. S.'" "Untitled," *Canadian Mute*, March 1, 1901, 3. For the purposes of this research I will credit G. F. Stewart as the author of the editorials between May 15, 1894, and December 15, 1902.
52. See, for example, J. B. Ashley, "Editorial: Personal Journalism," *Canadian Mute*, October 1, 1892, 2; William Nurse, "Home News," *Canadian Mute*, November 1, 1892, 5; William Nurse, "Home News," *Canadian Mute*, October 15, 1894, 5; William Nurse, "Home News," *Canadian Mute*, March 15, 1897, 5.
53. William Nurse, "Home News," *Canadian Mute*, February 1, 1897, 5.
54. Norah Lewis, *"I Want to Join Your Club": Letters from Rural Children, 1900–1920* (Waterloo, ON: Wilfrid Laurier University Press, 1996).
55. J. B. Ashley, "Editorial: Original Efforts," *Canadian Mute*, April 16, 1894, 2.
56. George Stewart, "Editorial," *Canadian Mute*, May 1, 1901, 2.
57. George Stewart, "Editorial: Technical Education," *Canadian Mute*, May 15, 1897, 2.
58. George Stewart, "Editorial: Learn a Trade," *Canadian Mute*, April 1, 1897, 4.
59. Galer, "A Friend in Need or a Business Indeed?" 19.
60. This was important in the face of a eugenic movement that had supporters such as Alexander Graham Bell arguing against marriage between the Deaf. The school newspaper was peppered

with marriage announcements among former students uniting in marriage and establishing families.
61. William Nurse, "Home News," *Canadian Mute*, December 15, 1897, 7.
62. "Poor Girls," *Canadian Mute*, June 1, 1893, 8.
63. William Nurse, "Home News," *Canadian Mute*, April 15, 1892, 5.
64. William Nurse made a habit of detailing the orders that came in and out of the shoe shop for various institutions, asylums, and prisons throughout the province in his Home News column throughout the years. See, for example, the "Home News" column for the following dates: November 15, 1892, 5; May 1, 1893, 5; April 16, 1894, 5; June 1, 1895, 7; December 2, 1895, 5; February 15, 1898, 6; November 1, 1901, 5.
65. William Nurse, "Home News," *Canadian Mute*, November 1, 1897, 5.
66. William Nurse, "Home News," *Canadian Mute*, November 15, 1892, 5.
67. William Nurse, "Home News," *Canadian Mute*, April 1, 1893, 5; D. Luddy, "Pupils' Locals—From the Boys' Side of the Institution," *Canadian Mute*, February 15, 1894, 4; William Nurse, "Home News," *Canadian Mute*, April 2, 1894, 5; William Nurse, "Home News," *Canadian Mute*, November 1, 1897, 5. William Nurse, "Home News," *Canadian Mute*, January 15, 1901, 5.
68. J. B. Ashley, "Editorial: Our School," *Canadian Mute*, March 1, 1894, 2.
69. George Reeves, "Pupils' Locals—From the Boys' Side of the Institution," *Canadian Mute*, May 1, 1893, 4.
70. "Pupils' Locals—From the Boys Side of the Institution," *Canadian Mute*, March 1, 1892, 3; George Reeves, "Pupils' Locals—From the Boys Side of the Institution," *Canadian Mute*, June 15, 1892, 3; William Nurse, "Home News," *Canadian Mute*, November, 1, 1892, 5; William Nurse, "Home News," *Canadian Mute*, May 15, 1893, 5; D. Luddy, "Pupils' Locals—From the Boys Side of the Institution," *Canadian Mute*, February 15, 1894, 4; H. Roberts, "Pupils' Locals—From the Boys Side of the Institution," *Canadian Mute*, May 1, 1894, 3; D. Luddy, "Pupils' Locals—From the Boys Side of the Institution," *Canadian Mute*, April 1, 1895, 4; William Nurse, "Home News," *Canadian Mute*, April 1, 1895, 5; William Nurse, "Home News," *Canadian Mute*, June 1, 1895, 7; William Nurse, "Home News," *Canadian Mute*, October 15, 1895, 5; William Nurse, "Home News," *Canadian Mute*, April 15, 1896, 5; "Little by Little," *Canadian Mute*, May 1, 1896, 2.
71. "Dish Breakers," *Canadian Mute*, May 16, 1892, 5; "Girls in the Laundry," *Canadian Mute*, May 16, 1892, 5; M. Lynch, "Pupils' Locals—From the Girls Side of the Institution," *Canadian Mute*, March 1, 1893, 4; "The Laundry," *Canadian Mute*, October 1, 1894, 4; William Nurse, "Home News," *Canadian Mute*, December 1, 1897, 5.
72. William Nurse, "Home News," *Canadian Mute*, May 15, 1894, 6; D. Luddy, "Pupils' Locals—From the Boys Side of the Institution," *Canadian Mute*, March 1, 1895, 3; William Nurse, "Home News," *Canadian Mute*, October 15, 1897, 5.
73. William Nurse, "Home News," *Canadian Mute*, April 15, 1897, 5.
74. "Untitled," *Canadian Mute*, March 1, 1894, 2. See also "Untitled," *Canadian Mute*, November 15, 1893, 2.
75. William Nurse, "Home News," *Canadian Mute*, May 15, 1896, 5.
76. George Stewart, "Editorial: Thirty-Second Anniversary," *Canadian Mute*, November 1, 1902, 2.
77. "Pupils' Locals," *Canadian Mute*, October 15, 1901, 2.
78. Elsie Garden, "Pupils' Locals— From the Girls' Side of the Institution," *Canadian Mute*, November 1, 1894, 3.
79. "Toronto Topics," *Canadian Mute*, March 16, 1896, 3.
80. "Pupils Locals'—Boys Side of the Institution," *Canadian Mute*, February 1, 1893, 3.

81. "Shop and Residence of Thomas Hazelton, Delta," *Canadian Mute*, March 1, 1901, 6.
82. William Nurse, "Home News," *Canadian Mute*, October 1, 1898, 2.
83. William Nurse, "Home News," *Canadian Mute*, April 1, 1898, 5.
84. George Stewart, "Editorial: Manual Training," *Canadian Mute*, February 1, 1895, 2.
85. William Nurse, "Home News," *Canadian Mute*, June 1, 1894, 11.
86. D. Luddy, "Pupils' Locals—From the Boys Side of the Institution," *Canadian Mute*, April 16, 1894, 4.
87. J. R. Bryne, "Former Pupils," *Canadian Mute*, May 16, 1892, 4.
88. A Graduate, "Peddling," *Canadian Mute*, February 15, 1895, 2.
89. A Graduate, "More about Peddling," *Canadian Mute*, April 15, 1896, 3.
90. William Nurse, "Home News," *Canadian Mute*, October 1, 1894, 4.
91. "Deaf-Mute Beggars," *Canadian Mute*, February 15, 1898, 4.
92. "Untitled," *Canadian Mute*, December 15, 1902, 3. See also L. Blatter, "Untitled," *Canadian Mute*, November 15, 1902, 5.
93. William Nurse, "Home News," *Canadian Mute*, May 2, 1898, 5.
94. William Nurse, "Home News," *Canadian Mute*, April 15, 1892, 5.
95. William Nurse, "Home News," *Canadian Mute*, April 15, 1901, 5.
96. B. Burdette, "Advice to a Young Man," *Canadian Mute*, April 1, 1895, 1.
97. William Nurse, "Home News," *Canadian Mute*, February 1, 1898, 5.
98. "Housework as Exercise," *Canadian Mute*, February 15, 1898, 8
99. "Pupils' Locals—Mr. Denys' Class," *Canadian Mute*, February 1, 1902, 5.
100. "Pupils' Locals," *Canadian Mute*, October 1, 1901, 4.
101. "Pupils' Locals—Mr. Coleman's Class," *Canadian Mute*, May 15, 1902, 3.
102. "Boissevain, Man," *Canadian Mute*, January 2, 1893, 3.
103. George Munro, "Pupils' Locals—From the Boys' Side of the Institution," *Canadian Mute*, January 15, 1896, 4.
104. H. Roberts, "Pupils' Locals—From the Boys Side of the Institution," *Canadian Mute*, February 15, 1897, 2.
105. Mary Lynch, "Pupils' Locals— From the Girls' Side of the Institution," *Canadian Mute*, June 15, 1892, 3.

BIBLIOGRAPHY

Primary Sources

Gallaudet University Archives. *Canadian Mute/The Canadian*. February 15, 1892–December 15, 1902.

Inspector of Prisons and Public Charities. *Annual Reports of Prisons and Public Charities of the Province of Ontario*, 1870–1902.

Minister of Education. "Report of the Minister of Education Province of Ontario for the Year 1905. Part I. Appendix L.—Report of the Superintendent and Principal of the Ontario Institution for the Deaf and Dumb."

Secondary Sources

Axelrod, Paul. *The Promise of Schooling: Education in Canada, 1880–1914*. Toronto: University of Toronto Press, 1999.

Baynton, Douglas. "Disability: A Useful Category of Historical Analysis." *Disability Studies Quarterly* 17 (1997): 82–96.

Baynton, Douglas. "Disability History: No Longer Hidden." *Review in American History* 32 (2004): 282–93.

Bennett, Paul. "Turning 'Bad Boys' into 'Good Citizens': The Reforming Impulses of Toronto's Industrial Schools Movement, 1883–1920s." *Ontario History* 78, no. 3 (1986): 77–101.

Bennett, Paul. "Taming 'Bad Boys' of the 'Dangerous Class': Child Rescue and Restraint at the Victoria Industrial School, 1887 to the 1920s." *Ontario History* 78, no. 3 (1988): 71–96.

Bradbury, Bettina. *Working Families: Age, Gender and Daily Survival in Industrializing Montreal.* Toronto: University of Toronto Press, 1993.

Brueggeman, Brenda Jo. "Think-Between: A Deaf Studies Commonplace Book." In *Signs and Voices: Deaf Culture, Identity, Language, and Arts*, edited by Kristin Lindren, Doreen DeLuca, and Donna Jo Napoli, 30–42. Washington, DC: Gallaudet University Press, 2008.

Bullen, James. "Children of the Industrial Age: Children, Work, and Welfare in the Late Nineteenth-Century Ontario." PhD diss., University of Ottawa, 1989.

Bullen, James. "Hidden Workers: Child Labour and the Family Economy in Late Nineteenth-Century Urban Ontario." In *Canadian Family History*, edited by Bettina Bradbury, 199–219. Toronto: Copp Clark Pitman, 1992.

Burch, Susan, and Ian Sutherland. "Who's Not Yet Here? American Disability History." *Radical History Review* 94 (Winter 2006): 127–47.

Carbin, Clifton. *Deaf Heritage in Canada: A Distinctive, Diverse, and Enduring Culture.* Toronto: McGraw-Hill Ryerson, 1996.

Chen, Xiaobei. *Tending the Gardens of Citizenship: Child Saving in Toronto, 1880s–1920s.* Toronto: University of Toronto Press, 2005.

Forestell, Nancy. "'And I Feel Like I'm Dying from Mining for Gold': Disability, Gender, and the Mining Community, 1920–1950." *Labor: Studies in Working-Class History of the Americas* 3, no. 3 (2006): 77–93.

Galer, Dustin. "A Friend in Need or a Business Indeed?: Disabled Bodies and Fraternalism in Victorian Ontario." *Labour/Le Travail* 66 (Fall 2010): 9–36.

Hogeveen, Bryan. "'You Will Hardly Believe I Turned Out So Well: Parole, Surveillance, Masculinity and the Victorian Industrial School, 1896–1935." *Histoire Sociale/Social History* 37, no. 74 (2004): 201–27.

Hogeveen, Bryan. "'The Evils with Which We Are Called to Grapple': Elite Reformers, Eugenicists, Environmental Psychologists and the Construction of Toronto's Working-Class Boy Problem, 1860–1930." *Labour/Le Travail* 55 (2005): 37–68.

Houston, Susan. "Victorian Origins of Juvenile Delinquency: A Canadian Experience." In *Education and Social Change: Themes from Ontario's Past*, edited by Michael Katz and Paul Mattingly, 83–109. New York: New York University Press, 1975.

Houston, Susan. "The Role of the Criminal Law in Defining 'Youth' in Mid-Nineteenth Century Upper Canada." *Historical Studies in Education* 23, no. 3 (1994): 39–55.

Jones, Alan, and Leonard Rutman. *In the Children's Aid: J. J. Kelso and Child Welfare in Toronto.* Toronto: University of Toronto Press, 1981.

Kealey, Greg. *Toronto Workers Respond to Industrial Capitalism 1867–1892.* Toronto: University of Toronto Press, 1980.

Kudlick, Catherine. "Disability History: Why We Need Another 'Other.'" *American Historical Review* 108, no. 3 (June 2003): 763–93.

Kudlick, Catherine. "A Profession for Every Body." *Journal of Women's History* 18, no. 1 (2006): 163–67.

Kudlick, Catherine, and Paul Longmore. "Disability and the Transformation of Historians' Public Sphere." *Perspectives* 44, no. 8 (November 2006): 8–12.

Lewis, Norah. *"I Want to Join Your Club": Letters from Rural Children, 1900–1920*. Waterloo, ON: Wilfrid Laurier University Press, 1996.

Longmore, Paul, and David Goldberger. "The League of the Physically Handicapped and the Great Depression: A Case Study in the New Disability History." *Journal of American History* 87, no. 3 (December 2000): 888–921.

McIntosh, Robert. *Boys in the Pits: Child Labour in Coal Mines*. Montreal: McGill-Queen's University Press, 2000.

Morrison, Terrance. "Reform as Social Tracking: The Case of Industrial Education in Ontario 1970–1900." *Journal of Educational Thought* 8 (1974): 87–110.

Osborne, Kenneth. "Citizenship Education and Social Studies." In *Trends & Issues in Canadian Social Studies*, edited by Ian Wright and Alan Sears, 39–67. Vancouver: Pacific Educational Press, 1997.

Palmer, Bryan. *Working-Class Experience: The Rise and Reconstitution of Canadian Labour, 1800–1980*. Toronto: Butterworth, 1983.

Parr, Joy. *Labouring Children: British Immigrant Apprentices to Canada, 1869–1924*. 2nd ed. Toronto: University of Toronto Press, 1994.

Prentice, Alison. *The School Promoters: Education and Social Class in Mid-Nineteenth Century Upper Canada*. Toronto: McClelland and Stewart, 1977.

Rennie, Rick. "The Historical Origins of Industrial Disease: Occupational Health and Labour Relations in the Flourspar Mines, St. Lawrence, Newfoundland, 1933–1945." *Labour/Le Travail* 55 (2005): 107–42.

Rooke, Patricia T., and R. L. Schnell. *Discarding the Asylum: From Child Rescue to the Welfare State in English Canada, 1880–1950*. Lanham, MD: University Press of America, 1983.

Rose, Sarah. "'Crippled' Hands: Disability in Labour and Working-Class History." *Labor: Studies in Working-Class History of the Americas* 2, no. 1 (2005): 27–54.

Sharman, Kael, and Larry Glassford. "The Appeal of Technical Education in Tough Times: A Comparison of the Toronto and Windsor Experiences, 1890–1930." *Historical Studies in Education* 23, no. 2 (Fall 2011): 54–71.

Stamp, Robert. "Urban Industrial Change and Curriculum Reform in Early Twentieth Century Ontario." In *Studies in Educational Change*, edited by Richard Heyman, Robert Lawson, and Robert Stamp, 11–87. Toronto: Holt, Rinehart & Winston, 1972.

Stamp, Robert. *The Schools of Ontario, 1876–1976*. Toronto: University of Toronto Press, 1982.

Sutherland, Neil. "'We Always Had Things to Do': The Paid and Unpaid Work of Anglophone Children between the 1920s and 1960s." *Labour/Le Travail* 25 (Spring 1990): 105–41.

Sutherland, Neil. "Children and Families Enter History's Mainstream." *Canadian Historical Review* 78, no. 3 (September 1997): 379–84.

Sutherland, Neil. *Children in English Canadian Society, 1880–1920: Framing the Twentieth-Century Consensus*. Toronto, 1976; reissued by Wilfrid Laurier University Press, 2000.

Taylor, Alison. "Education for Industrial and "Postindustrial" Purposes." *Educational Policy* 11, no. 1 (March 1997): 3–40.

Tomkins, George. *A Common Countenance: Stability and Change in Canadian Curriculum*. Toronto: Prentice-Hall Canada, 1986.

CHAPTER 6

"An Excuse for Being So Bold": D. W. McDermid and the Early Development of the Manitoba Institute for the Deaf and Dumb, 1888–1900*

Sandy R. Barron

Duncan Wendall McDermid, principal of the Manitoba Institute for the Deaf and Dumb (MIDD)[1] in Winnipeg, received a letter from the father of a 15-year-old student in March of 1891. James Wilkie had written to offer the institute $58 in lieu of tuition, as the newly founded school offered free admission, room, and board to deaf students. The money, Wilkie wrote, should be "applied towards forming a nucleus for a suitable Library for the D & D Institute," the lack of which was "to be regretted and which furnishes me an excuse for being so bold."[2] The principal endorsed Wilkie's gesture in his subsequent communication to the provincial government, and enclosed Member of the Legislative Assembly (MLA) Findlay Young's support for the money's contribution to a library fund.[3] The MIDD, called the Manitoba School for the Deaf (MSD) after 1912, faced a litany of institutional challenges beyond the procurement of a library in its first decade. McDermid's first decade of correspondence with the Minister of Public Works offers a glimpse into the difficulties confronting nineteenth-century public institutions that arose with the growing recognition of the deaf as citizens possessing civic and educational rights, rather than as recipients only deserving of private charity. After its founding in 1888, the school struggled to consolidate itself as a first-class publicly funded educational institution during a period in which the novelty of deaf education in pre-Confederation British North America had given way to an acceptance by the general public that it was a legitimate and necessary enterprise. Realizing Manitoba's recently enshrined goal of free education for deaf children, as well as the province's compulsory educational requirement for all deaf children of school age, remained difficult in the school's first few years in the face of a minimal provincial appropriation and the reluctance of some parents to send their children to the deaf residential school in Winnipeg. It is the purpose of this chapter to consider how the MIDD, despite these significant roadblocks, transformed from a school reliant on private and religious charity to one reliant on public funds, which allowed the school to incrementally improve its professional standing and bring its practices up to the emerging North American standard.

Deaf education in Canada has only recently been examined by academic historians, and most have chosen to focus on the methods debate between oralists and manualists that dominated printed sources from the late nineteenth and early twentieth centuries. Earlier work on deaf education presented the movement's history as divided into pre- and post–deaf education eras, and omitted consideration of the difficulties faced by provincial schools and governments to develop and consolidate effective educational institutions. The stories of schools, in other words, both began and ended with their founding or their adoption of oralism. Scholarly focus has taken an intellectual and national focus, with an emphasis on analysis of the words of administrators, in the service of understanding hearing dismissal of Deaf culture in the past.[4] This work has borne fruit, but attention to the difficulties of establishing and improving deaf schools has not been a central focus of study. Margret Winzer's work is a partial exception, as she focuses on the periods before deaf education was firmly established in Canada, as well as on the efforts of deaf and hearing North Americans to have education of deaf individuals recognized as a state responsibility, including institutional development after the founding of schools.[5] Winzer traces how nineteenth-century advocates for the pre-lingually deaf and hearing-impaired pursued childhood education as a primary goal, as well as the importance of the financial and moral support of clergy to the success of the deaf education movement. Most importantly for the scope of this paper, Winzer argues that reforms within institutions of special education almost exclusively came from both educators and individuals who were educated within them.[6]

While focused on the establishment of deaf and blind institutions in the Maritimes, Joanna Pearce has argued that the Halifax Asylum for the Blind and the Halifax Institution for the Deaf and Dumb represented a movement from a charitable institutional model to an educational, rights-based one, and that this transition was a key step in the emergence of what Mariana Valverde has called a "mixed social economy."[7] Pearce's research also points to the importance of the clergy and individual provincial legislators in establishing free deaf education as a provincial right in 1872, in the case of Nova Scotia. Other scholars have begun to focus on the difficulties and successes of the development of deaf schools over time. Stephane-D. Perrault, for example, has argued that the charitable model adopted by Quebec's three Catholic deaf schools allowed them to succumb after 1880 to political pressure to adopt oralism, or the exclusive use of lip-reading and speech as opposed to sign language, before other Canadian schools.[8] This chapter will argue that the primarily public model of funding for the Manitoba Institute for the Deaf and Dumb allowed the school to evolve and develop over time, albeit in opposition to rigid provincial budgets. The establishment of specialized educational institutions in late Victorian Western Canada was, then, a more complicated process than a diametrical model of progress in deaf education may suggest.

Some scholars have presented the development of institutions to serve people with disabilities in a simplistically negative light. While Veronica Strong-Boag, in her discussion of the transition of the care of disabled children from private to public support, correctly highlights how residential and "segregationist" schools like the MIDD quickly outstripped the fiscal expectations of provincial governments, she groups deaf schools with other coercive nineteenth-century public institutions.[9] These public bodies, she argues, became little more than "eugenic warehouses" that sought to offer limited training and support to disabled children in order to ameliorate the toll such care took on families and private charities.[10] Firstly, such a view of deaf educational institutions, which portrays deaf students and staff solely as victims, underestimates the limited agency that they increasingly exercised at the MIDD after 1890 in shaping the school's mission.[11] Principal McDermid's efforts to improve the school's material and educational standing and the Ministry of Public Works's acceptance of many of his requests also challenge Strong-Boag's assertion, albeit only in the limited context of the MIDD. McDermid firmly believed in the importance of provincial support for the school, and clearly sought to improve the institute's functioning through concerted lobbying for supplies, sign language–fluent employees, and building improvements that he felt were necessary to the development of a new type of specialized institution that had successful precedents throughout North America and Europe. "Surprise is frequently manifested by persons unacquainted with the need of an institution of this kind," McDermid wrote in his annual report for 1890. "We ... differ from ordinary schools."[12]

This chapter does not attempt to present a thorough picture of the school's fiscal circumstances from 1888 to 1900. Instead, it places singular importance on Duncan McDermid's appraisal of the school's needs and requirements communicated through his letters to James Smart and Robert Watson, the ministers of Public Works during the 1890s. Its conclusions are drawn from McDermid's correspondence with Smart, his annual reports to the Manitoba Legislature, a school history written by McDermid for the Chicago Exposition of 1893, and the institute's self-published newspaper, *Silent Echo*. Manitoba newspapers and the *American Annals of the Deaf* were also consulted to draw conclusions about the MIDD's larger political and social meaning in the province and in the continental Deaf community.

On January 13, 1888, Liberal Leader Thomas Greenway was called upon by the Lieutenant-Governor of Manitoba to form a government. The incoming administration was swept in on a wave of resentment towards the Canadian Pacific Railway monopoly in Western Canada, but quickly began to pursue other priorities. Greenway, with key ally and Brandon MLA James Smart, began to overhaul Manitoba's educational system. The goal was to ensure the government's fiscal control over education by seeking to eliminate the bilingual or "dual" system of French and English schools then in place and bringing schools under direct government supervision and responsibility.[13] The MIDD, while not directly linked to the "Manitoba Schools Question" that has dominated scholarship about Greenway's premiership, was certainly part of this larger movement of centralization in education. While notions of fiscal restraint may seem to be at odds with the establishment of a new institution to serve a small minority of the province's population, the Greenway government's endorsement of the MIDD can perhaps be best understood as a consolidation of provincial political power, rather than simply a charitable or altruistic enterprise. After early 1889, the MIDD was financed and overseen by the Ministry of Public Works, which also oversaw the province's emerging asylums and institutions.[14] Manitoba, as the first province in the Dominion to legislate compulsory deaf education, and only the third to offer free education to all deaf students, behind Nova Scotia and Ontario, created a uniquely difficult yet visionary system of deaf education. The Greenway government had taken sole accountability for deaf education, unlike in the rest of the country, where church and private contributions were central to the operating budgets of deaf schools in Ontario, Quebec, and Nova Scotia.[15]

In addition to the centralizing mission of the Greenway government, the MIDD originated as an outgrowth of an ethically motivated movement to address the needs of deaf children in the growing province. A survey carried out by the Manitoba Legislature in early 1888 by MLA Frederick H. Francis found that at least 37 pre- or post-lingually deaf children of school age were living in the province's Protestant communities alone.[16] The January 16, 1888, edition of the *Brandon Sun* remarked that "government assistance is required. There is no doubt that the number of deaf and dumb in the province is a large percentage, and that they should grow up without the advantages of an education is not desired."[17] After the City of Winnipeg refused to fund the school, the Winnipeg Ministerial Association (WMA), under the leadership of congregationalist minister Hugh Pedley, agreed to partially fund a small deaf school under the principalship of Hamilton native J. C. Watson, a former teacher at the Washington School for Defective Youth. The coalition's aim was to lobby the provincial government to take over the school in late 1888.[18] Pedley and Francis, along with Francis George Jefferson, a recent deaf immigrant, and Sarah McPhee, the mother of a deaf child, met with members of the Greenway government to argue for the establishment of a provincial school.[19] While the school operated in its first year under WMA support, it largely achieved financial solvency through Watson's personal financial contributions, as the WMA contributed only $100 in 1888.[20] After initially rejecting the initiative, the Liberal government of Thomas Greenway appropriated $25,000 to build and maintain the school in early 1889, and declared deaf education to be compulsory and free in the province by early 1891.[21] All spending appropriations were controlled by the provincial government. A group of five parliamentarians operated as an overseeing committee, receiving the school's concerns and monitoring its spending and progress.[22] The school operated under Watson in Winnipeg's Fortune Block until his resignation for health reasons in 1890, and his ultimate return to the Washington school. Duncan McDermid, a teacher working at the Iowa Institution, was hired as the school's principal. His wife, Mary, a deaf graduate of the Ontario Institute, was appointed as his assistant teacher. The school moved into its new building on the corner of Sherbrook Street and Portage Avenue shortly after McDermid's arrival.

The adoption of the MIDD for both the purposes of bureaucratic centralization and the amelioration of bleak employment prospects for deaf citizens reflects larger nineteenth-century North American trends in deaf education. American deaf schools emerged in the early nineteenth century from a climate of public and scientific fascination with the deaf that was an outgrowth of Enlightenment interest in the role of language in human development.[23] Interested French educators, including Charles-Michel de L'Epée and Roch-Ambrose Cucurron Sicard, developed methods for codifying existing sign languages and educating pre-lingually deaf citizens who were largely considered to be incapable of intellectual development before the Enlightenment. In 1817, Sicard's student Laurent Clerc helped found the first American deaf school in Hartford, Connecticut, which benefitted from the public's scientific fascination with deafness as well as their concern for the spiritual wellbeing of pre-lingually deaf people. Berger argues that during much of the antebellum period, the operation of a state-run school in the United States was a symbol of an individual state's power and benevolence.[24] Buildings were large, opulent monuments to modern educational science and state legitimacy, and remained so throughout the post–Civil War period, which was characterized by the growth of oralism, or the outlawing of sign language, in many American schools. Manitoba's legislators were motivated by this same mixture of moral concern and "province-building" during the late 1880s and early 1890s.

Duncan McDermid was born in 1858 in Martintown, Ontario. He began to work at the Ontario Institute in Belleville as a clerk and telegraph operator at 12 years old. From 1877 to 1882, he worked as a teacher at the school, and moved to the Iowa Institution as a teacher from 1882 to 1890. After arriving at the MIDD as principal, he quickly established close ties with Winnipeg's charitable and business communities, and worked hard to establish the school's connections with the community and increase public support for the nascent school. His association with philanthropic social groups like the Manitoba Club, of which he was president, and the St. Andrew's Society helped to increase the provincial profile of the MIDD.[25] He and his wife were key figures in the proliferation of sign language in Manitoba, and the McDermid family, including their two hearing children, Howard and Ruth, acted as teachers and interpreters for the deaf in court proceedings and church services for decades.[26] The MIDD largely resisted the wave of oralist education then sweeping the United States, a movement characterized by the prohibition of sign language on deaf campuses and the uniform determination to teach deaf children to speak and read lips in order to facilitate their greater integration into hearing society.[27] The McDermid family were tireless advocates for the employment opportunities of deaf Manitobans, and were formational figures in the early development of Deaf culture in Western Canada.[28] Duncan strove throughout his tenure as principal, as did Howard McDermid after his father's death, to establish and maintain links to the larger North American Deaf community through the establishment of a school paper and publication in the *American Annals of the Deaf*.

The establishment of a school for the deaf presented key differences from the founding of a school for hearing students. The Manitoba school taught students using the "combined method," meaning that pre-lingually deaf students were taught primarily through the medium of sign, and those students who had developed aural language abilities before their hearing impairment were taught lip-reading and elocution, or the oral teaching method. "Our object is to secure the greatest good to the greatest number and to accomplish this the use of the two systems of instruction seem [*sic*] necessary," McDermid wrote in 1891.[29] The annual report for 1890 shows that out of 29 students attending the school as of December of that year, 9 were "born deaf" or, by assumption, pre-lingually deaf.[30] While other students became deaf through childhood illness, the age at which they became hearing-impaired is not provided within McDermid's data, so it is not possible to determine with any degree of comfort the proportion of students involved in sign instruction and those in oral instruction. Attempts to teach students orally were likely rare and ad hoc before 1911, as the school only adopted a distinct oral educational stream that year. As we will see, McDermid felt that hiring employees who were proficient in sign was a key responsibility of his position and the Provincial Ministry of Public Works, so the distinction between the number of sign students and oral students is not a practically meaningful one. Sign language was the lingua franca of the school, and in order for employees to function there, they required receptive and expressive abilities in sign language. This chapter will categorize the specialized needs of the MIDD in the early 1890s in two ways: the infrastructural demands of a residential school, and the unique methods and demands of a school for the deaf.

From 1890 to 1900, McDermid kept up a vigorous correspondence with Public Works ministers Smart and Watson that highlighted the structural, fiscal, and practical problems that the principal likely felt were keeping the school from becoming a first-class institution. Among these were his concerns about the lack of qualified teachers and the Greenway Cabinet's unwillingness to pay competitive wages for them; the need to balance compulsory legislation with the fiscal needs of distant rural families; and the lack of adequate fire protection, sewage removal, filtered water capabilities, and medical attendance at the school. During the period under study, two of McDermid's fears were realized—1891 saw both a fire and a fatal scarlet fever outbreak at the school. A recurring theme in McDermid's letters was the need for the government to accommodate the unique nature of educational institutions for deaf students, and he repeatedly tried to frame his requests as being necessary to meet the demands of a new kind of residential educational institution. During McDermid's first two years as principal, the MIDD progressed slowly but incompletely toward meeting these goals.

Several of McDermid's most pressing problems with the new building challenged the developing school's role as a *residential* entity. McDermid requested on several occasions in his correspondence and personal interactions with the Ministry of Public Works that the school be afforded laundry and medical attendance in the building, which he argued was necessary to the operation of a residential school. "I feel that the interests of the Institution demand that you should understand more fully the straits we will be in if there is no provision made for laundry and medical attendance.… I fully believe that I will require altogether for Incidentals [*sic*] laundry and medical attendance more than $600 … no matter in what way you consider the question the expenses can not be reduced without seriously crippling our work."[31] Providing on-site laundry and medical support for the residential school would save the province money, he argued. An infirmary was added to the school shortly before a scarlet fever epidemic struck the school in late 1891, resulting in the illness of eight students and one student's death.[32]

Fire protection was another recurring infrastructural concern of McDermid's. On March 2, 1891, he wrote to Smart that "the protection of the building from the danger of fire and the inefficiency of the sanitary arrangements are so fully recognized as to their immediate necessity that further suggestions are out of place."[33] While it seems that the two men discussed the issue outside of their correspondence, adequate fire protection measures were not taken before fire gutted the upper floors of the Sherbrook and Portage building on the morning of October 27, 1891. The fire seems to have been helped by two overlapping problems of which McDermid complained—the shortage of water buckets to extinguish flames and the absence of a permanent medical attendant. The school's newly hired matron was fumigating a room with sulphur for a sick child, and her candles may have started the blaze, she admitted in a November 6th report.[34] The school was relocated to merchant A. G. B. Bannatyne's residence at Armstrong's Point for the next year, where McDermid's fire prevention requests were finally met. The infrastructural challenges to the establishment of a functioning residential school were only incrementally addressed by the Department of Public Works, often in response to related crises. Sewage disposal problems were addressed during the 1890s, but overcrowding and water filtration remained a problem at the school's numerous locations until its relocation in a newly built, permanent facility in Tuxedo Park in 1922. The problems in both quality and quantity of water are unsurprising, given Winnipeg's ongoing difficulties in ensuring a consistent citywide water supply under a private system that served the city until 1900 and drew from the polluted Red and Assiniboine rivers.[35]

McDermid's determination to improve the overcrowding at the school boiled over in an angry letter to new Minister of Public Works Robert Watson in 1893. The close proximity of residential students and staff promised that a general outbreak of communicable disease could be disastrous for the student body, as well as McDermid's own children. "I feel keenly upon the subject," he wrote; "I have two children of my own at tender ages—the time when they are most susceptible to such diseases as diphtheria, scarlet fever etc., and I fully realize the danger there is and has been to them in an outbreak." McDermid clearly felt that parents had not been fully notified about overcrowding issues during the past two years, and his writing betrays a sense of guilt over having to sell a cleaner bill of institutional health and safety to more distant parents than he thought the MIDD warranted at the time:

> It [speaking of his children earlier] will perhaps be some excuse for my speaking so directly upon this subject but I do not in any sense offer it as an argument in favor of something being done but more for the purposes of impressing upon you and other members of the government as parents the feelings which would naturally arise in the breasts of the parents of our pupils if they fully understood

how we are situated. The Camerons and Lonsdales of Headingly have made requests that they are to be notified at once if any infections or contagious disease breaks out so they may take their children home.... While this favor has been granted to these people, I fully recognize the injustice that is committed against other parents who would undoubtedly make the same request if they were in a position to know as much as the Lonsdales, Camerons, etc.[36]

Watson and the Liberal government began planning for a large school expansion early in 1894, likely due in part to McDermid's pressure and the newspaper reports of grand juries published during the period. The final expansion of a series of such initiatives was completed in 1901.

The principal devoted most of the space in his letters to Ministers Smart and Watson, however, to advocate for new expenditures to accommodate the specialized educational needs of deaf schools, rather than simply addressing the infrastructural shortcomings at the Sherbrook and Portage building. Throughout 1891, McDermid repeatedly requested that an additional teacher be hired. In his second annual report to the Manitoba Legislature, and in several letters to Minister Smart, he argued that the education of deaf students was a uniquely challenging enterprise that demanded a higher teacher-to-student ratio than the education of hearing students. "I have already explained verbally," McDermid wrote,

> that it is absolutely necessary to have a much larger percentage of instructors in schools for the deaf than in speaking and hearing schools, and the relative number of teachers to be employed cannot be decided by a comparison with the methods adopted in hearing schools. It would be considered extravagant and unnecessary to employ three or four teachers for forty speaking children, but on the other hand experienced instructors of the deaf would not consider such a number sufficient for forty deaf children. The explanation lies in the fact that the greater part of the instructor's time is taken on individual teaching.[37]

McDermid revealed that he had sought out a new instructor, and had settled on Augusta Spaight, a former assistant at the Ontario Institute, whose "services could be secured for $400 per annum with board and lodging."[38] This amount, McDermid admitted, was well below the market value for instructors of the deaf, who were difficult to attract to state and provincial schools in light of their small number and highly specialized training. Spaight, McDermid argued, had "limited schoolroom experience," but was "an expert signmaker and thoroughly understands the ways of the deaf." It would be, he wrote, "an easy task to train her in the methods of instruction peculiar to the deaf."[39]

While the Department of Public Works did consent to Spaight's hiring, McDermid's choice of a new teacher offers readers some insight into the financial strain that the school found itself under. Spaight's annual salary was at least $200 below the amount that a seasoned teacher would command, McDermid argued. In his second annual report, which covered January to December 1890, he provided a table that compared student-to-teacher ratios for selected North American deaf schools. For example, the American Asylum for the Deaf had 130 students to 16 teachers, the MacKay Institute in Montreal had 34 students to 4 teachers, and the Halifax Institution had 55 students to 5 teachers.[40] He quoted the unnamed principal of the Clarke Institute for the Deaf in Massachusetts to further bolster his argument that Manitoba would have to contribute more in order to ensure the success of the school's mission over time. "The number of persons employed as instructors," he quoted, "is determined with what is judged to be for the best interests of the pupils, rather than with reference to the expense incurred."[41] James Smart would have been able to quickly ascertain McDermid's point: the Manitoba Institute had a student-to-teacher ratio that was close to 20 to 1, while the schools he cited had ratios that were better than 10 to 1. In order to implement the province's vision of a self-sufficient deaf citizenry, the school had to bring down the student-to-teacher ratio. Between 1890 and 1900, increased hiring of teachers worked toward achieving this.[42]

Teaching staff were far from the only human resource problem faced by the MIDD in early 1891. McDermid wrote to Minister Smart on December 9, 1890, about the resignation of Archibald Ferguson, the institution's caretaker. This letter provided the principal with an opportunity to make two key points about the school's pressing needs—that caretaker and supervisor should be distinct positions, and that a supervisor should be proficient in sign language. Ferguson's shortcomings seem to have been in failing to communicate effectively with the children and balancing his caretaking and supervisory duties. "It is a difficult task," McDermid wrote, "to keep so many children out of mischief with proper supervision, but without this restraint it is like bedlam while they are at play." Deaf children, the principal argued, required "the constant direction of a person of good moral character," as the school served as a conduit of both educational and moral learning. According to McDermid, the residential setting presented moral danger to students, as "their conduct and progress in school are greatly influenced by their training out of school" and their socialization was occurring in a setting without parental guidance. McDermid assured Smart that the hiring of two new employees to accommodate distinct positions could be "filled satisfactorily within the present appropriation of fifty dollars per month."[43] The challenges of building a specialized educational institution were beyond the simple procurement of quantitatively adequate financial and human resources, though these were clearly important to McDermid. Employment at the MIDD necessitated specialized skills, principally in knowledge of sign language and teaching methods for the deaf. The principal's attempt to have Ferguson serve as both caretaker and supervisor had been "useless on account of other demands upon his time and partially on account of his ignorance of the sign language."[44]

McDermid also justified infrastructural requests solely upon the unique pedagogical needs of a deaf educational institution. "From the fact that all the recitations of deaf mutes are written it is very important to have large and superior blackboards," he wrote on March 9, 1891. "Those now in use are made of a rubbery cloth and are very unsatisfactory … [and] a great deal of dust is produced whenever they are used. This cannot be otherwise than unhealthful to both the teacher and pupil, and I would recommend that slate be purchased." He made similar arguments for the new building to be wired with electric light, as the education of pre-lingually deaf students depended on the medium of sight more than any other.[45] "As all knowledge comes to the deaf through the medium of the eye, the question of light is of unusual importance in a school of this kind, and I sincerely hope that you will succeed in introducing electricity. The light furnished by our lamps is insufficient, and at best they are unsafe ... as it is almost impossible to keep them [the children] from meddling with them."[46]

In the same letter, the principal argued that books for a suitable library had to be purchased. McDermid again based his plea upon the unique nature of deaf education and the needs of pre- and post-lingually deaf students. "I need not expand upon the value of reading matter for the deaf as an aid in their education ... it will require not less than $200 to procure a sufficient number of books to make the library of use to our school works."[47] There were donations given to a new library fund by private citizens, including the now-departed MLA Francis and the aforementioned James Wilkie, but these were not enough to ensure the building of a usable library. While there are certainly a few examples of private charitable giving in both contributions to the library fund and donations of Christmas presents for the students after the school's adoption by the province, it is clear that McDermid considered private contributions alone to be insufficient to support a specialized school and to allow it to develop.

Vocational education quickly became part of the MIDD's mandate under McDermid's leadership. The movement toward practical training in employable skills was an attempt to expand the merely educational opportunities offered to the deaf by the school into a wider integration into the adult workforce. Vocational training was, argues Margret Winzer, an attempt to inculcate a sense of Victorian self-sufficiency in the pre-lingually deaf, and reflected low expectations for deaf employment prospects held by hearing educators and administrators.[48] McDermid chose to hold classes in printmaking for male students and domestic labour for female students, as these were among the most frequent modes of employment practised by urban deaf North Americans and had been part of deaf school curriculums since the early nineteenth century in the United States and Britain.[49] The principal began calling for vocational programs in 1890. In his second annual report to the Legislature, McDermid argued that vocational training was a key component of fostering self-sufficiency for deaf adults after their school years. He argued that provincial spending on printmaking equipment would allow the "means of more perfectly educating our children and enabling them to become self-supporting members of society. The authorities of boarding schools and colleges are fully recognizing the benefits of manual training ... but how much more important is such an education to those that are deprived of hearing and speech."[50]

McDermid was able to secure funding for a printing class and newspaper by early 1892, again by arguing that vocational training was an integral part of the new type of specialized institution that he was charged with leading. The school developed a newspaper called *Silent Echo* in 1892 with the key purpose of giving students practical experience in the field and engaging other deaf communities in North America more generally. Printing was taught by both McDermid and Angus McIntosh, a deaf photo engraver for the *Manitoba Daily Free Press*, in the evenings. After 1893, printing became a full course with a new full-time deaf teacher, Joseph Reginald Cook. The program was successful enough that *The Voice*, the organ of the Winnipeg Trades and Labour Council, complained in 1897 that the MIDD "select[s] one or two trades, such as printing and blacksmithing, and in consequence increase an already too plentiful supply of men."[51] By 1905, McDermid had also succeeded in securing the employment of some students in civil service positions at the post office, after federal restrictions on deaf employment in the civil service were lifted that year.[52] In 1909, a *Silent Echo* editorial written by Cook expressed that "we are all proud of our printer boys. They all, with one exception, secured work at good wages in their home printing offices during their vacation. This speaks well for their attention and industry while at school, and, encouraged by their success during the summer, they have all returned to their places with renewed energy and a determination to more thoroughly master their trade during the present school year."[53]

The enforcement of the compulsory attendance rule proved to be difficult for the province. Though compulsory education for the deaf was strongly supported by McDermid and the Liberal government, it presented financial and logistical problems to not only the province, but also to parents of deaf children who lacked the fiscal means to send their children and perhaps lose their contributions on the family farm. In his annual report for 1890, McDermid was uncompromising in his view that the legislation should be enforced strictly. "I hope the government will consider the advisability of enforcing the provisions of the law, if parents will disregard the interests of their deaf children," he wrote, adding that the failure to educate pre-lingually deaf children led to the teaching of deaf adults, which he characterized as "the effort to train a mind that has been living in mental darkness for eighteen or twenty years." The experience of educating deaf citizens who were above school age was "one of the most annoying and discouraging things a teacher of the deaf has to contend with," McDermid wrote.[54] The statutory education law provided for a penalty of $25 or less than 30 days' imprisonment for violators.[55] There is, however, no evidence that legal measures were ever brought to bear upon the parents and guardians of truant students.

In a letter to Minister Smart from March 1891, McDermid's tone softened considerably. He had exchanged letters with rural families who pleaded that their non-compliance with the law was due to a lack of funds to send their children to Winnipeg and the economic blow of the loss of their children's farm labour. "Taking into consideration the difficulties that are presented to the teacher in instructing adult deafmutes and the chances against these children ever having the advantages of an education," he wrote, "I respectfully recommend that an appropriation be made to defray the railroad expenses and if need be the clothing expenses of indigent and orphan children."[56] McDermid and the Ministry of Public Works were contending with a new, perhaps unexpected expense of residential schools—the costs of transporting students to a metropolitan centre to reside in and attend school. The centralizing nature of the MIDD necessitated that the government offer new kinds of financial assistance to citizens outside of the metropolitan centre that ensured their ability to comply with the law without hardship. McDermid estimated that the number of deaf students who did not attend the school was between 15 and 20 in March 1891, and revised this number upward to 23 by the end of the year.[57] The only way to have those students attend the school in Winnipeg was for the province to shoulder some of the financial burden on behalf of rural and economically disadvantaged citizens. While it is unclear if the government did provide a small rail transport subsidy, the Canadian Pacific Railway lowered the cost of transportation for MIDD students in late 1891.[58]

For the rest of the century, the number of students in attendance rose, but truancy remained a problem, as the numbers of absent students did not fall in subsequent annual reports. Absenteeism was addressed only in an attendance table in McDermid's third annual report for 1891, and the problem was not given the prominent attention it had received in his second report for 1890.[59] This suggests that rural poverty was a stumbling block for the province's compulsory deaf education law, and perhaps that some young deaf Manitobans in rural communities were already receiving the training and experience they would need to carry out their lives as agricultural labourers or operators of family farms. It also suggests that many rural families valued their deaf members' contributions on the farm more than a potential education that would not necessarily add to their value as farmers and agricultural labourers. As Alison Prentice and Susan Houston have argued, *education* was not always synonymous with *schooling* in nineteenth-century Canada.[60]

The primarily urban origins of students, along with some students from areas between Winnipeg and Brandon, meant that the student body before 1900 was overwhelmingly British and Scottish in ethnic origin. Indigenous students did not attend the school until 1906, and intermittently thereafter. In June of 1890, Indian Commissioner Hayter Reed requested that the deaf son of Running Rabbit, the "Chief at Lower Blackfoot Reserve N.W.T," be admitted to the school.[61] While Reed, through a Winnipeg police inspector named McColl, inquired about cost, it appears that Running Rabbit's son did not attend. Deaf Indigenous youth faced bureaucratic, geographical, and citizenship hurdles to attendance, as "wards" of the federal government and non-citizens, who were subject to restricted movement under the pass system. Yet a request by Reed, an original designer of the pass system, shows that it was indeed possible for Indigenous youth to be considered for the school, even though it remains unclear whether Manitoba's legislators saw the 1891 Compulsory Deaf Education amendment as referring to Indigenous youth in Manitoba.

The advantages of public support and funding were cited by the principal in several sources. In his annual reports and letters, McDermid reflected on the differences between the prospects of success for private charity and public expenditure in funding new educational institutions. One of his statements about the desirability of public expenditure helps to place the incremental and ad hoc nature of the MIDD's financial and professional consolidation in context, and is worth quoting at length:

Experience has proved that when the State undertakes the responsibility of providing institutions for the care and education of its defective wards, that the most liberal and generous support has been supplied and every effort put forth to foster and promote the well being of those for whom the institution has been established. The need of an improvement or change has only to be stated and if proven to be a real and urgent necessity it is usually granted, thus permitting no backward step in the general progress of the work, as is the case where schools are supported by private contributions. The history of the Manitoba Institution is no exception to this rule.[62]

While there may have been an implied plea for increased provincial support in McDermid's words, it is more likely that his opinion was stated with a degree of real conviction. The principal's requests were often met, excluding the pleas for better fire protection and sewage disposal at the new building. The Manitoba Institute for the Deaf and Dumb of 1900 was a markedly different enterprise than Watson's school operating under church and private charity alone. It was more fiscally sustainable, largely due to the steady provincial appropriations under the compulsory education rule, in contrast to the private charitable funding model that was only made feasible through the use of Watson's personal funds. McDermid may have steadily argued for incremental building improvements and funding increases to bring the MIDD up to North American standards, but he certainly recognized that the school could not carry on without the province's funding and leadership.

One way to trace changes in financing methods for deaf schools in late Victorian Canada is to consider "exhibitions," as Pearce has done in her study of the origins of free education for the deaf and blind in Halifax.[63] Exhibitions, or examinations, were public events in which schools would publicize their efforts by publicly displaying the abilities of deaf students in order to strengthen charitable support. Pearce argues that public examinations and fundraising tours, where children would read or sign monologues and answer metaphysical questions to amaze crowds and seek charitable contributions from the public, were an important fundraising tool for the Halifax School during its consolidation in the 1860s and 1870s. In Manitoba, nearly 20 years later, there were exhibitions for members of the provincial parliament as late as 1892, as reported in the first edition of the school's newspaper, *Silent Echo*.[64] These exhibitions, however, were very different from those delivered in Nova Scotia 20 years earlier, or in Yorkshire, England, in the 1880s and 1890s, as described by Amanda Bergen.[65] First, they were not open to the public, but were a feature of Legislature members' visits to the school. They were not designed to solicit funds, but to "thank" parliamentarians for their support, as provincial commitment to the school was already securely enshrined in law. More importantly, the phenomenon of exhibitions for the deaf and blind, so popular in France, Britain, and the United States during the first 75 years of the nineteenth century, became more infrequent, perhaps due to the waning interest in deaf education as a scientific novelty or a "miracle" and the growing recognition of deaf education as a right supported by the state. England, in Bergen's example, remained a qualified exception to this trend in part because deaf education in northern Britain retained a private, charitable character into the twentieth century. McDermid, a strong supporter of the state's obligation to provide educational opportunity to its most vulnerable citizens, certainly saw the guarantee of public support for the education of the deaf as an end to the inconsistent returns and perhaps degrading pursuit of charitable funds from the public and churches through exhibitions.

Provincial funding, then, was central to the MIDD's mandate and operation and a key to its survival. Principal McDermid's prediction of a growing student body proved to be correct, and was especially aided by the explosive population growth of Winnipeg and the Canadian West during the "Laurier Boom" of 1896 to 1913. By the 1901–02 school year, the MIDD had enrolled 45 students from Manitoba and 13 from the Northwest Territories.[66] That year, 13 students also attended from British Columbia through an interprovincial agreement that saw the BC government pay tuition and room and board costs for student attendance.[67] The school's staff also expanded quickly throughout 1892 and 1893. McDermid's 1893 school history named 10 employees, including the distinct supervisor and caretaker positions, along with a night watchman and a permanent attending physician. By 1900, the school had added several deaf teachers, printing instructors, and supervisors.[68] These hires satisfied McDermid's earlier key demand to Minister Smart that the school staff be proficient in sign. While the professional development of the school and the achievement of effective specialization were incremental, 1890 to 1900 was a period of distinct improvement, and many of McDermid's requests were acceded to by the Department of Public Works. By 1918, there were 167 students at the school, including 93 from the other three Western Canadian provinces, as the renamed Manitoba School for the Deaf had solidified a regional reputation as the primary centre of the deaf education movement in the Canadian West.[69]

In its formative years, the Manitoba Institute for the Deaf and Dumb slowly and incrementally developed the specialized professional, pedagogical, and infrastructural standards that were necessary to the successful operation of a deaf school. Many of these improvements, especially in the key years under study of 1890 to 1900, were attributable to the pressure of Principal Duncan McDermid on the Ministry of Public Works to adopt the standards and human resources protocols common at longer-standing Canadian and American deaf schools. The hiring of deaf employees, beginning with McDermid's wife, Mary, and continuing with Angus McIntosh and John Byrne, assured the primacy of sign language and equal opportunity for communication at the school. The teacher-to-student ratio fell in 1892–93 and continued to fall for the rest of the century. Manitoba was slowly implementing the principle, adopted in early 1889, that deaf education should be free and compulsory for all of its residents. The structure of public funding allowed the school to build upon its gains, as the volatile pattern of funding through private and religious charity was replaced. Deaf education and vocational training were only prophylactic measures against a disempowered deaf citizenry, yet they represented a meaningful concentration of provincial will and resources during a period of low public investment in social spending in other areas. Deaf education may have lost its sense of "philosophical marvel"[70] and become an accepted part of the emerging Canadian public educational system, but it was far from assured a secure future in Manitoba in 1889–90. The protracted consolidation of the school's fiscal, infrastructural, and professional health was a complicated process that challenges a diametric depiction of deaf educational history into tidy pre-and post-deaf educational eras.

NOTES

* An earlier version of this paper was published in *Manitoba History* 77 (Winter 2015): 2–12.

1. This chapter will use the contemporary name for the school where applicable, despite its negative modern connotations.
2. "James P. Wilkie to Duncan McDermid, March 2, 1891." Ministry of Public Works Incoming Correspondence, Provincial Archives of Manitoba (PAM), GS 0123 GR 1607.
3. "Duncan McDermid to James Smart, March 8, 1891." PAM, GS 0123 GR 1607.
4. Canadian work on deaf education is still also heavily reliant on foundational American works, such as Douglas Baynton's *Forbidden Signs: American Culture and the Campaign against Sign Language* (Chicago: University of Chicago Press, 1996). An exception to a national narrative is Jason Ellis's work on deaf day schools in Toronto, a different context than provincial residential deaf schools as considered here. See Jason Ellis, "'All Methods—and Wedded to None': The Deaf Education Methods Debate and Progressive Educational Reform in Toronto, Canada, 1922–1945," *Paedagogica Historica: International Journal of the History of Education* 50, no. 3 (2014): 371–89.
5. Margret Winzer, *The History of Special Education: From Isolation to Integration* (Washington, DC: Gallaudet University Press, 1993); Winzer, "A Tale Often Told: The Early Progression of Special Education," in *Remedial and Special Education* 19 (July/August 1998): 212–18.
6. Margret Winzer, "Confronting Difference: An Excursion through the History of Special Education," in *The Sage Handbook of Special Education*, ed. Lani Florian (Thousand Oaks, CA: Sage, 2006), 22.
7. Joanna L. Pearce, "Not for Alms but Help: Fund-Raising and Free Education for the Blind," *Journal of the Canadian Historical Association* 23, no. 1 (2012): 134; Mariana Valverde, "The Mixed Social Economy as a Canadian Tradition," *Studies in Political Economy* 47 (1995): 33–60.
8. Stephane-D. Perrault, "Intersecting Discourses: Deaf Institutions and Communities in Montreal, 1850–1920" (PhD diss., McGill University, 2004), 108–9.
9. Veronica Strong-Boag, "'Children of Adversity': Disabilities and Child Welfare in Canada from the Nineteenth to the Twenty-First Century," *Journal of Family History* 32, no. 4 (October 2007): 422–23. Strong-Boag links the MIDD/MSD with institutions like the Ontario Asylum for Idiots and the Toronto Home for Incurable Children.
10. Strong-Boag, "'Children of Adversity,'" 423.
11. For a book-length discussion of the role of Deaf agency in resisting oralism in the United States, see Susan Burch, *Signs of Resistance: American Deaf Cultural History, 1900 to World War II* (New York: New York University Press, 2004).
12. Duncan McDermid, "Second Annual Report of the Manitoba Deaf and Dumb Institute," Deaf Heritage Room (DHR), Manitoba School for the Deaf (MSD).

13. Keith Wilson, *Thomas Greenway* (Winnipeg: University of Manitoba Press, 1985), 30.
14. The association with asylums did not have operational meaning. A Department of Education that could accommodate both mainstream schools and a deaf institution did not exist until the early twentieth century in Manitoba, when the MIDD was moved to the Department of Education.
15. Stephane-D. Perrault and Sylvie Pelletier, *L'institut Raymond-Dewar et ses institutions d'origine: 160 ans d'histoire avec les personnes sourdes* (Quebec: Septentrion, 2010), 53; Robert Mathison, "The Ontario Institution," in *Histories of American Schools for the Deaf, 1817–1893*, ed. Edward Allen Fay (Washington, DC: Volta Bureau, 1893), 8–10.
16. *Manitoba Daily Free Press*, October 2, 1888, 3.
17. *Brandon Sun*, January 16, 1888, 4. The *Sun* was a Liberal paper and thus supportive of the Greenway government. For example, the April 28, 1892, edition dismissed the Roblin opposition's allegations of improper hiring at the MIDD in two articles.
18. Duncan McDermid. "Manitoba Institution for the Education of the Deaf and Dumb," in *Histories of American Schools for the Deaf, 1817–1893*, ed. Edward Allen Fay (Washington, DC: Volta Bureau, 1893), 1–2.
19. Clifton Carbin. *Deaf Heritage in Canada: A Distinctive, Diverse, and Enduring Culture* (Toronto: McGraw-Hill Ryerson, 1996), 136. F. G. Jefferson came to Canada from the British Isles in 1884 as part of a deaf colonist scheme organized by Elizabeth Groom, a deaf evangelist and former teacher in Britain. For more detail about the Groom Expedition, see Jennifer Esmail, *Reading Victorian Deafness: Signs and Sounds in Victorian Literature and Culture* (Athens: University of Ohio Press, 2013), 150–62.
20. Carbin, *Deaf Heritage*, 137.
21. *American Annals of the Deaf* 35, no. 2 (April 1890): 165.
22. McDermid, "Manitoba Institution," 5.
23. Baynton, *Forbidden Signs*, 15–34.
24. Jane Berger, "Uncommon Schools: Institutionalizing Deafness in Early-Nineteenth-Century America," in *Foucault and the Government of Disability*, ed. Shelley Tremain (Ann Arbor: University of Michigan Press, 2005), 159.
25. Keith Wilson, "Duncan McDermid," in *Dictionary of Canadian Biography, 1901–1910*, ed. Ramsay Cook and Jean Hamelin (Toronto: University of Toronto Press, 1994), 622.
26. Carbin, *Deaf Heritage*, 140.
27. For a detailed discussion of the manual/oralist debate that was raging in the late nineteenth century, see Baynton, *Forbidden Signs*. Baynton links the rise of oralism to growing American nationalism in the post–Civil War period, and argues that oralism was adopted by most American schools in the late nineteenth century as a means of inculcating a sense of national identity in the deaf. For a more detailed discussion of the MIDD/MSD's resistance to adopting oralism, see Sandy Barron, "'Thinking It Savors of the Miraculous': The Manitoba Institute for the Deaf and Dumb and the Growth of Deaf Public Life in Manitoba, 1884–1909" (MA thesis, University of Calgary, 2016). For a detailed explanation of the Ontario Institute for the Deaf's movement toward oralism in 1905–06, see Alessandra Iozzo, "'Silent Citizens': Citizenship Education, Disability and d/Deafness at the Ontario Institution for the Education of the Deaf, 1870–1914" (PhD diss., University of Ottawa, 2015).
28. The convention of capitalizing the word "deaf" dates from the late twentieth century, and refers to a Deaf individual or group who self-identifies as *culturally* deaf. I use "deaf" when I am referring to historical individuals or movements, and "Deaf" when referencing modern Deaf culture.
29. Duncan McDermid. "Third Annual Report of the Manitoba Deaf and Dumb Institute," *Journals of the Legislative Assembly of Manitoba*, 24 (1892): 50.

30. McDermid. "Third Annual Report."
31. "McDermid to Smart, March 23, 1891." PAM, GS 0123 GR 1607.
32. Carbin, *Deaf Heritage*, 142.
33. "McDermid to James P. Smart, March 9, 1891." PAM, GS 0123 GR 1607.
34. "Matron Hossie, Statement Regarding October 27th, 1891 Fire." PAM, GS 0123 GR 1607.
35. Alan F. J. Artibise, *Winnipeg: A Social History of Urban Growth, 1874–1914* (Montreal and Kingston: McGill-Queen's University Press, 1975), chap. 12; David A. Ennis, "Pressure to Act: The Shoal Lake Aqueduct and the Greater Winnipeg Water District," *Manitoba History* 72 (Spring/Summer 2012): 13.
36. "Duncan McDermid to Robert Watson, December 7, 1893," 4. PAM, GS 0123 GR 1607.
37. "Duncan McDermid to James P. Smart, October 1, 1891." PAM, GS 0123 GR 1607.
38. "Duncan McDermid to James P. Smart, October 1, 1891."
39. "Duncan McDermid to James P. Smart, October 1, 1891."
40. McDermid, "Second Annual Report," 79.
41. McDermid, "Second Annual Report," 79. Though the Clarke Institute was an entirely oralist school, McDermid evidently felt that this distinction did not hamper his larger point.
42. After Augusta Spaight's hiring, most new hires were deaf women. McDermid likely hired deaf women, who commanded lower wages both because of their gender and their deafness, to help balance the school's books. The hiring of deaf teachers by the school well into the twentieth century reflects the fact that strict oralism was not instituted there before its closure in 1940.
43. "Duncan McDermid to James P. Smart, December 9, 1890." PAM, GS 0123 GR 1607.
44. "Duncan McDermid to James P. Smart, December 9, 1890."
45. "Duncan McDermid to James P. Smart, March 9, 1891." PAM, GS 0123 GR 1607.
46. McDermid, "Second Annual Report," 81.
47. McDermid, "Second Annual Report," 81.
48. Winzer, *The History of Special Education*, 145–46.
49. Robert M. Buchanan, *Illusions of Equality: Deaf Americans in School and Factory 1850–1950* (Washington, DC: Gallaudet University Press, 1999), 17; Carmen M. Mangion, "'The Business of Life': Educating Catholic Deaf Children in Late Nineteenth-Century England," *History of Education* 41, no. 5 (July 2012): 587. Agriculture remained the largest source of employment for rural deaf citizens in these countries.
50. McDermid, "Second Annual Report," 80.
51. *The Voice*, May 15, 1897, 4.
52. Wilson, "McDermid," 622.
53. *Silent Echo* 14, no. 1 (October 2, 1905), 5. DHR, MSD.
54. McDermid, "Second Annual Report," 77–78.
55. *American Annals of the Deaf* 35, no. 2 (1890), 165.
56. "McDermid to Smart, March 9, 1891." PAM, GS 0123 GR 1607.
57. McDermid, "Third Annual Report," 49.
58. McDermid, "Third Annual Report," 53.
59. McDermid, "Third Annual Report," 49.
60. Alison L. Prentice and Susan E. Houston, eds., *Family, School and Society in Nineteenth-Century Canada* (Toronto: Oxford University Press, 1975), 6.
61. "James Watson to James P. Smart, June 10, 1890." PAM GS 0123 GR 1607.
62. McDermid, "Third Annual Report," 49–50.
63. Pearce, "Not for Alms," 139–40.
64. *Silent Echo* 1, no. 1 (April 29, 1892). DHR, MSD.

65. Amanda Bergen, "The Public Examination of Deaf and Blind Children in Yorkshire, 1829–1890," *Northern History* 41, no. 1 (March 2004): 149–62.
66. Carbin, *Deaf Heritage*, 142. The Northwest Territories included, until 1905, the areas that became the provinces of Alberta and Saskatchewan.
67. Duncan McDermid. "Report of the Principal to Superintendent of Education, Victoria, B.C," *Thirty-First Annual Report of the Public Schools of British Columbia, 1901–1902* (Victoria, BC: Province of British Columbia, 1902), 278.
68. McDermid, "Manitoba Institution," 7.
69. Carbin, *Deaf Heritage*, 143.
70. Bergen, "Public Examination," 162.

BIBLIOGRAPHY

Primary Sources

American Annals of the Deaf, 1888–1890.
Annual Reports, Manitoba Institute for the Deaf and Dumb, 1891–1900. Deaf Heritage Room, Manitoba School for the Deaf, Winnipeg.
Brandon Sun
Manitoba Daily Free Press
Provincial Archives of Manitoba, Winnipeg.
Public Works Minister's Office, Correspondence Inward, 1888–1905. GS 0123 GR1607.
Silent Echo, Proofs, vols. 1–9 (1892–1899). Deaf Heritage Room, Manitoba School for the Deaf, Winnipeg.
The Voice

Secondary Sources

Artibise, Alan F. J. *Winnipeg: Social History of Urban Growth, 1874–1914*. Montreal and Kingston: McGill-Queen's University Press, 1975.
Barron, Sandy R. "'Thinking It Savors of the Miraculous': The Manitoba Institute for the Deaf and Dumb and the Growth of Deaf Public Life in Manitoba, 1884–1909." MA thesis, University of Calgary, 2016.
Baynton, Douglas C. *Forbidden Signs: American Culture and the Campaign Against Sign Language*. Chicago: University of Chicago Press, 1996.
Bergen, Amanda. "The Public Examination of Deaf and Blind Children in Yorkshire, 1829–1890," *Northern History* 41, no. 1 (March 2004): 149–62.
Berger, Jane. "Uncommon Schools: Institutionalizing Deafness in Early-Nineteenth-Century America." In *Foucault and the Government of Disability*, edited by Shelley Tremain, 153–71. Ann Arbor: University of Michigan Press, 2005.
Buchanan, Robert M. *Illusions of Equality: Deaf Americans in School and Factory, 1850–1950*. Washington, DC: Gallaudet University Press, 1999.
Burch, Susan. *Signs of Resistance: American Deaf Cultural History, 1900 to World War II*. New York: New York University Press, 2002.
Carbin, Clifton. *Deaf Heritage in Canada: A Distinctive, Diverse, and Enduring Culture*. Toronto: McGraw-Hill Ryerson, 1996.
Ellis, Jason. "'All Methods—and Wedded to None': The Deaf Education Methods Debate and Progressive Educational Reform in Toronto, Canada, 1922–1945." *Paedagogica Historica: International Journal of the History of Education* 50, no. 3 (2014): 371–89.

Ennis, David. "Pressure to Act: The Shoal Lake Aqueduct and the Greater Winnipeg Water District," *Manitoba History* 72, no. 2 (Spring/Summer 2012): 12–19.

Esmail, Jennifer. *Reading Victorian Deafness: Signs and Sounds in Victorian Literature and Culture*. Athens: Ohio University Press, 2013.

Iozzo, Alessandra. "'Silent Citizens': Citizenship Education, Disability and d/Deafness at the Ontario Institution for the Education of the Deaf, 1870–1914." PhD diss., University of Ottawa, 2015.

Mangion, Carmen M. "'The Business of Life': Educating Catholic Deaf Children in Late Nineteenth-Century England." *History of Education* 41, no. 5 (September 2012): 575–94.

Mathison, Robert. "The Ontario Institution." In *Histories of American Schools for the Deaf, 1817–1893*. Washington, DC: Volta Bureau, 1893.

McDermid, Duncan. "Manitoba Institution for the Education of the Deaf and Dumb." In *Histories of American Schools for the Deaf, 1817–1893*. Washington, DC: Volta Bureau, 1893.

Pearce, Joanna L. "Not for Alms but Help: Fund-Raising and Free Education for the Blind." *Journal of the Canadian Historical Association* 23, no. 1 (2012): 131–55.

Perrault, Stephane-D. "Intersecting Discourses: Deaf Institutions and Communities in Montreal, 1850–1920." PhD diss., McGill University, 2004.

Perrault, Stephanie-D., and Sylvie Pelletier. *L'Institute Raymond-Dewar et ses institutions d'origine: 160 ans d'histoire avec les personnes sourdes*. Quebec: Septentrion, 2010.

Prentice, Alison L., and Susan E. Houston, eds. *Family, School and Society in Nineteenth Century Canada*. Toronto: Oxford University Press, 1975.

Strong-Boag, Veronica. "'Children of Adversity': Disabilities and Child Welfare in Canada from the Nineteenth to the Twenty-First Century." *Journal of Family History* 32 (October 2007): 413–32.

Valverde, Mariana. "The Mixed Social Economy as a Canadian Tradition." *Studies in Political Economy* 47 (1995): 33–60.

Wilson, Keith. *Thomas Greenway*. Winnipeg: University of Manitoba Press, 1985.

Wilson, Keith. "Duncan McDermid." In *Dictionary of Canadian Biography, 1901–1910*, edited by Ramsay Cook and Jean Hamelin, 622. Toronto: University of Toronto Press, 1994.

Winzer, Margret. *The History of Special Education: From Isolation to Integration*. Washington, DC: Gallaudet University Press, 1993.

Winzer, Margret. "A Tale Often Told: The Early Progression of Special Education." *Remedial and Special Education* 19 (1998): 212–18.

Winzer, Margret. "Confronting Difference: An Excursion Through the History of Special Education." In *The Sage Handbook of Special Education*, edited by Lani Florian, 20–33. Thousand Oaks, CA: Sage, 2006.

CHAPTER 7

Remembering the Boys

Caroline E. M. Carrington-Decker

In *How to Treat the Criminal Classes*, published by the Ontario Board of Parole in 1896, Abott exclaimed, "A boy steals an apple from an orchard; steals a lot of apples; he keeps on stealing apples. What shall we do with him? We bring him before a magistrate and send him to a gaol and lock the door on him and forget about him."[1]

In 1921, the Special Committee of Enquiry assigned to investigate the Victoria Industrial School (VIS), in Mimico, Ontario, issued forth reports of thoughtlessness and sloppiness on the part of staff, for boys were lumped together: the "normal" with the "not very bright," the "criminals" with the "suffering."[2] This careless form of inclusion at the school on the outskirts of town not only shielded society from these wayward boys in the nineteenth century, but also was said to protect them from the bad influences of society.

This chapter will discuss the ethos that guided nineteenth-century industrial/training schools for wayward or deviant boys. I will provide a critical look into the selection and processing of boys to attend the VIS in Mimico, Ontario, and its geographical location in relation to the rest of society, the conditions under which these boys lived, and the institution's eventual downfall. It is my hope that the experiences of nineteenth-century boys (aged 7 to 14), whose voices were often suppressed or silenced, not be forgotten; what they endured and suffered at the hands of their "caregivers" should be exposed.

In 2008, Melanie Panitch discussed how Jo Dickey, a disability activist mother, shared her perception of why she was able to effect change: "It was because of my experience, you see? The only teacher we have is experience"; it was, in fact, not only her experiences that spurred societal change through the closure of institutions, but also the experiences of her son, who was a resident.[3] Stories from disability activist mothers in their campaign to close institutions are invaluable, for they demonstrate their years of challenges in fighting against what has been a powerfully persuasive and tightly structured social system: institutionalization. Radford and Park share that, in 1876 in Ontario, institutionalization became the solution for accommodating the "mentally deficient," a trend that had begun in parts of the United States and England. Institutions were portrayed socially as places that specifically catered to the needs of those with mental deficiencies.[4] It was becoming apparent that the "moulding of individual behaviour and personal expectations" for those labelled *mentally deficient* could also be applied to other disadvantaged groups or minorities.[5] The eventual solution (11 years later) to create the VIS as a means of moulding and shaping the young minds of the wayward boys of 1887 (from deviant to decent) should come as no surprise. DiMaggio explains that the "creation of new institutions is expensive and requires high levels of both interest and resources."[6] Therefore, those who were involved in this process for the wayward boys could be considered institutional entrepreneurs, who highly valued this so-called investment opportunity. Thus, much thought and care went into the creation of this new institution.[7]

The VIS was architecturally designed as a reformatory school to house delinquent, dependent, and/or neglected boys. Apart from providing these boys shelter, food, and clothing, the VIS also provided education and industrial training. The Archives of Ontario documents that this industrial/training school was governed by the Industrial Schools Act with its daily operations provided by the Industrial School Association of Toronto. The regulation of this school was through the Department of the Provincial Secretary until 1930, at which time the legal responsible body became the Department of Public Welfare.[8]

Under the *Rules and Regulations of the VIS* (1887), this school was described as follows:

> The intention of the school is to supply the place of a home for the boys; everything shall be done in the spirit and manner of a well regulated Christian Home, and every individual connected with the institution shall regard it as such, and shall seek in a wisely tempered Christian spirit to be all things to the boys, so as to make them happy, active and intelligent.[9]

The Archives of Ontario contain a report submitted to the minister of education (1894) seven years after the inception of the school in which the following was noted:

> The general influence of the school is excellent. The boys are provided with clean comfortable homes. They are trained to take proper care of their bodies. They are occupied busily throughout the day at profitable developing study and work. They are compelled to learn the lesson they specially need, the necessity for co-operative submission to constituted authority. They are made productive instead of destructive. They receive definite moral and religious training, and yet they have ample opportunity for recreation and amusement.[10]

Seemingly, this humanitarian approach to eradicating criminal behaviour from the streets, which was prompted by the need to "prevent further deviance," as shared by Hogeveen, was approvingly documented by the province as being "under control."[11] McCulloch states that such bureaucratic records, particularly those created by the state for the state, "present the perspectives of the elite, were less forthcoming concerning the effects of such deliberations on individuals and families, and were even less helpful for an understanding of social groups that were excluded or marginalized."[12] This necessity for the state to focus on each individual boy through a process of ownership, their being renamed as juridical subjects, was not an approach uniquely owned by the Industrial Schools Act; in fact, Read and Walmsley discuss this process of individualization being seen as early as the 1840s by Seguin.[13] Morley shares the following analysis of a southeast London, England, special school: "Picture the poor dullards in the old unenlightened days—locked up in lonely rooms, perhaps crouching in corners, turned out into the streets, the sullen, the mischievous, the stupid, the inarticulate—with asylum or workhouse surely looming in the distance. Picture them now!"[14]

Clearly, a cultural belief system began stirring globally, one that presented the individual as problematic, to be corrected and repudiated through institutionalization. Thus came the institutionalization process of the boys in the VIS, a practice that deconstructed the "backward" child through the concept of idealism. Davis argues that for Western society prior to the mid-nineteenth century, the concept of normalcy did not exist, but rather there was a "regnant paradigm" around the word "ideal."[15] Davis continues by stating that if one has a concept of "ideal," then a standard is established against which all humans exist with various levels of imperfection because they fall below the standard. This is used to affirm the point that in an "ideal" culture the absoluteness of physical imperfections is not seen but becomes "part of a descending continuum from top to bottom, for no one can have an ideal body, and therefore no one has to have an ideal body."[16] Using this premise, one could argue that the nineteenth-century individual in Western society risked being categorized as a less-than-ideal body, as argued by Davis.[17] Clearly, the shaping of the VIS boys was to articulate them into ideal men. This is laid out in a report to the Ministry of Education (1894) as it affirms the thesis that because of the aid of government the VIS is making "good, progressive, productive citizens out of those who would otherwise become a destructive and dangerous class," ultimately declaring that without this institution/training school the government would have to pay more to protect its citizens from such a potentially dangerous class.[18]

We can see this deviancy from "ideal" in the VIS case book files, which held documentation of each boy's history including a detailed description of each individual upon his commitment to the VIS.[19] Incorporated into the Personal Description category of case book 5 was room to comment on both the mental and physical condition of each boy. Although many of these youngsters were portrayed as being mentally "normal" and physically "good," there were still some who, under the heading "Mental Condition," were clearly characterized as being "rather delicate looking, undeveloped, apparently a simple-minded boy, not very bright, rather/somewhat simple, weak, fair but boy is backward, childish, seemingly deficient but possibly the result of deafness, bright but faulty, undeveloped but bright, dull, sub-normal, and below average." Under the heading "Physical Condition" (of this same case book) were descriptive terms such as "not very robust," "frail but healthy," "slight," "writes with left hand, has thumb missing on right hand," "slightly built but healthy," "good—only one leg," "manifested a murderous disposition," "rather delicate looking boy," and "good rather deaf."[20]

Students at the VIS were tested for their competency in reading, writing, and arithmetic; most had not attended school on a regular basis, and since many boys held down jobs it could be concluded that survival superseded an education. Parekh shares the conclusions she has drawn from her research that words used to describe mental condition became more biomedical, including terms such as "Mental Retardation, Moron, and Feeble Minded." It would have been during roughly this period of time—between 1919 and 1929—that the European concept of normalcy was originally reflected in Western society.[21] It was at the beginning of the nineteenth century, Davis reminds us, that the Europeans began developing the use of statistics from which arose the concept of the bell curve, otherwise known as the "normal curve."[22] Copeland discusses that this concept of normalization, as depicted by Foucault, worked to identify the deficient, dull, and backwards child; therefore, individuals were categorized into five processes: differentiation, homogenization, hierarchization, comparison, and exclusion. This distributing of groups socially through dividing processes worked to discover the "norm" of intellectual capacity.[23]

The first case book for the VIS (dated from 1887 to 1895) described the population of the school; notations were made of each boy's place of birth, religion, and nationality. Although not all 476 cases are legible enough to share, the following can be gleaned from those that are: in 134 case files of boys ranging in age from 7½ to 15, each boy's size was faithfully documented (size being weight, height, and waist) with the majority having their complexion and hair and eye colour noted as well. Complexions from fair, to ruddy, to slightly dark, to dark, to black, to sallow, to freckled, to swarthy, to clear were noted. Similarly, eye colour, which ranged from black, to light brown, to brown, to grey, to hazel, to blue, was also documented. Hair colours from black, to dark, to brown, to reddish or fair were also shared. In the later cases, complexion and hair and eye colour were not consistently recorded; however, the boy's size (height, weight, and waist) were religiously noted, leaving me to wonder if boys were being eyed for use as physical labourers.

Out of 134 cases it was noted that the majority of boys were born in Canada (Ontario) in cities such as Toronto (highest population), County York, Kingston, Barrie, Newmarket, St. Catharines, Brantford, Alliston, Aurora, Sault Ste. Marie, Caledonia, Guelph, Beamsville, Orangeville, Ottawa, Simcoe, and Brantford. Thereafter, their birthplaces included (from most to least noted) the following: England, Ireland, Scotland, the United States, Asia Minor, and Berlin. The majority of the boys held either an English or Irish nationality; others were Canadian, Scottish, Newfoundlander, Greek, African, German, Polish, and Welsh. Religions were also noted and these included Episcopalian, Baptist, Methodist, Presbyterian, Protestant, Roman Catholic, Salvation Army, Christian, Free Thinker, Greek, Christadelphian, Apostolic, Jew, Lutheran, Plymouth Brethren, and Congregational.[24]

Regardless of nationality or familial/religious background, one could only try to imagine the appearance this may have taken on the streets of Toronto at the time. It elicits shadows of young boys scurrying about with one another, caught up in a lifestyle of stealing, vagrancy, truancy, housebreaking, shopbreaking, indecent assault, and gambling, all considered crimes and all punishable by law.[25] Boys were either caught by officers or shopowners, were wards of the Children's Aid Society, or were turned over to the authorities by their own fathers, mothers, or siblings with committal to the VIS through a police magistrate or county judge.[26] Many sentences were indefinite.[27]

Perhaps there were conversations among citizens that led them to believe that industrial/training schools were actually in the best interest of wayward boys. Since the principal sources of income for these schools came from municipalities, dedication from the state to ensure its continued success may have contributed to this ruling of society, indicating financial benefits to these chools remaining in operation. One letter in particular, written by the superintendent of the VIS to a gentleman in Gananoque, clearly states that unless a child had a private hearing before a magistrate, there was no other way in which a boy could be committed.[28] Could it be that word of the influence of the VIS was spreading to other parts of Ontario and that parent(s) wanted their child to attend the VIS? What of sisters having their younger brothers incarcerated? How about an aunt having her nephew sent from Picton, paying for his maintenance in full? What of the father of an eight-year-old, bringing his son before a magistrate because the boy had stolen some money? How about a mother having her ten-year-old son committed to the VIS because she felt he was incorrigible? What is interesting is how the incorrigibility of this boy was defined: "Family was in better circumstances prior to death of the husband. George (her son) was sick for a long time after the accident which resulted in the removal of his leg and was spoiled; afterwards became a troublesome boy."[29] Were families relieved that the VIS existed and that it offered predictability and certainty for their child?

Life within the confines of this 50-acre parcel of good tillable land was planned on the "cottage system" with a capacity to house 225 boys (as affirmed by Inspector Chamberlain, 1894).[30] Hogeveen reminds us that it was located 20 kilometres west of Toronto and offered industrial training and an education to each boy.[31] According to Inspector Chamberlain (in his report) the industries that were carried out were tailoring, shoemaking, wood turning, carpentry, typesetting, knitting, and housecleaning. These young inmates were kept on a strict, regimented schedule which started at 6:30 a.m., with breakfast from 7:30 to 8:00 a.m. followed by half the boys attending school from 9:00 a.m. to 12:00 p.m. while the other half learned trades. There were two 15-minute breaks, one in the morning and one in the afternoon. After lunch and play (12:00 to 1:00 p.m.) the half that attended school in the morning now learned trades, and vice versa. Dinner was from 5:30 to 6:00 p.m., with the expectation that the boys were back to their cottages by 6:00 p.m. Once in their cottages they were expected to pursue their studies until lights out at 9:00 p.m. The reported success and excellence of work being done in each of the industrial departments, along with the half day of education they received, reflected well on the boys, for they were said to be happy, content, and doing well. The positive feedback received by the inspector (at the time of his report) from the superintendent of the school was that 80 percent of the boys who left the institution became good citizens.[32]

Beneath the surface of such promising reports laid the souls of these young boys. Prowling about even deeper than this was the late 1910 eugenics discourse (within Ontario) of Canadian psychiatric officials Dr. Helen MacMurchy and Dr. C. K. Clarke. The potential threat to the Anglo elite spurred medical doctors and psychiatrists to consider the possibility of juvenile deviancy as a product of defective genes and inferior breeding. Their solution was for judicial subjects to be permanently locked away from society, to be unable to reproduce, and for recent immigrants to be deported. It was a cleansing.[33] Erevelles and Minear reiterate this by stating that controlling the human species was to be considered for the "public good," as diseased bodies were portrayed as associated with the non-white population.[34] Erevelles and Minear share similar notations as Baynton and Gould that bodies of boys who were labelled with a mental illness or as being feeble-minded were seen in physical relation to those of an oppressive race.[35] It was as a result of this fear that such characteristics could be passed on that the need to protect the white race became an important mission. The call for such drastic measures may well have created a societal fear, as ownership now of deviant or wayward boys moved from the hands of the state to those of doctors and psychiatrists; however, still hiding behind the brick walls of the VIS were the youthful lads who had their own behaviours to monitor. There were no recorded accounts of punishment by Inspector Chamberlain in his December 11, 1894, report, because disciplining these boys was the accepted norm. Upon the inception of the VIS, the ministry cautioned in the 1887 *Rules and Regulations of the VIS* under article XVI that "all punishments shall be administered under the special authority of the Superintendent, and shall be duly recorded in books to be kept for that purpose, and produced at meetings of the Committee held in the school. No corporal punishment shall be inflicted except by the Superintendent, or in his presence and under his direction."[36]

Punishments were not public domain. They were kept as a private matter. This practice is also pointed out by Foucault, who states that "justice no longer takes public responsibility for the violence that is bound up with its practice" and that punishment will then have a tendency to become "the most hidden part of the penal process."[37] Therefore, the rearing of these inmates was left at the discretion of the superintendent—his own thoughts, ideas, and beliefs of what he deemed punishable and the character this punishment should take. Once these boys were committed to the VIS they became wards of the judicial system; parents or other relations were allowed to physically visit them once a month (on the last Saturday of every month), and they were allowed to correspond with them by letter only when the boys were deserving. Such communication with family was a privilege and could be easily revoked because of misconduct.[38] Although what may have seemed a good thing at the time (the maintaining of their sons), letters from parents requesting to see their sons outside of the VIS walls, scripted in a begging tone, record an impression of resentment on behalf of parents. One letter in particular, written by a father on behalf of himself and his wife, asks for a favour from the superintendent: to grant their son his Christmas holiday as he is a good boy and deserves to have his holidays. The father also states that the presence of his son at home will make the house more cheerful and that he promises to return him when he is so told. The father also shares his regret in keeping his son home last summer and begs for the discontinuation of punishment on his son for his actions. The letter concludes with the father's willingness to do whatever he needs to in order to make his request happen—his request was denied.[39]

This pleading leads one to wonder what families saw when they actually did have the privilege of visiting with their sons at the VIS. With allegations of abuse printed in the local newspaper, the public's skepticism grew.[40] The position of the school and its students on the outskirts of town had served well to hide the punishments of this penal system. It was the superintendent's idea of love and discipline that embodied the parameters of the VIS, since the way in which physical actions were exercised was at his discretion. According to the *VIS Register of Offences and Punishments* (1894–1902), boys were whipped between 1 and 13 times (at one sitting) and, in many instances, were made to walk for between 30 minutes and 2 hours, depending on the offence. This punishment of "walking" is interesting, for it meant that boys must "walk the line," parading through the gymnasium or around a tree (sometimes covering several kilometres) and making spectacles of themselves to provide a lesson for others. They were to walk like a bear, swaying back and forth and walking on their palms and feet.[41] Not only were the punished expected to walk the line, but they were also whipped.[42] Hogeveen shares the fact that intense offences were met with intense punishments; for example, any boys who ran away from the school were restrained by handcuffs (on both their wrists and ankles) to their beds, face down, and were whipped on both their backs and legs; afterwards, they were fed only bread and water for a month.[43] A list of recorded offences taken from the *VIS Register of Offences and Punishments* is as follows: generally troublesome, disturbance at the table, misconduct on the walk, laziness, misconduct in line, out of bounds, disobedience, throwing stones, not on walk, talking back, impertinence, neglecting work, scheming while off walking, talking in line, hat torn, breaking hoe, jumping in a window, stealing, lying, keeping what didn't belong to him, breaking broom, cutting pants, inattention, giving an exhibition of temper, being sulky, shuffling one's feet, laughing, reading a paper while in the bathroom, stealing apples and sugar, and wetting the bed.[44]

In 1895 the term "out of bounds" was used to describe boys who left school property, with this changing in the 1900s to the term of "running away." The *Register of Offences and Punishments* documented frequent whippings of boys who ran away or attempted to run away; this was a common occurrence. As an example of this, within one month from April 18 to May 18, 1900, a total of seven boys were whipped for "running away" and one boy was whipped because he "plotted to run away." Later indications in the register confirm that boys were also whipped if they knew that another boy or group of boys had planned on running away. The names of many different boys appeared in the register; however, there were several occasions when the same boy's name would be entered over a period of two weeks or more because he attempted to run away again even after being whipped for his first attempt.[45] For many boys the challenge of escaping such physical and emotional pain would have been worth the risk of the resulting punishment; however, they should not have been exposed to such challenges.

In 1904 the closing of the Penetanguishene Reformatory for Boys led to an increase in the population of the VIS; there was also an increase in the admittance of the feeble-minded, as they had few institutional options available to them. With the school bursting it became clear that what the VIS was originally intended for was being compromised, as there was not enough supervision and staff were improperly trained. Hogeveen points out that on February 29, 1912, the provincial government inquired into the conditions and overcrowding, but it wasn't until 1931 that the Industrial Schools Act was taken over by the Training Schools Act with complete responsibility being brought about by the government.[46] On November 2, 1938, the provincial secretary terminated the existence of industrial/training schools.[47]

Although the original intention of the VIS was to eradicate the potential downfall of the elite by removing the ill influences of boys who had gone astray, retraining them into ideal men and returning them safely into the community as contributing citizens, the end result demonstrated how immensely the system had failed the boys, their families, and society in general. Gleeson suggests that according to Foucault, these institutional power structures worked merely to produce "compliant subjects (docile bodies) for industrialising societies."[48] With increased attention being paid to the boys' mental condition and their renaming as inmates, as seen throughout the VIS archival files, it becomes clear that the state had concluded that it needed to warehouse these boys away from the rest of society since they were perceived to pose a threat. Although a lengthy time was spent committing each boy to the school, with great interest being paid to the child's familial history, this same consideration of time was not afforded to each boy after he passed through the doors of the VIS. Understanding, care, concern, and love were missing from each boy's life with any connections to such being on a privileged basis. With controlled visits from the outside world, what was deemed an offence and what punishment should fit that offence was left solely to those working within the confines of the VIS; they were accountable only to themselves.

CONCLUSION

What shall we do with these boys who steal apples? They were brought before the superintendent and whipped repeatedly and stole yet again. What was intentioned to be in the spirit and manner of a well-regulated Christian home endorsing a Christian spirit that would make these nineteenth-century wayward boys happy, active, and intelligent ended up proving to be questionable, even inhumane. The VIS offered society the sense that a warm home filled with laughter was provided for these boys; the irony of this is the documentation that supports laughter being met with punishment. The frequent attempts to run away were also met with punishment. It becomes apparent through the unpacking of history that the lives of those incarcerated in the VIS must not be in vain; rather, the spirits of those boys must be honoured through our resolve to ensure that we as a society never forget them and what they endured.

NOTES

1. *How to Treat the Criminal Classes, 1896*. Ontario Board of Parole. Record Group 8-56, 1895–1909. Archives of Ontario.
2. *Royal Commission to Investigate the Victoria Industrial School, Mimico (1920–1921)*. Archives of Ontario.
3. Melanie Panitch, "The Campaign to Close Institutions," in *Disability, Mothers and Organization: Accidental Activists* (New York: Routledge, 2008), 109.
4. John P. Radford and Deborah Park, "Historical Overview of Developmental Disabilities in Ontario," in *Developmental Disabilities in Ontario*, 3rd ed., edited by Ivan Brown and Maire Percy (Toronto: Ontario Association on Developmental Disabilities, 2003).
5. Radford and Park, "Historical Overview of Developmental Disabilities in Ontario."
6. DiMaggio quoted in Lynne G. Zucker, *Institutional Patterns and Organizations* (Cambridge, MA: Ballinger Publishing, 1988).
7. Gillian Parekh, "Disability, Eugenics, and the 'Boy-Problem' at the Victoria Industrial School" (paper completed for Critical Disability Studies: Geography of Disability course, York University, 2009).
8. Parekh, "Disability, Eugenics, and the 'Boy-Problem.'"
9. *Rules and Regulations of the Victoria Industrial School, Mimico, 1892*, Record Group 2-42, 1887. Archives of Ontario.
10. *Operational Correspondence of the Victoria Industrial School (1905–1930)*. Record Group 8-51, 1894. Archives of Ontario.
11. Bryan Hogeveen, "Accounting for Violence at the Victoria Industrial School," *Histoire Sociale/Social History* 42, no. 83 (2009): 147–74.
12. Gary McCulloch quoted in Jane Read and Jan Walmsley, "Historical Perspectives on Special Education, 1890–1970," *Disability and Society* 21, no. 5 (2006): 455–69, http://dx.doi.org/10.1080/09687590600785894.
13. Read and Walmsley, "Historical Perspectives on Special Education."
14. Charles Robert Morley quoted in Read and Walmsley, "Historical Perspectives on Special Education."
15. Lennard J. Davis, "The Rule of Normalcy: Politics and Disability in the U.S.A. (United States of Ability)," in *Bending Over Backwards: Disability, Dismodernism and Other Difficult Positions* (New York: New York University Press, 2002).
16. Davis, "The Rule of Normalcy."
17. Davis, "The Rule of Normalcy."
18. *Operational Correspondence of the Victoria Industrial School (1905–1930)*.
19. Victoria Industrial School Case Books, 1887–1929. Industrial Schools Association of Toronto, Record Group 8-51-7. Archives of Ontario.
20. Victoria Industrial School Case Books, 1887–1929.
21. Parekh, "Disability, Eugenics, and the 'Boy-Problem.'"
22. Davis, "The Rule of Normalcy."
23. Ian Copeland, "The Making of the Dull, Deficient and Backward Pupil in British Elementary Education 1870–1914," *British Journal of Educational Studies* 44, no. 4 (1996): 377.
24. Case Book 1, Victoria Industrial School Case Books, 1887–1895, Industrial Schools Association of Toronto, Record Group 8-51-7-1. Archives of Ontario.
25. Case Book 5, Victoria Industrial School Case Books, 1887–1895.

26. Letterbook 3, Victoria Industrial School Case Books, 1887–1895.
27. Case Book 5, Victoria Industrial School Case Books, 1887–1895.
28. Case Book 5, Victoria Industrial School Case Books, 1887–1895.
29. Case Book 5, Victoria Industrial School Case Books, 1887–1895.
30. Case Book 5, Victoria Industrial School Case Books, 1887–1895.
31. Hogeveen, "Accounting for Violence at the Victoria Industrial School."
32. Case Book 5, Victoria Industrial School Case Books, 1887–1895.
33. Case Book 5, Victoria Industrial School Case Books, 1887–1895.
34. Nirmala Erevelles and Andrea Minear, "Unspeakable Offenses: Untangling Race and Disability in Discourses of Intersectionality," *Journal of Literary & Cultural Disability Studies* 4, no. 2 (2010): 133.
35. Erevelles and Minear, "Unspeakable Offenses," 133
36. Erevelles and Minear, "Unspeakable Offenses," 133.
37. Michel Foucault, *Discipline and Punish* (New York: Vintage Books, 1977).
38. *Rules and Regulations of the Victoria Industrial School, Mimico, 1892.*
39. *Operational Correspondence of the Victoria Industrial School (1905–1930).*
40. Hogeveen, "Accounting for Violence at the Victoria Industrial School."
41. Hogeveen, "Accounting for Violence at the Victoria Industrial School."
42. *Victoria Industrial School Register of Offences and Punishments.* Record Group 8-51, 1894–1902. Archives of Ontario.
43. Hogeveen, "Accounting for Violence at the Victoria Industrial School."
44. *Victoria Industrial School Register of Offences and Punishments.*
45. *Victoria Industrial School Register of Offences and Punishments.*
46. Hogeveen, "Accounting for Violence at the Victoria Industrial School."
47. *Royal Commission to Investigate the Victoria Industrial School, Mimico (1920–1921).*
48. Brendan Gleeson, *Geographies of Disability* (New York: Routledge, 1999), 44.

BIBLIOGRAPHY

Primary Sources

How to Treat the Criminal Classes, 1896. Ontario Board of Parole. Record Group 8-56, 1895–1909. Archives of Ontario.

Operational Correspondence of the Victoria Industrial School (1905–1930). Record Group 8-51, 1894. Archives of Ontario.

Royal Commission to Investigate the Victoria Industrial School, Mimico (1920–1921). Archives of Ontario.

Rules and Regulations of the Victoria Industrial School, Mimico, 1892. Record Group 2-42, 1887. Archives of Ontario.

Victoria Industrial School Case Books, 1887–1895. Industrial Schools Association of Toronto, Record Group 8-51-7-1. Archives of Ontario.

Victoria Industrial School Case Books, 1887–1929. Industrial Schools Association of Toronto, Record Group 8-51-7. Archives of Ontario.

Victoria Industrial School Register of Offences and Punishments. Record Group 8-51, 1894–1902. Archives of Ontario.

Secondary Sources

Copeland, Ian. "The Making of the Dull, Deficient and Backward Pupil in British Elementary Education 1870–1914." *British Journal of Educational Studies* 44, no. 4 (1996): 377–94.

Davis, Lennard J. "The Rule of Normalcy: Politics and Disability in the U.S.A. (United States of Ability)." In *Bending Over Backwards: Disability, Dismodernism and Other Difficult Positions*, 102–18. New York: New York University Press, 2002.

Erevelles, Nirmala, and Andrea Minear. "Unspeakable Offenses: Untangling Race and Disability in Discourses of Intersectionality." *Journal of Literary & Cultural Disability Studies* 4, no. 2 (2010): 127–45.

Foucault, Michel. *Discipline and Punish*. New York: Vintage Books, 1977.

Gleeson, Brendan. *Geographies of Disability*. New York: Routledge, 1999.

Hogeveen, Brian. "Accounting for Violence at the Victoria Industrial School." *Histoire Sociale/Social History* 42, no. 83 (2009): 147–74.

Panitch, Melanie. "The Campaign to Close Institutions." In *Disability, Mothers and Organization: Accidental Activists*, 101–26. New York: Routledge, 2008.

Parekh, Gillian. "Disability, Eugenics, and the 'Boy-Problem' at the Victoria Industrial School." Paper completed for Critical Disability Studies: Geography of Disability course, York University, 2009.

Radford, John P., and Deborah Park. "Historical Overview of Developmental Disabilities in Ontario." In *Developmental Disabilities in Ontario*, 3rd ed., edited by Ivan Brown and Maire Percy, 3–5. Toronto: Ontario Association on Developmental Disabilities, 2003.

Read, Jane, and Jan Walmsley. "Historical Perspectives on Special Education, 1890–1970." *Disability and Society* 21, no. 5 (2006): 455–69.

Zucker, Lynne G. *Institutional Patterns and Organizations*. Cambridge, MA: Ballinger Publishing, 1988.

CHAPTER 8

"Someone in Toronto ... Paid Her Way Out Here": Indentured Labour and Medical Deportation— The Precarious Work of Single Women

Natalie Spagnuolo

Following World War I, pressure from the Canadian National Committee for Mental Hygiene (CNCMH) allowed for exclusionary strategies directed against perceived mental and moral "defectives" to be formalized through immigration legislation.[1] Eugenic immigration systems worked through prejudicial and pseudo-scientific assumptions to disenfranchise and exclude disabled people and specifically prevent people of colour from entering the country. Devised with the goal of replacing Indigenous peoples with a white settler population, these systems simultaneously supported genocidal practices. Domestic labour programs that recruited white immigrant women arose within this violent context. As has been well documented, domestic servants were predominantly sought from the British Isles, and preference was given to English-speaking women and to white women over women of colour. Marilyn Barber provides a history of these targeted recruitment efforts,[2] while Magda Fahrni explains how such values reflected white middle-class norms, writing that a "hallmark of a middle-class household was the financial ability to maintain at least one servant; the servant, then, was a status symbol."[3]

According to labour historian Jennifer Stephen, domestic service was the most popular occupation for women until about 1939.[4] This means that exclusions based on race would have profoundly limited many women's chances of gaining paid work in Canada. Historians have shown that 1920s racism was bound up with colonialism and fuelled by statements such as this one, attributed by Stephen to the psychologist Peter Sandiford: "the very survival of Canada is dependent upon its capacity to attract and retain the right stock of *white* British 'settlers.'"[5] As a reflection of both her employer's status and the future survival of the white settler nation, it is thus no surprise that domestic workers were closely scrutinized through eugenically informed standards. Archival evidence suggests that single white women who were recruited to work as servants during the 1920s were subjected to a form of monitoring and intervention that was influenced by a combination of eugenic preconceptions and white settler colonial ideals.

The practice of screening and testing foreign-born workers ultimately claimed to measure their value as labourers and predict their potential contributions to the nation. If they were suspected of posing any risk to the Canadian economy or the "Canadian public"—a notion that excluded Indigenous peoples and people of colour—they could be deported. This chapter will focus on several such deportation cases, while calling for further research into the history of immigration and disability that is attentive to colonial processes. Throughout this discussion, particular attention will be paid to the role of race and disability in selecting and discarding workers and shaping citizenship ideals. Case studies show how several white domestic workers, once "discarded" by their employers and removed from the labour market, were medicalized and labelled with psychiatric disabilities to facilitate their expulsion. Before turning to these examples, an analytic framework will be developed for understanding the construction of precarious work through deportation and the relationship between disability and migration.

DOMESTIC LABOUR AND DISABILITY TODAY: SETTLER COLONIAL ORIGINS AND HISTORICAL DISTINCTIONS

While certain parallels exist between the experiences of foreign-born women who currently perform domestic work and those from the 1920s, there are significant differences that prevent any straight lines from being drawn between these groups of workers. To begin, one must recall that opportunities for women to immigrate were, and in many ways still are, generally restricted to white people. During the period in question, the most preferred immigrants were white and English-speaking and originated from the British Isles. Ellen Scheinberg and others have noted that Canadian immigration officials directly targeted British rural areas, advertising domestic work as a desirable occupation to these prospective immigrant women.[6] Usha George, for example, has documented late nineteenth-century recruitment strategies that were at work in rural England, Scotland, Ireland, and Wales. George describes a form of positive eugenics that presented white working women as prospective mothers of the new Dominion.[7]

A more detailed discussion of the importance of race and country of origin can be found in Sedef Arat-Koç's comparative study of Caribbean domestic workers deported from Canada during the early twentieth century. Arat-Koç's research reveals the importance of race and place of origin in determining the treatment domestic servants received from their employers in Canada. As an example of this uneven and racially informed treatment, she describes the deportation of many Black women who were brought over through an "experimental" program initiated in 1911, known as the Guadeloupe agreement, which directed French-speaking women to Quebec. When Canada fell into a recession between 1913 and 1915, many of these Black domestic workers were expelled. Arat-Koç's account points to the fact that even while the Canadian government was recruiting Black women as domestic workers, it was not committed to transforming these women into citizens. In fact, Canadian officials anticipated a "better selection" of white domestics as result of World War I.[8]

As Sunera Thobani explains, this white-supremacist approach to Canadian citizenship is most evident in contemporary practices that position migrant labour as the main route to Canada for racialized people. Women of colour are even less welcome than men, evidencing a sexist form of racism that points to eugenic fears around the reproduction of people of colour.[9] Disability scholars have built upon this knowledge to show how settler colonialism, uneven relations between Global North and South, and disability oppression work in conjunction to shape Canadian immigration practices.[10] Distinguishing between the recruitment of migrant labourers and immigrants is key to understanding how contemporary forms of domestic work differ from past forms. Racist values have informed important changes to the structure of domestic labour and its relationship to citizenship, and unpacking these values allows us to better appreciate how domestic work has shifted from the realm of immigration to migrant labour. In 1973, for example, Canada began offering domestic workers—a category that includes caregivers—only "short-term permits rather than permanent resident status," according to Abigail Bakan and Daiva Stasiulis. This change marked a clear shift to a more disposable guest worker model and away from an interest in cultivating citizenship.[11] Commentators such as Bakan and Stasiulis suggest that these recent policy decisions have set back domestic workers and they emphasize the marginalized nature of this occupational group. Today, domestic work is indeed a highly gendered and racialized form of labour. As Ethel Tungohan shows, this work has been mostly carried out by women of colour from Global South countries, particularly Filipina women, who came to Canada as migrant workers through arrangements such as the Live-in Caregiver Program (LCP).[12] These transnational labour networks reinforce colonial relations between Global North and Global South and promote Canada's white settler vision.

While workers today may apply for permanent residency, the general trend is towards maintaining their outsider status.[13] For women who are part of programs like LCP, which was recently replaced with the Caregiver Program (CP), outsider status is enforced through processes that delay permanent residency and place caps on the number of applications approved. In resisting these practices, migrant activists are demanding permanent residency and membership upon arrival as a matter of both safety and justice.[14] In contrast to the treatment of these women of colour, white women who were recruited during the 1920s as domestic workers were expected to remain in Canada as immigrants. Thus, white settler ideals conferred a privileged status on these workers—a privilege that prevents any straightforward parallels between past and present forms of domestic work. Even though similarities may be found within some of the mechanisms used against women's claims to belonging, the application of these techniques took different forms against different groups. Medical inadmissibility is one such mechanism, and its use against migrants has long historical roots.[15] Recent examples of women of colour who arrived in Canada as workers being denied permanent residency show that this form of inadmissibility continues to play a critical role in preventing access to citizenship. As a concept, medical inadmissibility centres on ableist assumptions that allow for the use of services and supports by disabled people to be interpreted as an excessive demand.[16]

As previously suggested, disability discrimination and medical inadmissibility are applied against different groups in historically specific ways, and these take different forms when racism and white privilege are used to exclude people of colour. To begin, ableism intersects with racism in ways that have long justified the exclusion of racialized groups from Canada by presenting them as "inferior," "defective," and "unfit" for citizenship.[17] Medical deportations based on disability that target migrant women of colour ought to be read alongside programs like the LCP and CP and linked to actions that further limit the possibility of racialized people acquiring citizenship. The situation is so severe that migrant women today are forced to mediate what Bakan and Stasiulis call a "constant threat of deportation."[18] They also note that the temporary status of domestic work is one of the characteristics of this occupation that has endured through to our present time;[19] however, the medical dismissals discussed in the following sections must be distinguished from contemporary cases, as these older deportation mechanisms were applied against white women who were seen as "desired" immigrants and who were recruited as domestic workers from the British Isles. It is quite telling that during the same period, men of colour were often present in Canada under exploitative conditions as migrant labourers. Thus, deportation cases involving white domestic workers were based on forms of monitoring that were built upon the assumption that white women were suitable for membership, unless otherwise demonstrated.

MONITORING DOMESTIC SERVANTS: DEPORTING AND INCARCERATING THE "UNEMPLOYABLE"

White women originating from the British Isles who worked as domestic servants were viewed as desirable from a racial perspective, but they could still be rendered inadmissible and expelled from the country through the category of disability and through classist assumptions that linked poor and working-class immigrants with the public health crisis around "mental defectives." This was especially true when immigrants became unemployed, attempted to quit the domestic service occupation, or otherwise jeopardized their bond with their employer. Barbara Roberts's work demonstrates that deportation served both as a legal and extra-legal mechanism for "culling" the labour force, and as feminist historians have convincingly argued, the various forms of labour that took place in the private household were not exempt from these management efforts.[20] During the 1920s, medical institutions such as the Toronto Asylum[21] participated in this monitoring work and formed an important part of the deportation process for many women.[22] This link was made possible because the expulsion of domestic servants could be easily justified through medical diagnoses that were crafted by asylum doctors. These diagnoses placed inmates within the prohibited categories of immigrants and often framed them as "mental defectives." Such practices reflect Ameil Joseph's claim that Canadian colonialism and national identity are forged through the devaluation of those who are identified as inferior, specifically through "the creation of the savage and the mad."[23]

The importance of disability in Canadian deportation practices is further emphasized by Robert Menzies's analysis of immigration data, which estimates that between 1925 and 1935 at least 35,228 people were deported from Canada, 5,056 of which were for medical causes (half of whom were labelled as "feeble-minded" or "insane").[24] Given that domestic workers represented the highest category of women incarcerated at the Toronto Asylum during the early 1920s, there is good reason for considering the context of labour market access and regulation for this occupational group. The nexus of identity, normalcy, and employability is all too familiar to disability scholars. Working within this context, Marta Russell and Ravi Malhotra take the view that disability is an oppressive category that is peculiar to capitalist economic systems and to the ways in which work is structured within capitalism. The authors point out that as a product of the structure of capitalist society, disability "creates (and then oppresses) the so-called 'disabled' body as one of the conditions that allow the capitalist class to accumulate wealth."[25] Accordingly, the recognition or perception that someone is Mad or disabled tends to disqualify them from work. This creates a cache of people who are destined to remain unemployed. The "reserve army of labour" that Marxist analyses often present as a source of capitalist advantage over labour is thus enlarged by the category of disability, which helps designate individuals as "unemployable."

Indeed, unemployment has long been the subject of reform efforts by disability activists who would like to see greater economic equality and social inclusion. Some of these advocates have been critical of hiring practices that discriminate against candidates with disabilities,[26] while others have attacked the ableist standards that have shaped labour market participation to suit "standard bodies."[27] These critiques recognize that social membership is often dependent upon the perceived ability to labour—assumptions that become even more explicit when we consider the deportation of individuals who were deemed "defective" and unfit for work. Nevertheless, the medical categories of impairment that were invoked to expel individuals must be taken at face value, as these diagnoses functioned as legal categories that could be used to justify deportation for other unstated reasons. Along these lines, Russell and Malhotra emphasize the constructed nature of disability, linking the meanings assigned to different disabilities to their material context: "It is also evident that the definition of disability is not static but fundamentally linked to the needs of capital accumulation."[28]

Similarly, Nirmala Erevelles observes that people or groups who "prove to be counterproductive to the efficient logic of capitalism are marked as abnormal."[29] Thus, those who were deemed excessive to labour market needs, or who threatened those needs in some way, provide ready targets for intervention. There was a high demand for white domestic workers during the 1920s, but, at the same time, many women were seeking other employment options. Within this supply-and-demand context, women were often coerced into remaining in domestic service. Mariana Valverde has shown that church groups and women's organizations that provided settlement services also attempted to police the boundaries of the domestic work profession by facilitating the deportation of women who attempted to quit their jobs or who otherwise broke with dominant moral expectations—including through pregnancy, perceived sexual immorality, or illness.[30] These volunteer organizations would turn women over to immigration authorities upon suspicion of any violation. Domestic workers were not only expected to remain in their occupation and respond to labour market needs; they were also required to uphold white settler middle-class values while they performed their work. Their employability depended upon their perceived moral character as much as their actual capacity to work. Adherence to gender and sexual norms informed one aspect of these regulatory standards, while any failure to demonstrate compliance was interpreted in medical terms as evidence of intellectual deficiency. This last point takes us closer to specific monitoring practices and to the structural relations that sustained them.

Unemployment was often cited as a sign of mental deficiency and used as proof that an individual was "unemployable,"[31] while the opposite designation, employability, was the criteria for social membership. Stephen provides a detailed analysis of employability discourses and shows how these sought to assess more than simply a willingness to work. She reveals how gendered, racialized, class-based, and other standards worked to regulate the conduct of workers and shape women's employment options through deliberately designed screening processes during the World War II period. The belief that work-related aptitude testing could detect both "innate potential and pathology" reflects a clear link between labour market access and disability status.[32] Stephen notes that these employability discourses also had roots in 1920s anti-immigrationism, where prominent psychologists such as Sandiford linked intelligence to race and social problems such as unemployment to the supposed inferiority of certain immigrants.[33] Her findings suggest that the regulation of white women's work was structured through a racist and ableist belief system that overtly excluded women of colour from social membership.

The racialized nature of recruitment efforts and the explicit favouring of white settlers from the British Isles meant that many single British-born women serving as domestic workers during the early 1900s were granted membership as immigrants. At the same time, these domestic servants experienced a high degree of instability in their indentured work arrangements and this affected their status as Canadian residents. By centring colonialism and ableism in our analysis, we can better account for why certain white women were not fully included in the privileged category of "mothers of the race." Joseph's work is particularly instructive in this regard. He has shown that racialized people who are labelled as having mental health issues are disproportionately deported from Canada. He traces the racism that is evident in these practices to earlier forms of forensic psychiatry that were based upon "ideas of dangerousness and threat to Western civilization." According to Joseph, changes to immigration legislation have been motivated by these perceived threats and are thus enacted "to ensure the reproduction of a white, ableist, 'civilized' Canadian national identity."[34] Drawing attention to psychiatric diagnosis and disability confinement as a form of risk management can help account for the deportation of certain white women, showing how the asylum facilitated their medical deportation, as well as the deportation of other workers who were marked as different and undesirable.

As a site of confinement and as an official immigration station,[35] the provincially run Toronto Asylum can be viewed as a link between the household and the federally managed immigration system. In his research on the subject, Joseph argues that the very designation of an asylum as an immigration station was not as straightforward as it may at first appear. He has found that many of the processes that sustained this designation were arguably illegal and relied upon "the selective referencing of texts."[36] Nevertheless, the Toronto Asylum served an important function in this regard. As Barber points out, Toronto was a preferred destination for immigrant women working as domestic servants during the 1920s.[37] In fact, many women who were foreign-born were directly deported from the Toronto institution.

A survey of the asylum's records from the early 1920s supports Fahrni's claim that white women working as domestic servants represented a disproportionate number of women incarcerated during this period. In Fahrni's words, "the preponderance of domestic servants among convicted women offenders in this period is striking. For every year between 1880 and 1914 in which Kingston's Dominion Penitentiary recorded occupations for women inmates, servants and housekeepers were the most numerous"; she records similar trends for the Andrew Mercer Ontario Reformatory and the Toronto Jail.[38] At the Toronto Asylum during the 1920s, medical officials reporting to the provincial inspector provided occupational, marital, and other information about all inmates. During 1922, for example, the leading category was "Education and Higher Domestic Duties," which included 157 women, far outstripping the category "No occupation" which consisted of 59 women (who likely performed unpaid work in the home). "Education and Higher Domestic Duties" included the following roles: governesses, teachers, housekeepers, and nurses. A separate category representing waiters, cooks, and servants was labelled as "Domestic service"; it made up a significant occupational grouping nearly equal to women with "no occupation" with a count of 55 women.[39] Most of these inmates would have been white, having been born in England, Scotland, or Ireland. Importantly, the majority of the 151 women admitted that year were single (98 women); out of the 10 women deported, the majority were also single.

In 1919, the power of this medical deportation mechanism was enlarged when the residency requirement—that is, the number of years spent in Canada that could safeguard foreign-born individuals against deportation—was extended from three to seven years.[40] This change gave Canadian officials greater authority in expelling foreign-born individuals who resided in Canada. Even more leeway was given to them through the category of medical deportation, which undermined even the required seven years of residency by diagnosing individuals as permanently defective and claiming that because they were "defective upon arrival" (often an innuendo for congenitally or permanently disabled), their acquired years of residency were invalid.[41] As an authoritative source of psychiatric diagnosis, the asylum placed foreign-born inmates on the path to deportation, legitimizing their exclusion through ableist discourses.

"MOTHERS OF THE RACE": RECRUITING "HEALTHY" WHITE WOMEN FROM THE BRITISH ISLES

Incarceration represents a radical form of segregation that is connected to deportation not only when these practices are procedurally linked, such as through migration detention centres, but also through the very logic that permits them to exist. In this vein, Chris Chapman has astutely observed that incarceration flows from the logic of "the perfectibility of 'civilization.'" According to Chapman's survey, the diverse range of people considered defective, deviant, and "eliminable" were often grouped together in a variety of institutions. Many of these people were confined for real or perceived impairments, which were taken as evidence that they were "unemployable," or used to explain the fact that they had become unemployed. Chapman's research reminds us that in addition to serving an important economic function in capitalist societies by segregating individuals whose labour is considered useless or redundant, confinement also supports a moral imperative for improving the "quality" of the social body.[42] Such a moral imperative supports the settler colonial vision of a white and non-disabled society. Under these circumstances, the incarceration of domestic workers in asylums, jails, and reformatories is an example of the regulation of this occupational group that reflects the logic of perfectibility. Quite similarly, the role of deportation during the 1920s picked up the goal of perfecting the social body by removing individuals who were thought to be unfit for membership in Canadian society.

The general privileging of white women over women of colour and the special preference for white women from the British Isles were connected to notions of citizenship that emphasized "rationality." Recalling Joseph's observation that the idea of a civilized Canada was dependent on notions of "the mad" and "the savage," women of colour and Indigenous women were excluded from the nation on the grounds that they were less rational, less intelligent, and, therefore, less likely to behave according to dominant moral standards. Related to these racist assumptions is the sexist idea that women were inherently intellectually deficient and that poor and working-class women were prone to immoral behaviour. Picking up this theme, Angus McLaren has found that many hereditarians believed that poor British-born immigrants were also prone to defectiveness,[43] while Magda Fahrni has focused on the degree of anti-immigrationism among Canadians during the early decades of the twentieth century, pointing to negative perceptions of white, single working women from the British Isles.[44] In her study, Valverde explains how the fear that single woman immigrants were deviant was so strong that the Immigration Department created the Canadian Council for the Immigration of Women for Household Service in 1919 in order to manage the potential threat posed by these immigrants. By the 1920s, according to Valverde, officials were concerned with "defective" British women sneaking into Canada, and so the promise that white women would serve as "healthy mothers of the race" also required the monitoring of their moral and mental health.[45]

But this regulatory work was not necessarily carried out in the best interests of its targets. Indeed, Fahrni has shown that immigration officers were often unconcerned about the fate of their charges. Instead, they were interested in protecting the domestic servant's boss, and "appeared to be more concerned for the well-being of the employing households."[46] According to this reading, negative class relations and anti-immigrationism rendered suspect any woman who raised issues about her employer or her working conditions. Due to their status as poor people and immigrants, it was thought that some of these women "were clearly trying to escape lives that were materially and emotionally impoverished."[47] Stephen and Fahrni agree that what was commonly known as the "servant problem" was attributed to the supposed "low quality" of women entering the occupation, as well as to the fact that the work itself was unpopular and failed to attract an adequate supply of workers.

As Valverde has shown, many voluntary organizations were willing to help counter the "servant problem," monitoring workers' behaviour and reporting women who attempted to leave the occupation. Adding another layer to these interactions, the asylum can be viewed as an important site within a broad network of monitoring schemes and as a key source of authority within the deportation process. Archival evidence shows that asylum doctors were well positioned to respond to complaints about domestic workers from community members, such as the church and the women's group Valverde describes; however, it was not always the case that domestic workers were turned over to the asylum by these philanthropic groups. Another path to confinement arises when we consider employer motives. The practice of committing foreign-born workers to a total asylum allowed for a type of secrecy that benefitted employers when workplace conflicts arose. From an employer perspective, asylum confinement would have been further incentivized by the mechanism of deportation. As the final section of this chapter will show, deportation allowed employers to get rid of "troublesome" foreign-born women for good.

A case-by-case approach to this practice reveals these added layers of nuance, showing that psychiatric designations that justified confinement and expulsion could be shaped by interpersonal conflicts that occurred between the domestic servant and her employer, against whom she had very little leverage. The case studies explored in the next section expose the twofold nature of this problem, addressing both the perception of foreign-born domestic workers as "defective" and the oppressive nature of the working conditions they endured within the private household. The dismissal of women from this occupation, their confinement in the asylum, and their eventual removal from the country through medicalized labels points to the role of disability in the construction of citizenship. Just as disability itself is a complex concept, the medical evidence used to justify psychiatric confinement and deportation must be taken at face value. Instead, the social processes that lead to real or perceived impairments and/or that frame existing impairments as deficiencies should be brought to the forefront of our analysis. As Roberts notes, the legal causes cited for the removal of many foreign-born residents were often quite distant from the motivating factors.[48] A case-by-case approach such as Roberts suggests will enable a critical reading of the medical justifications given for the numerous deportations that took place from the Toronto Asylum. Two such cases are analyzed in the following section.

TWO CASE STUDIES: MARTHA T. AND SUSAN M.

A dramatic example of a domestic worker being deported as "defective" involves a woman named Martha T., who arrived in Canada in 1916. Martha was deported six years later at the age of 30 after having been sterilized and then confined at the Toronto Asylum.[49] She had worked in several occupations during World War I, including as a typist and a domestic servant, and at both a munitions factory and a book-binding factory. Following the war, she performed housework for a Mrs. Spiers, "but received little remuneration." Martha and Spiers had a difficult relationship, and it was at the behest of her employer that Martha was confined and diagnosed as "defective." When questioned about her experience as a servant, Martha is quoted as saying that her employer "was never satisfied no matter how hard you worked. She was always picking at you."[50] Martha explained that she went to work for Spiers when she became unemployed after the war and was having some difficulty: "This last year I met her at a church, and I was run down and she took compassion on me. She told me I wouldn't stick at anything."[51] Her medical record makes it clear that Spiers initiated Martha's confinement by reporting her "deviant" behaviour to a doctor. Martha describes the reason for her confinement as a misinterpretation of her actions by Spiers: "I tore up some sheets for dusters and she told the doctor. I had pains from shifting furniture and went to a doctor, but had no chance to explain. When told I was coming here, I decided to make no trouble."[52]

Martha's account, recorded by medical doctors and potentially edited by these authors, expresses regret at agreeing to work for her former employer ("It would have been better if I had never been dependent on her").[53] She describes an abusive situation to her examiners at the asylum and her account appears to have been taken as credible. Unfortunately, asylum authorities also interpreted Martha's willingness to endure the difficult situation for an entire year as a sign of her mental inferiority. Asylum staff recorded that while Spiers was abusive, Martha was responsible for her own care and failed in this regard, likely due to some inherent defect on her own part. They added that "it is unnatural to work a whole year without pay and receive abuse."[54] The apparent "unnatural" quality of Martha's commitment to Spiers was used as evidence of her mental inferiority and unemployability. Recalling that employability functioned as a moral criterion that was based on the absence of "inherent defects" rather than a willingness to work, we can see how the desire and ability to work was actually used against a domestic servant in this case.

Martha's medical record also suggests that she had been considered mentally inferior by medical authorities in Ottawa prior to her confinement in Toronto; the record mentions that she had been sterilized at St. Luke's Hospital in Ottawa four years prior—a treatment that was commonly used against "defective" women during this period.[55] The sterilization of so-called feeble-minded women has been well documented by historians who have linked the violence of these procedures to the same eugenic logic that permitted the mass confinement of many women.[56] Deportation for medical reasons operated on similar grounds, and Martha was deported under the explanation that she was mentally deficient, immoral, and unable to support herself (and likely to become a public charge). Given her lengthy residence in Canada (which was very close to the required seven years), it was necessary for her medical record to claim that she was inherently "deficient" and that she had been this way prior to her arrival. This reasoning placed Martha within a "prohibited class" of immigrant and, on these grounds, her deportation could be easily justified.

Interestingly, Martha's record notes that while she was thought to be "constitutionally inferior," she did not appear so and "would pass as sane."[57] Her appearance as "almost normal" would have worked against her, however, as it placed her in the more threatening category of women "defectives." As Erika Dyck explains, this "passing" group of women were viewed as more sexually threatening than any other class of so-called defectives. Martha's record reinforces Dyck's claim that any acts of sexual immorality committed by a poor woman, whether the result of violence or coercion, served as evidence of her intellectual inferiority.[58] Indeed, the brief note in her record indicating that she had worked as a prostitute before coming to Canada was likely intended to enforce the perception of her immorality. The observation that she was an apparently "normal-looking" but deeply defective woman would also have helped account for how she was able to pass the initial medical inspection at her port of arrival.

Asylum authorities justified Martha's deportation by suggesting that her immorality indicated "mental deficiency." According to dominant discourses around employability and disability, a "mentally deficient" person could not support herself in the labour market. These negative assumptions around Mad and disabled women echo the theory, summarized by Fahrni, that many British-born domestic workers had already proven their "deficiency" in their countries of origin and were simply "trying to escape lives that were materially and emotionally impoverished."[59] By drawing attention to Martha's work as a prostitute in England, the authors of her medical file are also appealing to a popular narrative described by Valverde, in which Canadian public health officials performed anti-prostitution work by "rescuing" foreign-born women and bringing them to Canada where they could work as domestic servants. This so-called rescue work also functioned as a form of policing and punishment. The Salvation Army, for example, "actively sought out fallen women, to train them in domestic work as way of improving their character … all with a view to future employment as servants."[60] Martha's encounter with Spiers at a church—typically thought of as a place of salvation—completes her rescue narrative.

Martha's record reports that she was eager to return to England. Whether or not this was the case,[61] the suggestion that Martha welcomed her deportation reminds us of the importance of considering inmates' perspectives and avoiding victim-centred approaches that deprive historical actors of the ability to resist oppressive systems or even use certain aspects of these systems to their advantage. Rather than minimizing or denying injustice and oppression, these more individualized accounts help illuminate how historical actors negotiated such issues in their lives. In fact, Franca Iacovetta has described a shift among historians away from an earlier interest in the recruitment of domestic servants (what she terms an outsider perspective) towards a more insider perspective that takes up the experiences of immigrants themselves.[62] Along these lines, Iacovetta rejects an immigrant-as-victim approach, or a straightforward economic causality that views immigration strictly as the flow of labour to capital. She suggests replacing these analyses with a concern for specific resources and motives and possible coping strategies that may have been practised within exploitative contexts.[63] Considering individual experiences, as more recent historical accounts have done, can lead to a clearer understanding of everyday conditions, revealing potential spaces of agency and resistance. These close readings also help identify how ableist and racist ideologies, among others, can complicate economic explanations, adding further layers to our understanding of how these systems operate by showing how different labour arrangements were deemed suitable for different groups at different times.

Along these lines, Arat-Koç offers a strong reminder that there was certainly a "reality of coercion" to domestic work that must be taken into account.[64] She explains how restrictive contracts were used to bind servants to their employers in order to limit their scope for resistance. She claims that conditions were so bad that the indentured nature of the work was the only way of keeping women in the job, and they often signed exploitative contracts with employers to gain passage to Canada.[65] The files of several asylum inmates surveyed for this chapter indicate that many women had in fact arrived in Canada through such indentured arrangements, which, as Arat-Koç explains, often involved employers providing a "loan" to the servant and paying the price of her passage. A representational example involves an inmate who explained that when she was 24 years of age, she left Ireland because "someone in Toronto, who wanted a servant paid her way out here."[66] Presumably, the inmate would have lived with her employer upon arrival. Indeed, Bakan and Stasiulis have identified the live-in requirement as one of the most oppressive and enduring features of domestic worker policy through to the 1990s. Such a requirement, which was only recently removed, helped sustain the indentured relationship between employers and workers.[67]

A broader reading of the context surrounding the incarceration of domestic workers at the Toronto Asylum reveals that in addition to those who interacted with these workers as "experts" through either the immigration or asylum system or as helping professionals, the general public would have also been aware of the issue of exploitative power relations reported by women such as Martha. Media stories reporting on these issues would have given the public at least some degree of insight into these abusive conditions. As Fahrni explains, at least part of the "crisis" of domestic work was attributed to the employer by contemporary observers. Fahrni cites a 1914 article from Toronto's *Evening Telegram*, which attributed the high turnover of servants to "the fact that the average woman is constitutionally incapable of attending to her own business, and she meddles and interferes and nags at her servants until it gets on their nerves so that they can't stand it."[68] So, even while dominant discourses and practices protected employers and offered little to women working in private households, the dangerous realities that these workers navigated were not so secret. When gender roles were involved, the influence of class and other forms of status became even more complex and uneven. The next case study directly addresses the indentured and precarious reality of domestic work by drawing attention to gender, sexuality, and class dynamics, along with their ability to shape Mad and disability identities. The experience of Susan M., a woman who came to Canada to work for a male employer and who was eventually deported to a workhouse in England after contracting a venereal infection from him, speaks to the power of assigning blame and medicalizing perceived moral failings.

Susan's record claims that she acquired gonorrhea as a result of her own sexual immorality. Not surprisingly, asylum authorities linked her sexual activities to mental deficiency, positioning her as an inherently "defective" woman. Her record suggests that her perceived mental inferiority was a permanent and untreatable condition, as it "looks as if she has always been subnormal mentally."[69] According to McLaren, it was common to view venereal infections as a cause of feeble-mindedness—and vice versa, as the sexual immorality of "feeble-minded" people was a rampant fear among anti-immigrationists, eugenicists, and public health reformers.[70] Susan, however, interpreted her infection as something that she contracted as a result of the working conditions she experienced as a domestic servant. She defended herself by explaining that she "came to Canada with a good character."[71] Further entries by asylum staff appear to discount Susan's character testament. The record undermines Susan's statement by highlighting her sexual appeal, describing her as "a buxom young woman," and "a good looking Scotch girl,"[72] further gendering the issue of her perceived sexual transgression by implying that she was to blame for what was possibly sexual assault by her male employer or, at best, a mutual relationship.

The crucial point is that no consideration was given to the male employer's role in the situation. The failure to reference his actions or character tacitly reinforces what has already been stated about Susan: that she is a "defective" woman who is entirely to blame for her own situation. The employer's treatment of Susan and possible violent exploitation of her position as an indentured worker living in his household is omitted from her file; however, the record does provide some insight into Susan's treatment by asylum staff and inmates, noting that she complained about the attitudes and behaviour of those around her and experienced stigma related to her infection.[73] Susan's marginalized status among other inmates is reflective of deeper undercurrents and divisions within the asylum. As Barber explains, domestic servitude carried its own stigma and was understood by British women as a form of "downward mobility" that was less preferred to factory and other forms of work.[74] Normative standards around gender and sexuality, in addition to her foreign-born status and the stigma of domestic work, may help account for the abuse Susan received at the asylum. After all, the belief that "defective" foreign-born women would "unfairly" tax Canadian-born residents with the cost of supporting them as public charges when their "deficiencies" landed them in institutions was common among asylum authorities.[75]

CONCLUSIONS

When framed as Mad or disabled, foreign-born women involved in the Canadian labour market as domestic servants could become the targets of confinement and medical deportation. Any difficulties that arose in their relationships with their employers could be attributed to their own "moral failings" and presented as a sign of "mental deficiency" and used as evidence of "unemployability." Ultimately, these claims worked to justify their deportation from the country. Psychiatric labels and medical inadmissibility criteria allow us to appreciate the role played by medical practitioners in the deportation process and to critically examine the nexus of labour, disability, and immigration during this period, as well as the effects of these relationships. Meanwhile, the presence of so many former domestic workers in the records of the Toronto Asylum suggests that further study of this inmate population would only add to our knowledge of indentured and working women, as well as to the broader role that disability plays in Canadian immigration history.

Close attention to pre-admission contexts will also be important in exposing the collusion between different sectors involved in public health monitoring. The case studies discussed in this chapter demonstrate how conflicts arising in the labour market brought certain women under the scrutiny of medical authorities, who then used eugenic testing methods to argue for the inherent "defectiveness" of these workers. Women such as Martha T., who was committed to the asylum by her employer, and Susan M., who experienced the indentured nature of domestic work, ended up in the asylum following negative encounters with the members of the households where they were employed. The experiences of these two women and the "proactive" nature of Martha's employer's intervention support Fahrni's observation that domestic workers were often subjected to uneven surveillance by police, medical, and other authorities. Fahrni also speaks to the role of gender, race, and class in structuring these encounters, writing that "in turn-of-the-century Canada, perceptions of class backgrounds, gender norms, immigrant status, and respectability intermeshed to ensure that many servants would come before the eye of the law, and that their defiance would sometimes be construed as criminal."[76]

As this chapter suggests, the practice of medically deporting domestic workers went beyond any straightforward economic causality. Eugenic and economic motives worked interdependently to facilitate the deportation of single Mad and disabled women, undermining the promise of immigration that went along with their status as white women from the British Isles. We have also seen how the promise of immigration through domestic work was denied when Canadians came to rely on the labour of women of colour from Global South countries. As Thobani and others have explained, discourses and practices that mobilize racist assumptions account for noticeable changes in domestic workers' status as this group has shifted from immigrants to migrant workers. Further research that incorporates race and disability, along with class, gender, and sexuality, will provide insight into how the current structure of domestic labour has been sustained and how the broader values supporting these systems have excluded and exploited certain groups and individuals. Ultimately, it was not only the nature of domestic labour that was at stake, but the broader settler colonial project and, along with this, the ideologies that would inform conceptions of Canadian citizenship.

NOTES

1. For a detailed discussion of the act and its amendments, see Ena Chadha, "'Mentally Defectives' Not Welcome: Mental Disability in Canadian Immigration Law, 1859–1927," *Disability Studies Quarterly* 28, no. 1 (2008).
2. Marilyn Barber, *Immigrant Domestic Servants in Canada*, Canada's Ethnic Groups Series (Saint John, NB: Canadian Historical Association, 1991).
3. Magda Fahrni, "'Ruffled' Mistresses and 'Discontented' Maids: Respectability and the Case of Domestic Service, 1880–1914," *Labour/Le Travail* 39 (1997): 69.
4. Jennifer Anne Stephen, *Pick One Intelligent Girl: Employability, Domesticity, and the Gendering of Canada's Welfare State, 1939–1947*, Studies in Gender and History (Toronto: University of Toronto Press, 2007). Stephen found that in 1939, 18.6 percent of women were employed as domestic servants; this number dropped to nearly half the following year (39).
5. Stephen, *Pick One Intelligent Girl*, 68–69; emphasis added.
6. Ellen Scheinberg, "Bringing 'Domestics' to Canada: A Study of Immigration Propaganda," in *Framing Our Past: Canadian Women's History in the Twentieth Century*, ed. Sharon Anne Cook, Lorna McLean, and Kathryn O'Rourke (Montreal: McGill-Queen's University Press, 2006).
7. Usha George, "Immigration and Refugee Policy in Canada," in *Canadian Social Policy: Issues and Perspectives*, ed. Anne Westhues and Brian Wharf (Waterloo, ON: Wilfrid Laurier University Press, 2012).
8. Sedef Arat-Koç, "From 'Mothers of the Nation' to Migrant Workers: Immigration Policies and Domestic Workers in Canadian History," in *Not One of the Family: Foreign Domestic Workers in Canada* (Toronto: University of Toronto Press, 1997), 72–74.
9. Sunera Thobani, "Closing Ranks: Racism and Sexism in Canada's Immigration Policy," *Race & Class* 42, no. 1 (2000): 35–55.
10. Yahya El-Lahib and Samantha Wehbi, "Immigration and Disability: Ableism, in the Policies of the Canadian State," *International Social Work* 55, no. 1 (2012): 95–108; Natalie Spagnuolo, "The Medical Inadmissibility of Intellectual Disability: A Postcolonial Reading of Canadian Immigration Systems," *Disability and the Global South* 3, no. 2 (2016): 1000–21; Ameil J. Joseph, *Deportation and the Confluence of Violence within Forensic Mental Health and Immigration Systems* (New York: Palgrave Macmillan, 2015).
11. Abigail B. Bakan and Daiva Stasiulis, "Foreign Domestic Worker Policy in Canada and the Social Boundaries of Modern Citizenship," *Science & Society* 58, no. 1 (1994): 13.
12. Ethel Tungohan, "Reconceptualizing Motherhood, Reconceptualizing Resistance: Migrant Domestic Workers, Transnational Hyper-Maternalism and Activism," *International Feminist Journal of Politics* 15, no. 1 (2013): 39–57.
13. For more on this issue, see Nandita Rani Sharma, *Home Economics: Nationalism and the Making of "Migrant Workers" in Canada* (Toronto: University of Toronto Press, 2006).
14. "Key Facts: Who Are Live-in Caregivers?" Caregiver Action Centre, updated 2017, http://caregiversactioncentre.org/permanent-status-now/.
15. Chadha, "'Mentally Defectives' Not Welcome."
16. Natalie Spagnuolo and Hadayt Nazami, "Canada's Dismal Treatment of Disabled Immigrants or 'How to Build a Disability-Free Country,'" Global Disability Watch, November 14, 2016,

http://globaldisability.org/2016/11/14/canadas-dismal-treatment-disabled-immigrants-build-disability-free-country.
17. Angus McLaren, *Our Own Master Race: Eugenics in Canada, 1885–1945* (2014).
18. Bakan and Stasiulis, "Foreign Domestic Worker Policy in Canada," 18.
19. Bakan and Stasiulis, "Foreign Domestic Worker Policy in Canada," 15.
20. Notably, Stephen, *Pick One Intelligent Girl*.
21. Known as the Ontario Hospital between 1919 and 1966. For an inmate-centred history of the institution, see Geoffrey Reaume, *Remembrance of Patients Past: Patient Life at the Toronto Hospital for the Insane, 1870–1940* (Toronto: University of Toronto Press, 2009).
22. For a more detailed discussion of Toronto Asylum deportations, see Natalie Spagnuolo, "Defining Dependency, Constructing Curability: The Deportation of 'Feebleminded' Patients from the Toronto Asylum, 1920–1925," *Histoire Sociale/Social History* 49, no. 98 (2016): 125–54.
23. Joseph, *Deportation and the Confluence of Violence*, 15, 41.
24. Robert Menzies, "Race, Reason, and Regulation: British Columbia's Mass Exile of Chinese 'Lunatics' Aboard the Empress of Russia, 9 February 1935," in *Regulating Lives: Historical Essays on the State, Society, the Individual, and the Law*, ed. John McLaren, Robert Menzies, and Dorothy Chunn (Vancouver: University of British Columbia Press, 2002), 203.
25. Marta Russell and Ravi Malhotra, "Capitalism and Disability," *Socialist Register* 38, no. 38 (2009): 212.
26. Robert D. Wilton, "From Flexibility to Accommodation? Disabled People and the Reinvention of Paid Work," *Transactions of the Institute of British Geographers* 29, no. 4 (2004): 420–32.
27. Claire Edwards and Rob Imrie, "Disability and Bodies as Bearers of Value," *Sociology* 37, no. 2 (2003): 239–56.
28. Russell and Malhotra, "Capitalism and Disability," 216.
29. Nirmala Erevelles, *Disability and Difference in Global Contexts: Enabling a Transformative Body Politic* (New York: Palgrave Macmillan, 2016), 158.
30. Mariana Valverde, *The Age of Light, Soap, and Water: Moral Reform in English Canada, 1885–1925*, Canadian Social History Series (Toronto: University of Toronto Press, 2008), 120–23.
31. See, for example, Stephen, *Pick One Intelligent Girl*; Spagnuolo, "The Medical Inadmissibility of Intellectual Disability."
32. Stephen, *Pick One Intelligent Girl*, 16.
33. Stephen, *Pick One Intelligent Girl*, 68.
34. Joseph, *Deportation and the Confluence of Violence*, 35, 53.
35. Archives of Ontario, Queen Street Mental Health Centre, patient case files, Q74, Patricia B., Immigration to Clare, 12 January 1922: "your institution having been designated as an Immigrant Station under Section 2, Sub-Section (s) of the Immigration Act." For further discussion of this designation, see Natalie Spagnuolo, "Defining Dependency, Constructing Curability"; and Joseph, *Deportation and the Confluence of Violence*.
36. Joseph, *Deportation and the Confluence of Violence*, 120–21.
37. Barber, *Immigrant Domestic Servants in Canada*, 15.
38. Fahrni, "'Ruffled' Mistresses and 'Discontented' Maids," 8.
39. All statistics for the Toronto Asylum are taken from the *55th Annual Report of the Inspectors of Prisons and Public Charities upon the Hospitals for the Insane Feeble-Minded and Epileptic: 1922*, Toronto, Ontario Sessional Papers, Vol. LVII, Part IV, Session 1923.
40. Valentina Capurri, "Canadian Public Discourse around Issues of Inadmissibility for Potential Immigrants with Diseases and/or Disabilities, 1902–2002," (PhD diss., York University, 2010), 97.

41. Spagnuolo, "Defining Dependency, Constructing Curability."
42. Chris Chapman, "Five Centuries' Material Reforms and Ethical Reformulations of Social Elimination," in *Disability Incarcerated: Imprisonment and Disability in the United States and Canada*, ed. Liat Ben-Moshe, Chris Chapman, and Allison C. Carey (New York: Palgrave Macmillan, 2014), 31.
43. McLaren, *Our Own Master Race*, 50–51.
44. Fahrni, "'Ruffled' Mistresses and 'Discontented' Maids," 75.
45. Valverde, *The Age of Light, Soap, and Water*, 125–26.
46. Fahrni, "'Ruffled' Mistresses and 'Discontented' Maids," 75.
47. Fahrni, "'Ruffled' Mistresses and 'Discontented' Maids," 77.
48. Barbara Ann Roberts, *Whence They Came: Deportation from Canada, 1900–1935* (Ottawa: University of Ottawa Press, 1988), 49.
49. All patient files for this study are part of Archives of Ontario (AO), series RG 10-270, Queen Street Mental Health Centre, and will hereafter be referred to simply by the patient's name and the container number where their file can be found, preceded by AO. Additionally, all patient names have been replaced with pseudonyms in order to protect the privacy of the individuals discussed; the container numbers, however, are accurate.
50. AO, RG 10-270, Queen Street Mental Health Centre, patient case files, Martha T., Q75, Clinical Record, 1 March 1922.
51. AO, Martha T., Q75, Clinical Record, 1 March 1922.
52. AO, Martha T., Q75, Clinical Record, 1 March 1922.
53. AO, Martha T., Q75, Clinical Record, 1 March 1922.
54. AO, Martha T., Q75, Clinical Record, 1 March 1922.
55. AO, Martha T., Q75, Clinical Record, 1 March 1922; AO, Martha T., Clinical Record, 27 March 1922. See Spagnuolo, "Defining Dependency, Constructing Curability," for further discussion of Martha's and Susan's treatment by asylum authorities.
56. Erika Dyck, *Facing Eugenics: Reproduction, Sterilization, and the Politics of Choice* (Toronto: University of Toronto Press, 2013).
57. AO, Martha T., Clinical Record, 27 March 1922.
58. Dyck, *Facing Eugenics*, 195.
59. Fahrni, "'Ruffled' Mistresses and 'Discontented' Maids," 77.
60. Valverde, *The Age of Light, Soap, and Water*, 102.
61. The existence of other records indicating vehement resistance to deportation by other inmates suggests that these details were not generally censored. Several case files of patients who escaped while awaiting their deportation explicitly address the threat of deportation. (AO, RG 10-270, Queen Street Mental Health Centre).
62. Franca Iacovetta, "Manly Militants, Cohesive Communities, and Defiant Domestics: Writing about Immigrants in Canadian Historical Scholarship," *Labour/Le Travail* 36 (1995): 243.
63. Iacovetta, "Manly Militants, Cohesive Communities, and Defiant Domestics," 228.
64. Arat-Koç, "From 'Mothers of the Nation' to Migrant Workers," 65.
65. Arat-Koç, "From 'Mothers of the Nation' to Migrant Workers," 66.
66. AO, Clare R., Q68.
67. Bakan and Stasiulis, "Foreign Domestic Worker Policy in Canada," 15.
68. Fahrni, "'Ruffled' Mistresses and 'Discontented' Maids," 78.
69. AO, Susan M., Q74, Medical certificate, 27 January 1922.
70. McLaren, *Our Own Master Race*, 40.
71. AO, Susan M., Clinical Record, January 1922.
72. AO, Susan M., Clinical Record, January 1922.

73. AO, Susan M., Clinical Record, 4 February 1922.
74. Barber, *Immigrant Domestic Servants in Canada*, 18.
75. See Ian Robert Dowbiggin, *Keeping America Sane: Psychiatry and Eugenics in the United States and Canada, 1880–1940*, Cornell Studies in the History of Psychiatry (Ithaca, NY: Cornell University Press, 2003).
76. Fahrni, "'Ruffled' Mistresses and 'Discontented' Maids," 87.

BIBLIOGRAPHY

Primary Sources

Archives of Ontario. Queen Street Mental Health Centre, Patient Case Files. RG 10-270.

55th Annual Report of the Inspectors of Prisons and Public Charities upon the Hospitals for the Insane Feeble-Minded and Epileptic: 1922, Toronto. Ontario Sessional Papers, Vol. LVII. Part IV, Session 1923.

Secondary Sources

Arat-Koç, Sedef. "From 'Mothers of the Nation' to Migrant Workers: Immigration Policies and Domestic Workers in Canadian History." In *Not One of the Family: Foreign Domestic Workers in Canada*, edited by Abigail Bakan and Daiva Stasiulis, 29–52. Toronto: University of Toronto Press, 1997.

Bakan, Abigail B., and Daiva Stasiulis. "Foreign Domestic Worker Policy in Canada and the Social Boundaries of Modern Citizenship." *Science & Society* 58, no. 1 (1994): 7–33.

Barber, Marilyn. *Immigrant Domestic Servants in Canada*. Canada's Ethnic Groups Series. Saint John, NB: Canadian Historical Association, 1991.

Capurri, Valentina. "Canadian Public Discourse around Issues of Inadmissibility for Potential Immigrants with Diseases and/or Disabilities, 1902–2002." PhD diss., York University, 2010.

Chadha, Ena. "'Mentally Defectives' Not Welcome: Mental Disability in Canadian Immigration Law, 1859–1927." *Disability Studies Quarterly* 28, no. 1 (2008).

Chapman, Chris. "Five Centuries' Material Reforms and Ethical Reformulations of Social Elimination." In *Disability Incarcerated: Imprisonment and Disability in the United States and Canada*, edited by Liat Ben-Moshe, Chris Chapman, and Allison C. Carey, 25–44. New York: Palgrave Macmillan, 2014.

Dyck, Erika. *Facing Eugenics: Reproduction, Sterilization, and the Politics of Choice*. Toronto: University of Toronto Press, 2013.

Edwards, Claire, and Rob Imrie. "Disability and Bodies as Bearers of Value." *Sociology* 37, no. 2 (2003): 239–56.

El-Lahib, Yahya, and Samantha Wehbi. "Immigration and Disability: Ableism in the Policies of the Canadian State." *International Social Work* 55, no. 1 (2012): 95–108.

Erevelles, Nirmala. *Disability and Difference in Global Contexts: Enabling a Transformative Body Politic*. New York: Palgrave Macmillan, 2016.

Fahrni, Magda. "'Ruffled' Mistresses and 'Discontented' Maids: Respectability and the Case of Domestic Service, 1880–1914." *Labour/Le Travail* 39 (1997): 69–97. doi.org/10.2307/25144107.

George, Usha. "Immigration and Refugee Policy in Canada." In *Canadian Social Policy: Issues and Perspectives*, edited by Anne Westhues and Brian Wharf, 333–54. Waterloo, ON: Wilfrid Laurier University Press, 2012.

Iacovetta, Franca. "Manly Militants, Cohesive Communities, and Defiant Domestics: Writing about Immigrants in Canadian Historical Scholarship." *Labour/Le Travail* 36 (1995): 217–52.

Joseph, Ameil J. *Deportation and the Confluence of Violence within Forensic Mental Health and Immigration Systems*. New York: Palgrave Macmillan, 2015.

McLaren, Angus. *Our Own Master Race: Eugenics in Canada, 1885–1945*. Toronto: McClelland and Stewart, 1990.

Menzies, Robert. "Race, Reason, and Regulation: British Columbia's Mass Exile of Chinese 'Lunatics' Aboard the Empress of Russia, 9 February 1935." In *Regulating Lives: Historical Essays on the State, Society, the Individual, and the Law*, edited by John McLaren, Robert Menzies, and Dorothy Chunn, 196–230. Vancouver: University of British Columbia Press, 2002.

Reaume, Geoffrey. *Remembrance of Patients Past: Patient Life at the Toronto Hospital for the Insane, 1870–1940*. Toronto: University of Toronto Press, 2009.

Roberts, Barbara Ann. *Whence They Came: Deportation from Canada, 1900–1935*. Ottawa: University of Ottawa Press, 1988.

Russell, Marta, and Ravi Malhotra. "Capitalism and Disability." *Socialist Register* 38, no. 38 (2009): 211–28.

Scheinberg, Ellen. "Bringing 'Domestics' to Canada: A Study of Immigration Propaganda." In *Framing Our Past: Canadian Women's History in the Twentieth Century*, edited by Sharon Anne Cook, Lorna McLean, and Kathryn O'Rourke, 336–42. Montreal: McGill-Queen's University Press, 2006.

Sharma, Nandita Rani. *Home Economics: Nationalism and the Making of "Migrant Workers" in Canada*. Toronto: University of Toronto Press, 2006.

Spagnuolo, Natalie. "Defining Dependency, Constructing Curability: The Deportation of 'Feebleminded' Patients from the Toronto Asylum, 1920–1925." *Histoire Sociale/Social History* 49, no. 98 (2016): 125–54.

Spagnuolo, Natalie. "The Medical Inadmissibility of Intellectual Disability: A Postcolonial Reading of Canadian Immigration Systems." *Disability and the Global South* 3, no. 2 (2016): 1000–21.

Spagnuolo, Natalie, and Hadayt Nazami. "Canada's Dismal Treatment of Disabled Immigrants or 'How to Build a Disability-Free Country.'" Global Disability Watch, November 14, 2016. http://globaldisability.org/2016/11/14/canadas-dismal-treatment-disabled-immigrants-build-disability-free-country.

Stephen, Jennifer Anne. *Pick One Intelligent Girl: Employability, Domesticity, and the Gendering of Canada's Welfare State, 1939–1947*. Studies in Gender and History. Toronto: University of Toronto Press, 2007.

Thobani, Sunera. "Closing Ranks: Racism and Sexism in Canada's Immigration Policy." *Race & Class* 42, no. 1 (2000): 35–55.

Tungohan, Ethel. "Reconceptualizing Motherhood, Reconceptualizing Resistance: Migrant Domestic Workers, Transnational Hyper-Maternalism and Activism." *International Feminist Journal of Politics* 15, no. 1 (2013): 39–57.

Valverde, Mariana. *The Age of Light, Soap, and Water: Moral Reform in English Canada, 1885–1925*. Canadian Social History Series. Toronto: University of Toronto Press, 2008.

Wilton, Robert D. "From Flexibility to Accommodation? Disabled People and the Reinvention of Paid Work." *Transactions of the Institute of British Geographers* 29, no. 4 (2004): 420–32.

CHAPTER 9

Service Clubs and the Emergence of Societies for Crippled Children in Canada: The Rise of the Ontario Society for Crippled Children, 1920–1940*

Roy Hanes

INTRODUCTION

Critical disability theory and histories of disabilities inform us that *disability* is a socially constructed category wherein disability definitions, paradigms, models, and theories are shaped and molded according to historical time, place, culture, and political economy, as well as societal values and beliefs. Over the past 100 or more years the disability category, at least in Western industrialized states, has been shaped or molded according to a number of paradigms and constructs,[1] including social welfare relief, medical, charity, moral, human rights, personal tragedy, and social oppression models.[2] One model that dominated most discourses pertaining to disability throughout the twentieth century, and that continues to do so, especially the framing of childhood disability (including the provision of medical care, support services, and educational opportunities, as well as opportunities for socialization and recreation) stems from the charity model, or what Canadian disability activist Jim Derksen (1980) framed as the "charity ethic."[3] The charity ethic has continued to dominate in terms of disability portrayal well into the twenty-first century despite the contested domain of the charity ethic and critiques made by disability activists and theorists whose ideology is linked to rights, inclusion, and accessibility expressed in social oppression models of disability.[4]

This chapter examines the early twentieth-century beginnings of the charity ethic's dominance pertaining to the provision of treatment and care of children with disabilities through the involvement of services clubs, especially the Rotary Club. The chapter pays particular attention to the rise of service clubs: why they came into existence when they did, what their purpose was, how they became involved with children with disabilities, and how and why they took on the responsibility of establishing programs for children with disabilities. The Rotary Club has had a lengthy relationship with children with disabilities, especially children with orthopedic impairments or, in the context of this chapter, crippled children. The Rotary Club movement in the United States and Canada was instrumental in establishing supports and services for needy crippled children beginning in the early years of the twentieth century. Rotary's involvement with crippled children emerges during an era wherein we find a growing societal interest in the plight of poor, abused, and delinquent children, which gave rise to children's aid societies, public education programs, child labour policies, and child reformatories. The interest in creating programs for children expanded throughout the United States and Canada so rapidly that the era has often been associated with the emergence of child saving.[5]

In other works,[6] this author addresses the ideological and philosophical connections between the rise of charitable relief programs for crippled children and other late nineteenth- and early twentieth-century "child saving" undertakings evidenced through the development of child labour laws, the introduction of compulsory public education for children and youth, and the rise of children's aid societies. Child saving principles and practices are rooted in what is commonly known as the Progressive Era, which emerged in the United States and was adapted to Canada between the 1870s and the 1920s.[7] The Progressive Era is noted for the rise of individual moral reform movements, such as temperance activities, as well as the focus on broader social reform activities including demands for public health services, supports and services for new immigrants, services for the urban poor, child saving, and improvements to the urban environment, such as the development of parks and green spaces.

Histories pertaining to the Progressive Era describe a number of important revelations regarding the concept of reformism of the time period, especially in terms of "moral and social reformers" and the targets or recipients of the reforms. Some notable observations include the race, ethnicity, education, class, religion, and gender makeup of those advocating for reforms in juxtaposition to the race, ethnicity, education, class, religion, and gender composition of those for whom the reforms were intended. For example, histories of the Progressive Era suggest that most well-known moral and social reform activists in Canada and the United States were white, middle-class, Protestant, well-educated, English-speaking women, and the targets of change were primarily poor, working-class, undereducated, Catholic, Eastern European, non-English-speaking newcomers. And while many poor and uneducated people's lives were improved through social reform movements and child saving efforts, an underlying ideology of those providing the service was to maintain the existing capitalist social order and to instill dominant white, Protestant, middle-class values in those who were identified as being subservient and in need of reform: "The child-saving movement grew in the Progressive period as reformers responded to the problems associated with rapid industrialization and massive immigration. Child savers believed that by alleviating the perils of poverty for the young and working to Americanize the children of immigrants, they could secure a better future for their nation."[8] While this observation is made about American social reform and child saving efforts, the same point can be made about child saving efforts emerging in Canada at the time; instead of Americanizing, the ideal was to "Canadianize."

Social reformists such as Jane Adams and Bertha Reynolds in the United States and Nellie McClung and Emily Murphy of Canada, who also advocated for the poor, especially poor children, were indicative of many social reformists who were primarily white, middle-class women. This is not to suggest that men were not involved in social reform activities of the late nineteenth and early twentieth centuries, because they were, but in terms of the initiation and development of grassroots child saving social reform movements such as community organizing, charity aid work, and friendly visiting activities, most individuals taking on this work were women.

When reviewing and researching histories of early twentieth-century social reform and child saving movements in the United States and Canada, it becomes evident that there are glaring differences between the work that was being done on behalf of non-disabled and disabled children. First, one is struck by the lack of historical investigation into child saving movements on behalf of children with disabilities (crippled children); just as significantly, one is struck by gender differences between the typical non-disabled child saviors and crippled child saviors. For example, whereas most persons involved in non-disabled child saving activities were women, most of the persons involved in crippled child saving efforts, aside from nurses, were men. These men were not merely a random group of urban-dwelling males interested in doing good deeds for crippled children; rather, these men represented a new breed of the late nineteenth- and early twentieth-century middle-class male in that they were all members of service clubs, in particular the Rotary Club. This shift from the established community-based reform efforts to service club and charity-based activities for crippled children presents a significant shift in early twentieth-century child saving, but, more importantly, the service club connection to children with disabilities provides the cement for the foundation of a secularized charity model of disability, which has existed for much of the past 100 years. It is this topic that will be explored in this chapter.

Borrowing from the works of social historians such as Platt, this author applies the term *child saving* to the work done on behalf of children with orthopedic impairments or, in the vernacular of the late nineteenth and early twentieth centuries, *crippled children*. The term *crippled child saving* is used to denote the early twentieth-century rise of services for a population of children who, for the most part, were associated with other outsider populations, such as delinquent and dependent children. It is this author's contention that the interest in and concern for crippled children was built on the same foundation of values and beliefs that had been applied to the development of programs and services for dependent and delinquent children, and that the rise of programs for crippled children was like the third leg in the three-D chair (the dependent, delinquent, and defective).

The crippled child saving movement, which emerged in the United States during the early twentieth century and was introduced to Canada in 1922, is closely linked to the rise of the service club movement, in particular the Rotary Club. Rotary played an instrumental role in establishing the first local Society for Crippled Children in Elyria, Ohio, and Rotarians established the Ohio Society for Crippled Children; this was quickly followed by the establishment of societies for crippled children in other states such as Michigan and New York. Once these state societies for crippled children were developed, Rotarians organized the National Association of Societies for Crippled Children in the United States.

Rotarians from the United States then helped fellow club members organize the Ontario Society for Crippled Children (OSCC) in 1922, the first society for crippled children in Canada. It was under the direction of American and Canadian Rotary Clubs that the National Association of Societies for Crippled Children joined with the Ontario Society to create the International Society for Crippled Children.

FAIRY GODFATHERS: SERVICE CLUB MEMBERS AS CRIPPLED CHILD SAVIORS

Defective child saving or crippled child saving was an extension of similar child saving work done for delinquent and dependent children during the late nineteenth and early twentieth centuries.[9] While there are numerous similarities to work being done on behalf of dependent, delinquent, and defective children,[10] there remains at least one striking difference: who carried out the work. The plight of delinquent and dependent children was primarily the concern of social reformers and involved social workers, charity aid workers, friendly visitors, educators, and penologists, as well as religious organizations such as the Salvation Army and women's groups. These groups included the National Council of Women, the Women's Christian Temperance Union, and various women's missionary societies.[11] For many years, the plight of crippled children was not a priority for these groups, and much of the work for crippled children was done by middle-class businessmen as part of their involvement in service clubs. By the mid-1920s, the community service work of club members became synonymous with the charitable work for crippled children and their families. This is not to suggest that charity aid groups were not involved with the provision of supports and services to crippled children, because they were, but the involvement was often connected to a service club activity or service club referral.

As noted above, the OSCC, which was established in 1922 and was the first such society to be developed in Canada, came into being as the direct result of Rotary's involvement. At the local level, service club members raised money for orthopedic appliances, helped to organize orthopedic clinics, provided transportation for crippled children and parents to and from hospitals or clinics, and visited children in hospital and when they were discharged to their family home. Service club members were involved in all aspects of crippled child saving work from international, national, state, provincial, and local initiatives to sponsoring and funding services and programs for individual crippled children. By the end of the 1920s, Rotary's involvement with crippled children had grown to such an extent that members referred to themselves as the "fairy godfathers to crippled children."[12] The term *fairy godfather* is quite interesting in that it underscores many social constructs that were applied to the crippled child at the time, including the connection between disability and charity, especially the relationship between the giver (fairy godfather/Rotarian) and the receiver (the defective crippled). In addition, the label *fairy godfather* also depicts the hierarchical relationship that existed between the child cripple and the adult non-cripple. Moreover, the phrase also suggests a spirit of benevolence on the part of the Rotarian through the act of giving; last but not least, the phrase *fairy godfather* conjures up the image that through the efforts of the Rotarians and other professionals the child's physical body and overall well-being could be changed for the better.

Once the societies for crippled children were established, it was service club members, particularly the Rotarians, who dominated the boards of directors. In this way, they had great influence over the philosophy underpinning the delivery of services to crippled children. Rotarians held the executive positions, therefore, directing the society, and, as part of their club dues, individual Rotarians paid fees that were used to maintain the society at the provincial level. Individual club members sponsored crippled children; through their sponsorship, Rotarians had to arrange for medical and surgical treatment and arrange payment for any needed appliances such as wheelchairs, braces, crutches, and orthopedic shoes. It is important to note that Rotarians were often in close contact with orthopedic surgeons and many of these surgeons often waived their fees for surgery and follow-up care, so a financial burden on the child's family was not a concern. In addition to the pre-hospital involvement and overseeing the hospital stay, which could have been weeks or months long, Rotarians carried out follow-up visits to the child and family in the child's home. It was their job to assess the family situation and to ensure that the child was using any necessary equipment.

In many ways, Rotarians were like the urban friendly visitors who went to the homes of dependent children to assess the situation and determine the actual level of destitution of the family and make recommendations as to whether or not the family qualified for charitable relief from local public and private authorities. In addition to the assessments, friendly visitors, as representatives of the middle and upper classes, used their interactions with poor and dependent families as an opportunity to set an example of good citizenship for both the child and the parents. In many ways, the activities of Rotarians mirrored the activities of friendly visitors in that Rotarians made home visits to assess the status of the family, determine the child's degree of improvement, and ensure that equipment that had been provided was being used. This interaction process changed little during the early years of the OSCC's existence, but by the late 1920s and early 1930s its services had spread across Ontario, and the expansion of services meant that Rotarians could no longer be heavily involved in the lives of crippled children and their families. By 1930, there was enormous growth in the numbers of crippled children that were being serviced by the OSCC; to keep up with the increased demand, there was a noticeable shift in Rotary's involvement with the OSCC, from a strictly charitable approach to an approach that was based on a corporate or business model. Because of the sheer number of children requiring assistance, Rotarians quickly realized the difficulty in continuing the work on behalf of crippled children. The group hired Reginald Hopper, a Rotarian from Ottawa, as the executive director of the OSCC, and, closely following Hopper's employ, Greta Ross was hired in 1935 as director of nursing for the OSCC. It was Ross who developed and implemented province-wide strategies aimed at offering services to all crippled children across Ontario. In addition to hiring Hopper and Ross, by the early 1930s Rotarians began to recruit physicians and surgeons to become part of the OSCC's board of directors. Despite the shift from a charity-based enterprise, the service club members did not lose control over the direction of the society.

FROM BUSINESSMEN'S FRATERNITY TO COMMUNITY SERVICE

Interesting, yet formidable, questions regarding the relationship between middle-class businessmen and crippled children emerge as we explore the rise of the crippled child saving movement in Canada: Why was it that middle-class businessmen became interested in the needs of dependent crippled children? What was it that service club members got out of their charitable work with crippled children, and how did crippled children benefit from the relationship? We examine in this section why, how, and where service clubs came into being; of significant importance is their community service work, which directly influenced the development of services provided to crippled children.

Rotary was introduced to Ontario in 1912 by James Pickett, general manager of the Imperial Life Assurance Company of Canada. Pickett learned of the Rotary Club while on a business trip in Winnipeg, where he was invited to attend a Rotary Club meeting. He was so impressed that he decided to start a similar club when he returned to Toronto. Pickett's enthusiasm for the Rotary Club is described by Scott Stockwell, who wrote that "this quiet and reserved man told his business associates that he had met the finest group of businessmen in Winnipeg that he had ever encountered in one group or gathering."[13] The first meeting of the Toronto Rotary Club was held on November 28, 1912, and William Peace, manager of the Toronto Branch of Imperial Life Assurance, was elected president. Ralph Waldo Emerson Burnaby, a real estate agent, was elected vice president. George Wark, secretary of Office Specialty Company, became the club's secretary, George Brigden of Brigden's Limited became treasurer, and H. C. Blanchford of H. & C. Blanchford Limited became registrar.[14]

The list of officers of Toronto's first Rotary Club provides an indication of the typical members of the clubs, as membership was based on social and economic status and members had to be businessmen or professionals. During the early years of the Rotary, only one representative of a business or profession could be a member of any one of the district Rotary clubs—this was done by design rather than coincidence. Membership in Rotary included "proprietor, partner, agent or manager in full charge of a legitimate profession, business calling or undertaking, or an officer in a company."[15] Membership was also restricted according to race, as the Rotary did not permit the membership of "coloured people."[16] Restricting membership to one member per business was a practice initiated when the Rotary Club was first established in Chicago in 1905, and it was not changed for many years: "This unique idea, since adopted by other organizations, precluded the take over of the club by any vocational clique and, at the same time each individual member came to be looked upon as a representative not only of his business but also of his vocation, in other words, the whole business or professional field of which his operation was a part."[17]

From their earliest days, Rotary clubs promoted fellowship among businessmen, and restricting membership along business and professional lines was designed to eliminate any competition that might undermine fraternal relations that existed between club members.[18] While service club fraternities such as the Rotary Club quickly became recognized for their charitable work, service was not the original purpose for the establishment of the clubs. On the contrary, the original purpose was to provide a "safe haven" for middle-class businessmen who felt their middle-class and Christian values and moral standards were rapidly eroding in an increasingly urbanized and morally corrupt society.

The population of Canada had not grown as rapidly as that of the United States, but by the late nineteenth and early twentieth centuries there was a period of rapid population growth, and most of that growth was in cities such as Montreal and Toronto. Between 1851 and 1921, the population had grown from just over 2 million people to close to 9 million (2.4 million in 1851, 4.3 million in 1881, and 8.7 million in 1921).[19] During this time, the population of Ontario increased by 81 percent. The vast majority of new immigrants were settling in Southern Ontario, and by the late nineteenth century, Ontario had become the industrial centre of Canada wherein most people in Ontario were urban dwellers living in and around Toronto.

Like cities in Britain and the United States, urban centres in Canada were fertile ground for the development of societies whose members were concerned with what they saw as urban decay and social unrest, which for many social reformers of the era was just about anything that challenged the values of Anglo-Saxon Protestants. Social reformers were concerned with such issues as "prostitution, divorce, illegitimacy, Indians and Chinese, public education, suppression of obscene literature, rescue of fallen women, and shelters for women and children."[20] Valverde has referred to the urban and social reform movement of late nineteenth- and early twentieth-century Canada as a social purity movement, "whose intent it was to raise the moral tone of Canadian society and in particular the urban working poor communities."[21] Alongside the social purity activists, there were also voluntary mutual support associations for middle-class men and women such as reading clubs, the YMCA, and Bible societies, which were actively encouraged and supported by the middle class, who saw these voluntary associations as surrogate families functioning to maintain traditional Protestant values through peer support, mutual aid, friendship, and moral guidance. Very often members of these voluntary societies were young adults from well-established families. Businessmen's clubs supported the same ideals, virtues, and interests, and initially the most distinctive feature of business clubs was that members were either professionals or businessmen.

The first of these businessmen's clubs was the Rotary Club, established in 1905. The club was founded by a young lawyer, Paul Harris, who had moved from rural Vermont to Chicago in 1896. Harris found Chicago very unfriendly and the opposite of his hometown in Vermont. Because he was lonely, Harris started a club with other professionals and businessmen who, like him, felt the need to promote the values of friendship and business.[22] From that beginning, "the Rotary Clubs began to organize in other large cities in the United States, and within a few years the Rotary Club spread to Canada and then overseas."[23] What began as a local businessmen's club in Chicago rapidly expanded, and by the early 1920s there were hundreds of Rotary clubs and other similar service clubs throughout the United States and Canada. Many middle-class businessmen felt their social order was rapidly disintegrating, and the clubs emerged as a safe haven for those who felt threatened by a rapidly changing social milieu. Charles contends that the service club provided a mechanism for maintaining many of the values of the small-town way of life that was disappearing through immigration, urbanization, and industrialization: "Through their meetings and activities they sought to recreate what they remembered as a warm friendliness and the booster spirit of the 20th century small town."[24] The term *businessmen's club* is applied to the Rotary, as it was overwhelmingly a male-only association at the local, national, and international levels. While there is some evidence of women's Rotary clubs in the United States as early as 1911,[25] the vast majority of the clubs disallowed membership for women until 1987, when the Supreme Court of the United States ruled that clubs could no longer ban women as members:

> The court decided that in the state of California, women could not be excluded from membership in Rotary solely because of their gender. The RI [Rotary International] Board had earlier decided that if they lost the California case, they would concede the U.S., rather than endure the costly expense of litigation in the remaining 49 states. Rotarians in the other 49 states immediately assumed that they could invite women to join in their states as well.[26]

Service clubs stressed the importance of friendship, fellowship, and ethical business practice, and many members joined primarily for the purpose of developing their business interests, as club members were expected to do business only with fellow members rather than with another member's competition. Club membership offered lucrative opportunities, especially since each club allowed only one member from any profession or business and, for many members, this was an important element of club membership. William Peace pointed out that "the best men in every line of business are members of the club." He emphasized the business opportunities available, concluding, "I would not take $10,000 for my membership in the Rotary Club of Toronto. I never did so much business since I became a Rotarian."[27] Peace's support for Rotary as a means of establishing business opportunities was not widely accepted, and more and more members complained of heavyhanded business during club meetings. Many members, in fact, felt they were under constant pressure to do business with men they had no desire to do business with, and as a result the original objectives of friendship and fellowship were often undermined by opportunism. To get back to the aims of fellowship and friendship, business transactions were prohibited at club meetings, and the focus changed to community service activities. The shift in focus from business to community service was captured in the slogan, "He profits most who serves best."[28] This slogan became the official motto of the Rotary Club in 1911, signifying a dramatic change from the club's original aim of developing business to the aim of serving the community.

Despite the replacement of business opportunism by principles of altruism and community service, the number of service clubs grew throughout the 1910s and 1920s as more men sought out the fraternalism and friendship offered through these clubs. It should be noted that while there may have been losses in terms of direct business transactions, membership and acts of altruism for needy populations did provide ample compensation, especially in terms of recognition through press releases and publicity campaigns.[29] Similarly, the shift to altruism and charitable work created a venue for men who wished to display their genuine concern for the "less fortunate" and who wanted to become involved in activities that were linked to Christian values of generosity and kindness; however, underpinning the focus on charitable relief through service was the paramount belief in personal change, self-improvement, and good citizenship; limited attention was paid to the greater inclusion of cripples in mainstream society if broader social, economic, and legislative change was required. Indeed, American researcher Frank Bowe noted that beginning in the early twentieth century, America became increasingly inaccessible to the point that the very environment of most towns and cities was designed in such a way as to handicap people with impairments; the same was true for Canada.[30]

FROM BOYS' WORK TO CRIPPLED CHILD SAVING

To appreciate the involvement of the Rotary Club with crippled children requires an examination of the Rotary's other community service work, for in this work is the philosophy underpinning the community service work for crippled children. Clubs such as the Rotary Club of Toronto became involved in community service activities prior to World War I, at which time club members began working with delinquent and dependent children. These altruistic activities flourished during the years following the war, as Rotary clubs became increasingly involved in larger scale charitable activities.

As noted earlier, service club members were very concerned with the social problems of urban life, and a major concern was delinquent and underprivileged boys. Rotary clubs established boys' committees to address problems of delinquency. It was through this community service work with delinquent and underprivileged boys that Rotarians came in contact with crippled children. In many instances, crippled boys were brought to the attention of Rotarians by community workers, teachers, and ministers, as well as other professionals. In other instances, crippled children were discovered by Rotarians during visits to the homes of boys who were already in programs sponsored by boys' committees. Rotary clubs across Ontario began purchasing appliances and equipment for crippled boys through the various boys' committees.[31] By the early 1920s, the Rotary was the primary service club working with needy crippled children and their families.

The focus of linking one Rotarian with one crippled child originates with the one-on-one community service work that Rotarians were doing with delinquent boys. For example, in some of the towns and cities such as Toronto, boys' committee members were assigned court duty on a regular basis, and when a boy came before the court, the boy was often assigned to a Rotarian. These Rotarians acted as quasi–probation officers, whose duty it was to provide guidance to the boy; such a responsibility meant regular meetings with the boy and his parents. The work also included getting the boy involved in constructive diversionary activities, such as Boy Scouts or the YMCA. This blueprint for interaction is quite evident in the crippled children's work, which was based on these same principles, including individual Rotarian sponsorship of a crippled child, home visits, and, when possible, the establishment of recreational programs and activities and the attendance of Rotarians at orthopedic clinics. Rotarians were expected to attend the clinics, and to follow up with crippled children and their families when they returned home.[32]

It appears that the work of crippled child saving undertaken by service club members was very similar to the child saving work for poor and delinquent children. To begin, assigning an individual Rotarian to a crippled child may have been based on pragmatic ideals, such as not wanting to overburden the same two or three club members with responsibility for large numbers of children. In addition, one-on-one work offered an opportunity for forming closer bonds to children, and for mentorship and role modelling, which was typical of moral reform and child saving activities of the late nineteenth century and early twentieth century. Moreover, it appears that when service club members became involved with crippled children, they adopted methods of intervention similar to those used by settlement house workers and friendly visitors who worked with urban poor and immigrant families. These similarities included the home visits and attempts at moral uplift that emphasized face-to-face contact, personal example, persuasion, and reporting. Preuter reports the following:

> Each member of the club is assigned a certain number of names.... It becomes his duty to visit the parents of the child assigned to him.... He endeavours to persuade the parents to bring the child to the clinic.... He does some valuable educative work in informing the parents as to the possibilities of successful remedial work of the most difficult crippling conditions.... He observes the condition of the home and the environment in which the child has its existence.... The information thus gathered is tabulated on a contact survey form and is forwarded to the secretary as a record for his files.[33]

Assigning one Rotarian per crippled child allowed the opportunity for home visits, which provided face-to-face contact, and allowed the Rotarian to evaluate the child's progress and determine whether or not the child was making use of any equipment or appliances purchased by the Rotary Club. In many ways, there was an element of mistrust on the part of the giver (service club members) toward the receiver (crippled child and family). This mistrust was indicative of the middle-class Protestant ethics of work, self-care, and self-responsibility that were part of service club ideals. In many ways, the desire for the face-to-face visit was linked to charitable relief assessments of the era wherein it was believed that personal contact was the best way to distinguish between the deserving and non-deserving poor and to institute possibilities of moral uplift by modelling good character. Members of the crippled children committees were expected to maintain direct contact with the children. For example, the first chairman of the Crippled Children's Committee of the Toronto Rotary Club, Charlie Collins, led by example, sponsoring 19 children himself. In 1925, Collins was replaced as chairman of the committee by Tom LeGras, Dominion consultant in orthopedic appliances, who, during his first year as chairman, sponsored 48 crippled children.[34] This procedure of sponsoring a crippled child and maintaining long-term contact with the child remained a central component of crippled children's community service for many years. But over time it was disbanded, as the number of crippled children sponsored by the Rotary Club through the OSCC increased to such an extent that direct contact could no longer be effectively maintained. By the mid-1930s, the OSCC recognized the difficulty that individual club members were having in maintaining direct contact with the children, and a visiting nurses program was established as a means of maintaining direct contact and follow-up visits with the children and their families.

Undoubtedly, during the era between 1900 and 1940 many hundreds of poor and needy crippled children were helped by service clubs, but while there were many benefits, there were also significant long-term negative consequences resulting from service provision and care that were rooted in charity. Of particular relevance was the image of the crippled child as a charity case; because of this close affiliation with charity, many services provided to crippled children and their families were provided as gifts, not as rights. It was not until the 1970s that the charity ethic was challenged by disability activists in Canada and abroad. Service clubs and charitable relief associations dominated the provision of care and relief for needy crippled children, while state-run programs remained basically overlooked until the rise of the modern welfare state; until that time, "arrangements for meeting the most pressing needs were haphazard at best and the welfare of even the most worthy recipients was sadly neglected."[35]

PROVIDING SERVICES FOR CRIPPLED CHILDREN

As indicated in the previous section, there were numerous links between the Rotary's work with delinquent boys and its work with crippled children. In some situations, the Rotary clubs' crippled children's committees grew directly out of the boys' committees. Many Rotary clubs in cities such as Windsor, London, Hamilton, Ottawa, and Toronto developed crippled children's committees through the course of their work with boys during World War I, and they continued to support crippled children's work following the war. In some ways this concern with helping crippled children may have influenced the Rotary's support for the OSCC beginning in 1922.[36]

Service club members were not necessarily concerned with broader social, economic, cultural, and political change, but they were concerned with the potential social problems presented by dependent youth, delinquent youth, and crippled children. They held the view that problem children grew up to become problem adults, and when it came to crippled children, the objective of making them into responsible and productive adults was a primary component of community service work: "The fact that Rotary was interested in preventive methods as well as curative activities and that its part in crippled children's work was at once beautiful and sublime—consorting in a mission of charity, philanthropy and altruistic effort to mend these cripples and to make them useful members of society."[37]

Although the crippled children's committees of local Rotary clubs played a very important role in the provision of community services for crippled children, the Rotary Club had no intention of replacing existing community charities or replacing existing public welfare organizations for children. Rotary clubs viewed their role as initiators of and co-leaders for service provision work, as the mission of the Rotary was to initiate programs and then pass the actual day-to-day operation of those programs on to the appropriate community organizations. And while Rotary clubs did not intend to replace existing charitable institutions or social welfare programs, the Rotary did hope that its community service work would instill in the community some degree of accountability for underprivileged populations. This approach was evident in the Rotary's work for crippled children, as much of this work was getting other community agencies, as well as municipal and provincial governments, involved in providing day-to-day medical care, supports, and services to crippled children. The crippled children committees of service clubs, such as the Toronto Rotary Club, were essential to the successful work carried out by the OSCC. In fact, it was the Rotary club movement that initiated charitable relief measures for crippled children, and it was the Rotary Club of Windsor, Ontario, that brought members together to establish the OSCC in 1922.

Despite the many challenges evidenced during OSCC's early years, it appears that the society evolved into a well-structured organization that functioned with military precision as it arranged supports and services for crippled children across Ontario. While the OSCC acted as the provincial umbrella organization for member clubs and agencies, it was the local service club, through its crippled children committee, that carried out the directives of the society. The crippled children committees worked with local hospital authorities to organize travelling clinics that went out from larger urban centres to smaller towns and villages for assessment and follow-up purposes. Similarly, it was the crippled children committees that arranged transportation for children and parents to and from hospitals and clinics, and raised funds to cover the cost of braces, crutches, wheelchairs, and artificial limbs for those who were unable to pay for these needed items. These committees also arranged for Rotarians and or others to visit the child when he or she was hospitalized, and arranged follow-up care.[38] "The Ontario Society for Crippled Children," suggested R. G. Cameron, "was organized for the purpose to serve as a medium through which all may cooperate who wish to assist in preventing and repairing the tragedies of nature and all accidents which are registered in the bodies of little children."[39] Simply put, without the charitable involvement and ongoing support of the crippled children committees, organizations such as the OSCC may not have come into existence when they did, nor would they have endured as long as they have.

DISCOVERING CRIPPLED CHILDREN

The provision of supports and services was a core element of the charitable relief activities of the crippled children committee, and another was locating or discovering crippled children who were in need of treatment. Crippled children's committees worked in close association with community agencies to conduct large surveys aimed at discovering crippled children. For example, the Crippled Children's Survey Committee of the Toronto Rotary Club, with the Neighbourhood Workers' Association and the Department of Public Health, conducted the first large-scale survey of crippled children in Canada in 1926, and this was followed by similar surveys in 1928 and 1929.[40]

The Toronto Rotary Club, by conducting these surveys with experts from other agencies, was actually applying protocol that had been part of the Rotary's approach to community service work since the years prior to World War I. When a Rotary club became involved in a particular community service project, it did so in a very systematic manner indicative of the attitude of scientific charity of the era. Regardless of the community service project, whether it was charitable work for impoverished children or community services for delinquent boys, the Rotary always conducted needs surveys first. The needs survey was a central component of the Rotary's community service work, and numerous needs surveys of crippled children were conducted throughout the 1920s, 1930s, and 1940s.[41]

Moreover, the use of outside experts was also a practice of community service work dating back to the years prior to World War I, as the use of outside expertise provided direction and credibility to community service work. Thus, many of the community service activities carried out by the Rotary included input from professionals such as doctors, social workers, educators, and church representatives; "reinforced by objective expertise, supported by an eager public, club members could feel confident of local goodwill, and more certain that they occupied a solid position in the community and the nation."[42]

ROTARIANS' CHANGING APPROACHES TO CRIPPLED CHILDREN WORK

While Rotarians played a significant role in establishing services for crippled children in Ontario, this did not necessarily mean that service club members held the children or their parents in high regard. Indeed, it can be argued that many service club members' attitudes toward crippled children and their families were, at best, very paternalistic. Similar to most of the populace of the time, most Rotarians viewed crippled children as pitiable creatures who were considered less human than "normal" children. For example, in a speech to the Ottawa Rotary Club, Ed Kelsey of Toledo, Ohio, vice president of the International Society for Crippled Children, referred to crippled children as "those twisted bits of humanity."[43] Other Rotarians viewed crippled children as a problem population and expressed concern that crippled children would grow up to become burdens on society, hence the desire to provide treatment at an early age so that these children had a chance of becoming productive citizens: "The children of today are the mothers and fathers of tomorrow and in their hands lies the destiny of the nation. That those children who are underprivileged in life's race and have the misfortune to be maimed, may have the same chance as other boys and girls, is one of the great aims of Rotary."[44]

While Rotary clubs were instrumental in establishing the OSCC and in starting local services for crippled children, long-term provision of services for crippled children was not always supported by every Rotarian. Many club members felt that continuous support for crippled children's programs was nothing more than charitable work and was, therefore, not the responsibility or the role of the Rotary Club. Many club members argued that the primary function of community service work was to initiate and demonstrate the need for a particular community service, and having demonstrated the need for the services, the service club's expectation was they would be taken over by other community organizations: "To continue such work as that for crippled children after demonstrating its value, is to carry on charity work … which definitely is not the role of a Rotary Club."[45] Opposing points of view such as these created debate among club members, and on many occasions Rotarians proposed discontinuing support for crippled children's programs and refocusing the work onto other needy populations: "The recommended and the established policy of Rotary with respect to service projects has been to find untouched fields of social and other public service, develop these fields, show their need and demonstrate successful methods of handling and pass them onto municipal or other agencies; and this done, to look for other untouched fields."[46] Other Rotarians, though, argued that the nature of community service work for crippled children required long-term involvement and, while this involvement went beyond the traditional boundaries of short-term charity work, it should nevertheless remain part of the Rotary's community service. Some members argued that the Rotary had become particularly identified with crippled children and to discontinue services would have a negative effect on programs for crippled children. "The established wide association of Rotary with the work," argued Dr. Robertson, "was a definite factor in its carrying on in its present proportions; that in the future more children probably would be reached and taken care of if the Rotary contact were maintained."[47] Other Rotarians discussed the pros and cons of the highly involved service work for crippled children, especially the consequence of losing face and credibility in the public domain if the Rotary withdrew its support for these services, warning "that the work had added to the club's prestige; that it would lose standing if it withdrew."[48] Despite the various debates, Rotary clubs expanded their community service work with crippled children and played a central role in establishing programs for crippled children across Ontario throughout the 1920s, 1930s, and beyond.

In addition to this direct community service work, increasingly, Ontario Rotary club members became politically active as they advocated for increased support for the children. As early as 1924, the executive of the OSCC met in Toronto to discuss the responsibilities the provincial government had in providing care for crippled children and what, if any, legislation there was pertaining to this population. R. G. Cameron said the following at the meeting of the Crippled Children's Committee of the Ottawa Rotary Club, on November 25, 1924:

With reference of getting further legislation and financial assistance from the Ontario Government a resolution was passed recommending that a committee be appointed at once with a view of finding out what legislation is now on the statute books and if necessary that the Society needs more legislation to carry on successfully to add to the present legislation.[49]

The primary role of the Rotary's crippled children's committees was to directly provide services to crippled children, but as time passed, the Rotary began lobbying the provincial government on behalf of crippled children. This lobbying of government was initiated by John Gibson, who was both a member of the Toronto Rotary Club and the president of the OSCC. Lobbying the provincial government represented a significant change in the delivery of services to crippled children as the committee argued that the care and treatment of crippled children was a provincial government responsibility, rather than a local responsibility.

The end of the 1920s ushered in a period of reorganization for both the OSCC and the various crippled children's committees. For example, beginning in 1928 and continuing through 1929, the Crippled Children's Committee of the Toronto Rotary Club established six subcommittees to oversee the work the club was doing on behalf of crippled children; these subcommittees oversaw surveys, transportation, purchasing, visiting, hospital admittance, and publicity. The Crippled Children's Committee of Toronto also initiated a new service delivery method, dividing the city of Toronto into nine districts and assigning a committee of three members to each district. These district committees worked in close association with the Toronto Hospital for Sick Children, the Department of Public Health, and the Neighbourhood Workers' Association. This was very much consistent with the Rotary's core philosophy of involving community agencies in its community service work.

Even though the shift toward some political involvement was not dramatic, organizing services at the local level and lobbying the government at the provincial level represented a significant change in the ideology underpinning service work. On the whole, the nature of the civic and charitable work carried out by Rotarians was aimed at maintaining fellowship among club members and a familiarity and trust that served them in business and community activities. The projects carried out by Rotarians, such as those for crippled children, were considered nonthreatening and apolitical, and were easily supported by club members because they did not disrupt the aim of overall fellowship within the club. But in many ways, acts of kindness and generosity were tinged with pity and a sense of good fortune and relief, with a "There but for the grace of God, go I" attitude. The minutes of the Ottawa Rotary Club in 1939 reflect this attitude: "The true meaning of service has been discovered and promoted by these loyal members who have carried out faithfully all tasks imposed on them by the Crippled Children's Committee. Certainly it has brought into the lives of these men new courage to face their own problems and a deep feeling of satisfaction in bringing practical help to others."[50]

CONCLUSION

In their capacity as friendly visitors, service club members could apply subtle yet powerful influence over crippled children and their families, as a primary function of the member was to evaluate the child's need for services and the family's capacity to purchase equipment, to ensure that equipment was being used, and to act as a role model for the parents and the child. Many of the friendly visitors from the service clubs were not unlike friendly visitor volunteers and workers who represented organizations such as Bible societies and religious tract societies, as well as secular organizations such as the YMCA and the YWCA, the Association for Improving the Conditions of the Poor, the Children's Aid Society, and charity organizations and settlement houses. The same ideologies underpinning earlier and contemporary social reform movements also gave direction to the service club's individual, familial, and community work for crippled children.

Even though most men and women involved in the early urban and social reform movement in Ontario saw the modern environment as a harsh and hostile place in which to live, they put limited emphasis on systemic social, political, and economic change, as most of their focus was on individual change, reform, and responsibility. Service club members held similar views toward cripples, and while they were heavily involved in paying for equipment and hospital stays, organizing hospital visits, and offering other supports for crippled children, they were not concerned with advocating for broader systemic change that would make the urban milieu more accessible and inclusive for crippled children. Indeed, the emphasis of the service work was on changing and reforming the individual, as individual stoicism and effort were highly valued, and, for all intents and purposes, crippled children and their families were expected to change or adapt as best as they could. As hard-working, middle-class Protestant men, many service club members considered the difficulties related to disability as a test from God for both themselves as service club members, good citizens, and good Christians, and the individual crippled child and their family. By providing services for crippled children, many service club members thought they had fulfilled their Christian duty, and as benevolent as their intervention was, that was most often the extent of their involvement with a child.

In addition to the strong influence of Protestantism, which directed the efforts of community service workers and most of their acts of charity, service club members were also deeply influenced by the ideology of rugged individualism. This ideology was particularly ingrained in businessmen who had worked hard and overcome many challenges to achieve their high-ranking social and economic status. By providing community service to needy populations, these businessmen felt not only that they were meeting their community responsibilities, but also that their efforts enhanced the lives of all needy citizens, including crippled children and their families. The objective was to make the "contest of life" fair for crippled children, but once the appropriate services were provided, it was up to the crippled child to become a productive and independent citizen. As a result, community service work was not instituted to rectify the inequalities of a hierarchical social order or address the restrictions created by an inaccessible social environment, but services were provided to temporarily assist needy crippled children and their families through difficult times. Adversity and life's challenges were often considered a test of one's character, and much of the work of crippled child saving was based on the principle that crippled children who exhibited strong moral character would succeed in life and, therefore, receive just rewards, while those with weak moral character were doomed to failure.

While there is no doubt that the service club members benefitted from their involvement in charitable activities, gaining public recognition and notoriety, many Rotarians were sincere in doing their community service work as acts of charity. Rotarians funded programs for underprivileged children; sponsored boys' clubs, the YMCA, and Scout troops; raised money to provide food and clothing for the poor; and developed programs for crippled children. Right or wrong, many of these middle-class service club members saw themselves as saviors of the downtrodden, especially crippled children, and they considered themselves to be the epitome of kindness and generosity and the torchbearers of progress, acting in the best interests of all. The focus on charity, including the belief in providing for those who could not provide for themselves, helping the downtrodden, and individual betterment, did not necessarily mean that service club members were concerned about significant societal, economic, and political changes that could have led to safer working conditions, improved living conditions, public education, higher wages, or the recognition of the rights of children and women. For the most part, charity was geared toward individual self-improvement, through which people in need, such as crippled children from poor families, could become productive and employable citizens. As Derksen reiterated, notwithstanding the good intentions of charitable organizations, charity and acts of kindness did not radically alter the social position of people with disabilities.[51] It was primarily through the political activism of people with disabilities from the 1970s onward that major changes were achieved in terms of accessibility and inclusion. Almost 100 years have passed since Rotarians became involved in providing services to crippled children and much of the ideology of involvement has shifted. While a charity ethic is still evident, more and more service clubs are taking on a greater role in advocacy for children with disabilities, but much more still needs to be done for children with disabilities and their families.

NOTES

*Throughout the chapter the author uses terms such as *crippled* and *defective* to denote children with physical impairments. These terms are not intended to be offensive but they are used because this is the language that was applied during the early twentieth century. Simply put, the terminology *children with physical impairments* did not exist at that time; to reflect history as accurately as possible the terms *crippled children* or *crippled child* are used.

1. G. DeJong, "Independent Living: From Social Movement to Analytic Paradigm," *Archives of Physical Medicine and Rehabilitation* 60, no. 10 (1979): 435–46; J. Sheer and N. Groce, "Impairment as a Human Constant: Cross-Cultural and Historical Perspectives on Variation," *Journal of Social Issues* 44, no. 1 (1988): 23–37; C. Liachowitz, *Disability as a Social Construct: Legislative Roots* (Philadelphia: University of Pennsylvania Press, 1988); S. Wendell, *The Rejected Body: Feminist Philosophical Reflections on Disability* (New York: Routledge, 1996); C. Brownlow and L. O'Dell, "Constructing an Autistic Identity: AS Voices Online," *Mental Retardation* 44, no. 5 (2006): 315–21; R. Schalock, R. A. Luckasson, and K. A. Shogren, "The Renaming of Mental Retardation: Understanding the Change to the Term Intellectual Disability," *Intellectual and Developmental Disabilities* 45, no. 2 (2007): 116–24; and C. Mercer and G. Barnes, *Exploring Disability* (Cambridge, UK: Polity Press, 2010).
2. M. Oliver, *The Politics of Disablement* (London: MacMillan Educational Press, 1990); P. C. Higgins, *Making Disability: Exploring the Social Transformation of Human Variation* (Springfield, IL: Charles C. Thomas, 1992); D. Marks, "Models of Disability," *Journal of Disability and Rehabilitation* 19, no. 1 (1997): 85–91; D. Pfeiffer, "The Philosophical Foundations of Disability Studies," *Disability Studies Quarterly* 22, no. 2 (2002): 3–23.
3. J. Derksen, *The Disabled Consumer Movement: Policy Implications for Rehabilitation Services* (Winnipeg: Coalition of Provincial Organizations of the Handicapped, 1980).
4. Oliver, *The Politics of Disablement*.
5. A. Platt, *The Child Savers: The Invention of Delinquency* (Chicago: University of Chicago Press, 1969).
6. R. Hanes, "The Rise of Services for Crippled Children in Canada: The Case Example of the Ontario Society for Crippled Children," in *The Routledge Handbook of International Histories of Disabilities*, ed. R. Hanes, I. Brown, and N. Hansen (London: Routledge, forthcoming).
7. Platt, *The Child Savers*.
8. P. S. Fass, *Encyclopedia of Children and Childhood in History and Society* (Farmington Hills, MI: Cengage Gale, 2003).
9. C. R. Henderson, *An Introduction to the Study of the Dependent, Defective and Delinquent Classes* (London: D. C. Heath, 1904).
10. Henderson, *An Introduction to the Study of the Dependent*.
11. Platt, *The Child Savers*; J. Gusfield, *The Culture of Public Problems: Drinking-Driving and the Symbolic Order* (Chicago: University of Chicago Press, 1981); L. Gordon, "The Politics of Child Sexual Abuse: Notes from American History," *Feminist Review* no. 28 (Spring 1988): 56–64; B. Carniol, *Case Critical: The Dilemma of Social Work in Canada* (Toronto: Between the Lines Press, 1987); M. Valverde, *The Age of Light, Soap and Water: Moral Reform in English Canada, 1885–1925* (Toronto: McClelland and Stewart, 1991).
12. "Rotary Voice," October 9, 1928. Files of the Toronto Rotary Club.
13. S. Stockwell, "Rotary's Heritage in Toronto: Its First Quarter Century 1912–1937," unpublished paper, 1970, 2. Files of the Toronto Rotary Club.
14. W. R. Carveth, "Address to the Rotary Club of Toronto," April 28, 1965, 3. Files of the Toronto Rotary Club.
15. E. C. Russell, *The Rotary Club of Ottawa: A History (1916–1981)* (Ottawa: Ottawa Rotary Club, 1981), 11.
16. Russell, *The Rotary Club of Ottawa*, 11.
17. Russell, *The Rotary Club of Ottawa*, 11.
18. Stockwell, "Rotary's Heritage in Toronto," 2.

19. Canada, Dominion Bureau of Statistics, *Canada Yearbook, 1922–1923, Official Statistical Annual of the Resources, History, Institutions and Social and Economic Conditions of the Dominion* (Ottawa: The Honourable Thomas A. Low, M.P., Minister of Trade and Commerce, and F. A. Acland, Printer to the King, 1924), https://archive.org/stream/canadbook19222300casouoft/canadbook19222300casouoft_djvu.txt; Government of Canada, *Statistical Abstract and Record, 1886* (Ottawa: Department of Agriculture and MacLean, Roger and Co.), http://publications.gc.ca/site/eng/9.838184/publication.html.
20. Valverde, *The Age of Light, Soap and Water*, 17.
21. Valverde, *The Age of Light, Soap and Water*, 17.
22. J. Charles, "Service Clubs in Twentieth Century America" (PhD diss., Johns Hopkins University, 1987).
23. Carveth, "Address to the Rotary Club of Toronto," 2.
24. Charles, "Service Clubs in Twentieth Century America," 9.
25. "History of Women in Rotary," Rotary International, updated 2017, https://www.rotary.org/en/history-women-rotary.
26. C. Jones, "A History of Women in Rotary International," presentation made at the Great Northland Breakfast, Los Angeles, California, June 15, 2008, https://www.rghfhome.org/first100/women/trustees/history.htm#.WQt9FInysfE.
27. Russell, *The Rotary Club of Ottawa*, 25.
28. Charles, "Service Clubs in Twentieth Century America," 80.
29. Charles, "Service Clubs in Twentieth Century America."
30. F. Bowe, *Handicapping America: Barriers to Disabled People* (New York: Harper & Row, 1978).
31. "History of the Crippled Children's Committee of the Rotary Club of Toronto, Fifty Years of Service, 1923–1972," 1972. Files of the Toronto Rotary Club.
32. *Ottawa Citizen*, April 29, 1927.
33. H. J. Preuter, *The Care and Education of Crippled Children in Ontario* (Toronto: Ontario Society for Crippled Children, 1937), 34.
34. "History of the Crippled Children's Committee of the Rotary Club of Toronto."
35. D. Guest, *The Emergence of Social Security in Canada* (Vancouver: University of British Columbia Press, 1980), 15.
36. Russell, *The Rotary Club of Ottawa*.
37. "Rotary Voice," October 9, 1928. Files of the Toronto Rotary Club.
38. R. Hopper, *A Brief History of the Crippled Children Committee of the Rotary Club of Toronto* (1953), 2.
39. "Minutes of the Crippled Children's Committee, Ottawa Rotary Club," December 1, 1924. Files of the Rotary Club of Ottawa.
40. Charles, "Service Clubs in Twentieth Century America."
41. Charles, "Service Clubs in Twentieth Century America."
42. Charles, "Service Clubs in Twentieth Century America," 139.
43. *Ottawa Citizen*, October 5, 1927.
44. *Ottawa Citizen*, September 17, 1928.
45. "Minutes of the Crippled Children's Committee, Ottawa Rotary Club," January 8, 1936. Files of the Rotary Club of Ottawa.
46. "Minutes of the Crippled Children's Committee, Ottawa Rotary Club," January 8, 1936. Files of the Rotary Club of Ottawa.
47. "Proceedings of the Open Meeting of the Crippled Children's Committee, Ottawa Rotary Club," January 8, 1936. Files of the Rotary Club of Ottawa.
48. "Proceedings of the Open Meeting of the Crippled Children's Committee, Ottawa Rotary Club," January 8, 1936. Files of the Rotary Club of Ottawa.

49. "Minutes of the Crippled Children's Committee, Ottawa Rotary Club," November 25, 1924. Files of the Rotary Club of Ottawa.
50. "Minutes of the Crippled Children's Committee, Ottawa Rotary Club," 1939, 16. Files of the Rotary Club of Ottawa.
51. Derksen, *The Disabled Consumer Movement*.

BIBLIOGRAPHY

Primary Sources

Canada, Dominion Bureau of Statistics. *Canada Yearbook, 1922–1923, Official Statistical Annual of the Resources, History, Institutions and Social and Economic Conditions of the Dominion*. Ottawa: The Honourable Thomas A. Low, M.P., Minister of Trade and Commerce, and F. A. Acland, Printer to the King, 1924. https://archive.org/stream/canadbook19222300casouoft/canadbook19222300casouoft_djvu.txt.

Government of Canada. *Statistical Abstract and Record, 1886*. Ottawa: Department of Agriculture and MacLean, Roger and Co. http://publications.gc.ca/site/eng/9.838184/ publication.html.

Files of the Ottawa Rotary Club.

Files of the Toronto Rotary Club.

The Ottawa Citizen.

Secondary Sources

Albrecht, G., and J. Levy. "Constructing Disabilities as Social Problems." In *Cross National Rehabilitation Policies: A Sociological Perspective*, edited by Gary Albrecht. London: Sage Studies in International Sociology, 1982.

Bowe, F. *Handicapping America: Barriers to Disabled People*. New York: Harper & Row, 1978.

Brownlow, C., and L. O'Dell. "Constructing an Autistic Identity: AS Voices Online." *Mental Retardation* 44, no. 5 (2006): 315–21.

Carniol, B. *Case Critical: The Dilemma of Social Work in Canada*. Toronto: Between the Lines Press, 1987.

Charles, J. "Service Clubs in Twentieth Century America." PhD diss., Johns Hopkins University, 1987.

DeJong, G. "Independent Living: From Social Movement to Analytic Paradigm." *Archives of Physical Medicine and Rehabilitation* 60, no. 10 (1979): 435–46.

Derksen, J. *The Disabled Consumer Movement: Policy Implications for Rehabilitation Services*. Winnipeg: Coalition of Provincial Organizations of the Handicapped, 1980.

Gordon, L. "The Politics of Child Sexual Abuse: Notes from American History." *Feminist Review* no. 28 (Spring 1988): 56–64.

Guest, D. *The Emergence of Social Security in Canada*. Vancouver: University of British Columbia Press, 1980.

Gusfield, J. *The Culture of Public Problems: Drinking-Driving and the Symbolic Order*. Chicago: University of Chicago Press, 1981.

Hanes, R. "The Medicalization of Disability: Crippled Child Saving in Ontario, 1880–1940." 1995.

Hanes, R. "The Rise of Services for Crippled Children in Canada: The Case Example of the Ontario Society for Crippled Children." In *The Routledge Handbook of International Histories of Disabilities*, edited by R. Hanes, I. Brown, and N. Hansen. London: Routledge, forthcoming.

Henderson, C. R. *An Introduction to the Study of the Dependent, Defective and Delinquent Classes*. London: D. C. Heath, 1904.

Higgins, P. C. *Making Disability: Exploring the Social Transformation of Human Variation*. Springfield, IL: Charles C. Thomas, 1992.

Hopper, R. *The First Twenty-Five Years*. Toronto: Ontario Society for Crippled Children. Ontario Easter Seals Society Files, 1947.

Hopper, R. *A Brief History of the Crippled Children Committee of the Rotary Club of Toronto*. 1953.

Hopper, R. "Reminiscences." Unpublished paper. Ontario Easter Seals Society Files. 1961.

Jones, C. "A History of Women in Rotary International." Presentation made at the Great Northland Breakfast, Los Angeles, California, June 15, 2008. https://www.rghfhome.org/first100/women/trustees/history.htm#.WQt9FInysfE.

Liachowitz, C. *Disability as a Social Construct: Legislative Roots*. Philadelphia: University of Pennsylvania Press, 1988.

Marks, D. "Models of Disability." *Journal of Disability and Rehabilitation* 19, no.1 (1997): 85–91.

Mercer, C., and G. Barnes. *Exploring Disability*. Cambridge, UK: Polity Press, 2010.

Oliver, M. *The Politics of Disablement*. London: MacMillan Educational Press, 1990.

Pfeiffer, D. "The Philosophical Foundations of Disability Studies." *Disability Studies Quarterly* 22, no. 2 (2002): 3–23.

Platt, A. *The Child Savers: The Invention of Delinquency*. Chicago: University of Chicago Press, 1969.

Preuter, H. J. *The Care and Education of Crippled Children in Ontario*. Toronto: Ontario Society for Crippled Children, 1937.

Russell, E. C. *The Rotary Club of Ottawa: A History (1916–1981)*. Ottawa: Ottawa Rotary Club, 1981.

Schalock, R., R. A. Luckasson, and K. A. Shogren. "The Renaming of Mental Retardation: Understanding the Change to the Term Intellectual Disability." *Intellectual and Developmental Disabilities* 45, no. 2 (2007): 116–24.

Sheer, J., and N. Groce. "Impairment as a Human Constant: Cross-Cultural and Historical Perspectives on Variation." *Journal of Social Issues* 44, no. 1 (1988): 23–37.

Valverde, M. *The Age of Light, Soap and Water: Moral Reform in English Canada, 1885–1925*. Toronto: McClelland and Stewart, 1991.

Wendell, S. *The Rejected Body: Feminist Philosophical Reflections on Disability*. New York: Routledge, 1996.

SECTION III

INTO THE MID-TWENTIETH CENTURY

From the early to mid-twentieth century, institutions for disabled people gained momentum as a place to warehouse people who were not like everyone else. These institutions became an industry in themselves, providing employment to non-disabled people. In addition, people began to categorize people who were different.

Malacrida's "Work, Education, and Privilege: An Alberta City's Parasitical Relationship to Its Total Institution for 'Mental Defectives'" uses the case example of the rise of the Michener Centre in Red Deer, Alberta, to examine the manner in which institutions for *mental defectives* came into being. Malacrida examines the rise of institutions for mental defectives by linking the development of the Michener Centre to the social, political, cultural, and economic context of the era. She makes the point that the rise of institutions for mental and physical defectives was very much linked to the political economy of the era—that is, the need for work and economic development in the community.

Turcotte's "Disability as Social Threat: Examining the Social Justice Implications of Canada's Eugenic History" discusses the historical roots of eugenics and sterilization laws to show how they had significant consequences for the development of Canadian disability policy. Turcotte's exploration of eugenics details the manner in which the hereditary sciences rooted in agriculture were applied to human beings. They were used as a mechanism of social control over persons identified as being part of nuisance or excess populations. This chapter explores the manner in which individuals, because of race, class, gender, or disability, were identified with all manner of social and economic ills in Canada during the late nineteenth and early twentieth centuries.

As Canada reached mid-century, technology had grown due to advancements in rehabilitation techniques after World War II.[1] Kaufert and Locker's "The Impact of Ventilation Technology: Contrasting Consumer and Professional Perspectives" emphasizes the importance of oral history and technology as part of disability history. This chapter contrasts the perceptions of technology among polio-impaired ventilator users and rehabilitation professionals. As part of this life history investigation, the authors present material from interviews with 10 people with post-polio respiratory impairment about their experiences with ventilator equipment and 10 professionals.

NOTE

1. Diane Driedger, *The Last Civil Rights Movement: Disabled Peoples' International*. London and New York: Hurst and St. Martin's, 1989.

CHAPTER 10

Work, Education, and Privilege: An Alberta City's Parasitical Relationship to Its Total Institution for "Mental Defectives"

Claudia Malacrida

The fates of individuals deemed to be "mentally incompetent" in Western modernity have been shifted in accordance with broader societal economic trends. In North America in the early 1900s, where there was great concern about citizenship, immigration, and nation-building, and a strongly perceived need to remove "non-productive" citizens from the public realm, large-scale institutions and institutionalization became the norm for people deemed unfit for life in their communities.[1] This move to institutionalization was driven partly by concerns about eugenics and race suicide, but it was also driven by an urgency to rebuild established states in America after the Civil War and by ambitions to colonize the West in both the United States and Canada.[2] Individuals with disabilities were seen as a burden to family members and as an impediment to non-disabled family members' capacity to engage in critically needed paid labour, so that institutions were seen as a way of providing "care" while relieving families of their dependents and freeing them up for the important nation-building tasks at hand.[3]

Economic concerns have persisted with regards to institutionalization in multiple ways; individuals were often institutionalized because of fears that they may not be able to take care of themselves or contribute economically to their communities.[4] Indeed, the rationale for the development of specialized institutions for "mental defectives" and "the insane" rested on the promise that such places could train people to become productive so that would not be reliant on the public purse.[5] Political support for the institutions rested on a belief that not only could they engender productivity and economic independence amongst people identified as defective, but also the institutions themselves were charged with being economically viable and were expected to operate without relying on state funding.[6] Thus, the new large institutions, drawing on progressivist rhetoric about individuals achieving their potential and becoming productive citizens, were also pushed to minimize their internal costs and to extract whatever they could from the "feeble-minded" under the guise of education and training.[7] Thus, the institutionalization of children was justified by characterizing them as "at risk" of becoming non-productive citizens, dependent burdens, or threats to the social order due to delinquency and indigence; at the same time, the institutions justified themselves as contributors to the economy through providing jobs for non-disabled citizens and producing enough so as not to burden the public coffers.[8]

In this chapter, drawing on archival documents and life history interviews with 21 ex-residents,[9] I argue that economic concerns were central to the establishment and continuance of the Provincial Training School (later known as Michener Centre), an institution for "mental defectives" in Red Deer, Alberta. I also posit that people with disabilities in the Province of Alberta during the twentieth century were not only expected to support themselves and pay their own way within the institution's walls, but they were also exploited to such an extent that the community surrounding the institution actually enjoyed a parasitical relationship to the institution and its residents, one that ultimately benefitted the local citizens over inmates and over other citizens across the province.

MICHENER AND EUGENICS

The Provincial Training School (PTS)[10] for "mental defectives" opened in 1923 in an imposing three-storey brick building located in parkland just outside the small city of Red Deer, Alberta. Prior to its opening, children with intellectual disabilities either remained in their communities, very often without services of any kind, or were housed along with individuals labelled as mentally ill in places like the Asylum for the Insane in Brandon, Manitoba, situated two provinces and almost a thousand kilometres from the Alberta border. Thus, PTS at the time was characterized as progressive because it segregated the "mentally retarded from the mentally ill," moved children closer to their families, and purportedly shifted the focus of services from incarceration to specialized and appropriate education.[11] For much of the twentieth century, PTS/Michener Centre was the only institution for children and adults labelled with intellectual and behavioural disabilities in Alberta, and while it "served" the entire province, its economic benefit was most directly felt by its host city of Red Deer.

While specialized training and education for residents were among the reasons given for PTS/Michener's existence, most residents of the institution did not in fact receive any education. Instead, eugenics concerns played a central role in establishing and sustaining the institution. During the first half of the twentieth century, a belief that "feeble-mindedness" could be attributed to poor genetic material prevailed in the minds of social reformers, government officials, and medical and scientific practitioners throughout much of the Western world.[12] At PTS/Michener Centre, institutionalization, segregation, and eugenics were intimately linked. The lifelong internment of "mental defectives" in a virtual fortress set at distance from a small rural town and the almost obsessive arrangements for sexual segregation within the Michener Centre functioned as a passive form of eugenics; "defective" individuals segregated in these ways posed little risk of "polluting" the social body with their genetic material.

More active eugenics programs also operated within the Michener Centre. In 1928, just five years after the opening of PTS, the Province of Alberta drew on eugenic rhetoric and commonly held public anxieties about undesirable immigrant groups to implement the Sexual Sterilization Act and establish the Alberta Eugenics Board. The board regularly convened meetings within the compound at Michener Centre, and although things started slowly with "only" 16 sterilizations performed in 1930, by the time the board was dismantled in 1972, it was approving between 30 and 40 involuntary sterilizations per year, most of them on Michener residents.[13] In 1937, in part because there were few volunteers for eugenic sterilization, the Sexual Sterilization Act was amended so that consent was no longer necessary to obtain in the case of people deemed mentally defective. The argument was that, due to their mental status, these people were incapable of providing such consent; "mental deficiency" was often (but not always) determined by IQ score or, in some cases, simply by visual examination within the institution itself.[14] This slackening of the act had profound implications for Michener residents who, along with those identified as "psychotic" or diagnosed with Huntington's chorea, were no longer required to consent to sterilization. In the end, the majority of those who were involuntarily sterilized came from Michener Centre.[15] While the eugenics doctrine swept the Western world during the first half of the twentieth century, it lost much of its steam after the excesses of Nazi Germany became clear; however, Alberta's eugenics program operated longer than many others, only ceasing with the repeal of the act in 1972.[16]

There is ample evidence of the racialized aspects of Alberta's eugenic activities. In the legislative discussions (which included little active debate and even less dissent) about the Sexual Sterilization Act, "problem populations" were frequently identified as people of Eastern European and Mediterranean origin, whose languages and Catholic religion set them apart from Alberta's dominant Anglo-Saxon settler society.[17] These discussions about eugenics were also tied to economic concerns; people who were deemed "unfit" to breed, once sterilized, would not be able to produce offspring that would presumably create a multi-generational drain on the public purse.[18] This helps explain why voluntary sterilization was implied in the act as a vehicle by which institutional inmates could gain release; in theory, once sterilized, residents no longer posed the threat of producing dependent or "defective" offspring. That said, sexual sterilization at Michener did not necessarily result in release; instead, sterilized inmates were frequently held in the institution. As I speculate elsewhere, it is feasible that this happened because many of those who were sterilized were categorized as "high-grade morons,"[19] and these people were useful within the institutional walls as helpers and workers, providing care and support to more needy inmates and to the broader community.[20] The complex interlacing of institutionalization and economic and eugenic concerns was expressed early on in the institution's history; in the first annual report and continuing through to the mid-1960s, admissions were reported in terms of inmates' ethnicity, religion, and family background, which included rankings from "comfortable" to "marginal" or "dependent." Those in the latter two categories were highly overrepresented in the Michener population.[21] The linking of eugenics and economic "threat" was expressly raised in the first annual report, whereby the superintendent seeks additional residential and training facilities to aid in the "control of the higher grades of deficiency, as it is this class that is the real menace economically, socially and eugenically."[22]

MICHENER AND POPULATION

The Provincial Training School/Michener Centre saw tremendous growth between its opening in 1923 and its heyday in the mid-1970s, expanding aggressively from an initial population of 105 to over 2,400 inmates at its peak in 1974.[23] Alberta's population also grew during these years, increasing almost threefold from 588,454 to 1,627,875 people. The population of Red Deer, where PTS/Michener was located, increased an astonishing twentyfold (in other words, at a similar rate to the institution itself) between 1921 and 1971. The growth of Red Deer during PTS/Michener's golden years did not reflect normal population trends. The years between 1921 and 1971 (both census years in Canada) saw a steady decline in the proportion of people living in rural areas and smaller centres in Alberta, with a constant migration from towns and small cities into the two major centres, Calgary and Edmonton. The two small cities that today are most similar in size to Red

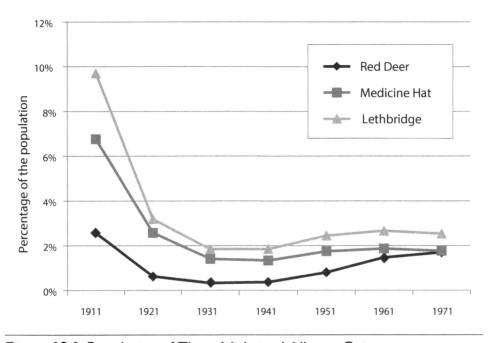

Figure 10.1: Population of Three Mid-sized Alberta Cities as a Proportion of the Province's Total Population (1911–1971)

Source: David George Bettison, John K. Kenward, and Larrie Taylor. *Urban Affairs in Alberta.* Vol. 2. Edmonton: University of Alberta, 1975.

Deer, Medicine Hat and Lethbridge, had 1921 populations of 11,907 and 9,634 respectively. By contrast, Red Deer at that time had only 2,328 citizens. By the early 1970s, Red Deer and Medicine Hat each had a population of approximately 30,000, while Lethbridge sat at around 40,000. Plotting these populations as a proportion of the provincial citizenry (see figure 10.1), it becomes clear that Red Deer is the only mid-range Alberta town that actually maintained its proportional share of the population over these decades, bucking the trend of losing population to urbanization in the two major centres.[24]

While one cannot prove that the sole reason for Red Deer's demographic success stems from its relationship to the institution, it is nonetheless clear from survivors' testimony and archival records that PTS/Michener played an undeniable role in the development of the town, and that Red Deer benefitted tremendously from a symbiotic relationship with this institution.

PRODUCTIVITY WITHIN THE INSTITUTION

Concerns about the economy, productivity, and dependency were clearly present from the very beginning of the institution's history. In its inaugural annual report to the Government of Alberta, the medical superintendent describes how maintenance costs were to be obtained for inmates of the facility.[25] He takes stock of payments from private family members, transfer funds from the residents' home municipalities, the sale of inmates' clothing to generate funds, and the labour contributions of inmates to renovations on the facility buildings and sustaining the facility farm. In sum, both private and public resources obtained at the levels of the individual, the individual's family, and the individual's home community were routinely funnelled toward the institution and, indirectly, to the community that housed it.

The government to whom the superintendent reported also placed a high value on inmates' productivity. Indeed, the Department of the Attorney General in Alberta established a specific branch to administer the estates of the "mentally incompetent," which included investing the assets of inmates while incarcerated; leasing out their real estate, farms, and businesses; and making decisions about the disbursement of assets in the case of discharge and/or death.[26] In a question period prior to Michener's opening, when Member of the Legislative Assembly Louise McKinney asked if service would be required of patients in "asylums," the governmental response was that inmates' work was considered an important part of treatment and would also offset patients' cost of maintenance, reducing costs to be covered by family members, home municipalities, or the inmates' assets.[27]

This focus on required labour was reflected in the experiences of the ex-inmates interviewed for this project, whose internment times cover the period from the late 1940s through to the early 1980s. Almost all of the survivors described working within the institution in a broad array of occupations. Roy Petrenko (all names are pseudonyms), who entered PTS in the early 1950s in middle childhood and spent more than 20 years there, related his experience:

Even as a kid you had to work.... In the Training School, if they figured if you were good [enough to work], they'd find you some kind of workshop job, you know. Shoe shop, cleaning up.... When I got a little older, I had some responsibility and that was just working in the kitchen ... where we would get everything ready to put in the dining room ... and eventually later on, the people who were older, they had to work out on the working crew outside. That was even worse because you had to shovel snow and there was always somebody around to watch if you worked out in the garden or something like that.

Male and female residents typically engaged in work that contributed to the operation of the institution, augmenting or replacing staff positions with their unpaid labour. Several of the survivors even described providing care to other inmates. Mary Korshevski, who arrived at the institution in 1955 at the age of 15 and remained for 21 years, worked doing housekeeping, cleaning, and food preparation. Eventually she was "promoted" to primary care work with other inmates. She describes this work in the following terms:

I ended up working with people that had real bad disabilities, but I went every day and worked on whatever ward I was told. And some of the wards that I worked on, it was some very sad cases. They had to be fed every meal and they had to be really taken care of. I went to feed people that couldn't feed themselves. I fed seven of them before it was my turn to eat.

Inmates' work, often under the guise of training or vocational therapy, served to offset the difficulties that the superintendent of the institution had in finding competent and reliable staff, a common complaint in the institutional reports. Inmates who could cook, clean, do laundry, and provide patient care could work under the supervision of fewer paid employees, and often took on the least desirable aspects of institutional work. Indeed, it seems that high quality levels of productivity were important, since several survivors described being punished or having privileges withdrawn if their work was not accomplished well.

In fact, the institution's annual reports intimate that inmate labour was critical to its operations. The reports provide lists of assets in the form of produce harvested from the gardens and work accomplished by resident workers. The scope of this labour was substantial. In 1957, for example, the garden and grounds sections of the annual report indicate that residents, under the tutelage of paid employees, accomplished the following:

An estimated total of some 25 acres [have been] seeded to lawn, 53,000 bedding-out plants were set out last Spring, all of which were started from seed in the School's greenhouse. Twelve hundred yards of black dirt were leveled in various areas.... Approximately 1,000 shrubs and trees were set out.[28]

There are recurring references to inmate labour in the annual reports. Inmates worked in the laundry, kitchen and storehouse; in seasonal occupations such as gardening or snow removal; and in the staff residences, where they were used as cleaners and servants. They also, as Mary indicated, accomplished much of the care, feeding, and cleaning of what were termed "lower grade" inmates.

Finally, inmate labour helped the institution's bottom line by selling the items produced during inmates' occupational therapy and vocational training, which included "furniture, tables, nut bowls, birdhouses and cabinets" made by the boys and "embroidery, knitting, weaving, leather and copper work, basketry, rug-hooking and other crafts" made by the girls.[29] Indeed, the 1962 Annual November Sale included almost 3,000 items provided by the institution's occupational therapy students.[30] It is not stated whether the proceeds of these sales went to the individuals who made the items, or if the profits were kept for other purposes, but survivors were insistent in their interviews that they did not typically receive money for any of their work or for the products they created.

As noted above, in addition to transfer funds from inmates' home municipalities, residents were also expected to cover the costs of their own upkeep from monies obtained from their families or estates. Records filed annually by the public guardian indicate that, at least until 1940, real estate belonging to inmates was held in trust, leased out, and actively farmed, with the resulting income used to offset institutional costs.[31] In its own published history, Michener Centre indicates that as late as 1985, better-off families were still obliged to cover the costs of their interned family members' upkeep.[32]

CONTRIBUTING TO THE COMMUNITY

In addition to supporting the internal economy of the institution, inmates who were deemed capable were expected to contribute their labour to the external economy of the city of Red Deer. Under the guise of educational and vocational training, inmates were regularly placed in jobs in the homes and businesses of Red Deer and its surrounding area. Guy Tremblay, who came into the institution in 1946 as a child and left the institution at 39 years of age in 1976, describes some of the work he and others did while living in Michener:

> I worked for a couple of farmers, and some of the boys worked at Jubilee Beverages in Red Deer. Some of them worked at a car wash … and at a place called Cosmos Enterprises. But they weren't getting paid, they were just working, making stuff. I worked there for a while.… We would go out there on a bus. There was a guy by the name of "John," who used to work at Michener, and he started the whole thing, and we would make things for trailers, for oil wells, too.

Guy thus describes a range of worksites, from local farms and businesses to suppliers for heavy industry, where he performed unpaid labour, some of which existed exclusively for the "vocational rehabilitation" of Michener inmates. The arrangement was that the businesses made contributions to the inmates' "training," while benefitting from a convenient pool of cheap (more often free) and compliant labour. Guy's narrative also intimates some of the indirect benefits that accrued when non-disabled Red Deer citizens worked as paid employees at Michener, as can be seen in the case of "John," who parlayed his Michener career into an ostensibly independent business venture that, in reality, relied upon subsidy in the form of inmates' unpaid or profoundly underpaid labour. It is interesting to note that some of these businesses continue to operate to the present day as "social enterprises" that rely in part on low-paid workers with disabilities and in part on government grants and incentives that support their operations.[33]

The blurring of "training" and "work" facilitated considerable economic abuse at Michener. When I asked Louise Roy about her earnings while at Michener, she replied that she hadn't been paid at all, "because they said that I can't make money when I'd be going to school." Thus, the ambiguous boundaries between "education" and "employment" that operated under the umbrella of vocational training were used to justify labour practices that were highly exploitative. This practice continued well into the 1980s. As part of a series of 1983 articles on deinstitutionalization in the local newspaper, the *Red Deer Advocate*, one writer described the working lives of Dorothy and Roland, who were among the "privileged few" from Michener Centre who participated in these workfare programs.[34] According to this article, despite the fact that they are paid well below the minimum wage, "Dorothy and Roland don't care. They would work for free." In the same article, Bob Greif, director of Michener's vocational services, who at the time coordinated work placements for over 400 residents, is quoted as defending below minimum-wage pay rates because "it is a training allowance and not payment for work. However … residents are encouraged to believe it is pay."[35]

Some interviewees like Jim Molochuk were not really sure of their pay status, because even though they were told they were being paid for their work, the money was deposited directly into a trust account managed by their legal guardian. Ironically, in Jim's case, as was the case for many institutionalized people, his legal guardian was the institution itself. Mary Korshevski, who worked as a nanny[36] and housekeeper for a family in Red Deer for many years, acknowledged that she was paid something for her work, but noted that she did not actually benefit from that pay because "when I got paid, I had to take it up to the office and they took care of it from there." In sum, while there seem to have been a variety of arrangements made to compensate inmates for outside employment, it is clear from the survivors' accounts that work performed in the community was undervalued at best and unpaid at worst. Conversely, employers, in the form of local families, farmers, and business people, must have enjoyed significant benefits from utilizing Michener's cheap (and often free) labour pool.

EDUCATION AND EMPLOYMENT FOR NON-INMATES

Until 1963, when it opened the doors of its community college, Red Deer offered no post-secondary opportunities for its residents outside of a three-year program for mental deficiency nurses (MDNs) that started at PTS/Michener Centre in 1937 as a way of dealing with chronic staff shortages.[37] Michener was the only place in Canada where young people could obtain such specialized education, and the institution's official history claims that students came from across the country to receive training that led to well-paid positions at Michener and other Canadian institutions.[38] Primarily, however, the training opportunities offered through Michener Centre were attractive to local people whose opportunities for full-time, unionized work were slim.[39] In a recent farewell article written upon his retirement, one former MDN had the following to say:

> When I first came to work in January of 1962 ... I had no idea 41 years later I would still be here when it came time to retire. I needed a job at the time and was told they were hiring at [Michener]. I applied not knowing what I was getting myself into.[40]

This man's story represents the experience of many local people trained at Michener Centre who enjoyed a lifelong career at one of the few places in the region where employment was available, offering a unionized workplace and the opportunity for secure employment.

Mental health workers such as MDNs were not the only occupational groups at Michener Centre. Over and above using inmate labour, the institution required a virtual army of unskilled and skilled outside workers to maintain its operations, from laundry and grounds supervisors to physiotherapists, occupational therapists, and cooks. In 1983, by which time the inmate population had been decreased by over a third (falling from 2,400 to only 1,500 inmates), the institution still employed almost 2,000 people.[41] Considering that the entire population of Red Deer in 1983 was only slightly more than 50,000, this indicates that, even as the institution was winding its operations down, as many as 1 in 25 people living in the Red Deer area were directly employed by the PTS/Michener. Less than a decade ago, with PTS/Michener housing only slightly over 250 people, 1 in 80 Red Deer citizens continued to hold highly coveted, well-paid, and relatively secure jobs at Michener Centre.[42]

In addition to jobs at the institution, the community of Red Deer gained other economic opportunities because of Michener Centre. Community businesses served the institution indirectly through service contracts for food delivery, uniform supply, stationery, office equipment, and furniture; in short, the community provided the institution with a vast array of items that could not be produced within the institution itself. Further, the landlords, realtors, and construction companies who produced housing in Red Deer benefitted from the influx of workers who came to work at the institution, and undoubtedly many shops and services were developed to serve the increased markets that the institutional workforce and the institution itself created.

Finally, workers were needed to build the place. By the time Michener reached its pinnacle in the 1970s, it comprised 66 buildings. These buildings included vocational training centres; workshops; laundry facilities; light manufacturing facilities; a small school; medical examining rooms for inmates; classrooms for MDN students; residences for inmates, staff, and MDN students, and dining facilities for each of these groups; a swimming pool (built in the 1970s for public use, not specifically for residents); a small gymnasium and school (built in the late 1950s in response to parental pressure); a house for the superintendent; industrial kitchens; administrative buildings; several group homes; storage facilities; a power plant; and greenhouses—in short, the workings of a small city were located on the 320-acre campus.[43] This infrastructure came into being as a result of a significant investment of government money into the community. It required construction workers and engineers to build it, and it demanded materials and supplies to support that construction. Inevitably, the construction of Michener Centre, over and above its everyday operations, benefitted the local Red Deer economy tremendously over the years, as goods and workers flowed through the institution's gates.

DISCUSSION

In the late 1960s, a number of events combined to initiate deinstitutionalization at Michener Centre. Most crucially, after considerable citizen complaints and some media exposure of the terrible conditions in the institution, the government sponsored an investigation into mental health services across the province; the resulting Blair Report called for the immediate closure of Michener Centre and a move to communitization.[44] In light of the importance of Michener Centre and its inmates to the local economy, however, it is not surprising that many members of the Red Deer community were—and remain—opposed to these recommendations. In addition to community members, the union representing Michener employees has vehemently opposed communitization. In 1994, the Alberta Union of Public Employees (AUPE) fought successfully to have Michener Centre run by an independent board of directors, rather than by the government that wanted to close it down. The union sought a board composed of residents' family members who would favour keeping Michener Centre open. To gather public support for this institution-friendly board, the union printed some 5,000 brochures, handing them out in shopping malls and other high-traffic areas.[45] The struggle has been ongoing; in 2004, the monthly AUPE bulletin called for its province-wide membership to keep the public aware of the "threats against Red Deer's Michener Centre" and encouraged its membership to call their local politicians to remind them of the "importance of this facility to this community."[46] When the Government of Alberta, under Conservative leadership, promised to close Michener's doors permanently by April 2014, a vigorous and ultimately successful grassroots and union-engaged lobbying effort resulted in a stay of execution.[47] With a pro-union NDP government winning the 2016 election in Alberta, closure seems unlikely.

Thus, the economic dependence of the citizens of Red Deer on the institution continues; while Michener Centre may no longer be providing the city with a standing army of unpaid workers for its farms, homes, and businesses, many of its ex-inmates continue to work in the "vocational training" enterprises that originated in Michener's exploitative work/training matrix. Of the 21 people interviewed for this project, 11 of them had worked at some point in community "social enterprises" such as the trailer manufacturing plant mentioned by Guy Tremblay (who worked there both prior to and following his release from the institution). Further, the institution is still a key employer in the area, and this function remains a linchpin in the argument over whether it should remain open, or, as the Blair Report of almost 50 years ago recommended, close its doors forever.

Regardless of the institution's future, however, we can safely say that without the PTS/Michener Centre and the contributions of its inmates, the city of Red Deer would certainly not have developed as favorably as it has over the last 75 years. It is ironic that eugenicists' worries about "mental defectives" as people who would be dependent on society formed the basis of establishing Michener Centre all those years ago when, in fact, over its many years of operation, the institution and the city that surrounds it have in so many ways depended on Michener's inmates to enrich their economy and their working lives. Thus, although it no longer exploits its residents economically as it once did, it remains a source of employment and economic benefit to the community. Further, its residents continue to be characterized as dependent, despite the ironies of the community's dependence on the institution and its residents for employment opportunities, and as major consumers of goods and services within the city. Finally, the historical arguments about disability and economics persist in debates concerning people with disabilities today. A central argument in current state welfare reform for people with disabilities in Alberta (as evidenced under reforms to Alberta's Assured Income for the Severely Handicapped program) rests on the assertion that such people should be encouraged to get off state support, cease depending on others for their sustenance, and start contributing to the economy.[48]

Such arguments are naive at best, pernicious and dangerous at worst. Almost 25 years ago, Gary Albrecht argued that the disability "service" industry is parasitical—that educated and well-paid social workers, psychologists, psychiatrists, and rehabilitation personnel benefit professionally and personally from keeping people with disabilities in relations of dependence, and that indeed the relationships between people with disabilities and their workers are more accurately characterized as interdependent at best.[49] In the ongoing history of PTS/Michener Centre, it is possible to take Albrecht's argument further and understand that it is not only those who are directly involved in working with disabled people that benefit from characterizing them as dependent burdens on society, but also entire communities such as Red Deer that have benefitted and continue to benefit from inaccurately characterizing disabled people as dependent individuals who require institutional "care" on the one hand, while treating them as exploitable resources on the other.

NOTES

1. Ian Dowbiggin, "Keeping This Young Country Sane: C. K. Clarke, Immigration Restriction, and Canadian Psychiatry, 1890–1925," *Canadian Historical Review* 76, no. 4 (1995): 598–627.
2. Dowbiggin, "Keeping This Young Country Sane"; Angus McLaren, "The Creation of a Haven for 'Human Thoroughbreds': The Sterilization of the Feeble-Minded and the Mentally Ill in British Columbia," *Canadian Historical Review* 67, no. 2 (1986): 127–50; James W. Trent, "To Cut and Control: Institutional Preservation and the Sterilization of Mentally Retarded People in the United States," *Journal of Historical Sociology* 6, no. 1 (1993): 56–73.
3. Trent, "To Cut and Control."
4. More draconian examples of the connection between productivity and the fates of intellectually disabled people arose in Nazi Germany, when discourses of nationalism, dependency, and the demands of a war-focused economy characterized disabled people as useless eaters, resulting in the drastic exploitation and annihilation of tens of thousands of them as a precursor to and prototype for the Holocaust. See Michael Burleigh, *Ethics and Extermination: Reflections on Nazi Genocide* (Cambridge, UK: Cambridge University Press, 1997); Florida Center for Instructional Technology, *Nazi Extermination of People with Mental Disabilities* (University of South Florida, 2005).
5. James W. Trent, *Inventing the Feeble Mind: A History of Mental Retardation in the United States* (Berkeley: University of California Press, 1994); Claudia Malacrida, *A Special Hell: Institutional Life in Alberta's Eugenic Years* (Toronto: University of Toronto Press, 2015).
6. Thomas E. Jordan, *The Degeneracy Crises and Victorian Youth* (Albany: State University of New York, 1993); Nicole Rafter Hahn, *Creating Born Criminals* (Urbana and Chicago: Illinois University Press, 1997); R. C. Scheerenberger, *A History of Mental Retardation* (Baltimore: Brookes Publishing, 1983). Trent, *Inventing the Feeble Mind*.
7. Geoffrey Reaume, "Patients at Work: Insane Asylum Inmates' Labour in Ontario, 1841–1900," in *Mental Health and Canadian Society: Historical Perspectives*, ed. James E. Moran and David Wright (Montreal: McGill-Queen's University Press, 2005).
8. Malacrida, *A Special Hell*.
9. The individuals involved in the study were interned at Michener during the late 1940s through to the 1980s, with ages ranging between 3 and 15 years old at internment, with an average stay of between 10 and 39 years, averaging 14 years. Many were sterilized during their stay in the institution, which may be attributed to their racial or ethnic status. Of the 21 individuals interviewed, 10 were of Mediterranean or Eastern European backgrounds, while 4 were Métis; these groups were targeted as undesirable in eugenic and populist discourse. No participants identified as First Nations; it may be that those children were more likely to be interned in Indian Residential Schools than in Institutions for Mental Defectives. All names of interviewees are pseudonyms. Pseudonyms have been chosen to reflect the ethnic/racialized categories relevant to those individuals. Mary Korshevski, Jim Molochuk, and Roy Petrenko all identified as Ukrainian, and Louise Roy and Guy Tremblay identified as Métis, for example.
10. In 1973 the institution was renamed the Michener Centre in celebration of Red Deer's most famous citizen, Roland Michener, a former athlete who became the governor general of Canada.
11. Government of Alberta, *Michener Centre: A History 1923–1983* (Edmonton: Alberta Government Publications, 1985), 2.
12. McLaren, "The Creation of a Haven for 'Human Thoroughbreds'"; Angus McLaren, *Our Own Master Race: Eugenics in Canada, 1885–1945* (Toronto: McClelland and Stewart, 1990).

13. Government of Alberta, *Michener Centre*; Deborah C. Park and John Radford, "From the Case Files: Reconstructing a History of Involuntary Sterilisation," *Disability & Society* 13, no. 3 (1998).
14. Joanne B. Veit, *Muir v. The Queen in Right of Alberta* (Ottawa: Canadian Legal Information Institute, Federation of Law Societies of Canada, 1996).
15. Malacrida, *A Special Hell*.
16. Jana Marie Grekul, "The Social Construction of the Feebleminded Threat: Implementation of the Sexual Sterilization Act in Alberta, 1929–1972" (PhD diss., University of Alberta, 2002); Jana Grekul, Harvey Krahn, and Dave Odynak, "Sterilizing the 'Feeble-Minded': Eugenics in Alberta, Canada, 1929–1972," *Journal of Historical Sociology* 17, no. 4 (2004); McLaren, "The Creation of a Haven for 'Human Thoroughbreds'" and *Our Own Master Race*; David J. Smith, *Minds Made Feeble: The Myth and Legacy of the Kallikaks* (Rockville, MD: Aspen Publications, 1985).
17. Although it has been suspected that eugenic involuntary sterilizations also targeted First Nations peoples, the evidence is only now coming to light. See Karen Stote, "The Coercive Sterilization of Aboriginal Women in Canada," *American Indian Culture and Research Journal* 36, no. 3 (2012); Karen Stote, *An Act of Genocide: Colonialism and the Sterilization of Aboriginal Women* (Black Point, NS: Fernwood Publishing, 2015); see Erica Dyck, *Facing Eugenics: Reproduction, Sterilization and the Politics of Choice* (Toronto: University of Toronto Press, 2013) and Malacrida, *A Special Hell*.
18. Both institutionalization and eugenic sterilization were also seen as ways to assuage concerns about racial and ethnic "pollution" in Alberta. The population at Michener Centre, which served as one of the main funnels to the Alberta Eugenics Board, was disproportionately populated by new immigrant groups, particularly Eastern Europeans and Mediterranean people (Malacrida, *A Special Hell*). While categories such as "Native" or "Métis" were not recorded at Michener, there is some evidence that First Nations and Métis people were disproportionately sterilized under Alberta's Sexual Sterilization Act (Jana Grekul, "Sterilization in Alberta, 1928–1972: Gender Matters," *Canadian Review of Sociology* 45, no. 4 [2008]; Grekul, Krahn, and Odynak, "Sterilizing the 'Feeble-Minded'"). As noted earlier, these racialized categorizations were disproportionately represented not only in Michener's population, but also in the survivors whom I interviewed.
19. "Moron" was the category used to describe individuals whose IQ scores fell just below the "normal" cut-off range of 70. To many eugenic advocates, this group was the most dangerous group because its members could pass as "normal" and hence could breed with "normal" people. Women identified as morons were perceived as sexually dangerous as they could "drag a good man down" because of their ability to pass and their presumed moral laxity.
20. Veit, *Muir v. The Queen in Right of Alberta*.
21. Malacrida, *A Special Hell*.
22. William McAlister, *Superintendent's 1923 Report to the Government of the Province of Alberta* (Red Deer, AB: Provincial Training School, 1924).
23. Government of Alberta, *Michener Centre*.
24. David George Bettison, John K. Kenward, and Larrie Taylor, *Urban Affairs in Alberta*, vol. 2 (Edmonton: University of Alberta, 1975).
25. McAlister, *Superintendent's 1923 Report*.
26. Henry G. Wilson, *The Annual Report of the Estates Branch: Official Guardian, Administrator of Estates of the Mentally Incompetent Consolidated Investment Fund* (Edmonton: Department of the Attorney General, Government of Alberta, 1940).
27. Louise C. McKinney, *A Return to an Order of the House re: Persons in the Asylums in the Province*. Government of Alberta, 1919.

28. Leonard J. LeVann, *Annual Report, 1957* (Red Deer, AB: Provincial Training School, 1957).
29. Leonard J. LeVann, *Annual Report: Provincial Training School, Red Deer* (Edmonton, AB: Department of Public Health, 1957).
30. Leonard J. LeVann, *Annual Report, Institutions for Mental Defectives* (Red Deer, AB: Provincial Training School and Deer Home, 1962).
31. Wilson, *The Annual Report of the Estates Branch*.
32. Government of Alberta, *Michener Centre*.
33. Anna Bubel, *Starting a Social Enterprise in Alberta*. Social Enterprise Series (Edmonton: Western Economic Diversification Canada, The Business Link, 2008).
34. Carolyn Martindale, "Work a Privilege Afforded to Few," *Red Deer Advocate*, August 15, 1983.
35. Martindale, "Work a Privilege Afforded to Few."
36. Mary's unpaid work as a nanny is bitterly ironic, as she was one of the hundreds of Michener female inmates involuntarily sterilized as "unfit" for motherhood.
37. D. L. McCullough, *Annual Report, 1938: Provincial Training School, Red Deer, Alberta* (edited by the Department of Mental Health, Government of Alberta, 1938).
38. Government of Alberta, *Michener Centre*.
39. Government of Alberta, *Michener Centre*.
40. Neil St. Denys, "Neil St. Denys Says Goodbye!" *Michener Messenger*, April 2003.
41. Government of Alberta, *Michener Centre*.
42. These numbers were found on the Michener Services website (http://www.pdd.org/docs/mich/michener_quickfacts.pdf; page no longer available). As I discuss in detail elsewhere, the Alberta Union of Public Employees, which represents the paid workers at Michener Centre, has been highly active and effective in lobbying successive governments seeking to shut Michener's doors (Malacrida, *A Special Hell*). At this writing, the institution continues to operate, albeit serving fewer than 150 residents.
43. Government of Alberta, *Michener Centre*.
44. W. R. N. Blair, *Mental Health in Alberta: A Report on the Alberta Mental Health Study 1968* (Edmonton: Human Resources Research and Development Executive Council, Government of Alberta, 1969).
45. Pat Roche, "Union Fears Michener Closure," *Red Deer Advocate*, January 8, 1994, B1.
46. Anonymous, "More Than 260 Central Alberta AUPE Members Brave Icy Conditions to Attend Joint AGM" (Alberta Union of Public Employees, 2004), http://www.aupe.org/in_the_news/PR2004/apr1504.php.
47. Julia Parrish, "Provincial Government Halts Closure of Red Deer's Michener Centre," *CTV News GO*, September 19, 2014.
48. Claudia Malacrida, "'The AISH Review is a Big Joke': Contradictions of Policy Participation and Consultation in a Neoliberal Context," *Disability & Society* 24, no. 1 (2009).
49. Gary L. Albrecht, *The Disability Business: Rehabilitation in America*. SAGE Library of Social Research (Thousand Oaks, CA: Sage, 1993).

BIBLIOGRAPHY

Albrecht, Gary L. *The Disability Business: Rehabilitation in America*. SAGE Library of Social Research. Thousand Oaks, CA: Sage, 1993.

Anonymous. "More Than 260 Central Alberta AUPE Members Brave Icy Conditions to Attend Joint AGM." Alberta Union of Public Employees, 2004.

Bettison, David George, John K. Kenward, and Larrie Taylor. *Urban Affairs in Alberta*. Vol. 2. Edmonton: University of Alberta, 1975.

Blair, W. R. N. *Mental Health in Alberta: A Report on the Alberta Mental Health Study 1968*. Edmonton: Human Resources Research and Development Executive Council, Government of Alberta, 1969.

Bubel, Anna. *Starting a Social Enterprise in Alberta*. Social Enterprise Series. Edmonton: Western Economic Diversification Canada, The Business Link, 2008.

Burleigh, Michael. *Ethics and Extermination: Reflections on Nazi Genocide*. Cambridge, UK: Cambridge University Press, 1997.

Dowbiggin, Ian. "Keeping This Young Country Sane: C. K. Clarke, Immigration Restriction, and Canadian Psychiatry, 1890–1925." *Canadian Historical Review* 76, no. 4 (1995): 598–627.

Dyck, Erica. *Facing Eugenics: Reproduction, Sterilization and the Politics of Choice*. Toronto: University of Toronto Press, 2013.

Florida Center for Instructional Technology. "Nazi Extermination of People with Mental Disabilities." University of South Florida, 2005.

Government of Alberta. *Michener Centre: A History 1923–1983*. Edmonton: Alberta Government Publications, 1985.

Grekul, Jana. "Sterilization in Alberta, 1928–1972: Gender Matters." *Canadian Review of Sociology* 45, no. 4 (2008): 247–66.

Grekul, Jana Marie. "The Social Construction of the Feebleminded Threat: Implementation of the Sexual Sterilization Act in Alberta, 1929–1972." PhD diss., University of Alberta, 2002.

Grekul, Jana, Harvey Krahn, and Dave Odynak. "Sterilizing the 'Feeble-Minded': Eugenics in Alberta, Canada, 1929–1972." *Journal of Historical Sociology* 17, no. 4 (2004): 358–84.

Jordan, Thomas E. *The Degeneracy Crises and Victorian Youth*. Albany: State University of New York, 1993.

LeVann, Leonard J. *Annual Report, 1957*. Red Deer, AB: Provincial Training School, 1957.

LeVann, Leonard J. *Annual Report: Provincial Training School, Red Deer*. Edmonton, AB: Department of Public Health, 1957.

LeVann, Leonard J. *Annual Report, Institutions for Mental Defectives*. Red Deer, AB: Provincial Training School and Deer Home, 1962.

Malacrida, Claudia. "'The AISH Review is a Big Joke': Contradictions of Policy Participation and Consultation in a Neoliberal Context." *Disability & Society* 24, no. 1 (2009): 5–18.

Malacrida, Claudia. *A Special Hell: Institutional Life in Alberta's Eugenic Years*. Toronto: University of Toronto Press, 2015.

Martindale, Carolyn. "Work a Privilege Afforded to Few." *Red Deer Advocate*, August 15, 1983.

McAlister, William. *Superintendent's 1923 Report to the Government of the Province of Alberta*. Red Deer, AB: Provincial Training School, 1924.

McCullough, D. L. *Annual Report, 1938: Provincial Training School, Red Deer, Alberta*. Edited by the Department of Mental Health, Government of Alberta, 1938.

McKinney, Louise C. *A Return to an Order of the House re: Persons in the Asylums in the Province*. Government of Alberta, 1919.

McLaren, Angus. "The Creation of a Haven for 'Human Thoroughbreds': The Sterilization of the Feeble-Minded and the Mentally Ill in British Columbia." *Canadian Historical Review* 67, no. 2 (1986): 127–50.

McLaren, Angus. *Our Own Master Race: Eugenics in Canada, 1885–1945*. Toronto: McClelland and Stewart, 1990.

Park, Deborah C., and John Radford. "From the Case Files: Reconstructing a History of Involuntary Sterilisation." *Disability & Society* 13, no. 3 (1998): 317–42.

Parrish, Julia. "Provincial Government Halts Closure of Red Deer's Michener Centre." *CTV News GO*. September 19, 2014.

Rafter Hahn, Nicole. *Creating Born Criminals*. Urbana and Chicago: Illinois University Press, 1997.

Reaume, Geoffrey. "Patients at Work: Insane Asylum Inmates' Labour in Ontario, 1841–1900." In *Mental Health and Canadian Society: Historical Perspectives*, edited by James E. Moran and David Wright, 271–87. Montreal: McGill-Queen's University Press, 2005.

Roche, Pat. "Union Fears Michener Closure." *Red Deer Advocate*, January 8, 1994. B1.

Scheerenberger, R. C. *A History of Mental Retardation*. Baltimore: Brookes Publishing, 1983.

Smith, J. David. *Minds Made Feeble: The Myth and Legacy of the Kallikaks*. Rockville, MD: Aspen Publications, 1985.

St. Denys, Neil. "Neil St. Denys Says Goodbye!" *Michener Messenger* (April 2003): 1–20.

Stote, Karen. "The Coercive Sterilization of Aboriginal Women in Canada." *American Indian Culture and Research Journal* 36, no. 3 (2012): 117–50.

Stote, Karen. *An Act of Genocide: Colonialism and the Sterilization of Aboriginal Women*. Black Point, NS: Fernwood Publishing, 2015.

Trent, James W. "To Cut and Control: Institutional Preservation and the Sterilization of Mentally Retarded People in the United States." *Journal of Historical Sociology* 6, no. 1 (1993): 56–73.

Trent, James W. *Inventing the Feeble Mind: A History of Mental Retardation in the United States*. Berkeley: University of California Press, 1994.

Veit, Joanne B. *Muir v. The Queen in Right of Alberta*. Ottawa: Canadian Legal Information Institute, Federation of Law Societies of Canada, 1996.

Wilson, Henry G. *The Annual Report of the Estates Branch: Official Guardian, Administrator of Estates of the Mentally Incompetent Consolidated Investment Fund*. Edmonton: Department of the Attorney General, Government of Alberta, 1940.

CHAPTER 11

Disability as Social Threat: Examining the Social Justice Implications of Canada's Eugenic History

Phillip B. Turcotte

PREFACE

Originally written in my fourth year of my undergraduate degree in human rights at Carleton University, this chapter (which was at the time but a term paper) attempts to understand how lawyers, politicians, and everyday people in Alberta got to the point where they believed it possible, and, in fact, rightful, to treat disability as a social evil and to seek to remove its existence through sterilization. While my chapter focuses primarily on the role of politicians and lawyers and the power exercised to create, legitimize, and enforce these laws, at the very heart of this work lie echoes of the real lived experiences of those who were subjected to Alberta's sterilization laws. When I first wrote this paper, I had no idea that it would be destined for publication as a chapter. My resources at the time did not allow me to speak directly to survivors and seek their input into my writings. I did my best, with the resources I had at the time, to understand survivors' stories and let that inspire my research and writing.

While we may study Canada's eugenics history from many angles and perspectives—and we must—it should always be remembered that the true experts on what took place in Alberta from 1928 to 1972 are the individuals who were institutionalized and sterilized; those who suffered through atrocities and whose lives were forever changed by pieces of paper, passed in a legislature and put into practice by medical professionals and lawyers, that allowed others to control their bodies and treat them as less than human. Those stories must never be lost and more must be done to bring them to light. It is only through the brave actions of survivors like Ms. Leilani Muir (whom I now consider to be a personal hero of mine) that we know the real human cost of Alberta's sterilization programs. Canada as a whole owes a great debt to all the survivors who spoke out and dared to share their stories.

I encourage you to learn more about survivors like Ms. Muir. Learn from and support projects like the Eugenics Archives (eugenicsarchive.ca) that are working to preserve and promote the stories of survivors and to ensure that we never again repeat these horrific wrongs of a not-so-distant past.

INTRODUCTION

The study of social justice issues within contemporary society is one that is challenging and requires both discipline and critical thought. Nowhere is this more important than within academia, where knowledge is produced, critiqued, and legitimized. While academics and researchers have made important contributions to the study of social justice, it can be said that from time to time these contributions lack an in-depth historical analysis. Without such an insight, studies, and recommendations that stem from them, have tended to provide short-term solutions to social justice issues. While helpful and practical, these short-term solutions result from studies that provide only a portion of a thorough analysis of what are complex situations of social justice.

When it comes to studying moments of social injustice, a more in-depth analysis is necessary in order to truly appreciate and account for the social, political, and historical factors that contributed to the creation of that injustice. This is especially important in situations where individuals, or members of a particular social group, were targeted as part of a law or program that sought to either control or eliminate their existence. Such laws or programs, and the processes of dehumanization, social construction, and regulation that sustain them, deserve some increased scrutiny. Such scrutiny is important, as it is likely to result in an increased awareness about the social circumstances that allowed for the perpetuation of injustice against particular social groups. With this knowledge and perspective in hand, it is possible to construct a rich critical framework from which academics, policy-makers, professionals, and the general public can ensure that injustices created through laws and governmental policies in the past won't continue in the present, and won't emerge in a new form in the future.

With this objective in mind, this chapter examines the popularity of the eugenics movement in Canada, with a particular focus on the use of sterilization laws in Alberta starting in 1928. Canada's history of eugenics is not well known. Indeed, the idea that our society could be made better by sterilizing marginalized groups, such as persons living with disabilities, immigrants, or Indigenous peoples, is something that would shock our modern way of thinking. It runs against our common perception of Canadian history to think that the foundational ideology behind the Nazi extermination programs—eugenics and the concept of creating a "master race"—was popular here in North America long before it was implemented en masse in Nazi Germany. And yet, eugenics did have a strong foothold in Canada and, to various degrees, provinces like Alberta put in place laws that sought to sterilize undesirable groups. That this part of our national history is largely unknown to the average Canadian is not to say, however, that Canada's eugenics projects have gone unstudied. On the contrary, scholars have, for decades now, attempted to account for the circumstances that led everyday citizens, politicians, and social elites alike to embrace a nationwide goal of defending Canadian "stock"[1] against the perceived threat of the continued procreation of persons living with disabilities, immigrant classes, Indigenous peoples, and others labelled as socially undesirable.[2]

It is an unfortunate and incontrovertible truth that Canada played an important role in legitimizing eugenics and sterilization as a viable final solution to the perceived social ills that different groups were thought to bring into their communities. As mentioned above, this history has been thoroughly documented by academics, social service professionals, and social justice activists alike. While this work of uncovering the past and documenting the realities of sterilization is of the utmost importance, such studies have tended to limit themselves to historical analysis, and do not expand their analyses to include how eugenics may still inform both social consciousness and public policy today.

Similarly to scholars studying eugenic history, Disability Studies scholars and others in critical disciplines have located their studies within a particular historical framework that tends to focus on contemporary realities, as is necessary, without considering possible deep historical roots that have led to these realities. Drawing on both the work of scholars and contemporary critical disciplines, the goal of this chapter is to show that Canada's eugenic past can serve as a case study to understand the ways in which disability has historically been constructed to as a threat to social order, and as a biological source for social problems. When disabled bodies and identities are perceived as threats to social order, they become the subject of regulation and control in the form of political and social intervention by governing authorities.

In order to demonstrate this, this chapter will first explore the implementation of eugenic policies in Canada. Second, the medicalization and professionalization of disability as part of Canada's eugenics past will be examined in order to account for the social construction of disability as problematic and worthy of state regulation. Third, various theories of social justice will be used to interpret the lasting impacts of Canada's eugenics period. Fourth, an analysis of Canada's eugenics period will be used to consider how it might be possible to create a counter-narrative to the still-popular view that disability is a source of social ills. Finally, this chapter will conclude by suggesting how a careful study of eugenics, combined with critical disability theories, might inform current debates about disability-related social issues.

WITNESSING CONTROL THROUGH LEGISLATION: UNCOVERING THE HISTORY OF CANADA'S EUGENIC STERILIZATION LAWS

The history of eugenics in Canada stretches over more than a hundred years. Early accounts show that the eugenics discussion gained popularity in Canada around the late 1800s. While it would be impossible to do justice to the movement's entire history within the confines of this chapter, what will be examined is the general ideology that underpinned most of the various eugenics theories that permeated social, political, and medical discourse from the late 1800s to the late 1970s. This particular time frame saw a specific correlation of social fears, political and social ambitions, and the emergence of hereditary science, which would together ultimately result in the successful implementation of sterilization legislation in British Columbia and Alberta, as well as mass campaigns to pass similar legislation in other provinces.

Canada's societal interest in eugenics began with its birth as a colony of the British and French empires. French and British colonial settlers came to the "New World" with a preconceived notion about the humanity of Indigenous peoples who inhabited the land. With this mentality came concerns about the preservation of a European way of life, and, in particular, a need to safeguard against Indigenous infiltration into European culture through a mixing of the "races." Settlers also arrived with a patronizing mission of "civilizing"[3] Indigenous societies, through which the control and "education" of Indigenous communities became a matter of public policy.

In fact, this assimilatory approach to Indigenous peoples migrated into eugenic thinking and sterilization policies. Arbitrary determinations of Indigenous intelligence and social worth led to Indigenous persons being labelled "feeble-minded." Being categorized as "feeble-minded," Indigenous peoples were then subject to sterilization, which was made possible through the passing of sterilization laws. Records have shown that of those who were sterilized, in Alberta in particular, Indigenous peoples were disproportionately represented with respect to the rest of the population. While this chapter does focus primarily on persons living with disabilities, it must be acknowledged that Indigenous peoples were deeply impacted and targeted by sterilization laws. It is hoped that the recommendations and arguments made in this chapter could be modified and used to further the cause of Indigenous rights in Canada.

The settler approach to Indigenous peoples demonstrates that Canada's various pre-Confederation colonies already held within them a practice of dealing with cultural and racial difference through public policy aimed at the coercive assimilation and removal of any form of difference that may be constructed as problematic to the ruling classes.[4] The same kind of nationalistic racial purity arguments emerged around the 1850s following the implementation of mass immigration programs aimed at populating Canada's vast territory, and especially the West. Urban centres such as Toronto saw their immigrant population double, and even triple, in decades.[5] Social fears began to emerge that these immigrants would start to diminish the largely white, Eastern European middle and upper classes. The middle and upper classes began to fear that they would no longer be the dominant social group.

At this point in time, no singular identity characteristic seemed to unite more Canadians in endorsing eugenic ideologies than that of racial solidarity. This social fear in its early stages manifested itself through the establishment and enforcement of strict immigration policies aimed at reducing the number of immigrants arriving into Canada. At this time, the social concern over the procreation of those who were seen to be socially "unfit" was at a particular high in Canadian society. A massive influx of immigrants came to North America from Europe in the early 1900s, creating a climate of national identity crisis. Those who viewed themselves as non-immigrants increasingly felt threatened by the arrival of a diversity of peoples from overseas.[6] What is perhaps the most effective in shaping this narrative of fear towards newcomers is the social perception of them, and how their outward physical appearances were used to construct them as being of a lower class, or a lower human status, than those who already lived in North America.

As a result of the dire conditions that immigrants left behind in their home countries, as well as the challenges of the journey to North America, they arrived on Canadian shores very malnourished, often sick, and dirty. This first impression made by immigrants provided the basis from which their prescribed identities would be formulated. Combined with their outward appearance, the fact that most immigrants spoke neither English nor French contributed to the anti-immigrant sentiment by allowing their opponents to believe that arriving immigrants were somehow mentally incompetent. These perceptions furthered the arguments from those who began to see immigrants as a social problem. Along with this developing social unease came the rise of eugenics, whose proponents argued that social "delinquency," "feeble-mindedness," and vagrancy were largely, if not completely, determined by biology and genetics.[7]

Concepts of social Darwinism, IQ testing, and biology were thus appropriated to help identify those who were biologically "unfit" to live within society and procreate. The agrarian lifestyle of most of Alberta's population also contributed to the evolution and popularity of eugenics ideologies. Farmers had used selective breeding techniques for generations to produce the best livestock. It was thus believed that the same process could be utilized to protect social "stock."[8] Because of this and other factors that will be explored later in this chapter, the concept of sterilization of the socially "unfit" gained an increasing amount of social popularity, and thus the Sexual Sterilization Act was created and passed to provide a means by which provincial resources could be utilized to both institutionalize and sterilize those determined to be "unfit" and a danger to the Albertan social "stock."

It should be noted that even in these early stages, persons with disabilities were singled out in particular and prevented from immigrating to Canada. However, these restrictions were mostly limited to cases of "visible" disabilities or impairments; the expansion of the concept of "feeble-mindedness" would emerge later on.[9] Anti-immigrant sentiment steadily grew, and was increasingly supported by politicians and the political elite. Social fears and calls for assimilation, which had begun with Indigenous populations, were now expanding to include immigrants from the Orient as well as Western Europe.[10]

With the constant increases in population came an escalation in poverty, crime, and behaviours believed to be socially "devious," such as prostitution and vagrancy. When it became clear that immigration policies were failing to contain the perceived immigrant threat, public pressure began to increase, with the worried masses looking for additional solutions. It is at this time that scientific notions of Darwinism emerge.[11] Scientific instruments such as Binet's IQ test were appropriated by Darwinist scientists and were utilized to measure social worth. This new scientific field found a niche in being able to attribute biological determinants to what was considered to be socially devious and undesirable behaviour. Vagrancy, poverty, sexual promiscuity, Indigeneity, and physical and psychological disabilities could now be explained away as consequences of inferior biological traits.

By virtue of this, all social ills began to be explained away as the result of inferior races that were bringing their inferior gene pools to Canada from overseas.[12] While a substantial scientific infrastructure emerged to broaden the establishment of eugenics and hereditarianism-based knowledge, this new explanation for social issues provided an overly simplistic interpretation of what were far more complex social issues. As will be discussed in a later section, what largely accounts for the propagation of hereditarian thinking is the lack of an effective counter-narrative. The targeted social groups were without effective agency, and were increasingly constructed as subhuman and thus not worthy of consultation or substantial representation. This discourse only further emboldened nationalistic, race-based sentiments. The survival of the "Canadian" race became an issue of patriotic duty.[13] If socially undesirable behaviours could be explained away by biological determinism, then eugenic logic demanded that these groups, and their "problematic" genes, had to be eliminated from the social gene pool.[14]

Under this racial banner emerged broad social campaigns for positive eugenics. Positive eugenics included proactive measures taken by individual citizens when it came to promoting proper racial and social "hygiene." Individuals from desirable social classes were encouraged to marry and procreate with each other in order to continue a racially "pure" line. Marriage protocols and laws were created and amended to prevent cross-racial pairings. Positive eugenics consisted mostly of mass public awareness campaigns to promote the ideals of racial purity and highlight the threat posed by those designated socially undesirable.[15] These campaigns were also expanded to encourage those "inferior" populations not to procreate, and to understand that while their inferiority was no fault of their own, it was nonetheless their responsibility to ensure that they did not pass on their "faults" to the next generation.[16] Positive eugenics remained popular throughout Canada well into the late 1900s, and it is worth noting that for many provinces, such as Ontario, eugenics projects went no further. This is partially due to strong Catholic beliefs within the population, especially in Quebec, which would not tolerate any form of coercive sterilization.[17]

British Columbia and Alberta embraced negative eugenics through the implementation of sterilization acts and other social control measures. Negative eugenics involves active intervention, through sterilization and other measures, to prevent the birth and reproduction of a particular social group. While British Columbia did sterilize persons believed to be racially inferior, historical records have shown that the province never resorted to coercive sterilization. In other words, sterilizations in British Columbia were never carried out without some form of consent by the person being sterilized, or someone authorized to make decisions on their behalf.[18] That being said, the fact that persons willingly subjected themselves to sterilization shows just how strong eugenic sentiment was, and how much pressure it put on those who were believed to be "undesirable" to sterilize themselves for the "betterment" of Canada.

In contrast to the rest of Canada, Alberta's sterilization project implemented forced sterilizations without consent, and did so quite vehemently. It is for this reason that Alberta's eugenic laws will be the particular focus of this chapter. Alberta's Sexual

Sterilization Act[19] is widely held as one of the most successful forced sterilization programs outside of those implemented by Nazi Germany.[20] What began the popularity of sterilization in Alberta was the convergence of anti-immigrant fears with hereditary science. The largely agrarian lifestyle of the population played an important role in this. Selective breeding had long been used to produce the most profitable and fit farm animals. At this time, various scientific and medical professionals began to argue that there existed a link between social "deviance" and biology. Given this, prominent Albertans began to believe that the practice of selectively breeding farm animals could be adapted to control the reproduction of human beings.[21]

Slowly, social discourse around eugenics began to shift from that of racial hygiene to the protection of "social stock," borrowing from the language of farming and animal breeding.[22] The Sexual Sterilization Act received royal assent on March 21, 1928, under the United Farmers of Alberta government. The United Farmers of Alberta (UFA), both the advocacy group, and then the political party, had long been part of the eugenics movement and had been a particular proponent of the idea that livestock breeding practices could be applied to human beings to prevent the procreation of the socially undesirable.[23] Alberta's scientific infrastructure at the time was not well established. This allowed for pro-eugenics individuals within influential scientific circles to lobby the UFA to adopt eugenics as a valid legislative matter.

Various scientific tests began to be administered to immigrants and individuals with physical or mental disabilities to determine their level of "feeble-mindedness." Through this emerging science, any form of socially undesirable characteristics began to be attributed mostly to "feeble-mindedness." With that, disability became understood as a source of "evil."[24] Everyday Canadians began to fear disability and persons living with disabilities. The social fear became so strong that persons living with physical disabilities and those determined through testing to be of "feeble" mind were soon interned in various institutions such as provincial training schools,[25] where they were kept out of sight, and, most importantly, prevented from reproducing.

Initially, sterilizations were performed only if a "resident" of an institution wished to be paroled or released. Their sterilization, which was a condition of their release, was seen as the final measure towards nullifying the social threat they presented.[26] This pre-release sterilization program soon proved to be unsatisfactory, as it was felt that "feeble-minded" persons were still too large a portion of society. In order to decrease their presence in future generations, the Sexual Sterilization Act was amended twice with the purpose of removing the consent requirement for sterilization, as well as to expand the categories of persons who could be sterilized.[27] Most importantly, the consent requirement was only ever removed for the "feeble-minded," who were most often persons with either physical, psychological, or intellectual disabilities. Alberta's sterilization program was halted in 1972, when its statute was repealed due to a loss of popularity for negative eugenics, and an increasing concern for human rights.[28]

THE MEDICALIZATION AND PROFESSIONALIZATION OF DISABILITY: LEGITIMIZING THE CONSTRUCT OF DISABILITY AS A SOCIAL THREAT

Having explored, in broad terms, Canada's eugenics history, further analysis is required to properly understand the way in which the medicalization and professionalization of disability was crucial to the idea that disability and "feeble-mindedness" were "evil," and thus worthy of extermination through selective breeding and forced or voluntary sterilization. Many of those who have studied eugenics in Canada, and in Alberta in particular, have intentionally moved away from understanding eugenics and sterilization as a practice akin to genocide and extermination. Many have pointed out, and quite fairly so, that while eugenics and sterilization represented the first part of Hitler's "final solution" and the Holocaust, that does not mean that other eugenic practices were similarly genocidal in intent.

It must be acknowledged that most eugenicists, and, in fact, the broad portion of Canada's population that supported positive eugenics, would not have supported negative eugenics, especially coerced sterilizations. A lack of intent is also stated as a defence against attempts to link eugenic programs to genocide. Researchers have claimed that "these cases have historically and recently been linked genocide, but although racist, were not genocidal, for one sees not an intention to eliminate the group as such but to 'improve it.'"[29] It will be the goal of this particular portion of this chapter to disagree with this statement. What is argued here, rather, is that this particular construction of disability as "evil" and the sterilization programs that sought to prevent the recurrence of disability were an attempt to exterminate a particular social group from the Canadian population. While academics are reluctant to suggest that sterilization could constitute a form of genocide, what is not refuted is the fact that what eugenics and genocides such as the Holocaust do have in common is "state intervention at the level of the population."[30]

The claim that eugenics was not genocidal because it sought only to "improve" a race is patently false. What the quoted statement above ignores is the fact that the "improvement" sought through sterilization applied only to a very specific portion of the population. As will be demonstrated below, sterilization procedures were not intended to "improve" persons living with disabilities; on the contrary, the procedures were quite clearly intended to prevent their future existence. Therefore, while those who endorsed forced sterilization did so with the belief that they would be improving the "Canadian stock," they did so at the expense of persons living with disabilities, who were actively constructed as needing extermination. The reluctance of academics and researchers to problematize the portrayal of disability as "evil" or in need of "correction" points to the fact that eugenic ideals still linger today. As critical as analyses of eugenics have been, they have left this assumption about disability largely intact. While the morality, ethics, and legality of eugenics have been questioned, its underlying assumption that promotes able-bodiedness, or not living with a disability, as natural and desirable has gone without criticism or analysis.

In this way, eugenics ideologies have persisted into the present, and continue to inform a commonly held belief that able-bodiedness is only natural, and that disability cannot be desired, or be a source of pride or of human diversity, and as natural as able-bodiedness.

Such an embedded and resilient construction of disability required a substantive intellectual and medical infrastructure to legitimize and sustain it throughout the eugenics period. This is especially key in Alberta, as this infrastructure bears the brunt of responsibility for the implementation of negative eugenics and coercive sterilization.[31] The most prominent advocates of eugenics came from the professional classes. They were medical doctors, psychologists, social workers, health care workers, and academics. Together they formed influential bodies such as the Canadian National Committee for Mental Hygiene (CNCMH), the Bureau of Social Research, and the Eugenics Society of Canada. The CNCMH is almost single-handedly responsible for publishing the studies that justified sterilization as the only feasible option to properly control the "undesirable" population.[32] Along with this, prominent social and political figures like Emily Murphy and Dr. MacEachran, a future Eugenics Board of Alberta chairman, used their social clout to legitimize eugenics and sterilization in particular. The United Farm Women of Alberta (UFWA) was an extremely influential group that had ties to the UFA; it led the charge to put social pressure on the government to pass the Sexual Sterilization Act.

In particular, the UFWA championed the idea that it was the patriotic duty of the "mothers of the nation" to advocate for the prevention of the procreation of mental defectives and other social undesirables in order to protect Canadian social stock.[33] The central idea underlying all of this was that the state was already suffering the "burden" of caring for those groups identified under the act, and that it was therefore within the province's obligation to go a step further by preventing their existence through sterilization, thus mitigating the social and economic "impacts" of the socially undesirable. The Eugenics Society of Canada tried unsuccessfully to raise enough political pressure to institute sterilization policies in other provinces, most notably Ontario.

While those attempts failed, the society did provide the central intellectual community for eugenic and sterilization proponents across Canada. The most prominent of its members published leaflets and held public talks on the dangers posed by the "feebleminded" and the solution eugenics provided. Those who studied hereditarianism and social Darwinism met with well-intentioned psychologists and social workers who sought new methods of "treatment" for the physically and intellectually disabled persons under their care.[34] The society's influence and success within the general population can be attributed to the broad social acceptance of the idea of positive eugenics and racial hygiene across Canada. Through these powerful lobby organizations, the discourse on disability as a social problem emerged.

The demonization of these professionals is not intended. Most did support eugenics through a misguided but well-intentioned belief that sterilization would provide a better alternative for some patients than a lifetime of institutionalization. As was mentioned above, sterilization offered a means by which patients could be "safely" reintegrated or "released" within society. It was also believed at the time that the experience of procreation or giving birth could psychologically and physically harm some patients. It must also be remembered that early sterilization required the consent of either the patient or their legal guardian. Where the medicalization and professionalization of disability becomes especially destructive and violent is the point at which consent was no longer required, and was seen rather as an impediment to progress. Here the patronizing notion that medical and social professionals knew better what was best for disabled persons than the individuals themselves turns away from the intent of care, and becomes a vessel through which the goal of extermination of disability from society could be achieved.

This shift in ideology is demonstrated by the creation of the Eugenics Board under Alberta's Sexual Sterilization Act; it was granted sole authority to determine whether or not a patient should be sterilized.[35] The board consisted of influential medical professionals and social elites who had ties to both the scientific and academic communities. Only 21 persons were appointed to the board in the 43 years of its operation;[36] most members held their positions for decades and had a vested interest in the promotion and evolution of eugenics and sterilization.[37] Without oversight, the board could, and did, exceed its authority and authorize sterilizations that could not be justified under the act.[38] The lack of checks and balances also allowed the board to decide how it would interpret the results of tests such as IQ tests in order to justify sterilization.

In all, an estimated 2,834 people were sterilized by order of the board.[39] The board recommended sterilization in 99 percent of the cases it oversaw, and spent an average of 13 minutes deliberating each case for sterilization before approving the procedure.[40] It is important to note that 89 percent of patients for whom consent was not required were eventually sterilized, versus 15 percent for those patients for whom consent was necessary. Of those for whom consent was not required, and who were determined to be "mentally defective" or were thought to have an intellectual disability, 77 percent were Indigenous.[41] The board reported to the minister of health only as a formality, and its reports were never made public.[42] It is only through eventual successful litigation brought forth by those sterilized that the board's activities were revealed to the public.[43]

Board members, through their authority, propagated a particular view of disability, and were instrumental in the application of sterilization procedures that were being used with the intention of exterminating disability.[44] Furthermore, many board members were active proponents of eugenics and lobbied the public for its support. Records also show that board members overstepped their authority and ordered sterilizations illegally, based on arbitrary determination of a patient's social worth. For example, as many as 15 men with Down's syndrome, who were sterile from birth, were forced to undergo a sterilization procedure by order of the board. Given that these men were sterile from birth, there were no apparent medical grounds to support their sterilization; nevertheless, they were sterilized. Historical documents reveal that the sterilization procedures carried out on these men were used as an excuse so their testicles could be harvested to further the research goals of one of the board members.[45]

For persons living with disabilities who were institutionalized, their fate, their humanity, was determined without their input, and they were provided no recourse to appeal the board's decisions. They were made to believe that they alone were the embodiment of social ills and thus that they were responsible for the propagation of social problems. Such a fundamental restructuring of disabled identities was only made possible by the willingness of the medical, professional, and academic establishments of the day to legitimize coercive sterilization. Canada's eugenic history cannot be explained away as simply a misguided attempt by a select few to "improve" the general population. On the contrary, the vast popularity of eugenics, and the political and social lobbying that made the adoption of Alberta's sterilization laws possible, are evidence of the fact that the dehumanization and attempted extermination of those who were constructed as a social threat by virtue of their living with disabilities became a part of Canadian social values. While contemporary society may not view disability so extremely today, much of our contemporary malaise with disability, and the dominant thought of disability as unfortunate, pitiable, and undesirable draws its roots from the days of eugenics.

What made eugenics and sterilization so successful in Canada in particular is the long-standing system of British governance that the provinces, with the exception of Quebec, inherited and adopted. The British Empire's focus on social welfare strongly influenced the level with which the issue of disability and other socially undesirable behaviours were institutionalized and seen as issues worthy of government intervention.[46] At the heart of this was the Elizabethan Poor Law of 1601, which provided for the "public responsibility for the relief of the dependent poor, financed and administered by the smallest unit of government."[47]

The Poor Law thus established a long history of governmental responsibility for the regulation of persons deemed to be a drain on the state and on society. When eugenicists first argued for the sterilization of persons living with disabilities and other individuals they believed to be "feeble-minded," it was already socially acceptable, thanks to the influence of the Poor Law, that the government would be responsible for the administration of these programs. Likewise, government authority over persons living with disabilities was already firmly established through this same history of government responsibility for social problems. It also stands to reason that the concept of deserving and undeserving poor played an important role in the initial arguments for sterilization. These distinctions of deservingness were by that point in time firmly established within the social imaginary. Much of the anti-immigrant rhetoric centred around socially undesirable behaviours such as vagrancy, criminality, begging, and poverty, which had all been targets of the Poor Laws.[48]

The regulation of undesirable behaviour through law strengthened the calls for tighter immigration policies to prevent the arrival of "undesirables" in Canada.[49] The Poor Laws certainly legitimized the patronizing approach that underlined the medicalization and professionalization of disability. Persons with disabilities were by default a governmental responsibility, and thus it would be up to governments, and the intellectuals and experts who advised them, to determine how best to deal with this particular "problem." That persons with disabilities could have been consulted or allowed to advocate for themselves would have run contrary to the dominant view of them as being rightfully dependent on the goodwill of the state. This patronizing approach was also in keeping with principles of retributive justice,[50] which called for the regulation of social problems and punishment for those who were seen as creating them.[51] In the case of eugenics, sterilization was indeed seen as a punishment for the wrongs that persons with disabilities were believed to be causing within society.

The growth of the welfare state in Canada, another British-inspired inheritance, only fuelled the sterilization rhetoric. Since the faith of those who were disabled was so firmly determined in terms of poverty and institutionalization, their continued existence was increasingly seen as a burdensome drain on public finances. Eugenic proponents used this public burden argument to justify the transition from institutionalization to sterilization.[52] Once the cause of disability and its perceived social ills could be attributed to hereditarianism and biology, then the logic of an early welfare state dictated that it would be more cost-efficient, and less burdensome to the public, to sterilize disabled individuals in order to prevent the future occurrence of disability, and thus the possibility of a continued drain on the state.

At this time it was widely believed, because of a scientific focus on genetics, that disability—and all its perceived negative traits—was something that one could inherit genetically. For proponents of eugenics who believed this, it was only "humane" to absolve persons living with disabilities of the "evil" within them, which was no fault of their own. It was seen as desirable to prevent the future occurrence of a disabled existence that had already been determined to hold none of the features of a life that was cherished and held to high esteem within society. In light of this, the welfare state as it existed at the time of eugenics only served to legitimize the cause for sterilization by providing an additional economic and patronizing justification for the elimination of disability.

The final contribution of the inherited British model is held within the division of powers between the provinces and the federal government. Section 92 of the Constitution Act[53] clearly establishes that provinces have jurisdiction over matters such as health care and institutions such as asylums and provincial training schools where persons living with disabilities were often institutionalized. This provincial responsibility helps explain the variance of eugenics policies across provinces. It also helps to explain why particular societal and political climates, like those of Alberta, had such a dramatic impact on the extent to which sterilization was implemented in a particular province. The lobbying of provincial governments by eugenic proponents such as the Eugenics Society of Canada and the CNCMH only served to further entrench the provincial jurisdictions over health care, and the adjoining responsibilities for resolving the "problems" posed by persons living with disabilities and the "feeble-minded." Most significantly, this division of power is responsible for the lack of a national sterilization policy, as such a project would not have been within the authority of the federal government.[54] That being said, the lack of federal authority in health care also slowed the emergence of a national counter-narrative to eugenics and the political and social movements that advocated for sterilization. The emergence of a national discourse on human rights is mainly what prompted the repeal of Alberta's Sexual Sterilization Act in 1972.

SOCIAL JUSTICE: EXPLORING THE IMPACTS OF EUGENICS AND STERILIZATION

If social justice is to be about addressing problems of inequality, then the Sexual Sterilization Act and the scientific and ideological premises that support the eugenic philosophy at its base are flawed in that they completely ignore the social factors that led to many of the despairing situations in which immigrants and disabled persons found themselves. Determinations of blame for social problems completely ignored the privileges and power imbalances that underlined society. Evidence has shown that, in fact, the act allowed for an abuse of power, and for certain highly placed members within society to profit from its implementation to the detriment of those under their care. The complete secrecy under which the Eugenics Board operated also suggests that even though the general population supported eugenics at the time, the truth about the extent of the program had to be hidden lest it be subjected to substantive criticism, as it indeed was when its operations were made public.

It is arguable then that from a social justice perspective, the Sexual Sterilization Act was malevolent. This is made evident by the litigation cases brought forth by those who had been sterilized and who felt deeply wronged in the process. The level of harm that the sterilization program caused to those who were subjected to it is a clear demonstration of the malevolency of the act. The fact that human rights instruments like the Canadian Charter of Rights and Freedoms[55] have put in place provisions that would, or at least should, prevent such programs from occurring again is also indicative of the fact that the act, by all reasonable standards, constituted a perversion of ideals of social justice, regardless of the intent of those who implemented and supported it. The Sexual Sterilization Act would seem to be a violation of the principle of human dignity itself.

Persons liable to sterilization under the Sexual Sterilization Act had virtually no means to access basic liberties, and they were certainly not comparable to those enjoyed by the able-bodied, white majority. Rather, it would seem reasonable to suggest that the rights of the majority were dependent, according to eugenics discourse, on the denial of rights to persons with disabilities. In this case, high offices of political or professional importance when it came to eugenics were reserved for only a select few, most of whom existed within self-appointing bodies. Targets of sterilization would certainly not have had access to those same positions.

As was demonstrated earlier, the whole premise of social good that underlined eugenic thinking, even amongst its most well-intentioned proponents, was so heavily biased against persons with disabilities that it could not be argued that even voluntary sterilization initiated at the request of a patient could be considered a benefit, regardless of how well such a suggestion could be defended. After all, what could be worse than being the target of extermination? Finally, redistributive justice was non-existent. The redistribution of the goods within society was not achieved for persons with disabilities at that time. Conceptualizations of the natural argued the opposite and encouraged the distribution of goods away from the most disadvantaged. Persons with disabilities were considered to be a drain on the system, an obstruction to the proper functioning of the welfare state, and thus underserving of redistribution.

CONCLUSION: OPENING THE SPACE FOR THE BROADENING CONTEMPORARY ANALYSES

If anything, the history of eugenics and sterilization in Canada demonstrates that any analysis of contemporary social issues and injustices must include a thorough historical examination of the problem's origins and the ways in which past events may still be influencing current discourses and policies. What the study of the sterilization of persons with disabilities contributes to contemporary disability rights questions is the origins of the medicalization, professionalization, and regulation of disability, as well as the conceptualization of disability as a social threat that requires intervention and regulation.

Drawing upon British Poor Laws, the links between disability and our contemporary understandings of social assistance and benefits, for example, can be explained through the long-established concept of the deserving and undeserving poor. The prevalence of eugenic ideologies combined with the existing patronizing approach to disability can help explain how easily identity can be constructed and how persons can be made to unjustly embody the blame for social problems. The study of eugenics, especially by organizations such as the CNCMH, the Eugenics Society of Canada, and the Alberta Eugenics Board, helps explain the ways in which disability discourses have been constantly dominated by medical and academic professionals, often without providing a space within which persons living with disabilities can self-advocate and enjoy self-determination. Perhaps the most important lesson to be learned from Canada's eugenic past is that the dehumanization and othering of individuals or social groups is not something that occurs as a fluke, or as a simple deviation from some nobler path. Occurrences of systematic oppression and social injustices cannot be explained away by simplistic rationalizations; rather, they demand a thorough analysis of the political and social circumstances that created them, and the social power relations that sustained those circumstances.

The field of Critical Disability Studies has begun the important work of critiquing contemporary conceptions of disabilities. By combining contemporary analyses with historical research, the field can only improve and provide a more compelling framework from which to question the underlying privilege of able-bodiedness that is still prevalent today. This seems particularly important given the re-emergence of eugenic ideologies within discussions of genetic testing and emerging reproductive technologies. This popular field risks evolving further without benefitting from the lessons of its eugenic past, and with the problematic assumptions it still holds with regards to the worth of individuals with disabilities. An example of this would be the inherited assumption that the majority of the challenges associated with living a life with disabilities is the result of the inherent nature of disability itself, and not the result of inaccessible and ableist social and built environments.

Finally, the participation of academics and universities in the dehumanization of persons living with disabilities, and the implementation of sterilization, should provide cause for concern. For far too long the academic community has been a vessel from which to perpetuate problematic understandings of diversity and disability, as made evident by some of the academic discourses presented in this chapter. Academia has inherited a problematic position of patronizing expertise and privilege. This academic freedom would be better utilized if exercised from a position of accountability and allyship, working together with various social groups to bring about positive and challenging discourses with the ultimate goal of redistributing the good within society and providing the greatest benefit to the least advantaged.

NOTES

1. Dirk Moses and Dan Stone, "Eugenics and Genocide," in *The Oxford Handbook of the History of Eugenics*, ed. Alison Bashford and Philippa Levine (New York: Oxford University Press, 2010).
2. Carolyn Strange and Jennifer Stephen, "Eugenics in Canada: A Checkered History, 1850s–1990s," in *The Oxford Handbook of the History of Eugenics*, ed. Alison Bashford and Philippa Levine (New York: Oxford University Press, 2010), 524.
3. Strange and Stephen, "Eugenics in Canada," 528.
4. Angus McLaren, *Our Own Master Race: Eugenics in Canada 1885–1945* (Toronto: Oxford University Press, 1990), 169.
5. Ian Robert Dowbiggin, *Keeping America Sane: Psychiatry and Eugenics in the United States and Canada, 1880–1940* (Ithaca, NY: Cornell University Press, 1997), 135.
6. National Film Board of Canada, *The Sterilization of Leilani Muir*, VHS (Montreal: National Film Board of Canada, 1996).
7. National Film Board of Canada, *The Sterilization of Leilani Muir*.
8. Jana Grekul, Arvey Krahn, and Dave Odynak, "Sterilizing the 'Feeble-Minded': Eugenics in Alberta, Canada, 1929–1972," *Journal of Historical Sociology* 17, no. 4 (2004).
9. Grekul, Krahn, and Odynak, "Sterilizing the 'Feeble-Minded,'" 143.
10. Dowbiggin, *Keeping America Sane*, 145.
11. National Film Board of Canada, *The Sterilization of Leilani Muir*.
12. National Film Board of Canada, *The Sterilization of Leilani Muir*.
13. Véronique Mottier, "Eugenics and the State: Policy Making in Comparative Perspective," in *The Oxford Handbook of the History of Eugenics*, ed. Alison Bashford and Philippa Levine (New York: Oxford University Press, 2010), 134.
14. Grekul, Krahn, and Odynak, "Sterilizing the 'Feeble-Minded,'" 362.
15. Grekul, Krahn, and Odynak, "Sterilizing the 'Feeble-Minded,'" 360.
16. McLaren, *Our Own Master Race*, 115–16.
17. Strange and Stephen, "Eugenics in Canada," 526.
18. Strange and Stephen, "Eugenics in Canada," 532.

194　Section III　Into the Mid-twentieth Century

19. The Sexual Sterilization Act, R.S.A. 1970, c. 341.
20. Grekul, Krahn, and Odynak, "Sterilizing the 'Feeble-Minded,'" 358–59; Strange and Stephen, "Eugenics in Canada," 530; National Film Board of Canada, *The Sterilization of Leilani Muir*.
21. Grekul, Krahn, and Odynak, "Sterilizing the 'Feeble-Minded,'" 361.
22. Moses and Stone, "Eugenics and Genocide," 199; Grekul, Krahn, and Odynak, "Sterilizing the 'Feeble-Minded,'" 361
23. Grekul, Krahn, and Odynak, "Sterilizing the 'Feeble-Minded,'" 362.
24. Strange and Stephen, "Eugenics in Canada," 532; McLaren, *Our Own Master Race*, 112.
25. National Film Board of Canada, *The Sterilization of Leilani Muir*.
26. Strange and Stephen, "Eugenics in Canada," 532; National Film Board of Canada, *The Sterilization of Leilani Muir*.
27. The Sexual Sterilization Act Amendment Act, 1937, S.A. 1937, c. 47 s. 5; The Sexual Sterilization Act Amendment Act, 1942, S.A. 1942, c. 48; Grekul, Krahn, and Odynak, "Sterilizing the 'Feeble-Minded,'" 361.
28. The Sexual Sterilization Repeal Act, 1972, S.A. 1972, c. 87.
29. Strange and Stephen, "Eugenics in Canada," 531–32; McLaren, *Our Own Master Race*, 107–15, 165.
30. Moses and Stone, "Eugenics and Genocide," 203.
31. Moses and Stone, "Eugenics and Genocide," 203.
32. McLaren, *Our Own Master Race*, 169; Strange and Stephen, "Eugenics in Canada," 534.
33. McLaren, *Our Own Master Race*, 109–10; Strange and Stephen, "Eugenics in Canada," 531; Grekul, Krahn, and Odynak, "Sterilizing the 'Feeble-Minded,'" 362.
34. Douglas Wahlsten, "Leilani Muir Versus the Philosopher King: Eugenics on Trial in Alberta," *Genetica* 99, no. 2–3 (1997): 191–92.
35. Dowbiggin, *Keeping America Sane*, x–xi.
36. Dowbiggin, *Keeping America Sane*, 189; Strange and Stephen, "Eugenics in Canada," 532; National Film Board of Canada, *The Sterilization of Leilani Muir*.
37. Grekul, Krahn, and Odynak, "Sterilizing the 'Feeble-Minded,'" 363.
38. Grekul, Krahn, and Odynak, "Sterilizing the 'Feeble-Minded,'" 363.
39. Wahlsten, "Leilani Muir Versus the Philosopher King," 190.
40. Moses and Stone, "Eugenics and Genocide," 203.
41. Grekul, Krahn, and Odynak, "Sterilizing the 'Feeble-Minded,'" 376.
42. Grekul, Krahn, and Odynak, "Sterilizing the 'Feeble-Minded,'" 366–76.
43. Grekul, Krahn, and Odynak, "Sterilizing the 'Feeble-Minded,'" 363.
44. National Film Board of Canada, *The Sterilization of Leilani Muir*.
45. Strange and Stephen, "Eugenics in Canada," 532.
46. Wahlsten, "Leilani Muir Versus the Philosopher King," 189; National Film Board of Canada, *The Sterilization of Leilani Muir*; Dowbiggin, *Keeping America Sane*, 133–39.
47. Karl De Schweinitz, "The Law of Settlement," in *England's Road to Social Security, from the Statute of Labourers in 1349 to the Beveridge Report of 1942* (New York: A. S. Barnes & Co., 1943), 57.
48. D. Guest, "The Colonial Inheritance," in *The Emergence of Social Security in Canada* (Vancouver: UBC Press, 1980), 9.
49. De Schweinitz, "The Law of Settlement," 57.
50. Dowbiggin, *Keeping America Sane*, 142–43, 154–55.
51. Dowbiggin, *Keeping America Sane*, 7; Andrew Webster, "SOWK 4703 Lecture Notes," Presentations 1, 2, and 7, Carleton University, Ottawa, May 2012.
52. Andrew Webster, Presentation 11 to SOWK/LAWS/SOCI 4703—Social Justice and the Residual Welfare State (Carleton University, Ottawa, June 13, 2012).

53. Dowbiggin, *Keeping America Sane*, 134–35; Mottier, "Eugenics and the State," 143; Moses and Stone, "Eugenics and Genocide," 203.
54. Constitution Act, 1867 (U.K.), 30 & 31 Vict., c. 3, reprinted in R.S.C. 1985, App. II, No.5. s.92(7).
55. Canadian Charter of Human Rights and Freedoms, Part 1 of the Constitution Act, 1982, being Schedule B to the Canada Act 1982 (UK), 1982, c.11.

BIBLIOGRAPHY

Primary Sources

Canadian Charter of Human Rights and Freedoms, Part 1 of the Constitution Act, 1982, being Schedule B to the Canada Act 1982 (UK), 1982, c.11
Constitution Act, 1867 (UK), 30 & 31 Vict., c. 3, reprinted in R.S.C. 1985, App. II, No.5.
The Sexual Sterilization Act, SA 1928, c. 37.
The Sexual Sterilization Act, RSA 1970, c. 341.
The Sexual Sterilization Act Amendment Act, 1937, SA 1937, c. 47.
The Sexual Sterilization Act Amendment Act, 1942, SA 1942, c. 48.
The Sexual Sterilization Repeal Act, 1972, SA 1972, c. 87.

Secondary Sources

De Schweinitz, Karl. "The Law of Settlement." In *England's Road to Social Security, from the Statute of Labourers in 1349 to the Beveridge Report of 1942*, 39. New York: A. S. Barnes & Co., 1943.
Dowbiggin, Ian Robert. *Keeping America Sane: Psychiatry and Eugenics in the United States and Canada, 1880–1940*. Ithaca, NY: Cornell University Press, 1997.
Grekul, Jana, Arvey Krahn, and Dave Odynak. "Sterilizing the 'Feeble-Minded': Eugenics in Alberta, Canada, 1929–1972." *Journal of Historical Sociology* 17, no. 4 (2004): 358–84.
Guest, D. "The Colonial Inheritance." In *The Emergence of Social Security in Canada*, 9. Vancouver: UBC Press, 1980.
McLaren, Angus. *Our Own Master Race: Eugenics in Canada 1885–1945*. Toronto: Oxford University Press, 1990.
Moses, Dirk, and Dan Stone. "Eugenics and Genocide." In *The Oxford Handbook of the History of Eugenics*, edited by Alison Bashford and Philippa Levine, 192–212. New York: Oxford University Press, 2010.
Mottier, Véronique. "Eugenics and the State: Policy Making in Comparative Perspective." In *The Oxford Handbook of the History of Eugenics*, edited by Alison Bashford and Philippa Levine, 134–53. New York: Oxford University Press, 2010.
National Film Board of Canada. *The Sterilization of Leilani Muir*. VHS. Montreal: National Film Board of Canada, 1996.
Strange, Carolyn, and Jennifer Stephen. "Eugenics in Canada: A Checkered History, 1850s–1990s." In *The Oxford Handbook of the History of Eugenics*, edited by Alison Bashford and Philippa Levine, 523–38. New York: Oxford University Press, 2010.
Wahlsten, Douglas. "Leilani Muir Versus the Philosopher King: Eugenics on Trial in Alberta." *Genetica* 99, no. 2–3 (1997): 185–98.
Webster, Andrew. Presentation 11 to SOWK/LAWS/SOCI 4703—Social Justice and the Residual Welfare State, Carleton University, Ottawa, June 13, 2012.

CHAPTER 12

The Impact of Ventilation Technology: Contrasting Consumer and Professional Perspectives

Joseph Kaufert and David Locker

This chapter contrasts the changing perceptions of polio survivors who are ventilator users and rehabilitation professionals who provided care during and after the polio epidemics of 1951 and 1953. Interviews were conducted with people with post-polio respiratory impairment to document the impact of their experience with changing ventilator technology. Respirologists, respiratory therapists, and respiratory equipment specialists involved in the care of ventilator users were interviewed to document their perceptions of user adaptation to changing technology.

Ventilator users' accounts emphasized adaptive strategies through which the benefits of each successive generation of technology were maximized and social costs minimized. Professional descriptions of the history of those who use ventilators focused primarily on periods of acute care and changes in independence and capacity. They also emphasized a more heroic representation of this life-saving technology and focused less on users' ability to access and control technology in the community.

CO-CONSTRUCTION OF HISTORY

Our interest in understanding the differences between user and professional perspectives on ventilators owes much to the vision and inspiration of the late Gini Laurie, who edited the *Rehabilitation Gazette* as a publication for people with polio-related disability, concentrating on alternative methods of risk management and technical data about new generations of ventilation technology. Laurie stressed user-controlled, independent, community-based living. She emphasized the importance of making clinical information accessible coupled with listening to experience-based information from users of technology.

Professional narratives made accessible clinical and technological information about mechanical ventilation, and the consumer contributed his or her personal experience. Gini Laurie noted that although current literature documented consumer perspectives, it had not documented the changing perspectives of respiratory rehabilitation professionals. She stressed that professionals could provide a historical sense of the development of technology and the evolution of community-based respiratory care.

We asked rehabilitation professionals to describe their experiences with succeeding generations of ventilator technology. We identified the network of respirologists, intensive care specialists, rehabilitation engineers, respiratory therapists, and technologists who were involved in providing respiratory support for the user group between 1952 and 1990. These professionals were interviewed to document the perspectives of those who provided technical support and care over the course of four decades.

VARYING PERSPECTIVES

In the past,[1] we have emphasized that ventilator users living with disability after the polio epidemics of the 1940s and 1950s are the first generation of technology users who have lived from childhood to late middle adulthood depending on mechanical ventilation for survival. We explore the cultural, technical, and logistical approaches that polio survivors use to live independently.

Conventional views regarding the social meaning of medical technology have emphasized two dominant themes. Professional and public perspectives on life-support technology frequently portray it as an expression of the power of science and the mastery by medicine of the process of life and death. More critical approaches from the social sciences and Disability Studies literature emphasize the hazards of medicalization and loss of control. Part of this literature characterizes medical technology as a negative force, transforming the nature of medical work and influencing both the user's and provider's experience of medical care.

Unfortunately, neither of these perspectives adequately describes the experience of ventilator users. Respirator users' and professionals' descriptions of the impact of ventilation technology upon life adaptations presented alternative and even conflicting interpretations. These contrasting narratives reflect the tension between enabling and disabling elements of technology. User strategies emphasize balancing advantages and disadvantages of successive generations of ventilators.[2] Interviews with professionals and ventilator users demonstrate how differences in the acceptance of new technology have been influenced by changes in knowledge base and values.

People with post-polio syndrome emphasized that some professionals have a selective awareness of the full scope of respirator users' adaptation during all phases of their use of ventilators. Less knowledgeable professionals were described by users as lacking a sense of continuity and awareness of the full range of options for treatment and independent living in community settings. These limitations may reflect the fact that physicians, respiratory therapists, and technologists were selectively involved in the polio survivors care adaptations.

The people interviewed were familiar with a variety of methods of mechanical respiratory support and had a shared experience with rehabilitation medicine and respirology. Some respondents had spent extended periods in hospital. Others spent the majority of their time in the community using home care services.

There were significant differences between users' and providers' perspectives on the quality and character of their everyday lives. Changing technology shaped consumers' biographies in that most small changes in their adaptation and perceived quality of life were described in relation to the advantages and disadvantages of each new generation of technology. Both consumers and professionals described how changes in their perceptions of "optimal use" of ventilators were influenced by their personal and professional values and priorities. For example, user values about maintaining control over maintenance led many to value reliable, user-friendly approaches to ventilators.

We encountered conceptual and methodological problems when comparing professionals' descriptions of adaptation with the users' descriptions of their long-term life experiences. Most professional involvement with post-polio ventilation problems was limited to restricted phases of each user's medical history. For example, respirologists initially involved during the polio epidemics in supporting people in iron lungs frequently had minimal experience with users' experience with respiratory home care.

Intensive care physicians and respirologists involved in caring for people with late-onset post-polio-related respiratory difficulty were often less familiar with and accepting of older ventilators. The perspectives of professionals who were selectively involved in providing care during sequential stages of technology development expressed their preference for specific types of ventilators and particular models of care provision (such as hospital-based respiratory care centres or user-directed respiratory home care). There were also differences between professionals who had experience before the implementation of Canada's comprehensive national health insurance in the 1960s and those involved in providing services under the universal national health insurance system.

In examining the priorities of professionals and technology users in descriptions of living with the support of a ventilator, we will examine how life priorities were transformed over the life course as a result of the interplay between the personal and contextual.

Professional and user descriptions of the impact of life-support technology upon quality of life during initial acute care emphasized themes of courage, strength, and individual sacrifice on the part of both users and caregivers. Pivotal events in users' interviews centred on the death of users in adjoining iron lungs and references to members of the attending clinical staff who acquired polio.

During the initial period of illness, which spanned from 3 to 18 months, during which the respondents were using an iron lung, the dominant priority was survival. The dominant theme in descriptions of this stage was uncertainty about the degree of recovery achievable and prospects for returning to community living. Several ventilator users described uncertainty about their prospects for recovery of functional capacity for mobility and self-care. They indicated that this initial experience had been crucial in dealing with the personal and clinical uncertainty that had shaped their more current response to the uncertainties of post-polio syndrome.

Two respirologists who had been involved in providing initial life support and respiratory rehabilitation during the 1952 and 1953 polio epidemics emphasized the logistical problems of providing ventilator support for over 200 people. They emphasized the reliability and effectiveness of the iron lung in acute care situations. Younger intensive care physicians and respiratory therapists who had become involved in ventilator care after 1970 stressed the efficacy of new ventilation technology. Among older physicians, acute care experience with the iron lung was described primarily in terms of initial emergency measures for life support.

Perceptions of efficiency and user-friendliness also varied with the generation of the clinician. For example, several of the younger respiratory therapists and intensive care physicians commented that they could not understand why patients continued to resist the adoption of more technologically sophisticated and physiologically efficient ventilators and rejected ventilation through the use of modern ventilator options, though the older physicians did not.

Professional narratives stressed the need for defining acceptable levels of risk and effectiveness for delivery of ventilator care in the community. These themes contrasted with the perspectives of ventilator users. Respirologists and one of the three respiratory therapists stressed the need to maintain standards for technological support and clinical standards for asepsis in home care settings at a level comparable to those maintained in intensive care units. In contrast, ventilator users and some older professionals emphasized that their long-term experience with first- and second-generation ventilators in home care settings had conditioned them to accept higher levels of risk and uncertainty that maximized patient control and allowed the user to self-direct his or her care within the community.

Following recovery from the acute phase, ventilator users entered a period of rehabilitation during which they and professional providers worked toward the recovery of vital capacity and independence in self-care and mobility functions. Interviews with both ventilator users and professionals emphasized the significance of initial acceptance of the rehabilitation model in terms of both quality of life and long-term adaptation. For both users and providers, the rehabilitation model provided a significant set of values that governed the relationship between the individual and technology and gave meaning and symbolic significance to both.

In their life histories, many ventilator users emphasized that acceptance of the rehabilitation model and decisions about alternative types of ventilators and home care options were largely controlled by professionals. Several ventilator users indicated that they felt the rehabilitation experience had imposed a single model of recovery and long-term life support. This model of successful recovery was perceived by ventilator users as not recognizing individual preferences or differences in functional capacity and economic or social resources.

Two respirologists and one respiratory therapist involved in post-acute rehabilitation described the survival and adaptation of a number of ventilator users in terms of commitment to the rehabilitation ethic. They emphasized the importance of being a "fighter or survivor" as the principal predictor of successful long-term adaptation among ventilator users. They also acknowledged that some elements of the rehabilitation ideology that emphasize avoiding dependence upon supportive technology became dysfunctional in terms of individual adaptations to the late effects of polio.

For both professionals and ventilator users, the rehabilitation model emphasized maximizing functional capacity, minimizing the use of various forms of support technology, and the importance of individual effort and perseverance in achieving personal and clinical goals.[3] The model also emphasized values such as independence and achievement, which aided both short- and long-term adjustment to ventilators; however, emphasis upon competition and total independence from support technology in rehabilitation also maximized the possibility of frustration, self-blame, and a sense of moral failure among individuals who did not achieve a high level of "functional recovery."

Most ventilator users recalled their initial commitment to the rehabilitation ethic and described how they set goals for themselves and persevered until those goals were realized. Weaning and transitioning to other forms of ventilators took place in rehabilitation hospitals that encouraged competition as a therapeutic tool. Emphasis on comparison and competition was perceived by both ventilator users and professionals as having positive and negative sides. Unrealistic expectations as to what an individual might achieve were accompanied by reported symptoms of depression among those who gauged their performance against the less severely impaired. One woman described being frustrated with her lack of progress: "I thought it must be something I'm doing wrong and other people are doing right."

During the rehabilitation phase, the major index of quality of life, for both ventilator users and professionals, was defined in terms of attainment of respiratory and functional independence. Relying on mechanical technology was sometimes perceived as an impediment to such independence, and as indicative of moral failure.

During the post-rehabilitation period, the level of many of the ventilator users' respiratory function remained relatively constant, although respiratory infections often necessitated a return to mechanical support and hospital care. Stable adaptations in the post-rehabilitation period often were not emphasized in the professionals' accounts because, after the closure of major respiratory centres, many former patients lived independently and had minimal contact with clinicians. For both providers and ventilator users, the primary formula for maintaining quality of life was the admonition to "use it or lose it." This value was later called into question as people began to experience post-polio syndrome.

The period of stability lasted approximately 10 to 15 years, after which most subjects entered a transitional phase characterized by an unexpected decline in respiratory capacity attributed to the post-polio syndrome. Declines in respiratory function associated with late polio-related aging effects brought into sharper contrast the assumptions of the initial rehabilitation model and the physiological and social imperatives of daily living. For ventilator users, this resulted in a change in attitudes, adoption of more effective and portable ventilators, and a fundamental reordering of life priorities.

Both ventilator users and professionals indicated that the acceptance of each new generation of ventilators, with their associated benefits and costs, depended on both parties rethinking some of the primary tenets of the early rehabilitation model. The adversarial position implied in patient and professional metaphors referring to "fighting disability" and avoiding dependence upon machinery or other people had to be modified. Emphasis on independence from life-support technology was replaced by emphasis on quality of life and recognition of the appropriate role of ventilators in achieving this goal.

Younger intensive care specialists and respiratory therapists who worked with ventilator users recently have indicated that they were initially puzzled by the reluctance of polio survivors to accept newer ventilators. Several such professionals indicated that they had subsequently learned to listen to users' experiences with older technology before prescribing new technology.

Among the ventilator users we interviewed, all had transferred to using new ventilation technology since 1983. Several developed customized "sip tubes" or facial masks rather than connection involving tracheostomies. With the exception of one individual, all users indicated that the benefits of the new equipment outweighed its cost.

In interviewing health professionals, marked generational contrasts were found between physicians and respiratory therapists who favoured tracheostomies and those who favoured other methods of connection. Some physicians with intensive care unit backgrounds were willing to provide ventilation only through a tracheostomy because it was perceived as more efficient. Another physician explained that he had gradually come to accept alternate approaches to connecting a person to the machine with a mask or mouth tube. He attributed his change in perspective to encountering people who had successfully used these methods.

SHIFTING RELATIONSHIPS WITH TECHNOLOGY

The final transition to modern portable positive pressure ventilation brought with it a different set of problems and constraints. Some of the costs and benefits are attributable to the new body/machine interface, while others are indirect, as the result of a changed relationship to the physical and social environment and to one's self. Those people who used portable positive pressure equipment talked of a new sense of bodily well-being. Both professionals and ventilator users emphasized that the individual's physical and psychological health improved substantially and, combined with increased mobility, transformed the quality of everyday life.

There were discrepancies between users and professional perspectives in terms of control of technology and training for equipment failure. The users emphasized that the new generation of portable respirators included improved safety features, such as backup systems and self-monitoring circuits controlled by microcomputers; however, many of these new technological innovations also brought new problems. It was reported that microprocessors malfunctioned in below-zero weather. In response to the uncertainty of technology, individuals learned to recognize problems before the crisis stage was reached. Users were sometimes taught little about these problems or the methods of managing them; rather, problems emerged in the course of daily experience and solutions were found by trial and error. As a consequence, the machine, and tending to the needs of the machine, became the central focus and activity of everyday life.

The accounts of both professionals and users regarding transitions to modern portable ventilators also emphasized many common themes. The difference in the perception of quality of life was so dramatic that portable ventilator users often tried to persuade other people with post-polio syndrome to make the transition to newer systems. A transformed sense of self accompanied the use of new equipment, as well as a changed relationship to the environment and the people in it. This shift to ventilator use coincided with the final rejection of the rehabilitation ethic that had been the guiding principle of the respondents' lives during the early years of disability.

CONCLUSION

This chapter explored the shifting relationships between changing systems of ventilation technology, changing user needs, and ideas. It illustrates the contradictory assumptions about using technology in rehabilitation ideologies, which often are modified as people develop adaptations to their changing needs. The contradictory themes in rehabilitation ideology of avoiding the use of aids and adaptations and accepting the liberating effects of life-support equipment were gradually reconciled as more "user-friendly" technology was adapted to the changing ventilation needs of aging users. For both the user and the professional, improved mechanical ventilation technology was appropriately seen as an effective way of restoring or enhancing respiratory capacity, improving energy levels, and ensuring survival in the short and long term.

However, the integration of technology and a chronic disabling condition involves balancing the freedoms and constraints imposed by life-support systems. While the benefits conveyed by positive pressure ventilators were substantial, they were only realized at a cost. Improvements in energy, mobility, and well-being were weighed against the imposition of new routines, new management strategies, and new worries and concerns. In most cases, these benefits and costs were balanced to produce significant and dramatic changes to the pattern of everyday life priorities and the broader experience of illness.

NOTES

1. D. Locker and J. Kaufert, "The Breath of Life: Medical Technology and the Careers of People with Post-respiratory Poliomyelitis," *Sociology of Health and Illness* 10, no. 1 (1988).
2. Locker and Kaufert, "The Breath of Life."
3. G. DeJong, "Defining and Implementing the Independent Living Concept," in *Independent Living for Physically Disabled People*, ed. N. Crewe and I. Zola (San Francisco: Jossey-Bass, 1983).

BIBLIOGRAPHY

DeJong, G. "Defining and Implementing the Independent Living Concept." In *Independent Living for Physically Disabled People*, edited by N. Crewe and I. Zola, 4–27. San Francisco: Jossey-Bass, 1983.

Locker, D., and J. Kaufert. "The Breath of Life: Medical Technology and the Careers of People with Post-respiratory Poliomyelitis." *Sociology of Health and Illness* 10, no. 1 (1988): 24–40.

SECTION IV

THE 1960S TO THE 1980S

Technology developed after the Second World War and the polio epidemics of the 1950s (related in Kaufert and Locker's chapter in the previous section) began to change the expectations of young disabled persons about living in society. People with mobility impairments had wheelchairs, ventilators, and better prosthetic limbs, and they began to see that society was built without their input. That is, stairs into buildings prevented people who were wheelchair and crutch users from participating in everyday Canadian life. People with disabilities were not content to be warehoused in institutions away from the public. They were not content to have societies for crippled children tell them what their reality was and that they were dependent on doctors, social workers, and their parents for their whole lives. They wanted to participate as independent citizens. This section provides examples of disabled people speaking for themselves, both banding together and working individually to bring about change in Canadian society. No longer were disabled people willing to sit on the sidelines, left out of the social and economic life of Canada. They began to exercise their citizenship rights.

Parent's "Je me souviens: The Hegemony of Stairs in the Montreal Métro" documents the systemic exclusion of disabled people from many aspects of daily life in Montreal due to lack of physical access for those with mobility impairments. Neutral public landscapes throughout the city assume a certain level of physicality or non-disability. Parent focuses on public transportation and traces the development of the Montreal subway system (or Métro) and the nearly 50-year struggle for access for people with disabilities.

Driedger's "Organizing for Change: The Origins and History of the Manitoba League of the Physically Handicapped, 1967–1982" provides a detailed depiction of the founding of this organization, a member of the national Coalition of Provincial Organizations of the Handicapped (COPOH). One could ask why is it important to explore the creation of one of many provincial advocacy associations run by and for people with disabilities. It is important to look at the manner in which grassroots organizations such as the Manitoba League of the Physically Handicapped came into existence and how they influenced disability rights and history in Canada.

D'Aubin's "The Council of Canadians with Disabilities: A Voice of Our Own, 1976–2012" documents the history of the council originally known as the Coalition of Provincial Organizations of the Handicapped (COPOH), which was founded in 1976 and was the first pan-Canadian cross-disability rights organization. D'Aubin traces the development of the organization from its inception, founding principles and concepts, and pioneering activism through to its key involvement with the development and signing of the United Nations Convention on the Rights of Persons with Disabilities.

Galer's "Building an Accessible House of Labour: Work, Disability Rights, and the Canadian Labour Movement" examines the rise of the disability rights movement in Canada and its relationship to organized labour. This chapter shows how disabled people began to work with the wider Canadian society and its institutions to advocate for employment for disabled persons, who wanted to be economic actors in Canada.

In McPhedran's "The Habeas Corpus of Justin Clark," the reader is provided with a personal account of a landmark trial in Canada wherein a young man took his parents to court to gain his freedom from a long-term care facility. As the title suggests, the story is about Justin Clark as he first attempts to gain legal control over his own life to leave the institution. This chapter is about challenging the system, advocacy, and, most importantly, gaining freedom.

CHAPTER 13

Je me souviens: The Hegemony of Stairs in the Montreal Métro

Laurence Parent

INTRODUCTION

Built during the Quiet Revolution (between 1960 and 1966), the Montreal Métro considerably changed the Montreal landscape and city life, and instantly became a major component of Montreal identity. The Montreal Métro was built in such a way that it could only be accessed by stairs. Because of that, many Montrealers whose mobility needs cannot be accommodated by stairs due to a lack of what are perceived as "normal" legs are excluded by the city Métro. In 2001, the historian Benoît Clairoux wrote a book dedicated to the history of the Montreal Métro. Clairoux's book is the only book focusing solely on this history. His book, *Le Métro de Montréal: 35 Ans Déjà* (*The Montreal Métro: 35 Years Already*), presents the Montreal Métro as a source of pride for Montrealers. The preface is written by Jacques Fortin, a former Société de Transport de Montreal (STM)[1] director. He claims, "We are proud of this jewel of Quebec's métropolis. Who has never heard that our métro is one of the most beautiful, clean and safe of métros of the world?"[2] *Montreal Souterrain: Sous le Béton, le Mythe* (*Underground Montreal: Under the Concrete, the Myth*) written by Fabien Deglise tells the history of and analyzes Montreal's past and present underground life.[3] However, one major architectural fact is ignored in both Clairoux's and Deglise's books: the Montreal Métro can only be accessed by stairs. Even though Clairoux's attention to detail is readily apparent throughout his book, the historian totally omitted the fact that access to the Montreal Métro is not granted to everybody. Clairoux's and Deglise's books illustrate how stairs in the Montreal Métro have been—and are still—largely understood as a neutral architectural structure that was not and is not problematic. The history of the exclusion of people who cannot be accommodated by stairs from the Montreal Métro has never been written. This paper will lift the veil on Quebec's walking-ableist society by exploring the history of the hegemony of stairs in the Montreal Métro from its conceptualization in the early 1960s to 1977, the year before the adoption of the Quebec law ensuring the rights of people with disabilities.

LA GRANDE NOIRCEUR

In 1948, Les Automatistes, a group of Quebec artists and intellectuals led by Paul-Émile Borduas, published *Le Refus Global*, a poetic manifesto that vigorously rejected the norms and values commended by the Quebec government and the Catholic Church. Borduas wrote this manifesto in reaction to the Grande Noirceur (Great Darkness) in which the Quebec population was plunged after the second election of Maurice Duplessis as Quebec premier in 1944. Well known for his frequent civil rights violations and his narrow collaboration with the Catholic Church, Duplessis's politics considerably delayed the emergence of the Quebec modern state. Under Duplessis's regime, artists and intellectuals were censored by the Catholic Church, which was acting like Big Brother. Even though the French-speaking population formed the majority of the labour force, they had little power in decision-making. The social areas of life were controlled by the French-speaking ecclesiastic elite, and the economic affairs were led mostly by English-speaking white men. The development of Montreal, the Quebec metropolis, was continually slowed down by Duplessis. A few months before his death, he declared the idea of implementing a metro system in Montreal ridiculous and unreasonable.[4]

Throughout the Grande Noirceur disabled people had been subjected to the most horrible treatments and kept in institutions. *La Grande Sortie*, a film on the history of disabled people in Quebec produced by the Office des personnes handicapées du Québec (OPHQ) in 1983 summarizes the lives of disabled people living in institutions. The film narrator repeats the following several times: "Exclusion, overprotection, lethargy and loneliness. This is what we will experience."[5] Murielle Larivière, one activist I had the opportunity to interview in 2009 for my master's thesis on the history of the exclusion of disabled people from the Montreal Métro, is a white disabled woman who lived in an institution during her childhood.[6] About life in institutions, she says, "I think life in an institution is empty of meaning."[7] The ecclesiastic power and some philanthropic groups ran the various institutions in the province. Boucher, Fougeyrollas, and Majeau write that the main mission of those institutions was to "educate or re-educate 'cripple, blind, deaf/mute children, etc.'"[8] Disability was seen as a private matter that was intrinsically horrible. Religion and charity were the only available supports.[9] Boucher, Fougeyrollas, and Majeau explain that it was common to see disabled bodies in places of pilgrimage waiting for a miracle that would "save" them from their impairments.[10]

While life in an institution was characterized by a perpetual immobilization within the institution's walls, life outside of the institution did not offer better opportunities for disabled people to be mobile and to participate in city life. Disabled people were rarely seen in public places. A clear method of segregation was inscribed in public spaces such as Montreal's public transit system. The private and public organizations providing transit in Montreal had always run a system that prevented access to people whose mobility needs could not be accommodated by stairs, a system in which stairs had always been hegemonic. However, one initiative put in place by the Montreal Tramways Branch No. 74

of the Canadian Legion of the British Empire Service League in collaboration with the Montreal Tramways Company must be acknowledged (though this initiative was based on charity principles and did not serve as a first opportunity to question the inaccessibility of regular public transit). One bus that looked like a school bus was retrofitted with a ramp. The adapted bus could fit 13 "wheelchair patients" and 4 of their attendants.[11] The bus was used for group trips, mostly to entertainment sites. One picture of the bus and some of its users reveals that it was probably primarily used by white men who acquired a physical disability. Even if the Montreal Tramway Company was involved in the operating of this bus, it was painted in the colours of the Canadian Legion. In the front of the bus, the word "special" was painted. This made obvious the distinction between the adapted bus and regular transit. While this adapted bus turned out to be the first initiative addressing the mobility needs of some wheelchair users, it also became the first example of the materialized segregation between "abnormal" and "special" users and regular transit users.

1960S: A TOO QUIET REVOLUTION

Maurice Duplessis's sudden death on September 7, 1959, symbolized the end of several Quebec conservative policies. In 1960, the newly elected Liberal government led by Jean Lesage started to metamorphose Quebec society. Elected under the slogan "Maîtres chez nous" (Masters of our own house), Lesage and its *équipe du tonnerre* (terrific team) challenged the hegemonic power of the Catholic Church and big corporations. They fashioned a welfare state and launched several ambitious projects that would mainly be managed by French-speaking men. The modification of social conditions—such as an increasing francization of economic affairs—removed some barriers that previously excluded the French-speaking population from participating in economic affairs. In Montreal, the Quiet Revolution was easily observable through radical change in the city landscape.[12] Montreal was experiencing significant urban growth that could be explained by rising employment in the service sector.[13] Linteau and colleagues explain that the construction of a metro system began to be seen as an urgent project.[14]

During the 1960 municipal election campaign, candidate Jean Drapeau promised that if his party were elected, Montreal would build its own metro system.[15] This promise, combined with the wind of optimism brought by the election of Lesage at the head of the Quebec government, incontestably contributed to the election of Jean Drapeau as the mayor of Montreal on October 24, 1960. A few months later, on January 26, 1961, the Quebec government amended the Charter of the City of Montreal, enabling the metropolis to build its own metro system.[16] Fifty years after the first metro projects were imagined and re-imagined for Montreal,[17] the city would finally have its metro within a few years. In April 1961, the City of Montreal created a committee dedicated solely to the construction of the metro, the Bureau du Métro. Lucien L'Allier was chosen as the engineer-in-chief and led the committee composed of architects and engineers.[18] They quickly designed a metro system in which stairs would be hegemonic, contributing to making it difficult—or near impossible—for people whose mobility needs cannot be accommodated by stairs to use it. Tremblay, Campbell, and Hudson explain that during the post-war period (1945–1970), elevators were primarily seen as serving to transport pianos, rather than humans, because "disability was considered a biomedical or rehabilitation issue, with solutions based on the adaptation of the individual to society."[19] On May 23, 1962, construction of the Montreal Métro, which would soon become one of the most important components of Montreal identity, started on Berri Street near Jarry Street. Reflecting on this important historical event, I wrote the following:

> During the night of August 12 to August 13, 1961, the German Democratic Republic started the construction of the Berlin Wall which will divide Berlin, Germany, and the world for over 28 years. Western history tells the Berlin Wall as a representation of power, control and fear. That day of May 23, 1962, the City of Montreal started the construction of my Berlin Wall.[20]

THE INAUGURATION OF THE MONTREAL MÉTRO: DIS-CITIZENSHIP FOR DISABLED MONTREALERS

October 14, 1966, the day of the inauguration of the initial Montreal Métro network, which numbered 26 stations, marked a significant moment in Quebec's modern history. Montreal became the seventh city in North America to own a metro system.[21] In the context of the Quiet Revolution, the opening of the Montreal Métro symbolized one of the first accomplishments by an elected government that served the needs of its citizens. For this reason, the inauguration is an important event to examine because it provides the definition of citizenship in Montreal. During the inauguration ceremony, Mayor Drapeau declared,

> Fifty years of patience, projects and studies. Fifty years of hope. Now it's done. My first thought goes to us, residents of this big city. We need to mutually congratulate each other to own such an underground transport system. We deserve it.... With its new métro, Montreal gains one more title among the greatest world capitals.[22]

One television reporter exclaimed: "Today the métro will live because there will be people in it!"[23] History that has been written and told until now presents this day as one of celebration that brought all Montreal citizens together, excited by the new possibility of mobility provided by the Métro.[24] Clairoux writes that "after the ceremony, the system is invaded by many thousands of Montrealers who discovered with wonder that their métro is even more beautiful and modern than they had imagined."[25] As I read this, I could not help but think,

Us. Residents. We Deserve It. People. Montrealers. Beautiful. Modern. Us? Who is us? Who are the Montrealers proud of their new métro?[26]

At first glance, this "us" seems to describe all human beings living on the Island of Montreal; however, this "us" as it was formulated during the inauguration of the Montreal Métro contributes to the construction and marginalization of disabled bodies—such as bodies that cannot use stairs. The needs of blind people and people with visual impairments were not taken in consideration either. The stations were built in such a way that put blind people and those with low vision in extremely dangerous situations. A total erasure of disabled bodies was needed in order to assert that the new Métro could be ridden by everyone—by "us." The inauguration of the Métro—understood as being a public space—tied the notion of being a Montrealer to the ability of riding the Métro. The status of citizen was granted upon the performance of a specific ability, judged by people in power to be a "normal" ability. It is important to note that all the people to whom the existence of the Montreal Métro is attributed are white, able-bodied men. Relph, a geographer, states that "modern landscapes seem to be designed for forty-year-old healthy males driving cars."[27] Vujakovic and Matthews assert that "decision makers are likely to infuse their work with their own values and meanings."[28] The inauguration of the Montreal Métro symbolizes the public consecration of the ability to use stairs as an essential ability. Consequently, the lack of this ability became sufficient to justify exclusion. Oliver defines "walkism" as the phenomenon that is "materialised in spatial structures that favour walkers over non-walkers."[29] The Montreal Métro silently became a space celebrating walkism; it became a walking-ableist space from which some people were excluded without shame.

I define *walkism* as the normative expectation that someone can walk and climb stairs. Favoured abilities that are at the heart of ableism according to Wolbring are not only seen as being preferable, but also as essential.[30] The hierarchy of abilities determines who will get to be fully recognized as a human being and who will not.[31] The abilities to walk and use stairs are cherished and valued in the hierarchy of abilities. Devlin and Pothier suggest that "because many persons with disabilities are denied formal and/or substantive citizenship, they are assigned to the status of dis-citizens, a form of citizenship minus, a disabling citizenship."[32] Drapeau's "we" represents the walking-ableist discourse that will write and tell the history of the Montreal Métro—a discourse that will, for the next decades, ignore and marginalize the exclusion of dis-citizens, a category in which people whose mobility needs cannot be accommodated by stairs belong.

THE CONSTRUCTION OF SEGREGATED MOBILITIES

The first years of operation for the Montreal Métro were characterized by the winds of change and optimism blowing in Quebec society. From April 28 to October 27, 1967, Montreal welcomed the world during Expo 67, which is still one of the most significant events that has happened in the Quebec metropolis. The Expo 67 theme, Man and His World, celebrated fraternity between nations. Godbout and colleagues describe Quebec during Expo 67 as a "Quebec between two worlds"[33]—between traditionalism and modernity.[34] Looking at Expo 67 is essential for the purpose of this research because, like the Montreal Métro, Expo 67 was an extremely ambitious project that changed the Montreal landscape and city life. Both projects are also intertwined. Their legacy to Quebec and Montreal history is monumental. It is part of our collective imagery, as expressed in a famous Beau Dommage song:[35]

> In sixty-seven everything was beautiful. It was the year of love, it was the year of the Expo. Everybody had their passport with their pretty picture. I wore flowers in my hair. How ridiculous was I![36]

In 1962, the City of Montreal decided to locate the site of the international exhibition in the middle of the St. Lawrence River. The city doubled the surface of Saint Helen's Island and built a completely new island of 600 hectares, Notre Dame Island, using the rock extracted from the ground to build the Métro tunnels.[37] Furthermore, Expo 67 boosted the expansion of the Métro system with the creation of the yellow line, which linked the Island of Montreal and the South Shore. A Métro station was inaugurated on Saint Helen's Island just in time for the beginning of Expo 67. Clairoux indicates that during Expo 67, 70 percent of 50 million visitors arrived by the Sainte-Hélène Métro station, which, like the other stations, was only accessible by stairs.[38] This statistic shows that the action of riding the Montreal Métro was part of the Expo 67 experience for millions of visitors.

The highest point of Expo 67 was reached in the summer, while French president Charles de Gaulle was visiting. De Gaulle's visit stimulated national pride and collective imagination based on the white, French-speaking identity. The mythic president chose to arrive by boat in Quebec City to remember the historical travel of Samuel de Champlain in 1608.[39] From there, he travelled in a convertible car to Montreal with Quebec premier Daniel Johnson. As they drove the 260 kilometres between Quebec City and Montreal, thousands of enthusiastic Québécois gathered along the Chemin du Roy—a historical road that runs along the St. Lawrence River—and cheered for De Gaulle. The road was paved with lilies, the symbol of Quebec's French heritage placed at the heart of the Quebec flag. People expressed their will to live in French with nationalist slogans such as "Québec en français" and by waving the flags of Quebec and France. Godbout and colleagues suggested that the president was profoundly touched and staggered by what he saw on his way to Montreal.[40] The ultimate destination of his exciting trip was Montreal's city hall. Inspired by the passionate crowd, De Gaulle exclaimed from the balcony: "Vive Montréal! Vive le Québec! Vive le Québec libre!"[41] De Gaulle's declaration galvanized nationalist inspirations. Canadian prime minister Lester B. Pearson, upset by the already historic declaration, cancelled De Gaulle's visit to Ottawa, which was supposed to take place only a few days later. After visiting Expo 67 and the Montreal Métro, De Gaulle went back to France, leaving behind him a young nationalist movement enthusiastically looking for its new identity.

Davis, a well-known critical disability scholar, argues that nationalism is based on normalcy.[42] He explains that "normalcy and linguistic standardization begin roughly at the same time," and that "language and normalcy come together under the rubric on nationalism."[43] The experience of riding the new Montreal Métro and visiting Expo 67 was recorded as a common experience at the very heart of Quebec nationalism. It became a normative experience, an experience understood through other social components, such as language, bodies, architecture, politics, and economics, that define what it means to be a Montreal citizen. Hillier and Hanson write that space is a "morphic language, and one of the means by which society is interpreted by its members."[44] The Montreal Métro as interpreted by its riders started to produce meanings and shape the limits of citizenship.

NATIONALISM AND THE NOTION OF THE AVERAGE CITIZEN (AKA THE CITIZEN WHO RIDES THE MONTREAL MÉTRO)

During the Quiet Revolution, the relationship between citizens and the state changed. The Quebec welfare state's definition of citizenship was based on equality of the average citizen, whose city life experiences were articulated around one unique narrative. In April 1969, the Quebec government confirmed its commitment to public transit by announcing the extension of the Métro.[45] The construction of new stations on the green line started in 1971. Once again, the hegemony of stairs in these stations has not been presented as an issue. At that time, the silent exclusion of disabled people received the state's sanction, since Quebec funded 60 percent of expenses related to the construction of the new stations.[46] The Quebec welfare state addressed the mobility needs of a specific and never-named category of the population: the able-bodied population. Imrie explains that "the (re)production of barriered and bounded spaces is as likely to be affected by the symbolic and cultural encoding of the city, particularly in seeking to reinforce the efficacy of 'civilised' and normal 'bodies.'"[47] Hugues and Kirby assert that "cultural practices based on notions of order, health, and normality still include tendencies of othering people, to confine, invalidate, exclude, and fix individuals and groups of people seen as having differences and deficiencies."[48] The development of the Montréal Métro as a collective project has the effect of othering disabled people.

Today, the Quiet Revolution is remembered for having created a space for a nation to define itself. The inscription of segregation in every Montreal Métro flight of stairs is not understood as a representation of the cohesive culture of normalcy. The concept of the average citizen, based on the marginalization of "uncivilized" and "abnormal" bodies, is explained by Davis, who claims that normalcy is hegemonic and exerts a tyrannical power over bodies.[49] Davis uses Foucault's terms and argues that bodies are disciplined and shaped to meet the needs of the bureaucratic and corporate state.[50] He asserts that the concept of equality among all individuals, which is at the heart of democratic and capitalist societies, is problematic. He argues that in order to postulate such a thing as the existence of equality, a notion of the average citizen is needed. Davis asserts that the average citizen who represents all citizens is the disembodiment of difference and hierarchy.[51] He is a "kind of fiction, a created character that fits the national mold."[52] The average citizen is a statistical figure central to the concept of the bell curve, which is also called the normal curve. Under the mathematical law of the normal curve, non-average citizens are needed to ensure that the curve has its perfect shape. Disabled people are relegated to these roles—with other marginalized groups—and are confined in the tails of the normal curve.

IF I CAN'T RIDE THE MONTREAL MÉTRO IS IT STILL MY REVOLUTION?[53]

Considering the Montreal Métro to be a representation of revolution, based on a nationalism cherishing normalcy and devaluing differences, it would be easy to think that disabled people did not experience any significant changes during this period of Quebec history; however, disabled people experienced what is called the Great Exit. The Great Exit is a movement of deinstitutionalization that happened during the 1960s and the 1970s. It started with patients' denunciation of treatments in Quebec psychiatric institutions.[54] In 1961, Jean-Charles Pagé, a psychiatric survivor, wrote the book *Les fous crient au secours* to raise awareness of the segregation and humiliation he had experienced. This book contributed to the development of the movement for the rights of people identified as mad and crazy.[55] In 1971, the Quebec state recognized, via the Castonguay-Nepveu Report addressing health issues, that disabled people should be considered citizens—as if disabled people were a new discovery. The authors of the report write, "The handicapped like any other citizens, should have access to goods and services necessary to his blossoming. He should be able to share the same hope and enjoy the principle of equality of opportunities in all areas of development."[56] In reality, disabled people who had been deinstitutionalized discovered that Quebec society was not expecting them. A city and a nation were being constructed without them. The narrator of the film *La Grande Sortie* explained this first shock upon encountering the outside world: "Every day, every minute, we were hitting barriers of all kinds."[57] Cresswell defines those barriers as "cultural signifiers that tell us if we are 'out of place.'"[58] Murielle Larivière, who has experienced deinstitutionalization, talks about how she felt when she arrived in mainstream society. She says, "What I found the most difficult when I started to go outside (of the institution), it was the pity I could see in people's eyes."[59]

The term used to describe the deinstitutionalization phenomenon itself—the Great Exit—suggests the existence of movements and mobility. In Montreal, for instance, many disabled people were trapped in institutions and homes in a city that was supposed to offer them possibilities and opportunities. Access to transport quickly became one of the first struggles of disabled people.[60] Larivière explained that the absence of accessible transport for people whose mobility needs could not be accommodated by stairs was particularly critical. She said, "without adequate transport, accessible or adapted, it is impossible to study, to work, to have leisure, go to the bank or to the food market, etc."[61] It is in this context that two brothers using wheelchairs who lived in Montreal funded the first para-transit service in Quebec. Jacques and Jean-Marc Forest had to find the funding necessary to create the service by themselves, since the Quebec state did not assume any responsibility regarding the transport of disabled. In 1973, the two brothers got a small grant from the Quebec government for their project and invested their own personal savings to create Minibus Forest. At its inception, the door-to-door service was provided by an adapted minibus in downtown Montreal only. The service was then extended to other sectors in the east of Montreal; however, Minibus Forest was unable to meet the needs of all members of this population. Larivière recalls Minibus Forest's first years of operation:

> They showed how the mobility needs of people using wheelchairs were urgent and a critical situation. Because of the lack of financial resources, the service served only the needs of a very small portion of the clientele. The administrators had to establish priorities for the type of clients and the reasons motivating their trips. Workers and students were the clientele that had priority. Even for this clientele, all the needs were not met.[62]

In 1976, the Forest brothers received their first government grant, which served to absorb an annual deficit of $51,540. This grant represents the first direct public intervention regarding the transport of disabled people.

The creation of a para-transit system led to a change of Montreal's landscape under the influence of hosting the 1976 Summer Olympic Games.[63] On a political level, the Quebec sovereigntist movement was gaining in importance. A few months after the Olympics, on November 15, the Parti Québécois, a nationalist party promoting Quebec sovereignty, was elected for the first time in Quebec history. The Quebec state was in the process of overcoming its own dependence on Canada. In Montreal, the expansion of the Métro network once again redefined the mobility habits of the average Montrealer. By 1978, the Montreal Métro included 43 stations.[64] Clairoux explains that the features of the new stations were an improvement upon the stations built during the 1960s: "The new stations are more spacious and the air circulation has been improved. Some stations are integrated with a park. The counters are closer to the platforms to facilitate the connection with buildings."[65] The first television advertising campaign in Montreal public transit history was broadcast in 1977. The aim of this campaign was to encourage Montrealers to use their Métro—as if riding it was a matter of choice. The advertisement showed six white, able-bodied male and female dancers from the Grands Ballets Canadiens de Montréal, all of whom represented the "ideal" body, dancing on the platform and in the car. The dancers sang an ode to the Montreal Métro titled "Il Fait Beau dans l'Métro" (It's Sunny in the Métro). The lyrics expressed a certain pride in the Montreal Métro: "Because we smile, our Métro is the most beautiful in the world."[66] Such a positive advertisement illustrates how the absence of people whose mobility needs cannot be accommodated by stairs from the Montreal Métro was not seen as something problematic. Instead, it was perceived as something normal that was not even worth mentioning. Considering the context in which people whose mobility needs cannot be accommodated by stairs have been constructed as abnormal and unfit citizens, the Forest brothers' initiative can be understood as an act of resistance and hope for disabled people who were trying to live in their community. In the film *The Great Exit*, the narrator explains that they are more mobile than they have ever been before. Because of the Forest brothers' initiative, disabled people started feeling that they were part of an ongoing powerful force and began investing in public spaces such as schools and workplaces.[67]

CONCLUSION

This short history of the hegemony of stairs in the Montreal Métro between 1960 and 1977 offers new perspectives on Quebec nationalism and Montreal citizenship by exposing the transit segregation experienced by many disabled people. The implementation of a public para-transit service in 1980 reinforced this segregation, which has historically been portrayed as a logical consequence of disabled people's impairments. The ultimate goal of this chapter is to acknowledge the history of an exclusion that has led to the categorization and construction of disabled people as outcasts from the locus of Montreal city life. To a greater extent, this shows that disabled people were excluded from the Quiet Revolution. In 2017, only 11 Métro stations out of 68 have a step-free access. A greater understanding of disability history is necessary for both disabled people and society to better advocate for change and fight against ableism.

NOTES

1. Because the Montreal public transit commission has changed its name several times since the 1950s, I decided to use one name (STM) to facilitate the reading of this major research paper. This name has been official since 2002.
2. Benoît Clairoux, *Le Métro de Montréal: 35 Ans Déjà* (Montreal: Hurtubise HMH, 2001), 7.
3. Fabien Deglise, *Montréal Souterrain: Sous le Béton, le Mythe* (Montreal: Héliotrope, 2008).
4. Clairoux, *Le Métro de Montréal*, 20.
5. Office des personnes handicapées du Québec, dir., *La Grande Sortie* (Quebec City, 1983).
6. Finding disabled people who have participated in the fight for an accessible Métro has proved to be challenging. All the people I have met or read about who were involved between 1960 and 1977 were white. This is one of the limitations of this research.
7. My translation of the original quote.
8. Normand Boucher, Patrick Fougeyrollas, and Pierre Majeau, "French-Speaking Contributions to the Disability Rights Movement in Canada and Internationally: From a Quebec Perspective," in *In Pursuit of Equal Participation: Canada and Disability at Home and Abroad*, ed. Aldred Neufeldt and Henry Enns (Concord: Captus Press, 2003), 170.
9. Office des personnes handicapées du Québec, *La Grande Sortie*.
10. Normand Boucher, Patrick Fougeyrollas and Charles Gaucher, "Development and Transformation of Advocacy in the Disability Movement of Quebec," in *Making Equality: History of Advocacy and Persons with Disabilities in Canada*, ed. Deborah Stienstra and Aileen Wight-Felske (Concord: Captus Press, 2003).

11. Regroupement des Usagers du Transport Adapté et Accessible de l'Ile de Montréal. *Article sur le Légion canadienne en 1950*, http://rutamtl.com/lcta-1950.pdf (page no longer available).
12. Paul-André Linteau et al., *Quebec Since 1930* (Toronto: Lorimer, 1991), 309.
13. Linteau et al., *Quebec Since 1930*, 392.
14. Linteau et al., *Quebec Since 1930*, 392.
15. Clairoux, *Le Métro de Montréal*, 21.
16. Clairoux, *Le Métro de Montréal*, 23.
17. Clairoux, *Le Métro de Montréal*, 23.
18. Clairoux, *Le Métro de Montréal*, 26.
19. Mary Tremblay, Audrey Campbell, and Geoffrey Hudson, "When Elevators Were for Pianos: An Oral History Account of the Civilian Experience of Using Wheelchairs in Canadian Society. The First Twenty-Five Years: 1945–1970," *Disability and Society* 20, no. 2 (2005): 113.
20. I wrote this on January 18, 2010.
21. Société Radio-Canada, *Le Métro de Montréal 35 Ans Déjà!* Television. 2001, http://archives.radio-canada.ca/economie_affaires/transports/clips/6920/.
22. Marc Guimont, *Montréal en Métro* (Montreal: Ulysse, 2007), 1. This is my translation of the original quote.
23. Société Radio-Canada, *Le Métro de Montréal ou la Sous-Terre des Hommes*. Television. 1966, http://archives.radio-canada.ca/economie_affaires/transports/dossiers/1246/.
24. Clairoux, *Le Métro de Montréal*; Société Radio-Canada, *Le Métro de Montréal*.
25. Clairoux, *Le Métro de Montréal*, 38. This is my translation of the original quote.
26. I wrote this on January 18, 2010.
27. Peter Freund, "Bodies, Disability and Spaces: The Social Model and Disabling Spatial Organisations," *Disability and Society* 16, no. 5 (2001): 695.
28. P. Vujakovic and M. H. Matthews, "Contorted, Folded, Torn: Environmental Values, Cartographic Representation and the Politics of Disability," *Disability and Society* 9, no. 3 (1994): 359.
29. Freund, "Bodies, Disability and Spaces," 695.
30. Gregor Wolbring, "Is There an End to Out-Able? Is There an End to the Rat Race for Abilities?" *M/C Journal* 11, no. 3 (2008), http://journal.media-culture.org.au/index.php/mcjournal/article/view/57.
31. Fiona Kumari Campbell, "Exploring Internalized Ableism Using Critical Race Theory," *Disability and Society* 23, no. 2 (2008): 153.
32. Dianne Pothier and Richard Devlin, *Critical Disability Theory: Essays in Philosophy, Politics, Policy, and Law* (Vancouver: UBC Press, 2006), 2.
33. My translation of the original quote.
34. Jacques Godbout et al., *Le Québec Entre Deux Mondes* (Montreal: Les 400 Coups, 2007), 83.
35. Beau Dommage, "Où Est Passé la Noce?" Capitol Records, 1975.
36. My translation of the original lyrics.
37. Clairoux, *Le Métro de Montréal*, 35.
38. Clairoux, *Le Métro de Montréal*, 40.
39. Godbout et al., *Le Québec Entre Deux Mondes*, 13.
40. Godbout et al., *Le Québec Entre Deux Mondes*, 13.
41. Godbout et al., *Le Québec Entre Deux Mondes*, 50.
42. Lennard J. Davis, "The Rule of Normalcy: Politics and Disability in the U.S.A. (United States of Ability)," In *Bending Over Backwards: Disability, Dismodernism and Other Difficult Positions*, ed. Lennard J. Davis (New York: New York University Press, 2002), 102.
43. Davis, "The Rule of Normalcy," 102.
44. Daphne Spain, *Gendered Spaces* (Chapel Hill: University of North Carolina Press, 1992), 198.

45. Clairoux, *Le Métro de Montréal*, 47.
46. Clairoux, *Le Métro de Montréal*, 50.
47. Rob Imrie, "Barriered and Bounded Places and the Spatialities of Disability," *Urban Studies* 38, no. 2 (2008): 233.
48. Michael J. Prince, *Absent Citizens: Disability Politics and Policy in Canada* (Toronto: University of Toronto Press, 2009), 56–57.
49. Lennard J. Davis, "Constructing Normalcy: The Bell Curve, the Novel, and the Invention of the Disabled Body in the Nineteenth Century," in *The Disability Studies Reader*, ed. Lennard J. Davis (New York: Routledge, 2006), 3.
50. Davis, "The Rule of Normalcy," 116.
51. Davis, "The Rule of Normalcy," 116.
52. Davis, "The Rule of Normalcy," 116.
53. This subheading is inspired by If I Can't Dance Is It Still My Revolution, a website promoting radical disability theory and politics. The website's name is inspired by the famous quote attributed to Emma Goldman, "If I can't dance it ain't my revolution." The author of this website is A. J. Withers, a disabled anti-poverty activist living in Toronto. He claims that disabled people have been and remain actively excluded from radical politics.
54. Boucher, Fougeyrollas, and Gaucher, "Development and Transformation of Advocacy," 140.
55. Henri Dorvil, "La psychiatrie au Québec: réalité d'hier, pratique d'aujourd'hui." 1981, http://classiques.uqac.ca/contemporains/dorvil_henri/psychiatrie_qc_hier_aujourdhui/psychiatrie_qc.html.
56. Québec. *Rapport (Castonguay-Nepveu) de la Commission d'enquête sur la santé et le bien-être social*, 7 vols., (Québec City, 1971).
57. Office des personnes handicapées du Québec, *La Grande Sortie*. This is my translation of the original quote.
58. Rob Kitchin, "'Out of Place,' 'Knowing One's Place': Space, Power and the Exclusion of Disabled People," *Disability and Society* 13, no. 3 (1998): 349.
59. Office des personnes handicapées du Québec, *La Grande Sortie*. This is my translation of the original quote.
60. Boucher, Fougeyrollas, and Gaucher, "Development and Transformation of Advocacy," 140.
61. Laurence Parent, "The Hegemony of Stairs in the Montréal Métro" (Major research paper, York University, 2010), 28. This is my translation of the original quote.
62. Parent, "The Hegemony of Stairs," 29. This is my translation of the original quote.
63. The Paralympic Games, which had previously been held in the same city as the Olympic Games (Rome 1960, Tokyo 1964), took place in Toronto in 1976. Since the Seoul Olympics in 1988, the Paralympic Games have been held in the same city as the Olympic Games (see "The History of the Paralympic Games" at https://www.paralympic.org/the-ipc/history-of-the-movement and "1976 Toronto" at https://www.insidethegames.biz/history/paralympics/1976-toronto).
64. Clairoux, *Le Métro de Montréal*.
65. Clairoux, *Le Métro de Montréal*, 50.
66. MysticMTL. "Il fait beau dans l'métro." Filmed November 2006. YouTube video available at http://www.youtube.com/watch?v=DcC31r1BxBY. This is my translation of the original lyrics.
67. Office des personnes handicapées du Québec, *La Grande Sortie*.

BIBLIOGRAPHY

Beau Dommage. "Où Est Passé la Noce?" Capitol Records, 1975.
Boucher, Normand, Patrick Fougeyrollas, and Charles Gaucher. "Development and Transformation of Advocacy in the Disability Movement of Quebec." In *Making Equality: History of Advocacy and Persons with Disabilities in Canada*, edited by Deborah Stienstra and Aileen Wight-Felske, 137–62. Concord: Captus Press, 2003.
Boucher, Normand, Patrick Fougeyrollas, and Pierre Majeau. "French-Speaking Contributions to the Disability Rights Movement in Canada and Internationally: From a Quebec Perspective." In *In Pursuit of Equal Participation: Canada and Disability at Home and Abroad*, edited by Aldred Neufeldt and Henry Enns, 169–95. Concord: Captus Press, 2003.
Campbell, Fiona Kumari. "Exploring Internalized Ableism Using Critical Race Theory." *Disability and Society* 23, no. 2 (2008): 151–62.
Clairoux, Benoît. *Le Métro de Montréal: 35 Ans Déjà*. Montreal: Hurtubise HMH, 2001.
Davis, Lennard J. "The Rule of Normalcy: Politics and Disability in the U.S.A. [United States of Ability]." In *Bending Over Backwards: Disability, Dismodernism and Other Difficult Positions*, edited by Lennard J. Davis, 103–12. New York: New York University Press, 2002.
Davis, Lennard J. "Constructing Normalcy: The Bell Curve, the Novel, and the Invention of the Disabled Body in the Nineteeth Century." In *The Disability Studies Reader*, edited by Lennard J. Davis, 3–16. New York: Routledge, 2006.
Deglise, Fabien. *Montréal Souterrain: Sous le Béton, le Mythe*. Montreal: Héliotrope, 2008.
Dorvil, Henri. "La psychiatrie au Québec: réalité d'hier, pratique d'aujourd'hui." 1981. http://classiques.uqac.ca/contemporains/dorvil_henri/psychiatrie_qc_hier_aujourdhui/psychiatrie_qc.html.
Freund, Peter. "Bodies, Disability and Spaces: The Social Model and Disabling Spatial Organisations." *Disability and Society* 16, no. 5 (2001): 689–706.
Godbout, Jacques, Marcel Jean, Michel Rivard, and Robert Saletti. *Le Québec Entre Deux Mondes*. Montreal: Les 400 Coups, 2007.
Guimont, Marc. *Montréal en Métro*. Montreal: Ulysse, 2007.
Imrie, Rob. "Barriered and Bounded Places and the Spatialities of Disability." *Urban Studies* 38, no. 2 (2008): 231–37.
Kitchin, Rob. "'Out of Place,' 'Knowing One's Place': Space, Power and the Exclusion of Disabled People." *Disability and Society* 13, no. 3 (1998): 343–56.
Linteau, Paul-André, René Durocher, Jean-Claude Robert, François Ricard, Robert Chodos, and Ellen Garmaise. *Quebec Since 1930*. Toronto: Lorimer, 1991.
MysticMTL. "Il fait beau dans l'métro." Filmed November 2006. YouTube video available at http://www.youtube.com/watch?v=DcC31r1BxBY.
Office des personnes handicapées du Québec, dir. *La Grande Sortie*. Quebec City, 1983.
Parent, Laurence. "The Hegemony of Stairs in the Montréal Métro." Major research paper, York University, 2010.
Pothier, Dianne, and Richard Devlin. *Critical Disability Theory: Essays in Philosophy, Politics, Policy, and Law*. Vancouver: UBC Press, 2006.
Prince, Michael J. *Absent Citizens: Disability Politics and Policy in Canada*. Toronto: University of Toronto Press, 2009.
Québec. *Rapport (Castonguay-Nepveu) de la Commission d'enquête sur la santé et le bien-être social*, 7 vols. Québec City, 1971.
Regroupement des Usagers du Transport Adapté et Accessible de l'Ile de Montréal. *Article sur le Légion canadienne en 1950*. http://rutamtl.com/lcta-1950.pdf (page no longer available).

Société Radio-Canada. *Le Métro de Montréal ou la Sous-Terre des Hommes*. Television. 1966. http://archives.radio-canada.ca/economie_affaires/transports/dossiers/1246/.

Société Radio-Canada. *Le Métro de Montréal 35 Ans Déjà!* Television. 2001. http://archives.radio-canada.ca/economie_affaires/transports/clips/6920/.

Spain, Daphne. *Gendered Spaces*. Chapel Hill: University of North Carolina Press, 1992.

Tremblay, Mary, Audrey Campbell, and Geoffrey Hudson. "When Elevators Were for Pianos: An Oral History Account of the Civilian Experience of Using Wheelchairs in Canadian Society. The First Twenty-Five Years: 1945–1970." *Disability and Society* 20, no. 2 (2005): 103–16.

Vujakovic, Peter, and M. H. Matthews. "Contorted, Folded, Torn: Environmental Values, Cartographic Representation and the Politics of Disability." *Disability and Society* 9, no. 3 (1994): 359–74.

Wolbring, Gregor. "Is There an End to Out-Able? Is There an End to the Rat Race for Abilities?" *M/C Journal* 11, no. 3 (2008): http://journal.media-culture.org.au/index.php/mcjournal/article/view/57.

CHAPTER 14

Organizing for Change: The Origins and History of the Manitoba League of the Physically Handicapped, 1967–1982

Diane Driedger

INTRODUCTION

Persons with physical disabilities, tired of being voiceless and powerless in making decisions about their own lives, decided to band together in the 1970s to struggle for changes in services and attitudes in society. They asserted that they were citizens with the same rights as all other citizens. In Manitoba, this led to the formation of the Manitoba League of the Physically Handicapped (MLPH) (later named the Manitoba League of Persons with Disabilities) in 1974. In the early years of the organization, 1974 to 1982, the MLPH fostered many changes in services and attitudes, developed businesses run by and for disabled persons, and expanded through rural branches. The MLPH was also involved in the formation of national and international coalitions of organizations of disabled people.

This chapter will trace the early years of MLPH and its origins. This is the history of disabled people's struggle to break out of the stereotype of "helpless cripples" who have nothing to contribute to society. As Jim Derksen reiterated in the MLPH newsletter in 1975,

> No longer can we remain the passive recipients of governmental and private helping programs. Let us reason together, let us deliberate on our problems and needs, let us consider our abilities, and when we have agreed on the problems and solutions let us articulate our opinions and ideas in a strong and united voice.[1]

DISABLED PEOPLE AFTER WORLD WAR II

The MLPH was formed due to a change in how people with disabilities expected to participate in society. In Canada, new medical and rehabilitation techniques after World War II meant that more disabled people survived and became more physically mobile;[2] however, they still did not make decisions about their own lives. Medical and rehabilitation experts evaluated what a disabled person could and could not do and treated that person as sick. Social workers reinforced this, and, in fact, labelled certain disabled persons "unemployable," while others were relegated to sheltered workshops to do repetitive work for two dollars a day. These experts often convinced parents that the best place for their blind, deaf, or mentally or physically disabled children was in separate schools and institutions. The 1940s and 1950s in Canada saw parents form organizations such as the Canadian Association for the Mentally Retarded, which were concerned with improving medical services and recreation facilities for their children. In the early 1950s, there was a major polio epidemic in Manitoba that disabled many children and young adults.[3]

The 1960s and 1970s can be viewed as an awakening for disabled people. New mobility aids, such as electric wheelchairs, ventilators, and better prostheses further increased the mobility of disabled persons. This meant that more disabled persons were surviving with their disabilities and they were becoming more mobile; this planted the seeds for people with disabilities to undertake their own struggle to participate in society.

AN AWAKENING

In the 1960s, Canadian disabled people watched the United States, where Ralph Nader's Raiders made consumers aware of their rights, and the black and women's rights movements increasingly protested. Disabled Vietnam War veterans started to protest for civil rights at the same time.[4] Soon, wheelchair sports associations were struck in Canada. Disabled people proved that they were fine athletes. Their sports associations were places where disabled people could meet to socialize and exchange ideas. These were the roots of the physically disabled people's movement in Manitoba.

In 1966, members of the Manitoba Wheelchair Sports Association suggested to the Pan American Games organizers in Winnipeg that there should be a parallel wheelchair sports event. Allan Simpson, one of the wheelchair sports association members, and others were told that it was against the rules.[5] They then proceeded to write to groups of wheelchair users in the United States, Mexico, Argentina, and Jamaica. In 1966, Simpson travelled to Mexico with a sports team and then to Jamaica and there was support for participation in the games. Finally, the Manitoba organization persuaded the Pan Am organizers that there was interest and Pan Am endorsed the wheelchair event, which would be held right after the Pan Am Games. The Manitoba group organized a Canadian wheelchair athletes' team and the wheelchair games were held after the Pan Am Games, as part of the event.

After the games, the Manitoba Wheelchair Sports Association continued to meet once a month. They began to realize that they had needs that were not being met and concerns that were not being addressed. They discussed the inadequate transportation for disabled persons who could not use regular bus systems because they could not board in wheelchairs or with crutches.

Indeed, a new consciousness was growing. In 1970, the federal minister of health and welfare, Marc Lalonde, reiterated in his speeches that social services had to start with agencies dialoguing with disabled persons themselves about their needs. The Canadian Rehabilitation Council for the Disabled (CRCD), an organization composed of rehabilitation organizations across Canada, decided to follow up on Lalonde's challenge.[6] Wilf Race, director of program services for the CRCD in Toronto, travelled to the council's member organizations in each province to promote the First National Conference of the Physically Disabled. This conference was to take place from November 4 to 7, 1973, at the Plaza Hotel in Toronto.[7] The CRCD hoped that this meeting would be the beginning of a national advisory committee to dialogue with and advise them, under the umbrella of their organization. Race asked each of the CRCD's provincial member organizations to send six delegates to the conference. Each disabled attendee would participate in workshops on one of six topics: housing, social integration, education, income maintenance, recreation, and transportation. All of these topics would be discussed in relation to the needs of disabled persons. The people selected were to represent disabled persons' concerns, not those of the rehabilitation agencies, and Race saw this as of the utmost importance, as he "stressed ... that although an agency might facilitate arrangements for a meeting, the actual appointment of delegates should be the prerogative of the handicapped persons themselves."[8]

The Society for Crippled Children and Adults of Manitoba, a member of the CRCD, organized the province's delegation. The director, Archie Carmichael, engaged the help of Tony Mann, a wheelchair user and director of the Canadian Paraplegic Association in Manitoba, and Janet Vickers, director of the Manitoba Wheelchair Sports Association, to find delegates with expertise in the different workshop areas.[9] The six delegates were Doug Boyles (education), Veronika Demereckas (housing), Charlie Grover (social integration), Jack Martin (income maintenance), Helen Smith (transportation), and Tim Thurston (recreation).[10]

At the 1973 conference in Toronto, the Manitoba delegates met people from Alberta and Saskatchewan who had recently formed self-help organizations of disabled people to lobby for change. In fact, Helen Smith, in a letter to R. S. Newman, director of administration at the Society for Crippled Children and Adults, dated November 15, 1973, wrote the following:

> The tenor of the Convention seemed to me to be one of strongly independent direction—that the physically disabled were highly dissatisfied with being considered, by the general public as adult Tiny Tims for whom said public feels vaguely sorry and forgets about as soon as it has done its duty by the United Way.[11]

Disabled persons agreed that their public image was not accurate and that education was needed, not only for the public, but also for disabled persons themselves, many of whom believed that they were helpless after having this ingrained by professional and public attitudes. Helen noted in a report on the conference that there was "a definite recognition of the fact that in order to achieve acceptance by society of the fact that one does not become a different person because of loss of mobility, the various obstacles that tend to set us apart[,] and one of the greatest is transportation and accessibility[,] must be rectified."[12] A national steering committee was formed at this meeting to work out the role of a disabled persons' advisory body in the CRCD.

The six delegates from Manitoba returned home and Helen wrote to a woman from the Saskatchewan disabled persons' group, the Voice of the Handicapped, asking for some information on their organization: "From the little you told me I formed the impression that it was an association which might well be worth knowing about before we have our general meeting here."[13] The six delegates called a meeting of disabled persons for January 28, 1974, to discuss the happenings of the convention. It appears that Tony Mann of the Canadian Paraplegic Association drew together the participants through phone calls and notices to other disability organizations, such as the CNIB, the Wheelchair Sports Association, and the Society for Crippled Children and Adults of Manitoba.[14] The meeting was held in a second-floor boardroom at the office of the society; between 50 and 60 people attended. The majority of those in attendance were wheelchair users, but there were also blind and hearing-impaired persons and some friends and relatives. The tone of the meeting was low-key and matter-of-fact. One theme that was reiterated throughout the meeting was that disabled persons should organize themselves in Manitoba. The delegates undoubtedly reported that groups had recently been formed in Alberta and Saskatchewan. They then discussed whether disabled persons should have an ongoing relationship with the Disabled Persons Committee of the CRCD. Instead of a motion on that issue, the group moved that a steering committee be set up to formulate a proposal outlining the workings, structure, function, and responsibilities of an independent, cross-disability self-help organization of disabled persons in Manitoba.[15] The steering committee would call another meeting of disabled people within a few months to accept the basic organizational structure, elect executive officers, and conduct any other business.[16] This motion was passed and people were asked to volunteer for this committee. Len Schmidt, one of the volunteers, was responsible for calling the new steering committee together.[17]

In all, the steering committee had 11 members: 7 men and 4 women, who were from European backgrounds. The committee met in the homes of its members every few weeks from February to June 1974. The committee discussed whether the new organization should be a structure of representatives from different organizations, such as the Muscular Dystrophy Association and the CNIB, or whether membership should be of individuals. Some people felt that service agency representation was preferable because then all the disability groups would be represented. In addition, some members felt that social service organizations should be included because disabled persons should be grateful for the services they had been given. One visually impaired person remembered when there were no services at all. Some individuals felt that perhaps disabled people should not ask for too many more privileges in society. Other people reiterated that the population was not just split into disabled and non-disabled persons; rather, everyone has disabilities and, therefore, there is no clear distinction between "us" and "them." There is a continuum of disabilities and so a line cannot be drawn with those on one side relegated to accepting less in the way of rights than those on the other side. The group also noted that each different service group might have its own mandate and, thus, it would be difficult for them to work together.

The group decided that the new organization would be one of disabled individuals or "consumers." Disabled persons are consumers of services and, therefore, they should have the right to identify their wants and needs regarding the services offered to them. This organization would also be able to approach government at all levels regarding problems and concerns. It would be non-partisan.

The questions of whether non-disabled persons and persons with intellectual disabilities could join were debated at length. It was decided that non-disabled persons who agreed with the aims of the organization could be associate members, who would be allowed to vote, but not to hold executive office or head a committee.[18] Regarding the membership of persons with intellectual disabilities, the members of the steering committee agreed that they did not wish to be identified with this group. Their view was that for so long society had viewed physically disabled persons as having intellectual as well as physical disabilities; therefore, they agreed that physically disabled persons must assert themselves as a separate group.[19] The organization would be open to any person "whose physical impairment from any cause, inhibits or prohibits his right and opportunity to full participation and the privilege of choice, usually due to a loss of normal physical mobility in varying degrees."[20]

The steering committee also decided that the organization would be based in Winnipeg and that rural branches would be established over time. The committee then debated the name of the organization, and decided to call it the Manitoba League of the Physically Handicapped. "League" was chosen because it referred to "a compact made between groups or individuals for mutual aid and the promotion of common interests."[21] It was also important that this be a league *of* disabled persons, as service agencies had been acting and speaking out *for* disabled persons.

The steering committee submitted its report to another general meeting of disabled persons at the Kinsmen Centre in early June of 1974, which was attended by 32 people. The report was accepted and an executive was elected with Len Schmidt as chairperson.[22]

ORGANIZING FORCES

During the summer of 1974, the MLPH planned for its first public meeting on transportation in November. The head of Winnipeg's Transit Department, Roy Church, the chairman of the Works and Operations Committee of the City, Gerald Mercier, and a federal representative on transportation named Avrum Riggestrof attended this meeting, which was attended by a hundred disabled persons. It was "the first concerted public protest by the disabled against the steadily worsening transportation situation."[23] Many disabled persons had no choice but to hire private wheelchair vans at $40 for a two-way trip. Many persons could not afford this at all. Medical appointments and social events were difficult enough to get to, but those trying to hold down full-time jobs in the community found it almost impossible. Thus, lack of access to transportation isolated disabled people and kept them out of public places. As Kitchener MP Peter Lang, member of the Committee on the Handicapped and Disabled, observed, "Never mind the back of the bus, the disabled still can't get on the bus."[24]

By the end of this public meeting, it was clear that public transportation was not usable for many disabled persons, and, in response, the members established a league transportation committee with Helen Smith as chairperson.[25] The purpose of this committee was to bring transportation needs to the attention of the proper municipal and provincial departments, the Works and Operations Committee of the city, and the provincial government's Department of Urban Affairs. The Transportation Committee met at least monthly and sometimes even more often to discuss and research the many aspects of transportation. Over the next few years, between 60 and 80 people attended some of its meetings. In the beginning they explored what the nature of a new system should be. Should it be contracted out to a private van operator and paid for by the city? It was decided over time that it would need to be a service subsidized by public funds and that it should be under the umbrella of city transit; it would be a parallel transit system. After all, disabled people were citizens who paid taxes for the regular bus system, which they could not even ride! Disabled persons, as citizens, were entitled to transportation. In the meantime, the league and the Works and Operations Committee of the City had openly communicated. The committee passed a resolution to investigate the situation and hired a firm of consultants to do so in December 1974.[26]

The league organized an open meeting on May 12, 1975, to discuss the progress made toward the goal of a city-subsidized transit system for physically disabled people. About 70 people, including city councillors McGonigal, Dixon, Zuken, and Corrin, attended the meeting. The councillors maintained that adequate transportation was a right of disabled citizens. There were indications at this meeting that a pilot project could be started within a year.

The summer of 1975 saw the hiring of the first league staff on a Secretary of State Summer Student Grant.[27] At first there was no office where the staff could work, but the MLPH soon found space on the main floor of the Kinsmen Centre in the office of the Society for Crippled Children and Adults of Manitoba, across from the reception desk. Near the end of the summer, the staff moved into a larger office on the second floor of the same building. The staff organized the office during the summer and began to work on a membership drive. They probably were also involved in the process of incorporating the MLPH.

The MLPH was incorporated on August 8, 1975.[28] Soon after, it moved to obtain a charitable status number. It appears the legal processes were not done without difficulty. A letter from staff person Brian Stewart thanking a person who contributed to the organization indicates these problems: "Unfortunately the League has had difficulty in getting the proper legal advice and the process of receiving one's tax number is a slow one. Hence we are unable at this time to give an official receipt for your cheque."[29] In a sense this reveals the inexperience of the group at this time. Everyone was new to this kind of organization. Jim Derksen, a wheelchair user, came into contact with the league in 1975 and wondered whether he wished to join such a naive group, which he felt "seemed to be very inexperienced and 'naive'! Secondly, the group was full of hope that somehow they would be able to effect change. Unfortunately, I succumbed to the temptation of thinking I was too busy to spend time working against complex problems with such an apparently inexperienced group."[30] Derksen later decided that disabled persons must have a unified voice to bring about changes and, even though he felt that he was more educated than a lot of the members, he joined the organization. In fact, he joined the MLPH as a volunteer under the Company of Young Canadians, a federal program, in August 1975 for a year. He was to assist in fundraising, public awareness, and branch development.

The summer of 1975 also saw the beginnings of a new branch in The Pas, which was founded in September. This group also identified transportation as one of the biggest problems in their community.[31]

Meanwhile, in Winnipeg, the league's lobby for transit continued. In late 1975, three members of the Transportation Committee met with the head of transit, the chairman of the Works and Operations Committee of the City, and senior staff from the city. A provincial official also sat in on this advisory group.[32]

Shortly before the formation of this group, the league held its fall conference and annual general meeting at the Convention Centre from October 10 to 12, 1975. The issues of the conference were housing, public education, architectural barriers, and human rights. The tone of the conference was one of being against charity images and campaigns, as Derksen reported in the newsletter, *Challenger*:

> The handicapped are tired of this kind of paternalism which is as rampant and visible towards our group as it is toward groups such as the Canadian Indians.... They (disabled people) are tired of fundraising campaigns which maintain the image of their being objects of charity only and especially of such campaigns into which they have little or no input as to how the money raised is going to be spent.[33]

A NATIONAL VOICE

The seeds of a new national organization also began to germinate in the midst of this conference. The MLPH had invited people from the Voice of the Handicapped in Saskatchewan and the Alberta Committee of Action Groups for the Disabled as resource speakers and observers. After the sessions during the day at the conference, league representatives met with them, and the idea of a "Western Alliance" of disabled people was discussed. They decided that they would meet early in the new year to look at the possibility of such a coalition.

The representatives of the three provinces met in January 1976 in Regina. It became apparent that a Western Alliance would not be able to have much of an impact on the federal government in Ottawa. Only a national federation of provincial organizations, speaking directly to the federal government, would have clout. They planned the framework for the Coalition of Provincial Organizations of the Handicapped (COPOH, now the Council of Canadians with Disabilities). By September 1976, British Columbia and Ontario had joined, and Prince Edward Island and Newfoundland were expected to join as well.[34] The seed planted in Manitoba had sprung into a national coalition and more provinces joined in the ensuing years.

Meanwhile, the MLPH continued to expand through membership and new branches. The membership of the league was more than 120 people by this time.[35] Ruby Miller, Peter Zacharias, and Henry Enns, the students hired to work for the league during the summer of 1976, successfully worked on branch development. The Brandon Branch had set up a steering committee by the fall of 1976. Steinbach, or Eastman Region, also founded a branch in August. The students also made contacts in Winkler and Altona.

LOBBYING FOR VICTORY

As a result of public demonstrations and lobbying, 1976 was a successful year for the MLPH. League representatives had been meeting with the advisory group on transportation since the fall of 1975. On April 26, 1976, in its presentation to the Works and Operations Committee of the City, this group recommended a transportation system for disabled persons. The league amassed a large delegation of its members and packed the boardroom where the meeting was taking place. Jim Derksen, research coordinator at that time, made a speech on behalf of the MLPH, reiterating that

> the City of Winnipeg now provides a "public transportation" system available to all non-handicapped persons who wish to use it during hours of operations.... It is therefore, an established city policy: a) to make public means of transportation available and, b) to charge only a minimal fare to the user.[36]

He also pointed out that disabled persons should enjoy the benefits of this policy for that would be consistent "with the principles of natural justice or equity or opportunities for all residents.[37] The Works and Operations Committee voted "to adopt the responsibility for transportation of the disabled and embark on a two-year demonstration project."[38]

After this decision, the league's Transportation Committee lobbied each city councillor individually on this resolution before the city councillors met in May. The league members appeared in full force at city hall for the council meeting on May 5, lending visible support once again to the transit proposal. The *Winnipeg Tribune* reported that "thirty persons in wheelchairs were crowded around the gallery doors and outside the chamber, unable to be accommodated in the gallery seats."[39] The council chamber was inaccessible for persons in wheelchairs. Allan Simpson, chair of the MLPH, and Elizabeth Semkiw, Transportation Committee chair, had to be carried down a set of stairs to the council chamber floor to make their presentations on behalf of the league. Simpson stated that disabled persons had been left out of the planning of services in societies and, therefore, their needs had not been met. After two years of meeting with city council, the MLPH felt that transportation needs could be met. Simpson also stated that the "Handi-Transit system would do more for the re-entry of disabled persons into the industrial and social mainstream of our community than all the billions spent on rehabilitation in recent years."[40] Indeed, increased mobility opens up employment, social, and educational opportunities for disabled persons. Semkiw also reminded the council that other centres across Canada had such transit systems and therefore it had been proven as a workable system.[41]

The city council unanimously approved the project and agreed to a $500,000 two-year demonstration project to be funded jointly by the city and the province.

The league's representatives continued to meet with the advisory group, which included the province and the city. They issued tenders for contracting out the Handi-Transit system to already existing van operators. No offers came, so the City of Winnipeg took responsibility for running the system, ordering buses, and training drivers. The system began operations in the summer of 1977. The MLPH had representatives on the newly formed Operations Advisory Committee of Handi-Transit, composed of the head of transit, the director of Handi-Transit, and a representative from city planning. They received comments and complaints about the system in Winnipeg.[42] On the rural scene, van transportation was achieved in The Pas in 1975. This transportation was funded through a federal Local Initiatives Program Grant and it continued to run through 1976 with no fare charged to disabled persons.[43]

The league also dealt with several other issues in 1976. A special general meeting was called on May 20, 1976, to discuss the Department of Health and Social Development's Rehabilitation Division proposals to segregate disabled persons with all kinds of mental and physical disabilities into combined sheltered employment workshops and training facilities. One hundred members showed up to voice their opinions against this proposal. The league believed that, first of all, disabled people should be in the community working, but those persons working in workshop situations should not all be lumped together. The government saw "integration" as integration of all disabilities together instead of being integrated into society! At the time, members of the MLPH did not wish to be classified with mentally ill and mentally handicapped persons in the same workshops. They felt that the public would then generalize that all persons in these workshops were mentally handicapped as well as physically handicapped. The MLPH passed a resolution calling for the provincial government to consult with the league and other groups and service agencies before adopting such a policy.[44] The government backed down on this issue and did not implement these workshops.[45]

The issue of integrated education for disabled children arose as well. In the past many disabled persons did not receive proper schooling because they were not integrated into the regular school systems. Often segregated schools were not available either. Jim Derksen wrote in the April 1976 *Challenger*, the newsletter of the MLPH, "I have talked to older members who never learned how to read or write because they were handicapped at a very early age during the time when it was thought that handicapped people had no need of education and when the school systems were unwilling to have them."[46] The provincial government passed Bill 58 in 1975, which stated that, "to the maximum extent practicable, handicapped children shall be educated along with children who do not have handicaps and shall attend regular classes."[47] This section met with opposition from parents of both disabled and non-disabled children, teachers, and school administrators because they felt that the regular school system did not have the aids needed to deal with this. For example, blind students would need Braille and tape resources. Schools that were not accessible, with many stairs and no ramps or elevators, would need to be revamped. To counter some of the opposition, Ben Hanuschak, minister of education, wrote to the Manitoba teachers saying that this bill would not be implemented until the classrooms were ready for disabled students. He also said that there was money available for each school to start the preparation process; however, the government did not impose a timeline for schools to achieve this goal. Thus, the bill was passed, but not proclaimed as law. The league formed a Bill 58 Committee to start to lobby to have the bill proclaimed, and then to have a timeline with different stages for gradual implementation of the measure.

EMPLOYMENT OPPORTUNITIES AND HUMAN RIGHTS

The league also formed an employment committee in 1977 to study the employment situation of disabled people. This committee was struck at the Fall Conference on Employment at the Convention Centre, which was held on October 16 and 17. According to Jim Derksen, anyone who attended the conference "couldn't miss feeling the ground swell [*sic*] of growing frustration and rebellion with their apparent rejection as significant potential contributors to productivity."[48] In Manitoba, 7 to 10 percent of the population was thought to be disabled at the time and their potential was being ignored. Many social workers told their clients that they were unemployable. Professionals and the public assumed that if a person could not walk, see, or hear they were incapable of using their hands, voice, and mind to work effectively.

In response to these issues, the MLPH's Employment Committee began to look into different employment concepts and models to further the integration of disabled persons into jobs in the community. The league learned of a federal program for job creation, a division of Manpower, and applied for a project to create businesses run by disabled persons. This project was to be called CONCEPT—Special Business Advisors,[49] and it would include coordinating a convention service called ManEvents, which would book halls and tours, organize meals, and do the paperwork for a convention. Another business under the umbrella of CONCEPT would plan socials for weddings and other events. VIP telephone services, which would do phoning for doctors and businesses, would also be included. Disabled people who had difficulty finding employment in the community would be hired to work in these businesses, and would make at least minimum wage. The government accepted this proposal and CONCEPT began operations in 1977 with a community board of directors—many board members were also members of the league. This project was then independent of the MLPH. The league, a lobby group, did not wish to be involved in providing services. It saw its role as being a monitor of service delivery systems. After several years of operation, the businesses under the CONCEPT umbrella had not made a profit and, thus, the convention and banquet services were suspended. A community training program then became a part of CONCEPT. Through the program, disabled persons would gain employment experience and skills in the community in preparation for more permanent employment in the community.[50]

The MLPH experienced other successes in 1977. The greatest of these was the amending of the Human Rights Act in Manitoba in May to protect physically disabled persons from discrimination in all areas of life including employment. Nine members of the league met with Attorney General Howard Pawley on the question of human rights on March 3, 1977. At this time, Pawley promised to do his best to include a human rights amendment into the current legislative session.[51]

The MLPH lobbied the government for three months before the passing of the act. The government agreed quite quickly to the league's request for an amendment.[52] The act was passed in the legislature in June 1977. Allan Simpson, chair of the MLPH, sent a telegram on behalf of the league to the Speaker congratulating the legislature on the passage of the bill, in which he observed that this "will mark the beginning of a new era for citizens who are physically handicapped which will permit us to accept our full opportunity and responsibilities in all levels of society."[53] This telegram was copied and passed out to each member of the Legislature on June 17, 1977.

SUCCESS AND EXPANSION

Many disabled persons were organizing for their rights over the summer of 1977. In July, a new branch, the Central Branch of the MLPH, was formed in the Altona/Winkler area. Summer staff working for the Eastman Branch organized a rural conference, which was held September 10 and 11. The conference brought together 80 representatives from The Pas, Brandon, Eastman, and Central branches to discuss architectural barriers, recreation, education (Bill 58), and rural transportation. The overall theme was integration and the conference was considered a great success.[54]

In the fall of 1977, the provincial election campaign was in process as well. The MLPH sent out a challenge ballot (titled "Our Challenge") to each of the candidates, asking them to state their position on disabled persons and their rights in education, employment, rural transportation, recreation, and home care. The rural transportation challenge (or question), for instance, read, "Are you prepared to support and commit government funds for a rural transportation policy and program for people with special transportation needs in the rural areas of Manitoba?"[55] Of the 40 candidates who responded to this, more responses came from NDP candidates than those representing any other party.[56]

The league continued its political challenges in 1978 when nine members of the league's council and office staff met with nine cabinet ministers on June 5. The MLPH presented a brief outlining its positions on housing, support services or home care, education, transportation, and architectural barriers. The government responded favourably to the league's request for an integrated approach in all of these areas. Each minister acknowledged the responsibility of their department to the physically disabled citizens in Manitoba. No longer would the Department of Health deal with all the needs of disabled persons, who had been seen as "sick" patients in the past.[57]

The MLPH also started a new employment venture in 1978. It received an Outreach Development Grant from Canada Employment and Immigration to set up E-Quality Employment for a six-month demonstration. Through this project, three people were hired to study the employment situation of disabled people, start a resource centre with data pertinent to the employment of disabled people, and prepare a proposal for longer term funding. E-Quality would provide seminars for disabled job seekers on how to look for work and write resumes, and would also undertake awareness-raising with employers in the community concerning the abilities of disabled workers.[58] This was not set up as a job placement service; according to the organization's pamphlet, "we do however, provide job seekers and employers with information that will help bring them together while preserving personal independence and individual responsibility."[59] This service was incorporated in March 1979 and continued its operations under the Outreach Development Grant. Again, this service was independent of the league and was monitored by a community board.

The MLPH also assisted COPOH in hosting the First Open National Conference on Employment in Winnipeg from June 23 to 25, 1978. This conference brought together disabled persons from across Canada. Employment was affirmed as a right of all persons during the sessions, and community-based employment was seen as the best alternative for disabled people. Bud Sherman, Manitoba health minister; Senator Joseph-Philippe Guay; Gordon Fairweather, Canadian human rights commissioner; and Terry O'Rourke, head of the American Coalition of Citizens with Disabilities were among the speakers at the conference. After the conference, COPOH produced a hundred-page report, which was sent out to government and other organizations around Canada. This exposure brought national attention to COPOH, a force to be reckoned with on the national level.

The MLPH had other successes of its own in 1978. The Eastman Branch received a Canada Works Grant in late 1977 to run their handi-van transportation service. They hired several drivers and operated several vans. Later, in September 1979, the handi-van received $15,000 from the provincial government to continue the operations of the van service.[60] At the same time, the van service started in The Pas in 1975 continued to operate.

The accessibility of buildings was an important issue at this time as well. The Stadium Committee of the league changed its name to the Community Access and Use Committee, or CAUSE. Early in 1978, after intensive lobbying of the owners of Winnipeg Stadium, Winnipeg Enterprises Corporation, the league received written commitment for 46 wheelchair-seating spaces on the top part of the lower deck in the east stands. This committee continued to lobby the provincial government to make the inclusion of wheelchair seating in public buildings, including theatres and entertainment places, binding under the Manitoba Building Code.[61]

CONFLICT: VOLUNTEERS VERSUS STAFF

Amidst these successes there was conflict between staff members and the executive, council and committee members, and membership at large working within the MLPH. The executive was concerned that volunteers were becoming reluctant to volunteer time in the office putting together the newsletter, typing, and doing general office work as they had done as recently as 1977, when Brian Stewart was the coordinator of the organization. The council wanted the staff to encourage volunteers to come to the office, and to make them feel wanted and welcome when they did volunteer. Staff argued that if a lot of different volunteers were in the office several times a week they would be disruptive and efficiency would decrease. The council decided that there had to be a balance worked out between staff and volunteers while still maintaining efficiency. In practice, this equilibrium was difficult to achieve. And, overall, it appeared that volunteerism was declining in the membership.[62] This led to questions about the structure and relationships of the council, its branches, and the members. The league had grown to a membership of 400 persons from a small core four years before and had established four new branches. Henry Enns, chair, wrote the following in the 1978 annual report:

> Can our existing structure accommodate the rapid expansion? How can we spread out the workload and get more membership involvement? Is there a feeling of alienation of the membership from the Provincial Council and if so how can this gap be bridged? How can we make the League truly a provincial organization and give due status to our branches?[63]

These problems continued in 1979. At this time the staff grew even larger. The MLPH received three simultaneous government grants for different periods of time. Most staff members were stationed in Winnipeg, with 14 people working at the different branches around the province. Staff were to act as research support persons for the Volunteer Committee, help put out the newsletter, and undertake fundraising projects and branch communications and development. A second office was opened up on Sargent Avenue to accommodate the extra staff hired to do the work funded by the grants. The three projects were all facilitated and monitored by one provincial coordinator who reported to the council and executive. This again created some problems for the members of the league. There was a high turnover of staff, and according to the grants, workers were hired for a year or even less. Volunteers often did not know the people in the office or who was in charge of what. This situation of confusion prompted Brian Stewart, chairman, to write in the 1979 annual report, "I am personally sorry about this, for as a volunteer also, I would have liked to see a steady staff who were well-versed to our needs. I think that as a Council we have realized that in the future we must be careful not to overload the League with staff."[64] After the year was over, Josie Concepcion, league secretary, was the only person to continue working, as her position had permanent funding.

The apparent shortcomings of the league's structure prompted the council to accept an offer from the Manitoba School of Social Work to conduct an organizational evaluation of the MLPH. The school researched and published *The Manitoba League of the Physically Handicapped: An Organizational Evaluation*. It provided background to the branches and committees of the league and identified its problems. First of all, the rural branches felt that the council was most concerned with Winnipeg's issues, and that communication between Winnipeg and their branches was insufficient. Another identified problem was the staff and volunteer participation in the organization. Volunteers were not participating in the organization as readily as in the early days of the MLPH. These problems were already recognized in annual reports and in the league's newsletter (now the *Update*, as *Challenger* had been too expensive to continue). In fact, some members, such as Bea Bardsley, felt that this evaluation was redundant: "It is obvious that these areas that are considered to be important by the Provincial Council and office staff are not as important to the general membership.... The Provincial Council, in their wisdom, decided that what the League really needed was to be analyzed and evaluated by a number of Social Work students."[65] Needless to say, the organizational problems were not solved within one year.

TAKING TO THE STREETS

In the midst of internal struggles, the MLPH reacted to external issues. The historic street crossing at Portage and Main was closed to overland pedestrian traffic and an underground concourse was opened in 1979. Persons in wheelchairs had a difficult enough time crossing this busy intersection before the opening of the concourse, but the situation was compounded now by the fact that there were only elevators down to the concourse crossing on two of the four corners. Organizations representing disabled persons, such as the Canadian Paraplegic Association, had asked for four elevators two years before. Their requests were met only halfway; thus, it would take a wheelchair user 20 minutes to cross to the other side of the street.

On Friday, March 9, 1979, some members of the MLPH joined Councillor Joe Zuken in an illegal overland crossing at Portage and Main. Zuken was upset that people could no longer cross this historic corner overland and he also supported the right of a disabled person to have proper access to a public crossing. At noon on that day, 25 people, including

6 persons in wheelchairs, crossed the intersection overland and made three circuits of the intersection with some aid from the police.[66] About 100 people watched in the −47 degree Celsius weather and police took down the names of the demonstrators. The city took no immediate action on this protest. Several disabled persons filed complaints with the Human Rights Commission concerning the crossing, but there was no action taken against the concourse development.[67]

In June, the MLPH once again organized into a protest. In 1979, the City Works and Operations Committee was evaluating Handi-Transit's two pilot years of operation. Winnipeg City Council was to set up a small ad hoc committee to review the service and hear briefs about the system. This committee was to provide the review needed for Works and Operations to give final approval to Handi-Transit under the City Transit umbrella. Soon after this ad hoc committee's first meeting on June 21, it was disbanded by city council. The city had received an offer from a private operator who claimed he could operate Handi-Transit more efficiently than the city under its regular transit system. City council opted to wait for the operator's final proposal in July instead of reviewing the current situation right away. The MLPH began to protest against this action. The league wanted Handi-Transit to continue under City Transit since disabled persons were citizens as deserving of city-run transit as other Winnipeg citizens. The MLPH's Transportation Committee organized a protest at city hall, and 40 wheelchair users packed the boardroom where the meeting of the Works and Operations Committee of the City was held. One person suggested that it would be a good tactic to totally encircle those meeting around the boardroom table since it would give the league members a psychological edge. The protesters adopted this tactic, and Mike Rosner, Transportation Committee chairman, presented a brief to the committee: "Handi-Transit would severely regress if taken from its rightful place under the Winnipeg Transit Department and we will not allow this backward development to take place, regardless of what council, what medium or what political level we must call upon."[68] The MLPH won its bid to have the ad hoc committee restored, and the review of the system commenced. The private operator's offer to operate the system was refused. Ultimately, Handi-Transit was approved as a permanent operation under City Transit.

Many issues were resolved in 1979, but the fate of Bill 58 and the right to integrated education was still pending. In fact, the new Conservative government in Manitoba introduced a wrinkle into the situation when it introduced Bill 22, a new Public Schools Act. Bill 58 still remained unproclaimed at that time. Bill 22 was not as progressive as Bill 58. The league's Education Committee met with the minister of education to lobby for more comprehensive legislation. As a result of the concerns expressed by the MLPH and other groups, the passing of Bill 22 was delayed to provide an opportunity for public hearings. The league presented its brief to the hearing in October. At this point, the Education Committee asked the league's membership to write letters to their MLAs about the bill. Committee members also appeared on CBC's *24 Hours*, a news and current affairs program, to publicize their views.[69]

This lobbying resulted in an amendment to Bill 22. Bill 31 was added to the proposed bill and again public hearings were held to allow concerned people input into the legislation. The MLPH presented its brief to the hearings in early July of 1980.

AN INTERNATIONAL VOICE, AN INTERNATIONAL YEAR

The relationship between league staff and volunteers continued to be contentious. The three grants had all run out by the summer of 1980 and seven summer student staff were hired to work in Winnipeg and at the various branches. It appeared that volunteer participation had fallen off almost completely in the office. Of course, many members continued to participate in committees, but now the committees seemed to meet less often. Staff complained of not having enough direction and help from the volunteer committees that they worked with.

The early summer of 1980, however, was an active time for the league's staff and volunteers as they participated in the World Congress of Rehabilitation International. Some league members attended as delegates. Rehabilitation International (RI) is an organization of social workers and rehabilitation professionals concerned with disability. Before the congress, COPOH became a member of this organization. COPOH is not an organization of professionals, but an organization representing disabled people; therefore its motives for joining RI and sending delegates were different than those of most of the other organizations represented at this congress. Representatives of the MLPH attended the COPOH Workshop on Rehabilitation in Ottawa in 1979. The people with disabilities there decided that rehabilitation services provided by professionals—including transportation, education, employment, and housing—should not encompass the lives of disabled people; rather, these should be provided in the community through the delivery systems set up for all citizens. Furthermore, at a COPOH conference in 1980 in Vancouver, the concept of disabled persons living in the community in the same manner as other citizens was endorsed by the delegates. COPOH's goal entering the RI congress was to promote the philosophy of independent living. Two of the COPOH representatives, Jim Derksen and Allan Simpson, who were also members of the league, presented papers on consumer self-help organizations of disabled people and traditional charity and medical ethics. These papers stressed that professionals in particular have seen disabled persons as sick people, unable to make decisions in their own lives, who are desperately in need of professional help.

Also attending the congress were 300 disabled professionals from over 40 countries. Manitoba league and COPOH staff and volunteers organized three consumer self-help sessions primarily for those disabled persons attending the congress. These sessions, held outside the RI sessions, allowed disabled persons to interact and share information about what was happening in their countries concerning disabled people. In addition, COPOH set up a "consumerism" office on the second floor of the Winnipeg Convention Centre to provide information and serve as a social gathering place for disabled delegates.

In the midst of this, the disabled delegates from Sweden introduced a resolution on the floor of the RI congress, asking for more participation of disabled persons in the decision-making of the organization. This resolution was defeated. This negative response caused "the handicapped people who were members of RI to become radicals outside RI."[70] When the resolution was defeated, a bond was created between the Canadian disabled delegates associated with COPOH and the other disabled delegates from around the world. These delegates broke away from RI to form a World Coalition of Disabled Persons at an after-session meeting organized by COPOH on June 25. The 300 disabled persons present elected a steering committee with representatives from the five regions of the world. Henry Enns of Canada, a league member, was elected chairman of the committee. This steering committee was to draft a constitution for the organization and plan for a cross-disability world congress of disabled people in 1981.

Disabled peoples' assertion of their right to speak for themselves on an international level was a fitting prelude to 1981, the United Nations International Year of Disabled Persons. The MLPH speculated on the potential impact of 1981 at its 1980 fall conference, entitled 1981 International Year of the Disabled Person: Will It Make Any Difference? Frank Rogodzinski, chairman of the league, observed that much had been gained in the previous decade, but there was much more to fight for:

> We must demand the right to be heard and accept the responsibility that these demands entail.... We now have a variety of integrated housing developments while at the same time we have persons with physical handicaps living in institutions. We have handicapped persons working more than ever before, while at the same time we have many unemployed or underemployed persons with physical handicaps who do not have the confidence to look for a job.[71]

Many disabled people did not have access to transportation in the rural areas of Manitoba going into 1981 either. After several years of lobbying, Don Orchard, minister of highways and transportation, approved a program designed to assist communities that had already initiated rural transportation services for disabled persons. This was the long-awaited victory of the Rural Transportation Committee. The province would grant monies to existing services in The Pas, Steinbach, and Neepawa.[72]

In this same year, The Pas branch sponsored a demonstration of the abilities of disabled people. Francis Mackay, a wheelchair user, wheeled 630 kilometres from The Pas to Winnipeg. The marathon created awareness and also raised $16,000 through sponsors. This money went towards making the buildings of The Pas accessible.[73]

The league was awarded a four-year Canadian Community Services Project entitled Handicapped Consumer Development for the '80s. The MLPH was able to hire four persons during 1981 under this grant. Again, staff were responsible for the office work, newsletter, and most of the research. Volunteers were still involved at the committee levels. It has been speculated that the drop in membership participation in the late 1970s and early 1980s had to do with the lack of specific tangible issues to rally around. The struggle to achieve Handi-Transit was a goal that a lot of people could identify with, and was also ultimately realized. Issues of public awareness and accessibility rarely showed tangible results—these were ongoing struggles.[74]

In December of 1981, the First World Congress of Disabled Persons was held in Singapore. The Steering Committee of the World Coalition of Disabled Persons, formed in 1980 and later renamed Disabled Peoples' International (DPI), organized the congress. Again, several members of the MLPH attended as delegates representing COPOH and others helped to organize the congress itself. At the congress, 400 delegates from 53 countries adopted the constitution and elected a world council and a chairperson, Ron Chandran-Dudley from Singapore. Henry Enns, a member of the league, was elected deputy chairperson. Canada was given the mandate by the world council to operate an office in Winnipeg to develop self-help projects of, for, and by disabled persons in the developing regions of the world.[75]

At the MLPH's 1982 fall conference, the concept of independent living was discussed. The idea discussed was that disabled persons should live in the community like other people in society, but there was often a lack of adequate services to enable many disabled persons, especially severely disabled persons, to do so. The provincial government provided support services, such as orderlies to help people get up in the morning and go to the washroom at various times of the day, but this was not enough help for some disabled people. The league looked at ways to lobby the government for a better home care or support services system in terms of both quantity of hours available and better-trained staff. Even if services were available, many disabled people in institutions would not know how to go about getting them. Disabled people also needed the confidence to move out on their own, and many disabled persons lacked that confidence. Thus, the MLPH began to consider the independent living centre concept that was in operation in the United States. These are resource centres run by disabled persons, who live on their own in the community. They conduct peer counselling for other disabled people on how to live in the community, and share information about services and contacts that enable a person to live more independently. Disabled persons saw that they had the right to have the opportunity to live their lives as independently as possible.

CONCLUSION

In 2014, the league (now renamed the Manitoba League of Persons with Disabilities) celebrated its 40th anniversary. The league continues to fight for changes in attitudes and public policies to ensure that people with all types of physical and mental disabilities are able to live and work in the community as full citizens. The MLPH fostered many changes in its early years that increased opportunities and independence for disabled people. Disabled persons united not only provincially, but also nationally and internationally, into a confident and insistent voice for change, as Jim Derksen wrote in 1975 in the *Challenger*,

To all I say, that even if we do not gain our personal aims, we may blaze a trail that will help future generations to a fuller, richer life. In so doing we will have made an extremely valuable contribution to our fellowmen [sic]. What would we have today if pioneers had not faced loneliness and weariness and pain to build what we now enjoy?[76]

NOTES

1. Jim Derksen, "Editorial Comment," *Challenger*, no. 1 (July 1975): 1.
2. *The Disability Myth*, a film directed by Alan Ayleward, Lauron Productions, 1982.
3. Henry Enns, "Canadian Society and Disabled People: Issues for Discussion," *Canada's Mental Health*, December 1981, 1–2; Diane Driedger, *The Last Civil Rights Movement: Disabled Peoples' International* (London and New York: Hurst and Co. and St. Martin's Press, 1989), 8–9.
4. Leah Morton, "From Nose Sprays to Nursing Shortages: Managing Epidemic Polio in Manitoba, 1928–1953," *Manitoba History*, no. 66 (Spring 2011): 20–21.
5. Val Ross, "Demanding Access for All," *Maclean's*, April 20, 1981, 50; Driedger, *The Last Civil Rights Movement*.
6. Peter Carlyle-Gordge, "No Handicap to Success," *Today Magazine*, January 10, 1981, 6.
7. Allan Simpson, interview, February 16, 1983.
8. "A Conference with a Difference," *ParaTracks* 2, no. 3 (July-August 1973): 7.
9. "A Conference with a Difference," *ParaTracks*.
10. The Society for Crippled Children and Adults of Manitoba, letter to National Conference of Disabled People participants, October 24, 1973.
11. Helen Smith, letter to R. S. Newman, November 15, 1973.
12. Smith, letter to R. S. Newman, November 15, 1973.
13. Helen Smith, letter to Jenny _____, November 16, 1973.
14. Helen Smith, letter to Wilf Race, January 3, 1974; Simpson, interview, February 16, 1983.
15. Mike Rosner, interview, February 24, 1983.
16. Steering Committee of the Manitoba League of the Physically Handicapped, "A Report Outlining the Purposes, Structure and Establishment of a Manitoba Organization of the Physically Handicapped" (unpublished report, May 1974), 2.
17. Rosner, interview, February 24, 1983.
18. Steering Committee, "A Report," 2–4.
19. Rosner, interview, February 24, 1983.
20. Steering Committee, "A Report," 7.
21. Steering Committee, "A Report," 7.
22. Simpson, interview, February 16, 1983.
23. Jim Derksen, "Editorial Comment," *Challenger* (August 1976).
24. Ross, "Demanding Access for All," 55.
25. Derksen, "Editorial Comment," *Challenger* (August 1976).
26. Elizabeth Semkiw, interview, February 28, 1983.
27. M. Thomson, letter to A. Carmichael, May 12, 1975.
28. "Letters Patent of Incorporation of the Manitoba League of the Physically Handicapped Inc.," August 8, 1975.
29. Brian Stewart, letter to Mr. Kristjanson, July 2, 1975.
30. Derksen, "Editorial Comment," *Challenger*, no. 1 (July 1975).

31. Mike Szadiak, "Report From The Pas," *Challenger*, no. 2 (September 1975): 8.
32. Elizabeth Semkiw, "Outline of the Steps towards Implementation of Handi-Transit in Winnipeg" (unpublished report, 1979), 1.
33. Jim Derksen, "The Philosophy of the MLPH," *Challenger* (December 1975): 3.
34. Manitoba League of the Physically Handicapped, "Chairman's Report," in *Annual Report of the MLPH, 1975–1976*, 1.
35. Brian Stewart, letter to Mr. McAuley, May 15, 1975.
36. Jim Derksen, "Speech to the Works and Operations Committee of Winnipeg City Council" (speech delivered at committee meeting, Winnipeg, April 26, 1976).
37. Derksen, "Speech to the Works and Operations Committee."
38. Elizabeth Semkiw, "Transportation Report," *Challenger*, no. 5 (August 1976): 1.
39. Tom Shillington, "Transit Plan Set for Disabled," *Winnipeg Tribune*, May 6, 1976, 1.
40. Allan Simpson, "Speech to City Council" (speech delivered to Winnipeg City Council, May 5, 1976).
41. Shillington, "Transit Plan Set for Disabled."
42. Semkiw, "Outline of the Steps," 1.
43. Szadiak, "Report from The Pas."
44. Manitoba League of the Physically Handicapped, *Annual Report of the MLPH, 1975–1976*, 4.
45. Rosner, interview, February 24, 1983.
46. Jim Derksen, "Can We Help Implement Bill 58?" *Challenger*, no. 5 (April 1976): 10.
47. Derksen, "Can We Help Implement Bill 58?"
48. *Challenger*, no. 6 (December 1976): 3.
49. Brian Stewart, interview, February 17, 1983.
50. Manitoba League of the Physically Handicapped, "L.E.A.P. Proposal by the MLPH," November 1977, 1–2.
51. "Human Rights Legislation to Change," *Challenger*, no. 7 (May 1977): 10.
52. Simpson, interview, February 16, 1983.
53. Allan Simpson, telegram to the Speaker of the Legislature, June 17, 1977.
54. Manitoba League of the Physically Handicapped, "Steinbach Conference Report," in *Annual Report of the MLPH, 1977*, 4–5.
55. "Our Challenge," an election challenge to the candidates in the provincial election, 1977, 3.
56. Elizabeth Semkiw, "Handi-Transit," *Challenger*, no. 9 (December 1977): 9.
57. Ruth Wiebe, "Pussycats in Lyon's Den," *Challenger*, no. 11 (July 1978): 9–10.
58. Frank Rogodzinski, "E-Quality Employment," *Challenger*, no. 13 (December 1978): 12.
59. *E-Quality Employment Opening Doors for Physically Handicapped Manitobans*, pamphlet, 1980, 3.
60. "Handi-Van Receives Provincial Grant," *Steinbach Carillon News*, September 9, 1979.
61. Dave Jenkins, "1977–1978 CAUSE Committee Report," in *Manitoba League of the Physically Handicapped Annual Report, 1978*, 7.
62. Rosner, interview, February 24, 1983.
63. Henry Enns, "Chairman's Report to the 1978 Annual Meeting," in *Manitoba League of the Physically Handicapped Annual Report, 1978*, 1.
64. Brian Stewart, "Chairman's Report to 1979 Annual Meeting," in *Manitoba League of the Physically Handicapped Annual Report, 1979*, 3.
65. Bea Bardsley, "The Members Speak," *Update*, March 1979, 1.
66. Tom Goldstein, "Handicapped Want Right to Cross Street," *Winnipeg Free Press*, March 10, 1979, 3.
67. Dave Jenkins, interview, February 28, 1983.
68. Tom Harper, "Handi-Transit Study Resuming," *Winnipeg Tribune*, July 10, 1979.

69. Derek Legge, "Education Committee Report," in *Manitoba League of the Physically Handicapped Annual Report, 1979*, 5.
70. Henry Enns and Allan Simpson, "Decade of Destiny Of and For Handicapped People," *Update*, August 1980, 7.
71. Frank Rogodzinski, "Chairman's Report to the 1980 Annual General Meeting," in *Manitoba League of the Physically Handicapped Annual Report, 1980*, 3.
72. "Transportation Grants to Help Rural Handicapped," *Winnipeg Free Press*, October 9, 1981.
73. Mary Penner, "MLPH The Pas Branch 1981 Annual Report," in *Manitoba League of the Physically Handicapped Annual Report, 1981*, 20.
74. Simpson, interview, February 16, 1983.
75. Driedger, *The Last Civil Rights Movement*, 48–57.
76. Derksen, "Editorial Comment," *Challenger*, no. 1 (July 1975).

BIBLIOGRAPHY

Primary Sources

Challenger. Newsletter of the MLPH. July 1975 to December 1978.
"Constitution of the Manitoba League of the Physically Handicapped Inc." Amended March 1979.
E-Quality Employment Opening Doors to Employment for Physically Handicapped Manitobans. Pamphlet. E-Quality Employment, 1980.
"Handi-Van Receives Provincial Grant." *Steinbach Carillon News*, Sept. 9, 1979.
"Letters Patent of Incorporation of the Manitoba League of the Physically Handicapped Inc." August 8, 1975.
Manitoba League of the Physically Handicapped. "L.E.A.P. Proposal by the MLPH." November 1977, 1–2.
Manitoba League of the Physically Handicapped. "Brief Re: Bills 31 and 19." Report submitted to the Study Committee on Privileges and Elections, July 2, 1980.
"Minutes of a Special General Meeting" (the first meeting of the membership). September 18, 1975.
Semkiw, Elizabeth. "Outline of the Steps towards Implementation of Handi-Transit in Winnipeg." Unpublished report, 1979.
Smith, Helen. "Report on Transportation Seminar." Canadian Rehabilitation Council for the Disabled Convention, Toronto, November 3–7, 1973.
Steering Committee of the Manitoba League of the Physically Handicapped. "A Report Outlining the Purposes, Structure and Establishment of a Manitoba Organization of the Physically Handicapped." Unpublished report, May 1974.
Update. Newsletter of the MLPH. March 1979 to February 1982.
Wiebe, Ruth. "MLPH—What Lies in the Future?" Unpublished report, 1978.

Secondary Sources

Carlyle-Gordge, Peter. "No Handicap to Success." *Today Magazine*, January 10, 1981.
D'Aubin, April. "'Nothing About Us Without Us': CCD's Struggle for the Recognition of a Human Rights Approach to Disability Issues." In *In Pursuit of Equal Participation: Canada and Disability at Home and Abroad*, edited by Henry Enns and Aldred H. Neufeldt, 111–36. Concord, ON: Captus Press, 2003.
Derksen, Jim, ed. *Report on An Open National Employment Conference*. Winnipeg: COPOH, 1978.

Derksen, Jim. *The Disabled Consumer Movement: Policy Implications for Rehabilitation Service Provision.* Winnipeg: COPOH, 1980.

Driedger, Diane. *The Last Civil Rights Movement: Disabled Peoples' International.* London and New York: Hurst and Co. and St. Martin's Press, 1989.

Enns, Henry. "Canadian Society and Disabled People: Issues for Discussion." *Canada's Mental Health*, December 1981.

Enns, Henry. "The Historical Development of Attitudes toward the Handicapped: A Framework for Change." Presented at the Fifth Canadian Conference on Family Practice, Banff, AB, May 24–29, 1981.

Ens, Frank. "Rural Transportation Resource Kit." Prepared for the Rural Transportation Committee of the MLPH, April 1, 1980.

Goldstein, Tom. "Handicapped Want Right to Cross Street." *Winnipeg Free Press*, March 10, 1979.

Harper, Tom. "Handi-Transit Study Resuming." *Winnipeg Tribune*, July 10, 1979.

Health and Welfare Canada. *Disabled Persons in Canada.* Ottawa: Minister of Supply and Services Canada, 1981.

Morton, Leah. "From Nose Sprays to Nursing Shortages: Managing Epidemic Polio in Manitoba, 1928–1953." *Manitoba History*, no. 66 (Spring 2011): 14–22.

ParaTracks. "A Conference with a Difference." Vol. 2, no. 3 (July-August 1973).

ParaTracks. Vol. 2, no. 4 (September/October 1973).

Prince, Michael J. *Absent Citizens: Disability Politics and Policy in Canada.* Toronto: University of Toronto Press, 2009.

Ross, Val. "Demanding Access for All." *Maclean's*, April 20, 1981.

Shillington, Tom. "Transit Plan Set for Disabled." *Winnipeg Tribune*, May 6, 1976.

Schmidt, Len. "Historical Outcomes." Unpublished report. 1979.

School of Social Work, University of Manitoba; The Community Social Work Collective; Barbara Bell, Marlene Hochbaum, Glen Schmidt, and B. D. McKenzie. *The Manitoba League of the Physically Handicapped: An Organizational Evaluation.* Winnipeg: School of Social Work, April 1979.

Simpson, Allan J. *Consumer Groups: Their Organization and Function.* Winnipeg: COPOH, 1980.

Winnipeg Free Press. "Transportation Grants to Help Rural Handicapped." October 9, 1981.

CHAPTER 15

The Council of Canadians with Disabilities: A Voice of Our Own, 1976–2012

April D'Aubin

INTRODUCTION

In 1976, people with disabilities laid the foundation for the Coalition of Provincial Organizations of the Handicapped (COPOH) and it "expanded to become a cross-disability national umbrella organization for self-representation."[1] It was founded as an organization of people with disabilities advocating for people with disabilities. In 1994, COPOH adopted the name Council of Canadians with Disabilities (CCD) and continued to operate as a pan-Canadian organization that brings people with various disabilities together at the national level to work with government and other sectors to advance the human rights of people with disabilities and to build an inclusive and accessible Canada.

In this paper, I refer to the organization as COPOH/CCD. I share highlights of some of the organization's activities that show how it has played three roles since its founding: convenor, innovator, and consensus builder. In the convening role, it brings together the disability community, government, and other sectors to focus on remedying barriers to the full and equal participation of people with disabilities. As an innovator, it promotes an understanding of the evolving concepts of access, inclusion, and equality. As a consensus builder, it promotes a shared vision of an accessible and inclusive Canada.

MANDATE AND STRUCTURE

In 1978, Consumer and Corporate Affairs Canada issued letters patent to COPOH/CCD, naming James Frank Derksen, Allan Simpson, and Henry Enns the first directors of COPOH/CCD. The letters patent identified the organization's objectives as follows: "(a) To create and provide opportunities and programs for, and to represent the needs and concerns of handicapped persons in Canada on a non-profit basis. (b) To engage in any activity pursuant to achieving the aims as set out in Clause (a)."[2] The organization's bylaws mandated it as a consumer-controlled cross-disability organization.

In a consumer-controlled organization, people with disabilities form the majority. A cross-disability group brings together people with various disabilities to address issues they have in common. As Henry Enns explained, "the philosophy of these organizations is one of 'self-representation' and a 'rights' orientation. They also believe that all disabilities united into one organization provides a stronger voice for change than each disability group speaking out separately."[3] Single disability organizations have been referred to as uni-disability groups.

In *The Disabled Consumer Movement: Policy Implications for Rehabilitation Service Provision* (1980), Jim Derksen elaborated on the concept of consumerism in the context of the disability community:

> The recent ascendency of the disabled consumer ethic is due to a number of causes. A general disillusionment with health care systems and professionals together with rising costs associated with these are part of the cause. The 1960s legacies of social activism and a growing consciousness with regard to discrimination in various forms and civil rights must also be credited as part of the etiology of the quickly emerging consumer ethic and its influence on governmental policies and programs. The recipient who defines himself as consumer is no longer the passive recipient but rather an active consumer participating in the decision-making about the production-provision/consumer relationship. The consumer claims as a right this active participation in decision-making....
>
> The consumer is aware of his[/her] role as consumer-citizen impacted upon [by] governmental legislation and policy development in which he[/she] claims the right of access. As there are a growing number and potentially, by self-definition, a massively greater number of consumers of rehabilitation services and mainstream community access than providers, the politician is most receptive to input from the consumer ethic through organized consumer groups. It follows that the bureaucrats are also receptive to such input.[4]

COPOH/CCD's members are organizations of people with disabilities. The first members were cross-disability provincial advocacy organizations. In 1993–94, COPOH/CCD amended its membership structure to admit national consumer-controlled advocacy organizations, thus becoming more inclusive; however, it set a cap on the number of national organizations that could join. The number of national members must be one less than the number of provincial members. The provincial organizations retained majority control on the National Council of Representatives, which governs COPOH/CCD.

In the 1990–91 annual report, chairperson Raleigh Orr explained that COPOH/CCD was undertaking structural reform to make the organization "stronger, more representative and more potent."[5] The organization began to use the name Council of Canadians with Disabilities in January 1994. In the 1993–94 annual report, Laurie Beachell, national coordinator, wrote the following:

From an organizational viewpoint, 1993/94 was a very good year: It was the year in which we changed from COPOH to CCD.... It was also the year in which we expanded our membership to include other national organizations. This action has greatly increased the cross disability nature of the coalition as well as ensuring representation from sectors that have not been involved previously. From a numbers standpoint, 1993/94 becomes the year in which we can truly say that we represent the largest coalition of persons with disabilities in Canada. Expansion of membership will continue and CCD can look forward to greater growth and inclusiveness.[6]

Over time a number of national organizations applied for and were granted membership in COPOH/CCD. By 2012, COPOH/CCD had 17 members—9 provincial, 1 territorial, and 7 national organizations. Its provincial/territorial members were British Columbia Coalition of People with Disabilities, Alberta Committee of Citizens with Disabilities, Saskatchewan Voice of People with Disabilities, Manitoba League of Persons with Disabilities, Citizens with Disabilities-Ontario, Confédération des Organismes de Personnes Handicapées du Québec (COPHAN), PEI Council of People with Disabilities, Coalition of People with Disabilities of Newfoundland and Labrador, Nova Scotia League for Equal Opportunities, and NWT Council of Persons with Disabilities. Its national members were Alliance for Equality of Blind Canadians, Canadian Association of the Deaf, DisAbled Women's Network Canada/Réseau d'action des femmes handicapées du Canada (DAWN-RAFH Canada), National Educational Association of Disabled Students, National Network for Mental Health, People First of Canada, and Thalidomide Victims Association of Canada.

The NWT Council of Persons with Disabilities was not admitted as a full member, because it was not a consumer-controlled advocacy organization. It was granted membership in recognition of the unique circumstances facing people with disabilities living in northern Canada, where there are barriers that work against the creation of separate service and advocacy organizations. For example, there are limited accessible transportation options available in remote and northern locations, so it is difficult for people with disabilities to get together to organize.

Each COPOH/CCD member organization appoints a representative to the National Council of Representatives, which governs the association. There are also two members-at-large elected by the members. The national council elects the chairperson and other members of the organization's Executive Committee. From 1976 to 2012, COPOH/CCD elected the following individuals to the office of chairperson: Michael Huck (1976–1977), Percy Wickman (1977–1979), Allan Simpson (1979–1982), Ron Kanary (1982–1984), Jim Derksen (1984–1986), Irene Feika (1986–1990), Raleigh Orr (1990–1992), Francine Arsenault (1992–1996), Eric Norman (1996–2000), Paul Young (2000–2002), Marie Ryan (2002–2010), and Tony Dolan (2010–2012). Other than Paul Young, the aforementioned were appointed to the National Council of Representatives by a provincial member group.

People First of Canada appointed Young as its representative to the council. As Young noted in "Finding My Voice," he was "the first person with a label to be the chair of the Council of Canadians with Disabilities."[7] Young explained the influence of COPOH/CCD's leaders on him:

> I was labelled "mentally retarded." I attended a segregated class and a sheltered workshop.... I was told I would never be able to: own a home; drive a car; get a job; love someone; be loved.... I got involved with a local chapter of the cross-disability group in Sydney. Ron Kanary invited me to a [COPOH] conference in Ottawa where I heard Ron, Allan Simpson and Jim Derksen speaking about the lack of accessibility and inequality for persons with disabilities. Before I heard them, I was taught to feel sorry for people with disabilities. There I saw very strong men talking about the issues. I was inspired by them and decided I wanted to get involved.[8]

The election of Paul Young, a representative from a national uni-disability organization, suggests that COPOH/CCD's structural reform had some limited success in assisting the organization to become more inclusive of the various perspectives in the Canadian disability community.

Mr. Young's comments about being inspired by *male* leaders is noteworthy. COPOH/CCD elected men to the position of chairperson for its first 10 years. Irene Feika was the first woman elected as chairperson. Women with disabilities felt marginalized in COPOH/CCD, as Pat Israel discussed at the founding meeting of DAWN-RAFH Canada, which was organized by women with disabilities to give them a unique and distinct voice at the national level:

> In the eighties I became a COPOH board member. At the time I met Yvonne Peters who is also a feminist. It was like meeting a long-lost sister. We were both frustrated by the disabled person's [sic] movement and the women's movement. Neither seemed interested in dealing with our concerns. We spent a lot of our time together discussing our issues as women with disabilities. We felt that in both groups, our priorities, problems and concerns were invisible and unimportant.[9]

DAWN-RAFH Canada became a member of COPOH/CCD and thus has a seat at COPOH/CCD's decision-making table. Within COPOH/CCD, DAWN-RAFH has been playing a leadership role, working to address the organization's lack of a gender lens.

Carmela Hutchison, a DAWN-RAFH appointee to the National Council of Representatives was elected as a COPOH/CCD vice chairperson in 2008 and has held other executive positions. Nevertheless, the power imbalance continues, as there is only one feminist organization at the decision-making table; however, with the encouragement of DAWN-RAFH Canada, COPOH/CCD has taken a step to become more gendered in its approach to disability issues. At its January 2011 meeting, the National Council of Representatives passed a motion that directed all COPOH/CCD papers to include a gender analysis and stated that COPOH/CCD should consult with DAWN-RAFH Canada when assistance on gender analysis is required.[10]

In addition to the Executive Committee, the National Council of Representatives establishes issue-specific committees that develop the association's initiatives. Its committees have focused on human rights, ending-of-life ethics, transportation, international issues, social policy (e.g., disability-related supports, employment, poverty, citizenship, and access and inclusion), and technology. Through its committees, COPOH/CCD has maintained a long-term relationship with a core of volunteer leaders with a high level of expertise, thus maintaining a direct connection to the original vision of the organization and enhancing expertise over time in a number of key areas. Take, for example, the first directors, Allan Simpson, Henry Enns, and Jim Derksen, who signed the letters patent. Simpson and Enns volunteered with the organization until their deaths in 1998 and 2002, respectively. Simpson advised the organization's Employment and Social Policy committees, and Enns remained involved in the organization's international work. Derksen's connection to the organization has been longer. He held the positions of national coordinator, chairperson of the National Council of Representatives, and chairperson of the Human Rights Committee. In 2012, he was a member of the Human Rights, International Development, and Ending of Life Ethics committees. Outside the disability community, the expertise of Simpson, Enns, and Derksen has been recognized, with Simpson receiving the Order of Canada in 1998, and Enns and Derksen receiving honourary doctorates in recognition of their work to improve the status of people with disabilities. Other examples are Pat Danforth and Yvonne Peters's volunteer careers with the organization. Danforth attended COPOH/CCD's second meeting on May 22 and 23, 1976.[11] She served as chairperson of COPOH/CCD's Transportation Committee, as a member of its Human Rights Committee, and, in 2012, was a member of the National Council of Representatives. Peters joined the COPOH/CCD National Council of Representatives in 1979. A human rights lawyer, she had a long-term involvement with the organization's Human Rights Committee, chairing it for periods in the 1980s and 2000s. She was also a co-principal investigator for a COPOH/CCD research project, *Disabling Poverty, Enabling Citizenship*, which began in 2008. More on these leaders' contributions is shared throughout this discussion of COPOH/CCD.

The organization's work is guided by a number of principles: citizenship, voice of our own/consumer control, equality and human rights, and universal design.

- Citizenship: People with disabilities have the same rights and responsibilities as Canadians without disabilities. Socially created barriers that prevent participation and discriminate against people with disabilities must be eliminated.
- Voice of our own/consumer control: Through the self-representational organiza-

tions that they control, people with disabilities must be involved in all stages of the development of disability services and policies, as well as the development of non-disability-specific laws, policies, and programs, as these too have an impact on people with disabilities.
- Equality and human rights: The *Charter of Rights and Freedoms* guarantees equal benefit and protection under the law and the *Canadian Human Rights Act* prohibits discrimination based on physical or mental disability. All legislation must conform to the demands of the Charter.
- Universal design: The structures of society should be developed in a manner that makes them usable by people with the widest possible range of functional abilities.[12]

The organization asserts that adherence to these principles will result in an accessible and inclusive Canada, where people with disabilities have full enjoyment of their human rights. Broadly speaking, COPOH/CCD engages in three main activities to prevent and remove barriers: law reform and litigation, awareness raising and education, and research and knowledge transfer.

WHY COPOH/CCD FORMED: HAVING A VOICE IN OTTAWA

On January 22, 1976, representatives from the Alberta Committee of Handicapped Action Groups, founded in 1973,[13] the Saskatchewan Voice of the Handicapped, which grew out of a provincial conference held in 1973,[14] and the Manitoba League of the Physically Handicapped, founded in 1975,[15] met in Regina, Saskatchewan, and decided to form an alliance of provincial organizations of people with various types of disabilities. The groups that sent representatives to the Regina meeting wanted to have a voice in Ottawa to influence federal laws, policies, and programs on disability issues.

In the minutes of the Regina meeting, the Saskatchewan Voice representative Michael Huck stated,

> Saskatchewan realizes no one province can make much headway in Ottawa. We need to develop national policies and approaches for presentation to Ottawa. This will require an organization for purposes of developing common policies as well as lobby strategies to be presented with authority.[16]

Even at this early stage, the participants had a political agenda: making their views known about "rehabilitation legislation now being prepared in Ottawa for presentation to Parliament in April 1976."[17] The meeting minutes noted "general concern that any new legislation that affects handicapped community services under the guise of rehabilitation legislation should first be presented to handicapped consumer groups for their reaction before being submitted to the final decision-making process in Parliament."[18] The participants decided to express their views in a telegram to Health and Welfare Minister Marc Lalonde.

Following the Regina meeting in 1976, COPOH/CCD worked to extend the fledging organization beyond western Canada to span the entire country. With a grant of $12,600 from the federal Secretary of State, COPOH/CCD undertook a membership development project, hiring Percy Wickman, of Edmonton, Alberta, as national development officer, to travel across Canada promoting membership in the new organization to provincial cross-disability organizations of people with disabilities.[19]

In 1978, COPOH/CCD hired Jim Derksen as national coordinator and he continued membership development. By June of 1978, COPOH had a membership that spanned southern Canada. It included the British Columbia Coalition of the Disabled, Alberta Committee of Action Groups of the Disabled, Saskatchewan Voice of the Handicapped, Manitoba League of the Physically Handicapped, United Handicapped Action Groups of Ontario, Comité de Liaison des Handicapés du Québec, PEI Council of the Disabled, and the HUB, Newfoundland. COPOH/CCD has never had a provincial member organization from New Brunswick.

Responding to Discrimination and Exclusion

The organization's members wanted a voice in Ottawa to advance the human rights of people with disabilities. In "Consumer Groups: Their Organization and Function," a paper prepared for the 1981 Rehabilitation International (RI) World Congress, Allan Simpson explained what a world where people with disabilities enjoyed their human rights would look like:

> For disabled citizens application of the civil rights legislation would mean accessible public services delivered via regular community or private delivery systems serving the general population. In other words, application of appropriate civil/human rights would eventually ensure integrated:
>
> - transportation via the regular transit public and private carriers
> - education via the public/private school systems
> - accessible housing, coupled with attendant care to assist in daily living
> - barrier free legislation re: all public use facilities
> - equal employment opportunities and job support systems
> - recreation in public and private community recreation facilities.[20]

At the time when people with disabilities were organizing COPOH/CCD, barriers were an everyday fact of life. Inclusion was not on the radar screen of society. A 1980 *Reader's Digest* article about COPOH/CCD shared the experience of Nova Scotian Laughlin Rutt, a wheelchair user who lost his job at Canada Manpower because it relocated to a building with stairs.[21] Allan Simpson and his friends wanted the 1967 Pan Am Games in Winnipeg to include a parallel wheelchair sports event, but were told it was against the rules.[22] Services to facilitate independent living were frequently unavailable. In *Life and Breath: A Love Story*, Theresa Ducharme, a polio survivor who used a wheelchair and respirator, described her career as a self-advocate seeking independent living services. In the mid-1970s, Ducharme wanted to marry and live with her husband, but disability-related supports were not available. Ducharme lobbied for supports to be available in her home. She recalled one of the proposals she received from the Manitoba government:

> I could move to the King George Hospital after my wedding and go home to Clifford on his days off. This hardly seemed a better alternative; to be an institutionalized wife at great expense to the taxpayer, and live with my husband only two days a week, just so they could avoid changing a policy and hiring an attendant. This was unacceptable.[23]

To make Manitoba more accessible and inclusive, Ducharme became a member of the Manitoba League of the Physically Handicapped (MLPH), one of COPOH/CCD's founding organizations. She commented,

> Viewed as a whole, difficulties in these areas amounted to a denial of the rights of handicapped people to be full human beings, and so they had to be dealt with through the legal system and through changes in legislation. Viewed separately, they were a series of obstacles or roadblocks which had to be tackled one by one, through political action, in order to have them changed or removed. Underlying everything were problems of attitude and a lack of awareness, which had to be corrected through the press, radio and television.[24]

Like Ducharme, people with disabilities across Canada joined COPOH/CCD's member organizations to work on the issues of exclusion and discrimination. Some policy analysts were also identifying the exclusion experienced by people with disabilities. In *A Hit or Miss Affair: Policies for Disabled People in Canada* (1977), Joan C. Brown explained the policy origins of many of the barriers encountered by people with disabilities. She identified four main responses to the concerns of people with disabilities: (1) behaving as if people with disabilities did not exist, (2) classifying people with disability as welfare cases in need of charity, (3) offering rehabilitation, and (4) tinkering with existing services.[25] Brown explained that the first two approaches provided a way for service providers to avoid making their services usable by people with disabilities. She noted that with the development of more robust social programming, it became more difficult to outright exclude people with disabilities and the service system responded by developing band-aid solutions rather than devising comprehensive models that addressed the service needs of people with disabilities throughout the lifecycle. She explained,

> Thus the Illness Benefit is strung on to Unemployment Insurance. Disability Pensions are included as an often inferior version of Retirement Pensions. A department may organize a division for the handicapped, primarily for the

mentally retarded, and will then add on disabled people. Institutional and home care services are organized for the aged and people with short-term illness and the disabled are fitted in. Senior citizen's housing units are built and the disabled allocated a proportion of the units. In none of these cases are the basic rules developed in relation to disabled people. They are planned around the larger population group and disabled people must simply fit in, whether or not this produces a satisfactory result.[26]

Brown criticized the voluntary organizations that had been lobbying in support of and creating services for people with disabilities because they prioritized rehabilitation services, but were less aggressive regarding the "many issues which are the key to independent living for disabled people, issues such as income, housing, support services and matters related to the human rights of disabled people."[27]

In "The Disabled Consumer Movement: Policy Implications for Rehabilitation Service" (1980), published by COPOH/CCD, Jim Derksen also critiqued the service environment, particularly rehabilitation. He argued that people with disabilities were disempowered by the services provided to them, because the service systems had removed decision-making authority from disabled people and vested it in the professionals who delivered the services. Derksen explained that organizations like COPOH/CCD were seeking "active participation in the decision-making"[28] about services.

In 1976, when the Prairie organizations of disabled people decided to form a national alliance controlled by people with various disabilities, there were few similar organizations. Deaf Canadians organized the Canadian Association of the Deaf in 1940.[29] Following World War II, disabled veterans organized the Canadian Paraplegic Association, which developed a service model and services for people with mobility impairments. As a consumer-controlled cross-disability advocacy organization, COPOH/CCD was unique. Since 1976, people with disabilities have formed many more organizations. Other cross-disability advocacy organizations have emerged, such as DAWN-RAFH Canada, the National Educational Association of Disabled Students, and the Canadian Multicultural Disability Centre. Along with the other disability organizations that have emerged, COPOH/CCD, working as a convener, innovator, and consensus builder, has been promoting an accessible and inclusive Canada.

CONVENER

Organizing at Rehabilitation International Congress

In the convening role, COPOH/CCD brings together the disability community, government, and other sectors to focus on remedying barriers to the full and equal participation of people with disabilities. Through the leadership of Allan Simpson, Jim Derksen, and Henry Enns, COPOH/CCD played a pivotal role at the 1980 Rehabilitation International

(RI) Congress, organizing a variety of opportunities whereby the voice of people with disabilities could be heard by conference participants, including government officials at the event and the media. At that time, RI was a global organization made up mainly of health care professionals focused on rehabilitation. The Canadian Rehabilitation Council for the Disabled (CRCD), which spoke out on disability issues in Canada from a medical model perspective, was part of this organization. Through its activities at the RI Congress, COPOH/CCD positioned itself and its consumer philosophy as a counterpoint to organizations like CRDC that worked from the medical model perspective. COPOH/CCD undertook a number of activities at the RI Congress aimed at promoting people with disabilities and their self-representational organizations as the legitimate spokespersons on disability issues.

The organization published a newsletter, the *COPOH Newsline*, which critiqued conference events and speakers' presentations, awarding stars to speakers who supported the independent living aspirations of people with disabilities and dinosaurs to those who promoted traditional rehabilitation. The *Newsline* was delivered to the hotel rooms of conference participants and to the media. People with disabilities in attendance at the conference were invited to events facilitated by COPOH/CCD where they had the opportunity to come together, express their views, and make plans for how they wanted to work with the rehabilitation sector. At the RI conference, COPOH/CCD created both actual physical spaces, and philosophical and conceptual spaces, where people with disabilities felt comfortable making plans for an international organization of their own that would be the global voice of people with disabilities. This is an important early example of COPOH/CCD in its convening role. At the RI Congress, people with disabilities in attendance resolved to found their own global organization. Disabled Peoples' International (DPI) was officially founded in 1981 in Singapore; Henry Enns was elected its first vice chairperson and Jim Derksen was hired as its chief development officer.

The decision to form an international organization of people with disabilities was spurred by RI's decision not to welcome people with disabilities as partners in the RI decision-making structure. Under the headline "No Voice for the Handicapped," the *COPOH Newsline* commented:

> The delegate assembly of Rehabilitation International refused to recognize service consumers as equal partners in their structure by a vote of 37 for, 61 against and 2 abstentions.... Canadian delegate Yvonne Peters of COPOH was appalled at Rehabilitation International's refusal to recognize the need for affirmative action.[30]

In a press release, COPOH/CCD expressed its dismay at the RI decision. It explained that the decision was the result of RI not understanding that exclusionary social structures were at the root of problems experienced by the disability community. National coordinator

Jim Derksen commented, "They [rehabilitation providers] often assume that our disability is the focus of the problem, but the crucial blocks to independence are other environmental barriers, inadequate community services, and the general public's perception of us as objects of charity."[31] Simpson explained that the people with disabilities were promoting independent living as an alternative to the traditional rehabilitation service model: "Consumers here have a major task to limit rehabilitation to medically related needs and to promote independent living. Independent living is a process designed to provide resources in the community to make a full and meaningful lifestyle possible for the disabled."[32]

COPOH/CCD's leadership at the RI Congress was recognized by some outside the disability community. Ann Darnbrough wrote the following in the *Nursing Mirror*:

> A group known as COPOH (Coalition of Provincial Organizations of the Handicapped) was conspicuously active and well organized. They placed bilingual news releases on the desks of all hotels before 07.00h and notices of their meetings were posted up everywhere. Under the very noses of the "establishment," COPOH was behind what may well be remembered as the most significant event of this 1980 Congress—the setting up of a steering committee to establish an International Coalition of Disabled Persons.[33]

National Action Plan/End Exclusion

The *National Action Plan*/End Exclusion was another example of COPOH/CCD working in the role of convenor. Marie Ryan, a former deputy mayor of St. John's, Newfoundland, chaired COPOH/CCD for eight years, and chaired its Social Policy Committee. Ryan played a key leadership role in the development of the disability community's *National Action Plan* and in End Exclusion, a community forum on disability issues. In 2006 and 2007, working in collaboration with the Canadian Association for Community Living and other organizations, COPOH/CCD facilitated the disability community's creation of *From Vision to Action: Building An Inclusive and Accessible Canada: A National Action Plan on Disability*. Sharing both short- and long-term recommendations, the *National Action Plan* called for the federal government to implement a national strategy on disability issues, focusing on disability-related supports, employment, poverty, citizenship, and access and inclusion. At the End Exclusion event that was held in Ottawa in 2007, over 300 people from the disability community gathered in support of the *National Action Plan*, which was shared with federal cabinet ministers. The endorsement of the *National Action Plan* by 103 civil society organizations, primarily from the disability community, demonstrated that the Canadian disability community had a unified plan for the creation of access and inclusion.

INNOVATOR

From 1984 to 2012, the COPOH/CCD International Committee was chaired by Henry Enns, Irene Feika, Francine Arsenault, and Steven Estey. The organization also appointed them to governance structures of Disabled Peoples' International (DPI), such as the North American Caribbean Regional Council. With their guidance and that of the International Committee, COPOH/CCD worked as an innovator in the field of inclusive development and international human rights.

Inclusive Development

In 1984, COPOH/CCD's International Committee secured a Public Participation Program project from the Canadian International Development Agency (CIDA) to deliver development education to its member groups and Canadian development agencies.[34] The goal of this work was to encourage people with disabilities to become involved in the international development sector and to encourage international development organizations to include people with disabilities in their programming. COPOH/CCD joined the Canadian Council for International Co-operation (CCIC), which brings together Canadian organizations engaged in international development, and encouraged CCIC member organizations to make the inclusion of people with disabilities a criterion for the funding of international development projects. The International Committee developed public education materials on disability and development to share with the development community. The high point of its educational work in support of inclusive development was the publication in 1996 of *Across Borders: Women with Disabilities Working Together*, which explored the efforts of women with disabilities in developing countries to address sexism and ableism and to overcome barriers. Diane Driedger, Irene Feika, and Eileen Girón Batres edited *Across Borders*. In 1991, the International Committee made working with women with disabilities in developing countries a priority.

Policies in Support of Inclusive Development
The International Committee encouraged CIDA to develop a policy on disability and development. It recommended a "twin-track" approach like the one used in the United Kingdom. The twin-track approach seeks to take account of people with disabilities' needs and rights in mainstream development initiatives, as well as specific undertakings aimed at the empowerment of people with disabilities. As of 2012, CIDA had not adopted a policy on disability development.

Leading by Example

From 1985 to 2000, COPOH/CCD undertook international development projects with southern members of DPI. It began by encouraging the twinning of COPOH/

CCD member groups with organizations of people with disabilities in other countries. A COPOH/CCD member group, the Saskatchewan Voice of the Handicapped (as it was then known) twinned with the Organization of Disabled Revolutionaries in Nicaragua; PUSH Ontario twinned with the Combined Disabilities Association of Jamaica; and the Manitoba League of the Physically Handicapped (MLPH) (as it was then known) partnered with the Guyana Coalition of Citizens with Disabilities (GCCD). Twinning functioned as a partnership between equals, with both groups expecting to benefit from the relationship. Susan Deane, staff person for the MLPH International Committee, described the expectations surrounding the MLPH-GCCD twinning:

> At the start of the partnership, the MLPH Committee wished to learn from Guyana about: international perspectives on disability, societal attitudes towards disabled people in Guyana, role of the family, particular issues and needs faced by disabled people, how they are resolved, and most important how do disabled people function in the context of a less developed country. The [International] committee on the other hand hoped to share information on self-help techniques, models like the Independent Living Resource Centre, Manitoba League of the Physically Handicapped (MLPH) support models, and information on different disabled people's groups working together. It also helped to share ideas on management skills, fundraising, advocacy and literature on disability. Material aid such as wheelchairs and crutches, where appropriate, was also to be extended.[35]

The success of the twinning projects led COPOH/CCD itself to undertake development projects with DPI members. Reductions in CIDA funding to COPOH/CCD forced it to draw to a close its development projects. This cutback points to one of the organization's long-term challenges: diversifying its funding. Throughout its history, COPOH/CCD has relied upon different federal government departments for funding and has not developed robust additional revenue streams. The organization has rejected the type of fundraising that reinforces stereotypical images of people with disabilities, preferring fundraising consistent with its message of citizenship, human rights, and the voice of people with disabilities. For example, it has informed potential donors about the opportunity to contribute to its litigation fund.

COPOH/CCD Campaigns for International Treaties

The COPOH/CCD International Committee became involved in the campaign to ban landmines that led to the 1997 Mine Ban Treaty. Its work on the landmine issue was consistent with its 1985 adoption of the 1982 Disabled Peoples' International Peace Statement, which urges the countries of the world to cease producing weapons. In association with people with disabilities in other countries, COPOH/CCD worked to ensure that people disabled by landmines were not forgotten during the landmine treaty negotiation process. COPOH/CCD held that in addition to funding for demining, funding was needed to support the independent living goals of landmine survivors. At the invitation of Foreign Affairs Minister Lloyd Axworthy, Henry Enns chaired the session on survivors' issues at the Winnipeg Landmines Conference in January 1997. COPOH/CCD International Committee member Irene Feika, who was also on the World Council of DPI, and Steven Estey, who was then staffing the International Committee, were also speakers. Feika stated,

> Landmine survivors must have equal rights.... We recognize and applaud the Canadian government for its role in stopping the further development of landmines. However, we strongly recommend a unilateral ban of any further productions in the future of landmines, a ban on stockpiling of landmines, and a ban on any future use of landmines. We would also recommend a multilateral program of rehabilitation be developed for and with landmine survivors.[36]

Following Canadian ratification of the landmines treaty, the COPOH/CCD International Committee worked with the Cambodian Disabled People's Organization (CDPO) to develop self-help projects to assist landmine survivors, and became a member of Mines Action Canada (MAC), an international leader in the efforts to eliminate landmines.[37] Steven Estey served on the MAC board of directors from 2001 to 2007 and as MAC chairperson from 2003 to 2006. Mary Reid, a former member of the COPOH/CCD International Committee, also served on the MAC board.

COPOH/CCD and the Convention on the Rights of Persons with Disabilities

In 2001, following a proposal from Mexico, the United Nations (UN) General Assembly established an ad hoc committee to study proposals for a convention to promote and protect the human rights of persons with disabilities. The UN adopted the Convention on the Rights of Persons with Disabilities (CRPD) on December 13, 2006, and it entered into force on May 3, 2008. On March 11, 2010, Canada ratified the CRPD. Speaking as a guest at the Provincial/Territorial Meeting of Ministers Responsible for Disability Issues and Human Rights on March 15, 2011, in Winnipeg, Jim Derksen, a member of the COPOH/CCD International Committee, described the importance of the CRPD to Canadians with disabilities:

> There is no doubt that the progressive changes that we have seen over the past forty years have come about because people with disability have spoken out and called for improvements. The disability community has been the catalyst for change. We know things cannot change all at once, but we do expect continued and accelerated efforts to integrate us into the economy and the full life of the community. We view the CRPD as a new opportunity to generate renewed

commitment and action that will result in us being able to realize our full and equal citizenship. We cannot accept the status quo and we will be vigilant to resist further barriers and inequities.[38]

The International Committee took the lead for COPOH/CCD on activities related to the CRPD. Through its work on the landmines treaty, the committee had already developed some expertise related to international treaties. During the negotiation stage, COPOH/CCD undertook three main activities related to the CRPD: informing its members about the CRPD, participating on the Canadian delegation that helped draft the wording of the CRPD, and informing the Canadian CRPD delegation about the disability community's views on the draft wording of the convention. Once the CRPD was adopted by the UN, COPOH/CCD began to push for its ratification by Canada. Following ratification, COPOH/CCD began urging Canada to adopt a robust implementation and monitoring strategy.

Sharing Information on the CRPD

To share information with its members and the general public, COPOH/CCD used a variety of methods. In 2004, COPOH/CCD produced a background paper titled "The UN Convention on the Human Rights of Disabled People: What Canadians Need to Know," which explained why the International Committee would be participating in the development of a new international treaty on the rights of people with disabilities. The paper stated,

> the process of drafting these focused conventions has served to raise awareness and build capacity among both governments and non-governmental organizations concerned with human rights issues pertaining to these various populations. Once the treaties have entered into force, they provide a forum for the consideration of human rights issues insofar as they pertain to the treaty, and serve as a focal point for the human rights initiatives of governments and non-governmental organizations, spurring developments in national laws and highlighting best and worst practices.[39]

In 2005, when International Committee member Mary Ennis went to the UN ad hoc committee meeting, COPOH/CCD circulated an email newsletter sharing Ennis's firsthand account of the proceedings. In her fourth report, Ennis shared a statement drafted by the International Disability Caucus (IDC) as their last intervention at the meeting. The IDC elaborated its expectations with regard to the CRPD: "We would like to state our firm commitment to any methodology which will allow us to advance and finalize the Convention in the very near future; however, we are strongly opposed to any meeting, even if it is defined as technical, which does not include representation from IDC."[40] COPOH/CCD was in agreement with these goals and worked both in Canada and New York to see them realized. The organization continued to share information on the CRPD. In 2010, COPOH/CCD began a three-year education project on the CRPD, with Vangelis Nikias as its staff person. Nikias had been a government representative on the Canadian delegation that contributed to the writing of the convention's text.

Participating on the Canadian Delegation
The inclusion of people with disabilities on the Canadian delegation was a priority for COPOH/CCD because it was essential to have the benefit of the disability community's expertise on human rights. Along with other organizations in the disability community, COPOH/CCD successfully made the case for inclusion to Human Resources Development Canada, Foreign Affairs, Heritage Canada, and Justice Canada. The Government of Canada invited Dulcie MacCallum, a lawyer from the Canadian Association for Community Living (CACL), and first Mary Ennis and then Steven Estey from COPOH/CCD to participate on the Canadian delegation. Estey was invited by the government to be on hand at the UN when Canada signed and ratified the CRPD. The participation of Canadians with disabilities in the drafting of the CRPD had an influence on the convention. Former CACL staffer Anna McQuarrie commented,

> Canada's imprint on the CRPD is substantial and substantive. Uniquely Canadian concepts—like inclusive education and supported decision-making—are now, for the first time, entrenched in international law. The leadership from Canada's delegation and the Canadian disability community on Article 12 will have—and already is having—resounding impact around the world.[41]

Informing the Canadian Delegation about the Disability Community's Perspective on the Draft CRPD Text
The COPOH/CCD International Committee hosted community consultations, funded by Human Resources and Skills Development Canada, where representative organizations of people with disabilities provided input to the Canadian delegations that worked on the text of the CRPD. Steven Estey, chairperson of the International Committee, chaired the community consultations. The 2004 community consultation identified the following areas where there was consensus:

> The Canadian delegation should include broad representation from the disability community. Disability NGOs in Canada want to have their voices heard in future consultations on the convention. The convention should include a strong statement on the duty to accommodate, which should be defined as outlined in Canadian law, where the responsible party must provide accommodation up to the point of undue hardship. There must be a strong monitoring mechanism—otherwise the convention may not have a significant impact.[42]

At the 2005 community consultation on the CRPD, there was interest in having the wording of the CRPD article on the Right to Work worded as strongly as the Convention on the Elimination of Discrimination against Women (CEDAW) provisions on the right to work. Throughout the negotiation process, COPOH/CCD made Canadian officials working on the CRPD aware of the disability community's perspective on the concepts that should be included in the articles contained in the CRPD. Canada's delegations went to the UN with an awareness of what elements Canadians with disabilities expected to see included in the convention.

COPOH/CCD's CRPD Work Post-ratification
Following ratification, the COPOH/CCD International Committee focused on Canada's implementation and monitoring of the CRPD. On March 11, 2011, the first anniversary of the ratification of the CRPD, COPOH/CCD, along with the CACL, organized the disability community to make a collective call to action in support of robust implementation and monitoring. Joining COPOH/CCD and CACL were 130 organizations from the disability community, who called for federal and provincial/territorial governments to work with persons with disabilities and their organizations to fully implement the CRPD and to remove barriers experienced by Canadians with disabilities. In particular, there was a call for the federal government to

- Develop national mechanisms for implementation, monitoring and reporting.
- Establish a high-level federal focal point and coordination mechanism to implement the CRPD.
- Demonstrate federal policy leadership on key priorities (i.e., the *National Action Plan*) of the disability community.
- Create a parliamentary committee for input and leadership.
- Ensure an independent monitoring mechanism to measure progress and impact.
- Establish a process for Canada's first Comprehensive Report to the United Nations on progress made. This report will be submitted in 2012.[43]

In keeping with the priority that COPOH/CCD places on the voice of people with disabilities, the call to action emphasized the need for the federal government to develop a participation strategy in keeping with the obligations outlined in Article 4 to "consult with and actively involve persons with disabilities, including children with disabilities, through their representative organizations" in implementing the CRPD. The call to action also urged the federal government to adopt a national action plan that would elaborate methods for collaboration, benchmarks for monitoring and reporting, and strategies for priority areas for action the disability community had identified, including access to disability-related supports, poverty alleviation, participation in the labour force, accessibility and inclusion, and international co-operation.

When ratification occurred, there were two disappointments for the Canadian disability community: Canada did not ratify the Optional Protocol to CRPD, and it ratified the CRPD with reservations on Articles 12 and 33. On December 3, 2009, the Honourable Peter MacKay, on behalf of the Government of Canada, tabled the CRPD in the House of Commons. At that time, the Government of Canada reported that

> Canada would enter an interpretive declaration to Article 12 (2) and (3), to clarify its understanding that Article 12 reflects a presumption of legal capacity and permits supported and substitute decision-making arrangements, much as guardianship and powers of attorney. Canada would also enter a reservation to protect its ability (in the event of a contrary interpretation of international law) to continue the use of substitute decision-making arrangements in appropriate circumstances and subject to appropriate and effective safeguards.... Canada would enter a limited reservation to preserve its right to maintain the supported and substitute decision-making arrangements that are not subject to regular review by an independent authority, where such measures are already subject to review or appeal.... Article 33 (2) ... enter an interpretive declaration, stating it understands that the Article's requirements ... accommodates Canada's federal/provincial/territorial structure.[44]

In the call to action, COPOH/CCD and the other endorsing organizations urged Canada to establish a timeline and process for reviewing the country's position on Article 12 and the Optional Protocol. Since ratification, COPOH/CCD has worked in support of effective monitoring of the CRPD; it has urged that the Canadian Human Rights Commission (CHRC) be named as the Canadian monitor of the CRPD and appropriately resourced to undertake the work. In recognition of Canada's federal and provincial jurisdictions, COPOH/CCD promoted an approach whereby the CHRC would work in partnership with provincial and territorial commissions to monitor the implementation of the CRPD. In keeping with its belief in the "voice of our own" principle, COPOH/CCD also called for development of an engagement strategy which would include the organizations of people with disabilities in the monitoring of the convention. New Zealand developed an approach similar to what COPOH/CCD recommended. Along with CACL, COPOH/CCD discussed with the Canadian Association of Statutory Human Rights Agencies how organizations of people with disabilities and commissions could collaborate on the monitoring of the CRPD.

Inclusion of Disability Rights in the Charter of Rights and Freedoms

Another example of the organization's work as an innovator is COPOH/CCD's efforts to have disability included in Section 15 of the Charter of Rights and Freedoms. On November 3, 1980, Yvonne Peters participated in a demonstration on Parliament Hill in support of the inclusion of people with physical and mental disabilities in the Equality Rights Section of the Charter, because people with disabilities had been left out. Following the demonstration, Peters and Ron Kanary, COPOH/CCD vice chairperson, met with key politicians to seek a hearing before the Joint Committee on the Constitution. Peters commented,

> Our appearance before the Joint Committee marked a turning point for COPOH's Constitutional lobby. The public protest and the appearance before the Committee gave our issue profile and credibility.... Thus, on January 28, 1981, the Joint Parliamentary Committee on the Constitution unanimously accepted an amendment of the Charter, which, at long last, included the ground of both "physical or mental disability" in Section 15, now known as the guarantee of equality in the Canadian *Charter of Rights and Freedoms*.[45]

After Section 15 of the Charter of Rights and Freedoms came into force in 1985, COPOH/CCD intervened in a number of court cases, where it explained equality rights in the context of disability. For a number of years, Peters chaired the COPOH/CCD Human Rights Committee, which guided the organization's litigation in support of human and equality rights.

Disabling Poverty/Enabling Citizenship

The Community-University Research Alliance (CURA) Disabling Poverty/Enabling Citizenship research project was another example of COPOH/CCD working as an innovator. Yvonne Peters and Michael J. Prince were co-principal investigators for this research project, which was funded by the Social Sciences and Humanities Research Council. Of the 92 CURA grants awarded over the years, only 10 were community-led and the COPOH/CCD project was one of them. Because this project was awarded to COPOH/CCD, the control and direction of the project was vested in a consumer-controlled disability organization and not an academic institution. The organization argued that it was very important for a consumer-controlled organization to determine the research process, because the research was a component of the organization's wider disability rights agenda. The project used a disability lens to investigate poverty as it affects persons with disabilities and to formulate strategies for reducing poverty in the disability community and develop recommendations for policy reform.

CONSENSUS BUILDER

Working for an Accessible and Inclusive Canadian Museum for Human Rights

Monitoring the environment for barriers and undertaking activities in support of barrier prevention and removal by COPOH/CCD helps to ensure that the voices and concerns of people with disabilities are not overlooked. The organization's work with the Canadian Museum for Human Rights (CMHR) illustrates how COPOH/CCD has worked as a consensus builder in support of access and inclusion. The CMHR, which was established by the Government of Canada through amendments to the Museums Act in 2008, is a museum focused on the promotion of human rights. The CMHR developed an advisory committee of people with various disabilities that it consults on how to deliver its programming in an accessible manner. John Rae, a COPOH/CCD vice chair, and Jim Derksen, a Human Rights Committee member, served on the advisory committee, along with others from the disability community. Laurie Beachell, COPOH/CCD national coordinator, was a member of a content advisory committee, which assisted the CMHR to focus its message. Derksen also served on an advisory committee to the CEO of the CMHR. COPOH/CCD worked to build consensus about the importance of access and inclusion with the museum's decision-makers.

After the announcement of the founding of the CMHR, COPOH/CCD monitored each stage of the museum's progress. If public events related to the museum were inaccessible or discussions were silent on disability, COPOH/CCD drew the CMHR's attention to how it was excluding people with disabilities. COPOH/CCD explained to the museum why it needed to adhere to the principles of universal design and provided examples of other museums' strategies on accessibility. The UN Convention on the Rights of Persons with Disabilities defines universal design as "the design of products, environments, programmes and services to be usable by all people, to the greatest extent possible, without the need for adaptation or specialized design. 'Universal design' shall not exclude assistive devices for particular groups of persons with disabilities where this is needed."[46] COPOH/CCD worked with the Allan Simpson Memorial Fund to host two public events that brought representatives of the CMHR together with the disability community to learn about the disability community's human rights story.

Transportation Access

Through its Transportation Committee, COPOH/CCD has worked to build consensus on transportation issues in the disability community and beyond. For example, in June 2007, COPOH/CCD held a workshop on transportation for representatives of disability organizations. From that meeting, COPOH/CCD developed the document "Building an Inclusive and Accessible Canada Policy Statement by Council of Canadians with Disabilities (CCD) Re: Transportation Access," which was endorsed by 45 organizations. Through this policy statement, people with disabilities called for

1. Accessibility regulations similar to the United States regulatory model for all federally regulated modes of transportation and federally regulated transportation service systems (airports, stations, station-based ground transport, information systems, etc.).

2. A Disability Organizations Advisory Committee on Accessible Transportation that is resourced to undertake research and provide advice to the Minister of Transport for advancing access and inclusion of persons with disabilities.
3. The rebuilding of the capacity of the Accessibility Unit within Transport Canada to develop a national action plan on accessible transportation.
4. The Transport Development Centre to engage in research related to identifying new means of advancing accessibility and universal design.
5. The Government of Canada must attach a strong access standard/universal design principle to all infrastructure initiatives.
6. Enforcement of accessibility must be strengthened by providing the Canadian Transportation Agency (CTA) with the powers to grant interim injunctions related to purchase of any new equipment that would create new barriers, ensuring that CTA can make interim awarding of cost and award human rights remedies.
7. Legislative reforms to ensure that accessibility remains one of the principle objectives of the National Transportation Act.[47]

Assessing the impact of people with disabilities on the transportation system, Pat Danforth commented,

> Looking back it is hard to believe that 30 years ago many people living with disabilities were being denied basic transportation.... Nationally we have won great victories by voicing our concerns and championing for change. In the late 1980s, we helped put in place the Canadian Transportation Act.... The Act entrenched the concept of equal access by recognizing obstacles to our mobility, and includes investigating complaints, developing regulations plus codes of practice and conducting compliance reviews.[48]

Danforth, who has worked with the Saskatchewan Human Rights Commission, disability community organizations, the National Transportation Agency, among others, has had a significant involvement in COPOH/CCD. As chairperson of the COPOH/CCD's Transportation Committee, Danforth had a key role in directing the organization's successful legal challenge to VIA Rail's purchase of inaccessible passenger rail cars for service in Canada. The Supreme Court of Canada ordered VIA Rail to make its passenger cars accessible, and Judge Abella, who wrote the decision, commented that service providers like VIA Rail have a responsibility not to create new barriers. This decision was celebrated by the disability community.

CONCLUSION

The voice of people with disabilities has been a catalyst for change in Canada. People with disabilities are moms and dads, learners and workers, old and young, gay and straight, newcomers and First Nations. People with disabilities are Canadians. People with disabilities are not Other. Indeed, most Canadians will eventually experience disability either personally or through the experience of a family member. As new laws and programs are developed and existing ones reformed, COPOH/CCD will continue to advocate so that the voice of Canadians with disabilities will be heard.

NOTES

1. Coalition of Provincial Organizations of the Handicapped, (brochure, undated), COPOH/CCD files.
2. Consumer and Corporate Affairs, "Letters Patent (Coalition of Provincial Organizations of the Handicapped)," 1978, 34.
3. Henry Enns, "The Role of Organizations of Disabled People: A Disabled Peoples' International Discussion Paper," Independent Living Institute, undated, http://www.independentliving.org/docs5/RoleofOrgDisPeople.html.
4. Jim Derksen, *The Disabled Consumer Movement: Policy Implications for Rehabilitation Service Provision* (Winnipeg: COPOH, 1980), 11–12.
5. Raleigh Orr, "National Chairperson's Report," in *COPOH Annual Report, 1990–1991*, 2.
6. Laurie Beachell, "National Coordinator's Report," in *CCD Annual Report 1994*, 2–4.
7. Paul Young, "Finding My Voice," in *Celebrating Our Accomplishments* (Winnipeg: CCD, 2011), 27.
8. Young, "Finding My Voice," 27–28.
9. DAWN Canada, "National Organizing Meeting of the DisAbled Women's Network Report," 1987, 14.
10. Council of Canadians with Disabilities, "Minutes of the January 28 and 29, 2011 Meeting."
11. Coalition of Provincial Organizations of the Handicapped, "Minutes of the May 22 and 23, 1976 Meeting."
12. Council of Canadians with Disabilities, "About CCD," 2013, http://www.ccdonline.ca/en/about/.
13. Voice of Albertans with Disabilities, "A Proud History," 2017, http://vadsociety.ca/about-vad/a-proud-history.
14. Saskatchewan Voice of People with Disabilities, "About Us," 2014, http://saskvoice.com/about/who-we-are/
15. Diane Driedger, "Speaking for Ourselves: A History of COPOH on Its 10th Anniversary," in *COPOH Annual Report, 1985–1986* (Winnipeg: COPOH, 1986), 17–23.
16. Coalition of Provincial Organizations of the Handicapped, "First Meeting of Planning Committee for a 'Coalition of Provincial Organizations of the Handicapped,'" 1976, 34.
17. Coalition of Provincial Organizations of the Handicapped, "First Meeting," 34.
18. Coalition of Provincial Organizations of the Handicapped, "First Meeting," 34.
19. *St. John's Evening Telegram*, "Group Seeking National Voice for Handicapped," undated.
20. Allan Simpson, "Consumer Groups: Their Organization and Function" (Winnipeg: COPOH, 1980), 3–4.
21. Julianne Labreche, "The Disabled: Rebels with a Cause," *Reader's Digest*, June 1980, 123.
22. Kathy Newman, "#27: Allan Simpson," *50 Years, 50 Stories* series, Canadian Wheelchair Sports, 2017, http://www.cwsa.ca/70-50-40/allan-simpson.
23. Theresa Ducharme and Eric Jensen, *Life and Breath: A Love Story* (Winnipeg: Theresa Ducharme, 1987), 54.

24. Ducharme and Jensen, *Life and Breath*, 70.
25. Joan C. Brown, *A Hit-and-Miss Affair: Policies for Disabled People in Canada* (Ottawa: CCD, 1977), 452–53.
26. Brown, *A Hit-and-Miss Affair*, 452–53.
27. Brown, *A Hit-and-Miss Affair*, 454–55.
28. Derksen, *The Disabled Consumer Movement*, 11.
29. Canadian Association of the Deaf (CAD), "About CAD," http://www.cad.ca/about_cad.php.
30. Coalition of Provincial Organizations of the Handicapped, *COPOH Consumer Newsline*, no. 1, June 23, 1980.
31. Coalition of Provincial Organizations of the Handicapped, "Disabled Consumers Demand Voice at World Congress" (press release, undated).
32. Coalition of Provincial Organizations of the Handicapped, "Disabled Consumers Demand Voice."
33. Ann Darnbrough, "Miracles for Many," *Nursing Mirror*, August 14, 1980, 29.
34. Coalition of Provincial Organizations of the Handicapped, "Public Participation Program," *Info COPOH*, vol. 2 (1984).
35. Susan Deane, "Twinning with the Guyana Coalition of Citizens with Disabilities," in *Sharing Our Voices*, ed. Diane Driedger (Winnipeg: CCD, 1994), 4.
36. Council of Canadians with Disabilities, "CCD Participates in Winnipeg Landmine Conference," *International Developments*, March 3, 1997), 2.
37. Mary Reid, "Nothing about Us, without Us: Landmine Survivors Turning the Tide," in *Celebrating Our Accomplishments* (Winnipeg: CCD, 2011), 165.
38. Jim Derksen, "Disability Community Priorities and Expectations" (presentation made at the Provincial/Territorial Meeting of Ministers Responsible for Disability Issues and Human Rights, Winnipeg, March 15, 2011), http://www.ccdonline.ca/en/international/un/canada/jim-derksen-march2011.
39. Council of Canadians with Disabilities. *Final Report: Council of Canadians with Disabilities Community Consultation* (Winnipeg: CCD, 2004), 8.
40. Council of Canadians with Disabilities, "Mary Ennis's 4th Report from the UN." CCD International Developments UN Convention Series, August 12, 2005 (CCD Files).
41. Anna MacQuarrie, "The New Convention on the Rights of Persons with Disabilities: A New Era of Disability Rights," in *Celebrating Our Accomplishments* (Winnipeg: CCD, 2011), 146.
42. Council of Canadians with Disabilities. *Final Report*, 2.
43. Council of Canadians with Disabilities and Canadian Association of Community Living, "A Call to Action on the UN Convention on the Rights of Persons with Disabilities," 2011.
44. Council of Canadians with Disabilities, "CCD Chairperson's Update," November–December 2009.
45. Yvonne Peters, "A Missed Wedding, a Landmark Protest, and a Legal Victory," in *Celebrating Our Accomplishments* (Winnipeg: CCD, 2011), 137–39.
46. UN, Convention on the Rights of Persons with Disabilities (Ottawa: Department of Canadian Heritage, 2010), 4.
47. Council of Canadians with Disabilities, "Building an Inclusive and Accessible Canada," Policy Statement by Council of Canadians with Disabilities re: Transportation Access (Winnipeg: CCD, 2007).
48. Pat Danforth, "Moving Forward—Looking Backwards," in *Celebrating Our Accomplishments* (Winnipeg: CCD, 2011), 45.

BIBLIOGRAPHY

Beachell, Laurie. "National Coordinator's Report." In *CCD Annual Report 1984*, 2–4. Winnipeg: CCD, 1994.

Brown, Joan C. *A Hit-and-Miss Affair: Policies for Disabled People in Canada*. Ottawa: Canadian Council on Social Development, 1977.

Coalition of Provincial Organizations of the Handicapped. "COPOH." Brochure, undated. CCD files.

Coalition of Provincial Organizations of the Handicapped. "Disabled Consumers Demand Voice At World Congress." Press release, undated.

Coalition of Provincial Organizations of the Handicapped. "First Meeting of Planning Committee for a 'Coalition of Provincial Organizations of the Handicapped.'" 1976, 1.

Coalition of Provincial Organizations of the Handicapped. *COPOH Consumer Newsline*, no. 1, June 23, 1980.

Coalition of Provincial Organizations of the Handicapped. "Public Participation Program." In *Info COPOH*, vol. 2, 1984.

Consumer and Corporate Affairs. "Letters Patent (Coalition of Provincial Organizations of the Handicapped)." 1978, 2.

Council of Canadians with Disabilities. "Building an Inclusive and Accessible Canada," Policy Statement by Council of Canadians with Disabilities re: Transportation Access. Winnipeg: CCD, 2007.

Council of Canadians with Disabilities. "CCD Participates in Winnipeg Landmine Conference." *International Developments*, March 3, 1997.

Council of Canadians with Disabilities. "CCD Chairperson's Update." Winnipeg: CCD, November–December 2009.

Council of Canadians with Disabilities. *Final Report: Council of Canadians with Disabilities Community Consultation*. Winnipeg: CCD, 2004.

Council of Canadians with Disabilities. "Mary Ennis's 4th Report from the UN." CCD International Developments UN Convention Series. August 12, 2005.

Council of Canadians with Disabilities and Canadian Association of Community Living. "A Call to Action on the UN Convention on the Rights of Persons with Disabilities." 2011.

Danforth, Pat. "Moving Forward—Looking Backwards." In *Celebrating Our Accomplishments*, 45–46. Winnipeg: CCD, 2011.

Darnbrough, Ann. "Miracles for Many." *Nursing Mirror*, August 14, 1980.

DAWN Canada. "National Organizing Meeting of the DisAbled Women's Network Report." 1987.

Deane, Susan. "Twinning with the Guyana Coalition of Citizens with Disabilities." In *Sharing Our Voices*, edited by Diane Driedger, 3–8. Winnipeg: CCD, 1994.

Derksen, Jim. *The Disabled Consumer Movement: Policy Implications for Rehabilitation Service Provision*. Winnipeg: COPOH, 1980.

Derksen, Jim. "Disability Community Priorities and Expectations." Presentation made at the Provincial/Territorial Meeting of Ministers Responsible for Disability Issues and Human Rights, Winnipeg, March 15, 2011. http://www.ccdonline.ca/en/international/un/canada/jim-derksen-march2011.

Driedger, Diane. "Speaking for Ourselves: A History of COPOH on Its 10th Anniversary." In *COPOH Annual Report, 1985–1986*, 17–23. Winnipeg: COPOH, 1987.

Driedger, Diane, Eileen Giron Batres, and Irene Feika, eds. *Across Borders: Women with Disabilities Working Together*. Charlottetown, PEI: Gynergy Books, 1996.

Ducharme, Theresa, and Eric Jensen. *Life and Breath: A Love Story*. Winnipeg: Theresa Ducharme, 1987.
Enns, Henry. "The Role of Organizations of Disabled People: A Disabled Peoples' International Discussion Paper." Independent Living Institute, undated. http://www.independentliving.org/docs5/RoleofOrgDisPeople.html.
Labreche, Julianne. "The Disabled: Rebels with a Cause." *Reader's Digest*. June 1980, 124.
MacQuarrie, Anna. "The New Convention on the Rights of Persons with Disabilities: A New Era of Disability Rights." In *Celebrating Our Accomplishments*, 145–47. Winnipeg: CCD, 2011.
Newman, Kathy. "#27: Allan Simpson." *50 Years, 50 Stories* series. Canadian Wheelchair Sports, 2017. http://www.cwsa.ca/70-50-40/allan-simpson.
Orr, Raleigh. "National Chairperson's Report." In *COPOH Annual Report, 1990–1991*, 1–2.
Peters, Yvonne. "A Missed Wedding, a Landmark Protest, and a Legal Victory." In *Celebrating Our Accomplishments*, 137–39. Winnipeg: CCD, 2011.
Reid, Mary. "Nothing about Us, without Us: Landmine Survivors Turning the Tide." In *Celebrating Our Accomplishments*, 165–66. Winnipeg: CCD, 2011.
Simpson, Allan. "Consumer Groups: Their Organization and Function." Winnipeg: COPOH, 1980.
St. John's Evening Telegram. "Group Seeking National Voice for Handicapped," undated.
UN, Convention on the Rights of Persons with Disabilities. Ottawa: Department of Canadian Heritage, 2010, 4.
Young, Paul. "Finding My Voice." In *Celebrating Our Accomplishments*, 27–29. Winnipeg: CCD, 2011.

CHAPTER 16

Building an Accessible House of Labour: Work, Disability Rights, and the Canadian Labour Movement*

Dustin Galer

A central player in a changing labour market, the Canadian labour movement reflected the extent to which disability rights penetrated the world of work from the mid-1970s onward. The emergence of disability rights in Canada coincided with unprecedented changes in the organization of work and the transformation of union membership. Among union leaders, these changes facilitated purposeful dialogue about the role of disability rights in the workplace and within union structures; however, as social institutions embedded in local communities, unions reflected an understanding that disability affected the individual rather than being a manifestation of exclusionary socio-cultural systems. Inherent divisions in the broader disability community also manifested themselves in unions. Core union practices, such as advocacy on behalf of injured workers, reinforced the medical pathology of disability, which undercut declarations in support of disability rights. The business of union work increasingly ran up against a new generation of labour activists championing social justice and the extension of civil rights to traditionally marginalized groups. In an attempt to combine union business with social movement activism, the Canadian labour movement struck a fine balance in its support of medical authority and the social model of disability. What follows is an investigation of the Canadian labour movement's changing response to disability rights and the ideological dilemmas elicited by this response. We begin with a reflection on the importance of work in the discourse of disability rights.

DISABILITY RIGHTS AND THE SIGNIFICANCE OF WORK

Exclusion and marginalization with respect to the economic dimension of citizenship has been a consistent feature in the history of disability rights as activists have emphasized the need to integrate disabled persons into the workforce. Disability rights activists channelled energy from other social movements at home and abroad by articulating their critique of employment practices using the language of civil rights. In 1975 the UN Declaration on the Rights of Disabled Persons stated, "Disabled persons have the right to economic and social security and to a decent level of living. They have the right, according to their capabilities, to secure and retain employment or to engage in a useful, productive and remunerative occupation and to join trade unions."[1] The following year, the 31st session of the United Nations General Assembly resolved that 1981 would be the International Year for Disabled Persons (IYDP). The theme of the year would be "full participation" and the promotion of "all national and international efforts to provide disabled persons with proper assistance, training, care and guidance, to make available to them opportunities for suitable work and to ensure their full integration in society."[2] Where the IYDP promoted greater inclusion and participation of disabled persons in the workforce, the UN's Declaration on the Decade for Disabled Persons ([UNDDP] 1983–1992) provided a more realistic time frame for the implementation of measures identified during the IYDP. While these were not enforceable or binding resolutions, they set in motion a course of events in Canada that effectively plucked disability rights from the margins of public consciousness and thrust it to the centre. Unfortunately, however, disabled people would have to wait another 30 years for the sustained attention and concerted action on employment issues necessary for meaningful and lasting change.[3] Achievement of "full participation" in the workforce was a formidable goal because disabled people were consistently half as likely to be employed as the able-bodied population, while unemployment rates were even higher for those with "severe" disabilities.[4]

Many persons with disabilities were considered members of a "surplus population" whose difficulty selling their labour for wages at once permanently marginalized them in the realm of competitive paid employment and made them dependent on the "productive" able-bodied population.[5] This dependency took a number of forms including charitable benevolence, forced institutionalization, and, from the mid-twentieth century in Canada, state-sponsored income support. Disabled people found themselves excluded from the social expectation to engage in paid work that developed in the industrial period when people increasingly relied on wage work for survival.[6] Exclusion from paid work reinforced the belief that disabled people were incapable of productive remunerative work and therefore required charitable support rather than equitable opportunity in the labour market. Restrictive standards of physical and mental ability formed the underlying basis for a variety of barriers to paid employment that prevented most people with disabilities from achieving financial autonomy and the full expression of their economic rights. Willing and able to work, many disabled people found that inaccessibility pervaded the social order, making it difficult or impossible to attain paid employment. Blocked participation in education, job training, affordable housing, health care, and other services, as well as employer resistance to hiring disabled workers, kept many disabled people out of the labour market and forced them to live in poverty.[7] Unemployment and dependency among disabled people were largely the result of a self-fulfilling prophecy engendered by the convergence of prejudicial social attitudes, cultural practices, public policies, institutional arrangements, and inaccessible systems of production, movement, and exchange.

The medicalization of disability stigmatized disabled people in the labour market. Most hiring practices were shaped by an employer's calculation of potential productivity or profitability against the costs of training and compensation—factors that often stacked up against prejudice surrounding disabled people.[8] Rosemarie Garland-Thompson explains that the social categorization of disability informed interactions with the economy and the labour market. "The problem of how to formulate disability as a social category," she writes, "arises from a conflict between the need to preserve a social hierarchy linked to individual economic condition and the need to recognize the freedom from divine intervention that makes individual achievement tenable."[9] Disability highlighted tension surrounding formulations of the "working body" and an uncompromising ethic of individualism that underpinned industrial and post-industrial capitalism. Labour market status—so fundamental in the process of self-definition in modern capitalism—branded those whose bodily or mental difference kept them under- or unemployed and reinforced the belief that disability and economic marginalization were natural correlates. By the late 1970s, however, forces were at play to mitigate these negative perceptions and bring about greater economic integration for disabled people.

NEW LANDLORDS IN THE HOUSE OF LABOUR

The Canadian labour movement underwent a remarkable transformation in the post-war period. Initially made up of "blue collar" civil servants, public sector unions secured progressive wage increases for their members who staffed expanding government bureaucracies and who, by the early 1960s, began to pull ahead of their "white collar" counterparts in the private sector.[10] Clerical workers, professionals and para-professionals, hospital workers, social service employees, teachers, and others flocked to unions by the thousands as relations with management became increasingly impersonal. Federal and provincial legislation passed between the mid-1960s and 1970s encouraged unionism in the public sector by granting the right to certification, collective bargaining, and to strike, thus bringing public sector labour relations in line with the private sector.[11] Union growth in the public sector coincided with the declining strength of private sector unions as employment shrunk in core unionized sectors and employers went on a vigorous offensive.[12] By 1975 the Canadian Union of Public Employees (CUPE) was the largest union in Canada, followed by the Public Service Alliance of Canada (PSAC) and the National Union of Public and General Employees (NUPGE).[13] Public sector unions breathed new life into the Canadian labour movement by breaking down the long-standing domination by American unions and imparting a reinvigorated sense of militancy gained by a new position of strength and national leadership. By the 1970s, women represented roughly half the membership of public sector unions and steadily filled key leadership positions. These changing gender dynamics, alongside the predominance of the public sector, dramatically altered the labour movement's course of evolution. For example, CUPE elected the first female national union president in 1975, established a National Women's Task Force in 1981, held a National

Women's Conference in 1984, and created the "Rainbow Committee" in 1988 to coordinate efforts to promote employment equity.[14] Craig Heron explains, "Women played a crucial role in sensitizing their union leaders to the fact that not all members were white, English-speaking, heterosexual men."[15] The democratic structure of unions meant that women used their strength in numbers to initiate an energetic and decisive dialogue on equality. A new generation of labour activists nurtured the idea that the labour movement should prioritize a reconnection with its roots in social movement activism at a time when unions were dealing with the emerging threat of neoliberal politics.[16]

The growth of unionized public sector work presented new opportunities for disabled persons in terms of available work, type of workplace, and nature of employer. The expansion of government bureaucracies, schools, hospitals, social services, and affiliated work created an extraordinary demand for workers in a variety of workplaces. On the one hand, most of this work was presumably out of reach for disabled persons because public sector workplaces were just as likely to be physically inaccessible and unaccommodating to those with cognitive or developmental disabilities (particularly given the education and training requirements for many jobs). On the other hand, public sector employers were often leaders in developing employment equity and accommodation policies as they were held to a higher standard than the private sector in terms of the visibility and political pressure affecting public sector employment. For example, Metro Toronto was one of the first "equal employment opportunity employers" in Canada to declare its support in 1980 for the principles of employment equity. In a study of disability policy development in the Canadian labour movement, Rayside and Valentine found that, exceptions aside, "Union federations and public sector unions are more likely than others to respond favourably. White-collar unions are generally more advanced than blue-collar; female-dominated unions more than male-dominated."[17] The public sector, then, provided a climate that was especially ripe for the development of responses to the economic dimension of disability activism.

By the early 1980s, the discourse of equality evolved toward the notion of equity with its more comprehensive focus on securing equal opportunity for women, visible minorities, Aboriginals, and persons with disabilities. The 1984 report of the Royal Commission on Equality in Employment (otherwise known as the Abella commission) coined the term *employment equity* as part of a move away from the implications of job quotas that were associated with the existing term, *affirmative action*. Employment equity carried a greater focus on addressing and eliminating workforce barriers while allowing for special measures and accommodations in accordance with the differences between target groups. Over the course of the 1980s and 1990s, it became increasingly clear that a "hierarchy of equity" had developed in the labour movement whereby women's equality was strategically prioritized over other target groups. Ruth O'Brien explains, "Unlike women and people of color, persons with disabilities did not have equal standing with the rest of society. Persons with disabilities had to demonstrate that they could work before any demands could be imposed on employers."[18] Unionists felt compelled to focus on the most attainable and least divisive goals in a period of concerted attacks on unionized jobs. One early CUPE education manual explained that "to attack all problems at once may result in none being solved. Furthermore the large number of women in CUPE suffering from discrimination assures us that concentrating our energies on them—at least for the time being—will bear the most fruit."[19] This pragmatic approach to social justice issues in the labour movement was determined by strength in numbers, which at the outset favoured large groups of unionized women.

Practical calculations aside, Canadian labour organizations reflected the developing consensus on employment equity and disability rights by issuing a series of policy statements and forging new coalitions with disability activists. In 1980, the Canadian Labour Congress (CLC) called on the labour movement to encourage and support the employment of disabled people.[20] The following year, the Ontario Federation of Labour (OFL) issued its Statement on Employment of the Disabled, noting, "Labour's goal must be the same as the personal goal of every disabled person: total social integration and well-being. We all know a job is important. For the disabled, it is a precious right, long-denied."[21] The OFL pointed to discriminatory hiring practices and attitudinal barriers as the principal culprits for high unemployment rates and recommended that the statement be interpreted as a guideline for unions to identify and eliminate workforce barriers for disabled workers.[22] In 1983, NUPGE and the Council of Canadians with Disabilities (CCD; known at the time as the Coalition of Provincial Organizations of the Handicapped) issued a joint report entitled *Together for Social Change*, which represented the culmination of an unprecedented collaboration between disability rights activists and the labour movement.[23] The report was intended to promote awareness of workforce barriers faced by disabled people and included a set of recommendations that would serve as a framework for policy-makers, unionists, and disability activists undertaking a more informed plan of action to increase the employment of persons with disabilities. In particular, the report recommended the enactment of employment equity legislation, development of accessibility policies, more education on disability rights, and a commitment toward ongoing co-operation. As important as the collaboration was, its ad hoc nature was revealed as there appeared to be no follow-up reports or similar collaborations with other unions and disability activists.

More than a decade later the CCD pointed out that "there were many more instances when unions appeared to be more interested in getting involved with charity boosting, even to the extent of supporting telethons, than they were in making their employers sit down at the bargaining table and hammer out employment equity provisions."[24] At a conference held in 1994, echoing the CCD/NUPGE collaboration, but involving the Manitoba Federation of Labour and the Manitoba League of the Physically Handicapped, there was observed "an underlying tension that, in spite of all the good will [sic] in the world, is bound to exist between 'haves'—those with jobs, trade unionists in this case—and 'have nots,' the vast majority of the population of people with disabilities."[25] The tension and disappointment articulated by disability rights activists reflected their frustration with the lack of change in unemployment rates of people with disabilities and with their irregular and noncommittal relationship with the labour movement.

Upon closer examination it appears that the developing consensus on disability rights conflicted with the inner workings of the labour movement that compelled unions to reinforce the medicalization of disability.

WALKING THE LINE: MEDICALIZATION VERSUS SOCIAL CONSTRUCTION

The conventional understanding of disability as a medical impairment that afflicted the individual was challenged by disability rights with its underlying commitment to seeing disability in terms of the socio-cultural construction of barriers and arbitrary notions of able-bodiedness. Many disability rights activists held that to perceive disability as individual impairment was to reinforce the medicalization of disability while ignoring or minimizing the role of social processes. The Canadian labour movement was unique in that it simultaneously represented both the individual and social model of disability. On the one hand, injured workers endorsed the medical categorization of their impaired bodies in order to qualify for access to workers' compensation, job accommodations, and seniority entitlements, and to facilitate dialogue on occupational health and safety issues. Meanwhile, workers with pre-existing or congenital disabilities within and outside the union movement were more interested in drawing attention away from their individual disabilities to focus on systemic barriers to employment faced by all disabled people regardless of the origin of one's disability; however, disability rights were often lumped into a larger equity agenda in which advocates competed for attention alongside other equity-seeking groups. In the end, unions chose to deal with measures that largely affected injured workers because they felt compelled to focus on practical union matters in a climate of progressive government cutbacks, outsourcing, and a coordinated assault on contract provisions.

The relationship between injured workers and other disabled persons reflected broader tensions in the disability community between those with congenital disabilities and others who acquired their disabilities later in life. Within some disability circles, especially out of the United Kingdom and United States, a "hierarchy of disability" placed paraplegics and other wheelchair users on top and persons with developmental and intellectual disabilities somewhere near the bottom.[26] This hierarchy reflected differences in the experience of disability according to the magnitude of barriers, public visibility and popularity, political influence, and organizational funding. The disability hierarchy also extended to labour market experiences where persons with physical disabilities were often seen as more employable than those with intellectual or psychiatric disabilities.[27] While the politics and discourse of the disability hierarchy are beyond the scope of this chapter, it is imperative to consider how this hierarchy might have influenced relationships between labour leaders and disability activists as well as disabled workers within the union movement.

In the 1990s and early 2000s, unions and labour federations established disability caucuses with the express purpose of building a strong and progressive dialogue on equity issues that affected disabled people. Delegates at labour conventions were required to self-identify as having a disability in order to attend meetings and vote on pertinent matters. It is not clear that disability caucuses were the most attractive venue for most injured workers as they had their own groups to attend. Many injured workers likely did not even see themselves as disabled in the sense that they identified with or shared a common purpose with the larger disability community. Many injured workers likely preferred to see themselves as "fallen workers" instead of internalizing a new identity as a disabled person. Part of this likely reflected the natural process of psychological readjustment in self-awareness accompanying the "loss" of ability;[28] however, many disabled workers were part of a community of injured workers, often brothers and sisters in the union movement, who shared a common set of ethics that informed their self-identity. Robert Storey explains that in developing a "master frame of injustice," the injured worker developed a new self-identity as the "proud but beaten man who, because of a disabling workplace injury, could no longer provide for his family as he wanted and was supposed to do."[29] Preoccupied with their experience of disease or injury and drawing strength from their peers in the union movement and injured workers' associations, injured workers aligned themselves with a collective outlook that was quite distinct from the identity associated with disability rights and equity activism.

Injured workers in Toronto led a movement during the late 1970s and early 1980s against perceived attempts to dismantle the existing system of pensions for disabled workers.[30] An increasing number of industrial accidents put pressure on the workers' compensation system that led to a stiffening of payment and benefit structures by the early 1980s, provoking protest from a vocal cohort of injured workers.[31] Injured workers formed their own unions while energizing labour activism on a number of relevant issues, including job accommodation, modified work schemes, and workplace accessibility. Injured workers also drew attention to the fact that disabled bodies were still working bodies who had a "right to work" with entitlements to compensation and accommodation. Activism by injured workers in Canada reached back in labour history to the origins of workers' compensation at the turn of the twentieth century, but its contemporary resurgence had excellent timing alongside an upsurge in disability rights activism; however, injured workers were far better organized and insinuated within union culture than a smaller and less influential minority of workers with self-identified pre-existing and/or congenital disabilities.[32] Unions were obliged to negotiate on behalf of their members for higher disability pensions and modified work schemes. Workers' Compensation Boards drew up payment schedules that ascribed monetary figures to the loss of digits, limbs, range of motion, and other physical disabilities identified by medical professionals. As Ruth O'Brien observes, "Disability rights activists abhorred the idea that people must compensate for their disabilities, particularly so that they can accommodate the so-called normal workplace."[33] The idea that physical disability was somehow a loss in need of financial reimbursement or could be so plainly quantified through medical testing was clearly at odds with the ideologies underpinning disability rights that also empowered disabled people to reconsider their self-identity and social roles.

There was widespread uncertainty among unionists about how seniority provisions in collective agreements would interact with employment equity and disability rights more generally. Despite the strategic incorporation of social justice issues into a larger plan of action, the labour movement remained rather cool to the implementation of concrete measures to increase workforce participation rates of disabled people. Many unionists felt that the duty to accommodate disabled workers engendered certain conflict with seniority rights.[34] In 1987, the OFL assured its members, "We believe that we do not have to give up seniority in order to achieve affirmative action. In fact, women and minorities need stronger seniority clauses to break out of job ghettoes. A weakening of seniority would be of no benefit to them."[35] However, without the benefit of a critical mass of vocal disability activists in the labour movement, the social model of disability had trouble gaining adherents given its apparent complexity and the obscure threat it posed to conventional union priorities. Many unionists wondered whether employment equity was in fact a veiled attempt by legislators and employers to override seniority provisions and erode the power of collective agreements. As a result, they mounted a successful campaign to ensure that the Ontario Employment Equity Act would treat seniority arrangements as paramount.[36]

Another hurdle for disability activism in the labour movement was that Canada's Charter of Rights and Freedoms—one of the key vehicles ensuring protection of disability rights in Canada after 1985—was seen by unionists as an attack on the collective rights of labour unions and a move to undermine the foundation of the Canadian labour relations system. Section 15 of the Charter included the provision of equality rights that stipulated, "Every individual is equal before and under the law and has the right to the equal protection and equal benefit of the law without discrimination and, in particular, without discrimination based on race, national or ethnic origin, colour, religion, sex, age or mental or physical disability."[37] Many observers, particularly Canadian leftists, worried about the unintended effects of the Charter in practice, with its promise of routing individuals and organizations through expensive legal proceedings in the hopes of achieving social change.[38] Unionists argued that the Charter advanced a particularly individualistic notion of rights that was incompatible with the collective basis that unions relied upon to represent workers. The case of *Lavigne v. OPSEU* manifested these concerns when Lavigne, a member of the Ontario Public Service Employees Union, reasoned that when the union used part of his dues to finance political campaigns he did not necessarily agree with, his personal right to freedom of association under the Charter was curtailed. The case essentially pitted the linchpin of the post-war labour relations system—union security—against the Charter. Although the case eventually failed at the Supreme Court of Canada, it aroused serious concern among labour leaders about how legislation in the name of equity and human rights might be used against unions. The OFL reflected upon these general concerns, noting that the Charter, then, could turn out to be a two-edged sword. The leading edge may well carve out decisions that end discrimination against disadvantaged groups of people, or complete the economic and political freedoms of public sector workers now denied both the right to strike and political activity as citizens. The trailing edge of the sword, however, when wielded by reactionary minorities would cut down the whole framework of modern industrial society within which trade unions have helped to build a more humane environment.[39]

Unionists argued that the Charter should provide a "proper balance between collective and individual rights" rather than weighing heavily on individual rights and undermining the basis of collective action in a democratic society.[40] Disability rights commitments in union policy statements therefore raised an underlying concern about how those rights might be exercised to the detriment of the labour movement.

CONCLUSION

At the end of the UNDDP in 1992, CUPE concluded, "As the decade started out ... there was a rise in expectations—that there would be an increasing awareness about disabilities, leading to meaningful change, especially in the area of employment. This has not been the case, and the persistent realities in the lives of disabled persons have given way to new levels of bitterness and frustration."[41] A 1998 background paper for the CLC concluded, "The question of income security for persons with disabilities, regardless of their origin, has been waning and waxing in Canada for at least two decades.... While CLC interest in this issue has been consistent over time, it has also been a relatively low priority."[42] Also in conjunction with the end of the UNDDP, disability activist Yvonne Peters submitted a report commissioned by CUPE concluding that there were indeed union members with disabilities and some locals were devising strategies to address the needs of these members, but most locals needed more resources and information on strategies and methods for protecting the rights of members with disabilities.[43]

The labour movement was larger, more stable, and better funded than the loose coalition of volunteers leading the Canadian disability rights movement. These differences in structure and size meant that labour organizations tended to solicit the input of disability activists and rights organizations when the opportunity arose and forced the terms of these momentary partnerships to fit within an existing set of priorities. Disability activists in the labour movement also pointed to this unidirectional power relationship as the source of inherent tension and chronic inaction on disability rights.[44] As a result, the labour movement afforded intermittent attention to disability rights until the late 1990s, when union education departments expanded and the concerted efforts of a new generation of labour activists began to implement real action on disability rights.

The political discourse of disability rights directly influenced the heavily unionized public sector where it combined with existing pressure from women and visible minorities in both public and private sector unions to prioritize employment equity. Social activists and equity-seeking groups pushed against the traditional organizational culture of unions in order to create space for traditionally marginalized groups, including disabled workers; however, women's equality soon took precedence in a "hierarchy of equity," while disabled persons and others competed for attention. The union version of the "hierarchy of disability" devoted more attention to issues and organizations serving injured workers than the alternative of building stable and enduring connections with disability rights organizations. A gradual turn toward social unionism within parts of the Canadian labour movement afforded greater opportunities for disabled workers and for the advancement of disability rights. In a study of how Canadian unions responded to social movement activism, Carroll and Ratner argued that the labour movement carried a certain amount of responsibility by virtue of its dominant position in terms of size and funding.[45] They discovered a labour movement still in the process of reinvention in 1995, presumably balancing its long-standing objectives with the cross-coalitional grassroots action demanded by diverse social movements.[46]

By the turn of the century, labour organizations began to realize that passive and impromptu relationships with disability rights activists and organizations did not result in productive and valuable partnerships.[47] Malhotra and Thomas found that Canadian unions used the arbitration process to protect disability rights in the workplace as part of an ongoing transition to affirmative commitment and decisive action regarding disability rights issues.[48] In 2000, the CLC held its first Disability Rights Conference, bringing together labour leaders and disability activists to establish a more formal dialogue on disability rights in the labour movement. The result was an ongoing campaign entitled MORE (Mobilize, Organize, Represent, and Educate), which culminated in the publication of the aptly named *The MORE We Get Together: Disability Rights and Collective Bargaining Manual*.[49] The manual was intended to facilitate further understanding of persons with disabilities and the discourse of disability rights, while guiding union locals as to the best means of identifying and lowering workplace barriers. The opening segment of a 2007 union education film by the CUPE Persons with Disabilities National Working Group acknowledged, "Disability rights are a mainstream issue for our union in much the same way as contracting out or workplace safety and health issues."[50] These encouraging signs remind us that consistent attention and concerted action concerning the exclusion and marginalization of disabled people are necessary to achieve greater social and economic integration within the workforce and broader community.

NOTES

* Special thanks to Rob Hickey, David Kidd, Duncan MacDonald, David Lepofsky, and Lynn Carlisle for their advice and guidance. Thanks to Manda Vranic at the Toronto Archives as well as Debbie Rebeiro and other staff at the CUPE Equality Branch for assistance in locating resources. My sincere gratitude to Ian Radforth, Rob Hickey, and Andy Vatiliotou for reviewing earlier drafts of this paper. Any errors that remain are the author's responsibility.

1. United Nations General Assembly, *Declaration on the Rights of Disabled Persons*, Resolution 3447, December 9, 1975.
2. United National General Assembly, 31st Session, Resolution 31/123, "International Year for Disabled Persons," December 16, 1976, 104.
3. Michael Prince, *Absent Citizens: Disability Politics and Policy in Canada* (Toronto: University of Toronto Press, 2009), 18.
4. Emile Tompa et al., "Precarious Employment and People with Disabilities," in *Precarious Employment: Understanding Labour Market Insecurity in Canada*, ed. Leah F. Vosko (Montreal: McGill-Queen's University Press, 2006).
5. James Charlton, *Nothing about Us without Us: Disability Oppression and Empowerment* (Los Angeles: University of California Press, 2000), 149.
6. Sharon Snyder and David Mitchell, *Cultural Locations of Disability* (Chicago: University of Chicago Press, 2006), 51.
7. David Lepofsky, "The Long, Arduous Road to a Barrier-Free Ontario for People with Disabilities: The *Ontarians with Disabilities Act*—The First Chapter," *National Journal of Constitutional Law* 15 (2004): 134.
8. Marta Russell, "What Disability Civil Rights Cannot Do: Employment and Political Economy," *Disability & Society* 17, no. 2 (2002): 128.
9. Rosemarie Garland-Thompson, *Extraordinary Bodies: Figuring Physical Disability in American Culture and Literature* (New York: Columbia University Press, 1997), 47.
10. Craig Heron, *The Canadian Labour Movement* (Toronto: Lorimer, 1996), 95.
11. Heron, *Canadian Labour*, 96.
12. Employment in forestry, mining, and manufacturing all declined during this period. See Desmond Morton, "Government Worker Unions: A Review Article," *Labour/Le Travail* 35 (Spring 1995): 299.
13. Heron, *Canadian Labour*, 98; Morton, "Government Worker Unions," 298.
14. Canadian Union of Public Employees, "Topics," accessed March 26, 2013, http://cupe.ca/topics.
15. Heron, *Canadian Labour*, 147.
16. William Carroll and Murray Shaw, "Consolidating a Neoliberal Policy Bloc in Canada, 1976 to 1996," *Canadian Public Policy/Analyse de Politiques* 27, no. 2 (2001): 195–217.
17. David Rayside and Fraser Valentine, "Broadening the Labour Movement's Disability Agenda," in *Equity, Diversity, and Canadian Labour*, ed. Gerald Hunt and David Rayside (Toronto: University of Toronto Press, 2007), 178.
18. Ruth O'Brien, "From a Doctor's to a Judge's Gaze: Epistemic Communities and the History of Disability Rights Policy in the Workplace," *Polity* 35, no. 3 (April 2003): 339.
19. Canadian Union of Public Employees, *Equal Opportunity at Work: A CUPE Affirmative Action Manual* (Ottawa: CUPE Education Department, 1976), 3.
20. Canadian Labour Congress, *Policy Statement on the Disabled* (Ottawa: Canadian Labour Congress, 1980).
21. Ontario Federation of Labour, *Statement on the Employment of the Disabled* (November 1981), 1.
22. OFL, *Statement on the Employment of the Disabled*, 4.
23. Derek Fudge and Patty Holmes, *Together for Social Change: Employing Disabled Canadians* (Ottawa: Coalition of Provincial Organizations of the Handicapped and National Union of Provincial Government Employees, 1983).
24. Council of Canadians with Disabilities, "Labour and Disability," *Abilities* (Fall 1994).
25. CCD, "Labour and Disability."

26. Snyder and Mitchell, *Cultural Locations of Disability*, 166; Jay Dolmage and Cynthia Lewiecki-Wilson, "Refiguring Rhetoric: Linking Feminist Rhetoric and Disability Studies," in *Rhetorica in Motion: Feminist Rhetorical Methods and Methodologies*, ed. Eileen Schell and K. J. Rawson (Pittsburgh: University of Pittsburgh Press, 2010), 33.
27. Brigida Hernandez, Christopher Keys, and Fabricio Balcazar, "Employer Attitudes toward Workers with Disabilities and Their ADA Employment Rights: A Literature Review," *Journal of Rehabilitation* 66, no. 4 (2000): 4.
28. S. Michelle Driedger, Valorie Crooks, and David Bennett, "Engaging in the Disablement Process over Space and Time: Narratives of Persons with Multiple Sclerosis in Ottawa, Canada," *Canadian Geographer* 48, no. 2 (2004): 120.
29. Robert Storey, "'Their Only Power Was Moral': The Injured Workers' Movement in Toronto, 1970–1985," *Histoire Sociale/Social History* 41, no. 81 (2008): 128.
30. Storey, "'Their Only Power Was Moral,'" 114.
31. Storey, "'Their Only Power Was Moral,'" 120.
32. A policy statement from the OFL in 2001 spoke of the need to continue to develop close relationships with disability organizations and how the labour movement had been much more successful in developing formal institutional links with injured workers' organizations such as the Canadian Injured Workers Alliance, Ontario Network of Injured Workers, and affiliate organizations than with disability rights organizations. Ontario Federation of Labour, "Persons with Disabilities: Labour's View," December 2, 2001, 5, 8.
33. O'Brien, "From a Doctor's to a Judge's Gaze," 328.
34. M. Kaye Joachim, "Conflicts between the Accommodation of Disabled Workers and Seniority Rights" (MA thesis, University of Toronto, 1997), 67.
35. Ontario Federation of Labour, "A Statement on Equal Action in Employment" (statement made at the 31st Annual Convention of the OFL, November 1987), 2.
36. For example, in August 1993, CUPE's Equal Opportunities Department submitted a recommendation to the Ontario government recommending that Bill 79 (regarding employment equity) be amended to ensure seniority rights were better respected. Other unions and labour federations filed similar petitions, and in a February 1994 bulletin CUPE Ontario reported that Bill 79 was amended to reflect better seniority entitlements. Toronto Archives, Fonds 1011, Box 431328, Canadian Union of Public Employees Local 79.
37. Canadian Charter of Rights and Freedoms, Section 15(1).
38. Sarah Armstrong, "Disability Advocacy in the Charter Era," *Journal of Law & Equality* 2, no. 1 (Spring 2003): 38–40.
39. Ontario Federation of Labour, "Labour and the Charter" (statement made at the 29th Annual Convention, November 1985), 4.
40. Canadian Union of Public Employees, "Collective Rights," in *Jeff Rose: Worth Fighting For; Selected Speeches and Articles, 1983–1991* (Ottawa: Canadian Union of Public Employees, 1991).
41. Havi Echenberg, *Income Security and Support for Persons with Disabilities: Future Directions* (Ottawa: Canadian Labour Congress, 1998), 2.
42. Echenberg, *Income Security and Support*, 2.
43. Yvonne Peters, "Survey on People with Disabilities," CUPE Equality Branch, 1992, 2.
44. Rayside and Valentine, "Broadening the Labour Movement's Disability Agenda," 178–79.
45. William Carroll and R. S. Ratner, "Old Unions and New Social Movements," *Labour/Le Travail* 35 (Spring 1995): 218.
46. Carroll and Ratner, "Old Unions," 196.
47. One policy statement in 2001 from the OFL—a leader of sorts on the discourse of disability in the Canadian labour movement—spoke about labour's long history of social unionism and in

particular with disability organizations, but followed with the reminder, "Any such relationships are not static and should be re-examined from time to time to ensure that the needs of all participants are being met." Ontario Federation of Labour, "Persons with Disabilities," 3.
48. Mark Thomas and Ravi Malhotra, "Is Solidarity Accessible?: Disability Rights, Trade Union Democracy and the Politics of Inclusive Workplace Representation" (conference paper, Society for Disability Studies, June 2001), http://www.ee.umanitoba.ca/~kinsner/sds2001/proceed/pdocs/htms/17.HTM.
49. Canadian Labour Congress, *The MORE We Get Together: Disability Rights and Collective Bargaining Manual* (Ottawa: Canadian Labour Congress, 2004).
50. Canadian Union of Public Employees Persons with Disabilities National Working Group, "Challenging Attitudes," [video] (Ottawa: CUPE National Equality Branch, 2007).

BIBLIOGRAPHY

Armstrong, Sarah. "Disability Advocacy in the Charter Era." *Journal of Law & Equality* 2, no. 1 (Spring 2003): 33–91.

Canadian Labour Congress. *Policy Statement on the Disabled*. Ottawa: Canadian Labour Congress, 1980.

Canadian Labour Congress. *The MORE We Get Together: Disability Rights and Collective Bargaining Manual*. Ottawa: Canadian Labour Congress, 2004.

Canadian Union of Public Employees. *Equal Opportunity at Work: A CUPE Affirmative Action Manual*. Ottawa: CUPE Education Department, 1976.

Canadian Union of Public Employees. "Collective Rights." In *Jeff Rose: Worth Fighting For; Selected Speeches and Articles, 1983–1991*. Ottawa: Canadian Union of Public Employees, 1991.

Canadian Union of Public Employees Persons with Disabilities National Working Group. "Challenging Attitudes." [Video]. Ottawa: CUPE National Equality Branch, 2007.

Carroll, William, and R. S. Ratner. "Old Unions and New Social Movements." *Labour/Le Travail* 35 (Spring 1995): 195–221.

Carroll, William, and Murray Shaw. "Consolidating a Neoliberal Policy Bloc In Canada, 1976 to 1996." *Canadian Public Policy/Analyse de Politiques* 27, no. 2 (2001): 195–217.

Charlton, James. *Nothing about Us without Us: Disability Oppression and Empowerment*. Los Angeles: University of California Press, 2000.

Council of Canadians with Disabilities. "Labour and Disability." *Abilities* (Fall 1994).

Dolmage, Jay, and Cynthia Lewiecki-Wilson. "Refiguring Rhetorica: Linking Feminist Rhetoric and Disability Studies." In *Rhetorica in Motion: Feminist Rhetorical Methods and Methodologies*, edited by Eileen Schell and K. J. Rawson, 23–28. Pittsburgh: University of Pittsburgh Press, 2010.

Driedger, S. Michelle, Valorie Crooks, and David Bennett. "Engaging in the Disablement Process over Space and Time: Narratives of Persons with Multiple Sclerosis in Ottawa, Canada." *Canadian Geographer* 48, no. 2 (2004): 119–36.

Echenberg, Havi. *Income Security and Support for Persons with Disabilities: Future Directions*. Ottawa: Canadian Labour Congress, 1998.

Fudge, Derek, and Patty Holmes. *Together for Social Change: Employing Disabled Canadians*. Ottawa: Coalition of Provincial Organizations of the Handicapped and National Union of Provincial Government Employees, 1983.

Garland-Thompson, Rosemarie. *Extraordinary Bodies: Figuring Physical Disability in American Culture and Literature*. New York: Columbia University Press, 1997.

Hernandez, Brigida, Christopher Keys, and Fabricio Balcazar. "Employer Attitudes toward Workers with Disabilities and Their ADA Employment Rights: A Literature Review." *Journal of Rehabilitation* 66, no. 4 (2000): 4–16.

Heron, Craig. *The Canadian Labour Movement*. Toronto: Lorimer, 1996.

Kaye Joachim, M. "Conflicts between the Accommodation of Disabled Workers and Seniority Rights." MA thesis, University of Toronto, 1997.

Lepofsky, David. "The Long, Arduous Road to a Barrier-Free Ontario for People with Disabilities: The *Ontarians with Disabilities Act*—The First Chapter." *National Journal of Constitutional Law* 15 (2004): 125–333.

Morton, Desmond. "Government Worker Unions: A Review Article." *Labour/Le Travail* 35 (Spring 1995): 297–307.

O'Brien, Ruth. "From a Doctor's to a Judge's Gaze: Epistemic Communities and the History of Disability Rights Policy in the Workplace." *Polity* 35, no. 3 (April 2003): 325–46.

Ontario Federation of Labour. *Statement on the Employment of the Disabled*. November 1981.

Ontario Federation of Labour. "Persons with Disabilities: Labour's View." December 2, 2001.

Peters, Yvonne. "Survey on People with Disabilities." CUPE Equality Branch, 1992.

Rayside, David, and Fraser Valentine. "Broadening the Labour Movement's Disability Agenda." In *Equity, Diversity, and Canadian Labour*, edited by Gerald Hunt and David Rayside, 156–80. Toronto: University of Toronto Press, 2007.

Russell, Marta. "What Disability Civil Rights Cannot Do: Employment and Political Economy." *Disability & Society* 17, no. 2 (2002): 117–35.

Snyder, Sharon, and David Mitchell. *Cultural Locations of Disability*. Chicago: University of Chicago Press, 2006.

Storey, Robert. "'Their Only Power Was Moral': The Injured Workers' Movement in Toronto, 1970–1985." *Histoire Sociale/Social History* 41, no. 81 (2008): 99–131.

Thomas, Mark, and Ravi Malhotra. "Is Solidarity Accessible?: Disability Rights, Trade Union Democracy and the Politics of Inclusive Workplace Representation." Conference paper, Society for Disability Studies, June 2001. http://www.ee.umanitoba.ca/~kinsner/sds2001/proceed/pdocs/htms/17.HTM.

Tompa, Emile, Heather Scott, Scott Trevithick, and Sudipa Bhattacharyya. "Precarious Employment and People with Disabilities." In *Precarious Employment: Understanding Labour Market Insecurity in Canada*, edited by Leah F. Vosko, 3–40. Montreal: McGill-Queen's University Press, 2006.

CHAPTER 17

The Habeas Corpus of Justin Clark

Marilou McPhedran[*]

Rights ... is still deliciously empowering to say. It is the magic wand of visibility and invisibility, inclusion and exclusion, power and no power. The concept of rights, both positive and negative is also the marker of our citizenship, our relation to others.[1]

Rights of mobility, physical access and equality under Canadian law were central to the political agenda of the disability movement. In a context in which disabled citizens were routinely denied access to many spaces of social life and thus suffered extremes of isolation, this liberal rights agenda spoke in a very immediate way to what it was like to be disabled in Canada.[2]

INTRODUCTION

Dear Reader:

I know this is a textbook on the history of disability in Canada, but it's a sunny Saturday afternoon—why am I in my office writing to you about events of decades ago? Well, in 2011, I was delighted to have been invited to give a lecture on disability rights law for an intensive university credit course co-directed by Dr. Michelle Owen and Dr. Nancy Hansen, offered by the University of Winnipeg Global College.[3] I had quite a legalistic lecture prepared and in it a brief reference to the landmark legal battle cited as *Clark v. Clark* in Ontario that began in 1981, which was designated by the UN as the International Year of Disabled Persons (IYDP). As a young man, Justin Clark—with no freedom and no money—had to get to court to fight his parents and the government for his right to choose where and with whom he wanted to live, although he had clearly attained the age of majority.

On that summer day in that class, for the first time "on the public record," I found myself confessing to conduct that I chose as a young lawyer—knowing it would likely have been considered unbecoming to the profession of law and might have resulted in my disbarment, had it become known at the time. Two of the editors of this book, Nancy Hansen and Roy Hanes, put out a call for "untold stories," and after that class, Nancy asked me to write about my role in the Justin Clark case as one such story for this book—and that is how this rather long letter to you came to be. This story will not become legalistic, but to tell it, I must situate Justin's dilemma in its legal context at the dawn of the 1980s—*before* anyone could rely on disability rights in Section 15 under "Equality Rights" in the Canadian Charter of Rights and Freedoms entrenched in the Constitution Act, 1982, because a moratorium had been placed on Section 15 until 1985.

To write this, I dredged my memory and as much of the media coverage of the trials from 30 years ago as I could find, as well as files in my own archives from 1981 when I was on Justin Clark's legal team. I'd like to tell you about the story behind the story told by these documents, and to share some of my observations on Justin's triumph. I'm writing this in 2017, the 35th anniversary of the definitive court case that liberated Justin and set a new freedom standard for people with disabilities in Canada, using the oldest remedy for unjust detention in Commonwealth law: the ancient writ of *habeas corpus ad subjudicium*—the right to appear before a judge for a determination of whether imprisonment is unlawful.

For reasons explained in this chapter—for the first time in print—my role in the Justin Clark case changed abruptly, and I turned into a potential witness to testify in support of Justin's legal quest for his "lived rights." I hadn't thought of this term back then, but it certainly applies—as I tell my students today, *lived rights* are the crucial difference between words online or on paper in a display case, and *actual positive changes in the lives of disadvantaged people* that make it possible to live in peace and realize full human potential.

My transition from Justin's lawyer to Justin's witness was necessitated by the fact that it was imperative that his voice be heard in the legal battle to determine whether he could live his life as a free man. For Justin to be heard by a judge, his voice had to be in the format respected by the courts: a sworn affidavit based on Justin's competence to express his preferences, particularly his passionate longing for emancipation from forced detention in the Rideau Regional Centre (RRC) in Smiths Falls, Ontario, the government-run institution to which he had been consigned as an infant by his parents.

The Right Honourable Beverley McLachlin, Chief Justice of the Supreme Court of Canada, explained that

> the oldest human right is the right to be free from arbitrary arrest and imprisonment. Chapter 33 of the *Magna Carta* of 1215 banned arbitrary arrest and imprisonment and established the right to call upon a judge to be freed—the right of *habeas corpus*.[4]

Justin insisted on his right to "produce the body" (habeas corpus) in order to have a judge assess whether detention against his will by his parents and the government officials who ran the RRC was illegal. Justin and his legal team also had to prove he was mentally competent and, to do this, they relied on Canada being a country with the "rule of law"—a term that we may often hear, but probably don't appreciate until things start to go wrong and people are stopped from living their rights. In that same speech, Chief Justice McLachlin connected habeas corpus as essential to the rule of law, which

> stands ... for four values that are as important in times of crisis as in times of peace—legitimacy, universality, rights protection and accountability. Legitimacy: the principle that power must be exercised according to law and not arbitrarily. Universality: the principle of one law for all, and that none are excluded in a discriminatory fashion. Rights protection, the principle that rights must be sustained and can be attenuated only when this is demonstrably necessary to the greater collective interest. Accountability: the principle that all those who exercise power are accountable for that exercise through the law as applied in independent courts.[5]

When Justin and his supporters reached out to the Advocacy Resource Centre for the Handicapped (ARCH) in Toronto, they engaged all four of these values in the rule of law and deeply challenged our legal system. In most legal proceedings, preparing and swearing an affidavit is commonplace and relatively easy—but not for Justin Clark. The first affidavit that Justin gave in his long legal battle was taken by me in secret in Justin's room on a weekend, using the Blissymbolics board on his wheelchair (before I was escorted out by security personnel at the RRC). As a counsellor at a summer camp run by the Society for Crippled Children and Adults of Manitoba (now the Society for Manitobans with Disabilities) in the 1960s, I had used Blissymbolics. Thus, I was the lawyer in the office who could most readily interview Justin to gather the information needed and attest to his affidavit. I got in to see Justin that day (for the first and last time while he was at the RRC) by not telling the truth about why I was there and what I intended to do. I made my way to the centre in knowing contravention of the decision by the Ontario government and Justin's parents to block Justin's access to legal counsel from ARCH, where I was employed at that time. For my chosen actions on that day, I took (and continue to take) full personal responsibility, but I can't say that I've been unworried about the possible ramifications to my professional reputation until now—no longer a practising lawyer or member of a regulatory body for lawyers—even though my name as a lawyer for Justin never appeared in media coverage of the case. Sometimes being a lawyer following the rules does not serve justice.

In a letter to ARCH to my attention in early October 1981, the Legal Services Branch of the Ontario Ministry of Community and Social Services advised that Justin's request to see his medical reports was denied:

> The Ministry's position is that the record is the property of the Ministry and will only be released when there is a legal requirement to do so. As far as I know, there is no provision in our law which entitles a resident to see his record.... Justin Clarke [sic] is considered to be incompetent and incapable of managing

his affairs.... He is, as far as this Ministry is concerned, incapable of consenting to the release of records and of instructing Counsel and thus, in the absence of any legal requirements, the Ministry is unable to accede to your requests.[6]

In an interview that Justin's parents gave to a reporter from the *Ottawa Citizen* on March 9, 1982, Justin's father, Ottawa lawyer Ronald H. Clark, said that his son Justin was "retarded" and that he based his opinion on medical reports he and his wife had received from the authorities running the RRC. Having filed in 1981 to obtain legal guardianship over his son, even though Justin was over 18, his father indicated surprise when he was opposed by his son's legal team in court. In his affidavit, Justin told the court about his life in the RRC, about the friends that were being blocked access to him, that his parents had not visited him for 16 years after putting him into the RRC, and that, after learning Blissymbolics, Justin had conveyed requests to his parents to visit or phone him but they did not answer for years. Justin's father indicated to the reporter that he doubted Justin's affidavit, and was quoted in the article as saying, "I would expect my son would not be capable of recalling the details and I think the people who assisted in the preparation (of the affidavit) were not knowledgeable of the facts.... I believe it would be very difficult if not impossible, for my son to communicate with a solicitor."[7]

I want to share with you exactly what Justin said to me in his first affidavit, sworn before me on October 19, 1981, because nothing I can tell you will be as compelling as Justin's own words. As I write this, I am holding a copy of Justin's first affidavit, addressed to the Supreme Court of Ontario, which states:

IN THE MATTER OF THE HABEAS CORPUS ACT, R.S.O. 1980, C.193;

AND IN THE MATTER OF AN APPLICATION BY JUSTIN CLARK FOR A WRIT OF HABEAS CORPUS AD SUBJICIENDUM AND FOR A WRIT OF CERTIORARI

BETWEEN:

JUSTIN CLARK

APPLICANT

- A N D -

DR. NESA LYSANDER, ADMINISTRATOR OF THE RIDEAU REGIONAL CENTRE

RESPONDENT

AFFIDAVIT

I, JUSTIN CLARK, OF THE RIDEAU REGIONAL CENTRE, IN THE TOWN OF SMITHS FALLS, IN THE PROVINCE OF ONTARIO, MAKE OATH AND SAY AS FOLLOWS:

1. I am nineteen years of age, a Canadian citizen, having been born in the City of Ottawa ... son of Mr. and Mrs. Ronald H. Clark of Ottawa. My present place of residence is on Ward 3-A at the Rideau Regional Centre in Smiths Falls, Ontario.
2. Ever since I was two (2) years old I have lived at the Rideau Regional Centre. My parents visited me once after I was admitted and did not visit me again for over sixteen (16) years.
3. When I was about twelve years old I went to a summer camp and started to learn how to use a method of communication called Blissymbolics.
4. After that summer camp was over, I went back to the Rideau Regional Centre and that fall I met my friend Carol MacLaughlan who had come to work at the Centre in order to teach us how to use our "Bliss Boards." This was very important for me because up until then I had had lots of trouble talking to people and getting them to understand what I was saying. Carol helped me to use more and more symbols and because I saw her every day at school, we became good friends.
5. Because I could talk to Carol with my Board I told her that I wanted to write to my mother and father. In order to do this, I pointed to the symbols that told her how I was feeling and she wrote the letters to my parents. In these letters I asked my parents to visit me or if they did not want to visit me, to phone me. I told my mother and father that I loved them and sometimes I asked Carol to send them pictures of me. For a long time my mother and father did not answer.
6. For many years, Carol was my teacher and my friend and sometimes I would leave the Centre to go to Carol's house and I sometimes stayed overnight. Now, Carol does not work here, but she phones me and she comes to visit me. Right now, I am having problems because I want to go on outings with Carol and my other friends but I have to stay inside the Centre unless somebody who works here takes me out.
7. I have another friend who used to work here named Normand Pellerin. Normand used to be a teacher here at the Centre and while he was working here, we became good friends. I think Normand is probably my best friend. Normand has taken me to visit his family at Christmas time. Last Christmas I was able to go to the farm where Normand lives to stay overnight and to have a good time with everybody else on the farm for three (3) days. I have asked Normand if I can spend Christmas at his house again this year and he told me that we have to wait and see. It seems like a long time since Normand could come into the Centre to see me. Sometime he calls me on the

telephone and we talk but I know that Normand is not being allowed in to visit me. Nobody has explained to me why Normand cannot come here, but I think it might be because of the vacation we had planned this summer.

8. My friend (WM) lives on the same ward as I do. Normand asked us if we would like to go on one (1) week holiday to Quebec City. We really wanted to go, and for the first time, I signed the request form to get permission from Dr. Earl. Later Normand came to see me and told me that Dr. Earl had changed his mind. I asked Normand to tell me why Dr. Earl had changed his mind and we decided to go to Dr. Earl's office and ask him ourselves.

9. I remember going with Normand to meet Dr. Earl. There was still time for me to go with (W) and Normand and Normand's father. I could not understand why Dr. Earl had changed his mind and so Normand asked Dr. Earl to tell us why. That was when Dr. Earl told us that my father had refused permission for me to go on this vacation. Dr. Earl told us that it was up to my father to change his mind or else I could not go to Quebec City.

10. After I saw Dr. Earl, Normand and I returned to the ward and we decided that we should call my father. Normand telephoned to my father and I heard Normand ask my father to change his mind. I heard Normand tell my father that I was with him by the telephone. I do not know exactly what my father said to Normand, but I know that he would not change his mind and that I had to stay behind while (W) and the others went to Quebec City. This made me feel sad and it also made me feel angry.

11. I have written to my father for many years and I have told him that I love him. It made me feel sad to know that my father would not let me go with my friends even though I had often gone on outings with them before and nothing bad had happened.

12. I was supposed to go to Quebec City in July but I had to stay behind. Since that time, I have not been allowed to go outside of the Centre with any of my friends who used to work here. When Normand got back from Quebec City, we talked about what we could do and Normand explained to me that I had the right to have my own lawyer so that I could leave the Centre with a volunteer who was a friend. On July 24, 1981, I signed a paper that made it clear that I wanted a lawyer to help me. A few days later my lawyer, David Baker, came to see me at the Centre. David and I talked about my problems and I showed him on my Board that I was very worried that my parents or maybe someone else would try to keep me inside even when I wanted to go out with my friends. David explained what he thought we could do and I told him that I wanted him to go ahead and take legal action to permit me to leave the Centre without requiring my parents' permission.

13. David and I went to see Dr. Lysander and Dr. Earl together. They would not speak to him with me present. David left their office and was going to leave the Centre. I asked him to see them without me, which he did. Nothing changed after that meeting.

14. I have another friend named Danielle Allen who still can come to visit me here. I used to be able to go out with Danielle and some of my other friends who live here but now I cannot go out with her any more. I know that Danielle asks if I can go with her every chance that she gets, but they always say no. None of my other friends who live here have to stay behind. I do not think this is fair.

15. Danielle told me that she asked if I could go with Betty and Germain and Delsie and Mary and Robert to dinner at Danielle's house and then to a dance on Saturday, October 17, 1981. It made me very sad to be left behind again. I love my mother and father and I do not want to get them into trouble, but I do not think that they should be able to stop me from seeing my friends.

16. I have wanted to see my mother and father ever since I can remember. For over sixteen (16) years they didn't answer my letters or come and see me. After my lawyer became involved this changed. In August, my mother and father came to see me here at the Centre. On my birthday, September 21st, I was nineteen (19) years old and my mother and father brought me a present. I am glad that my parents are coming to see me. I want to be able to see my mother and father but I do not think I should be stopped from seeing and going out with my friends as well.

17. I have lived at the Rideau Regional Centre for a long time. It is the only home that I know. I do not want to leave here until I have another place to go to. I think I should be able to visit other places where I might want to live so that I can see for myself what they are like. Right now, I am not being allowed to go anywhere unless I am with a member of the staff. That is not the way it used to be and that is not the way that I think it should be.

18. Nobody has told me why Dr. Earl and Dr. Lysander and my mother and my father have decided that I must stay at the Rideau Regional Centre all the time while my friends who live here are free to leave as before.

19. I am now nineteen (19) years old and I can communicate very well with my Bliss Board. Because I have cerebral palsy I use my Board to talk. By pointing to symbols I am able to make sentences. I have no problem understanding what is said to me. I am doing well in school. Now shown to me and marked as Exhibit "A" to this my Affidavit is a copy of my Bliss Board.

20. I have seen several doctors and psychologists recently. They told me they thought I was able to make decisions for myself. I wish that people who think I cannot decide things for myself would take the time to talk to me so that they could understand how much I really know.

21. I know Dr. Lysander and Dr. Earl run the Rideau Regional Centre. I do not want to interfere with their job. Dr. Earl told me I could not go out of the Centre because my father would not let me. I have been given no other reason for keeping me in here. I do not think my father should be able to stop me from seeing my friends. I do not think that Dr. Lysander and Dr. Earl should follow my father's instructions because I am old enough to make these decisions for myself.

22. I love my mother and father and I hope that they will still come and visit me. I do not want to hurt their feelings but I also do not want to stay inside all the time and not be able to see my best friend at all. I believe that keeping me here in this way should not be allowed and I have asked my lawyer, David Baker, to do something about this as soon as he can.

HOW JUSTIN FOUND HIS VOICE THROUGH THE MEDIA

Justin's legal team agreed that Justin needed media attention to augment his lonely voice against the powerful resources and controls held by his father and the government officials working to keep him away from his friends and detained at the RRC. But we were also concerned that media attention too soon would damage Justin's chances to have a judge deliberate fully and fairly on how he was being held against his will and whether he was mentally competent to make his own choices.

Days after I prepared and witnessed Justin's affidavit, a courier delivered a package to the home of one of Canada's most famous journalists, Michele Landsberg of the *Toronto Star*. It was still 1981, the same year in which equality seekers in Canada lobbied long and hard to strengthen the rights protections in the Canadian Constitution and, based on my experience with Michele following the Ad Hoc Women's Constitutional Conference earlier that year, I believed she was the only member of the media who could be trusted completely to keep her word that the information we gave her about Justin's struggle would stay "off the record." The package I sent to Michele was not in a proverbial unmarked brown envelope, but it was marked "personal and confidential," and it contained the major components of our case, including the draft affidavits of our most important witnesses in support of Justin's argument that he was being unlawfully detained. Mishandled, that package could have destroyed Justin's chance at freedom.[8]

Instead, Michele went quietly to the courtroom in Perth, Ontario, near the RRC where Justin was being detained; she was the only member of the media present for what would be the first of many hearings before Justin's case was determined. Michele's first article in November 1981 broke the case open and she was back in the courtroom a year later when Judge John Matheson finally read out his decision:

> With incredible effort, Justin Clark has managed to communicate his passion for freedom, as well as his love of family, during the course of this trial.... We have recognized a gentle, trusting, believing spirit and very much a thinking human being who has a unique part to play in our compassionate, interdependent society. Therefore, in a spirit of liberty, the necessity to understand the minds of other men and the remembrance "that not even a sparrow falls to earth unheeded," I find and declare Mathew Justin Clark to be mentally competent.[9]

CONCLUSION

As our Indigenous leaders teach, life is a circle. Without knowing how to understand Justin using his Blissymbolics board, I could not have surreptitiously drafted his first affidavit. When I was still a teenager, I came in from rural Manitoba to attend the University of Winnipeg and there I met another student, David Steen, recently retired as the chief executive officer of the Society for Manitobans with Disabilities, the organization that ran the summer camp where I learned to use the Blissymbolics board. Steen has reflected on the impact of the IYDP in 1981, which may well have influenced Justin's friends to reach out for his legal representation that year. As Steen put it, "IYDP heightened our expectations of what was possible and it made us hungry for more. It encouraged us to dream our dreams of a better, more inclusive and caring world."[10]

Justin Clark is now a man in his mid-fifties, who has lived the majority of his life in the community, with his friends as his chosen family. Justin has achieved what he set out to do and more. He lives a "normal" life: he has a job that he travels to and from, he takes vacations outside of Canada, he goes for dinner with friends and family. Justin—in an extraordinary manner—lives an "ordinary" life, free of de facto institutionalized incarceration, as he continues to inspire others by sharing the remarkable story of his journey to freedom launched by using the ancient remedy of habeas corpus. In 2014, Justin was the recipient of an award from Celebration of People for his advocacy on disability rights. The following is an excerpt from an interview with Justin by journalist Kelly Egan of the *Ottawa Citizen*:

> He extended his right hand, flat and twisted, a little web-like, and smiled mightily. He has brown eyes and no hint of grey hair. Clark, who lives in a group home in the south end, communicates with a tablet-like device that is pre-loaded with words and symbols, and fixed to his wheelchair. It can take as long as five or ten minutes for him to tap out a short answer, which is then read by a voice synthesizer. It unnerved me at first.... But he trained me to wait and listen. I had to adjust to his rhythm, muster some patience, accept his way of being, be still. Perhaps this has been his life's struggle: for the harried world to pause, accept this different form of expression, see beyond the strange noises and kicking feet.[11]

Justin and other persons with disabilities—with their allies—deserve the strongest possible rights framework that those of us who make laws can deliver. In 1982, Justin's legal team had to use a very old legal remedy to win his freedom, also setting in motion the eventual closure of that institution. But in 2010, the United Nations International Convention on the Rights of Persons with Disabilities (ICRPD) came into force in Canada; however, Canada has still not ratified the Optional Protocol to the ICRPD, which is an essential tool for effective advocacy. As a recently appointed senator, I remain convinced that Canadian governments are obligated to ensure that all Canadians, including those with disabilities—like Justin—have the tools they need to live their rights to the fullest extent possible.

Justin's struggle for his freedom of choice, his freedom of movement, and his freedom to live his rights happened in a small place, but with his circle of chosen family, Justin has demonstrated that those rights have meaning far beyond. He embodies the aspiration that all of us share: to live in dignity.

The picture below was taken near the end of 2017 when I visited Justin at his workplace and we caught up on each other's lives. Justin seemed amused that the lawyer who slipped past institutional guards to take his affidavit decades ago is now a senator. As I finish this letter to you, Justin and I are planning for his introduction to the Senate of Canada. Perhaps unsurprisingly, the logistics are proving to be somewhat of a challenge because—well, because the Senate visitors gallery is not accessible. Undaunted, we see more advocacy opportunities for disability rights in the heart of government, right up here on Parliament Hill.

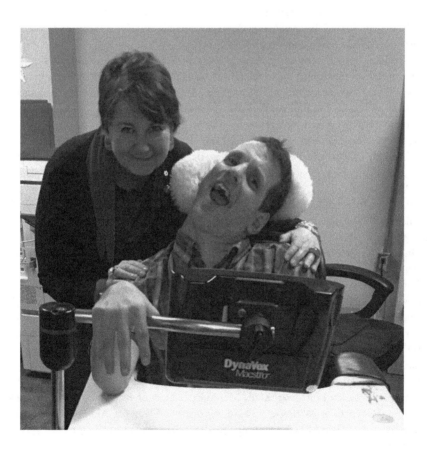

NOTES

* The author is a human rights lawyer, professor, and activist, appointed in November 2016 as an independent senator for Manitoba in the Parliament of Canada. She was an influential leader at the 1981 Ad Hoc Committee of Canadian Women on the Constitution Conference, the grassroots social movement of women across Canada resulting in stronger equality rights in the Constitution. With Patricia Israel, she coordinated Canada's first national conference on disability rights under the Canadian Charter of Rights and Freedoms in 1982. She is also a co-founder of several widely recognized non-profit Canadian organizations including the Women's Legal Education and Action Fund (LEAF), which has conducted constitutional equality test cases and interventions for more than 30 years; the Metropolitan Action Committee on Violence Against Women and Children (METRAC); and the Gerstein Crisis Centre for homeless discharged psychiatric patients. She wishes to express appreciation to Cathy Lin, a JD candidate at the University of Ottawa Faculty of Law, for her resourceful research assistance.

1. Patricia Williams, *The Alchemy of Race and Rights* (Cambridge, MA: Harvard University Press, 1991), 164.
2. Vera Chouinard, "Legal Peripheries: Struggles over DisAbled Canadians' Places in Law, Society, and Space," in *Rethinking Normalcy*, ed. Tanya Titchkosky and Rod Michalko (Toronto: Canadian Scholars' Press, 2009), 217.
3. The Re-Imagining Disability Summer Institute provided three university credits in an intensive course that ran from July 4 through 15, 2011, at the University of Winnipeg. More information can be obtained through Professor Michelle Owen, director of the Global College Institute on Health and Human Potential (m.owen@uwinnipeg.ca), and requests can be made to access the video records of lectures.
4. The Right Honourable Beverley McLachlin, "Remarks of the Right Honourable Beverley McLachlin, P.C. to the Vietnam-Canadian Business Association" (speech delivered in Ho Chi Minh City, November 28, 2003), http://www.scc-csc.ca/judges-juges/spe-dis/bm-2003-11-28-eng.aspx.
5. McLachlin, "Remarks of the Right Honourable Beverley McLachlin, P.C. to the Vietnam-Canadian Business Association."
6. Rosemary J. McCully, Solicitor, "Letter from the Legal Services Branch of the Ontario Ministry for Community and Social Services to the Advocacy Resource Centre for the Handicapped," October 2, 1981, McPhedran fonds 2007/031/104(8), York University Clara Thomas Archives and Special Collections.
7. Roswitha Guggi, "Parents Believe Their Son Just Can't Grasp What's Going On," *Ottawa Citizen*, March 9, 1982, 39.
8. Marilou McPhedran, "Memo to Michele Landsberg," October 21, 1981, in McPhedran fonds 2007/031/104(8), York University Clara Thomas Archives and Special Collections.
9. Clark v. Clark, 40 OR (2d) 383, 1982 CanLII 2253.
10. David Steen, "The Times, They Were A'changing," in *The Voice of People with Disabilities: Making a Difference in Manitoba*, ed. Manitoba League of Persons with Disabilities, Social Planning Council of Winnipeg, Disabilities Issues Office of Manitoba, and Council of Canadians with Disabilities (Winnipeg: Manitoba League of Persons with Disabilities, 2012), 19.
11. Kelly Egan, "32 Years after Landmark Case, Justin Clark a Free Spirit, Loud and Clear," *Ottawa Citizen*, December 7, 2014.

BIBLIOGRAPHY

Primary Sources

Clark v. Clark, 40 OR (2d) 383, 1982 CanLII 2253.

Secondary Sources

Chouinard, Vera. "Legal Peripheries: Struggles over DisAbled Canadians' Places in Law, Society, and Space." In *Rethinking Normalcy*, edited by Tanya Titchkosky and Rod Michalko, 217–26. Toronto: Canadian Scholars' Press, 2009.

Egan, Kelly. "32 Years after Landmark Case, Justin Clark a Free Spirit, Loud and Clear." *Ottawa Citizen*, December 7, 2014.

Guggi, Roswitha. "Parents Believe Their Son Just Can't Grasp What's Going On." *Ottawa Citizen*, March 9, 1982.

Steen, David. "The Times, They Were A'changing." In *The Voice of People with Disabilities: Making a Difference in Manitoba*, edited by Manitoba League of Persons with Disabilities, Social Planning Council of Winnipeg, Disabilities Issues Office of Manitoba, and Council of Canadians with Disabilities, 19–24. Winnipeg: Manitoba League of Persons with Disabilities, 2012.

Williams, Patricia. *The Alchemy of Race and Rights*. Cambridge, MA: Harvard University Press, 1991.

SECTION V

TO THE END OF THE TWENTIETH CENTURY AND BEYOND

After the 1980s, people with disabilities continued their pursuit of full participation and equality in Canadian life. This took place through their own organizations, and it was bolstered by technology that increased the well-being and independence of people with all types of disabilities.

Enns, Koskie, Bomak, and Evans provide a concise, well-rounded examination of activities of the Deaf from the mid-1980s to the mid-1990s in "Winnipeg Community Centre of the Deaf: Program Development as Community Development." The chapter examines how the Winnipeg Community Centre of the Deaf (WCCD) became involved in community development, which, at the time, was a major shift in the focus of activities for the organization. The chapter reveals how the rise of a strong cross-disability rights community in Winnipeg influenced WCCD, and traces how the rise of Deaf people's activism manifested in the organization.

Wolbring and Ball write about the role of scientific discovery and technological advancement in the lives of people with disabilities in "History of Science and Technology and Canadians with Disabilities." They note that there are approximately 290 technological and scientific discoveries that have (to a greater or lesser degree) affected the lives of people with disabilities over the last hundred years. Wolbring and Ball suggest that scientific and technological advances fall into three primary domains, including the development of tools that allow people with disabilities to address day-to-day challenges without actually changing their "biological reality." In this regard, this element of scientific discovery and technology focuses on environmental issues. The other two elements of scientific and technological advances, Wolbring and Ball suggest, fall under diagnosis and treatment, thus altering the individual's "biological reality." Such discoveries and technologies appear to be based on medical model notions of disability that view people with disabilities as being deficient or defective.

Chouinard's "'Like Alice through the Looking Glass' II: The Struggle for Accommodation Continues" provides a detailed auto-ethnographic account of the author's own struggles for accommodation in her workplace. She describes how her work life changed following the onset of rheumatoid arthritis in the early 1990s; she then realized that her university environment was no longer accessible, as her needs had changed. Chouinard describes her encounters with university administration and the university's subsequent reaction as she advocated for environmental changes so that her workplace could become more accessible.

In "Triple Jeopardy: Native Women with Disabilities," Demas describes the situation of Native women with disabilities in Canada, pointing to the governmental jurisdictional issues related to receiving needed supports to live independently. This chapter was originally written in the late 1980s, and the situation has not changed much regarding Indigenous women. Since the original publication of this chapter, Jordan's Principle has been accepted as policy by the provincial and federal governments to solve the wrangling over which government pays for accommodations and medical treatment for Indigenous children with disabilities. Jordan's Principle was named in honour of Jordan River Anderson, who died after spending two and a half years in the hospital unnecessarily due to the inability of provincial and federal government officials to decide who would pay for him to return home to live in his community. Jordan's Principle says that the government that has first contact with a First Nations child with disability should pay for that child's treatment and supports. There are still issues that arise in applying this policy, as governments at both levels have set a very narrow criteria as to who qualifies under this policy; thus, it has not been applied to many situations concerning Indigenous disabled children, and, under the policy, children do not continue to receive support once they become adults. The need to solve these issues and to support Indigenous people with disabilities remains.

Lutfiyya, Kendel, and Schwartz trace the closure of a long-term care facility for people with cognitive impairments in "The Community Inclusion Project in Manitoba: Planning for the Residents of the Pelican Lake Training Centre." The authors describe the transition of the centre's residents from institutional to community-based living, and the vital role that the Association for Community Living, Manitoba, played in ensuring that this transition would be as stress-free as possible. The authors note that the reasons for writing this chapter were twofold: to challenge current debates that promote the continuation of institutional accommodation for people with cognitive impairments, and to reveal that the process of moving a group of people with cognitive impairments from an institution to the community can take place when proper planning and supports are provided.

McGillivray's "Living in the Midst: Re-imagining Disability through Auto/biography" is the final chapter of *Untold Stories*. Her piece is a fitting end to our survey of disabled people's history in Canada since 1867. She discusses how she, as a woman with a disability, is using the tools of feminist and disability theory to write her own life story as a Canadian with disability. She affirms the movement of people with disabilities, from recipients of charity and pity to actors in their own lives, who play an important part in the history of Canada. We encourage the uncovering of disabled people's history in our communities and hope that these histories will look first to the voice of disabled people as defining their own experiences as we move further into the twenty-first century.

CHAPTER 18

Winnipeg Community Centre of the Deaf: Program Development as Community Development

Charlotte Enns, Bruce Koskie, Rita Bomak, and Gregory Evans

The decade from 1985 to 1995 was an important one for the Winnipeg Deaf community. This was a time when the disability rights movement as a whole was gaining momentum. Such momentum provided the context for empowering a variety of minority groups typically viewed as deficient.[1] In particular, Deaf people were establishing themselves as members of a cultural and linguistic minority in Canada and throughout the world.[2] The increased awareness of signed languages, and specifically American Sign Language (ASL) as a legitimate and sophisticated language,[3] resulted in a greater understanding of cultural identity, which in turn significantly strengthened community organizations.

The focus of this chapter is the work of one such community organization: the Winnipeg Community Centre of the Deaf, Inc. (WCCD), which took an active role in the development of programs and services for linguistically and culturally Deaf people in Winnipeg, Manitoba, during the late 1980s and early 1990s. Despite a relatively small active membership (approximately 200 to 250 members), WCCD was able to contribute significantly to the development of a number of unique programs and services that were specifically designed to meet Deaf people's and the Deaf community's needs and goals. The programs included for the purpose of this discussion are as follows:

1. The Deaf Human Service Worker Training Program (DTP), a post-secondary diploma program that used ASL as its language of instruction and trained Deaf adults to work in organizations that provided services for the Deaf community.
2. The Deaf Literacy Program (DLP), a community-based literacy program for Deaf adults incorporating a bilingual approach to teaching and learning using both ASL and written English as its languages of instruction.
3. Sign Talk Children's Centre (STCC), an ASL/English bilingual daycare for hearing and Deaf children.

BACKGROUND

The centre was the pivotal organization of the local Deaf community. It served as the community's focal point for cultural, social, political, educational, and recreational activities. Its primary purpose was to increase and support self-determination for Deaf people. The roots of this organization are found on a hockey team, the Silent Hockey Club, established in 1908. The organization was renamed the Winnipeg Association of the Deaf (WAD) in 1914 to better reflect its function as both an athletic and social club. In 1939, WAD purchased and renovated its own building, and when the new building opened, the organization became known as the Winnipeg Community Centre of the Deaf.[4] The organization was incorporated under that name in 1967. It is important to note that WCCD achieved many of its goals and accomplishments through the work of dedicated volunteers. The value of volunteering is an important element in the cultural identity of Deaf communities and dedicated volunteers are responsible for the development and maintenance of numerous Deaf clubs, activities, and organizations throughout the world.[5] The important role that volunteers have played in Deaf community development strongly emphasizes the collective nature and focus on group goals within these communities.

The Winnipeg Deaf community, similar to many linguistically and culturally Deaf communities, has long operated as a collective. In a collective, the community's goals are more important than individual goals.[6] People work for the betterment of the community, as opposed to individual achievement. In more individualistic societies, such as standard Canadian culture, each person's talents and potential are typically highlighted, and personal achievements are important indicators of success. In contrast, collective communities emphasize co-operation and a shared responsibility for group accomplishments. The valuing of the group over individual needs also has an impact on decision-making processes.[7] Typically, in individualistic cultures, decisions are made by the majority rule. The process is democratic in that everyone has a vote and is entitled to their individual opinion, but in the end the decision goes to the majority. In a collective, decisions are made by consensus and efforts are made to include minority opinions. This process can involve extended dialogue where all parties are expected to listen and respectfully consider differing points of view until a position is reached where everyone is in agreement.

These two cultural patterns, individualistic and collective, are not "better/worse" or "right/wrong," but rather reflect different perspectives and values.[8] Collective values provide the context for how the members of WCCD operated their organization and why some of the decisions they made and procedures they implemented were unique and differed significantly from general societal standards. The collective cultural pattern of the Deaf community is frequently the primary source of identity, even for those Deaf people with other racial, ethnic, and Indigenous heritages.[9] The Winnipeg Deaf community during the 1980s and 1990s reflected the general diversity of the Winnipeg population—mainly Euro-Canadians, with some Indigenous and Asian Canadian (Japanese and Filipino) members; however, Deaf identity and membership in the Deaf community is based on being Deaf and communicating in ASL. Other racial, ethnic, or Indigenous affiliations were not considered relevant to belonging to the group. In this way, being Deaf serves as a great equalizer; however, the result is that not much information is available regarding the diversity of the Deaf community during this formative time (the late 1980s and early 1990s), as the focus was on shifting away from the deficit of "not hearing" and embracing the difference of "being Deaf."

As the central Deaf organization in Winnipeg, WCCD developed a number of processes that ensured all Deaf people had access to information about events, programs, and services and were involved in making decisions. It was essential that these decision-making processes were accessible in order to allow for the maximum amount of input by Deaf community members. As in other collective societies, WCCD decisions were made by consensus.

In 1985, WCCD, with the Children's Home of Winnipeg, co-sponsored a Deaf Culture and Pride workshop. This event played a major role in determining the organization's activities for the next decade. The workshop, attended by 230 participants, focused on developing the pride, identity, and confidence of Deaf individuals; promoting awareness of ASL and the Deaf experience; and providing recommendations to assist in Deaf community development. At this workshop, a number of recommendations were made that directed WCCD to focus its activities in three areas: culture, family, and education.

The Deaf Culture and Pride workshop offered an example of how programs were initiated within the Deaf community. Deaf people identified the issues and a WCCD subcommittee was established to gather information, develop an action plan, and secure the resources necessary to realize the goal. As each initiative took shape, Deaf people became more familiar with the process, made more contacts in the community that could assist them, and established clearer guidelines for how a cultural and linguistic minority group could work more effectively within the context of the majority culture.

The Deaf Human Service Worker Training Program (DTP) was a direct result of two issues that were identified at the Deaf Culture and Pride workshop: (1) that Deaf individuals were often the recipients of services that were not culturally and linguistically sensitive, and (2) that traditional post-secondary education programs were unable to satisfactorily meet the needs of Deaf adults for whom English functioned as a second language. The DTP was funded through a federal government grant obtained jointly by WCCD and the Children's Home of Winnipeg and was administered through the New Careers Program of the Manitoba government. Similar to other new careers programs, the DTP followed a co-operative learning model where participants would alternate between two weeks of classroom learning and six weeks of on-the-job learning. Both the classroom and field training were individualized and geared specifically to the needs of the Deaf participants. This was accomplished by hiring two instructors, one Deaf (Len Mitchell) and one hearing (Greg Evans), who were both fluent in ASL and had experience working between the Deaf and hearing worlds.

The first teaching module for all DTP participants, regardless of their job placement, focused on developing their understanding of culture and language, specifically

Deaf culture and ASL. Although many of the Deaf participants had intuitive knowledge of their cultural values and linguistic abilities, in many cases this was the first time they were able to discuss these concepts and reflect on the impact the concepts had on their lives. Once these foundational skills were in place, more specific instruction and experience could be directed to facilitate the participants' success in the DTP. Success in the program was not measured by completing academic papers or passing written tests, but by gaining the competencies to carry out their jobs effectively in the workplace. Through this program, Deaf people successfully took on the roles of counsellors, early childhood educators, recreation directors, group-home workers, and community developers.

The Deaf Literacy Program (DLP) addressed the important need for appropriate education, and more specifically improved literacy levels, within the Deaf community. The low reading and writing abilities of Deaf students graduating from high school has been well documented;[10] however, the reasons for these poor results have often been attributed to Deaf students' inability to develop spoken language skills. The approach of the DLP was to incorporate a bilingual teaching model that recognized the Deaf students' abilities in their first language, ASL, and build on this foundation to enhance their skills in written English. This perspective builds on the theoretical premise that bilingual individuals have underlying mental concepts that are common to both languages and that development in either language contributes to this common core.[11] A teaching approach that recognizes the concepts Deaf students can express in ASL, and systematically teaches these to them in English, takes advantage of this prior knowledge and common understanding. Although the teaching approach implemented in the DLP incorporated a bilingual perspective using ASL and English, there were no established curricula for the instructors to follow. As a result, the instructors, also one Deaf (John Gibson) and one hearing (Kirk Ferguson), adapted curricula from other bilingual and English as an Additional Language (EAL) programs to meet the needs of their learners. The individualized and flexible approach of the DLP also allowed for the incorporation of materials and activities that were relevant to the students, such as reading work-related manuals or writing letters to friends or businesses.

By ensuring that instructors were fluent in both ASL and English, and familiar with bilingual teaching strategies and visual learning techniques, the curriculum developed for the DLP was ideally suited to meeting the needs of Deaf people. The program was open to all members of the Deaf community and was provided at no cost, thereby making it completely accessible as well as educationally appropriate. The DLP, implemented through Red River College, continues to be a community resource for Deaf people in Winnipeg.

Sign Talk Children Centre (STCC) was another unique program that was developed based on the recommendations made at the Deaf Culture and Pride workshop, particularly in the areas of culture and family. The needs of Deaf families were often not being met in regular daycare centres, both in terms of communication between parents and child care workers, and the roles assumed by parents and children. Most Deaf parents give birth to hearing children;[12] due to educational and societal influences, many of these Deaf parents believed that "hearing is better" and "speech is better" than being Deaf and signing. As a result, children were not developing appropriate language skills, either spoken or signed, and parents lacked confidence as their children's language and social role models. The STCC provided a place where being Deaf and using ASL was normal and valued. The staff included both Deaf and hearing people working together as a caring team. Staff members were fluent in ASL and could easily communicate with parents, keeping them informed of their child's progress and development. The centre supported the children's home language, ASL, but also exposed them to spoken English so they were prepared for school. It allowed for open communication between parents and caregivers, as well as among the children themselves. The STCC supported the uniqueness of Deaf culture and encouraged children of Deaf parents to grow up with a healthy pride in their parents' culture and the necessary self-esteem to make their contribution to the broader community.

Community support for programs such as the DTP, the DLP, and the STCC was strong because the programs met needs specifically identified by Deaf people. The programs were also successful because WCCD followed a number of unique criteria and processes.

WCCD'S ROLE IN PROGRAM DEVELOPMENT

The WCCD Board of Directors acted as a "clearing house" for new programs or services. Ideas for new programs were brought to the board for approval; the board could either approve the development of the program or set up a meeting to obtain consensus from the community. This type of meeting, known as a town hall meeting, was an open, public forum where the community received and provided information and acted as a decision-making body.[13] If there was sufficient support for a new idea, WCCD would establish a subcommittee to gather information and develop an action plan. The subcommittee could be made up of only WCCD members, or a combination of WCCD members and representatives from relevant outside agencies or organizations. Subcommittees were ad hoc committees that reported informally to the general membership on a quarterly basis at WCCD general meetings and formally at the annual general meeting. Once the program was running, WCCD would appoint representatives to sit on a program's board of directors, or steering or advisory committee. In general, all programs and services that involved Deaf people in Winnipeg had advisory committees. Representatives were expected to keep WCCD members informed of developments within programs and services, either through submissions to the monthly WCCD newsletter or presentations at the general meetings held four times each year.

WCCD's role as a clearing house offered a number of advantages to both program developers and consumers: (1) it helped to prevent duplication of services or waste of resources, (2) it ensured that the programs met the needs of the Deaf community, (3) it offered program support and input from the Deaf community, and (4) WCCD could and would lobby on behalf of the programs at the local, provincial, and federal government levels.

PROGRAM STANDARDS

It should be noted that the actual number of participants in the newly initiated programs was small. Specifically, 12 people were enrolled in the DTP for a one-time, two-and-a-half-year period; approximately 25 people attend the DLP at any given time, for varying lengths of time; and the STCC had spaces for 20 children between the ages of two and five years. Because of the collective nature of the Winnipeg Deaf community, programs were expected to benefit not only their participants, but also the wider Deaf community. Programs were required to achieve a number of informal standards that were monitored by WCCD:

1. **Programs and services must be culturally and linguistically sensitive.** Because program needs were identified from within the Deaf community, the use of ASL and culturally sensitive methodologies were essential components. With educational programs such as the DTP, the DLP, and the STCC, curriculum was designed to meet the needs of its participants. The organization also emphasized this philosophy with the Manitoba School for the Deaf and supported the shift to a bilingual/bicultural approach through representatives on the school's Bilingual Bicultural Committee. In addition, people who worked for services like the Manitoba Relay Service, a 24-hour telephone/TTY relay service, were strongly encouraged to participate in training in Deaf culture provided by members of the Deaf community.
2. **Program development and monitoring must involve public discussion.** As stated earlier, through town hall meetings, WCCD subcommittees, and advisory committees, Deaf community members were encouraged to give input at any stage of program or service development. Individuals with concerns or feedback could at any time meet a program or service's WCCD representative and their opinions would be forwarded to the appropriate people.
3. **Programs must be seen as benefitting the Deaf community as a whole.** Programs and services were often established with a limited number of participants, but all participants were encouraged to be involved in activities that benefitted the Deaf community as a whole. These activities could include co-sponsoring workshops or providing workshops to the Deaf community. Programs operated under the mandate of providing service to the community as a whole, not only to program participants. When programs were evaluated, a major consideration was the Deaf community's perception of the program and its effectiveness; these views were taken seriously by the service agency administrators.
4. **Program staff were expected to be contributing members of the Deaf community.** Program staff, both Deaf and hearing, were expected to be actively involved in the Deaf community. This expectation had two effects: (1) it ensured that program staff were aware of community issues and concerns, and (2) it provided members of the Deaf community with access to program staff.

BENEFITS OF WCCD'S PROCESSES

The involvement of the WCCD in the development of programs and services ensured that participant and community needs were met. Trial and error was often the guide to identifying processes that worked within the Winnipeg Deaf community, yet the processes and standards that were successful provided a model for other communities. By actively involving the Deaf community in identification of issues, gathering information, and developing action plans, WCCD helped to remove the stigma of Deaf people as "recipients" of services. WCCD was approached to appoint consultants to programs and services because government and agency administrators were recognizing that the people who knew what was best for the Deaf community were Deaf people themselves. This process often involved volunteer work on the part of Deaf people, but the benefit was the extensive connections and increased understanding regarding the needs and abilities of Deaf people gained within the broader society. In addition, these activities also benefit the individual Deaf volunteers by increasing their awareness of ASL, and developing their access to information and self-advocacy skills. By emphasizing a collective approach, WCCD enabled Deaf and hearing people to develop models of bilingual/bicultural teamwork at both programmatic and organizational levels.

TODAY'S CONTEXT

With consideration to the important programs and services that were established in the early 1990s, some have changed or no longer exist, but others continue to have an influence on the Winnipeg Deaf community today. Although the DTP was a one-time offering, many of the program's participants continue to work in their roles in a variety of organizations and to provide access to these services for Deaf people. The DLP has become a regular offering at Red River College and as such is supported under its budget. The STCC no longer exists; however, this may reflect the empowerment of Deaf parents and their ability to ensure appropriate communication in ASL with their children and their children's caregivers, rather than a decreased need for Deaf community services. Deaf parents have gained an understanding that ASL can provide the important first language foundation for children just as effectively as spoken English, so they are comfortable and confident interacting in ASL with their preschool children. Parents also advocate for the use of ASL-English interpreters when communicating with hearing caregivers at local daycare centres to ensure full access to information for and about their children.

The name of WCCD has also changed to the Manitoba Deaf Association to reflect a broader focus. Ironically, the success of these programs has actually resulted in diminishing or changing the role of members of the Deaf community. For example, mental health services were typically not available or accessible to Deaf people in the past, so members of the Deaf community were much more personally and directly involved in supporting and caring for Deaf people in non-professional ways, such as visiting or bringing meals. Now that professional counselling services are accessible to Deaf people through non-Deaf agencies, this kind of personal care is no longer as critical a function of the Deaf community. Similarly, increased access to technology, including text messages, videophones, and the Internet, has decreased the need for face-to-face contact; therefore, social events, town hall meetings, and other gatherings no longer occur as frequently in the Deaf community. The town hall meeting structure is still valued and continues to be a key function prior to the annual general meeting; however, it now typically happens only once a year. The influence of inclusion and technology are changing the function of Deaf community organizations, and it will be interesting to see how Deaf people will respond to these new challenges.

NOTES

1. Doris Fleischer, *The Disability Movement: From Charity to Confrontation* (Philadelphia: Temple University Press, 2001); Gerald Hales, *Beyond Disability: Towards an Enabling Society* (Thousand Oaks, CA: Sage, 1996); Duane Stroman, *The Disability Rights Movement: From Deinstitutionalization to Self-Determination* (Lanham, MD: University Press of America, 2003).
2. Clifton Carbin, *Deaf Heritage in Canada: A Distinctive Diverse and Enduring Culture* (Toronto: McGraw-Hill Ryerson, 1996); Harlan Lane, Robert Hoffmeister, and Ben Bahan, *A Journey into the Deaf-World* (San Diego: Dawn Sign Press, 1996).
3. Edward Klima and Ursula Bellugi, *The Signs of Language* (Cambridge, MA: Harvard University Press, 1979); William Stokoe, "Sign Language Structure: An Outline of the Visual Communication Systems of the American Deaf," *Studies in Linguistics*, occasional paper no. 8 (Buffalo, NY: Department of Anthropology and Linguistics, University of Buffalo, 1960).
4. Carbin, Deaf Heritage in Canada.
5. Carbin, *Deaf Heritage in Canada*; John Vickrey Van Cleve and Barry Crouch, *A Place of Their Own: Creating the Deaf Community in America* (Washington, DC: Gallaudet University Press, 1989).
6. Richard Brislin and Tomoko Yoshida, *Improving Intercultural Interactions: Modules for Cross-Cultural Training Programs* (Thousand Oaks, CA: Sage, 1994).
7. Sana Reynolds, Deborah Valentine, and Mary Munter, *Guide to Cross-Cultural Communication*, 2nd ed. (Boston: Prentice Hall, 2011).
8. Kenneth Cushner and Richard Brislin, *Intercultural Interactions: A Practical Guide*, 2nd ed. (Thousand Oaks, CA: Sage, 1996).
9. R. Greg Emerton, "Marginality, Biculturalism, and Social Identity," in *Cultural and Language Diversity and the Deaf Experience*, ed. Ila Parasnis (New York: Cambridge University Press, 1998), 136–45.
10. Des Power and Greg Leigh, "Principles and Practices of Literacy Development for Deaf Learners: A Historical Overview," *Journal of Deaf Studies and Deaf Education* 5, no. 1 (January 2000); Barbara Schirmer and Sarah McGough, "Teaching Reading to Children Who Are Deaf: Do the Conclusions of the National Reading Panel Apply?" *Review of Educational Research* 75, no. 1 (March 2005).
11. Jim Cummins, *Negotiating Identities: Education for Empowerment in a Diverse Society* (Los Angeles: California Association for Bilingual Education, 1996).

12. Raymond Trybus and Carl Jensema, *Communication Patterns and Educational Achievement of Hearing Impaired Students*, series T, no. 2 (Washington, DC: Office of Demographic Studies, Gallaudet College, 1978).
13. Sarah Stitzlein, "Democratic Education in an Era of Town Hall Protests," *Theory & Research in Education* 9 (March 2011).

BIBLIOGRAPHY

Brislin, Richard, and Tomoko Yoshida. *Improving Intercultural Interactions: Modules for Cross-Cultural Training Programs*. Thousand Oaks, CA: Sage, 1994.

Carbin, Clifton. *Deaf Heritage in Canada: A Distinctive Diverse and Enduring Culture*. Toronto: McGraw-Hill Ryerson, 1996.

Cummins, Jim. *Negotiating Identities: Education for Empowerment in a Diverse Society*. Los Angeles: California Association for Bilingual Education, 1996.

Cushner, Kenneth, and Richard Brislin. *Intercultural Interactions: A Practical Guide*. 2nd ed. Thousand Oaks, CA: Sage, 1996.

Emerton, R. Greg. "Marginality, Biculturalism, and Social Identity." In *Cultural and Language Diversity and the Deaf Experience*, edited by Ila Parasnis, 136–45. New York: Cambridge University Press, 1998.

Fleischer, Doris. *The Disability Movement: From Charity to Confrontation*. Philadelphia: Temple University Press, 2001.

Hales, Gerald. *Beyond Disability: Towards an Enabling Society*. Thousand Oaks, CA: Sage, 1996.

Klima, Edward, and Ursula Belugi. *The Signs of Language*. Cambridge, MA: Harvard University Press, 1979.

Lane, Harlan, Robert Hoffmeister, and Ben Bahan. *A Journey into the Deaf-World*. San Diego: Dawn Sign Press, 1996.

Power, Des, and Greg Leigh. "Principles and Practices of Literacy Development for Deaf Learners: A Historical Overview." *Journal of Deaf Studies and Deaf Education* 5 (January 2000): 3–8.

Reynolds, Sana, Deborah Valentine, and Mary Munter. *Guide to Cross-Cultural Communication*. 2nd ed. Boston: Prentice Hall, 2011.

Schirmer, Barbara, and Sarah McGough. "Teaching Reading to Children Who Are Deaf: Do the Conclusions of the National Reading Panel Apply?" *Review of Educational Research* 75 (March 2005): 83–117.

Stitzlein, Sarah. "Democratic Education in an Era of Town Hall Protests." *Theory & Research in Education* 9 (March 2011): 73–86.

Stokoe, William. "Sign Language Structure: An Outline of the Visual Communication Systems of the American Deaf." *Studies in Linguistics*, occasional paper no. 8. Buffalo, NY: Department of Anthropology and Linguistics, University of Buffalo, 1960.

Stroman, Duane. *The Disability Rights Movement: From Deinstitutionalization to Self-Determination*. Lanham, MD: University Press of America, 2003.

Trybus, Raymond, and Carl Jensema. *Communication Patterns and Educational Achievement of Hearing Impaired Students*. Series T, no. 2. Washington, DC: Office of Demographic Studies, Gallaudet College, 1978.

Vickrey Van Cleve, John, and Barry Crouch. *A Place of Their Own: Creating the Deaf Community in America*. Washington, DC: Gallaudet University Press, 1989.

CHAPTER 19

History of Science and Technology and Canadians with Disabilities

Gregor Wolbring and Natalie Ball

INTRODUCTION

Science and technology (S&T) products and their governance have throughout history impacted the lives of everyone, including Canadians with and without disabilities. The move from hunter-gatherer, to agrarian, industrial, knowledge-based, post-industrial, and post-knowledge societies was and is enabled by scientific and technological advancements. Each of these societies favoured different abilities, and societies in the future will continue to do so.[1] As such, these developments directly impact people with disabilities who tend to be more vulnerable to ability judgments.[2] Indeed the term *ableism* was coined by the disabled people's rights movement in the United States and Britain during the 1960s and 1970s to question species-typical, normative body ability expectations,[3] and the resultant prejudice and discrimination experienced by people whose body ability functioning was labelled as impaired, in need of being fixed as much as possible towards the species-typical.[4] *Ableism* is also a term used by Canadian Disability Studies scholars and the Canadian disability movement.[5] The direction, advances, and policies regarding S&T usage, research, and development (which themselves are founded upon particular intentions, purposes, and actions) embody the perspectives, purposes, prejudice, particular objectives, and cultural, economic, ethical, moral, spiritual, and political frameworks of different social groups and society at large within which these human activities take place.[6] On the one hand, S&T usage, research, and development follows social norms, expectations, and markets; on the other hand, S&T usage, research, and development changes and influences the quality of our lives, our perception as to what is a "good life," and our ability to pursue "the good life."[7] There are different types of S&T interventions that impact people with disabilities, their perceptions of a "good life," and their ability to pursue "the good life":

> S&T may develop tools to adapt the environment in which disabled people live and give disabled people tools that would allow them to deal with environmental challenges. These forms of S&T would make the life of disabled people more

livable without changing the identity and biological reality of the disabled person. S&T may develop tools that would diagnose the part of disabled people's biological reality seen by others as deficient, defect and impaired thus allowing for preventative measures. S&T may develop tools that would eliminate that portion of disabled people's biological reality seen by others as deficient, defect, impaired.[8]

Research and developments in S&T have the potential to be liberating for people with disabilities if the right frameworks are in place; however, S&T are often developed and implemented in ways that encourage and exhibit forms of ableism that presume normative abilities and the perception that people with non-normative abilities are lacking in their ability capacities. Many S&T developments have, as such, historically led to *disablism*,[9] the discriminatory, often oppressive, non-accommodating, or abusive behaviour of people with the "required" abilities toward those who are judged as lacking certain abilities. Many emerging S&T developments, such as advancements in robotics, have the potential to exhibit the same problem.[10] Indeed, being literate in S&T is a prerequisite for being able to influence S&T policies and research and development.[11] Being employed as a person with disability in S&T gives one a chance to expose people within S&T to disability issues and to influence research and development. This chapter starts with an evaluation of lists of innovations and missed opportunities, and continues to highlight the impact of various S&T developments on the lives of Canadians with disabilities. It concludes by evaluating the situation of Canadians with disabilities being educated in S&T topics and employed in S&T areas.

HISTORY OF INVISIBLE ACHIEVEMENTS: S&T AND DISABLED PEOPLE

Various lists of innovations exist. The About.com section on innovations lists 289 innovations starting in 1900 and ending in 2010.[12] Each of these 289 innovations affects people with disabilities in different ways; some have little impact, some only impact certain groups of people with disabilities, and some impact all people with disabilities. Of the 289 innovations, the authors submit that blind people are impacted by 87, Deaf people are impacted by 32, people with cognitive differences are impacted by 42, and people with physical difference are impacted by 75. Of those listed, 12 of the innovations could be classified as medical, which target the body and aim to fix impairments. Only 2 could be classified as tools that people with certain non-normative abilities could use to navigate the world (Braille glove, e-legs exoskeleton). Lists of innovations exist on the Web that cover more non-medical innovations related to disabled people; however, they are separate from the general innovation lists. The website Trendhunter.com has a list of 53 innovations for blind people,[13] 21 for deaf people,[14] 16 for and of disabled people.[15] Another webpage lists mobile apps for disabled people.[16] Many of these innovations are actually usable by so-called non-disabled people. Of the innovations for blind people, those mentioned by Young that can be seen to have utility for non-blind people are as follows: braille tattoo, textured Rubik, braille watches, avatar for the blind (virtual world using 3D sound to create a sense of space), blind photographers, camera for the blind (records sounds and transfers images via 3D embossing technology so that people who can't see will still have a recording of the sounds of an event and be able to use their sense of touch to "see" the image), dining in the dark (Montreal restaurant O.Noir, where your visual senses are taken from you the moment you step inside; eating in the dark changes how one experiences the flavour of food), voice stick (portable text scanning tool, utilizing the optical character recognition [OCR] function to identify text and convert this information into voice), braille graffiti, braille wallpaper, braille t-shirts, painting for the blind, braille architecture, sign-voice-language translator (converts gestures into audible voice as well as voice into text), and braille jewellery.[17]

Of the innovations listed for deaf people,[18] the following might all be useful for non-disabled people: hearing aids that might soon move to have abilities not existing in normal ears; a concept ballet shoe, called the music-toucher, that has a sole equipped with a vibrating module that will register musical rhythms and transfer them as rhythmic vibrations to a dancer's feet; and wristbands that translate sound to images. Vibration is already used in many devices used by the hearing. As for those innovations listed for physically disabled people,[19] the following can be used by others: animatronic suits, which are powered suits that support disabled or elderly individuals in their physical activities, the universal toilet, and the disabled-friendly gym. Various forms of brain-machine interfaces were not listed, but could be included in this category. As for the mobile apps for disabled people,[20] the "ThinkContact" mobile application, which allows people to place a phone call by using their minds; mobile OCR; V-braille; audio tactile graphics; and eyes-free speech-enabled mobile apps might also be of utility to so-called non-disabled people. Innovations for and by disabled people deserved to be mainstreamed. Many of the innovations may be too new for people to realize how widely they are applicable, but perhaps it is more likely that we are still at the level of discourse where disabled people and their life experiences are not seen to have any utility for the so-called non-disabled.

S&T AND CANADIANS WITH DISABILITIES IN EDUCATION AND EMPLOYMENT: HISTORY OF GAPS

Education and employment are two areas in which S&T play an increasingly influential role, primarily in the form of adaptive technologies that enable people with disabilities to partake in education and work. Indeed, according to three Canadian empirical studies, the "overwhelming majority of students with disabilities use computers and the Internet, but ... 41% of them need some type of adaptation to use computers effectively."[21] A 2010 report titled *Success in STEM: Studying and Pursuing a Science or Technology Career as a Post-Secondary Student with a Disability* by the Canadian group the National Education Association of Disabled Students (NEADS) includes a section called "Technology Matters:

Creating Usable Working Environments,"[22] which highlights the potential for assistive technology to remove some of the traditional employment barriers for disabled persons and outlines steps to determine appropriate assistive technology to enhance job performance; however, Canadians with disabilities still face many barriers in accessing needed devices in their education endeavours at the primary, secondary,[23] and post-secondary levels.[24]

HISTORY OF ENDANGERMENT: S&T AND EUGENIC GOALS

Science and technology usage, research, and development are human activities that are often articulated in terms of human betterment, though the question is what the notion of human betterment means for people with disabilities. Much of S&T development provides space for the negative judgment of particular ways of being and living. The philosophy of eugenics (the idea of bettering the human race through genetic improvements)[25] is founded upon very concrete ability expectations and judgment of what human betterment is. Many S&T developments could and can be used for eugenic purposes.[26] In Canada, for example, sexual sterilization, genetic prenatal testing linked to abortion, and pre-implantation testing linked to in vitro fertilization are S&T that have been used for eugenic goals. Other developments on the horizon include gene therapy and genetic enhancement, as well as synthetic genomics linked to an artificial womb.[27]

A few quotations from the *Globe and Mail* and the *Canadian Medical Association Journal* over the years demonstrate that there was support for the use of S&T for eugenic purposes and highlight some issues that were raised regarding its detrimental nature for people with disabilities. In 1924, the *Globe and Mail* reported that "the subnormal are producing two or three times as rapidly as the mentally normal. It is a pitiful reflection on our intelligence that we allow a condition of that kind to go on. It must be stopped."[28] The following was included in the same article: "On the one hand, it was claimed that unless society took steps to protect itself against the rapid multiplication of mental subnormals, civilization would drift toward another dark age. On the other it was argued that both sterilization and birth control were anti-social and anti-Christian."[29]

In 1969, Kaufman of the *Globe and Mail* stated, "I note representatives of church, government and the legal profession do not approve compulsory sterilization of parents unfit to have children. Evidently none of them expressed any concern about compulsion on the unfortunate descendants of a poor heredity doomed from infancy to bear throughout a miserable life the handicaps of incompetence and disability. Do they think unborn children would choose such parents? If they dislike compulsion, why impose it on innocent unborn children? Have unborn children no human rights?"[30] Kaufman also wrote the following: "I agree with Dr. R. B. McClure that parents incapable of caring for children properly should be sterilized by compulsion if necessary."[31]

The *Canadian Medical Association Journal* included the following quotes in relation to this issue: "As for the feeble-minded and their progeny, society for its own protection cannot permit their present unrestrained rate of reproduction" (1934)[32]; "This group of defective, socially valueless or socially dangerous people could be largely eliminated if sterilization were courageously employed, as is done in the province of Alberta" (1947)[33]; and "Although the mentally defective or mentally ill population has increased six and a half times, the cost of caring for them has increased well over ten times" (1934).[34]

In general, Canadians with disabilities did not occupy any role in the discourse around the promotion of sterilization that took place in Canada from the beginning of the 1900s up to the 1970s, and the eventual demise of the practice. A similar absence is felt in the discourse and practice of genetic testing, abortion, and genetic counselling for eugenic purposes. People with disabilities were not members of the Royal Commission on New Reproductive Technologies, which tabled its report, *Proceed with Care*, in 1993, and the report exhibited a systemic absence of a positive narrative of disabled people. Instead, it set up a dichotomy of ethical boundaries by asking for sex selection to be outlawed, while no such prohibition demand was evident in the report in relation to de-selection based on ability preferences. Indeed, the distinction between sex and ability preference selection is widespread in the genetic testing discourses.[35] Groups such as the Council of Canadians with Disabilities denounced the two-tiered system of judgment regarding the use of prenatal testing in the debate around the passing of the Canadian Assisted Human Reproduction Act.[36] The result of their intervention, alongside women's groups, was that the existing reproduction law in Canada is non-discriminatory at the level of the fetus (a women can abort independent of reason), but discriminatory at the level of the embryo (one cannot choose an embryo with a certain sex, but one can decide against an embryo based on ability-related characteristics).

RACING BEHIND: THE HISTORY OF COMMUNICATION

Innovations in communication have a long history, from the development of an alphabet by the Phoenicians and cuneiform writing by the Sumerians (3500 BC to 2900 BC) to the development of the Internet.[37] Canada was and is at the forefront of developing communication tools.[38] The addition of writing as a communication tool posed a unique challenge to blind people. Some writing could be identified through tactile means, such as *khipu* used by the Inka, but most could not. Tactile enabled forms of writing do not lead to a gap in communication abilities between the blind and non-blind; however, any writing that is not identifiable through tactile means leads to an ability gap between blind and non-blind people. When photography was invented, it led to another communication gap between blind and non-blind people. Television, motion pictures, and computers and the Internet are recent challenges to blind people. The telephone led to problems for deaf people. Deaf people may be able to compensate for oral communication using lip reading and sign language, which they might have set up as part of living in a community where there is face-to-face communication; however, this compensation was not possible with the newly invented telephone, which therefore led to a gap in communication abilities between deaf and non-deaf people. Additionally, some communications tools (such as texting options for phones) are problematic for those who have certain non-normative physical abilities, such as not being able to write. Conversely, different communication innovations also make it easier for some people with disabilities even if it makes it more difficult for others. A typewriter, for example, might help people who cannot hand-write, but does not help blind people. A telephone might be great for blind people, but not for deaf people.

The following is a timeline of communication innovations in the Canadian context:[39]

- March 23, 1752—Canada's first newspaper, the weekly *Halifax Gazette*, appears.
- October 30, 1869—Georges Desbarats publishes the first issue of his *Canadian Illustrated News*, the world's first periodical to use the halftone technique to reproduce a photograph.
- July 26, 1874—Alexander Graham Bell first describes his idea for the telephone to his father at the family home on the outskirts of Brantford, Ontario. In June of 1875, Bell's first functioning telephone is demonstrated in Boston.
- August 10, 1876—Alexander Graham Bell makes the world's first long-distance phone call, from the Bell residence in Brantford to a shoe and boot store in nearby Paris, Ontario.
- May 20, 1920—The Canadian Marconi Company's experimental radio station XWA hosts the first scheduled radio show in North America, and possibly the world, broadcasting a music program from Montreal to a meeting of the Royal Society of Canada in Ottawa. This became the station CFCF on November 4, 1920, which is reputed to be the oldest radio station in the world.
- July 6, 1924—William Stephenson from Winnipeg sends the first wire photo across the Atlantic, to England from New York, by radio; the first of his wire photos was published by the *Daily Mail* in December 1924.
- 1927—The first coast-to-coast radio network broadcast celebrates the Diamond Jubilee of Confederation.
- November 2, 1936—The new Canadian Broadcasting Act creates the Canadian Broadcasting Corporation and CBC Radio takes to the air.
- September 6, 1952—Canadian television broadcasting begins as CBFT-TV in Montreal (part of CBC's French network Radio-Canada) starts transmitting with a broadcast of Jean Cocteau's drama *Oedipus Rex*; two days later, English-language CBLT-TV starts broadcasting in Toronto. Both stations launch with 18 hours of programming a week.
- October 1, 1966—CBC TV introduces first colour broadcasts.
- 1975—TV cameras are allowed in the House of Commons for the first time.
- 1990—Canada has the world's largest contiguous cellular network.
- 1995—Consumer Internet service is launched.

Although adaptation tools came much later, communication is a good example of an area in which science and technology not only disadvantages people with disabilities, but also enables them. The lapses between the implementation of disabling communication tools and an enabling accessibility innovation seem to be steadily decreasing. In 1829, blind Frenchman Louis Braille invented Braille, a tactile system of raised dots representing letters of the alphabet. Canadian Roland Galarneau invented computerized Braille in 1972. The telecommunication device for the deaf (TDD) was invented by James C. Marsters and Robert Weitbrecht, two deaf people, in 1964. The first closed-captioning decoders for televisions were sold in the United States in 1980.[40] Beyond innovation, the availability and penetration of these technologies is also an issue. The World Wide Web Consortium (W3C) gives clear guidance on Web accessibility, but in 2006, 97 percent of all websites were deemed inaccessible.[41]

MISSED APPLICATION OF EXISTING INNOVATIONS

We highlight two areas in this section: (1) access to sanitary facilities and (2) access to transport. There have been many accessibility enabling innovations in both areas; however, people with disabilities still experience lack of access to sanitary facilities and transportation today.

Sanitation

Sanitation is a critical area of innovation, with constant change in the area of toilets and washrooms;[42] however, many Canadians and non-Canadians with disabilities have no access to sanitation despite existing innovations and S&T products that allow for completely accessible washrooms.[43] A 2008 report titled *Design for Independence and Dignity for Everyone* by the Safety Codes Council of Alberta recognizes, for example, that barrier-free paths to washrooms and accessible soap and towel dispensers are needed,[44] yet many washrooms fail in both regards. Existing S&T solutions are not employed consistently in Canada to fix restroom accessibility problems. Some doors have buttons allowing them to open automatically, but they are rare and scarcely implemented, leaving many washrooms doors too heavy to open. Similarly, a Calgary report states that "controls, dispensers and receptacles shall not require the use of two hands, or two simultaneous movements by one hand to operate;"[45] however, many do require arms of normal length and two hands to use—a problem for those whose arms or hands function non-normatively.[46] Many more examples exist that could be highlighted here.

Transport

Transport is essential for people with disabilities in Canada and elsewhere to partake in nearly every aspect of their lives. Many accessibility problems for people with disabilities, including Canadians with disabilities, are reported in general and particular around air, bus, and rail.[47] The goal of accessibility has still not been achieved in Canada. A 2006 article on Abilities.ca states,

Transit accessibility in major cities has improved in recent years, even if it is often at a snail's pace. Transportation providers are purchasing low-floor buses that accommodate wheelchairs, retrofitting subway stations with elevators and adding vehicles to their paratransit fleets, for example. However, it's not uncommon for people to be left without a ride for the day and, in places with poor transit accessibility, such as parts of the Maritimes and Saskatchewan, people with disabilities must either plan out their lives in advance in order to use a paratransit service or, in the worst-case scenario, stay home because they live outside the area serviced by accessible transit.[48]

Indeed, advocating for access is a main area of activity for the Council of Canadians with Disabilities.[49] Various scientific and technological solutions exist to make accessible transport a reality, but they are rarely implemented by companies and governments.[50]

CANADIANS WITH DISABILITIES AND S&T EDUCATION AND EMPLOYMENT: HISTORY OF NO DATA AND LITTLE INITIATIVE

The positive and negative impacts of S&T on the lives of Canadians with disabilities is one aspect of this field. Another is how many Canadians with disabilities are employed in S&T research and development and S&T policy development, and how many Canadians with disabilities learn S&T-related topics in post-secondary education. It seems we have a history of no numbers, no empirical data. This lack of numbers in Canada is well recognized. In 2006, a report from the Hypatia Association provided data from Statistics Canada as to how many Nova Scotians employed in technical occupations in natural and applied sciences and in trade were women, Aboriginal people, and visible minorities;[51] however, no numbers were presented for people with disabilities, including Indigenous people with disabilities. Indeed, their report stated that "the lack of reliable data on the employment of persons with disabilities in these occupations makes it very difficult to analyze their participation."[52]

In the 2010 report titled *Success in STEM: Studying and Pursuing a Science or Technology Career as a Post-Secondary Student with a Disability* produced by NEADS, one reads the following:

> Indeed research on the number of Canadian scientists with disabilities currently employed is next to non-existent. According to the most recent Participation and Activity Limitation Survey (PALS) conducted by Statistics Canada, 96,610 people with disabilities work in Canada's professional scientific and technical services industry. But this sector includes people working in legal services, accounting, architecture and engineering, management, scientific and technical consulting and last, but not least, scientific research and development.[53]

The NEADS report highlights further that in general it is difficult to locate peer-reviewed Canadian literature relevant to the employment of Canadians with disabilities in S&T,[54] which includes numbers on Indigenous people with disabilities. At the same time, the report states that "there is unquestionably a larger body of US-funded and US-focused research and literature relating to the representation of persons with disabilities in the science and technology fields."[55] The report, therefore, focused mostly on US initiatives in regards to S&T and people with disabilities, many of which it might be worthwhile to employ in Canada; however, the report also contained 27 interviews of Canadians with disabilities. From these 27 interviews, the following were identified as the most frequent barriers to increased representation of people with disabilities in S&T employment: lack of opportunities, lack of awareness and promotion of opportunities, lack of support, lack of knowledge and awareness around accommodation, lack of adequate accommodation, requirements of full-time study and other time aspects, resistance amongst employers toward arranging remote working situations, and lack of examples/role models/mentors.[56] The report also highlights that numbers for S&T education of Canadians with disabilities also do not exist,[57] which makes it difficult to ascertain how many people with disabilities would be qualified to apply for a STEM (science, technology, engineering, and mathematics)-related job.

The conclusion of the 2010 NEADS report states the following:

> One notable exception to the dearth of Canadian programs working to improve the representation of persons with disabilities in science and technology sectors is the Toronto Rehab Scholarship in Rehabilitation-Related Research for Students with Disabilities. This $20,000 renewable scholarship is open to Masters and Doctoral students in the following rehabilitation-related fields: biomedical physics, chemical engineering, computer engineering, management of technology, mechanical engineering, physical sciences, physics, systems engineering, telecommunications, technology, medical biophysics, materials engineering, biotechnology, biochemistry, biochemical engineering, computer networks and chemistry. Other Canadian institutions should follow the lead of Toronto Rehab and undertake initiatives that actively support students with disabilities in science and technology fields while helping to raise the profile of young scientists.[58]

CONCLUSION

Science and technology have the potential to have a positive and negative impact on Canadians with disabilities in many areas. More work has to be done to increase the positive effects and decrease the negative effects. For example, various negative aspects around the emerging application of robotics in employment and education have not been dealt with and, indeed, are rarely a topic of investigation.[59] In addition, the numbers and visibility of Canadians with disabilities, including Indigenous people with disabilities, educated and employed in S&T areas has to increase. For this to occur, we first need data on how many people with disabilities in Canada, including Indigenous people and women with disabilities, are employed in STEM jobs and how many were and are presently educated in STEM. Furthermore, work to eliminate the barriers identified by the 27 interviewees in the NEADS report must begin.

NOTES

1. Gregor Wolbring and Sophya Yumakulov, "Education through an Ability Studies Lens," *Zeitschrift für Inklusion* 10, no. 2 (2015), http://www.inklusion-online.net/index.php/inklusion-online/article/view/278/261.
2. Gregor Wolbring, "Ability Privilege: A Needed Addition to Privilege Studies," *Journal for Critical Animal Studies* 12, no. 2 (2014); Gregor Wolbring, "Employment, Disabled People and Robots: What Is the Narrative in the Academic Literature and Canadian Newspapers?" *Societies* 6, no. 2 (2016); Gregor Wolbring and Lucy Diep, "The Discussions around Precision Genetic Engineering: Role of and Impact on Disabled People," *Laws* 5, no. 3 (2016); Gregor Wolbring, "Obsolescence and Body Technologies Obsolescencia Y Tecnologías Del Cuerpo," *Dilemata International Journal of Applied Ethics* 2, no. 4 (2010).
3. Gregor Wolbring, "Expanding Ableism: Taking Down the Ghettoization of Impact of Disability Studies Scholars," *Societies* 2, no. 3 (2012).
4. Wolbring, "Expanding Ableism"; Wolbring, " Obsolescence and Body Technologies."
5. James Overboe, "Vitalism: Subjectivity Exceeding Racism, Sexism, and (Psychiatric) Ableism," *Wagadu: A Journal of Transnational Women's and Gender Studies* 4, no. 2 (2007).
6. Gregor Wolbring, *The Triangle of Enhancement Medicine, Disabled People, and the Concept of Health: A New Challenge for HTA, Health Research, and Health Policy*, HTA Initiative #23 (Edmonton: Alberta Heritage Foundation for Medical Research, Health Technology Assessment Unit, 2005), 1.
7. Wolbring, *The Triangle of Enhancement Medicine*, 1.
8. Gregor Wolbring, "Innovation for Whom? Innovation for What? The Impact of Ableism," *2020 Science* (blog), 2009, http://2020science.org/2009/12/14/wolbring/.
9. Paul Miller, Sophia Parker, and Sarah Gillinson, *Disablism: How to Tackle the Last Prejudice* (London: Demos, 2004), http://www.demos.co.uk/files/disablism.pdf.
10. Sophya Yumakulov, Dean Yergens, and Gregor Wolbring, "Imagery of Disabled People within Social Robotics Research," in *Social Robotics*, ed. ShuzhiSam Ge et al. (Berlin Heidelberg: Springer, 2012); Gregor Wolbring and Sophya Yumakulov, "Social Robots: Views of Staff of a Disability Service Organization," *International Journal of Social Robotics* 6, no. 3 (2014); Wolbring, "Employment, Disabled People and Robots"; Lucy Diep, John-John Cabibihan, and Gregor Wolbring, "Social Robots: Views of Special Education Teachers," in *Proceedings of the 3rd Workshop on ICTs for Improving Patients Rehabilitation Research Techniques* (New York: Association for Computing Machinery, 2015).
11. Wolbring and Diep, "The Discussions around Precision Genetic Engineering."
12. Mary Bellis, "Modern Inventions: Inventions from 2000–2009," *ThoughtCo*, updated April 17, 2017, http://inventors.about.com/od/timelines/a/ModernInvention.htm; Mary Bellis, "20th Century Timeline 1900–1999: 20th Century—the Technology, Science, and Inventions,"

ThoughtCo, updated February 14, 2017, http://inventors.about.com/od/timelines/a/twentieth.htm.
13. Meghan Young, "53 Innovations for the Blind," *Trendhunter*, January 26, 2010, http://www.trendhunter.com/slideshow/innovations-for-the-blind.
14. Brian G. Randles, "21 Innovations for the Deaf," *Trendhunter*, updated August 4, 2011, http://www.trendhunter.com/slideshow/innovations-for-the-deaf.
15. Andrew Robichaud, "16 Innovations for & from the Disabled," *Trendhunter*, updated June 22, 2011, http://www.trendhunter.com/slideshow/innovations-for-and-from-the-disabled.
16. Sarah Perez, "Amazing Innovation: Mobile Apps for the Disabled," *Readwriteweb*, August 6, 2010, http://readwrite.com/2010/08/06/amazing_innovation_mobile_apps_for_the_disabled/.
17. Young, "53 Innovations for the Blind."
18. Randles, "21 Innovations for the Deaf."
19. Robichaud, "16 Innovations for & from the Disabled."
20. Perez, "Amazing Innovation: Mobile Apps for the Disabled."
21. C. S. Fichten et al., "Access to Educational and Instructional Computer Technologies for Post-Secondary Students with Disabilities: Lessons from Three Empirical Studies," *Journal of Educational Media* 25, no. 3 (2000): 191.
22. Gladys Loewen, "Technology Matters: Creating Usable Working Environments," *National Educational Association of Disabled Students (NEADS)*, 2010, http://www.neads.ca/en/about/projects/stem/stem_Technology.php and http://www.neads.ca/en/about/projects/stem/.
23. Government of Canada, "Chapter 3: Learning," in *Government of Canada's Annual Report on Disability Issues, 2010* (Ottawa: Human Resources and Skills Development Canada, 2010), http://www12.hrsdc.gc.ca/servlet/sgpp-pmps-pub?lang=eng&curjsp=p.5bd.2t.1.3ls@-eng.jsp&curactn=dwnld&pid=3875&did=1.
24. C. S. Fichten et al., "Accessible Computer Technologies for Students with Disabilities in Canadian Higher Education," *Canadian Journal of Learning and Technology/La revue canadienne de l'apprentissage et de la technologie* 29, no. 2 (2003).
25. Francis Galton, *Hereditary Genius and Inquiries into Human Faculty and Its Development* (originally published in 1883), http://galton.org/books/human-faculty/text/human-faculty.pdf; Francis Galton, "Eugenics: Its Definition, Scope, and Aims," *American Journal of Sociology* 10, no. 1 (1904); Natalie Ball and Gregor Wolbring, "Portrayals of and Arguments around Different Eugenic Practices: Past and Present," *International Journal of Disability, Community & Rehabilitation* 12, no. 2 (2013).
26. Ball and Wolbring, "Portrayals of and Arguments around Different Eugenic Practices."
27. Ball and Wolbring, "Portrayals of and Arguments around Different Eugenic Practices."
28. *Globe and Mail*, "Health Officers Debate Curbing of Birth Rate," *The Globe (1844–1936)*, May 21, 1924.
29. *Globe and Mail*, "Health Officers Debate."
30. A. R. Kaufman, "Sterilization," *Globe and Mail (1936–Current)*, May 3, 1969.
31. Kaufman, "Sterilization."
32. W. L. Hutton, "Tendencies in Human Fertility," *Canadian Medical Association Journal* 30, no. 1 (1934).
33. G. H. Stevenson, "Mental Hygiene Related to Psychosomatic Disorders," *Canadian Medical Association Journal* 57, no. 5 (1947).
34. M. T. Macklin, "Genetical Aspects of Sterilization of the Mentally Unfit," *Canadian Medical Association Journal* 30, no. 2 (1934).
35. Gregor Wolbring, "Disability Rights Approach towards Bioethics," *Journal of Disability Studies* 14, no. 3 (2003).

36. Standing Committee on Health, Parliament of Canada, "Minutes of Meeting," November 29, 2001, http://www.parl.gc.ca/HousePublications/Publication.aspx?DocId=1041224&Language=E&Mode=1&Parl=37&Ses=1.
37. Mary Bellis, "The History of Communication," *About.com* (2011), http://lifein24.com/wp-content/uploads/2010/09/timeline_-_history_of_communication1.pdf.
38. United Nations International Telecommunication Union, "Historical Timeline of Canadian Telecommunications Achievements," http://www.itu.int/newsarchive/wtsa2000/english/media/timeline.pdf.
39. United Nations International Telecommunication Union, "Historical Timeline."
40. Jamie Berke, "Deaf History: History of Closed Captioning," *Verywell*, updated April 11, 2017, https://www.verywell.com/history-of-closed-captioning-1046543.
41. "97% of Websites Still Inaccesible," *456 Berea Street*, December 15, 2006, http://www.456bereastreet.com/archive/200612/97_of_websites_still_inaccessible/.
42. Cecilia Biemann, "45 Toileting Innovations to Celebrate World Toilet Day," *Trendhunter*, November 20, 2008, http://www.trendhunter.com/slideshow/45-toileting-innovations-to-celebrate-world-toilet-day#2; Andrew Robichaud, "100 Wonderous Washroom Innovations," *Trendhunter*, July 23, 2009, http://www.trendhunter.com/slideshow/100-wonderous-washroom-innovations.
43. Jacqueline Noga and Gregor Wolbring, "The Economic and Social Benefits and the Barriers of Providing People with Disabilities Accessible Clean Water and Sanitation," *Sustainability* 4, no. 11 (2012); Gregor Wolbring, Verlyn Leopatra, and Sophya Yumakulov, "Climate Change, Water, Sanitation and Energy Insecurity: Invisibility of People with Disabilities," *Canadian Journal of Disability Studies* 1, no. 3 (2012); Verlyn Leopatra, "Able People Disabling World: Water Access Inequality and Disabled People, Part 1," video, 14:32, http://www.youtube.com/watch?v=YCFbgaBy-tE; Verlyn Leopatra, "Able People Disabling World: Water Access Inequality and Disabled People, Part 2," video, 14:55, http://www.youtube.com/watch?v=gs-W_6DUrDg.
44. Safety Codes Council, *Barrier-Free Design Guide: Design for Independence and Dignity for Everyone* (Edmonton: Safety Codes Council and Government of Alberta, July 2008), http://www.safetycodes.ab.ca/Public/Documents/2008_SCC_BFDG_FINAL_protected.pdf.
45. Advisory Committee on Accessibility, City of Calgary, *Access Design Guidelines* (Calgary: Advisory Committee on Accessibility, January 2002), http://www.calgary.ca/PDA/pd/Documents/development/access_design_guidelines.pdf.
46. Leopatra, "Able People Disabling World, Part 1."
47. "Transportation," *Council of Canadians with Disabilities*, http://www.ccdonline.ca/en/transportation/.
48. Aaron Broverman, "In Transit: Public Transit Moves toward Accessibility," *Abilities Magazine*, Summer 2006, http://www.webcitation.org/query?url=http%3A%2F%2Fwww.abilities.ca%2Findependent_living%2F2006%2F08%2F16%2Fin_transit%2F&date=2011-08-20.
49. "Transportation," *Council of Canadians with Disabilities*.
50. Broverman, "In Transit."
51. Nan Armour, Cathy Carmody, and Donna Clark, *In the Picture ... A Future with Diversity in Trades, Science and Technology*, vol. 3 (Halifax: Hypatia Association, 2006), http://womenunlimitedns.ca/images/uploads/In-the-PictureVol3.pdf.
52. Armour, Carmody, and Clark, *In the Picture*.
53. National Educational Association of Disabled Students, "Success in STEM: Results of the Project Research Phase," *National Educational Association of Disabled Students (NEADS)*, 2010, http://www.neads.ca/en/about/projects/stem/stem_Research.php and http://www.neads.ca/en/about/projects/stem/, 9.

54. National Educational Association of Disabled Students, "Success in STEM."
55. National Educational Association of Disabled Students, "Success in STEM."
56. National Educational Association of Disabled Students, "Success in STEM."
57. National Educational Association of Disabled Students, "Success in STEM."
58. National Educational Association of Disabled Students, "Success in STEM."
59. Yumakulov, Yergens, and Wolbring, "Imagery of Disabled People"; Wolbring and Yumakulov, "Social Robots"; Wolbring, "Employment, Disabled People and Robots"; Diep, Cabibihan, and Wolbring, "Social Robots."

BIBLIOGRAPHY

Advisory Committee on Accessibility, City of Calgary. *Access Design Guidelines*. Calgary: Advisory Committee on Accessibility, January 2002. http://www.calgary.ca/PDA/pd/Documents/development/access_design_guidelines.pdf.

Armour, Nan, Cathy Carmody, and Donna Clark. *In the Picture ... A Future with Diversity in Trades, Science and Technology*. Vol. 3. Halifax: Hypatia Association, 2006. http://womenunlimitedns.ca/images/uploads/In-the-PictureVol3.pdf.

Ball, Natalie and Gregor Wolbring. "Portrayals of and Arguments around Different Eugenic Practices: Past and Present." *International Journal of Disability, Community & Rehabilitation* 12, no. 2 (2013).

Diep, Lucy, John-John Cabibihan, and Gregor Wolbring. "Social Robots: Views of Special Education Teachers." In *Proceedings of the 3rd Workshop on ICTs for Improving Patients Rehabilitation Research Techniques*, 160–63: New York: Association for Computing Machinery, 2015.

Fichten, C. S., J. V. Asuncion, M. Barile, M. Fossey, and C. De Simone. "Access to Educational and Instructional Computer Technologies for Post-Secondary Students with Disabilities: Lessons from Three Empirical Studies." *Journal of Educational Media* 25, no. 3 (2000): 179–201.

Fichten, C. S., J. V. Asuncion, C. Robillard, M. E. Fossey, and M. Barile. "Accessible Computer Technologies for Students with Disabilities in Canadian Higher Education." *Canadian Journal of Learning and Technology/La revue canadienne de l'apprentissage et de la technologie* 29, no. 2 (2003). https://www.cjlt.ca/index.php/cjlt/article/view/26549/19731.

Galton, Francis. *Hereditary Genius and Inquiries into Human Faculty and Its Development* (originally published in 1883). http://galton.org/books/human-faculty/text/human-faculty.pdf.

Galton, Francis. "Eugenics: Its Definition, Scope, and Aims." *American Journal of Sociology* 10, no. 1 (1904): 1–25.

Globe and Mail. "Health Officers Debate Curbing of Birth Rate." *The Globe (1844–1936)*, May 21, 1924, 11.

Government of Canada. "Chapter 3: Learning." In *Government of Canada's Annual Report on Disability Issues, 2010* (Ottawa: Human Resources and Skills Development Canada, 2010). http://www12.hrsdc.gc.ca/servlet/sgpp-pmps-pub?lang=eng&curjsp=p.5bd.2t.1.3ls@-eng.jsp&curactn=dwnld&pid=3875&did=1.

Hutton, W. L. "Tendencies in Human Fertility." *Canadian Medical Association Journal* 30, no. 1 (1934): 73–77.

Kaufman, A. R. "Sterilization." *Globe and Mail (1936–Current)*, May 3, 1969, 6.

Loewen, Gladys. "Technology Matters: Creating Usable Working Environments." *National Educational Association of Disabled Students (NEADS)*, 2010. http://www.neads.ca/en/about/projects/stem/stem_Technology.php; http://www.neads.ca/en/about/projects/stem/.

Macklin, M. T. "Genetical Aspects of Sterilization of the Mentally Unfit." *Canadian Medical Association Journal* 30, no. 2 (1934): 190–95.

Miller, Paul, Sophia Parker, and Sarah Gillinson. *Disablism: How to Tackle the Last Prejudice.* http://www.demos.co.uk/files/disablism.pdf.

National Educational Association of Disabled Students. "Success in STEM: Results of the Project Research Phase." *National Educational Association of Disabled Students (NEADS)*, 2010. http://www.neads.ca/en/about/projects/stem/stem_Research.php; http://www.neads.ca/en/about/projects/stem/.

Noga, Jacqueline, and Gregor Wolbring. "The Economic and Social Benefits and the Barriers of Providing People with Disabilities Accessible Clean Water and Sanitation." *Sustainability* 4, no. 11 (2012): 3023–41.

Overboe, James. "Vitalism: Subjectivity Exceeding Racism, Sexism, and (Psychiatric) Ableism." *Wagadu: A Journal of Transnational Women's and Gender Studies* 4, no. 2 (2007): 23–34.

Safety Codes Council, *Barrier-Free Design Guide: Design for Independence and Dignity for Everyone.* Edmonton: Safety Codes Council and Government of Alberta, July 2008). http://www.safetycodes.ab.ca/Public/Documents/2008_SCC_BFDG_FINAL_protected.pdf.

Stevenson, G. H. "Mental Hygiene Related to Psychosomatic Disorders." *Canadian Medical Association Journal* 57, no. 5 (1947): 468–72.

United Nations International Telecommunication Union. "Historical Timeline of Canadian Telecommunications Achievements." http://www.itu.int/newsarchive/wtsa2000/english/media/timeline.pdf.

Wolbring, Gregor. "Disability Rights Approach Towards Bioethics." *Journal of Disability Studies* 14, no. 3 (2003): 154–80.

Wolbring, Gregor. *The Triangle of Enhancement Medicine, Disabled People, and the Concept of Health: A New Challenge for HTA, Health Research, and Health Policy*, HTA Initiative #23. Edmonton: Alberta Heritage Foundation for Medical Research, Health Technology Assessment Unit, 2005.

Wolbring, Gregor. " Obsolescence and Body Technologies Obsolescencia Y Tecnologías Del Cuerpo." *Dilemata International Journal of Applied Ethics* 2, no. 4 (2010): 67–83.

Wolbring, Gregor. "Expanding Ableism: Taking Down the Ghettoization of Impact of Disability Studies Scholars." *Societies* 2, no. 3 (2012): 75–83.

Wolbring, Gregor. "Ability Privilege: A Needed Addition to Privilege Studies." *Journal for Critical Animal Studies* 12, no. 2 (2014): 118–41.

Wolbring, Gregor. "Employment, Disabled People and Robots: What Is the Narrative in the Academic Literature and Canadian Newspapers?" *Societies* 6, no. 2 (2016): Article 15.

Wolbring, Gregor, and Lucy Diep. "The Discussions around Precision Genetic Engineering: Role of and Impact on Disabled People." *Laws* 5, no. 3 (2016): Article 37.

Wolbring, Gregor, Verlyn Leopatra, and Sophya Yumakulov. "Climate Change, Water, Sanitation and Energy Insecurity: Invisibility of People with Disabilities." *Canadian Journal of Disability Studies* 1, no. 3 (2012): 66–90.

Wolbring, Gregor, and Sophya Yumakulov. "Social Robots: Views of Staff of a Disability Service Organization." *International Journal of Social Robotics* 6, no. 3 (2014): 457–68.

Wolbring, Gregor, and Sophya Yumakulov. "Education through an Ability Studies Lens." *Zeitschrift für Inklusion* 10, no. 2 (2015). http://www.inklusion-online.net/index.php/inklusion-online/article/view/278/261.

Yumakulov, Sophya, Dean Yergens, and Gregor Wolbring. "Imagery of Disabled People within Social Robotics Research." In *Social Robotics*, edited by ShuzhiSam Ge, Oussama Khatib, John-John Cabibihan, Reid Simmons, and Mary-Anne Williams, 168–77. Berlin Heidelberg: Springer, 2012

CHAPTER 20

"Like Alice through the Looking Glass" II: The Struggle for Accommodation Continues*

Vera Chouinard

INTRODUCTION

It was in 1993, three years after being diagnosed with rheumatoid arthritis, that I first began to write about my struggles for accommodation as a disabled female professor in a Canadian academic workplace. I did so out of a sense of outrage and disbelief that an institution of higher learning and research, instead of setting a positive example on this crucial human rights issue, seemed to operate in ways that, perversely, made my job immeasurably more difficult to do than I could have ever imagined as an able-bodied female scholar. This is saying something, since even before becoming ill my job had been made difficult enough by marginalizing behaviours on the part of some colleagues. I was not only the only female professor in my department at the time, but was also working in newer areas of human geography (radical and feminist) that were not well understood or valued by some colleagues. I was also outspoken rather than being the quiet and deferential woman at least some of my male colleagues preferred.

It was at the urging of a colleague at another university that I decided to share the story of my struggle for accommodation in an academic workplace. The early years of my struggles are recounted in the 1995–96 article entitled "Like Alice through the Looking Glass: Accommodation in Academia," published in *Resources for Feminist Research*.[1] Although I had referred in passing to certain aspects of those struggles elsewhere, it was in the Alice article that I found, for the first time, the courage to begin to write openly about the enormous personal and professional toll that these struggles for accommodation had taken.

The decision to write the first Alice article was not an easy one. Not only was I making an intensely personal and traumatic set of experiences public, but I was also conscious of the very real possibility of backlash from administrators and others who might have preferred that women such as myself remained silent. It was a risky decision and one that in some ways made me vulnerable to further discrimination. And it is fair to say that I have been punished at times in my workplace for not remaining silent. If anything, however, efforts to intimidate me into silence have only made me even more aware of how important it is that disabled women speak out about their lives in academic and other workplaces. Intolerance toward women with illnesses and impairments compounds and deepens the other disadvantages women face in academic and other settings. The end result is that women already struggling to deal with serious physical and psychological challenges, such as limited mobility and chronic pain, are forced to contend with a multiplicity of daunting barriers to doing their jobs, barriers arising from socio-spatial practices of devaluation, marginalization, and exclusion.

Although some at my university may disapprove, it is for these reasons that I have decided to write a sequel to the Alice article. I would like to share some of what I've experienced and learned about being a disabled woman in academic workplaces since the mid-1990s and to encourage others to speak out and help in the vital work of making our academic and other work environments more supportive and inclusive of disabled women and diverse people in general.

AN AUTOETHNOGRAPHIC ACCOUNT

As in the original Alice article, I adopt an autoethnographic approach, reflecting on my personal experiences of struggling for accommodation and of being devalued and constructed as "out of place" in the academy as a result of illness and impairment, and trying to understand those personal experiences in a wider social and cultural context. While definitions of and approaches to autoethnography vary,[2] here I use the term in a manner consistent with how autoethnography is defined in the *Sage Dictionary of Qualitative Inquiry*: "a particular form of writing that seeks to unite ethnographic (looking outward at a world beyond one's own) with autobiographical (gazing inward for a story of oneself) intentions."[3] My account aims, in other words, to draw readers into my personal story of being constructed as negatively "other" in an academic workplace (in the evocative sense) and to try to begin to make at least some sense of why it is that such workplaces remain resistant to full inclusion of persons with illnesses and impairments who need accommodation.

OF HOLLOW VICTORIES AND ONGOING STRUGGLES

By the time the first Alice article was written, I had begun to suspect that my struggles for accommodation of my needs as a disabled professor might go on indefinitely. I had also learned that there is a perverse illogic to the norms and practices of ableness that govern our work environments, in which privileges associated with being able-bodied, such as being assumed to be a productive worker who "belongs" in the workplace, are lived as taken-for-granted entitlements of "normality" and discriminatory acts toward those unable to approximate able norms are re-represented as fair, impartial, and appropriate treatment. I have likened the experience of that illogic to Alice's experiences through the looking glass: experiences of a topsy-turvy world in which arguments are no longer rational or fair although they are represented as such. Being a disabled woman struggling for accommodation in an academic workplace is rather like being at a "mad" tea party that stubbornly refuses to end. Indeed, a picture of Alice at the Mad Hatter's table hangs in my office to remind me, should I ever forget, of exactly that point.

After an initial accommodation agreement was reached in 1994, I gradually realized that my "victory" in continuing to be allowed to do my job was a highly qualified one. The seemingly mundane fact that I was still visibly in a workplace in which at least some colleagues regarded me as "not belonging" and "out of place" was in some ways a hollow victory since it set the stage for less obvious, more insidious forms of devaluation, exclusion, and discrimination than I had faced before (e.g., tangible physical barriers such as access to the building in which my office was located). It was only once these more obvious, tangible barriers to doing my job had been removed (at least temporarily) that what disability scholars refer to as the pervasive social barriers facing disabled people (arising from practices that devalue and discriminate against persons with disabilities) emerged more clearly into view.

I noticed, for example, that an ongoing problem in my home academic unit was annual evaluations of my academic performance that were always "below par," seemingly irrespective of my productivity on the duties I remained responsible for under the accommodation arrangement (i.e., research and service work, and graduate but not undergraduate teaching). When I questioned this I was reminded that I was in a very "productive" academic unit (quite true, at least as measured in simple ways such as research grant dollars) and so "of course" would come up short in comparison. I discovered, however, that there was more to my seemingly dismal performance than that; in fact, I was being evaluated *as if* I was still responsible for the same set of duties as my able-bodied colleagues. In other words, I was not being evaluated on the basis of duties that I remained responsible for under the accommodation agreement but for those *and those I would have been responsible for had I not been accommodated*. I would argue, drawing on the wider literature concerned with how "fictionalized" identities are constructed in relation to disabled workers, that this is one of the important ways in which disabled academic women such as myself can be constructed as less capable and less valuable members of an academic workplace.[4] These parallel modes of devaluation are experienced by others who embody "difference" in the academy; for example, assumptions encountered by faculty who are women of colour that they are not in academic workplaces because of their abilities and talents but as a result of affirmative action initiatives.[5]

While it is, in hindsight, so obviously unfair to evaluate an employee for work they are no longer expected to do that it seems bizarre that this would happen—it is like giving a worker one job description and then evaluating them on the basis of another—I was placed in a situation in which I could not possibly win; however, my inevitable below-par rating did benefit my immediate co-workers because in the par system of evaluation (an inherently divisive system that compares individual performances and allocates set salary increments accordingly), poor evaluations of my academic performance meant that there were more salary increments that could be distributed amongst the able majority. That year, my dean once, to his credit, adjusted my performance to a par rating in response to the concerns I continued to express about how my academic performance was being evaluated. This meant, had recommended salary increases ever been processed in my case during the 1990s (which they were not), then I might have at least had a little financial incentive to do what I was already doing because I loved my work. That was, as medication and my illness permitted, doing my best to work at my modified duties full-time despite assessments of my functional abilities (physical abilities to move, walk, and so on) by medical experts that concluded that it was admirable that I was continuing to work at all, since, on a purely medical basis, I qualified as fully disabled.

It is difficult to convey how draining my struggles to have inequities such as this addressed became as a result not only of the university's prolonged failure to act in any systematic way to correct them, but also, and in some ways most importantly, because of the hostility and ill will I encountered from some of those in positions of administrative authority as a result of raising such valid accommodation issues. I recall, for example, a meeting that took place after the dean of science had, on a one-time basis, made the adjustment to my performance evaluation. The meeting was an annual meeting (required as part of the 1994 agreement) to discuss accommodation matters among myself, the dean of science, the director of my home academic unit, and the university equity officer in attendance. It was an extremely tense meeting, with a visibly angry director expressing frustration, resentment, and more than a little hostility toward me and the dean as a result of the dean's decision to override the performance evaluation of the school committee that year. Accusing the dean and me of having struck some sort of "special deal," which, the Dean correctly said, was not the case, the director sarcastically retorted something to the effect of "Well, why bother to assess her performance at all.... Why not simply always judge it as par?" The tension in the room escalated when I correctly pointed out that there were problems with such an approach, notably that it dismissed the possibility that, in fact, my performance might sometimes be above par as well. This, as it turned out, would be a relatively mild example of situations in which I or my graduate students were punished for speaking out on accommodation issues (as well as those who took even limited steps to address the issues I raised).

SPATIAL AND SOCIAL EXCLUSION

Another facet of the marginalization that disabled workers experience in our contemporary workplaces is spatial and social exclusion,[6] taking forms such as isolated office locations and being avoided by co-workers who feel uncomfortable interacting with a disabled person. One form of social and spatial exclusion that I experienced on an ongoing basis in my home academic unit was the fact that faculty meetings and other school events, including Christmas parties and welcome-to-term events, were located in places I could not physically access as someone who had to use an electric scooter to get around. Although an automatic door opener had been placed upon the door of the room used for faculty meetings, staff had to remember to turn it on so that I could get into the room on my own (the whole logic of course behind having automatic door openers in the first place). This was never done and so I was reduced to banging on the door until someone opened it and cleared my way in—obviously more disruptive and awkward for me than had the device been turned on. And although I repeatedly raised concerns with the school administrator about the location of school events in places that could only be accessed by stairs (which, obviously, my scooter could not do), nothing was done, and so I was forced not to attend many events at which my graduate students, in particular, would have appreciated my presence. When I finally (and somewhat uncharacteristically) gave up on raising objections to these locations, my graduate students did object, only to be told in no uncertain and unsupportive terms, "Oh well, Vera would get in if she really wanted to." How someone whose mobility was so limited that she used a scooter would do this was beyond me—unless, as I joked with my graduate students, it was by parachute!

SYSTEMIC SALARY DISCRIMINATION

Then there was the vexing issue of prolonged systemic salary discrimination. When I became ill, in 1990, my salary was frozen at the low associate professor level I was earning at the time. This was followed, as I explained in the first Alice article, by the accommodation arrangement of 1994, whereby the university would pay one-half of this frozen salary and the university insurer would pay the other half as disability benefits. Unfortunately, the plan did not include any provisions for salary increments, even though I was working full-time at my modified duties, continued to have my performance annually reviewed, and my faculty dean forwarded recommendations for annual salary increases accordingly. When I repeatedly inquired as to how this salary discrimination would be remedied, the response from our human resources benefits administrator was always the same: it was impossible to increase my salary because if the university did so, then the insurance company would simply claw back a corresponding amount of the benefits portion of my salary. The outcome then was a salary frozen at 1990 levels seemingly in perpetuity. There was obviously more than a little something wrong with this scenario, as I kept insisting to senior university administrators; however, nothing was done.

By 1998, when I was promoted to full professor, I had decided that this long-standing financial discrimination was intolerable and unjust, and had to be addressed. If I could perform my duties under the accommodation agreement at a level that warranted promotion to this senior level of the academy, surely I also deserved to earn more than I had almost a decade earlier!

On May 26, 1998, I sent a memo to the provost and vice-president of the university, outlining the facts of my case, my mounting concerns regarding the ongoing systemic salary discrimination I had then been experiencing for eight years, and the future salary discrimination that I would face were the university to adopt a human resources proposal for paying my salary in the future (the outcome of time-consuming and, on my part, very frustrating internal negotiations). I noted that human resources and the university generally had effectively acknowledged salary discrimination in my case by agreeing to a one-time lump sum payment in partial compensation for wages lost from 1990 to 1998 (a payment of a little over $11,000 made in October 1998). I explained the systemic discrimination and violations of disabled faculty's rights that were embedded in the new proposal for my salary emanating from the human resources department:

> The proposed scheme was a "deal" with the insurer allowing [the Insurance Co.] to claw back 20% of any salary increases received (through reductions in disability benefit payments) and exemption from their responsibility to cover salary increases earned since 1990 in the event of increased or total incapacity to work. The scheme discriminates against disabled faculty in the following ways: a) by making all earned salary increases 20% less than those earned by non-disabled faculty[,] b) by allowing the insurer to eventually halt payment of all disability benefits even if the disabled faculty member's capacity to work has not increased[,] c) by providing no insurance coverage for salary increases earned after accommodation of special needs[,] and d) thus imposing financial penalties on disabled faculty in order to benefit able-bodied faculty through lower disability insurance premiums.

I went on to outline how the handling of my case was in violation of Canadian human rights law: it breached the principle of equal treatment in employment irrespective of differences such as race, gender, disability, and age, and the Canadian Human Rights Act's explicit statement that discrimination in employment consists in any act that adversely differentiates an employee, on a prohibited ground, in the course of her or his employment. The memo closed with a list of proposed remedies for the salary discrimination experienced to date including adjustment of my salary to at least the base level received by a full professor at the university, and financial compensation for lost salary and interest that would have accrued from same since 1990.

It was over a year later, on August 23, 1999, that I received an interim response to my stated concerns in a memo from the provost to the dean of science, head of human resources, a vice-president dealing with financial aspects of the university, and myself. In that memo, the provost acknowledged that looking into my case had been a complex but educational task (noting, in particular, learning about the elements and structures of the university's long-term disability benefits plan). He stated that it was important that the university recognize the significant career advancement entailed in my promotion to full professor through an appropriate salary increase. He went on to note that my case raised the question of whether or not a partial disability benefits plan should be considered by the university in its negotiations with the faculty association. He also voiced concern about my lack of insurance coverage in the unfortunate event that I became fully disabled at some point in the future. He outlined the steps he was prepared to take to address the issues in my case. These were to increase my salary to a level recommended by the dean of science;

support human resource's recommended 80/20 split of this increased salary between the university and its insurer, which was the inequitable plan discussed in my 1998 memo to him; and suggest that disability arrangements for faculty be examined. He asked us for any additional input we might have and indicated that he would write a final memo on the matter by September 10, 1999.

My first response to the August 1999 interim memo was outrage that, after several years of ongoing discussion and negotiations around these matters, the university was prepared to entrench salary discrimination as an ongoing feature of my life as a disabled female professor. Surely, through almost a decade of discussions about disability, equity, and human rights, we had learned better than that. Moreover, as an institution of higher learning, surely it was everyone's responsibility as part of the university community to stand firm against discriminatory, exclusionary, and, quite frankly, illegal practices! Although I appreciated the provost's efforts to become better informed about my case and disability issues generally—after all, I knew first-hand how complex my case had become as too many years of inaction passed—I could not condone continued violation of my, and presumably other disabled workers', rights on campus.

A few days after receiving this memo, I decided to act on recommendations that I get a lawyer with expertise in human rights. I drove to an imposing office tower in downtown Toronto for an appointment with an eminent Canadian lawyer who had headed the Ontario Human Rights Commission before returning to private practice. I remember the deep sense of outrage and fury that precipitated my decision to take legal action. I had tried at this point for almost a decade to work in a collegial way toward a fair accommodation of my disability. I had even spent two years in the mid-1990s working with a large number of faculty and staff to draft an accommodation policy that the university could be proud of and use to guide its handling of cases of disability and other needs arising from diversity in the future. It was three years after this policy had been drafted, however, that it was passed by the university senate in August 1998. Apart from minor wording changes requested by the faculty association, the only apparent reason for such a lengthy delay in approving the policy was that the draft policy had sat on administrators' desks for some time. Ironically, while it did so, some other Canadian universities had used our policy as a model for their own. At least we were playing a leadership role and making a positive difference on other campuses!

The office tower where I met my lawyer for the first time was an impressive structure inside and out. With my battered old professor's briefcase and sandals I felt a little … well … out of place. My discomfort dissipated quickly, however, as I noted that this lawyer was bright and quick to get to the point in our discussions, but at the same time clearly compassionate in learning about what I had been going through for so many years. After we discussed some of the key facts in my case he looked me in the eye and said, "You know there is no way you should have to hire a lawyer on your own?" He was referring to the fact that our faculty association had at that time refused to take action on my case. Without hesitation, I replied, "I know." We then discussed how a poorly paid professor whose salary had been frozen since 1990 could afford the legal costs that would accrue if he represented me, and worked out a viable arrangement.

Leaving the office tower I felt, for the first time in many years, that there might be hope of a fair resolution to my case—perhaps even one that would allow me to do the work I loved to do without constantly being forced to contend with the systemic barriers to fair treatment and inclusion that human rights laws are meant to address.

LEGAL STRUGGLES

Taking legal action against an employer is never easy, particularly in cases where an individual is up against a large, powerful institution such as a university. But after nine years of futile struggles to have accommodation issues addressed through internal channels, I was convinced that I had been left with no other choice. While a university-wide accommodation policy had been adopted, and I had even worked on developing parallel policies for groups such as graduate students, my case and others indicated that it was one thing to have such policies "on the books" and quite another to ensure that they were implemented.

At the end of August 1999, my lawyer notified the provost that he was representing me in my legal dispute with the university and that he hoped we could move toward a swift resolution of this matter. To his dismay, it was not until he sent a second letter that he finally received a reply on November 10th from the provost. This was followed two weeks later by a letter dated November 24th in which the provost outlined the university's proposed revised accommodation plan.

After outlining aspects of the history of my case, the provost's letter stated the university's position on its handling of my accommodation case: because my initial 1994 accommodation agreement had released me from undergraduate teaching, and undergraduate teaching was, in their view, an essential duty of a professor, "the arrangements that have been made with you since your disability have exceeded the University's duty to accommodate your disability. However, because of the history and particular circumstances of your case, the University is prepared to continue to make an individual arrangement with you on a gratuitous basis." This statement clearly put a very interesting spin on the university's duty to accommodate a disabled professor. Apparently, not only had the university *not* violated my human rights for almost a decade, it had done *even better* at accommodating me than the law required! I could almost envisage a university lawyer waggling his finger at me in a scolding and patronizing manner and saying something such as, "Now *really*, Dr. Chouinard, what *could* you have been thinking in claiming that your human rights have been violated?!" This image became sharper as I contemplated the related implicit message that any accommodation arrangement with me was being made out of kindness to an individual faculty member and not because the university had any legal obligation to do so.

Before I concluded in despair that I really was, like Alice, stuck at some perversely mad tea party, my lawyer provided some reality checks on the university's portrayal of my case. He quickly noted that claims about undergraduate teaching being an essential duty of a professor's job would not stand up in a court of law precisely because case law on accommodation clearly shows that a modification of the range and types of duties done by employees can be a fair and reasonable response to disabled workers' accommodation needs. Further, the only way in which a large employer such as a university could plausibly argue to have exceeded their legal duty to accommodate is in a situation where either the costs of doing so would be unreasonable or the rights of all employees to health and safety in the workplace would be jeopardized. As the latter didn't pertain in my case, the university could only have "exceeded its duty to accommodate" my disability if the costs associated with doing so threatened the viability of the entire enterprise. This is a difficult criterion to satisfy in any accommodation case (particularly since accommodation costs are usually minimal), but it is especially difficult in cases where large employers are involved.

Having spun the university's prolonged failure to adequately accommodate a disabled professor into a contrary, highly benevolent image, the provost's letter went on to outline the university's proposals for my future accommodation in the workplace. These included a modest salary increment and assurances that my performance would be evaluated on the basis of duties I remained responsible for. It also proposed, however, that because of what was referred to as a "reduced workload" (rather than a full-time modified one) the monetary value of any earned career progress merit increments would be reduced by 50 percent. It was noted that there might be an LTD (long-term disability insurance) component to my remuneration but was not clear about whether or not this would involve the 80/20 clawback arrangements I had criticized as unfair in my earlier memo to the provost.

One of the interesting things about legal battles is how important language is in framing positions taken and representing discriminatory acts and inactions as anything but. At first glance, for instance, it might seem logical and reasonable that an employee on a so-called reduced workload should be denied one-half the monetary value of any salary increments earned through career progress. On closer scrutiny, however, such an argument implicitly treats the accommodation of a disabled employee, through measures such as modified duties or hours of work, *as if* this is the same as an employee who voluntarily elects to change their contractual relationship with an employer by working fewer hours or at altered duties. In doing so, it fails to recognize that disabled employees face systemic barriers to equality in employment vis-à-vis their able counterparts, and that therefore different treatment may be required to help ensure more equitable employment outcomes. In this context, one might reasonably ask why an employer would be justified in compounding the disadvantages a disabled worker faces by denying her or him earned salary increases. If it is acknowledged, further, that it is possible for a disabled employee to work full-time at a range of duties modified in order to accommodate disability, then any apparent "fairness" to denying them earned salary increases quickly evaporates: after all, this would amount to enshrining permanent salary discrimination into an accommodation plan, something which is clearly an oxymoron!

In my experience, unravelling the logic, illogic, rhetoric, and reality in such arguments is a constant challenge in struggles for fair and reasonable accommodation in the academic workplace. This may in part be attributed to the fact that universities and employers generally are often learning as they go when accommodation issues arise because we are not yet at the point where inclusive and fair responses to needs associated with diversity are a taken-for-granted part of our working lives. But there is also an element of hard-nosed negotiating aimed at limiting, as opposed to recognizing and taking responsibility for, the duty to accommodate in practice in cases such as mine.

In a December 17, 1999, letter responding to the university's latest proposals on dealing with my case, my lawyer outlined our objections in detail. The letter stressed the need to view my workload as a different but not an inherently lesser or reduced one and pointed out that modification of duties was a common legal remedy in accommodating disabled workers. It noted that the provost's proposals failed to respond to the outstanding issue of salary shortfalls since 1994 resulting from a salary frozen in 1990, shortfalls in excess of those covered by the 1998 one-time lump sum payment made to me by the university. Nor did it provide assurance that my salary would not be reduced by 20 percent of any future earned increments under the proposed clawback scheme with the university insurer. Qualifications in how the provost's letter discussed methods to bring my salary to a fair and equitable level, notably the phrase that this would occur in a manner consistent with "the standards generally expected of Professors" at the university, were flagged as vague and confusing. The letter went on to note that the university's position on its duty to accommodate in my case would be very difficult to defend as a matter of law, for the legal reasons already outlined above, and cited a recent Supreme Court case reiterating that legal standard for accommodating workers with disabilities required every possible accommodation to the point of demonstrable undue hardship, "whether that form takes the form of impossibility, serious risk or excessive cost."[7] Before outlining an alternative proposed accommodation plan that did not contain the discriminatory elements proposed by the university, the letter expressed concern about the university's failure to acknowledge its duty to accommodate disabled workers:

> It was disappointing that your letter chose not to acknowledge the University's duty to accommodate disabled faculty and the related fact that accommodation of special needs is a term and condition of employment at ... [the] University under its own institutional policies. It is misleading, in this context, to suggest that any accommodation agreement reached with Dr. Chouinard is an individual or gratuitous arrangement. I believe it is also short-sighted since, with an aging population, the incidence of disability is on the rise. [The University] will have to find ways of accommodating disabled faculty in the future and the longer this is delayed the worse the repercussions on the institution will be.

An intense year of such legal struggle would ensue before, on December 5, 2000, a decade after my struggles for accommodation had commenced, I reached an out-of-court legal settlement with the university. According to that settlement, the university agreed to act upon its legal duty to accommodate disabled employees by working out the details of an accommodation plan with me, compensating me for past lost wages, and adjusting my salary to a level appropriate to my status as a full professor (without the discriminatory 20 percent clawback provisions). And I agreed to have "some involvement in undergraduate teaching." There is no doubt that the settlement was a formal victory in terms of human rights—at long last there was formal recognition of the university's duty to provide reasonable accommodation of my needs as a disabled professor and employee and efforts to enshrine ongoing discriminatory salary provisions had failed. What was much less clear was whether or not it would turn out to be a substantive victory.

FROM FORMAL TO SUBSTANTIVE RIGHTS: THE STRUGGLE FOR AN ACCOMMODATION AGREEMENT CONTINUES

After a decade-long, difficult, and personally costly struggle for a reasonable and equitable accommodation, it was tempting to see the legal settlement of late 2000 as marking a fundamental turning point in my relations with my university employer—as opening a new, more hopeful, and less adversarial chapter in efforts to work out the details of a reasonable accommodation plan. And it was in such a frame of mind that I initially contemplated meeting with colleagues in positions of administrative authority to finally work out details of a new accommodation plan.

To my dismay, despite repeated requests on my part and on the part of the university's anti-discrimination officer for an initial meeting on this matter, it was eight months before the acting provost finally called such a meeting in August of 2001. The meeting, which included the new head of our human resources department, the acting dean of science, the acting director of my home academic unit (then known as the School of Geography and Geology), the university's anti-discrimination officer, the acting provost, and myself, focused on the sometimes contentious issue of how I would fulfill my commitment to do "some form of undergraduate teaching." This was an ongoing source of contention between me and the university because, with an activity-sensitive illness such as rheumatoid arthritis, I was limited in the amount and type of undergraduate teaching I could do (needing, for example, to work at home for a significant proportion of any given workweek to manage pain and fatigue). The university was demanding that I take on a large proportion of a "normal," able undergraduate teaching load (of three courses in my home academic unit).

If I had had any illusions that things were going to be different in terms of my experiences of accommodation, these were, at least for the short term, dashed at that meeting. It was quickly apparent that the sole focus of the meeting would be how I would fulfill my commitment to have "some form of involvement" in undergraduate teaching rather than also on my accommodation needs (as the legal settlement required). Equally problematic were the facts that, due to staff turnover (including the departure of the university's equity officer who had previously assisted in my case), the only two persons in the room familiar in detail with the facts of my case were the acting provost (formerly the dean of science under whose authority my home academic unit fell) and myself. This in part helps to explain why most of those in positions of authority sat silently around the table, as a clearly hostile and angry acting provost dismissed every suggestion that I, with the help of the anti-discrimination officer, put forward in terms of undergraduate teaching (e.g., for a distance education course) with the same unhelpful comment: "Oh, that will never work." With little support from those around the table, apart from the anti-discrimination officer, and after an hour or so of being subjected to this over and over again, tears of frustration, anger, and disappointment welled in my eyes and spilled down my cheeks. I remember how impassively almost all of those around the table reacted to my obvious, and humiliating, distress and how alone this made me feel. As the meeting mercifully finally drew to a close, I remember composing myself and insisting to the acting provost afterwards that we had to work more constructively to resolve this matter. Nonetheless, I left feeling deeply angered and frustrated at the destructive nature of the proceedings.

In hindsight, and after a discussion with a female colleague who had had similar experiences as a result of speaking out on different issues at the university, I realized that I was in some ways being punished for being outspoken for so many years on accommodation issues and for taking legal action against the university. Perhaps more importantly, at least some of those in senior positions of authority were continuing to construct my own and others' efforts to press for my reasonable accommodation as a negative "problem" as opposed to part of a much-needed solution. Needless to say, the persistence of such negative constructions of disability advocacy is another powerful way in which disabled faculty and their allies are marginalized and sometimes silenced.

The meeting described above served as an important reality check on my hopes for a more collegial resolution to my accommodation as a disabled faculty member. I was beginning to realize that even with a legal settlement in place, the university administration was not necessarily going to co-operate in efforts to work out the reasonable accommodation plan the law required. As the anti-discrimination officer and I continued to press unsuccessfully for the follow-up meeting that had been agreed to at the August meeting, the chances of a purely internal resolution grew steadily more dim. In November 2001, I contacted my lawyer to voice my concerns about the university's non-compliance with the legal settlement. By this time I was working full-time, and without an accommodation plan in place, as acting director of the Women's Studies program, a position I had accepted both because of my enthusiasm for the program and because it offered a more collegial and supportive environment for myself and my graduate students than we had experienced in my home academic unit. This unaccommodated situation was, however, seriously taxing my health and my capacities to manage symptoms such as pain and fatigue.

From the fall term of 2001 to the fall term of 2002, the only accommodation-related discussions I had were with the director of the School of Geography and Geology and these concerned only what I would contribute to the school in terms of undergraduate teaching when I was no longer acting director or director of Women's Studies (the latter a five-year appointment that I accepted in 2002–03). The acting provost and subsequently once again the dean of science had apparently washed his hands of any further accommodation discussions—resolving this matter had been left in the hands of the director of the school.

By the fall of 2002, the director was proposing the following undergraduate teaching arrangement: I would financially compensate the school on an annual basis for costs associated with the teaching of a three-unit undergraduate course and I would teach two three-unit courses (bringing the total with financial compensation for the three-unit course to the nine units normally taught by faculty). One of the interesting things about this proposal, as the anti-discrimination officer observed, was that it was about accommodating the university's needs rather than mine. My lawyer agreed, noting that the duty to accommodate was the university's legal obligation, not mine, and that he had never heard of the beneficiary of an employment accommodation being required to financially compensate an employer for fulfilling their legal obligation—another reminder, although I no longer needed any, that whatever the intentions of those involved, responses to struggles for accommodation in academia at least sometimes take on a perverse illogic all of their own.

At my lawyer's suggestion, I approached the Canadian Association of University Teachers (CAUT) to see if they would be willing and able to provide legal advice in my ongoing efforts to negotiate an accommodation plan with the university. They agreed, noting that my case was a particularly severe one and encouraging me to also try once again to work with my faculty association. I had tried for many years to enlist the association's formal support in my struggles for accommodation, but whenever I did so, they refused, reiterating the administration's position that this was an individual, private affair between me and the university, comparable to early retirement. One of the problems with this position (aside from the fact that my struggles were about employment not retirement) was that it failed to recognize the university's legal duty to accommodate any disabled faculty person. Moreover, after the university's accommodation policy was passed by its senate in 1998, this position failed to recognize that accommodation was a term and condition of employment under the institution's own policies! For reasons I don't fully understand, although these certainly included an association president who seemed resolved to help me get the right thing done, this time I was finally able to enlist the formal support of the faculty association. This support was important not only in providing another impetus to efforts to get a new accommodation plan in place in my case, but also because it (at least I hoped) signalled that other faculty were now prepared to treat accommodation of diversity as a matter of collective concern and entitlement.

With the advice and assistance of CAUT, and the support of the university faculty association, we were finally able to bring the relevant persons in positions of administrative authority back into the discussion of what a new accommodation plan would look like (those persons included the new provost of the university, the dean of science, the director of my home academic unit, the new head of human resources, and the anti-discrimination officer). A year of negotiations would take place until finally, in late 2003, three years after the legal settlement and thirteen years after my struggles for accommodation had begun, an accommodation plan had been developed that the university and I were prepared to sign. That plan acknowledged the university's obligations to provide reasonable accommodation of my needs as a disabled faculty member in accordance with its own institutional policies, the legal settlement of December 2000, and the Ontario Human Rights Code. It was agreed that my workload would be a modified one that placed greater emphasis on research and graduate teaching than undergraduate teaching and service activities. My undergraduate teaching load would consist of one undergraduate course (taught for the Women's Studies program as long as I was director and subsequently for my home academic unit). The plan provided, in partial compensation for the toll that protracted conflict had taken on my capacities to engage in research work, a one-year research leave. I had also experienced difficulties in getting the university (via the dean of science) to provide lab space for one of my research projects and so the plan committed the university to providing accessible space for this. Other difficulties in my home academic unit, such as meetings and events in inaccessible locations and failure to notify me when important and time-sensitive materials arrived for me in the main office, were also addressed. Importantly, the plan provided for sensitivity training for faculty, staff, and students on accommodating the needs of disabled faculty and employees more generally.

The signing of an accommodation plan in late 2003 was without a doubt a milestone on the long and difficult road to accommodation. It was hard-won, through the determination and persistence not only of myself but also of those others who came to my assistance along the way. And it provided a framework through which we could at least begin to translate formal human rights into substantive practices. Did it resolve all of the accommodation issues that I faced? No. Did it ensure that I would have an accommodated workload? Only in part. Did it mean that at long last I would no longer have to fight for the right to reasonable accommodation? Unfortunately not.

For the fight for accommodation of disability and other aspects of diversity will necessarily remain an ongoing and unfortunately never-ending one until everyone in every workplace (and beyond the workplace as well) is prepared to acknowledge that those of us who are different from able and other norms still "belong" and can make equally important, if in some ways different, contributions—that, for example, having faculty who are disabled provides important opportunities to learn from first-hand knowledge (and, in my case, through research on disability issues as well) about the challenges disabled people face and what can be done to diminish these. As human rights and equity specialists know, when those who are "different" face barriers to inclusion and well-being, different (not special) treatment may be required to ensure equality of outcome. And different is not inherently lesser or a problem—it is oftentimes simply different. When all of us take those lessons to heart we will be well on the way to building the more inclusive world that everyone deserves.

EPILOGUE 1

A part of me wishes I could end this story on a happily ever after note. But that, unfortunately, would be a fiction. So instead I will say a little about what has happened since 2003 and what, if anything, we can learn from it. Directing the Women's Studies program (a position from which I stepped down in July 2007) was in many ways an exciting and fulfilling experience. Although I had been part of the Women's Studies Advisory Committee from the inception of the program, being the director brought me into more regular contact with enthusiastic and dedicated feminist scholars and students and provided me with a work environment that was more supportive than what I had known previously (which over the years had had many elements of what experts refer to as a "poisoned work environment," which made my working life and struggles for accommodation especially difficult); however, it was an often stressful challenge to direct a program that, despite its importance in providing a safe and supportive space for women and feminist inquiry on campus, remained very marginalized in terms of not only resources but also, in some ways, respect. In 2004, the challenging politics of directing the program combined with the strains of having to continue to struggle for accommodation and a largely unadjusted workload took their toll, and I slipped into a deep depression from which it would take me two long years to gradually recover. It was at this time that I was diagnosed with a second chronic, debilitating illness: bipolar disorder (sometimes referred to as a mood disorder or manic depression), which is often characterized by a vulnerability to prolonged periods of depression and brief episodic periods of agitated thought and behaviour. I was devastated by this diagnosis for many reasons—not the least being the knowledge that, if disclosed, I was likely to be constructed as even more negatively different than in the past, in light of the extreme stigma that still attaches to any form of mental illness. More positively, however, it has taught me first-hand about how marginalizing and silencing such stigmas remain and how important it is that we challenge them. I was also interested to learn, from the writings of a psychiatrist with manic depression, that this illness is often associated with gifted accomplishments in fields as varied as music, writing, painting, and research.[8] Who knows? Maybe being different from the norm isn't always such a entirely bad thing!

I returned to directing the Women's Studies program in the 2006-07 academic year, stepping down in July 2007 to take a regular six-month research leave (primarily to start research on disabled women's and men's lives in the developing nation of Guyana). I am now preparing to return to my position in what is now the School of Geography and Earth Sciences. As part of those preparations, I recently met with the acting director of the school to discuss what my undergraduate teaching might consist of. It was a collegial meeting and I was convinced that he was willing to learn more about the university's accommodation policy and my own accommodation situation. Nonetheless, one of his comments, although clearly well intentioned, worried me: "Well, if you can't do the job [i.e., the full load of 'normal' undergraduate teaching], why not go on disability benefits [and just do research]? Life's too short." There were eerie echoes here of earlier claims that being disabled meant I no longer "belonged" in the regular academic workplace. He was absolutely right that life is too short, but is it too short to stand up for our human rights? I hope not. By the way, anyone for tea?

CHALLENGING ABLEISM IN AN EXCLUSIONARY WORLD (EPILOGUE 2)

It is April 2017 and I've been asked to update this account of my struggles for accommodation and inclusion. Where should I start? Perhaps by saying that, as with my first epilogue, I wish this story ended on an unambiguously upbeat note; however, at best I can say that it has been a difficult journey, for myself and others, and that the outcomes in terms of building a more inclusive academy have been mixed—moving forward in some ways, but backward in others. For example, my access to disabled parking on campus remains precarious. Yes, there are more parking spots around the building I work in than in the past, but others need these as well and so they are frequently full when I try to access campus and my office.

Over the past seven years, I have also continued to be subjected to what I regard as systemic salary discrimination. Although administrators, as noted above, tried and failed to formally enshrine financial discrimination as a condition of my employment, another avenue for such discrimination has been implementation of our career progress merit evaluation system. To reiterate, this system compares the performances of individual professors to each other and most generously rewards those who outperform their colleagues in terms of largely quantitative measures (e.g., numbers of publications, research grants, and so on). In this competitive system, particularly within the neoliberal university with increasing pressures on individuals to "produce," it should be recognized that disabled professors who are accommodated cannot be assessed on the same bases as their able counterparts. Not only do bodily and mental experiences of such aspects of impairment as pain, fatigue, and mental distress often result in "slower scholarship," but disabled professors' contributions also need to be assessed differently with recognition given to their distinctive contributions to enriching university life—whether this be mentoring of disabled students, teaching about marginalization and exclusion, advocacy on disability issues, or efforts to develop more accommodating modes of academic life These contributions include the often exhausting extra work of struggling for accommodation.

When I reflect on my own experiences of struggling for accommodation and inclusion, I am reminded of how crucial it is that we tackle, together, the still pervasive ableism that informs our society and spaces of daily life. By *ableism* I refer to a regime of power that values and privileges those who most closely approximate normative expectations of the able body and mind.[9] These normative expectations include productivity, strength (particularly for men), engaging in paid work, and achieving economic independence. In what follows, I briefly speak to two experiences and what they illustrate about the workings of ableism in the academy.

Ableism is, unfortunately, a regime of privilege and a vantage point on the world that, too often, all of us internalize and not just those of us with mind and body differences. So, for example, and despite my determination to help challenge ableism and exclusion, there have been many times where experiences such as poor performance evaluations have made me feel that I don't "belong" in the academy and that I am somehow inferior to able others. One way I've tried to counter this is to focus on the different but still important contributions disabled professors make to the academy and the project of making it more inclusive. But it is an uphill struggle given how pervasive ableism is in and outside the academy. As an instructor and supervisor of undergraduate and graduate work by disabled students, I also find it heartbreaking to watch these students grapple with ableist forms of oppression in their lives—whether it be faculty and students who devalue their abilities or contributions or lashing out in frustration because they believe that their academic success is entirely dependent upon the accommodations they receive. In terms of the latter, it is critical to acknowledge that although they may need to perform academic work differently, these students also have many gifts and talents.

It is important to remember that ableism often finds expression in mundane everyday attitudes and practices. For example, I recently gave a virtual plenary talk at a conference as I am physically unable to travel alone to conferences. I was absolutely delighted that the organizers accepted my offer to give this talk virtually—perhaps a small step toward inclusion but nonetheless a progressive one! This was, in my mind, an excellent example of trying to do academic conferences differently and a reminder that different isn't necessarily lesser. I had also had a disheartening response to another offer I made to present virtually to the same conference in a panel dealing with human rights and diversity issues. In this instance, there was no response whatsoever—not even a polite no thanks, just silence. Whether intentional or not the implicit message was that doing things in ways that accommodated disabled colleagues was not desirable or "normal."

Despite technical problems with running the video component of Skype, people at the plenary talk seemed to engage with it in positive ways. There is a caveat though, which is that at least two members of the audience indicated to me that it was "too bad" that I couldn't be there in person. While they meant this in a supportive way, one implicit message was the ableist one that this different way of presenting was lesser than in-person contributions to conference proceedings. Being "able" to participate in person, in other words, trumped the goal of creating a more inclusive conference environment. I was actually reminded of a talk that I gave at the University of Saskatchewan on what I called "the war on disabled women in Canada." Because of joint pain and fatigue I sat rather than stood to give this talk. Afterwards a professor, no doubt with good intentions, commented on how it was "too bad" that I was unable to stand. The implicit message being, of course, that my contribution was less effective than if I had been able to stand to deliver the presentation. What is sobering and cause for reflection/concern is that this happened in 1999 or almost two decades ago! They say that history has a way of repeating itself and it is critical that we keep this in mind when trying to challenge ableism in society and space.

To end on a more positive note, I am encouraged by the exciting work going on in Disability Studies including in geographies of disability. There is also much work to celebrate in terms of disability activism. We have learned a lot, I think, about creating more inclusive environments and the oppressive costs of not doing so. But we also live in disturbing and neoliberal times and this means that there are especially severe challenges to creating more enabling societies and spaces of everyday life. In this context, we need to continue to insist that all lives matter and that doing things differently is not inherently lesser, but can be progressive in terms of challenging the pervasive ableism of the academy and society.

We need, in short, to re-imagine our worlds in ways that can help us to embrace the differences in ability that we embody and to celebrate academic and other accomplishments (e.g., disability law), and yet still remain resolved to combat ableist norms, attitudes, and practices. This is urgently needed, especially given developments such as attacks on disabled people's income, support, and services (in the United Kingdom, for example). Together we will propel progressive change—it will continue to be a long and difficult struggle, but we will get, as Martin Luther King put it in the context of the US civil rights movement, "to the promised land." Here ableism and the ableist norms and practices that sustain it, such as measuring productivity primarily or exclusively in quantitative terms and only with regard to paid work, will rightly be regarded as outdated and oppressive. It will also be recognized that living this type of oppression, from the vantage point of disabled people, is at least partly about having one's different contributions rendered invisible at worst and less valuable at best. And we need to recognize that no one's lives are untouched by ableism—we all have stakes in building a world in which all lives matter and are valued and supported.

NOTES

* An earlier version of this chapter was published in *Resources for Feminist Research* 33, no. 3/4 (2010).

1. Vera Chouinard, "Like Alice through the Looking Glass: Accommodation in Academia," *Resources for Feminist Research* 24, no. 3/4 (1995–96).
2. For discussions of autoethnography, see Carolyn Ellis, "Evocative Autoethnography: Writing Emotionally about Our Lives," in *Representation and the Text: Reframing the Narrative Voice*, ed. William G. Tierney and Yvonna S. Lincoln (Albany: State University of New York, 1997), 116–39; Carolyn Ellis and Arthur P. Bochner, "Autoethnography, Personal Narrative, Reflexivity: Research as Subject," in *Handbook of Qualitative Research*, 2nd ed., ed. Norman K. Denzin and Yvonna S. Lincoln (Thousand Oaks, CA: Sage, 2000), 733–68; Kathryn Besio and David Butz, "The Value of Autoethnography in Field Research in Transcultural Settings," *Professional Geographer* 56, no. 3 (2004): 350–60; Kathryn Besio, "Telling Stories to Hear Autoethnography: Researching Women's Lives in Northern Pakistan," *Gender, Place and Culture* 12, no. 3 (2005): 317–31; Mike Crang and Ian Cook, *Doing Ethnographies* (London: Sage, 2007).
3. Thomas A. Schwandt, *Sage Dictionary of Qualitative Inquiry* (Los Angeles: Sage, 2007), 16.
4. For discussion of the role of fictionalization and negative ascribed identities in marginalizing disabled workers, see Pamela M. Robert and Sharon L. Harlan, "Mechanisms of Disability Discrimination in Large Bureaucratic Organizations: Ascriptive Inequalities in the Workplace," *Sociological Quarterly* 47, no. 4 (2006): 599–630.

5. Minelle Mahtani, "Mapping Race and Gender in the Academy: The Experiences of Women of Colour Faculty and Graduate Students in Britain, the U.S. and Canada," *Journal of Geography in Higher Education* 28, no. 1 (2004): 91–99.
6. Robert and Harlan, "Mechanisms of Disability Discrimination."
7. *British Columbia, Superintendent of Motor Vehicles v. British Columbia, Council of Human Rights*, No. 26481, para 32, cited in private communication.
8. Kay R. Jamison, *Touched with Fire* (New York: Simon and Schuster, 1996).
9. See also Fiona K. Campbell, *Contours of Ableism: The Production of Disability and Ableness* (London: Palgrave Macmillan, 2009).

BIBLIOGRAPHY

Besio, Kathryn. "Telling Stories to Hear Autoethnography: Researching Women's Lives in Northern Pakistan." *Gender, Place and Culture* 12, no. 3 (2005): 317–31.

Besio, Kathryn, and David Butz. "The Value of Autoethnography for Field Research in Transcultural Settings." *Professional Geographer* 56, no. 3 (2004): 350–60.

Campbell, Fiona K. *Contours of Ableism: The Production of Disability and Ableness*. London: Palgrave Macmillan, 2009.

Chouinard, Vera. "Like Alice through the Looking Glass: Accommodation in Academia." *Resources for Feminist Research* 24, no 3/4 (1995–96): 3–10.

Crang, Mike, and Ian Cook. *Doing Ethnographies*. London: Sage, 2007.

Ellis, Carolyn. "Evocative Authoethnography: Writing Emotionally about Our Lives." In *Representation and the Text: Reframing the Narrative Voice*, edited by William G. Tierney and Yvonna S. Lincoln, 116–39. Albany: State University of New York, 1997.

Ellis, Carolyn, and Arthur P. Bochner. "Autoethnography, Personal Narrative, Reflexivity: Research as Subject." In *Handbook of Qualitative Research*, edited by Norman K. Denzin and Yvonna S. Lincoln, 733–68. Thousand Oaks, CA: Sage, 2000.

Jamison, Kay R. *Touched with Fire*. New York: Simon and Schuster, 1996.

Mahtani, Minelle. "Mapping Race and Gender in the Academy: The Experiences of Women of Colour Faculty and Graduate Students in Britain, the U.S. and Canada." *Journal of Geography in Higher Education* 28, no. 1 (2004): 91–99.

Robert, Pamela M., and Sharon L. Harlan. "Mechanisms of Disability Discrimination in Large Bureaucratic Organizations: Ascriptive Inequalities in the Workplace." *Sociological Quarterly* 47, no. 4 (2006): 599–630.

Schwandt, Thomas A. *Sage Dictionary of Qualitative Inquiry*. Los Angeles: Sage, 2007.

CHAPTER 21

Triple Jeopardy: Native Women with Disabilities*

Doreen Demas

It is estimated that in some Native communities, more than 40 percent of the population lives with a disability of some kind. In Northern Canada, otitis media is a persistent problem. In many communities, this middle ear infection affects 80 percent of the individuals at some time during their life. This infection is a major cause of hearing impairment. Fully one-third of all deaths among status Indians and Inuit are alcohol related, while over 60 percent of the Native children in care arrive in that situation as a direct result of alcohol abuse. The number of Native children who attend school until the end of secondary level is 20 percent, compared with the national rate of 75 percent. Native unemployment is about 35 percent of the working age population, and in some areas it reaches as high as 90 percent.

People with disabilities are disadvantaged in the areas of education, access, transportation, housing, employment opportunities, recreation, cultural opportunities, and so on. Women with disabilities speak of double jeopardy. I believe that Native women who have a disability are in a situation of triple jeopardy. You may be familiar with many of the concerns that Aboriginal people in Canada have—poor housing conditions, lack of adequate medical care, and substance abuse. When you add disability and being female to this, you have a situation of extreme disadvantage.

As an example, when it was time for me to start school, I had to leave my home in Manitoba to attend a special school for visually impaired children in Ontario. Not only did I have to leave my family, but I was also living in a different culture with its own language and norms. Like all the children there, I experienced the negative effects of being educated in a segregated institution, but for me there was the additional burden of being in a different culture. This is still happening today. There are many Native children from remote communities in the North who must come to the South for educational or rehabilitative services.

WHO WE ARE

Native people are not a homogeneous group. Just as you cannot talk about "the disabled" with any clarity, you must remember that Canada's Aboriginal population can be divided into the following groupings: status, non-status, treaty, Métis, and Inuit. Aboriginal people are urban and rural dwellers; some live on a reserve while others live off the reserve; and many still live in the North. This means that there are many varying circumstances and realities for Canada's Aboriginal population.

SELF-GOVERNMENT

Self-government is the number one priority for Aboriginal people. It is seen as the best way to improve their status in Canadian society. While Native persons with disabilities are in agreement with self-government, there is the concern that their needs as persons with disabilities may not be included in the process of self-government. I saw evidence of this when doing the interviews that comprise the Coalition of Provincial Organizations of the Handicapped (COPOH) report titled "Disabled Natives Speak Out."

JURISDICTIONAL PROBLEMS

It is often said that for disadvantaged groups, education is the key to escaping poverty, dependency on welfare, unemployment, and so on. Natives with disabilities are being denied access to the services that would enable them to get the education that assists in obtaining employment. Employment is crucial if an individual is to have an independent and financially secure lifestyle.

What is denying us that access? That access is being denied by jurisdictional quagmires. Those of us who have status or treaty rights have always been viewed by service agencies as the responsibility of the federal government. This means that provincial rehabilitation resources that are available to other Canadians with disabilities are not always available to us. For example, in Manitoba, the Society for Manitobans with Disabilities (formerly the Society for Crippled Children and Adults) does not include people with status in its mandate. This makes it very difficult for Native people to get needed services.

I have my own personal example in this area. I was told by one worker at the Canadian National Institute for the Blind (now CNIB), in response to my request for a closed-circuit TV reader, which I needed for my education, that as a Native person with status I was not eligible for Vocational Rehabilitation for the Disabled Program (VRDP)–allocated equipment, and that VRDP students had first priority to these devices. The worker told me that as a Native person I was not eligible for VRDP, and as a status Indian I was the responsibility of Indian Affairs and it was to them that I should make the request; however, not more than two days prior to that I had been told by someone from the education department of Indian Affairs that there was no money in their budget for these devices and that I was registered with and should make my request to CNIB. This is just one example of a situation where the lack of clarity and the bureaucratic runaround prevent Natives with disabilities from getting adequate services.

Now that Native people have started to set up their own education services, the whole situation has become just that much more complex. Despite the fact that Indian Affairs has a policy on Native people with special needs, this policy is not clear or well understood by many of these organizations. As a consequence, they do not know how to access the funds that are theoretically available to meet the rehabilitation needs of Native persons with disabilities. So who is the loser in all this? It is ultimately the person with the disability, of course.

Just as there is a lack of clarity in the education area, there is a lack of clarity in the area of medical services. I have come across many situations in which a person with a disability whose health is stabilized and who is eligible for assistance from other programs is rejected by those programs because those programs assume that medical services should be taking care of all their needs. We are running up against the domination of the medical model. This is something that non-Native people with disabilities were fighting in the early 1970s when the consumer movement was born. Native people with disabilities are still fighting that battle. Often, these people end up going home to their reserve with nothing, because none of the programs would accept responsibility for them.

These are just a few examples of the bureaucratic problems that Native people with disabilities encounter when they attempt to access necessary services. Add to that coming from a different culture, speaking a different language, and having to deal with non-Native bureaucrats, and you will get an idea of some of the obstacles encountered by Native people with disabilities and why I am talking to you about a situation of triple jeopardy.

ISOLATION

Recently, I attended a conference that focused on the concerns of parents of children with disabilities from the North. There were a number of women at the conference who were single parents. These women felt that their needs, and the needs of their disabled children, were not being met. For the most part, these women were living in poverty and it was difficult for them to meet the dietary needs of a child with a disability. At this conference, I heard many accounts from parents whose children were living in Southern institutions. These children have come from Northern isolated communities to Southern settings to get needed services that are unavailable in the North. I heard about how these children lose contact with their families and their communities. The length of time spent away from family and community can be months and even years. The only way for parents to see their children is to fly South, which is very expensive. It is impossible to make frequent trips. This is particularly true if you have a low income or are on social assistance. The end result is that you lose contact with your child. You really have no choice in that matter, because there are no services in your community. If the child is to get those services, she/he must come South.

TRANSITIONS

People can become disabled as children or later in life. If you have a disability as a child and you have to leave your community to get access to services or for education, the more time spent away from your community and family, the more assimilated into white culture you become. Earlier I made a reference to going away to school. I spent six and a half years of my childhood away from my family and community, and during that time I lost most of my language, a lot of my cultural roots, and, perhaps most devastating to me, I lost family contacts and bonds. While language and culture are important, these are something I think one can relearn. But not growing up in a family atmosphere is not something that you can make up for in later years. Being assimilated into another culture makes you a stranger in your own culture, but it does not make you belong in the other—in a sense you belong in neither culture. Ultimately, if you have different norms and values than your family, it makes it more difficult for you to be part of your own family, so you tend to be isolated.

When you are disabled as an adult, you have to learn to adjust to your disability while simultaneously adjusting to white culture in order to receive services. If you need services to assist you with these adjustments, they are very difficult to find. There are very few service providers that have the necessary understanding of both the cultural factors and the disability factors to assist a person in coping with the transitions they are experiencing in their life.

Non-Native disability organizations do not always have culturally appropriate programs to help people who are Native. Native organizations do have these programs, but they often do not have the understanding of disability issues.

We need to aim some of our attention at Native women's organizations, so that they become sensitive to the issues and concerns of their Native sisters who have disabilities.

CONDITIONS ON RESERVES

I have met a number of Native women and men with spinal cord injuries at Ten Ten Sinclair, which is a housing project in Winnipeg for disabled people. These women and men were preparing for a life in Winnipeg, because there are no options at home on their reserves. There are no accommodations on their reserves to assist them to live in that setting with their disability—ramps into buildings, modified living units that are accessible, accessible transportation, and so on. The condition of existing facilities on reserves can make independent living difficult. For example, gravel roads that are poorly maintained are difficult to travel on when using a wheelchair. These individuals had no choice but to live in the city.

People who live in isolated communities in the North get into the community either by winter road or by air. During spring when the ice is breaking up, there is total isolation, because the winter roads are not usable and you can't fly in. You are stuck either in or out.

That makes it difficult for a person with a disability. It doesn't make it easy for you to live in your community. Situations such as this also force people into urban settings.

SUBSTANCE ABUSE

It is well known that the high rate of substance abuse leads to disabilities. For example, children born with fetal alcohol syndrome can have learning disabilities. People become disabled in accidents that are brought on by substance abuse. Furthermore, drug dependency does not end with disablement. Many treatment facilities are inaccessible. This is particularly true when it comes to women's treatment facilities. We need to work to see that these facilities become accessible and have programs that are culturally appropriate for Native women with disabilities.

Substance abuse is a contributor to domestic violence. Many Native women are survivors of violence. As the DisAbled Women's Network (DAWN) report indicates, violence can lead to disability. Shelters for abused women need to be made aware of the needs of Native women with disabilities. Non-Native shelters for abused women need to be encouraged to have culturally appropriate programs for Native women with disabilities.

MEDICAL CONDITIONS

Native people are susceptible to certain kinds of diseases and medical conditions, such as diabetes, which can cause loss of limbs, blindness, and other serious issues. These medical conditions are exacerbated and triggered by poor living conditions on reserves, including malnutrition and poor housing. Many reserves still have poorly constructed houses that lack plumbing, water systems, and adequate heating systems. These living conditions make it difficult for a person with a disability to live independently, and it is particularly difficult for women who are raising children. You can imagine how difficult it is for a Native woman who is a wheelchair user to raise her children in a house that does not have indoor plumbing.

Inadequate health services on reserves compound the problem. There are examples of people who are more disabled than they need to be because they were treated by people who were poorly trained and underqualified in limited facilities with poor diagnostic equipment.

It would seem to me that clarity of jurisdiction, clear lines of responsibility, and a better internal understanding of the lines of responsibility would improve the situation immensely. Some recommendations are as follows:

- Clarify methods for accessing services and make this information well known at the individual level. If consumers better understand how to access services, it is easier for them to get the services that they are looking for.
- Decentralize services. Services should be available on reserves so the people living there would not have to leave their community.

- Improve access on reserves. For example, schools could be made accessible.
- Make access to people with disabilities a priority everywhere—including on reserves.
- Develop information programs, so that the people who need this information can get access to it. Native organizations need to have an understanding of the funding process so they can get the funds to provide the services they require.

We must do public education with Native women's organizations, so they become aware of the issues and concerns of Native women with disabilities. We must also encourage non-Native women's organizations to provide culturally appropriate programs that meet the needs of Native women with disabilities.

NOTE

* An earlier version of this chapter was published in the Women and Disability Issue of *Canadian Woman Studies*, 13, no. 4 (1993): 53–55.

CHAPTER 22

The Community Inclusion Project in Manitoba: Planning for the Residents of the Pelican Lake Training Centre*

Zana Marie Lutfiyya, Dale C. Kendel, and Karen D. Schwartz

INTRODUCTION

In 2006, the United Nations Convention on the Rights of Persons with Disabilities was adopted. Canada signed the convention in 2007 and ratified it in 2010. Some of the general principles in Article 3 of the convention are

a. Respect for inherent dignity, individual autonomy including the freedom to make one's own choices, and independence of persons;
b. Non-discrimination;
c. Full and effective participation and inclusion in society;
d. Respect for difference and acceptance of persons with disabilities as part of human diversity and humanity.[1]

Article 19 specifically stresses that "States Parties to this Convention recognize the equal right of all persons with disabilities to live in the community, with choices equal to others, and shall take effective and appropriate measures to facilitate full enjoyment by persons with disabilities of this right and their full inclusion and participation in the community."[2]

Notwithstanding that Canada is a signatory to the convention, some people with intellectual disabilities continue to be confined to institutions in Manitoba and other parts of Canada. Authors of the online newsletter *Institution Watch* argue that "progress toward the closure of the last large institutions for persons with intellectual disabilities in Canada remains unacceptably and frustratingly slow despite ongoing efforts by families, self advocates, and organizations working on their behalf."[3] The current conditions echo the findings of the *Community Inclusion Survey Report* (1998):

> Many people with disabilities do not have the opportunity to live ordinary lives.... [They] cannot aspire to even an ordinary life if they are not included in a

community. For most people, community inclusion just happens, but for people with disabilities, being included requires considerable effort just to overcome the barriers that keep them isolated and excluded.[4]

In 2010, People First of Canada, the national advocacy organization representing people with intellectual disabilities, filed a Human Rights complaint against the Province of Manitoba on behalf of the residents of the Manitoba Developmental Centre (MDC) in Portage La Prairie, Manitoba. The parties settled just over a year later with an agreement that the province would move 49 individuals out of the MDC over the next three years. This would reduce the population at the MDC to about 150 individuals; however, both the MDC and the St. Amant Centre in Winnipeg would remain open.[5]

In response to the Government of Manitoba's determination to maintain its policy supporting institutional living for its citizens, our purpose in writing this chapter is to reflect back on an ACL-Manitoba (Association for Community Living-Manitoba) initiative in the late 1990s that focused on planning for residents at the Pelican Lake Training Centre (PLTC), located in Ninette, in the southwest corner of the province. It is important to remember and document the history of a group of citizens that has been consistently marginalized. It is our hope that such a reflection will encourage Manitobans, and other Canadians, to recognize the importance and possibility of community living for all people, regardless of their disability.

THE COMMUNITY INCLUSION INITIATIVE

In 1997, the Government of Canada allocated 3 million dollars for a Community Inclusion (CI) initiative to support Canadians with intellectual disabilities, their families, their caregivers, and their communities. Administered by Human Resources Development Canada (HRDC; now Human Resources and Skills Development Canada) through the Social Partnerships Division, the CI initiative used a model of change based on action, advocacy, collaboration, and networking. These efforts were to be guided by the CI initiative objectives, which included (a) expanding opportunities to build capacity for inclusion in communities, (b) improving the quality of supports and services available for individuals with intellectual disabilities and their families, and (c) basing these supports on practices that facilitate inclusion. Other goals also included (a) opportunities to learn about self-advocacy, (b) developing and maintaining a network of co-operative partnerships among stakeholders, and (c) creating opportunities to share lessons learned.

After a period of development and consultation, a number of demonstration projects were funded. These projects were identified and funded through the Canadian Association for Community Living (CACL) and its provincial and territorial counterparts, as well as People First of Canada. In all, 67 projects were funded across Canada, involving 219 communities. The CACL (now Inclusion Canada) is a national organization that advocates for the interests of individuals with intellectual disability and their families, which has chapters in all Canadian provinces and territories. This organization promotes community living and personalized supports. People First of Canada is a national self-advocacy organization of people with intellectual disabilities.

In Manitoba, the provincial Association for Community Living (ACL-Manitoba) began its project by identifying the major barriers that limited the full participation and involvement of individuals with intellectual disabilities in community life. An extensive consultation process was undertaken with individuals and organizations, and 20 meetings were held on a variety of topics in various communities across the province. At each meeting, the discussion was initiated by asking a series of questions. After these meetings were concluded, ACL-Manitoba staff organized all of the feedback into themes. One of the significant themes was institutionalization. Deinstitutionalization had been and continues to be a long-standing goal of ACL-Manitoba. Notwithstanding these efforts, approximately 750 Manitobans with intellectual disabilities continued to reside in institutions in the late 1990s. In light of their findings and their commitment to community living, ACL-Manitoba decided to pursue this issue as one of its five areas of change.

PLANNING FOR RESIDENTS AT THE PELICAN LAKE TRAINING CENTRE

In 1998, ACL-Manitoba became involved in an initiative to design individualized plans for 69 people who were residents of the PLTC. According to a website about the PLTC,

> The purpose of the Centre was to house and train selected mentally challenged residents of the Manitoba Developmental Centre in Portage La Prairie that had become very overcrowded. The people selected were those deemed capable of learning to care for themselves and their living quarters. The aim was to help them develop to a point where they could live in foster homes in the community.[6]

To facilitate the planning, it was decided to use a person-centred planning process, known as Planning Alternative Futures with Hope, or PATH.[7] Planning is "person-centred" when it is "rooted in respect for the person and a commitment to build inclusive communities. The process takes its lead from sustained, careful listening to the person, in whatever ways the person communicates."[8] Themes of person-centred planning include "(a) creating vision, (b) developing capacity, (c) developing supports, (d) sharing resources, and (e) building community."[9] A team of four provincial staff members, known as the "Transition Team," was hired or seconded to help organize and implement this process. The team began to identify PATH facilitators, contact families, and set up planning sessions.

Unexpectedly and before any planning had actually taken place, the provincial government announced the closing of the PLTC in February 1999.[10] All participants involved with the initiative were surprised and unprepared. While ACL-Manitoba was pleased with this decision, the centre's staff and some families of residents were not. Staff members were clearly concerned about their employment possibilities, while some families worried about what provisions would be made for their relatives. In response to the announcement, the Transition Team faced a barrage of questions, worry, frustration, and outright hostility as they continued with the planning process. Public meetings for families were held. Staff and many families worked against the closure. The provincial government tempered its initial announcement and, in May 1999, reversed it.[11] Confusion reigned.

A profound lack of trust among virtually all of the parties and changing government priorities maintained the fraught atmosphere. Many of those who facilitated PATH felt that the process was being sabotaged by a lack of clear parameters, fearmongering, and worry. With a few months of hindsight, one participant felt that the concerns of most parties were simply being ignored. Staff of the PLTC were not told directly about programmatic concerns at the institution and only read about them in the newspapers. They were concerned about their jobs and their future. Those families who maintained contact with their sons or daughters were worried about where and with whom they would end up being placed. Others felt that many of the residents were effectively silenced during the planning. Although facilitators thought many participants were well prepared, the administration at the PLTC was described as increasingly absent from the process.

Despite the emotional turmoil, the planning process, which was mandated by law, was completed. The result was the creation of plans for 69 individuals living at the PLTC. Most of the plans included moving to the community, or at least exploring the option to do so. By the end of 2000, about 20 people had left the PLTC. By the end of 2001, 49 people left for homes in communities such as Brandon, Boissevain, Dauphin, Grandview, Rivers, Virden, and Winnipeg. Two people moved to Toronto and one to Calgary, allowing for both community placement and family reunification.

As things unfolded, the process of actualizing the PATH and moving to the community was a careful and thoughtful one. Before selecting a new home, individuals visited between two and four communities that had been identified during the planning process. The Transition Team paid attention to both verbal statements and non-verbal behaviours to help them identify a good match between people, supports, and the home community. All placements were individualized, meaning that people moved into small group homes with no more than three residents, or apartments with either one or two residents. During the first year, all people received an individualized day program designed to help them get to know their new community. This was done by support staff who were hired to help people learn about available resources and opportunities.

At a press conference on March 9, 2000, the Manitoba family services minister finally announced the closing of the PLTC.[12] He noted the following: "As we worked through the plans for the residents at Pelican, approximately 54 of the 70 [sic] have indicated a preference for community living." He continued with the observation that there were people being supported to live in the community who were more disabled than many of the residents living at the PLTC. Members of People First of Manitoba who had already become involved with former PLTC residents as they moved into the community attended the press conference and released a statement of their own. Donna Smith, then president of the organization said, "It is exciting to see people at Ninette finally get a chance to live in the community. I have met some of the people.... I have welcomed them ... and hope they are happy."

VIGNETTES

This chapter would not be complete without the inclusion of several personal stories that capture the experiences of some of the people who moved from the PLTC into Manitoba communities. The first author was contracted by ACL-Manitoba to collect qualitative data from those individuals who had been involved in this effort. The second author assisted with some of the focus groups that were conducted. Please note that the names of the individuals and locations have been replaced with pseudonyms.

A Welcoming Speech

An unanticipated result of the planning process was the involvement of two People First members in a neighbouring community. Aware of the public debate about closure, these individuals attended a public forum and tried to talk about the benefits they enjoyed as a result of leaving another institution several years earlier. They made a video that depicted their lives, their homes, possessions, jobs, friends, neighbours, and community activities. Despite the homemade quality of the production, the video was a poignant testimony to the extraordinary importance of ordinary opportunities in our lives. Residents at the PLTC watched this video and found it to be personally helpful. One viewer expressed surprise at the realization that perhaps he could own a pet in his new home. The two People First members became very involved in welcoming the individuals who left the PLTC to live in their community. They helped newcomers to unpack and set up house and hosted a housewarming party and, later, a birthday party. One woman made a welcoming speech that the newcomers framed and hung in their living room. In part, it stated, "I would like to welcome you both to the community. We wish you all the best. This move was made possible from ... the support of People First ... if you see us in the street, be sure to say hi."[13]

Moving to Lakeside

Anthony's plan called for him to visit several communities so that he could make a decision about where he wanted to live. He travelled to Lakeside, a small town, with a member of the Transition Team. He arrived at a group home, toured the house, returned to the living room, sat on the couch, and smiled. The staff person accompanying him later said that he almost fell over as he could see that Anthony had found his home.

After a few visits, Anthony moved to his new home, which he shares with three other people. During these visits he chose his bedroom furniture including his bed, dresser, lamp, clock, bed linens, and television. He also selected a full-length mirror. He stood in front of this mirror for a long time in the store, and the staff realized that he wanted it for his new room. Anthony showed an interest in horses by buying framed prints and other items. His spacious bedroom already had a futon in it, which Anthony chose to keep as a couch. He draped an afghan that he had brought with him from the PLTC over the futon. A few days later, he replaced that afghan with one he had received as a "welcome to Lakeside" gift.

When Anthony first moved to Lakeside, he came with a picture board for communication purposes, as he did not speak. This was thrown away two days later when he began speaking in words and phrases, which were quickly replaced with simple sentences. According to the staff, Anthony seemed agitated for the first couple of days after his move. While they didn't know why this was so, he soon relaxed. Right from the beginning, he seemed to enjoy car rides and exploring his new territory. His initial agitation continued only when driven on the highway he had to take from Ninette to Lakeside. His staff used back roads for six weeks until Anthony calmed down.

After six months, Anthony enjoyed going to movies, hockey games, and concerts. He had a wonderful time at the 25th anniversary party of the agency that supported him. He found work with several other people cleaning local businesses and facilities such as a hardware store and skating rink. He also had a daily paper route, which he enjoyed. All of this was an enormous change for the 40-year-old man who had been institutionalized for 25 years. But for Anthony, there was no looking back.

Home in Big Valley

"We are very pleased to have these women in our community," Eva began, "and we have an especially welcoming community." Eva worked for a residential support agency in Big Valley. She helped to welcome three women who moved from the PLTC. She and another staff person went to the PLTC to meet six people who were considering a move to Big Valley. Her job was to choose which individuals would move; however, she and her co-worker refused to make that choice and decided instead to "say welcome to the first people we met."

And so, three women moved to live in Big Valley in late February 2000. Because of the long distance between Big Valley and Ninette, there were no opportunities for visits ahead of the move. The people in Big Valley wanted to make sure that these women really wanted to live there. Two of the three women indicated their approval almost right away, while the third woman took a week to make her decision. They now share a home together.

Although the furniture was supposed to arrive just before they did, the basics arrived two days later, which meant that they had to camp out for a few days. When the furniture finally arrived, the women went about decorating their new home. During their first week after the move, the women were reportedly a bit anxious. Then they went shopping for bed linens, lamps, and towels. As the cashier rang up and bagged their items, one of the women kept retrieving her purchases in order to keep them in plain view—she wanted to keep an eye on her new things! Afterwards, they ate lunch at a fast food restaurant, an apparent first for them. The day was a great success. All three of these women had lived in institutions for many years. One of them had spent 55 of her 62 years at the MDC and the PLTC.

The women spent those first days learning how to take care of themselves and their home. They enjoyed doing housework, baking, and cooking, as well as making a variety of crafts. One woman made herself an apron. They also learned their way around town and were pleased to meet people. They began spending time at a bakery. Managed by the agency that supports them, many people have been employed there baking and serving lunches. The bakery represents one of many opportunities for people with intellectual disabilities living in the community.

"1958 Boots"

In December 1999, three men living at the PLTC met with staff from a residential support agency in Princeton. Due to the distance involved, they agreed to visit the town for three or four days. On the second day of the visit in January 2000, the men made it clear that they were not going back to the PLTC. One man unpacked in about "two and a half minutes," the program administrator reported. "He said 'my home' and that was it." When the program administrator visited the home after a five-day absence, another of the men took her by the arm and said, "My room. My house. Come with me." They had found a new home.

These men picked out bed linens, curtains, and other things to go with their new bedroom furniture. They also purchased virtually an entire wardrobe, replacing clothing that was old and not always in good shape, including a pair of "1958 boots." One of the gentlemen chose Western wear and came home with denims and a jean jacket. Another indicated that he wanted to buy a ring. They visited a stylist and proudly showed off new haircuts. The men were happy hosts during an open house, eager to display their new home. One man's birthday was celebrated with a big bash.

The only difficulty they demonstrated during the initial settling period was their reluctance to get in the car. They did not want to go anywhere. When asked if they wanted to return to the PLTC to see anyone, one man named a friend whom he had not seen in many years. It turned out that this individual had been living in Princeton for the past 10 years, and the friends were quickly reunited.

The men took part in a home-based day program at the outset. The men learned to take care of their home, to bake, and to cook. They especially loved to be in the kitchen, earning the collective nickname "the Mr. Moms." The program administrator recalled, "One night they had made trifle in individual glasses. There is always fresh baking every time you stop by … their house always smells so good."

Two of the men had lived in institutions for more than 30 years each, while the younger man had spent the last 20 of his 30 years in two different institutions. They now live in their own home, help take care of it, and do things in the community on a daily basis. One man likes to swim, and does so two or three times a week. The program administrator concluded, "We're excited and grateful to be a part of their lives." She was eager to welcome and support others who might choose to move to Princeton in the future.

The Keys to His Castle

Keith and Eric were among the first to leave the PLTC. They moved to Hayden in early December 1999. Over several visits beforehand, these two men picked out all of the furniture for their apartment and met people over lunch. On their first visit, Keith indicated that he wanted the keys to the apartment saying, "My apartment, my keys." In response, his support worker gave him a set of keys. Residents were not allowed to keep any keys at the PLTC, so Keith had to return them to the support worker at the end of the visit. This made him visibly upset. Over subsequent visits, the support worker made sure that he was always at the apartment to welcome Keith and Eric, avoiding any obvious use of the keys. Notwithstanding this effort, Keith still asked about the keys on every visit. His support worker told him that he would have his own keys once he moved into the apartment.

On December 2, 1999, the two men moved into their apartment. Unfortunately, the night before the move the keys were stolen from a staff person's car. Keith was upset the next morning, as his support worker had apparently broken his promise. All was forgiven when the locks were rekeyed and the two men were presented with their own house keys later that morning.

Keith attended a press conference in late March when the minister of family services announced the closure of the PLTC. When asked by a reporter where he liked to live, Keith replied, "My apartment." When asked if he would like to go back to the institution, Keith replied, "No. My apartment. My keys." Both Keith and Eric have refused opportunities to return to the PLTC to visit friends, although they have expressed an interest in visiting individuals who had already moved to the community.

Family Reunion

Keith's sister, Anya, and several other siblings were institutionalized at the same time. While service providers were not clear about how many siblings there were and where they all lived, they did know that one brother lived in a foster home just outside of the small town where the PLTC is located. Anya moved to Hayden, in an apartment next door to Keith and Eric. Although Keith and Anya had lived at the PLTC for years, recognized each other, and knew that they were related, there had been little encouragement for the two to stay in touch with each other or any of their other siblings. When Anya moved to Hayden in March 2000, she and Keith had little interest in each other. After their move into the community, they enjoyed a much closer relationship as staff members actively provided them with opportunities to spend time together and to get to know each other. The staff members made plans to ensure that Keith and Anya would visit and keep in touch with their siblings in the future.

LESSONS LEARNED

The Community Inclusion Project, with its focus on planning for residents at the PLTC, contributed to ACL-Manitoba's understanding of how to help people move from institutional to community life. A number of lessons were learned that can assist in planning for current institutional residents.

First, stakeholders felt that a clear and coherent statement of the planning process was essential, along with the resources to actually carry out the plans. In the case of the PLTC, the invitation to plan, followed closely by a public announcement to close the centre, caught people by surprise. Later statements only added to the overall confusion. Anxiety and tension, which naturally accompany new planning processes, was exacerbated by the changing policies over closure.

The planning process itself must be conducive to the situation. In the case of the PLTC, there was a lack of information about the residents coupled with the fact that family and staff felt threatened by the closure announcement. In order to plan successfully with PATH, certain conditions must be present; however, in this case, crucial gaps in information and insight affected at least some of the planning sessions.

The Transition Team devised some helpful ways of moving the planning process forward in the face of some opposition to community options. This allowed for the development of plans that would contribute to more positive futures for the individuals involved, avoided power struggles, and built receptivity to discuss difficult issues. Once the topic of community living was broached, it became possible to include "baby steps" towards community involvement. These steps included the commitment to explore certain options in the community before coming to a final decision, at least opening a new set of possibilities for people to consider. In fact, several families and individuals explored community options and subsequently decided to go ahead with moving out of the PLTC.

Finally, once plans are developed, there must be some way to implement them. Neither the staff nor the administration at the PLTC had made a clear commitment to the planning process, let alone carrying out the action steps. In addition, because there was a lack of staff time, those designated to certain tasks did not actually carry them out. This left the Transition Team with the responsibility of carrying out the PATH goals, along with their other responsibilities.

CONCLUSION

While several Canadian provinces have made the decision to close institutional settings for individuals with intellectual disabilities, the Province of Manitoba remains committed to institutional care for at least some of its citizens. Making a decision to close an institutional setting remains contentious. The closure of the PLTC provides a "made in Manitoba" case study to consider. Despite the initial confusion regarding closure, the commitment of the Transition Team, a person-centred planning process, and the movement of resources from the PLTC to community-based service providers resulted in a relatively orderly process. Individual residents had some opportunity to choose where and with whom they wanted to live. At the time the case study was conducted, both staff members and residents who were interviewed reported an overall satisfaction with the transition process. Former PLTC residents were satisfied with their new homes. Those who had re-established relationships with family and friends were particularly grateful. The only "difficult" behaviours that were noticed appeared when former residents seemed to think that they might be returning to the PLTC. At the end of the day, the former residents of the PLTC moved to what might be described as "ordinary homes" in different communities across the province. With support, they began to make a new life for themselves.

NOTES

* Human Resources Development Canada—Employability and Social Partnerships Division, the Association for Community Living Manitoba (ACL-Manitoba), and the Canadian Association for Community Living (CACL) provided financial support for this study. The views expressed are the authors, and do not necessarily reflect those of HRDC, ACL-Manitoba, or the CACL.

1. United Nations, Article 3, Convention on the Rights of Persons with Disabilities, A/RES/61/106, (December 31, 2006), http://www.un.org/disabilities/documents/convention/convoptprot-e.pdf.
2. United Nations, Article 19, Convention on the Rights of Persons with Disabilities, A/RES/61/106, (December 31, 2006), http://www.un.org/disabilities/documents/convention/convoptprot-e.pdf.
3. *Institution Watch*, "Editorial," June 3, 2011, http://www.cacl.ca/publications-resources/institution-watch-volume-6-no-1-summer2011.
4. Human Resources & Development Canada, *Community Inclusion Survey Report* (1998), iii.
5. Province of Manitoba, "Province Announces Human Rights Complaint against Manitoba Developmental Centre Settled," news release (November 25, 2011), http://news.gov.mb.ca/news/index.html?item=12683.
6. Erna Kurbegovic, "Pelican Lake Training Centre," *Eugenics Archives*, April 5, 2014, http://eugenicsarchive.ca/discover/institutions.
7. Marsha Forest, John O'Brien, and Jack Pearpoint, *PATH: A Workbook for Planning Positive and Possible Futures* (Toronto: Inclusion Press, 1993).
8. John O'Brien and Jack Pearpoint, *Person-Centered Planning with MAPS and PATH: A Workbook for Facilitators* (Toronto: Inclusion Press, 2004), 7.

9. O'Brien and Pearpoint, *Person-Centered Planning with MAPS and PATH*, 6.
10. Province of Manitoba, "Residents and Staff Priorities in Closure of Pelican Lake Centre," news release (February 4, 1999), http://news.gov.mb.ca/news/?item=23805&posted=1999-02-04-27k-1999-02-04.
11. *Winnipeg Free Press*, "Pelican Lake Training Centre," May 6, 1999.
12. Province of Manitoba, "Pelican Lake Centre to Close Dec. 31," news release (March 9, 2000), http://news.gov.mb.ca/news/?item=24396&posted=2000=03-09-26k-2000-03-09.
13. This is used with permission on the condition that the author remains anonymous (personal communication, 2001).

BIBLIOGRAPHY

Forest, Marsha, John O'Brien, and Jack Pearpoint. *PATH: A Workbook for Planning Positive and Possible Futures*. Toronto: Inclusion Press, 1993.

Human Resources and Development Canada. *Community Inclusion Survey Report*. 1998.

Kurbegovic, Erna. "Pelican Lake Training Centre." Eugenics Archives, April 5, 2014. http://eugenicsarchive.ca/discover/institutions.

Lutfiyya, Zana Marie, and Dale C. Kendel. *Outcomes from the Community Inclusion Project in Manitoba*. Research report submitted to the Canadian Association for Community Living and Human Resources Development Canada—Social Development Partnerships Division, 2000.

O'Brien, John, and Jack Pearpoint. *Person-Centered Planning with MAPS and PATH: A Workbook for Facilitators*. Toronto: Inclusion Press, 2004.

Province of Manitoba. "Residents and Staff Priorities in Closure of Pelican Lake Centre." News release, February 4, 1999. http://news.gov.mb.ca/news/?item=23805&posted=1999-02-04-27k-1999-02-04.

Province of Manitoba. "Pelican Lake Centre to Close Dec. 31." News release, March 9, 2000. http://news.gov.mb.ca/news/?item=24396&posted=2000=03-09-26k-2000-03-09.

Province of Manitoba. "Province Announces Human Rights Complaint against Manitoba Developmental Centre Settled." News release, November 25, 2011. http://news.gov.mb.ca/news/index.html?item=12683.

Winnipeg Free Press. "Pelican Lake Training Centre." May 6, 1999.

CHAPTER 23

Living in the Midst: Re-imagining Disability through Auto/biography

Kelly McGillivray

"When are you going to write your autobiography?" I have been asked multiple times, as though simply by virtue of being disabled, I have a story to write. What are people expecting from my autobiographical utterance, I wonder? But I already know the answer.

Increasingly I find myself living within a Western culture that centres on individualism, valorizes independence, and enacts and reiterates the normative practices, processes, and discourses contained therein. This neoliberal fixation on independence, individualism, and normalization is enacted frequently and consistently in disability autobiography. This chapter engages with, and ultimately unravels, such hegemonic notions of the independent, autonomous, rational self as it is constructed in relation to disability, particularly in/through autobiography. I do so using strategies of autoethnography and by drawing on critical disability studies, feminist theory, and auto/biography theory. It is my hope and my intention to challenge problematic autobiography expectations and representations, and to open up radical possibilities for change, moving away from everything we have been taught and internalized about illness and disability—disconnection, isolation, fear, individualism—and towards stories that are more compassionate, stories that connect us and that embody community.

In attempting to respond to autobiographical queries, I surveyed the growing field of disability autobiography, and I observed gaps and systemic problems within the literature. In the face of a long history of oppression, there are a multitude of narratives by people with disabilities who have heeded calls to write their own stories, on their own terms, that have entered the public discourse in the last two decades. Through examining many of these accounts, it quickly becomes obvious that people with disabilities have inherited discourses and patterns—of autobiographical writing and of disability—through which they must tell their lives, their stories, and their bodies. So, while the inclusion of disabled people's stories in the autobiography genre has been considered revolutionary, access has only been granted peripherally, on limited and conditional bases (*so as to not upset the order of things*). G. Thomas Couser points out that disabled people's prose licenses carry restrictions upon entry into the literary marketplace. They may enter the marketplace on the condition that their stories conform to preferred paradigms. Couser refers to this as the "tyranny of the comic plot"—that is, disability, which is often considered to be depressing and downbeat, may be represented so long as the story takes the form of the "narrative of overcoming."[1]

This overcoming story takes root at the intersection between neoliberal constructions of self, disability, and normalcy. Critiques of the genre place their focus here, recognizing that "autobiography as a genre emerged out of a distinctive set of interacting cultural, historical, economic, social, technological and political trends related to the growth and consolidation of" modern capitalism, including the neoliberal concept of the rational, independent, and autonomous individual.[2] David T. Mitchell uses Leonard Kriegel's autobiographical work, *Flying Solo: Reimagining Manhood, Courage, and Loss*, as an example: "While championing angst-ridden models such as T. S. Eliot's J. Alfred Prufrock or Emersonian platitudes about sublime solitude, Kriegel sets himself up as heir-apparent to a male tradition of self-imposed alienation from community."[3] As Mitchell says, Kriegel presents his disability experience as an isolated affair, ripe with obstacles and bodily limitation that must be overcome. What is established in this piece is the notion that a worthy life—of both living and of writing about—conforms to the standards of normalcy. It is disability-as-a-problem that propels the narrative forward, making it something that must be resolved or overcome. This configuration plays out time and time again, so much so that at times we seem hopelessly trapped in this script. As people with disabilities, our autobiographies often end up reiterating problematic constructions of self and of normalcy, rather than dismantling the medicalization and troping of disability as isolation and personal tragedy.[4] People with disabilities continue to be oppressed by this individual model of thinking about disability, by history, and by the regulatory norms of disability and normalcy, which set up a dominant system of meaning, scripting people with disabilities as dependent, deviant, other, worthless, monstrous, less than human, and abnormal. Not considered *bodies that matter*,[5] let alone lives and stories worthy of being told, people with disabilities have been marginalized from, and silenced in, autobiographical practices traditionally exalting the white, male, individual writer.

Certainly, life writings by people with disabilities have occupied a somewhat ambiguous position within the field of disability studies for these reasons,[6] for they have traditionally been written and read—that is, presented, represented, understood, and reproduced—in very specific and traditional ways. They are generally in written form, as opposed to oral, visual, or other accessible texts. They follow a linear trajectory, with a beginning (diagnosis, trouble), middle (a series of obstacles), and an ending where the autobiographer usually overcomes their disability in some way. The normative, neoliberal discourse that is established participates in, creates, and sustains the larger socio-cultural story of disability—where overcoming narratives predominate, disability is Other, an individual experience, and exhaustively referred to "as a troublesome difference, a problem, as a way to refer to other problems, or as a problem that has been undergone, overcome, managed, or dissolved."[7] In the process, rigid hierarchical demarcations remain intact: healthy/ill, normal/abnormal, able/disabled, before/after, mind/body, triumph/tragedy, pedestal/pity, us/them, independent/dependent, strong/weak, self/other. In effect, this locks and fixes people into categories and locations. Disability/illness remains "over there," as something that happens to "other" people, making it difficult to relate to or imagine. We are inundated with particularly narrow notions of illness/disability that continually reflect these larger socio-cultural messages, from conventions that call for quick fixes and cures, health promotion, overcoming, and bravery, to ones replete with pity, fear, uncertainty, and anxiety. In short, these conventions are about disconnection, and they express a kind of distancing from disability and illness in our everyday encounters. These deeply rooted discourses and patterns are, and create, the *expected* stories. And they are generally devoid of the inclusion of Indigenous experiences or any meaningful consideration of the ways in which disability intersects with gender, race, class, sexuality, culture, and other socially produced categories of difference.

These are powerful stories. Our stories are *powerful*. We come to the experience of disability—our own and others'—with fully formed ways of knowing (or assuming we know) what it means to be disabled in Western society. We have all heard these stories. They come to us through our readings, the images we see, the language and metaphors we use, the television shows and films we watch, discussions we have with friends, conversations around the water cooler, news reports, culture, history, the assumptions we make about others, and the very stories we tell about our own lives, our selves. We are constantly telling our stories; this is, as Marlatt suggests, how we make sense of, and make real, our lives to ourselves and the other people in our lives, and how we come to know and perpetuate what is important to us.[8] We take up these stories, grant them meaning, and redistribute them, solidifying them into deeply entrenched conventions from and through which we act in the world. As Tanya Titchkosky emphasizes, "we are active participants in making up the meaning of people."[9] That is, we *create* disability in the telling of these stories, in the iterations, the repetitions, and the ways "we narrate the intersections of human diversity."[10] We are meaning-makers.

Thus, it is critical that we explore the ways we have been grounded and positioned in complex systems of power relations and cultural inscriptions, the scripts we have been given to write and speak our stories, and the ways we make meaning. The usefulness of examining the conflicts and contradictions that surround our particular inheritances cannot be emphasized enough, for unravelling the dominant cultural and autobiographical codes can, as Carol Thomas insists, help "inform the generation of new knowledge,"[11] and also help us understand "what knowledge is and how it is produced."[12] Joan Borsa's feminist work on the "politics of location" is instructive in negotiating locations of not only gender, but also disability, race, class, sexuality, and other intersections, and how we can utilize the locations we occupy as sites of resistance and representation: "On the one side we seem hopelessly trapped, fixed into inherited systems and structures, and on the other we appear reactive, engaged in revisionary tactics, offering new stories as if in themselves they can set things right."[13] Indeed, sometimes we seem fixed and trapped in these autobiographical patterns.

I do not intend to criticize other people's stories, and I am not necessarily saying that particular patterns are problematic on their own, but I am concerned with the one-dimensional nature and singularity of the scripts, the very limited and narrow discourses we have inherited to articulate our experiences. We are not a society very practised at simply *being with* illness/disability, without setting it in opposition to normalcy, without trying to cure it or overcome it, without reducing it to a set of symptoms and problems, without responding with fear or anxiety. Instead we are inundated with discourses of individualism, separation, disconnection, and Otherness; these discourses isolate, marginalize, categorize, medicalize, segregate, hierarchize, and oppress. It is a language that disconnects us from others, the earth, our bodies, our selves, our lived experiences, our stories. This is the world view from which we, as a society, act in the world. It has real-world, everyday consequences in terms of how we treat each other, how we include and exclude, and how we create, sustain, and break barriers and systems of power and oppression. And it misses rich dimensions of the human experience.

I recognize that we are all, in some way, complicit in this larger system. But I have also been conscious of not wanting to share my own story in a way that reinforces and reiterates the dominant neoliberal overcoming script by simply adding my story into the large fold of other disability memoirs. Repeating the dominant narrative perpetuates inequalities and allows the status quo to thrive. So, yes, I could tell you that I became ill out of the blue 28 years ago when I was 14, dramatically and profoundly separating my life into before and after. I could tell you that the barriers, challenges, abuses, and silences have been plentiful, and often unbearable. But I don't want to tell an overcoming story with a beginning, middle, and end. And I also don't want to tell a story of pity or unattainable aspiration/inspiration. I find that, with all of this distancing from illness/disability that we do daily, we are left with a picture that is very different than the lived reality I have come to experience over the past 28 years. I have struggled to find my own story in the midst of these larger scripts. I have not overcome my illness/disability and achieved greatness; I'm not a "happy cripple"; I'm not bitter or angry; most days I wouldn't rather be dead than disabled (as some people have suggested to me); my illness/disability was not caused by sin and cannot be cured by attending church (as other people have suggested); I am not "tragic but brave [or] helpless and dependent";[14] I haven't been cured by a miracle drug. I didn't trek to the North Pole or climb a mountain despite my illness. I didn't climb a mountain at all, for that matter. And I don't live in isolation from community. I am simply an ordinary woman, living each day with illness and disability as a part of my being-in-the-world. *Living in the midst*. Living with uncertainty, in an unstable and fluid self and body, facing challenges and joys, anxieties and desires, just like everyone else. The everyday stuff of life. I wonder how this simple acknowledgement—this different way of knowing and being in the world—could question, unravel, and carve space to rebuild the larger disability story through our personal narratives.

And so I wish to ask: What if we could rethink, re-imagine, and tell the story differently? What would that mean? What would that look, sound, and feel like? What would that mean for voice, for agency? Here is what I have gathered. There are gaps and spaces in the narrative repetitions to question and re-imagine our engagement with disability, for "disability transforms the tale, utterly."[15] In fact, the very presence of disability—the disruption of difference—can be a teacher, as Tanya Titchkosky makes explicit, giving us opportunities to rethink our socio-cultural and institutional practices and policies.

Timothy Barrett focuses on reading strategies to rethink the concept of individualism in life writing by people with disabilities. He says "that researchers can negotiate or mitigate the problem of individualism in a number of ways: by seeing the social in the personal; by recognising individualism as a social trend; and by paying attention to the slippery boundary between autobiography/biography."[16] I am in agreement; however, not everyone has the tools (or access to the tools) for such critical reading strategies. I contend that it is not simply *what* we write, but the very processes through which we read and write that can be transformative. It is not enough to simply add more disability autobiographies to the genre. Couser suggests that "simply having a narrative grounded in one's lived experience is by no means a guarantee that it will offer either a politically grounded or counter-discursive portrayal of disability."[17] Indeed, the "I" in autobiography can only express itself through the language available to it.[18] Thus, we must start looking for spaces and places to tell a different kind of story and thinking about how we write them: "How do we shift those stories across language, culture, community? And once translated, who listens and how?"[19] Eli Clare writes that "certainly it's necessary to tell it…. But by itself, story isn't enough."[20] "We need to tell, talk, translate the marrow. Tell it as trouble…. Tell it as joy," Clare insists. "Talk it as postmodern theory, teasing those ideas out of the bramble, or as a training ground for health-care providers. Translate it as history, policy, fierceness, rebellion, civil rights, a poem sung in the streets."[21] Yes. And here, I wish to also tell it as community. As living in relation. As interdependence and as intersectionality.

The autobiography that I would wish to write would embody community, would use accessible and inclusive forms, and would use feminist post-structuralist strategies to "blow up the Law," "knock the wind out of the codes," and "cross, or even double-cross"[22] the conventional scripts of genres and locations. These "jams" work to "crip"—to critique and disrupt[23]—the reigning paradigms by creating space for disabled people's writing, unsettling the notion of the universal, individual, normative subject,[24] and challenging the very notion of representation itself, the very ways we see and read and write. In this way, "cripping" is understood as a strategy "to re-imagine conceptual boundaries, relationships, communities, cultural representations, and power structures."[25] Thus, to return to Joan Borsa's politics of location, rather than remaining hopelessly fixed in inherited systems—such as culture, history, gender, race, sexual difference, and identity—disabled autobiographers may "appear reactive, engaged in revisionary tactics, offering new stories as if in themselves they can set things right."[26] As I invited earlier, if we are to read and write the story differently—and I believe we must—what might that look, sound, and feel like?

Let us pause for a moment. Let us step back from the conventions, from everything we think we know about illness and disability—all the layers of meaning and metaphor, language and form, oppression and silence, expectation, fear, and anxiety. Let the women and texts that follow show us what it means to be ill/disabled, but in a different way, by creating a space—a rupture in the master scripts—for agency and something different to unfold. I am interested in self-stories that ask us to take a moment, to slow down the process, to stop, to think, to be present, to read differently, and to question habitual and power-laden practices and discourses and our relationship to them.

I envision the auto/biographies of Nancy Mairs, Sandra Butler and Barbara Rosenblum, Georgina Kleege, and Bonnie Sherr Klein as examples of modelling ways to tell the story anew. These women take up and make manifest wonderfully creative revisionary tactics in their work. Their texts "destabilize our dominant ways of knowing disability,"[27] as they try to find alternate spaces to speak and experience disability through autobiography, through the very stories we tell about our lives. Stories that connect us, that are more compassionate, layered, open-ended, circling, in process, and dynamic with radical possibility; ones that are less individualized, isolating, disconnecting, and reductive. In doing so, I imagine and re-imagine community as *a way of being in the world*, not simply the places or spaces we occupy or groups to which we belong. Community, conceptualized in this way, draws from Indigenous world views in which the "primary mode of existence is communal, involving 'all my relations' human, animal, plant, spiritual and elemental."[28]

Against a tradition of absence, marginalization, and silence, these women's texts explode binaries and boundaries through *processes*, by challenging fixed notions of genre, narrative timeline, authorship, form, medium, and self/subjectivity, always questioning received notions of "history," "truth," and "knowledge," and falling both within and beyond the printed page. Separately and together, all of these texts are "auto/biographies," that is, they are concerned with "the shifting boundaries between self and other, past and present, writing and reading, fact and fiction … within the oral, visual, and written texts that are biographies and autobiographies."[29] They are auto/biographies, recognizing that people with disabilities are part of social networks, which Liz Stanley makes explicit. She writes that it "is a very rare autobiography that does not contain within its pages many, shorter or longer, biographies of other people who figure, in different times and places, in the subject's life."[30] Hence her use of the term *auto/biography*, for "autobiographers are almost inevitably also biographers."[31]

All these auto/biographies, in relation to each other, are important texts that weave together various forms, layers, and textures. Through their multi-voiced, multi-genred, collaborative approaches, they *require* different reader engagement, challenging the very *processes* through which we see and read and write. They allow for a pause. And they challenge the binary operations defining disability and illness in opposition to non-disability, health, and normalcy, as well as the hierarchies within the categories of illness and disability.

To begin, Sandra Butler and Barbara Rosenblum—two voices—collaboratively compose a narrative of *Cancer in Two Voices*. Through letters and alternating journal entries, the process is a dynamic exchange and collaboration between and among the women, offering two interlocking perspectives that shed light on a shared experience of cancer.

They write about what it is like to be in the experience together. Butler and Rosenblum construct an "us" in the process. It is an "us" that powerfully exemplifies the auto/biographical significance of two women coming together as "mother, lover, friend, confidant, partners, playmates" to each other.[32] This is their story, as they "lived it together," writes Butler.[33] Together, they unsettle dominant metaphors of illness/disability as individual experiences that *one* must overcome and bridge gaps between established binaries. Butler and Rosenblum invite their community into the dynamic as active participants in the process, as witnesses and companions. Through healing circles, a commitment ceremony, and reaching out through letters, they create a space for their experience to unfold differently: in solidarity, in community. In the acknowledgements of the text, Butler writes, "My life with Barbara was embedded in friendship, in connectedness, in community. Those we loved were the cushion upon which we rested and strengthened ourselves." Their story of illness/disability, and the broader story of their love, and of "living expansively, openheartedly, joyfully in the face of our inevitable death,"[34] unfolds within this context of community. Illness/disability—cancer, in this case—is a shared experience, a "collective experience,"[35] Sandra Butler reminds us.

Like *Cancer in Two Voices*, *Shameless: The Art of Disability* embodies the notion of intersubjectivity, that "the narration of a life or a self can never be confined to a single, isolated subjecthood. Others are an integral part of consciousness, events and the production of the narrative."[36] Like a dynamic postmodern pastiche of layers, textures, and blended forms, filmmaker Bonnie Sherr Klein's text weaves together the visual, the oral, the written, and beyond. It is at once a video documenting part of Klein's disability/illness journey, the stories of four other people with varying disabilities through multiple art forms, and a meditation on traditional scripts of disability/illness. As a collaborative endeavour, *Shameless* unsettles the notion of single authorship and ownership. The "self" of disability/illness is constructed in relation to others, in community, among fellow travellers, teachers, mentors, and friends. In the process, this text ends up implicitly suggesting that the more perspectives, genres, formats, and mediums—*processes*—that can be brought to bear on the disability/illness experience, the more we can shift how it is received and perceived, and thus shift our routinized ways of conceptualizing and being with illness/disability. Reading and writing fuller, richer, multi-dimensional accounts can lead to greater understanding and connection, and less distance and separation, between people who are disabled/ill, those who are not, and everyone in-between.

Also focusing on processes, Georgina Kleege's *Sight Unseen*, unlike most contemporary narratives by women with disabilities, is more an indictment of negative representations of blindness, ways of knowing and seeing, and of *normal* behaviour, than it is the story of losing her sight, as Susannah B. Mintz outlines. Kleege minimizes autobiographical details, insistently *looking* outward, for rather than getting caught up in the intimate details of her blindness, she is more interested in ways of *knowing* and *seeing*, and of blurring conventional binaries of seer and seen, subject and object, male and female, disabled and the norm, the literal and the representational.[37] This is not the typical linear story of the isolated disabled/ill individual who overcomes and triumphs over adversity. In fact, Kleege deliberately writes in circular motion, taking what we know of autobiography and blindness, and dismantling them, in form and content, at every turn.

Nancy Mairs also tells the story differently than the usual script. In fact, she literally tells the story differently in her auto/biography, *Waist-High in the World: A Life among the Nondisabled*. The collection unfolds as a series of separate but interlocking essays. Through these essays, Mairs attempts to discover "what physical, emotional, moral, and spiritual elements shape the 'differences' founded by disability," so she structures her tale around a "welter of questions" focusing on several themes: language, rights, caregiving, bodies, and the larger community.[38] She chooses the essay format because it allows her to ruminate on these issues, and because the process is "contemplative, exploratory, even equivocal, not definitive. If there are absolute answers to the kinds of questions I ask, I don't know them."[39] She raises questions about identity, self, embodiment, normalcy, and narrative form. There can be agency in the gaps facilitated by the essay structure. Because they are open-ended and non-linear, Mairs offers no neat and tidy beginnings, endings, or answers to the questions she poses. Instead, she writes everything in between. She is, in fact, what Mintz calls a "serial autobiographer."[40] She always has more to write; her story is ongoing, shifting, changing, in process. She does not claim to be sharing the whole of the experience; she shares just a fragment, which is part of something larger. And she refuses to fix an ending, instead leaving us in the midst of her journey (rather than an overcoming ending), while on vacation in England with her husband, George, in the closing pages of her text.

Nancy Mairs, like the other women and their texts, attempts to take us to a new place—a potentially unfamiliar place, and yet a hospitable place, in her auto/biography. She is not seeking to be "a member of the inspirational class," and she is not, as she says, writing a "feel-good book."[41] She is creating an opening, a path. She invites us, the readers, on her journey: "I ask you to read this book, then, not to be uplifted, but to be lowered and steadied into what may be unfamiliar, but is not inhospitable, space. Sink down beside me, take my hand, and together we'll watch the waists of the world drift past."[42] It is a form of what she refers to as "taking care,"[43] an accompanying process. She is asking us to compassionately engage the world among people with disabilities and illnesses in new and sometimes unfamiliar ways. She reminds us that we can focus on our connections without effacing difference:

> There are readers—not a lot of them, but even one is enough—who need, for a tangle of reasons, to be told that a life commonly held to be insufferable can be full and funny. I'm living the life. I can tell them.... This is no piteously deprived state I'm in down here but a rich, complicated, and utterly absorbing process of immersion in whatever the world has to offer.[44]

Mairs's auto/biography is also what Beth A. Ferri calls a "counter-narrative," one that brings the lived experience of people with disabilities to the centre of the research. It is a piece that "talks back" to,[45] instead of reinforcing or reiterating, the dominant script—of overcoming, of individualism, of independence, and of normalization—and allows us to question society's taken-for-granted assumptions about disability. The implications of this kind of analysis have real world, everyday consequences in terms of how we construct difference; how we create, sustain, and break barriers and systems of power and oppression; how we tell the stories of our lives and our selves. Telling narratives as/with community challenges the neoliberal idea of the self and creates new imaginaries for disability. This is just the beginning of understanding the power of our stories to engage in creative re-visionary tactics that allow a larger picture of the illness/disability experience to emerge, exceeding the narrow frames of traditional disability autobiography. I suggest that all of these women—Nancy Mairs, Barbara Rosenblum and Sandra Butler, Georgina Kleege, and Bonnie Sherr Klein—and so many other disabled auto/biographers among us, offer different ways of knowing and being in the world, by deconstructing and rebuilding the disability story, and asserting "that their bodies have tales to tell, stories that rethink fundamental questions about subjectivity, community, and the construction of difference."[46] It *is* possible to re-imagine and rethink our engagement with disability and illness in and through our auto/biographies. And in the process, rather than valorizing independence, we can draw strength and wisdom from each other in our interdependence. An intersubjective "living together."[47]

NOTES

1. G. Thomas Couser, "The Empire of the 'Normal': A Forum on Disability and Self-Representation; Introduction," *American Quarterly* 52, no. 2 (June 2000): 307–8.
2. Timothy Barrett, "De-individualising Autobiography: A Reconsideration of the Role of Autobiographical Life Writing within Disability Studies," *Disability & Society* 29, no. 10 (2014): 1571.
3. David T. Mitchell, "Body Solitaire: The Singular Subject of Disability Autobiography," *American Quarterly* 52, no. 2 (June 2000): 315.
4. See, for example, Susannah B. Mintz, "Dear (Embodied) Reader: Life Writing and Disability," *Prose Studies* 26, no. 1/2 (August 2003): 131–52; Barrett, "De-individualizing Autobiography."
5. Judith Butler, *Bodies That Matter: On the Discursive Limits of "Sex"* (New York: Routledge, 1993). Judith Butler theorizes that the self is an effect of the telling, produced through iterations. In her work on "gender performativity" and regulatory norms, Butler explicates the *process* by which some bodies come to matter. She argues that language "expects" us. There is a social code into which we are born—the "naming" of a "girl," for example, in sonograms—and we constitute ourselves as social beings by imitation, by *repeating* the code. It is the way we come into being. We are constantly "performing" our "sex"; we become so *practised* at gender roles that, through repetition, they become internalized, incorporated, part of our subjectivity and materiality, and re-enacted, so that they seem *natural*, just the "way the world is." For Butler, then, "performativity is thus not a singular 'act,' for it is always a reiteration of a norm or a set of norms" (12). In this way, she says that "construction of gender operations

through exclusionary means—against the inhuman—establishes boundaries, norms" (8). So we end up with some bodies that "matter" and some that do not, which, in part, institutionalizes the "heterosexual regime." This binary structuring of society by gender norms—male/female—has a hegemonic hold on us. Operating in a similar way, I suggest that "able-bodied" or "non-disabled" norms are just as "compulsory," that they establish what Alison Kafer calls the "political institution of able-bodiedness" (77). To explain, Shildrick and Price succinctly argue that, "the body as abled/disabled has historicity and is constructed, not by once-and-for-all acts, not yet by intentional processes, but through the constant reiteration of a set of norms. It is through such repetitive practice that the body as abled/disabled is both materialized and naturalized" (Margrit Shildrick and Janet Price, "Breaking the Boundaries of the Broken Body," Body & Society 2, no. 4 [1996], 94). Thus, a world view—a hegemonic master script—materializes through our stories about disability/illness.

6. Barrett, "De-individualizing Autobiography," 1570.
7. Tanya Titchkosky, *Reading & Writing Disability Differently: The Textured Life of Embodiment* (Toronto: University of Toronto Press, 2007), 9.
8. Daphne Marlatt, *Readings from the Labyrinth* (Edmonton: NeWest Press, 1998), 63.
9. Titchkosky, *Reading & Writing*, 6.
10. Titchkosky, *Reading & Writing*, 6.
11. Carol Thomas, *Female Forms: Experiencing and Understanding Disability* (Philadelphia: Open University Press, 1999), 68.
12. Thomas, *Female Forms*, 69.
13. Joan Borsa, "Towards a Politics of Location: Rethinking Marginality," in *Canadian Woman Studies: An Introductory Reader*, ed. Nuzhat Amin (Toronto: Inanna, 1999), 38.
14. Colin Barnes, Geof Mercer, and Tom Shakespeare, *Exploring Disability: A Sociological Introduction* (Cambridge, UK: Polity Press, 1999), 193.
15. Nancy Mairs, *Waist-High in the World: A Life Among the Nondisabled* (Boston: Beacon Press, 1996), 182.
16. Barrett, "De-individualizing Autobiography," 1570.
17. Couser in Beth A. Ferri, "Disability Life Writing and the Politics of Knowing," *Teachers College Record* 113, no. 10 (October 2011): 2269.
18. Butler in Ferri, "Disability Life Writing," 2269.
19. Eli Clare, *The Marrow's Telling: Words in Motion* (Ypsilanti, MI: Homofactus Press, 2007), 73.
20. Clare, *The Marrow's Telling*, 89.
21. Clare, *The Marrow's Telling*, 89.
22. Helene Cixous, "The Laugh of the Medusa," in *The Critical Tradition*, ed. David H. Richter (London: St. Martin's, 1989), 1098; Sidonie Smith, *Subjectivity, Identity, and the Body: Women's Autobiographical Practices in the Twentieth Century* (Bloomington: Indiana University Press, 1993), 2.
23. Emily Hutcheon and Gregor Wolbring, "'Cripping' Resilience: Contributions from Disability Studies to Resilience Theory," *M/C Journal* 16, no. 5 (August 20, 2013), http://journal.media-culture.org.au/index.php/mcjournal/article/view/697.
24. Smith, *Subjectivity, Identity, and the Body*, 2.
25. Hutcheon and Wolbring, "'Cripping' Resilience."
26. Borsa, "Towards a Politics of Location," 38.
27. Titchkosky, *Reading & Writing*, 5.
28. Lovern in Heather Norris, "Colonialism and the Rupturing of Indigenous Worldviews of Impairment and Relational Interdependence: A Beginning Dialogue towards Reclamation and Social Transformation," *Critical Disability Discourse/Discours Critiques dans le Champ du Handicap* 6 (2014): 71.

29. Liz Stanley, "From 'Self-Made Women' to 'Women's Made-Selves'? Audit Selves, Simulation and Surveillance in the Rise of Public Woman," in *Feminism and Autobiography: Texts, Theories, Methods*, ed. Tess Cosslett, Celia Lury, and Penny Summerfield (New York: Routledge, 2000), 41.
30. Stanley, "From 'Self-Made Women,'" 47.
31. Barrett, "De-individualizing Autobiography," 1576.
32. Sandra Butler and Barbara Rosenblum, *Cancer in Two Voices* (San Francisco: Spinsters Book Company, 1991), 8.
33. Butler and Rosenblum, *Cancer in Two Voices*, iii.
34. Butler and Rosenblum, *Cancer in Two Voices*, iii.
35. Butler and Rosenblum, *Cancer in Two Voices*, iii.
36. Tess Cosslett, Celia Lury, and Penny Summerfield, eds., *Feminism and Autobiography: Texts, Theories, Methods* (New York: Routledge, 2000), 4.
37. Susannah B. Mintz, "Invisible Disability: Georgina Kleege's Sight Unseen," *NWSA Journal* 14, no. 3 (Fall 2002): 157, 172.
38. Mairs, *Waist-High in the World*, 17.
39. Mairs, *Waist-High in the World*, 17.
40. Susannah B. Mintz, *Unruly Bodies: Life Writing by Women with Disabilities* (Chapel Hill: University of North Carolina Press, 2007), 4.
41. Mairs, *Waist-High in the World*, 18.
42. Mairs, *Waist-High in the World*, 18.
43. Mairs, *Waist-High in the World*, 84.
44. Mairs, *Waist-High in the World*, 10–11, 18.
45. Ferri, "Disability Life Writing," 2268.
46. Mintz, "Dear (Embodied) Reader," 131–32.
47. Cosslett, Lury, and Summerfield, *Feminism and Autobiography*, 7.

BIBLIOGRAPHY

Barnes, Colin, Geof Mercer, and Tom Shakespeare. *Exploring Disability: A Sociological Introduction*. Cambridge, UK: Polity Press, 1999.

Barrett, Timothy. "De-individualising Autobiography: A Reconsideration of the Role of Autobiographical Life Writing within Disability Studies." *Disability & Society* 29, no. 10 (2014): 1569–82.

Borsa, Joan. "Towards a Politics of Location: Rethinking Marginality." In *Canadian Woman Studies: An Introductory Reader*, edited by Nuzhat Amin, 36–44. Toronto: Inanna, 1999.

Butler, Judith. *Bodies That Matter: On the Discursive Limits of "Sex."* New York: Routledge, 1993.

Butler, Sandra, and Barbara Rosenblum. *Cancer in Two Voices*. San Francisco: Spinsters Book Company, 1991.

Cixous, Helene. "The Laugh of the Medusa." In *The Critical Tradition: Classic Texts and Contemporary Trends*, edited by David H. Richter, 1090–1102. London: St. Martin's, 1989.

Clare, Eli. *The Marrow's Telling: Words in Motion*. Michigan: Homofactus Press, 2007.

Cosslett, Tess, Celia Lury, and Penny Summerfield, eds. *Feminism and Autobiography: Texts, Theories, Methods*. New York: Routledge, 2000.

Couser, G. Thomas. "The Empire of the 'Normal': A Forum on Disability and Self Representation; Introduction." *American Quarterly* 52, no. 2 (June 2000): 305–10.

Ferri, Beth A. "Disability Life Writing and the Politics of Knowing." *Teachers College Record* 113, no. 10 (October 2011): 2267–82.

Hutcheon, Emily, and Gregor Wolbring. "'Cripping' Resilience: Contributions from Disability Studies to Resilience Theory." *M/C Journal* 16, no. 5 (August 20, 2013). http://journal.media-culture.org.au/index.php/mcjournal/article/view/697.

Kafer, Alison. "Compulsory Bodies: Reflections on Heterosexuality and Able-bodiedness." *Journal of Women's History* 15, no. 3 (Autumn 2003): 77–89.

Kleege, Georgina. *Sight Unseen*. New Haven, CT: Yale University Press, 1999.

Klein, Bonnie Sherr, dir. *Shameless: The Art of Disability*. National Film Board of Canada, 2006.

Mairs, Nancy. *Waist-High in the World: A Life among the Nondisabled*. Boston: Beacon Press, 1996.

Marlatt, Daphne. *Readings from the Labyrinth*. Edmonton: NeWest Press, 1998.

Mintz, Susannah B. "Dear (Embodied) Reader: Life Writing and Disability." *Prose Studies* 26, no. 1/2 (August 2003): 131–52.

Mintz, Susannah B. "Invisible Disability: Georgina Kleege's Sight Unseen." *NWSA Journal* 14, no. 3 (Fall 2002): 155–77.

Mintz, Susannah B. *Unruly Bodies: Life Writing by Women with Disabilities*. Chapel Hill: University of North Carolina Press, 2007.

Mitchell, David T. "Body Solitaire: The Singular Subject of Disability Autobiography." *American Quarterly* 52, no. 2 (June 2000): 311–15.

Norris, Heather. "Colonialism and the Rupturing of Indigenous Worldviews of Impairment and Relational Interdependence: A Beginning Dialogue towards Reclamation and Social Transformation." *Critical Disability Discourse/Discours Critiques dans le Champ du Handicap* 6 (2014): 53–79.

Shildrick, Margrit, and Janet Price. "Breaking the Boundaries of the Broken Body." *Body & Society* 2, no. 4 (1996): 93–113.

Smith, Sidonie. *Subjectivity, Identity, and the Body: Women's Autobiographical Practices in the Twentieth Century*. Bloomington: Indiana University Press, 1993.

Stanley, Liz. "From 'Self-Made Women' to 'Women's Made-Selves'?: Audit Selves, Simulation and Surveillance in the Rise of Public Woman." In *Feminism and Autobiography: Texts, Theories, Methods*, edited by Tess Cosslett, Celia Lury, and Penny Summerfield, 40–60. New York: Routledge, 2000.

Thomas, Carol. *Female Forms: Experiencing and Understanding Disability*. Philadelphia: Open University Press, 1999.

Titchkosky, Tanya. *Reading & Writing Disability Differently: The Textured Life of Embodiment*. Toronto: University of Toronto Press, 2007.

CONTRIBUTORS

Natalie Ball completed her BHSc at the University of Calgary under the supervision of Dr. Gregor Wolbring. Her research interests include critical disability studies and social justice. She is currently studying occupational therapy at the University of Alberta.

Sandy R. Barron is a Vanier Scholar and doctoral student in the History Department at Carleton University. His research concerns the politics and social history of deafness and Deaf communities in Western Canada from 1880 to 1930. He completed his master's thesis on the Manitoba School for the Deaf at the University of Calgary in 2016.

Rita Bomak has been a key member of the Deaf community all of her life. She has represented Canada in the Deaflympics in curling and served as team manager on three occasions. Rita was also a delegate of the Canadian Deaf Sports Association to attend the International Congress of Sports for the Deaf (ICSD). Rita participated in the Deaf Human Service Worker Training Program and since graduation (1990) has worked as a community counsellor in the Deaf Adult Services Department at the Society for Manitobans with Disabilities.

Caroline E. M. Carrington-Decker, now an elementary teacher, reflects back to her years as a master's student researching the wayward boys of downtown Toronto during the late 1800s. Her curiosity to discover circumstances surrounding such waywardness was fuelled by her 10 years of working "in the trenches" with our wayward boys of today. It became Caroline's passion to ensure that the voices of those wayward boys of the 1800s were honoured and shared with today's society.

Vera Chouinard is a professor of geography at McMaster University. She is a feminist and social geographer who has written extensively on disability issues. Her publications include work on disability and legal struggles in Canada, the impacts of state restructuring on disabled women's lives, experiences of mental ill health and place, and disabled people's lives in the Global South. Vera has also been disabled by barriers to accommodation and inclusion throughout her academic career and has written on those experiences to illuminate ableism in the academy.

Kathryn Church is director of and associate professor in the School of Disability Studies at Ryerson University, Toronto. Since 2002, she has been part of key initiatives that have brought the school's "vision, passion, action" message to life across the university and in the public eye. Kathryn has been allied with the Mad movement since the 1980s, and is a foundational contributor to the emerging field of Mad Studies. A critical ethnographer, she is author of *Forbidden Narratives: Critical Autobiography as Social Science*, and co-curator of two award-winning national exhibits: *Fabrications: Stitching Ourselves Together* (with her mother, Lorraine) and *Out from Under: Disability, History and Things to Remember*. Recognized for teaching excellence and curriculum innovation, Kathryn has been honoured with a Woman of Distinction award from the Ontario Confederation of Faculty Associations, and a David C. Onley Award for Leadership in Accessibility.

April D'Aubin is engaged in the disability community through work (Council of Canadians with Disabilities [CCD]), volunteering (Winnipeg Independent Living Resource Centre; Canadian Association of Independent Living Centres, now known as Independent Living Canada; Canadian Centre on Disability Studies; and the Manitoba League of Persons with Disabilities), and study (disability studies).

Doreen Demas was born and spent her early years living in her home community of Canupawakpa Dakota Nation in Manitoba, but has made Winnipeg her home for many years. She attained a degree in social work from the University of Manitoba. She has been involved in the First Nations, disability, and women's movements for more than three decades. She has worked with First Nations organizations, provincial and federal governments, and persons with disabilities as a consultant, researcher, policy analyst, and writer on issues related to Indigenous persons with disabilities. An award winner, she has travelled and published and spoken provincially, nationally, and internationally on perspectives of Indigenous persons with disabilities.

Diane Driedger has been involved in the disability rights movement in Canada and internationally since 1980. She is author or editor of nine books, including *The Last Civil Rights Movement: Disabled Peoples' International* (Hurst, 1999). She is also a poet and visual artist. Her latest publication is *Red with Living: Poems and Art* (Inanna, 2016). She holds an MA in history and a PhD in education and lives in Winnipeg.

Charlotte Enns is a professor in the Faculty of Education at the University of Manitoba. Her work as a researcher was launched through her involvement in monitoring the bilingual acquisition (ASL and English) of the children attending Sign Talk Children's Centre. Charlotte's research continues to focus on the assessment and development of language and literacy skills in deaf children.

Gregory Evans has served the Deaf community locally and nationally as an interpreter and interpreter trainer. He was also an instructor in the Deaf Human Service Worker Training Program. He continues to be involved in the Deaf community in various ways, and since 2010 has been the principal lawyer and owner of Evans Family Law firm in Winnipeg.

Catherine Frazee is one of three curators of the groundbreaking exhibit *Out from Under: Disability, History and Things to Remember*. She is a professor emerita at Ryerson University's School of Disability Studies; her work as a writer, educator, and activist explores the human rights, precarious citizenship, and cultural resistance of disabled people.

Dustin Galer received his PhD in history from the University of Toronto. He completed a post-doctoral fellowship at York University in conjunction with the Centre for Research on Work Disability Policy. His research explores relationships between disability, work, activism, and poverty. He is the founder of MyHistorian (www.myhistorian.ca), where he works as a personal historian.

Roy Hanes, PhD, is an associate professor of social work at Carleton University in Ottawa. He is recognized for his work in the area of disability history, disability policy, teaching direct social work practices with individuals and families with disabilities, and community organizing. He is a founding member of both the Persons with Disabilities Caucus of the Council on Social Work Education and the Canadian Disability Studies Association. He is an active promoter of disability studies in Canada and is involved with advocacy organizations such as the Council of Canadians with Disabilities. He has presented and published widely on disability issues relating to immigration, education, social work, theory, family, civil rights, cross-cultural concerns, ableism, and violence.

Nancy Hansen is associate professor and director of the Interdisciplinary Master's Program in Disability Studies at the University of Manitoba. She obtained her PhD (human geography) from the University of Glasgow. Her current research interests are disability and post-conflict, disability history, access to primary care, medical ethics, and eugenics.

Alessandra Iozzo-Duval completed her PhD in the Faculty of Education at the University of Ottawa. She is currently a post-doctoral fellow at the Nursing History Research Unit in the Faculty of Health Sciences at the University of Ottawa. Alessandra teaches part-time in the Institute of Interdisciplinary Studies at Carleton University and part-time at the University of Ottawa in the Faculty of Social Sciences and Interdisciplinary Health Sciences. Her current research interests include the history of health and disability, particularly in educational contexts, as it intersects with gender, citizenship, and racialization.

Joseph Kaufert, PhD, is professor emeritus in the Department of Community Health Sciences in the College of Medicine, University of Manitoba. He is a medical anthropologist and public health researcher, teacher and disability studies scholar. His research has supported innovations fostering culturally safe communication and reduction of cultural-structural barriers to access to health care and community living for disabled Canadians and Indigenous peoples. He developed community-based, participatory frameworks for ethical research practice and examined issues in disability and consumer advocacy. He developed and co-taught consumer-led course modules focusing on disability rights and the impact of the independent living and social models of disability.

Dale C. Kendel enjoyed a diverse 40-year career in the field of intellectual disability and community development, as a liaison with government and NGO planning. Dale retired as executive director of Community Living Manitoba in 2009, a position he held for 34 years. In 2012, Dale was the recipient of the Honorary Life Member Award from the Canadian Association for Community Living. In retirement, Dale continues to be selectively involved in issues such as Barrier Free Manitoba and Manitoba Marathon, and consults with disability-related groups in Manitoba and Saskatchewan. He is actively involved in Trinity United Church and has been involved in the Manitoba NW Ontario conference, serving on several committees.

Bruce Koskie has been an active member of the Deaf community all his life. He has served as a board member for a variety of local organizations and worked on numerous committees to plan educational, advocacy, and social activities. Bruce has worked as a vocational rehabilitation counsellor in the Deaf Adult Services Department at the Society for Manitobans with Disabilities for almost 30 years.

Phaedra Livingstone is a museologist with extensive international experience developing, delivering, and evaluating museum and university-based programs. Prior to joining Centennial College in 2017, she spent a year as a senior museum consultant on a new national museum project in Dubai, United Arab Emirates. From 2008 through 2015, she was a professor at the University of Oregon, where she directed the Museum Studies concentration and graduate certificate.

David Locker (1949–2010) was associate dean of the Faculty of Dentistry, University of Toronto. A graduate of the University of Sheffield with a PhD in sociology, Dr. Locker was a researcher deeply committed to community-centred, innovative health service delivery. An accomplished award-winning author and speaker, he wrote numerous books and 19 book chapters, and presented 250 papers.

Zana Marie Lutfiyya is a professor in the Faculty of Education at the University of Manitoba in Winnipeg. In her research, she has focused on the factors that help or hinder the social participation of individuals with intellectual disability.

Claudia Malacrida is a professor in sociology and the associate vice president of research at the University of Lethbridge in Alberta. She is the author of several books on disability, health, and the body, including *Mourning the Dreams: Miscarriage, Stillbirth and Early Infant Death* (Left Coast Press), *Sociology of the Body: A Reader* (Oxford University Press), *Cold Comfort: Mothers, Professionals and ADHD* (University of Toronto Press), and *A Special Hell: Institutional Life in Alberta's Eugenic Years* (University of Toronto Press). She is engaged in two ongoing research projects: "Eugenics to Newgenics in Alberta" explores the continuities and disjunctures between historical eugenic actions and current responses to disabled people's sexuality and reproduction, and "Childbirth and Choice" examines the cultural, structural, moral, social, and discursive contexts that both constrain and produce women's childbirth experiences.

Kelly McGillivray is a King's University College graduate based in London, Ontario. Working at the intersection of critical disability studies and feminist auto/biography, her research weaves arts-based approaches with autoethnography to challenge barriers and problematic representations of disability, and to explore ways of re-imagining society's engagement with difference through autobiography. Kelly is a writer, researcher, teaching assistant, disability advocate, and artisan.

Marilou McPhedran is a Member of the Order of Canada, a human rights lawyer, professor, and activist, appointed in 2016 as an independent senator to the Parliament of Canada by Prime Minister Justin Trudeau. She co-founded several internationally recognized non-profit Canadian organizations and was the founding principal (dean) of the University of Winnipeg Global College. In 1981–82, she was a lawyer with the Advocacy Resource Centre for Handicapped Persons and, with Pat Israel, she coordinated Canada's first national conference on disability rights and the Canadian Charter of Rights and Freedoms. In 1985, she co-founded the Women's Legal Education and Action Fund (LEAF) to implement a high-impact litigation strategy on the intersectional equality rights of women and girls.

Melanie Panitch is an associate professor at Ryerson University, where she holds the John C. Eaton Chair in Social Innovation and Entrepreneurship in the Faculty of Community Services. She was founding director of the School of Disability Studies (1999–2011). She co-curated *Out from Under: Disability, History and Things to Remember*, a groundbreaking exhibit on activist disability history in Canada, now on permanent display at the Canadian Museum for Human Rights. Her research, published as *Disability, Mothers and Organization: Accidental Activists* (Routledge, 2008), is a gendered history of activist mothering in the Canadian Association for Community Living.

Laurence Parent is a PhD candidate in humanities at Concordia University. She holds an MA in critical disability studies from York University and a BA in political science from Université du Québec à Montréal. She lives in Montreal and is passionate about disability activism, disability history, and mobility. Laurence's academic work and artwork has been featured at numerous conferences and exhibitions in Canada, the United States, and England. In 2016, she was selected by the Canadian Disability Studies Association (CDSA-ACEI) as the recipient of the Francophone Tanis Doe Award for Canadian Disability Study and Culture.

Geoffrey Reaume created the first university credit course on Mad People's History in 2000, which he introduced and taught at the University of Toronto (2000), Ryerson University (2002–03), and York University (since 2004), where he also teaches a course on Critical Interpretations of Disability History in the critical disability studies graduate program.

Karen D. Schwartz is a social sciences and humanities research facilitator at the University of Manitoba. Her research interests focus on issues facing people with intellectual disabilities. In particular, she is trying to better understand the role that historical and contemporary ideas of personhood and humanness play in advancing or precluding a meaningful and valued life for these individuals. Most recently she has been examining the meaning of human rights and social justice for adults with intellectual disabilities.

Natalie Spagnuolo is a doctoral candidate in critical disability studies at York University. Her research interests are in public policy and biopolitics, often taking a historical perspective. She has contributed articles on a range of topics related to disability, including migration, custodialism, political participation, and labour. Her work is supported by the Social Sciences and Humanities Research Council.

Phillip B. Turcotte is a disability advocate who works towards creating disability-positive communities and spaces where disability is welcomed, included, and celebrated as an essential part of diversity. A lawyer, Phillip received his Juris Doctor from the University of Ottawa's Faculty of Law. In his studies there, he focused on human rights compliance and enforcement as well as dispute resolution. Phillip received his Bachelor of Arts Highest Honours in Human Rights from Carleton University. There, his studies focused on disability theory, disability justice, and sexuality. He has received several awards in recognition of his advocacy work: Dr. John Davis Burton Award (2014), Legal Leaders for Diversity Trust Fund Scholarship (2016), and Advocacy Award–Celebration of People Awards (2016).

Vanessa Warne is a member of the Department of English, Film, and Theatre at the University of Manitoba. Her research explores the nineteenth-century history of visual disability, with particular emphasis on literacy. She is the co-curator, with Sabrina Mark, of *Books Without Ink*, a 2016 exhibit exploring the first century of blind people's experiences of tactile reading and writing. She is also the co-organizer, with Dr. Hannah Thompson, of *Blind Creations*, a 2015 international conference and micro-arts festival on visual disability, creativity, and accessibility.

Gregor Wolbring is an associate professor in the Cumming School of Medicine, University of Calgary, specializing in community rehabilitation and disability studies.

COPYRIGHT ACKNOWLEDGEMENTS

Sandy R. Barron, "'An Excuse for Being So Bold': D. W. McDermid and the Early Development of the Manitoba Institute for the Deaf and Dumb, 1888–1900." *Manitoba History* 77 (Winter 2015): 2–12. Permission granted by Manitoba Historical Society.

Vera Chouinard, "'Like Alice through the Looking Glass' II: The Struggle for Accommodation Continues." *Resources for Feminist Research*, Volume 33, Nos. 3/4 (2010). Permission granted by *Resources for Feminist Research*.

Kathryn Church, Melanie Panitch, Catherine Frazee, and Phaedra Livingstone, "'Out from Under': A Brief History of Everything." From *Re-Presenting Disability: Activism and Agency in the Museum*, edited by Richard Sandell, Jocelyn Dodd, and Rosemarie Garland-Thomson, copyright 2010, Routledge, reproduced by permission of Taylor & Francis Books UK.

Doreen Demas, "Triple Jeopardy: Native Women with Disabilities." *Canadian Woman Studies*, Women and Disability Issue, 13, no. 4 (1993): 53–55. Permission granted by Doreen Demas.